African American Historic Places

AFRICAN AMERICAN HISTORIC PLACES

National Register of Historic Places

Edited by Beth L. Savage

Editorial Director
Carol D. Shull

Editorial Assistant
Rama Ramakrishna

National Park Service
United States Department of the Interior

The Preservation Press
National Trust for Historic Preservation

National Conference of State Historic Preservation Officers

The Preservation Press
National Trust for Historic Preservation
1785 Massachusetts Avenue, N.W.
Washington, D.C. 20036

Printed in the United States of America
97 96 95 94   5 4 3 2 1

Library of Congress Cataloging-in-Publication Data

African American Historic Places / National Register of Historic
   Places, National Park Service; edited by Beth L. Savage;
   editorial director, Carol D. Shull; editorial assistant,
   Rama Ramakrishna.
      p.   cm.
   Contains a listing of properties from the National Register and
   essays relating to the sites.
   Includes index.
   ISBN 0-89133-253-7 : $24.95
      1. Afro-Americans—History. 2. Historic Sites—United States.
   I. Savage, Beth L. II. Shull, Carol D. III. National Register of
   Historic Places.
   E185.A2534   1994   94-33218
   973' .0496073—dc20   CIP

Design by J. Scott Knudsen

CONTENTS

ACKNOWLEDGMENTS

This book represents a monumental collaborative venture by the National Park Service, the National Conference of State Historic Preservation Officers, the National Trust for Historic Preservation, and others. It would not have been possible without the contributions of countless individuals.

We thank Director Roger G. Kennedy and Associate Director, Cultural Resources, Jerry L. Rogers of the National Park Service, U.S. Department of the Interior, for their support of this project.

We appreciate the contributions of James O. Horton of the American Studies Department, George Washington University; Elizabeth Clark Lewis of the Public History Program, Howard University; and Sharon Harley of the Afro-American History Department, University of Maryland, College Park who provided sage advice as project consultants and intern sponsors for the three graduate students who worked on the project.

We thank the National Conference of State Historic Preservation Officers for its support. We especially recognize Eric Hertfelder, Nancy Miller, Andra Damron, Eleanor O'Donnell, Larry Karr, Tanya Velt, and Brenda Olio for their efforts.

We thank the contributors for their planning, researching, and writing of articles.

We appreciate the cooperation of the state historic preservation officers and their staffs who reviewed the significance synopses for the historic places in their states.

Chief Historian Edwin C. Bearss, History Division, National Park Service, U.S. Department of the Interior, and his staff provided helpful comments. Jenny Masur, staff Ethnographer, Applied Ethnography Program, Anthropology Division, National Park Service, U.S. Department of the Interior, offered additional insight.

We are grateful to our colleagues of the Interagency Resources Division, National Park Service, U.S. Department of the Interior, especially former Chief Lawrence E. Aten, Diane Miller, John Byrne, and all members of the National Register staff, for their support and assistance.

Catherine Lavoie, Joseph Balachowski, Jet Lowe, Jack Boucher, and Paul Dolinsky of the Historic American Buildings Survey/Historic American Engineering Record, National Park Service, U.S. Department of the Interior; Carol Ahlgren; Howard S. Berger; Lynn Bjorkman; George Carney; Tom DuRant; James Lockhart; Linda McClelland; Arleen Pabón; William Rasdell; and Nancy Todd assisted with obtaining illustrations.

Special thanks are due the staff of the Preservation Press, National Trust for Historic Preservation, especially Buckley Jeppson, Janet Walker, Pete Lindeman, and Margaret Gore Johnson.

INTRODUCTION

Carol D. Shull

African Americans have made profound contributions to American history, many of which have been previously overlooked. The story of African Americans in this country is at the very heart of our heritage. Contained herein are the more than 800 tangible places recognized in the National Register of Historic Places that reflect importance in such diverse areas as social history, community development, education, science and medicine, the arts and literature, women's history, military events, and civil rights. All Americans can benefit from the documentation and preservation of the places where we can learn firsthand what the African American experience means to our nation.

African American Historic Places begins with articles that weave listed places and their special values into the larger framework of American history and heritage preservation and suggest additional readings about the topics. The articles are followed by descriptions of all of the listings organized by location within the states and territories. Finally, there are several indexes to assist readers in identifying places in a specific location or relating to a variety of subjects. The book is an educational resource and a reference for teachers, students, and travelers.

Maintained by the National Park Service, the National Register of Historic Places is our nation's inventory of historic districts, sites, buildings, structures, and objects significant in American history, architecture, archeology, engineering, and culture. The National Historic Preservation Act of 1966 gave the Secretary of the Interior the authority to expand and maintain the National Register to assist in recognizing and preserving historic places as living parts of our communities. The National Register includes nationally significant historic areas of the National Park System designated by Congress, such as the Mary McLeod Bethune Council House National Historic Site, and exceptionally important National Historic Landmarks designated by the Secretary of the Interior, like the Ralph Bunche House, the Little Rock High School, and the Sweet Auburn Historic District. But most of the listings are added to the National Register as a result of state and federal agency nominations, and over 90 percent are of state and local significance. The places in this book highlight the accomplishments of such well-known individuals as Frederick Douglass, Booker T. Washington, and Maggie Walker and the equally important history of ordinary people as recorded in churches, social institutions, schools, banks, businesses, houses, neighborhoods, and archeological sites. They illustrate the events, people, designs, and information from our past that document black history in 42 states and two territories. The articles use listed properties to illustrate significant historic contexts on the role of communities, migration, women, the arts, the struggles for freedom and civil rights, and heritage preservation. They pay powerful tribute to the spirit of African Americans in our past and provide stimulating dialogue for our future contemplation.

To be eligible for listing, each place must meet the National Register Criteria for Evaluation, which are explained in the "How to Use This Guide" section. Listing honors the property by recognizing its importance to a community, a state, or the nation. National Register properties are often recognized in publications, tourism literature and activities, and in other ways. They are sometimes protected by state and local laws and financial incentives. About 76 percent of listed properties are privately owned and usually not open to the public, but many are within historic districts that can be visited; others are publicly owned and open to the public, such as the units of the National Park System, which are identified.

Private owners of listed properties can do anything they wish with their properties. They have no obligation to open them to the public, to restore them, or even to maintain them. However, federal agencies whose projects may affect a listed or eligible property must give the Advisory Council on Historic Preservation, established under the National Historic Preservation Act, an opportunity to comment on the project and its impacts on the property. Owners may also be able to obtain federal historic preservation funding when money is available, and federal investment tax credits for rehabilitation and other provisions may apply.

Like the National Register, which is itself a partnership among federal agencies, states, local governments, American Indian tribes, Alaska Natives, Native Hawaiians, and private preservationists, this book has been created through a partnership. Conceived by the National Park Service and edited by the National Register staff, the book has been written by distinguished Americans with expertise in African American studies and historic preservation. The descriptions of each place have been compiled by graduate students of African American history from George Washington University, Howard University, and the University of Maryland, College Park. Authors of the articles and the students worked under contract to the National Conference of State Historic Preservation Officers, the organization representing state officials who nominate properties to the National Register on behalf of the states. The book is published by The Preservation Press of the National Trust for Historic Preservation.

For nearly thirty years we Americans have been documenting and recognizing our common heritage through listings in the National Register. The National Park Service expands the National Register; maintains registration documentation on each listing, including a description, statement of significance, maps, and photographs; and operates an automated index to listings, the National Register Information System. The National Register is a rich source of information for planning and public education. This book is part of an ongoing effort to make information about historic places available to the public to encourage their protection and interpretation and to enhance the study of the diverse cultural groups that have built our nation. The National Park Service urges all Americans to use the National Register and to recommend places for inclusion. It belongs to all of us.

How to Use This Guide

The buildings, sites, districts, structures, and objects in this volume are among the more than 62,000 listed in the National Register of Historic Places to date. They represent only a portion of the existing properties important in African American history nationwide; there are many more that have yet to be nominated. The historic places included in this book were identified using the National Register Information System database to search for properties coded for significance in African American heritage that were listed by December 31, 1993. State historic preservation officers were consulted on the places in their states. After the summaries of historical significance were completed, index terms were ascribed to each entry using the Integrated Preservation Software (IPS). Analysis of the frequency of use and the historical patterns reflected by the indexing terms helped guide the content of the articles. The general format of the book and its indexes were generated using IPS.

ARTICLES

The significance of any single place cannot be fully understood without some knowledge of its historical and cultural context. The authors of the first six articles use listed places to illustrate broad historical and cultural currents. The final two articles speak to the importance of historic preservation in communities. Together, they set the framework for understanding the importance of both the everyday and the extraordinary places whose descriptions follow.

AFRICAN AMERICAN HISTORIC PLACES

The information on each entry is based on the National Register registration documentation. Nomination documentation is prepared by multitudes of individuals and submitted by more than 100 different state and federal preservation officers, and it reflects various approaches to and levels of information regarding the significance of historic places.

Each entry is headed by a banner containing the name of the place as it appears in the National Register, followed by the street address and town or city. For historic districts, approximate street boundaries are given under street address. The summaries are organized by county within each state and alphabetically by name within county. Some large cities, such as Richmond and St. Louis, are not considered a part of any county. These independent cities are subheaded within states the same way counties are. Alphabetical indexes by place name and by city follow to further assist readers in locating specific properties.

The text explaining the place's significance in African American history follows. At the end of each entry is a line containing several pieces of information:

Thematic Resource (TR), Multiple Resource Area (MRA), or Multiple Property Submission (MPS), if applicable, under which the property was nominated. 194 of the listed properties are registered as part of multiple property groups, under which places sharing common historical or architectural themes are individually listed.

Additional Documentation (AD), if applicable, indicates that supplemental information was added to the nomination documentation after a property's initial listing in the National Register.

National Register Criteria for Evaluation under which the property is listed. The National Register Criteria, indicated by the letters A,B,C, and D, are listed at the end of this section.

Listing Date

National Park Service (NPS) and National Historic Landmarks (NHL) indicators. Properties that are units of the National Park System are designated as such by Congress and are open to the public. National Historic Landmarks are nationally significant properties exhibiting exceptional importance that are identified and evaluated within the context of specific themes in the nation's history. They are designated by the Secretary of the Interior and simultaneously listed in the National Register of Historic Places.

Identification Number

The 8-digit number identifying the property in the National Register Information System database.

The National Register Criteria for Evaluation

The quality of significance in American history, architecture, archeology, engineering, and culture is present in districts, sites, buildings, structures, and objects that possess integrity of location, design, setting, materials, workmanship, feeling, and association, and:

•That are associated with events that have made a significant contribution to the broad patterns of our history (Criterion A); or

•That are associated with the lives of significant persons in our past (Criterion B); or

•That embody the distinctive characteristics of a type, period, or method of construction, or that represent the work of a master, or that possess high artistic values, or that represent a significant and distinguishable entity whose components may lack individual distinction (Criterion C); or

•That have yielded or may be likely to yield, information important in history or prehistory (Criterion D).

Criteria Considerations

Ordinarily cemeteries, birthplaces, graves of historical figures, properties owned by religious institutions or used for religious purposes, structures that have been moved from their original locations, reconstructed historic buildings, properties primarily commemorative in nature, and properties that have achieved significance within the last 50 years shall not be considered eligible for the National Register. However, such properties will qualify if they are integral parts of districts that do meet the criteria or if they fall within the following categories:

•A religious property deriving primary significance from architectural or artistic distinction or historical importance; or

•A building or structure removed from its original location but that is primarily significant for architectural value or that is the surviving structure most importantly associated with a historic person or event; or

•A birthplace or grave of a historical

figure of outstanding importance if there is no appropriate site or building associated with his or her productive life; or

•A cemetery that derives its primary importance from graves of persons of transcendent importance, from age, from distinctive design features, or from association with historic events; or

•A reconstructed building when accurately executed in a suitable environment and presented in a dignified manner as part of a restoration master plan and when no other building or structure within the same association has survived; or

•A property primarily commemorative in intent if design, age, tradition, or symbolic value has invested it with its own exceptional significance; or

•A property achieving significance within the last 50 years if it has exceptional importance.

CROSS-REFERENCING

Many entries are cross-referenced to other entries in the book. Cross-references appear in parentheses in the body of the each entry as follows: (see also [name of property, location]). Properties are cross-referenced if they share a common significant association with a notable individual, historical event, or pattern of events. Properties that are only tangentially associated (for example, theaters where Duke Ellington played, Rosenwald schools, churches in Georgia, doctor's offices) may be located through the name, subject, place, and occupation indexes.

INDEXES

All indexes are arranged alphabetically. The **name index** includes notable individuals and organizations associated with each place, (for example, Duke Ellington, National Association for the Advancement of Colored People). The proper names of individuals that appear as part of the National Register listing name are alphabetized by surname. The **subject index** includes building types, events, and patterns of events (for example, schools, World War I, Rosenwald Fund, slave rebellions). The **occupation index** includes traditional as well as nontraditional categories. The **city index** is arranged by city within each state. Also included is an **index of National Register listing names** as they are entered in the National Register.

Both cross-referencing and indexes are included to help readers interested in a specific subject locate pertinent information. The records of the National Register are open to the public. Readers may obtain copies of National Register documentation, which includes a physical description, statement of significance, bibliography, map, and photographs, to learn detailed information about specific places. Together with the suggested readings that follow the articles, the narratives of these individual properties form a rich and compelling record of the contributions of African Americans to our history as a nation.

NEWSPAPE

according to Act of Congress in the year 1859, by FRANK LESLIE, in the Clerk's Office of the District Court for the Souther

NEW YORK, SATURDAY, NOVEMBER 5, 1859

RACY.

trations of
ry. In an
ently con-
a certain
ched, with
the negro
his fellow
ny black,
York ; he
conflict.
wa ; he is

t graphic
gine-house
rs, under
side were
s, consist-
the door-
some are
s outside.
rced, and
e ground,
the burial
f conflict.
eral rites
g-place.

Y.

event has
ver before
tary servi-

HARPER'S FERRY INSURRECTION—BURYING THE DEAD INSURGENTS.

SOCIAL HISTORY AND THE AFRICAN AMERICAN EXPERIENCE

James O. Horton

TWO GENERATIONS of Americans have grown up with a Muppet friend Kermit, a little green frog, who was smart and a little devilish and who sang a song with lyrics and a melody that lifted our spirits and embedded itself in our minds—"It's not that easy being green." Green, we were told, was so unexciting, so common, so ordinary when contrasted with the radiance of more spectacular colors. We listened and smiled, and most of us identified with the little frog and wanted to reassure him and ourselves that green was not so very inconsequential after all. Ironically, at this very moment scholars were engaged in the process of lifting ordinary people out of historical obscurity and making ordinary not only consequential but central to our understanding of our past and present society and culture.

"History from the bottom up" some scholars called it. This study of everyday things and ordinary people broadened our notion of what history was and of who

made it. It was a departure from what in the late 1960s some called traditional history, which focused on powerful politicians, dashing military commanders, and brilliant philosophers. For most of our national life these have been the focal points of historical attention. They marked the path and formed the substance of the things, the events, and the people worth studying, and they even defined the terms of the historical debate. Even today most of us think of an American history divided into periods determined by the traditional questions asked and the traditional heroes considered—the colonial era, the Revolution, the Jeffersonian and Jacksonian periods, antebellum America, or the era of the Civil War and Reconstruction, these demarcations lead us through the first half of almost any survey course in U.S. history. They determine the break for standard two-volume textbooks and dictate fields of specialization for most students of American history. Similarly, presidential

"Harpers Ferry Insurrection, burying the dead" in Frank Leslie's Illustrated Weekly Newspaper, New York, Saturday, November 5, 1859. Courtesy of the Library of Congress.

elections, wars, and major economic upheavals delineate the 20th century in the minds of Americans.

Historians still refer to the progressive period, the pre- or post-war years, the Great Depression, and the cold war era automatically, seldom feeling the need to justify the use of these historical markers. While it is true that all Americans were affected directly or indirectly by these significant events, historians have too often explored these issues and events only at the level of national policy. Most Americans experienced these things at very personal levels of family and community, and although the politics of policy formation was assumed to be history, until recently the impact of that policy on the lives of ordinary people was not. From the standpoint of most people, American history is based largely on distant, sometimes artificial issues of our national experience, issues most relevant to a small minority—almost all male, white, well-educated northerners, except during the era of the Civil War, and almost all eastern and affluent. Traditionally, these are the central actors in the American drama.

Social history, as a field of study, predates the 1940s. Yet until the end of the 1950s, it consisted largely of what many scholars considered a quaint fascination with the household trivia of history. Most historians focused on the politics, the economics, and the military events of history, disdaining social history as what some called "pots and pans" history. Before the 1960s, most social historians focused on many of those left out of scholarly history but generally did not take them seriously as important actors on the national stage. Then came the civil rights movement with its reliance on the power of mass organization. On television screens across the country we witnessed ordinary people becoming the focus of national attention. Maids, gas station attendants, sharecroppers, and housewives linked arms with ministers, teachers, and students, and they were eventually joined by doctors, lawyers, and even politicians, all unquestionably forcing a change in national policy, all making history in the streets. Black people, women, the poor, the rural folk, voices that had been silent in the pages of history were now singing out in unmistakably discordant tones. By the late 1960s social history was taking a turn toward a broader vision of the American past, asking if those regional, economic, gender, and racial groups so obviously involved in the national life of contemporary society could be discovered as actors in earlier periods. Black Americans were highly critical of the fact that they were excluded from American history except as minor supporting, racially stereotyped characters and that the important factor of race was almost totally absent.

In 1968 a ground-breaking series of articles appeared in an anthology edited by Barton J. Bernstein under the title *Toward a New Past: Dissenting Essays in American History*. The essays in this volume attempted to redress the imbalance in the study of history, focusing on many of the groups long ignored in the standard story of America and analyzing American history from a different angle of vision. Hot on the heels of Bernstein came a number of revisionist studies that broadened the telling of America's story. Black history, women's history, the history of Native Americans and of American ethnic groups, these were the new directions of historical inquiry by the early 1970s. They posed different questions, told a different story, and even demanded new methods of research.

The new historical information being produced was often called data and was subject to a new standard of analysis. The new urban history and the new labor history moved in an even more interdisciplinary direction, incorporating anthropology, literature, and sociological theory into their historical analyses. Cliometricians used economic theory and mathematical models aided by computers, the new history tool, to gather and evaluate enormous quantities of quantifiable data taken from public and private records—all this in order to write a more inclusive American history.

Clearly the new history emerging during the late 1960s was chipping away at many of the old assumptions, challenging perceptions of an American consensus that two generations had come to accept. These perceptions were represented in the popular culture by *Ozzie and Harriet*, *Father Knows Best*, and dozens of other family television shows and symbolized by terms like *melting pot* or *mainstream* that had worked their way into the language of social science and the humanities during the 1940s, 1950s, and early 1960s. They were based on notions that equal opportunity actually existed in America, that Americans shared an analysis of their society and held a common vision of the past and present. Many scholars of this era were consumed by the search for "the American national character" or "the American experience."

The new history strongly suggested that these terms and the supposition that supported them were incomplete and largely incorrect. It suggested that the history that often masqueraded as the American experience was in fact but one of a number of American experiences, each different and each colored by a different historical perspective. Both generals and privates go to war, but they often experience the conflict very differently. The generals' experience, however, is more likely to define the formal history passed down to later generations. Privates are often forced to suppress their historic memories and to accept a perspective bearing little resemblance to their own. Similarly, America's privates, more likely to be people of color, poor people, the non-elites of our society, often feel a disjunction between their lives and history— the distinction that many people make between the world of books or the "ivory tower" and "the real world." Social history seeks to bring the two worlds together without minimizing the importance of either.

The National Park Service has an important role to play in documenting a broad American history and making it available to the widest audience. The vast number of National Park historic sites and properties listed in the National Register of Historic Places incorporate an array of histories. A visit to any of these historic places can illuminate the lives of countless ordinary people. Most historic places in the National Register are recognized for their local significance and are especially suited for telling the grassroots story. The historic properties listed in this volume focus on various aspects of the African American experience. They provide a critical context not only for a fuller understanding of black history, but for a multifaceted and consequently more realistic look at all of America's past.

It is almost impossible to focus on the history of black people without calling conventional interpretations of America into question. Thus, a social history perspective is particularly suitable to the study of black history. An innovative approach to the selection and analyses of historic properties can also supply a rich spatial context that is both instructive and exciting. These developments encourage a process of inquiry well underway. During

W. E. B. Du Bois (1868–1963), Harvard-trained teacher, author, editor, scholar, Pan-Africanist. Photo courtesy of the Library of Congress (C. M. Battey).

the 1960s voices raised on behalf of African American history issued one of the earliest and strongest challenges to American historians. Although its immediate moral and political power sprang from the civil rights movement, the intellectual roots of African American history had been planted at least a century earlier. Long before the Civil War black Americans published histories of their American experiences, and they continued to do so throughout the 19th century. During the 20th century, Harvard-trained scholars like W. E. B. Du Bois and Carter G. Woodson, whose homes are listed in the National Register of Historic Places and included in this volume, were joined by Charles Wesley and other scholars in defining the emerging field of what was then called Negro history. Their hundreds of books and articles form the foundation of today's African American studies. By

the 1950s and 1960s when John Hope Franklin, Benjamin Quarles, Eric Foner, and others were making their substantial contributions, American scholarship was poised for dramatic change and black studies was a critical component.

On many majority white university campuses black students, present in significant numbers for the first time, demanded not only that the history of African American people be taught but that a curriculum of black studies be established to educate contemporary American society on the contributions of black people and the significance of race to the nation's development. This black studies movement, as it came to be called, was a direct outgrowth of the civil rights movement and the emerging militancy of the black power movement that was supplanting it in the early 1970s. Like the women's studies movement and the American Indian studies movements that followed, the black studies movement was highly political. Heated debates among African American students and scholars centered around who should take black studies courses, who should teach them, and ultimately what themes should define and structure the field.

African American history resists comfortable incorporation into the traditional American story. The black historical experience challenges the validity of that story and demands that it be altered significantly. Even more than social history generally, African American history forces us to confront the less admirable aspects of our national experience. The preservation and interpretation of historic places like Harpers Ferry National Historical Park are no simple proposition. From the vantage point of black history, the John Brown raid, the event for which the site is most widely known, was a heroic attempt to free slaves. Traditional history has most

THE GALLANT CHARGE OF THE FIFTY FOURTH MASSACHUSETTS (COLORED) REGIMENT.
On the Rebel works at Fort Wagner Morris Island near Charleston July 18th 1863 and death of Colonel Robt G. Shaw

Currier and Ives lithograph of the Fifty-fourth Massachusetts Regiment at Fort Wagner. The Fifty-fourth Massachusetts was one of the first black regiments raised for service to see battle in the Civil War. It is among the best-known black regiments, and its military contributions were featured in the film Glory. *Courtesy of the Library of Congress.*

often held Brown to be a madman, an evil murderer engaged in a diabolical plot to foment racial violence. Reconciling these opposing interpretations requires a commitment to serious scholarship and a great deal of sensitivity and courage, for viewing America through the racial lens is to risk potentially explosive controversy.

Thus initial efforts to "integrate" American history into texts and into the National Register have generally amounted to little more than the inclusion of a careful selection of those places and characters that have most closely conformed to traditional interpretations. Slaves who rose from the depths of bondage to national and international acclaim confirmed an uplifting story and could be fitted into the myth of American social mobility. It was not difficult to include a

few sentences on Booker T. Washington, former slave and famous black educator who favored a nonconfrontational approach to racial progress. His home could be included as a national historic site without undue controversy. Black war heroes, athletes, inventors, anyone who struggled to success could be included so long as questions about the nature and the reasons for their struggle were not closely considered. This was the brand of "contribution"-oriented African American history that was least challenging to the historical status quo. But this narrow focus on exceptional African Americans and this limited level of inquiry could not be maintained for long.

Debates in black studies paralleled those taking place among historians generally and questions raised by social history were also relevant to an understanding of African American history. Despite obvious commonalities, there have been a variety of African American histories distinguished by gender, class, region, and other specifics that shape individual and community experiences. It is just as misleading to attempt to understand black history by focusing exclusively on the experiences of significant black political, economic, and social leaders as it is to focus exclusively on the great men of American history. The life of Frederick Douglass is instructive, for it broadens our understanding of the inhumanities of slavery, the complexities of freedom, and the difficulties and the promise of interracial cooperation. Frederick Douglass's Cedar Hill home in Washington, D.C., is a part of the National Park System and listed here among the significant historic places, but his life cannot and should not be expected to stand for the total experience of millions of women and men in a variety of economic, political, and regional 19th-century settings.

For every Cedar Hill there are a hundred sites like Goodwill Plantation in South Carolina. Most of the almost 1,000 slaves who were held there during the Civil War never escaped slavery but were freed only after the surrender of the Confederacy. Without land and with few employment opportunities, even after the war, many remained on the plantation. Claiming their former place of bondage as their home, they became day laborers and sharecroppers. Theirs is not a narrative of triumph in the conventional sense, but it is a more common story of struggle and survival in the face of overwhelming odds. It is a story that speaks to the vast majority of human beings who have overcome adversity not through the high drama that traditional history often demands, but through common, ordi-

nary, everyday acts of cooperation and perseverance. These were people well worth remembering with lives worth celebrating. There are many such stories of ordinary people to be told through the testimony of the historic properties listed in this volume, which set an important new context for understanding our nation and the struggles of its people.

Great black man history, like great white man history, is limited; it reveals only part of the story. Mary Ann Shadd Cary, abolitionist, newspaper editor, women's rights advocate, and the first black woman to receive a law degree and to practice law in the United States, was also a mother and wife who found it necessary to live separately from her husband in order to pursue her profession. Her 19th-century experience has relevance for every 20th-century working woman in America. A visit to her historic house will add an important dimension to the African American story and to the story of American women.

No individual biography can stand alone but must be set in the context of the wider narrative of the black community. Many of the listings here encourage a broad community focus. Philadelphia's Mother Bethel AME Church and Boston's African Meetinghouse were two of the first black churches organized in America and among the most important meeting places for the community and for black and white abolitionists during the 19th century. Recognizing the importance of the black community story, scholars are increasingly finding that a social history approach to African American studies is needed for full comprehension of that area of study.

The historic places found here bear witness to the strength and endurance of ordinary people and to their relevance for our understanding of the complex

American experiences. For example, the Jackson Ward Historic District in Richmond, Virginia, was the home of that city's free black community in the decades before the Civil War. It was a vital social and economic center that became one of the most important African American business and professional hubs in the country. The fate of Jackson Ward during the 1950s is instructive, for it parallels that of many black urban communities of the period. Community life was severely disrupted when the district was bifurcated by the construction of a highway. Later, many of its buildings were razed, replaced by several public buildings. Yet the community was not totally destroyed and even today survives as an important black residential and business area. This is not only the saga of Jackson Ward, it is an experience of urban renewal and change familiar to many ethnic communities across the nation.

Other historic places also tell the story of cooperative struggle. The historic buildings that make up the Daufuskie Island Historic District in South Carolina document a thriving post-Civil War black community that arose on the site of antebellum slave plantations. Freedom, to a formerly enslaved people, meant the opportunity to establish institutions which would serve their collective needs. The district's churches and schools attest to the faith these people held in the promise of American society, if not for themselves then surely for their children. Yet these black Americans had not totally abandoned their African roots. Perhaps the island's isolation encouraged the maintenance of many old-world traditions exhibited in the community's Maryfield Cemetery in the form of traditional African grave decorations, such as household crockery and personal items that belonged to the deceased in this world and were thought to be of value to them in the next. This island, still isolated with but a tiny population today, represents an important part of America's African heritage.

These historic places can also expand our vision of better-known aspects of American history, and no figure is more symbolically American than the cowboy. The One-hundred-and-one Ranch in Ponca City, Oklahoma, is central to our understanding of the real American cowboy. Established in 1879 by George Washington Miller, the ranch sponsored a Wild West show featuring many black cowboys, among them Henry Clay, who taught Will Rogers to do rope tricks; trick rider George Hooker; and one of the best-known black cowboys of his day, Bill Pickett, the man who invented bulldogging. This historic ranch illuminates a little-known fact about one of our most enduring national symbols: throughout the 19th and early 20th centuries there were more cowboys of color—that is black, Indian, and Mexican cowboys—than there were white cowboys. On the historic cattle range, John Wayne was a minority.

It took a wide variety of people to make American history, and without knowledge of their experiences our vision of America's past is much too narrow. We too easily lose sight of the wide-ranging strength of the cultural interaction that produced the multicultural foundation of our nation. As historians grapple with the complexity of the American experience there are concerns about what some have called its cultural fragmentation. Arthur Schlesinger, in his *Disuniting of America: Reflections on a Multicultural Society*, warns that without a strong cultural center America is in danger of cultural disintegration. This concern currently animates

First Union African Baptist Church, Daufuskie Island Historic District, Beaufort County, South Carolina. Photo courtesy of South Carolina Department of Archives and History (Rebecca Starr).

the debate among scholars focusing on gender, ethnicity, or any of the various fields of study that have concerned historians intent on providing a more complete view of our national past. Recently the term multicultural has been applied to the effort to view the kaleidoscope of American histories. Some find the notion of historical variety disturbing, fearing that without a synthetic past America can have no unified and robust future. Yet a growing number of scholars are arguing

that it is America's diversity that makes for a stronger, more vital, more interesting culture. Moreover, an appreciation of our multifaceted history provides a usable, more recognizable past that holds relevance for the masses of Americans who presently do not consider themselves a part of American history.

The historic districts and properties listed herein provide a foundation for ordinary people to rediscover portions of the American past missing from much of

General store, offices, and bank of the One-hundred-and-one Ranch, near Ponca City, Kay County, Oklahoma. Photo courtesy of the National Park Service (Peavler and Associates).

the history taught in the educational institutions of our country. Even today, American history remains a prisoner of traditional assumptions about what is and what is not worthy of historic designation. Certainly a significant change has taken place over the last generation, and it will continue to take place, but only if the ordinary people of America take the telling of history into their own hands. Our American experiences are not all the same, but they are all significant and necessary to America's complete story. Moreover, their variety provides needed points of comparison that will allow us to judge not only the contrasting but also the common elements of an American experience. Only through an inclusive history can we reach a realistic understanding of what America has been, what it is, or what it ought to become.

Red Bird City Hall, Red Bird, Wagoner County, Oklahoma, listed as a component of the thematic group of Historic Local Government Buildings in Oklahoma's All-Black Towns. Photo courtesy of the Oklahoma Historical Society (Bryan Brown).

FROM PLACE TO PLACE: AFRICAN AMERICAN MIGRATION & HISTORIC SITES

James R. Grossman

FOR MUCH OF THE PAST two centuries, migration has symbolized to African Americans both the promise and the limitations of American opportunity. Slavery began as a forced migration; the dream of freedom would later inspire such migratory metaphors as the Underground Railroad and crossing the River Jordan. As slaves, many African Americans suffered forced migrations with the attendant heartbreaks of separation from family and community. As freed men and women they seized upon spatial mobility as one of the most meaningful manifestations of their newly won emancipation. Subsequently, black southerners sought to better their condition by moving within the rural south, to southern cities, and finally to northern cities and the West Coast in a frustrating quest for equality and opportunity.

Not only the actual paths and processes of migration, but also migration themes in African American culture are readily associated with particular places. In some cases these represent transfer points, whether for slaves being bought and sold, escapees following the North

Star to freedom, or 20th-century migrants seeking opportunity in industrial cities. Or, sites can recall men and women who worked as "conductors" on the Underground Railroad, went west during the California gold rush, participated in the building of "black towns," or played central roles in encouraging and facilitating movement north during the Great Migration.

African American migration begins with forced emigration from Africa. The numbers remain hazy, but recent estimates suggest that approximately 10 million Africans were brought by European traders to the Western Hemisphere; at least 2 million more died along the way. The areas now incorporated into the continental United States constituted a relatively minor market, importing perhaps six percent of the captured Africans, most of whom were destined instead for plantations in the West Indies or South America. In some cases, the West Indies served as a way station, its merchants buying human cargo from transatlantic traders and selling to the North American market, most of which lay in the southern

Harriet Tubman (c. 1821–1913), fugitive slave, abolitionist, nurse, spy, and social reformer. One of the most famous conductors of the Underground Railroad, she was widely known as the Moses of her people. Photo courtesy of the Library of Congress.

colonies of Maryland, Virginia, the Carolinas, and Georgia. The Danish colony of St. Thomas—now part of the Virgin Islands—was among the largest slave trading centers in the Caribbean, and the Charlotte Amalie Historic District provides a glimpse into the world of a port deeply enmeshed in human commerce.

The first significant internal migration of African Americans followed the American Revolution and the subsequent opening of the trans-Appalachian west to settlement by slaveholders. The enormous expansion of cotton cultivation in the early 19th century, combined with the closing of the foreign slave trade in 1808, soon transformed a forced migration dominated by planters carrying their own slaves westward to one increasingly characterized by the professional slave trader and the central slave market. The Old Slave Mart in Charleston, South Carolina, now a museum of African American history, was the site of regular slave auctions, advertised as far as New Orleans, Memphis, and Galveston. Although the Chesapeake remained the major source for the interstate slave trade, after 1830 North and South Carolina, Kentucky, Tennessee, Missouri, and eventually Georgia also became "exporters" of slaves. The plantations of Alabama, Mississippi, Louisiana, Florida, Arkansas, and Texas were worked largely by these early black "migrants" and their children.

The volume of the domestic slave trade remains uncertain, but it is likely that more than 1 million black southerners were forcibly relocated between 1790 and 1860. The firm of Franklin & Armfield, which bought and sold more human beings than any other slave trading enterprise within the United States, has also left the most visible traces. The firm's Alexandria, Virginia, headquarters, a National Historic Landmark (other offices were in Natchez, Mississippi, and New Orleans, Louisiana), still spans one-half block, although its slave pens were removed after the Civil War. At the peak of its activity in the 1830s, the firm shipped upward of 1,000 slaves annually from this site to markets in Louisiana and Mississippi. The fruits of Isaac Franklin's entrepreneurial spirit remain visible today near Gallatin, Tennessee, where his plantation, Fairvue, is now a designated National Historic Landmark.

Although most African Americans who moved from place to place before the Civil War did so by compulsion, others sought new homes either as escaped slaves or as participants in broader trends of migration toward the city or to the West. Runaways had plagued slaveowners as long as the system had existed, but until emancipation in the northern states after the revolution escapees tended to head to remote areas in hopes of remaining isolated from Anglo-American life. By the 19th century, however, the Ohio River represented a dividing line between slavery and freedom, and an extensive—though mainly informal—network developed in northern African American communities to help slaves who sought to defy the odds and make their way to freedom.

This "underground railroad" also included white abolitionists, such as Levi Coffin, whose home in Indiana was a popular way station, with possible hiding places that remain visible to modern tourists. The homes and barns of white abolitionists are more likely than those of less affluent African American activists to remain standing; moreover, for a century after the Civil War the predominantly white amateur and professional historians continued the abolitionist tradition of depicting heroic reformers coming to the aid of long-suffering escaped slaves. More commonly, runaways sought refuge in northern black communities, a process appreciated most tangibly through visits to 19th-century black churches in communities from Chicago, Detroit, and the District of Columbia to Indianapolis and Terre Haute in Indiana and Ithaca and Tarrytown in New York. Only a small minority of slaves, however, sought to escape. That the will was there, if not the opportunity, is suggested by the impact of the Civil War on black migration. Thousands of slaves fled toward the advancing army. Many slaveholders, recognizing that they risked losing their property, took their most valuable slaves in the opposite direction, toward the up-country in the eastern states or from the Deep South to Texas and Arkansas. This latter group of African Americans in many cases migrated back to their original homes after the war, searching for family from whom they had been separated. For a generation, newspapers across the South would contain advertisements from former slaves trying to locate their kin.

Former slaves continued to move away from plantations after the war ended. Although family reunification probably was the greatest impetus, for many the act of moving constituted a test of the meaning of emancipation. Much of the movement grew out of a search for favorable social, political, and economic conditions, especially the chance for "independence," which was closely associated with landownership. The flurry of migration generally involved short distances, often merely to the next plantation or a nearby town or city.

Southern cities offered former slaves the protection of the Freedmen's Bureau and Union Army, black institutions, political activity, freedmen's schools, and wages exceeding what most rural workers could earn. But under pressure from whites—and often faced with the prospect of starvation—many of the thousands who moved cityward soon returned to the plantations. Urban whites considered the black city dweller a threat to social order, and planters sought to stabilize and reassert dominance over their labor force. Vagrancy laws provided a temporary mechanism, and even after the legislative reforms during Reconstruction, the economic structure of the cities limited the urbanization of the black population. Few jobs outside the service sector were available to blacks, and black men especially found that survival was easier in the countryside.

Black southerners continued to migrate to cities, but in modest numbers. By 1910 less than one-fourth lived in communities larger than 2,500. In towns and cities from Wilson, North Carolina, to Montgomery, Alabama, and Waxahachie, Texas, National Register historic districts continue to provide glimpses into the black communities that did develop through a combination of enforced segregation and migration from the countryside. These districts are better able to suggest the life of the small black middle class than they do the life of the far more transient African American working class. Many people moved back and forth, mainly between farm and small town, following seasonal labor patterns. And most remained in the South as economic opportunities in the North remained scarce, and newspapers and even legislation proclaimed the fervent wish that African Americans remain a predominantly southern people.

Like other Americans in the late 19th century, African Americans looked to the West beyond the Mississippi for new opportunities. Before the Civil War a handful of black northerners had tried their hand at frontier farming or entrepreneurship, but lack of capital and racism generally limited these opportunities. Perhaps because of the unusually ethnically and racially diverse population it attracted, gold rush California appears to have constrained African Americans less than elsewhere. The Moses Rodgers House in Stockton, for example, honors a successful African American mining engineer—though one still unable to secure adequate capital. The Sugg House in Sonora documents the home life of one black pioneer, while reminding visitors of other methods by which African Americans could participate in the California boom: William Sugg was brought from North Carolina as a slave, occupying common frontier roles as a muleteer and bullwhacker along the trail.

On the whole, however, westward

migration was an alternative to few African Americans, and a limited alternative at that. Nearly 10,000 black Kentuckians and Tennesseans made their way to Kansas during the mid-1870s, many under the leadership of Benjamin "Pap" Singleton. An escaped slave, Singleton had returned home to Nashville after Emancipation. Responding to the frustrated ambitions of ex-slaves to become landowners, Singleton turned his mind to places outside the South and to the possibility of African Americans settling among themselves. The potential of homesteading and the formation of black towns was central to his enthusiasm for migration to Kansas. In 1877 and 1878, migrants from Lexington, Kentucky, brought the same impulse west and founded what remains the most notable black settlement—Nicodemus, Kansas. Surviving buildings, some dating back to the town's earlier years, now constitute a National Historic Landmark District.

Nicodemus, along with two towns founded by Singleton himself and four other black settlements, were doing well by the end of the 1870s, when a new stream of migration to Kansas emerged. As Reconstruction collapsed under the pressure of white violence, thousands of black southerners—especially in Mississippi and Louisiana—were caught up in "Kansas fever." But only 12,000 actually relocated, many never making it beyond St. Louis or even the east bank of the Mississippi. It was the same old story: too little capital, too little of the vaunted frontier hospitality and community feeling from white neighbors on the prairie.

If the Kansas Exodus left in its wake more frustration than hope, it hardly spelled the end of westward ventures based on the lure of open land and the promise of independence. More than 7,000 African Americans participated in the 1889 Oklahoma land rush, and over the next two decades, approximately 100,000 more followed. Expanding on what had been only a minor theme in the Kansas Exodus, many of these pioneers participated in the organization of towns established, developed, and inhabited exclusively by blacks. Strategies in the quest for land and both political and economic self-determination, black towns had proliferated in the South during Reconstruction. Of these earlier ventures, none lasted as long as Mound Bayou, Mississippi, where a home built in 1910 by town founder Isaiah T. Montgomery testifies to the town's spirit.

Two generations after the establishment of Mound Bayou in 1865, similar ventures emerged in Oklahoma. The largest of these was Boley, founded in 1903, where fourteen buildings in the original downtown business district still stand. Taft, Oklahoma, established the same year as Boley, offers the visitor only one early 20th-century structure, but it is the City Hall, the focus of not only government, but a variety of other community activities as well.

Promoters of black towns linked the ownership of property—particularly productive land—to the attainment and protection of full citizenship. Segregated communities represented not rejection of American identity, but what their historian has called "the promise of eventual entrance into the mainstream of American life complete with economic prosperity and full social and political rights for all." The approximately 25 black towns in Oklahoma established between 1891 and 1910 promised, in this sense, one solution to the eternal dilemma that W. E. B. Du Bois referred as the "twoness" of being both black and American.

But if Oklahoma's black towns offered economic and political autonomy unavail-

Fairvue, Gallatin, Sumner County, Tennessee. Photo courtesy of the National Register of Historic Places (Jack Boucher).

able anywhere else in the United States, these struggling communities also suffered disappointment, disillusion, and hardship. Economic difficulties plagued them from the beginning, and the transition to statehood in 1907 led to disfranchisement accompanied by racial violence. Even as African Americans were still streaming into Oklahoma during the early 20th century, despair had driven many earlier settlers to look outside the United States for refuge.

Although prospective emigrants considered other destinations, Africa occupied the focus of the most enduring, and perhaps quixotic, migration project involving black Americans. Before the Civil War, the American Colonization Society, comprising mainly philanthropic—if usually Negrophobic—whites, had transported 12,000 black colonists to Liberia. Although most black leaders opposed the society's efforts, considering colonization akin to deportation and

Liberia "a mere dependency of southern slaveholders," some accepted emigration as a legitimate alternative to the limited freedom available in the United States. During the half-century after the Civil War, each successive low point in American race relations—first the end of Reconstruction and later the passage of Jim Crow laws and the upsurge of lynchings during the 1890s—stimulated renewed interest in Liberia among black Americans. Not only was land available, but neither economic nor political structures required interaction with whites. Only 1,000 black southerners actually sailed to Liberia during the 20 years after 1890, but thousands others participated by buying shares in joint stock companies that promised passage across the Atlantic, joining emigration clubs, listening to speeches, or reading newspapers advocating emigration. But with the bulk of its appeal in the poorest areas of the rural Deep South, emigration to Africa remained financially impossible. Few historic places remain that recall the enthusiasm Liberia aroused at the turn of the century. The role of African Americans in Colonization Society activities is recalled by the birthplace of Lott Cary, an ex-slave who led a group of Virginia free blacks to Liberia in 1821 and later served a short term as governor of the colony.

If most black southerners either could not or did not wish to leave the South, they did not passively remain in one place awaiting salvation; like white Americans they were remarkably mobile during the half-century after the Civil War. Kansas and Liberia captured the imaginations of thousands of black southerners hungry for land and autonomy, but less exotic destinations within the South provided more practical outlets for dissatisfaction, restlessness, and even hope. Worn-out lands in the Carolinas and Georgia were abandoned for the Mississippi Delta and other areas in the gulf states. By the 1890s, one black southerner in twelve would cross state lines during the decade in search of the still unfulfilled promise of emancipation. Local moves remained even more frequent. In most cases, however, migrants found social and economic relations similar to what they had left behind.

The direction and historical impact of black migration shifted dramatically during World War I. Northern industrialists, previously reluctant to hire blacks when they could draw upon the continuing influx of white immigrants, turned their attention southward as immigration ceased and production orders began pouring in. Some sent recruiters into the South, but news about opportunities and conditions in the North more often traveled across a network within the black community. Black southerners read (or listened to readings of) northern black newspapers (especially Robert Abbott's

Chicago Defender) and letters from earlier migrants; they talked to railroad workers; they visited friends and relatives or attended fraternal conventions in northern cities. Observers and subsequent scholars offered various catalogs of economic and social factors that pushed migrants from the South and pulled them toward the North. Floods, boll weevil infestations, and credit contractions contributed to the urge to move to northern cities offering higher wages than those available to black southerners. Jim Crow, lynching, disfranchisement, and discrimination in the legal and educational systems contrasted with seemingly more equitable and flexible race relations in the North. Most migrants left because of a combination of motivations, which they often summarized as "bettering my condition." For the first time, however, thousands of black southerners looked to industrial work, rather than landownership in their hopes to enjoy the prerogatives of American citizenship.

Nearly one-half million black southerners headed north between 1916 and 1920, setting off a long-term shift that would leave only 53 percent of black Americans in the South by 1970, compared with 89 percent in 1910. Nearly all of these migrants went to cities, first in the Northeast and Midwest, and later in the West. Most followed the longitudinal routes of the major railroads, although by World War II, California was drawing thousands of migrants from Texas, Oklahoma, Arkansas, and Louisiana. At the same time, black southerners moved to southern cities, which by 1970 contained two-thirds of the region's black population. Even the massive urban unemployment of the Great Depression only moderately slowed the continuing flow northward, and movement accelerated to unprecedented levels during World War II and the following decades.

The Victory Sculpture, Chicago, Cook County, Illinois, listed as a component of the thematic group on the Black Metropolis. Photo courtesy of the Commission on Chicago Landmarks (Henry Reuel).

Since 1970 migration has leveled off, and there has been some evidence of a return to the South.

The Great Migration transformed both American urban and Afro-American society, as migrants adapted to urban life while retaining much of their southern and rural culture. It was not unusual for southern communities to reconstitute themselves and their institutions in northern cities. Frequent visiting between relatives in the South and North has contributed to this interchange between regional cultures, and the South is still "down home" to some northern black urbanites. Visits to historic sites that commemorate music history, whether the 18th and Vine area of Kansas City, the Jewell Building in Omaha, or the Chicago neighborhood once known as the Black Metropolis, not only locate an important component of the Great Migration, but also remind us of the dynamic relationship between South and North, rural and urban, in the shaping of African American cultural expression.

In this sense, all of the historic places mentioned in this essay evoke both the worlds that African Americans have created for themselves and the oppression that has limited their choices and their access to American institutions. If slave markets remind us of circumscription, the Underground Railroad documents the spirit that underlay escape and resistance. The entrepreneurial spirit embodied in black towns speaks through commercial structures, public buildings, and pioneer homes. Similarly, places commemorating the Great Migration testify to ambition and cultural dynamism in the face of limited opportunities. To visit these places is to gain a greater appreciation of this central tension in African American history, this recurring theme of adaptation and resistance to injustice and oppression.

THE AFRICAN AMERICAN LEGACY BENEATH OUR FEET

Theresa A. Singleton

AFRICAN AMERICAN archeology is a specialization within archeology that attempts to understand the diverse experiences of African Americans through the study of tangible material remains. It is concerned with addressing questions such as: How did African Americans create a culture that was different from European Americans? What role did African Americans play in shaping American life as a whole? How did the experience of enslavement, emancipation, poverty, and racism structure the lives of African Americans?

Archeologists became interested in African Americans during the revitalization of black heritage studies that took place in universities, museums, and historic preservation programs as a consequence of the 1960s civil rights movement. As a part of this renewed effort to examine African American life, archaeological investigations were launched in 1968 at the Kingsley Plantation, a property listed in the National Register that is now part of the Timucuan Ecological and Historic Preserve, located outside of Jacksonville, Florida. The goal of this exploratory project was to recover information on the daily lives of enslaved African Americans that had not been emphasized in the historical literature of slavery and to examine how an African heritage influenced the creation of African American culture.

Building upon these objectives, archeological studies of African Americans have developed along three directions: (1) studies that examine how an African heritage was integrated or reinterpreted in America; (2) studies of slavery and plantation life; (3) studies of African American communities in social contexts other than plantations.

Archeologists initially studied plantation slavery to recover artifactual evidence of an African heritage. No objects suggestive of African origins were found at the first sites excavated, and few have been identified from subsequent investigations. What the archeological record has provided are insights into practices that may have been influenced by an African heritage, such as the ways in which pottery was made and used to prepare foods and medicines, houses were constructed, or objects were used in healing, in divination, and other folk practices.

Pottery used for preparing, serving, and storing food is the most frequently recovered artifact presumably produced by African Americans. In the United States this pottery is known as colonoware—a low-fired, unglazed earthenware recovered primarily in South Carolina and Virginia. The use of this pottery suggests that African Americans prepared their food to suit their own tastes, perhaps incorporating aspects of traditional African cuisines. Thus, some African customs associated with preparing and serving food may have been maintained during enslavement. Slaves also used this pottery to prepare food for their masters. Consequently, the culinary techniques used by slaves influenced the local cuisine of southern whites as well.

Another area in which an African heritage appears to have influenced the material world of African Americans is in the construction of housing. Several written sources describe African-styled housing built by enslaved African Americans, but archeological excavations can provide detailed information as to size, materials, construction techniques, and floor plans. Excavations at two 18th-century plantations in South Carolina have uncovered the earliest archeological evidence to date of African-styled housing on a southern plantation. These quarters consisted of mud walls, presumably covered with thatch palmetto leaves, similar to thatched roof houses used even today in many parts of Africa.

Perhaps the most puzzling archeological finds are objects that provide clues about aspects of African American folk beliefs and practices. Through conjuring or divining, African Americans sought to understand and control the world around them. Although archeologists can only speculate about the original association of these artifacts, their presence in a diverse group of sites suggests that such activities were commonplace and were a source of strength as well as creativity for many African Americans.

Oral histories taken from former enslaved African Americans and other historical sources support that cowrie shells, pierced coins, and other small trinkets were used as charms or in conjuring and in divining. Pierced coins were tied on strings and worn around the ankle or neck for good luck and to prevent rheumatism. Cowries—a traditional form of currency in many parts of Africa—were used as decorative elements on clothes and ritual objects, in divination, and as gaming pieces; small brass charms known as *figas* that depict a clenched fist were believed to keep the witches away.

An understudied area of research in African American archeology is the investigation of industrial sites where black laborers once worked. Industrial sites have been excavated, but the African American contribution to these industries has been virtually unexplored. For example, future excavations of the alkaline-glazed stoneware factories, such as the National Register site of the Trapp and Chandler Pottery in South Carolina, could recover evidence of how African Americans influenced this industrial craft. At the Trapp and Chandler factory, and at other antebellum, alkaline-glazed factories, enslaved and free African Americans took part in every aspect of the pottery manufacture. They also appear to have exerted their influence on a distinctive category of forms—the face vessels. The images resemble African carvings and may be related to arts of the Kongo cultures in central Africa. The face jars were made in a variety of sizes and forms including jugs, pitchers, lidded jars, cups, and water carriers. Some very small face jars appear to have had no practical use, and may have served some symbolic or ritual purpose.[1]

Marked alkaline glazed sherds recovered from the Trapp and Chandler Pottery Site, Greenwood County, South Carolina. Photo courtesy of South Carolina Institute of Archeology and Anthropology (Gordon Brown).

Another objective for the archeological study of slavery has been to better document and understand how enslaved people survived the rigors of everyday life. Like written records, archeological data provide primary sources of information on slave life. Much of the historiography of slave living conditions has been drawn from provision records kept by slaveholders. These records, when available, contain information on slaveholder provisions—usually housing, clothing, blankets, and food allotments. Archeological findings can amplify the information contained in such records by supplying detailed information on housing, foodways, health care and hygiene, clothing, adornment, and recreational items. More significantly, however, the archeological record tends to preserve the remains of housewares, personal possessions, and food acquired through the slaves' own efforts. Such items are often absent from planters' records. Archeology can also shed light on how plantation resources were distributed, utilized, and recycled.

In the study of slave living conditions, archeological investigations frequently recover information on the quarters used to house enslaved people. These findings, together with architectural studies of extant slave dwellings, have documented temporal, regional, and other variations in slave quarters. Houses were generally of log or frame construction and occasionally brick, but along the southeastern coast, slave quarters were often built of a substance known as tabby, a crude concrete made of crushed shells, sand, and lime.

Tabby proved to be extremely durable and weather-resistant, and examples of such slave quarters survive at the National Register sites of Kingsley Plantation in Florida and Hamilton Plantation in Georgia. Slave quarters also varied in floor plans, and most antebellum houses were either single-family structures that housed one family unit or multiple-family structures that housed two or more family units. At the National Register site of Horton Grove in Durham, North Carolina, the enslaved community occupied a unique, multiple-family structure—a two-story quarter divided into four units. Similar two-story slave dwellings have been excavated at the Somerset Plantation in Creswell, North Carolina.

In addition to slavery, the archeological study of plantation life has examined the transformation from slavery to emancipation, which includes both newly formed communities of black landowners as well as the reorganization of slave-worked plantations into tenant plantations. Such studies permit comparisons between antebellum and postbellum living situations. For example, at Fish Haul, an archeological site in the National Register, the community of Mitchellville was created in 1862 as part of the Union army's Port Royal experiment settling former slaves on the South Carolina sea islands. The archeological assemblage at Mitchellville, compared with that of nearby slave sites, shows marked differences in artifacts and food remains. The inhabitants of Mitchellville purchased expensive items such as furniture, silver utensils, and fancy jewelry and consumed more domestic meat than did slaves. Emancipation for the freedmen and -women at Mitchellville undoubtedly meant greater access to material goods than they had experienced as slaves.[2]

Not all former slaves fared as well as the residents of Mitchellville. Many were forced onto lands that were barely arable and had to eke out a living the best way they could. In some cases, their material conditions were not much better than they had been under slavery. The freedmen and -women who founded the settlements in the listed historic district of High Point-Half Moon Bluff in Camden County, Georgia, were forced off the plantations where they once worked as slaves. They acquired squatters rights, built simple huts for shelter, and eventually became a community of landowners who could transfer land and properties to their descendants.

Beyond the southern plantation, archeologists have studied numerous African American sites. These investigations range from the individual homes of prominent individuals such as W. E. B. Du Bois to entire towns such as Allensworth, California, or Buxton, Iowa. The Buxton Historic Townsite, a National Register site, was the first extensive archeological study of a 20th-century town with a large black community. Excavations revealed that black residents of this short-lived coal-mining town established in 1900 and abandoned by 1926 had a rich material life and access to most conveniences of the day. Former residents interviewed for the study described Buxton as a "black utopia," a peaceful place to live with no racial problems.

In multicultural communities, archeologists attempt to understand the interaction between African Americans and other cultural groups. Sometimes this interaction produced a harmonious community, as at the Lighthouse Archeological Site—a National Register property that was once a settlement of African Americans, European Americans, and displaced Native Americans. Founded

Tabby slave cabins and garden at the Hamilton Plantation, St. Simons Island, Glynn County, Georgia. Photo courtesy of the Department of Natural Resources (James R. Lockhart).

in 1740 and abandoned by 1869, this village in northwestern Connecticut raised crops and made baskets to sell to nearby white settlers.

More often, however, the interaction between whites and blacks resulted in racial tensions. For example, at the Sandy Ground Historic Archeological District—an oystering community of blacks and whites established before the Civil War in Staten Island, New York—the equality African Americans had achieved in oystering and in the community began to collapse because of the capitalization of oystering and the rise of Jim Crow at the end of the 19th century. The archeological record at Sandy Ground suggests that black Sandy Grounders responded to both new competition in the labor market and increased racism by moving away from material expressions of ethnic identity to ones emphasizing their similarity to white households of comparable occupation and class. Perhaps they chose this strategy to cope more effectively with their changing world.[3]

A growing area of archeological research is the study of African American cemeteries. Although archeologists avoid excavating burials whenever possible because of legal, religious, and moral considerations, unmarked cemeteries are sometimes inadvertently uncovered or intentionally excavated when subject to land redevelopment. Studies of African American cemeteries have been conducted at sites in northern and southern, rural and urban contexts. The African Burying

Mold blown and machine made bottles recovered from the Sandy Ground Historic Archeological District, Richmond County, New York. Photo courtesy of the Department of Parks, Recreation and Historic Preservation (Bill Askins).

Ground, a National Historic Landmark site located in lower Manhattan, is the largest investigation to date of a slave cemetery. It was used during the 18th century, and more than 400 individuals were recovered from the excavations. Analysis of both the human remains and recovered artifacts is ongoing, and examination of the burials should provide information on the nutrition, disease, physical stress, and injury of this population, as well as on funerary practices.

More efforts have been directed toward the public interpretation of African American archeology than in many other areas of archeology. This focus is due primarily to the social and political pressures that gave rise to this research in the 1960s and to subsequent demands of black communities for a more inclusive public history. Museum exhibits

and historic site interpretation have been important vehicles for presenting this research to broad audiences. These exhibits include the Slave Quarter exhibition at Carter's Grove, a historic property owned and operated by the Colonial Williamsburg Foundation; the traveling exhibition "Before Freedom Came: African American Life in the Antebellum South," organized by the Museum of the Confederacy and recently revamped by the Smithsonian Institution Traveling Exhibition Service (SITES); "Buttons, Bottles, and Bones: Archeology and the Black Experience," sponsored by the Historic Annapolis Foundation and the Banneker-Douglass Museum; the University of Maryland's "African American Life in Annapolis, Maryland"; and "To Witness the Past: African American Archeology in Alexandria,

Uncovering archeological materials from Portici Plantation. Photo courtesy of the National Park Service, Manassas National Battlefield Park.

Virginia," recently exhibited at the Alexandria Archeology Museum.

In addition to these exhibits and many others in progress, several films have featured archeological research at African American sites, including the Public Broadcasting System's "Other People's Garbage," the British Broadcasting Corporation's "Digging for Slaves," and South Carolina Public Television's "Strength of These Arms: Black Labor-White Rice." There have also been numerous popular articles, radio programs, and public lectures. South Carolina held an archeology week with African American archeology as its theme.

Yet, despite the growing interest in African American archeology in both professional and public sectors, many significant aspects of African American life have received little or no archeological atten-

tion. For example, few sites associated with black soldiers have been studied. The Bullis Camp Site, a National Register site that served as a base camp for Lieutenant John L. Bullis and his Black-Seminole Indian scouts and the registered Indian Hot Springs sites associated with the Tenth Cavalry Buffalo Soldiers could reveal information on camp life among these regiments that is missing from other historical sources.

The study of slave flight and rebellion is another underexplored area of archeological research. Future investigations at the listed site of Fortsberg in the Virgin Islands could yield information on the slave rebellion launched there on November 23, 1733. Investigations of the 18th-century frontier outpost of Gracia Real Santa Teresa de Mose located just north of St. Augustine, Florida, represent the only major archeological study of a community of self-liberated (runaway) slaves in the United States. Fort Mose was occupied by former slaves who had escaped from plantations in South Carolina to Spanish Florida, where they were granted their freedom. In the Great Dismal Swamp of North Carolina and Virginia, a preliminary survey and testing were undertaken to locate sites once occupied by maroons (self-liberated slaves who established their own independent communities). The Great Dismal Swamp was home to one of the largest maroon communities in the United States.

The detailed information recovered through archeological research often complements written documents and oral histories. In other cases, archeology may be the only source of information about African American communities that are poorly documented or about sites that reflect little-known aspects of African American life. In either case, archeology is undeniably an essential tool for studying and preserving the African American heritage.

Notes

1. John M. Vlach, "International Encounters at the Crossroads of Clay: European, Asian, and African Influences on Edgefield Pottery," in *Crossroads of Clay: The Southern Alkaline-Glazed Tradition*, ed. Catherine W. Horne (Columbia, S.C.: McKissick Museums, 1990), p. 29.

2. Michael Trinkley, ed., "Indians and Freedmen: Occupation at the Fish Haul Site, Beaufort County, South Carolina," in *Research Manuscript Series 7* (Columbia, S.C.: South Carolina Institute of Archaeology and Anthropology, 1986), pp. 268–78, 310–11.

3. William V. Askins, "Sandy Ground: Historical Archeology of Class and Ethnicity in a Nineteenth-Century Community on Staten Island (New York)" (Ph.D. diss., City University of New York, 1988).

"LIFTING AS WE CLIMB": AFRICAN AMERICAN WOMEN AND SOCIAL ACTIVISM (1800–1920)

Carla L. Peterson

THE HISTORY OF African American women in the 19th century has most often been associated in the popular imagination with the system of slavery. Black women are seen to exist primarily within the plantation economy—as field hands, house slaves, or managers of domestic spaces in the slave quarters—and, less frequently, in urban slavery as domestic workers. In fact, from the very beginning of the 19th century and perhaps even earlier, black women fulfilled many other roles in many different geographic areas of the United States—the South, North, Midwest, and, increasingly after the Civil War, the West.

A cultural and social history of African Americans in the 19th century that takes into account the important contributions made by black women would need to underscore the great complexity of the roles they played. Throughout the period from approximately 1800 to 1920, black women were often obliged to adapt their activities to the larger movements of American political and social history—slavery, the politics of Reconstruction, the racial violence of the post-Reconstruction

period—as well as to decisions and actions of the black male leadership. Yet even during this period black women were able to develop their own forms of social activism within their communities. And in the decades after the Civil War, they started building national institutions of their own to address social issues of vital importance to their own welfare and that of all African Americans. In their fulfillment of their social and cultural goals as well as in our reconstruction of the activities of African American women, place—whether it be birthplace, home, schoolhouse, or site of community activism or entrepreneurship—becomes of tremendous importance, standing as a testament to their efforts and accomplishments. Many of these places are listed in the National Register of Historic Places.

At the beginning of the 19th century, the majority of black women were engaged in forms of unskilled or semiskilled labor, as field or household workers in the southern slave system and as domestics, laundresses, seamstresses, or keepers of boardinghouses under conditions of freedom in both the North and the South. Even at this early date women leaders were starting to emerge from within the black community. The black male leadership in urban centers such as Boston, New York, and Philadelphia had already begun the slow process of creating social institutions that would provide intellectual and political direction to all African Americans. Within the local communities, the most important of these institutions were benevolent and reform associations, antislavery organizations, and literary societies; on a broader national level, they were Masonic lodges, the church, the press, and the annual conventions. As arenas established to debate public civic issues and to determine public policy nationally, these latter organizations remained closed to black women, who were expected to confine their activities to the domestic spheres of home and community. Thus, antebellum black women formed their own local literary, benevolent, and antislavery associations. Throughout the 1830s female literary societies were created in Boston, New York, Philadelphia, and many other cities. In addition, benevolent societies whose members pledged to care for one another in times of need sprang up in a number of communities, large and small. For example, in 1842 black women in Washington, D.C., organized the Female Union Band Society. Its cemetery, listed in the National Register of Historic Places as part of the Mount Zion Cemetery, testifies to the important role played by mutual aid associations in the lives of antebellum black women.

Black women who sought to carry their social activism to a broader national level were obliged to do so primarily outside of institutional structures. Thus, rather than minister officially in the newly created "African" churches, women evangelists like Sojourner Truth, Jarena Lee,

and Zilpha Elaw labored as itinerant exhorters, traveling throughout the northeastern and mid-Atlantic states to preach the Gospel. In Boston Maria Stewart, a protégé of William Lloyd Garrison, was undoubtedly present at many events at the African Meetinghouse, a property recognized in the National Register. In 1832 she decided of her own accord to lecture publicly on issues of racial uplift to Boston's black community, becoming the first African American woman to speak to a "promiscuous assembly." To the extent that black women did work within national institutional networks, they most often did so through the antislavery organizations and activities of white women, such as the Anti-Slavery Conventions of American Women in 1837, 1838, and 1839, in which white women insisted that black women join their ranks. One such white abolitionist leader was Abbey Kelley whose home, Liberty Farm, a property listed in the National Register, served as a station on the Underground Railroad.

Education was perhaps the most important component of the African American community's racial uplift program in the antebellum period. Black women were able fully to participate in these educational efforts as teachers in the African Free schools located in all the major northern urban centers, as well as in Sunday schools affiliated with churches of different denominations. Sarah Mapps Douglass, for example, started the first female academy for black girls in Philadelphia in the 1830s and later headed the girls' preparatory department of the Philadelphia Institute for Colored Youth when it opened in 1853. At times, the work of these black women was supplemented by that of remarkable white women who dedicated their lives to the education of black youth. Particularly

Mount Zion Cemetery (which includes the Female Union Band Society Graveyard), Washington, D.C. Photo courtesy of the National Capital Planning Commission (William Edmund Barrett).

important were Prudence Crandall, whose Connecticut school for black girls was forced to close in 1834 after being attacked by the local population, and Myrtilla Miner, who started a teacher-training school for black girls, the Miner Normal School, in Washington, D.C., in 1851. These two schools, listed in the National Register, underscore the cooperative efforts of antebellum white and black women in the field of education.

During and after the Civil War, the development of black educational institutions in the South became a major concern of all African Americans. In the 1860s, and even well into the 20th century, their efforts were supported by federal, state, and private white philanthropy. For example, the Freedmen's Bureau provided a building for Henry Tupper's North Carolina school, which later changed its name to Shaw University and in 1873 established the Estey Seminary for women; Estey Hall is listed in the National Register. At the height of the Civil War, two white women funded by the Pennsylvania Freedmen's Relief Association, Laura Towne and Ellen Murray, settled on St. Helena Island in South Carolina and opened the Penn School, a property recognized in the National Register, where they were soon joined by Charlotte Forten, a young black teacher from Philadelphia. Finally, at the turn of the century, Anna T. Jeanes, a wealthy Philadelphia Quaker, established

Virginia Randolph Cottage, Glen Allen, Henrico County, Virginia. Photo courtesy of the National Park Service.

a fund to support teachers in black rural schools in the South. In 1908 Virginia Randolph became the first Jeanes teacher and worked at the Virginia Randolph Training School until her retirement in 1949. Now a museum, the Virginia Randolph Cottage has been designated a National Historic Landmark.

But African Americans did not need, nor did they wish, to rely on outside philanthropy to further their work in the field of education. Indeed, even while the Freedmen's Bureau was still in existence, black educators were seeking ways to establish schools that would operate independently of white control. Thus, the C.M.E. High School (later known as Lane College) was first established under the aegis of the Colored Methodist

Episcopal Church and was supervised by Bishop Lane's daughter; Charlotte Hawkins Brown's Palmer Memorial Institute was closely associated with the American Missionary Association. Both of these schools are recognized in the National Register.

These examples underscore the degree to which education was both a possible and a desirable profession for 19th-century black women. Indeed, in the postbellum period teaching became an increasingly important field for many women whose mission was to educate the newly emancipated slave population in the South. In adopting the teaching profession, these women were simply following a tradition started by their antebellum foremothers. Building upon the

Hampton-Tuskegee tradition that emphasized vocational training for black youth, many educators such as Charlotte Thorn, Mabel Dillingham, Elizabeth Evelyn Wright, and Mary Mcleod Bethune established "industrial schools"—the Calhoun Colored School, Vorhees Industrial School, and Daytona Normal and Industrial School for Negro Girls, all of which are listed in the National Register. In contrast, Lucy Addison's Harrison School in Roanoke, Virginia, sought to provide academic training to secondary school age black children.

In the 19th century a number of black women reached a degree of literacy that enabled them to become writers. None of them have achieved the fame accorded to Harriet Beecher Stowe, who wrote *Uncle Tom's Cabin* in the early 1850s from her home in New Brunswick, Maine, designated a National Historic Landmark. But, from the mid-1850s until her death in 1911, Frances Ellen Watkins Harper, who established residence in Philadelphia in the 1870s, published many volumes of poetry (*Poems on Miscellaneous Subjects*, 1854; *Sketches of Southern Life*, 1872; *Atlanta Offerings*, 1895; and others) and wrote several novels, notably *Iola Leroy* (1892), while also working and speaking on behalf of the abolitionist, women's rights, and temperance movements. A less public figure, Charlotte Forten Grimke wrote poems, travelogues, and art appreciations that were published in both the abolitionist and mainstream press of her time. Her best-known work was "Life on the Sea Islands," an account of her life on St. Helena Island, which appeared in the *Atlantic Monthly* in 1864. After her marriage to Francis Grimke in 1878, Grimke's Washington, D.C., home became a salon that attracted many members of the Washington elite. Both Harper's and Grimke's homes have been

Harriet Beecher Stowe (1811–96).
Courtesy of the Library of Congress.

designated National Historic Landmarks.

In the postbellum period, black women continued the antebellum tradition of community activism, organizing benevolent and reform associations as well as literary societies, many of which were housed in properties listed in the National Register. Toward the end of her life, Harriet Tubman, the "Moses of her people," established a Home for the Aged in New York State, while Rebecca Bullard opened the Mattie V. Lee Home to house young black working women in Charleston, West Virginia, in 1915. The Phillis Wheatley YMCA, a vital center providing a wide range of community services to the black population of Washington, D.C., was started in 1905 by a black women's literary group. Many

Charlotte Forten Grimke House, Washington D.C. Photo courtesy of the National Park Service (Walter Smalling, Jr.).

in the National Register, reflect such community efforts.

The most important development in the history of black women occurred at the end of the 19th century, when their leaders came together to create their own national organizations. The impetus underlying this movement was the increasing frustration of black women over the fact that neither the organizations of white women nor those of black men were capable of addressing the specific problems black women faced at the end of the century. After the Civil War, the women's suffrage movement, many of whose members had been active abolitionists in the antebellum period, had gradually come to place issues of gender above those of race, opposing the Fifteenth Amendment and forging an alliance with white southern women. Black men, in turn, had found themselves politically empowered by the franchise at the beginning of the 1870s and had begun to seek economic empowerment through the creation of all-male labor unions.

Thus, by the 1890s black women decided to come together to combat the virulent attacks by post-Reconstruction racists against their "virtue" and to resist their continued relegation to menial jobs despite their rise in educational and professional status. Women like Ida B. Wells-Barnett and Mary Church Terrell, whose homes have been designated National Historic Landmarks, worked in many different states of the union to organize black women's clubs designed to ameliorate the condition of black women, provide education to black children, and generally address the "Negro problem." These clubs were eventually grouped together in state federations and finally in 1896 into the National Association of Colored Women, whose motto was

of these benevolent associations sprang up in towns like Bastrop, Texas, where the local population's determination to ensure community stability and prosperity was enhanced by significant black home ownership at a time when relatively few blacks could afford to own their own homes. Bastrop's Kohler-McPhaul, Harriet and Charlie McNeil, Beverly and Lula Kerr, and Jennie Brooks Houses, all recognized

"Lifting As We Climb"; Mary Church Terrell was the association's first president. Several properties listed in the National Register bear witness to the importance of the club movement among black women: the Jefferson Franklin Jackson House in Montgomery, Alabama, which housed the City Federation of Colored Women and Youth Clubs, and the Minor House in Indianapolis, which served as the headquarters of the Indiana State Federation of Colored Women's Clubs.

Black women were able to take this crucial step toward institutional autonomy at the end of the 19th century because of the tremendous strides they had made, and would continue to make, both in the professions and in entrepreneurship. Such strides were facilitated by the Great Migration, through which black men and women congregated in increasing numbers in the cities of the North and Midwest. Although the majority of black women worked as unskilled laborers in domestic service or in factories, others were able to take advantage of the educational, professional, and commercial opportunities offered by these urban centers. If Mary Ann Shadd Cary had been the only black woman newspaper editor in the antebellum period, publishing the *Provincial Freeman* from Toronto, Canada, during the 1850s, she was joined in the postbellum period by women like Ida B. Wells-Barnett, editor of the *Memphis Free Press* in the early 1890s.

Shadd Cary was also one of the first black women to receive a law degree, graduating from Washington, D.C.'s Howard University Law School in 1883 and paving the way for other black women lawyers like Lena Smith from Minneapolis. Both these women's homes are properties recognized in the National Register. Still more significant perhaps was the entrance of black women into the medical profession. Even before 1870, black women were receiving degrees from medical colleges for women located in the major northeastern cities, and by the turn of the century they were practicing in states as far west as Colorado. The Justina Ford House in Denver, listed in the National Register, is indicative of the geographic expansion of black women's medical practice.

A final area in which black women sought to fulfill their aspirations toward economic autonomy was in the establishment of local businesses, many of whose buildings are properties listed in the National Register: the Elizabeth Harden Gilmore House in Charleston, West Virginia, which was once a funeral home; the Kilby Hotel in High Point, North Carolina; the Alston House in Columbia, South Carolina, which was used as a dry goods store; and the St. Luke Building and the Maggie Lena Walker House in Richmond, Virginia, which are associated with Maggie Walker, president of the St. Luke Penny Savings Bank. This trend toward entrepreneurship is perhaps best exemplified by the career of Madame C. J. Walker, who made a fortune in the field of black cosmetology and whose Walker Building in Indianapolis has been designated a National Historic Landmark. Villa Lewaro, her residence at Irvington-on-Hudson, also a National Historic Landmark, and her Harlem home became central meeting places for black intellectuals, artists, and entrepreneurs during the Harlem Renaissance.

It is women like Madame Walker who exemplify the important contributions made by African American women both to their communities and to American history generally. The places they lived and worked serve as living reminders of these important contributions.

*From the living room to the library room in the Evans-Tibbs House, Washington, D.C.
Photo courtesy of the D.C. Historic Preservation Division (Gary Griffith).*

FROM THE "MYSTIC YEARS" TO THE HARLEM RENAISSANCE: ART AND COMMUNITY IN AFRICAN AMERICA

A. Lynn Bolles

DURING THE "MYSTIC YEARS," as W. E. B. Du Bois called the era of Reconstruction, African American culture flourished. African Americans expressed this new freedom through their emancipated bodies, auditory and literary voices, kinetic expressions, and visual arts. Well into the 20th century, the artistry of black America took art in new directions and to new heights. African American artistic expressions commented on community events and situations in the society at large. Through their creativity, black artists became visionaries for a new future.

After the Civil War, African Americans migrated out of the South to the North and the West in search of hospitable locales. To new black neighborhoods and sections of town, black migrants brought southern-based social and cultural conventions. Because of legally enforced segregation in the South and the West and de facto segregation in the North, blacks found or created educa-

tional, employment, and business ownership opportunities by and for themselves in their own communities.

Many African American institutions and other locations where African American artists lived and worked are listed in the National Register of Historic Places. To demonstrate the contributions African Americans made to their communities and the society at large, owners of many of these sites have preserved or restored them, and some sites are open to the public. These places allow visitors to walk through the door of a building and experience the historic environment where black geniuses created beauty, style, and art forms that future generations can continue to admire and appreciate. The historic properties associated with African American artists and listed here form an important part of the black legacy in the United States.

The development of African American culture in new environments had two primary sources: traditions forged in slavery

Jubilee Hall at Fisk University, Nashville, Davidson County, Tennessee. Photo courtesy of the National Historic Landmarks Program (Horace J. Sheely).

and, after emancipation, the availability of formal education. Through opportunities ranging from elementary to postgraduate study in the humanities and the professions, African Americans finally could get the education that been denied them during slavery. These two forces kept the black performing arts and literary worlds at the forefront of artistic discovery.

Just after the Civil War, a number of institutions were founded that would affect generations of black musicians, writers, and visual artists. The music conservatories established at this time trained countless black musicians and vocalists. In addition to predominantly white institutions, black colleges, universities, and institutes, such as Lane College, Fisk and Howard Universities, and Bethune-Cookman College, trained African

American artists. One graduate of Howard University's music program was Lillian Evans Tibbs, pioneer opera diva and founder of the Negro National Opera. "Madame Evanti" (Tibbs's professional name) was popular in Europe, and her career flourished even when she returned home to a segregated United States. Her home in Washington, D.C., was a meeting place for the city's black intelligentsia. Listed in the National Register in 1986, it is now restored as a museum dedicated to her life and art.

Fisk University owes its very existence, in part, to its choir, the Jubilee Singers, which toured the country to raise funds to erect school buildings on its Nashville campus. Today Jubilee Hall, a designated National Historic Landmark, stands as a tribute to the choir's efforts.

Students at the Edwin M. Stanton School, Jacksonville, Duval County, Florida, c. 1882. James Weldon Johnson (1871–1938) is in the front row, far right. Photo courtesy of the Jacksonville Historic Landmarks Commission.

One direct result of the establishment of these educational institutions to train African Americans in the arts was the founding of the Peabody Fund in 1867. The Peabody Fund was the first philanthropic fund aimed at advancing black education. Later, John F. Slater (1892), the General Education Board (funded by John D. Rockefeller, 1902), and the Julius Rosenwald Fund (1912) took up the cause of supporting black institutions and creative artists. African American artists could work freely and diligently with the financial backing of these leading benefactors. Competition for funding from these sources was fierce, for life for black artists was a constant struggle to overcome the odds.

A segregated society meant that African Americans had to create their own institutions. One of these, the Edwin M. Stanton School in Jacksonville,

Florida, was established in 1868 as the first public school for African Americans in that city. The gifted writer James Weldon Johnson was a graduate of Stanton, and for a time the school's principal. Of equal importance to the black community of St. Louis, Missouri, was Sumner High School. Founded in 1875 after years of contention with whites, the institution became a source of pride and a symbol of achievement to the African American community it served. These schools, and numerous others listed in the National Register, are representative of the responsive environment where artists learned the basics of their craft and were encouraged to continue to develop those talents.

In addition to schools, African Americans organized civic and fraternal organizations and recreational areas in black communities to provide for their

Rear orchestra and mezzanine of the Lincoln Theater, Washington, D.C. Photo courtesy of the D.C. Government, Office of Business and Economic Development.

own social needs. During Reconstruction, religious life provided not only spiritual sustenance for African Americans, but it also enabled them to establish networks of community-based support and self-help organizations. One example of a black community where such organizations were formed is Freedman's Town, in Houston, Texas, the city's first settlement of freed slaves. Because of its pivotal role at the center of the city's black community development in the late 19th and early 20th centuries, the neighborhood is referred to as the "Mother Ward for Black Houston." The National Register historic district includes the area's black business district and residential neighborhood, the Antioch Missionary Baptist Church, the original Colored High School, and the black Carnegie Library.

Individual artists found their callings in religious settings as well. John William "Blind" Boone was an internationally renowned black concert pianist and composer at the turn of the century who began his career as a church musician. Overcoming the challenges of blindness and racism, Boone performed a range of music from classical to camp songs to popular compositions. Boone's numerous fundraising concerts benefited various black churches, schools, and other organizations.

Because the church was such an important black institution, sometimes a family's upward mobility within it afforded family members opportunities for high levels of achievement. In 1866 the Reverend Benjamin Tucker Tanner moved his family from Pittsburgh to Philadelphia, where he became a bishop of the African Methodist Episcopal Church. His son, Henry Ossawa Tanner, grew up in this middle-class religious environment and studied painting under Thomas Eakins at the Philadelphia Academy of Fine Arts. After living and teaching in the South, he became an expatriate in France, where he was the first black visual artist to win international recognition and one of the few American artists to receive the Legion of Honor of France. Henry Ossawa Tanner's house in Philadelphia is a National Historic Landmark.

Also connected with the urban middle-class black church was Harry T. Burleigh. For more than 40 years Burleigh was the soloist at St. George's Episcopal Church in Manhattan, a property listed in the National Register. Rising from poverty, Burleigh became an internationally acclaimed composer, arranger, and artist at the beginning of the 20th century. Burleigh's work elevated the Negro spiritual and helped it become accepted by classical musical artists.

The black church also gave rise to a new form of secular music called the blues. The blues is characterized by free solo expression of lyrics centered on individual pain and plight. Most blues compositions are based on a special musical structure. By the early 20th century, the predominant pattern contained three lines of four measures each. It consists of two phrases (A and B) arranged in the pattern AAB. The first two lines (A) describe the situation and restate it, emphasizing the importance of the situation, the seriousness or the possible consequences, or the necessity for solution. B is a contrasting phrase explaining the consequences or offering a solution to the problem. This now well-known 12-bar AAB pattern is found in such blues ballads as "Stagolee" and "Boll Weevil."

Known as country, rural, folk, or primitive blues, the earliest style of blues is characterized by spontaneity, improvisation, simple instrumental self-accompaniment, moans, and spoken commentary. Typically, the instrumental accompaniment extended the vocal statement to form a call and response pattern.

Although the blues developed in the rural South, blues musicians traveled to the urban, industrialized centers of the South, Midwest, and West as African Americans migrated in search of jobs and social justice. In the urban environment, the blues lost many of its folk characteristics and the lyrics changed. City blues described the problems of city life. W. C. Handy popularized the blues by publishing his world famous "St. Louis Blues" in 1914. The Beale Street Historic District in Memphis, a National Historic Landmark, includes the recording studio and the clubs where Handy made his style famous. It was, however, women blues singers who really claimed this art form as their own.

In *Blues People*, Leroi Jones (Amiri Baraka) states a number of reasons women became the best classic blues singers. Until the emergence of the black theater, women sang in churches or sang their personal sadness over washtubs. Minstrelsy and vaudeville not only gave women singers an arena to sing the very secular blues songs, but also helped to develop the concept of the professional black female entertainer. Minstrelsy was one of the most popular forms of entertainment in the United States between 1845 and 1900. Originally, minstrelsy consisted of white performers in blackface who performed crude characterizations of African Americans in plantation settings singing, dancing, and playing the fool. Black minstrel shows, featuring black performers in whiteface, did not appear until after the Civil War. As minstrel shows died out, blues singers, tap dancers, and comics soon replaced "darky" portrayals on the stage.

Gertrude Pridgett "Ma" Rainey was the pioneer "Mother of the Blues." She began her career as a blues singer with her husband, William "Pa" Rainey, in minstrel shows at the beginning of the century. After the duo disbanded, Ma continued touring the country, making her first recording in 1924. Of her 932 recordings, many were her own compositions. She often sang about the stormy relations between men and women, a taboo subject in late Victorian America. Her life and work are memorialized in her house in Columbus, Georgia, which was entered in the National Register in 1993. Ma Rainey was the principal teacher of Bessie Smith, who became perhaps the most famous classic blues singer.

The blues made way for another musical innovation from black America. Beginning in the 1890s, songwriters made increasing use of syncopation in new pieces called rags. Also based on syncopated rhythm, a new dance form called the Essence became the first popular dance for professionals from the African American tradition. For many years, rag music was found only in African American musical settings. But in 1898, largely in connection with a new dance—the Cakewalk—ragtime took America by storm. Ragtime differed from many other styles of African American music in that it

was intended to be played as written. Many of ragtime's originators, including Scott Joplin, were accomplished pianists who both read and notated their music. Often, a ragtime pianist was called "little professor" because of this ability to read music.

Scott Joplin wrote operas based on a combination of Midwestern folk songs and African American melodic rhythm traditions. Joplin was more than just a "little professor." When the ragtime craze swept the country, Scott Joplin was able to publish his syncopated music. His works include "Peacherine Rag" and "The Entertainer," later the theme for the movie *The Sting*. Most sources cite 1917, the year of Joplin's death, as the date by which ragtime had ended as a major musical style. Joplin's St. Louis home, a National Historic Landmark, houses a museum that testifies to his contribution to American music.

African American cultural traditions gave birth not only to blues and ragtime but also to jazz. Before World War I, the main center for jazz was New Orleans. The year 1917 marked a transition in American music: Scott Joplin's death marked the end of ragtime, and the closing of the country's largest club and red-light district in New Orleans dispersed many jazz performers to other cities, including Kansas City. Concentrated in the Kansas City's 18th and Vine Historic District, listed in the National Register in 1984, buildings such as the Mutual Musicians' Foundation Building, the Lincoln Building, and the Gem and New Rialto Theaters recall the city's jazz scene in the 1920s and 1930s. The Mutual Musicians' Foundation Building, a designated National Historic Landmark, is immortalized in the song "627 Stomp," one of the original boogie-woogie tunes by jazz greats Pete Johnson and Joe Turner. As the influence of Kansas City jazz waned in the late 1930s, some of the city's most prominent musicians, such as Charlie "Bird" Parker and Count Basie, left for Chicago and New York.

Associated with the culmination of New York's jazz scene in the 1940s, Minton's Playhouse in Harlem's Cecil Hotel is recognized in the National Register as a pivotal property fundamental to the transformation of jazz composition from a simple, melodic, and harmonic style to a distinctly sophisticated and virtuosic form. Minton's Playhouse is a tribute to jazz musicians and their experimental jam sessions, and to the foresight of its owner, Harry Minton, who played a significant role in integrating the musicians' union and improving the professional status of black musicians.

Jazz dance forms evolved with jazz music. According to Marshall and Jean Stearns's *Jazz Dance*, in the years between 1910 and 1920 America went dance mad. Dances such as the Turkey Trot, Ballin' the Jack, and Eagle Rock emerged as creations of African American professional dancers. Much of the music that accompanied these dances was also composed by black musicians. Pioneering composer Will Marion Cook used his classical musical training to help open Broadway to black entertainment. At the turn of the century, he teamed up with some of the great talents in the field, including entertainer Bert Williams. In 1911 Cook helped James Reese Europe organize the Clef Club's Syncopated Orchestra, a 125-member ensemble that performed at Carnegie Hall in 1912. In 1914 the orchestra signed a recording contract with Victor Record Company, signaling the industry's appreciation of black musicians and their music. As the dance craze swept America, the Clef Club profited from the fad and played all the best places for the cream of society.

Numerous halls and theaters featuring black entertainment throughout the first half of the 20th century are represented in the National Register. As minstrel shows died out, many theater circuits focused on productions featuring blues singers, bands, vaudeville acts, and other forms of entertainment. By the turn of the century hundreds of black theatrical troupes were traveling the country. The most famous agency booking these productions was the Theater Owners' Booking Agency (T.O.B.A.), or, as it was known in the trade, "Tough on Blacks." T.O.B.A. arranged tours, usually one-night stands, in the larger southern and midwestern cities.

The Lyric Theater in Miami, Florida, was built by a prominent black entrepreneur, Gedor Walker, in 1915. Starting in 1910, the Howard Theatre in Washington, D.C., was at the forefront of black entertainment, and it remained so for more than 50 years. Also located in the nation's capital is the Lincoln Theatre, which showed primarily first-run movies for black patrons. Situated in the U Street commercial corridor, Washington's Black Broadway, the Lincoln was the finest theater in the area. Its Colonnade Ballroom was a favorite venue for nationally known black performers such as Bessie Smith.

Another mecca for African American entertainment was the Apollo Theater in New York City. The Apollo was renowned as the proving ground for black entertainers because critical New York audiences expected excellence. In the Midwest, the Classic Theater in Dayton, Ohio, was that city's first black-owned and -operated theater. And in Georgia, the Liberty Theater in Columbus was one of a few houses built for African Americans and served as the principal black entertainment center for half a century. In all of these theaters, the great names of black dance, music, drama, and musical comedy provided entertainment for black audiences. Many of the theaters and ballrooms that flourished in the early and mid-20th century closed in the 1950s and 1960s after segregation was ended in public facilities. These buildings are important reminders of the rich cultural legacy engendered, in part, by segregation.

Harlem, which became a fashionable place for white New Yorkers to see black entertainment, also gave its name to one of the most celebrated American artistic and literary movements—the Harlem Renaissance. The Harlem Renaissance evolved from the migration of African Americans to New York in search of opportunities. Many college-educated African Americans came to New York during the period. They were what W. E. B. Du Bois called the "talented tenth" of the population, who were in a position to lead the race to new political and cultural heights. Black artists already in New York encouraged others to join them there, and the coming together of the vanguard in one location—Harlem—was unprecedented.

Historians date the beginning of the Harlem Renaissance era from various events: the arrival of James Weldon Johnson in Harlem in 1914; the move by the black congregation of St. James Presbyterian Church from West 51st Street to uptown; the return of the New York National Guard 15th Regiment, a black regiment, from overseas in 1919 and its triumphant march uptown; or the publication of seminal literary works. Whatever the chronological referent point, Harlem became a mecca for some of the greatest creative minds of the United States in the 20th century, and

these geniuses were African American.

In 1925, Alain Locke, the first black Rhodes scholar and professor of philosophy at Howard University, edited *The New Negro*, in which he writes of the importance of recognizing the African legacy in African American cultures. Locke beseeched African Americans not simply to dwell on race and social problems, but to set their own agenda and to seek their own solutions. The volume marked a critical moment in black intellectual thought, as people of the arts and letters were implored to reach beyond conventional intellectual boundaries.

Included in *The New Negro* is an early work of Zora Neale Hurston. Born in Eatonville, Florida, at the turn of the century, Hurston was an anthropologist and folklorist who became the most celebrated black woman writer of the Harlem Renaissance. She received a degree from Barnard College; studied under Franz Boas, the father of American anthropology at Columbia University; and was a recipient of Rosenwald and Guggenheim fellowships. A writer of short stories, essays, and scholarly works, her most successful book was *Their Eyes Were Watching God* (1937). The last house in which she lived and worked, located in Fort Pierce, Florida, is listed in the National Register.

Harlem was not only the locale, but also the subject, of some of the literature of this period by Claude McKay, James Weldon Johnson, and Langston Hughes. Hughes's poetry spoke of the sights and sounds of the city. "It was a period when local and visiting royalty were not at all uncommon in Harlem. And when the parties of A'Lelia Walker, a Negro heiress, were filled with guests whose names would turn any Nordic social climber green with envy. . . . It was the period when the Negro was in vogue." Harlem,

Florence Mills House (center), New York County, New York. Photo courtesy of the National Park Service (Walter Smalling, Jr.).

wrote Langston Hughes, "made a poet black and bid him sing."

Jamaican-born Claude McKay was one of the most outstanding prominent literary figures of the Harlem Renaissance. He is best known as the first black novelist to reach the best-seller list with his book *Home to Harlem* (1928) and for his autobiography *A Long Way from Home* (1937). James Weldon Johnson made notable contributions in writing, music, diplomacy, and public affairs. His song "Lift Every Voice and Sing" was adopted by the National Association for the Advancement of Colored People (NAACP) as the black national anthem. The Harlem residences of McKay, Johnson, and Hughes are all National Historic Landmarks.

The consummate renaissance man,

Paul Robeson also made Harlem his home during the era. Born in New Jersey, Robeson graduated as a Phi Beta Kappa and a football all-American from Rutgers. He attended Columbia University Law School and set up practice in 1922 in New York. It is, however, for his skills as a concert artist, stage and screen actor, athlete, scholar, and, later, humanitarian that Robeson is known. During the Harlem Renaissance, his friend dramatist Eugene O'Neill cast him in leading roles in *All God's Chillun Got Wings* and *Emperor Jones*. Robeson's residence is also a designated National Historic Landmark.

Another Harlem writer of the era was Arna Bontemps, whose poetry was published in *Crisis*, the journal of the NAACP, and who was awarded the magazine's Alexander Pushkin Poetry Prize in 1927.

Bontemps wrote and coedited works with other notable Harlem Renaissance figures, such as Langston Hughes. His early boyhood home in Alexandria, Louisiana, is in the National Register and has been restored as a museum.

Harlem's music and musicians created the city's jazz scene. The dilettantes of modernism from downtown came uptown to go "slumming"—that is, to enjoy the nightlife of Harlem. Big cabarets such as the Cotton Club, where Bill "Bojangles" Robinson danced, and dozens of other night spots brought sightseers to hear bands and to be titillated. There were battles of the bands at the Savoy Ballroom. It was the Cotton Club Orchestra, however, led by the young Edward Kennedy "Duke" Ellington, that drew the crowds of noisy and excited dancers and party goers. Considered one of America's greatest composers, Ellington began his tenure at the Cotton Club in 1927. He attained international stature as a musician, composer, and conductor, and his band was once called "probably the hottest band this side of the equator!"

Although music created by African Americans was becoming ever more popular, black dancers remained virtually unknown until 1921. J. Levbrie Hill had produced a show called *Darktown Follies* that opened in Washington, D.C., in 1911 and moved to the Lafayette Theater in Harlem a few years later. Although the show featured a variety of innovative dancing, it remained in relative obscurity. When showman Florenz Ziegfield purchased *Darktown Follies,* he made no mention of Hill, and he hired none of the black dancers who taught his chorus line the steps.

Black dancers emerged from obscurity, however, with the 1921 opening of the Broadway show *Shuffle Along*, a mon-

umental Harlem Renaissance event. Conceived, organized, and produced by four talented black men—Flournoy Miller, Aubrey Lyles, Noble Sissle, and Eubie Blake—*Shuffle Along* was the first major black musical to play white theaters from coast to coast, and it was a financial success for its creators. The show made stars of entertainer Florence Mills and a newcomer, Josephine Baker. Mills, whose New York house is a designated National Historic Landmark, became one of the most acclaimed entertainers of the era. In addition to getting star billing in *Shuffle Along*, she appeared in *Plantation Revue, From Dover Street to Dixie,* and *Blackbirds of 1926.*

During the 1920s the Black Bottom become a dance craze, second only to the Charleston. The dance-song composer of the Black Bottom was Perry Bradford, who wrote the instructions to the dance in the lyrics of the song of the same name in 1919. Four years after Bradford's dance-song appeared, the Charleston, based on the Black Bottom, reached a large public in the all-black show *Runnin' Wild*. With its beginnings as a black dance, the Charleston wiped out the distinction between popular dances to watch and dances to dance. Further, ballroom and tap dancing merged on the professional level as tap dancers created a tap Charleston.

Bill "Bojangles" Robinson was "discovered" with the 1927 opening of *Blackbirds of 1928*, an all-black revue. A veteran dancer in vaudeville and the T.O.B.A. circuit, Robinson was well known among black audiences for his Stair Dance. Robinson became the first black dancing star on Broadway in *Blackbirds of 1928*. Three years later, the second most important black musical on Broadway, *Brown Buddies*, opened. Showcasing Bill Robinson's talent, the show ran for 113 performances. The popularity of tap dancing was never higher.

On January 1, 1928, the Harmon Foundation held its first "Exhibit of Fine Arts Productions of American Negro Artists" at the International House near Columbia University and close to Harlem. The list of awardees from the 1929 and 1930 shows reads like a who's who of Harlem Renaissance African American visual artists. Given the success of the exhibitions and competitions, the Harmon Foundation continued as a primary supporter of black artists from the 1920s to the 1940s.

Postemancipation African American art forms reached their zenith during the Harlem Renaissance. The arts, as reflections of the cultures that produce them, tell their contemporary viewers something about themselves and serve as historical points of reference for succeeding generations. Starting during Reconstruction, black visual, performing, and literary artists reached out to a growing number of audiences, as newly won freedom allowed African Americans the right to travel and pursue new activities. Migrants from the "black belt" in the Deep South moved not only northward, but also westward, where segregation was all too familiar. Even though northern towns and cities afforded African Americans new opportunities, de facto segregation was the unwritten rule.

Taking these limits as challenges, African Americans created their own communities and institutions and celebrated their own arts. They welcomed and supported concerts, musical revues, literary works, and visual arts. Only when the black arts were viewed by integrated audiences did the popularity of these art forms move onto the larger social scene. More often than not, however, the original African American creators were not recognized when their arts "crossed over."

Look back on the successes of African American popular dance in the mainstream, particularly the Charleston and tap. We readily envision the Charleston, but it is not a sepia flapper that comes to mind. Likewise, although we know that the consummate tap dancer wore a top hat and tails, we remember the Euroamerican pupil who gained fame and fortune but not the black mentor. Clearly receiving acclaim for their creativity and originality, especially in the realm of popular culture, is a relatively recent development for African American artists.

An important goal, therefore, is to find a way to reclaim, appreciate, and celebrate the creative forces of black artists within black communities from Reconstruction through the Harlem Renaissance. An understanding of the cultural sources and the environments that spawned the outflow of black talent and creativity in the arts is necessary to fully appreciate the achievements of African Americans. Part of that understanding may be gleaned from physically entering the world of creativity by visiting the historic properties where the notes, the lyrics, the syncopation, the jokes, and the drama took shape in the mind and then came to life on the stage, on a recording, as a performance, in writing, or as a work of visual art. By preserving these historic properties as a living legacy, we honor the artists as they continue to inspire and elate future generations.

John Lewis making his speech at the March on Washington, August 28, 1963. Photo courtesy of the author.

THE POWER OF HISTORIC PLACES: MY CIVIL RIGHTS EXPERIENCES

Congressman John Lewis

I BELIEVE DEEPLY in the importance of historic preservation—so that we understand where we are going as a people, as a nation, and as a society. The United States is a diverse nation with a proud history. The nation's character comes not from one ethnic, racial, or national group; rather, it has resulted from the contributions of many groups. It is important that we all know our collective history—that the contributions of African Americans, Hispanics, Native Americans, Asian Americans are recognized and included. Historic preservation must represent every community.

I believe that we need to increase the number of properties commemorating African American history and culture and that we are already making great progress. By sharing the rich information about tangible historic properties collected in the National Register of Historic Places over nearly 30 years, efforts such as this book contribute meaningfully to our understanding of the diversity of our pasts by illustrating what has been accomplished thus far and by providing direction for the future.

The National Park Service is charged with preserving the nation's natural and cultural heritage. As the federal partner of the national historic preservation program with other federal agencies, state historic preservation offices, local governments, and the public, the park service leads the National Register program. In keeping with the American tradition of diversity, the National Park Service commemorates the history of African Americans through its numerous sites devoted to the preservation of black history. The National Park System preserves America's cultural heritage by maintaining the monuments, lands, and historic sites designated to honor events and persons important in American history. The more than 62,000 properties listed in the National Register convey the stories of countless Americans and their lives. The historic preservation and conservation work of the National Park Service is important because the nation's culture and history are crucial to the continued development of this country.

I remember clearly the inspiration I felt when, as a young boy, I learned about famous African Americans. While attending a segregated school during Negro History Week, my classmates and I were required to make scrapbooks that contained the pictures of famous African Americans such as Frederick Douglass, Harriet Tubman, Booker T. Washington, W. E. B. Du Bois, Joe Louis, and Ralph Bunche. These individuals inspired us to dream of a better life—a more just life. We felt a yearning for freedom and justice that stirred and beckoned us. Some of the properties in this book are connected with these famous, inspirational Americans; but, equally important, about half of the places herein are historically related to locally renowned people, social institutions, and businesses that exist as parts of living communities.

As a participant in the civil rights movement, I have spent a great deal of time telling others about the history of the movement. Its roots were humble. Even after the Civil War and the abolition of slavery, black citizens across the South continued to be deprived of their basic civil and political rights. The majority of black Americans found themselves exploited in feudal-like conditions and living in grinding poverty. With virtually no rights and second-class status as human beings, black southerners barely eked out a living between the late 19th century and the time of the civil rights movement.

My early family life was typical of many black southerners. I come from a small town in southeast Alabama called Troy. My parents were sharecroppers, and our family raised cotton, corn, chickens, hogs, and soybeans on a little farm. I had 10 brothers and sisters, and we spent much of our childhood doing back-breaking work in the hot sun and dusty fields.

Life in rural Alabama was hard and unforgiving. The signs of discrimination and segregation were everywhere. I saw signs that said White Men, Colored Men, White Women, Colored Women, White Waiting, and Colored Waiting. There

were two different worlds: a white world and a black world.

I have been particularly impressed with how many historic properties have been recognized in the National Register related to the history of the movement. In Montgomery, Alabama, just 50 miles from my hometown of Troy, Alabama, one can see the Dexter Avenue Baptist Church and its Pastorium. The church was the base from which Dr. Martin Luther King, Jr., organized the Montgomery bus boycott. Dr. King, then a young Baptist minister, attracted worldwide attention for the protest that launched his career as a civil rights leader.

Out of the churches, civic organizations, and colleges in the black community, the movement emerged. We must not lose sight of the fact that the movement was born from the conditions of the black community. Although it grew to embrace millions of Americans of all races, the style, the leadership, and the strategy of the movement were clearly African American in nature.

It was one of the great privileges of my life to witness, just 50 miles from my home in the heart of the Deep South, a bright ray of hope—the birth of the civil rights movement. I first heard about the civil rights movement when I was 15 years old and in the 10th grade. I heard and read about Dr. King, a son of the South, working for freedom and justice through nonviolence and love.

Dr. King was a product of southern black traditions and institutions. The son of a minister, Dr. King grew up in the black church and was nurtured in the heart of the black community. He had been educated in black Atlanta public schools and at Morehouse College, a historically black college founded in 1867 that is listed in the National Register as part of the Atlanta University Center

Historic District. This district is home to six institutions of higher learning: Atlanta University; Clark, Morehouse, Morris Brown, and Spelman Colleges; and the Interdenominational Theological Center. These schools have graduated scores of prominent African Americans, in addition to Dr. King.

In Atlanta, historic sites honoring African American history are numerous. The Martin Luther King, Jr., National Historic Site (NHS) and Preservation District is one of the most frequently visited units of the national park system in the country, with nearly 3 million visitors annually. Within an area of several blocks are the birthplace, church, and grave site of Dr. King. The King NHS overlaps with the Sweet Auburn Historic District, a flourishing black commercial district surrounding Auburn Avenue, which was described as the "richest Negro street in the world" during much of the early part of the century. Sweet Auburn anchored Atlanta's black middle class, providing a source of jobs and a home to scores of black-owned businesses and social institutions, including the nation's first black daily newspaper, the *Atlanta Daily World;* the headquarters of the Southern Christian Leadership Conference and the Atlanta Urban League; the Butler Street YMCA; the Atlantic Life Insurance Company; and the Royal Theater of the Auditorium Building and the Royal Peacock, where Ma Rainey, Bessie Smith, Nat "King" Cole, and Cab Calloway, among others, performed.

In 1961, I went to Washington for the first time, as a 21-year-old civil rights activist. I journeyed there to begin the Freedom Rides, a series of protests in which interracial groups rode buses to test compliance with desegregation laws on public transportation. Two years later, I became chair of the Student Nonviolent Coordinating Committee (SNCC), and I returned to Washington to help organize the March on Washington. The event culminated in a rally at the Lincoln Memorial at which Dr. King delivered his famous "I Have a Dream" speech. Through the years, the Lincoln Memorial has been a favored site for civil rights rallies because of its symbolic importance in the civil rights movement. The Lincoln Memorial is listed in the National Register and is a component of the National Mall, a unit of the national park system.

I had gotten my start in the movement as a student helping to lead sit-in protests in Nashville, Tennessee, where I had been attending a Baptist seminary. I later transferred to Fisk University, also in Nashville. Chartered in 1867, Fisk University was founded by the American Missionary Association (AMA) and the Western Freedmen's Aid Commission and is historically significant for its role as one of the foremost black universities in the country. Of the many religious organizations that supported black education after the Civil War, the AMA established more schools, staffed them with better teachers, and provided them with more lasting support than any other organization. The importance of Jubilee Hall, the Carnegie Library, and the buildings of the Fisk University Historic District is underscored by their listing in the National Register.

SNCC was formed in 1960 as a result of the student sit-ins in cities across the South. The National Register recognizes the Downtown Greensboro Historic District, in Greensboro, North Carolina, which features the Woolworth's department store where the widely publicized lunch counter sit-in occurred. As the site of that 1960 sit-in, which was the impetus for similar protests across the South,

The March on Washington near the Lincoln Memorial was characterized as the greatest peacetime assembly in U.S. history. Photo courtesy of the National Park Service History Collection.

John Lewis being arrested after a sit-in demonstration in Nashville, Tennessee, in the early 1960s. Photo courtesy of the author.

Civil rights leaders resting during the march from Selma to Montgomery, Alabama, March 7, 1965. Left to right: John Lewis, Ralph Abernathy, Martin Luther King, Jr., two unidentified people, and Andrew Young (front with back turned). Photo courtesy of the author.

the Woolworth's building is a significant landmark of the civil rights movement. The sit-in participants were students enrolled at the nearby Agricultural and Technical College of North Carolina (now North Carolina Agricultural and Technical State University), North Carolina's first black land grant university. The college's five oldest surviving buildings are also listed in the National Register.

The preservation of historic properties relating to the civil rights movement is an ongoing process. In 1989, I introduced legislation in the Congress to study the road from Selma to Montgomery, Alabama, for designation as a national historic trail. The road from Selma to Montgomery was the symbolic last leg in the journey to the Voting Rights Act of 1965, which removed the last hurdle to the legal right for all Americans to vote. Designation of this trail is especially important to me because I was honored to lead the march across the Edmund Pettus Bridge, in Selma, Alabama, on Sunday, March 7, 1965, in an effort to dramatize the need for voting rights legislation. Approximately 525 people attempted to march the 54 miles from Selma to Montgomery, but when we reached the apex of the Pettus Bridge in Selma, we were attacked by police dogs and state troopers. Scenes from what became known as Bloody Sunday sent shock waves around the world, raised the nation's consciousness, and convinced political leaders that the time had come for voting rights legislation.

In response to events culminating in the Selma to Montgomery march, President Lyndon B. Johnson urged Congress to pass the Voting Rights Act of 1965 with the following words:

> I speak tonight for the dignity of man and the destiny of democracy. . . . At times history and fate meet at a single point and a single place to shape a turning point in man's unending search for freedom. . . . So it was at Lexington and Concord. So it was a century ago at Appomattox. So it was last week in Selma, Alabama.

Presently two Selma churches, First Baptist Church and Brown Chapel African Methodist Episcopal Church, are listed in the National Register for their associations with the renowned Selma to Montgomery march. Imagine the powerful symbolism of the 50 miles of the highway between Selma and Montgomery associated with the march embodied in a national historic trail.

In recent years the National Park Service has extended its arms to embrace minority representation in its own programs and permanent sites, and such representation will continue to be important for the National Park Service as a major institution in American society. By the year 2000, for every non-Hispanic white child born, a black, Hispanic, or Asian child will be born in this nation. Our National Park System and the historic properties listed in the National Register of Historic Places must increasingly reflect this diversity as demographic changes alter American society. Our history is a precious resource. We must do all that we can to preserve it and to ensure its accuracy by including the history of all Americans. By experiencing historic places and seeing them with our own eyes, we keep alive our rich and varied history. A better understanding of the full range of American history embodied in these buildings, sites, structures, districts, and objects has the power to inspire and uplift present and future generations of Americans.

Excerpts of this essay were previously published in John Lewis, "Keeping Our African-American Heritage Alive," *Historic Preservation Forum* 7 (January/February 1993): 27.

THE PRESERVATION MOVEMENT REDISCOVERS AMERICA

Elizabeth A. Lyon and Frederick C. Williamson

LONG-HELD VIEWS of American history are changing to include persons, places, and events previously overlooked. When the National Historic Sites Act was passed in the 1930s, Americans had little doubt about what constituted the heritage of a nation and its people. In the minds of most, it was the magnificent edifices and places associated with monumental events of war and peace and the great personages that had shaped the direction of the nation since its beginning. That the predominant European groups that settled particular sections of the country were to be honored for their contributions to our heritage was an accepted principle.

However, from the passage of time and the experience gained in the administration of the National Historic Preservation Act of 1966 by the National Park Service (NPS) and the state historic preservation officers at the state and local level, a new perspective has evolved on what constitutes the heritage of this nation. We have begun to recognize that large and diverse ethnic and racial groups, plus the indigenous Native American population, have left a rich and varied legacy of accomplishments and historic places that cannot be ignored.

The preservation movement has started to respond to this evolving historical perspective. African American heritage, along with the legacy of other ethnic and racial groups that make up America, is increasingly coming to the forefront of preservation activity nationwide. It was early in the 1970s that some in the national preservation movement first began to recognize gaps in the documentation of our legacy. History texts had generally overlooked the significant presence, before the nation's beginning, of African Americans and their contributions to the nation's development, other than references to the unseemly manner of their passage to America and their influence on the American Civil War. Dependable archival material that could document this history was unavailable from conventional record-keeping sources. The omissions and indifference reflected the pervasive de facto and de jure patterns of segregation of more than three centuries that divided America into two separate communities—one black and the other white.

Then, as a consequence of the pressures rising from the civil rights struggles of the 1950s and 1960s and the questions from a people thirsty for knowledge of their own racial heritage, Afro-American studies programs began to appear in many colleges and universities. These black studies programs fostered research and more inclusive interpretations of American history. Meanwhile, the history profession, which at one time considered local history to be less worthy of research attention than politics, war, and great men, developed a new and broader focus. Architectural history, too, began to give scholarly attention to everyday buildings, the vernacular architecture and cultural landscapes that provide the character of our communities. Most important, private black heritage societies and a growing number of African American museums began to explore new sources of information and use new techniques, such as oral history, to make up for deficiencies in conventional recorded history. These groups began combing their neighborhoods, churches, fraternal organizations, and family records to develop archival and oral history records that could provide a basis for a more complete understanding of the nation's history. They developed exhibits and promoted black heritage trails to the places associated with African American history in their communities.

During the 1970s and early 1980s, there were sporadic efforts to use historic preservation strategies both to fill in the gaps in our view of history and to improve the quality of community life. Spurred by the Bicentennial, the NPS contracted with an African American consulting group to identify potential National Historic Landmarks associated with black history. Working with the Rhode Island State Historic Preservation Office, for example, the consultants rec-

ommended the site of the August 1778 Battle of Rhode Island in the town of Portsmouth, where the First Rhode Island regiment, all black except for its officers, fought valiantly as part of the American revolutionary forces. Other sites, such as the Martin Luther King, Jr., Historic District in Atlanta, were also designated as landmarks at this time. The NPS then added National Historic Sites associated with prominent black historical figures like George Washington Carver and Booker T. Washington, and later Frederick Douglass and Maggie Walker, to its system. The Kansas Historical Society in 1977 published a report, "Black Historic Sites: A Beginning Point." Neighborhood housing programs in Cincinnati and Pittsburgh, encouraged and assisted by the National Trust for Historic Preservation (NTHP), preserved historic neighborhoods. In Brooklyn, the Society for the Preservation of Weeksville and Bedford-Stuyvesant History set out to preserve the remains of a 19th-century African American community in the midst of an urban renewal project. The number of local African American museums increased and state historic preservation officers (SHPOs) nominated larger numbers of African American properties to the National Register.

By the late 1980s, the black community's surge of interest in the relationship of its patrimony to the preservation movement motivated both the National Trust, representing the private nonprofit sector, and the National Conference of State Historic Preservation Officers (NCSHPO), representing public programs in the states, as well as the NPS, to step up efforts to involve a more diverse constituency in historic preservation. Through various meetings and committees convened over the decade to address this issue, it had become clear that extra-

Students at the Frederick Douglass National Historic Site, Washington, D.C. Photo courtesy of the National Park Service History Collection.

ordinary efforts were needed if the full sweep of the nation's history was to be preserved. The National Trust, as the private, nonprofit organization chartered by Congress to encourage public participation in the preservation of historically significant sites and buildings, has been actively engaged in funding and encouraging African American preservation activities, especially in inner-city neighborhoods. In addition to several special meetings to address issues of cultural diversity, recent national conferences of the National Trust have brought attention to the issues, projects, and success stories of African American historic preservation efforts and have increased the diversity of conference participation through a scholarship program. Through these opportunities for learning and interaction, statewide and local organizations, such as the Indiana Landmarks Foundation, have been encouraged to set up special projects to involve African Americans. The Trust also published an Information Series Booklet[1] and a special edition of *Historic Preservation Forum* to go along with the 1992 conference theme of Cultural Diversity in Historic Preservation.

The National Park Service, as administrator of the federal government's historic preservation program, has undertaken several special initiatives, such as this book, that address needs of particular ethnic groups. The Historically Black Colleges and Universities project, underway for several years in the Department of the Interior, is an example. This initiative provides technical assistance in defining rehabilitation needs for significant campus buildings and funding for work on these buildings to selected colleges. Additional NPS-sponsored initiatives and activities targeted at Historically Black Colleges and Universities have included student internships, an architectural measured drawings course, historic preservation and planning curriculum development, and a variety of training opportunities in professional cultural resources management.

The National Conference of State Historic Preservation Officers has also addressed the issues of cultural diversity. As administrators of the national program in the states, SHPOs are responsible for identifying, evaluating, and preserving the broad patterns of the nation's history as it is found in the historic properties of their

Virginia Hall at Hampton Institute, Hampton, Virginia, was identified as a potential rehabilitation candidate in the Historically Black Colleges and Universities Project. Photo courtesy of the National Park Service.

states. It is, therefore, critical that they and their staffs be able to understand the fullest range of that history. In 1988, concerned about the issues and questions being raised in various preservation forums and confronted with increasing requests for cultural preservation and broader recognition, the NCSHPO established a Task Force on Minority Participation in State Programs, chaired by this article's authors, to undertake a two-year study of the issues. The task force recognized that several SHPOs had begun initiatives to increase minority representation in their programs but knew that these special actions were not widely publicized. Task force members realized that programs in the states needed assistance, possibly based on the development of networks of support. They were convinced that concentrated efforts were needed to bring groups outside the traditional preservation network together with the public and private programs that could assist their community revitalization efforts.

One of the initial ventures of the NCSHPO task force, supported by the National Trust through a Critical Issues Fund grant, was a plenary session during the 1989 annual meeting of the NCSHPO. There a panel of SHPOs, African Americans, and other ethnic representatives active in state and local preservation presented some of the issues they had encountered to a national audience of preservation professionals and interested citizens. The task force continued to sponsor workshops and special sessions at national meetings to educate professionals and address perceived barriers. Its final report to the NCSHPO included recommendations for minority professional development in the preservation field as well as the results of a survey of minority program activity in states that identified African Americans and Native Americans as the predominant cultural groups with whom the states were working.[2]

The special initiatives of the National Trust, NPS, and NCSHPO to assess the status of diversity in the historic preservation movement and to encourage broader participation from African Americans have brought to light a remarkable variety of current activity. Recent endeavors include cultural resource surveys, National Register nominations, contextual and planning studies, building rehabilitation projects, and community development projects. Museums seem to have been the first response to the impetus to make America's black heritage visible. Black heritage museums across the country display the full panorama of this history, from the 1619 landing of 20 Africans in Virginia as indentured servants to the civil rights movement in Montgomery, Birmingham, and elsewhere. More important, the built environment is offering an ever expanding view of the life of African Americans, with such buildings as the Prudence Crandall House, New England's first female black academy, in Canterbury, Connecticut; the Madame C. J. Walker Building in Indianapolis, Indiana, the site of a successful hair products company; and the Great Plains Black Museum in Omaha, Nebraska. Many, like William F. Drake Hall at Alabama A. & M University, an archives and museum, or the Smith-Robertson Museum and Cultural Center in a former school building in Jackson, Mississippi, are located in restored historic buildings. Several are in historic churches, like the African meetinghouses in Boston and Nantucket and the South Dakota Black History Museum in an early African Methodist Episcopal church. Recent examples that seek to display history and culture and interpret historic buildings include the Beach Institute African American Cultural Center in a 1869 missionary school building in Savannah, Georgia, and the Delta Cultural Center in the restored 1915 Missouri Pacific depot in Helena, Arkansas, where the culture of the Delta region, including blues music, agriculture, the Civil War experience, and the African American experience, is exhibited.

In many states, the interpretation of existing historic sites is being revised and amplified to include all of the ethnic and cultural groups associated with the site's history. Williamsburg, for example, now includes black history and slave culture in its interpretive program, as do many plantation sites in southern states. Somerset Place, a state historic site in North Carolina has attracted national attention for its homecoming celebrations, which bring together descendants of the slaves who lived and worked there. In addition, a growing number of tour guides serve the increasing interest in African American places. Alabama, Georgia, and Ohio, in joint ventures between state offices of historic preservation and tourism, have produced tour brochures. The National Trust has included black history promotions in its Heritage Tourism initiative. The Pepperbird Foundation in Hampton, Virginia, a nonprofit organization for multicultural heritage, produces heritage brochures for several southern states. Michigan published "Pathways to Michigan's Black History" to point the way to African American historic places in that state. Florida's state historic preservation office recently published a statewide guide to black heritage sites that presents historical narratives containing little-known information about the long history of African Americans in that state. In many states one can find a growing number of local black history tours and trails, such as Rhode Island's Freedom Trail and the Negro history trails in Boston and Savannah. The number of special conferences, such as Pennsylvania's annual black history conference, is growing. Local and statewide heritage education programs

The Webster Telephone Exchange Building in Omaha, Douglas County, Nebraska, now houses the Great Plains Black Museum. Photo courtesy of the Nebraska State Historical Society (D. Murphy).

increasingly include African American history components.

The expansion of interest in places where African Americans lived and worked would not be possible without the data and research produced by the preservation movement. As this book illustrates, most of the states have recognized significant African American buildings and neighborhoods through National Register listings and Determinations of Eligibility. The federal project review process occurs when a federally financed or licensed project threatens older areas where African Americans lived, such as rural farms and plantations or urban neighborhoods. Because SHPOs must consider a variety of resources as they assess the effects on the built environment through this review process, they have begun to see a broader picture of that environment. As questions are raised about traditional survey and research methodologies, SHPOs are encouraging and supporting surveys and new types of historical context studies designed to find and evaluate African American resources. In fact, there seems to be an explosion of special black heritage surveys. They are both statewide, as in California, Indiana, Ohio, New York, and Washington, and regional and local, as in Allegheny County, Pennsylvania; Okmulgee County, Oklahoma; North Omaha, Nebraska; Minneapolis, St.Paul, and Duluth, Minnesota; Little Rock, Arkansas; Thomasville, Georgia; and Newport, Rhode Island. Recent special studies include "Invisible Hands," a study and traveling exhibit produced by a local preservation organization in Macon, Georgia, that identifies the work of more than 6,000 African American craftsmen, designers, and builders who contributed to the building of the city. The *Florida Black Heritage Trail* is not just a traveler's guidebook but a compilation and analysis of new historical information. The project's impetus was the discovery of an archeological site near St. Augustine, Fort Mose, established in 1738 as the first legally sanctioned free black community in what was to become the United States. Posters featuring Alabama's historically black college campuses and a calendar of the historic black churches of the state were possible because of surveys and National Register nominations encouraged by the Alabama Black Heritage Council. *African-American Historic Places: Buildings, People and Culture,* a resource guide from a Georgia project of statewide workshops, focused attention on the cultural associations of historic properties and the people they represent. Archeological investigation, initiated in response to a federal construction project at Foley Square in New York City, has brought to light the earliest history of the city in a large, long-forgotten African American burial ground.

Making communities aware of this history through surveys and National Register nominations, tour guides, heritage education exhibits, and museums makes it more likely that the contributions of all citizens will be considered in planning and development. Buildings that represent black history are being rehabilitated and adaptively reused in many communities. For example, the Murphy-Collins House in Tuscaloosa, Alabama, the home of one of the first licensed black embalmers in Alabama, now serves as the office of the Tuscaloosa County Preservation Society and a museum of African American heritage. A home in Birmingham, Alabama, built to house orphaned and elderly African Americans now serves as a nursery for underprivileged children. A 1935 gymnasium in a black school district in Nevada County, Arkansas, now serves as a community and social center. A restored 1850s cottage in Natchez, Mississippi, contains a gallery and shop featuring African American arts and crafts. Historic residential buildings are providing affordable housing. Shotgun houses in Macon and Augusta, Georgia, and Shreveport and New Orleans, Louisiana, have been rehabilitated using tax incentives and creative financing by local governments and non-profit housing and preservation organizations assisted by their state historic preservation offices. The contributions that historic preservation can make to neighborhoods was recognized early in places like Cincinnati and Pittsburgh. Now, activity can be seen from New Orleans's Lower Garden District to Chicago's Black Metropolis and from Baltimore and Washington, D.C., Jacksonville and Tampa, Florida, to St. Louis, Missouri. The connection between community development programs, many funded through the Department of Housing and Urban Development (HUD), and historic preservation is one of our greatest unfulfilled opportunities to make the history of African Americans and other ethnic groups relevant to contemporary life. The National Trust and the NCSHPO, working with HUD and the President's Advisory Council on Historic Preservation, in 1993 initiated new efforts to encourage the use of historic resources in housing and community development programs.

Even such a cursory sampling of preservation activity demonstrates a growing awareness throughout the country of the buildings and sites of African American history that had for so long gone unnoticed and a rising concern on the part of African Americans that these places not be lost. As the chairman of Georgia's Minority Historic Preservation Committee wrote, "Preservation is personal. A story, an event or a family connection becomes a reasons to get involved in the restoration of a building, a neighborhood, or a town."[3] African Americans are increasingly and personally concerned about historic places and are making efforts to preserve them. Unfortunately, many African Americans have been working in isolation, either unaware of the larger preservation movement or believing it was irrelevant to them. The growing attention to African American historic resources by both professional programs and citizen organizations suggests this is changing.

Our understanding of our history and of what is worth preserving has grown. Through the surveys and studies, the exhibits and tours, and the growing interest in the preservation of all of our history, we have begun to see the imprint of many peoples on our cultural landscape and to develop a broader view of the development of our communities, both urban and rural. At the 1991 conference of the National Trust, author David McCullough aptly described this phenomenon as the lights on a stage coming up to reveal all of the people who had been there all of the time.[4]

These changes have not happened without extraordinary measures on the part of both preservationists and other interested citizens. It has been necessary to locate and explore new sources of information and documentation, to expand our methodologies and research questions. In this process the contributions of African American museums and black heritage societies have been notable. Further progress will not be possible without continued expansion of our horizons and without special measures that bridge the gaps between traditional preservation organizations and other organizations and community groups. Black heritage councils, like the one estab-

lished in Alabama in 1984, and special committees, like Georgia's Minority Historic Preservation Committee, set up in 1989, are springing up in many states, especially in the Southeast, where Kentucky, Mississippi, and South Carolina have recently established special committees. In other states such as Maryland, Michigan, Oklahoma, and Pennsylvania existing black history advisory committees are expanding their attention from documents and artifacts to historic places. The attention of the more recent African American preservation committees to the built environment, the physical imprint of history on the land and in the community, is an important new development. These committees thus bridge earlier concerns that history be made visible through research and exhibits of the material culture of African Americans and preservation concerns that are increasingly coming to the forefront. They can serve as the community forums that bring collective interest and concern to the attention of agencies and organizations that provide technical assistance and support, like the SHPOs, statewide and local preservation organizations, and their national counterparts, the NCSHPO, the National Trust, and the NPS.

How we understand our history is important to the preservation of that history. When we set aside a portion of our history as distinct, through such mechanisms as Black History Month, and fail to connect it to our other national celebrations, such as the Fourth of July, our understanding is incomplete. That we have made a substantial beginning in "rediscovering America," as one of the authors directed us several years ago,[5] is evident in the African American activities and information chronicled here. Much remains to be done. The context of our history is infinitely richer and more

The Eighth Regiment Armory, Chicago, Cook County, Illinois, was listed in the National Register as a component of the thematic group on the Black Metropolis. Photo courtesy of the Commission on Chicago Landmarks (Henry Reuel).

complex than we had previously realized, and the historic places that embody that rich history deserve to be preserved. Indeed, the role of preservation is expanding into wider areas of contemporary life. As the mosaic of the nation's people becomes more diverse, we are on the threshold of even greater opportunities to connect historic preservation to broader social, economic, and cultural objectives that truly represent our full national heritage.

Notes

1. Elizabeth A. Lyon, *Cultural and Ethnic Diversity in Historic Preservation,* Information Series, no. 65 (Washington, D.C.: National Trust for Historic Preservation, 1992).

2. National Conference of State Historic Preservation Officers, "Minority Participation in State Historic Preservation Programs Task Force Report" (Washington, D.C.: National Conference of State Historic Preservation Officers, 1991).

3. See Janice White Sikes in *African American Historic Places and Culture: A Preservation Resource Guide for Georgia* (Atlanta: Minority Historic Preservation Committee and the Office of Historic Preservation, Georgia Department of Natural Resources, 1993).

4. See David McCullough, "A Sense of Time and Place," in *Past Meets Future: Saving America's Historic Environments* (Washington, D.C.: The Preservation Press, 1992), pp. 29–35.

5. See "Task Force Report."

My mother, Juliana St. Bernard Cooper; myself at age 4; and my father, John Walcott Cooper, c. 1933. Photo courtesy of the author.

WHERE CHILDREN'S DREAMS BECAME REALITY: THE SOCIETY FOR THE PRESERVATION OF WEEKSVILLE AND BEDFORD-STUYVESANT HISTORY

Joan Maynard

In 1968 James Hurley, a historian and photographer from Boston, and Joseph Haynes, a New York engineer and aviator, made an important discovery. From their two-seater plane, they located part of a long-forgotten early 17th-century path, along which stood four tiny peak-roofed cottages miraculously nestled in a thicket of unremarkable early-20th-century rowhouses. The path turned out to be a portion of the colonial Hunterfly Road, which ran along the eastern edge of the 19th-century black settlement of Weeksville in what is now central Brooklyn.

The discovery led to the founding of the Society for the Preservation of Weeksville and Bedford Stuyvesant History (the Weeksville Society) in 1968. The Weeksville Society was chartered by the New York State Education Department in 1971 to research, preserve, and disseminate the heritage of African Americans living in central Brooklyn, and particularly in Weeksville.

Weeksville was named for James Weeks, a pioneer in Brooklyn's African American community, who acquired part of the vast Lefferts family estate in 1838. The four historic houses are about one-quarter mile from the James Weeks homesite. By 1849, the tiny village had been dubbed Weeksville. In the following year, the Brooklyn directory listed people as living near the Hunterfly Road at Weeksville. Founded around 1837 after the abolition of slavery in New York, Weeksville is the earliest documented black community in an area now populated predominantly by African Americans.

The Hunterfly Road Houses, which date from between 1841 and 1883, were among the last buildings erected in Weeksville and are the oldest known existing buildings in the Bedford-Stuyvesant area of Brooklyn.

My interest in black history prompted me to join the Weeksville Society. I was born to two extraordinary people who had held a keen understanding of their heritage and who passed that understanding on to me. They taught me that black history began not with slavery, but with the African culture, which has made significant contributions to world civilization in areas of agriculture, metallurgy, government, and philosophy. The same pride that I felt led the children from P.S. 243, the local public school that succeeded the Colored School #2 of Weeksville, to suggest fixing up the old houses and creating a black history museum. This simple mandate continues to fuel the Weeksville Society's preservation and restoration efforts.

In June 1970, children, teachers, parents, and members of the fledgling Weeksville Society attended a New York City Landmarks Commission hearing, requesting that the four old homes located at 1698–1708 Bergen Street be designated city landmarks. The petition was successful. The Hunterfly Road Houses District was designated by the New York City Landmarks Commission in August 1970 and was subsequently listed in the National Register of Historic Places (under the name Houses on Hunterfly Road District). These events were nurtured by the preceding decade of civil rights awareness and a "need to know" that acted as a catalyst to action in the black community.

By 1977 the Weeksville Society had purchased the four historic houses with the assistance of the Bedford-Stuyvesant Restoration Corporation, the Vincent Astor Foundation, funds from a gala Salute to "Roots" Dinner, and a Federal Historic Preservation Fund matching grant awarded by New York State. In 1981 the society began the restoration of the historic houses using Federal Community Development Block Grant funds. The Pratt Center for Community and Environmental Development, an early and steadfast supporter of the society and a source of valuable technical assistance, introduced the society to William H. Cary, a highly qualified and sensitive restoration architect. A graduate of Columbia University and a former Peace Corps volunteer, Cary was well prepared to meet the preservation challenges at Weeksville. He assembled a restoration team consisting of two master craftsmen and two neighborhood apprentices. After several years of daunting preservation work, the team completed the restoration of the first building. It opened to appreciative visitors in May 1985.

Thereafter, diminished funding in the recessionary climate severely slowed the restoration process. However, following an episode of theft and vandalism at the end of 1991, the society was revived with generous assistance from the New York State Council on the Arts, the New York Landmarks Conservancy, Brooklyn Borough President Howard Golden, the Brooklyn Downtown Development Corporation, other foundations, and private and community contributions.

Archeology has been a unique feature of the project. The earliest dig, in 1969 to 1971, was in the center of Weeksville. Many people worked on that dig, including James Hurley; William "Dewey" Harley, an aged resident with roots in the community; Youth-in-Action, Boy Scout Troop #342; the New York University Field School in Archeology; and even

Before—The houses on Hunterfly Road, c. 1968. Photo courtesy of the Weeksville Society (Jim Hurley).

After—The houses on Hunterfly Road, 1985. Photo courtesy of the Weeksville Society (Jack Jupp).

Children from the Weeksville Houses, New York City Housing Authority, c. 1975. The Weeksville Society office was located in the housing complex from 1974 to 1980 when it moved to the historic site. Carol Jackson is dressed as the "Weeksville Lady," the symbol of the society. Seated at front, far left, is resident Benora Winfield, who now works as the assistant coordinator of youth programs at the Brooklyn Children's Museum. Photo courtesy of the Weeksville Society (the author).

The Weeksville Society staff, myself (center), and others at the tree planting honoring benefactor Arthur Ashe, August 1993. Photo courtesy of the Weeksville Society (Marty Markowitz).

children from the Weeksville School, who participated during their recess period. In the 1980s, a five-year summer field school dig was conducted on Hunterfly Road by City College of New York. Several proposals are currently being developed to complete further archeological research on the property. The proposals are aimed at incorporating archeological components into the permanent educational programs of the society with continuing community participation. Teachers from local high schools have expressed enthusiasm about cooperating with the society to conduct activities for motivated students such as a lab for the cataloging of the 40 boxes of artifacts already recovered from the site.

A 1990 grant from the National Endowment for the Humanities supported an institutional self-study report for the Weeksville Society. This study was directed by Claudine Brown, deputy assistant secretary for museums at the Smithsonian Institution, and drew upon the talents of other outstanding professionals in architecture, education, and museum programming. The study provided a valuable three-year development plan. Recommendations included staff expansion, public programming, and possibly construction of a supportive educational facility for the historic houses on the adjacent city-owned land.

We have almost completed the adaptive reuse of one of the four buildings, which will significantly increase the public space needed to accommodate visiting school classes. An average of 3,000 children visit each year to observe the restoration "works in progress" and learn about historic Weeksville. This phase of our work was made possible by a grant from the New York City Department of Cultural Affairs and funds from the New York State Natural Heritage Trust.

Today, Weeksville is situated in Brooklyn, New York, a city that has the most diverse population of people of African descent in the world, representing the vast geographic, cultural, and linguistic spectrum of the African diaspora for the past 500 years. The Weeksville African American Museum will serve as a resource for all present-day New Yorkers by sharing the special story of the early Weeksville pioneers who survived against great odds. To interpret the site, the society tells its story of preservation and museum development through two media: a constantly upgraded slide presentation and a 50-page illustrated booklet entitled *Weeksville, Then and Now*. A cut-out book, *Let's Make a Landmark*, was designed for a younger audience. Both publications have been reprinted and widely distributed.

A host of contributors including governments, private foundations, businesses, educational institutions, churches, museums, historical societies, and neighbors—like the residents of the Kingsboro Housing Project, who maintained the Society Green Thumb garden next to the historic houses for six years—continue to help make the children's dream a reality.

The restoration process itself, with its peaks of progress and valleys of setbacks, represents the general situation of our home community here in the inner city. The successful completion of the preservation project and its continuance as a museum symbolize for many the use of historic preservation as a powerful tool. It is imperative that the lessons learned through preservation benefit not only the affluent, but all people. The Society for the Preservation of Weeksville and Bedford-Stuyvesant History fulfills an important need. It preserves old buildings, but, more than that, it saves a tangible part of the past and brings history alive to the people of Bedford-Stuyvesant.

Chronic problems and recent disturbing events in our nation's cities may have helped more people to see the Weeksville Society's vision of the relationship between preservation, education, history, pride, hope, and positive motivation for all members of our society, especially our children. It is essential that places like Weeksville, where the human spirit survived and succeeded, be preserved for future generations to see, touch, and celebrate.

Hunter House, Mobile County (Anne Sieller).

ALABAMA

BALDWIN COUNTY

Lebanon Chapel AME Church
Intersection of Young and Middle streets
Fairhope

This church is the finest example of a religious building constructed of concrete block in Baldwin County. Construction of the building began in 1923 when the church had only 20 members. The building project was supervised by church member Warren B. Pearson, a mechanic and builder who lived north of Fairhope in Volanta. Throughout its history the Lebanon Chapel African Methodist Episcopal Church has played a vital social and religious role in the local black community. [Rural Churches of Baldwin County TR, C 8/25/88, 88001351]

Twin Beach AME Church
South Side of County Route 44
Fairhope

The congregation of Twin Beach African Methodist Episcopal Church was formed in 1867 by African Americans living in the vicinity of Battles Wharf. After the Civil War, the black population of freed slaves was supplemented by other African Americans who moved into the area to farm. The small congregation held services in a brush arbor until a frame building was constructed years later. A

fire and storm later destroyed the building. In 1925 the present church was constructed by Axal Johnson, a black craftsman, to the specifications of the 200 church members: concrete blocks molded to resemble stone, a popular building material used in Fairhope from c. 1905 to c. 1935 for residences, businesses, and churches. When it was listed in the National Register, the church congregation numbered approximately 150 members. [Rural Churches of Baldwin County TR, C 8/25/88 88001358]

BUTLER COUNTY

Butler Chapel AME Zion Church
407 Oglesby
Greenville

Organized in 1867, this church's congregation is the earliest social institution fully controlled by African Americans in Greenville. And the church itself, built in 1913, is associated with the oldest known independent black congregation in Greenville. The congregation's wide-ranging influence in the community is most evident in the establishment of Butler County's earliest known black high school, Greenville High School, at Butler Chapel African Methodist Episcopal (AME) Zion Church in 1893. The original building provided classroom space for the school from its inception in 1893 until 1898 when the present site of the school was purchased.

The church is also important as a local manifestation of the AME Zion Church Extension Program, which during the early 20th century provided financial relief to its struggling local churches. When the original Butler Chapel building burned in 1911, the program assisted in erecting the current building on the site of the original within two years. Today Butler Chapel remains the first and only AME Zion Church in Greenville. Its location in the city's more affluent early black neighborhood reflects the church's important role in the community. [Greenville MRA, CA 9/4/86, 86001755]

First Baptist Church
707 South Street
Greenville

Built in 1908, First Baptist Church, also known as the First Missionary Baptist Church, is Greenville's earliest known black missionary Baptist congregation and the town's oldest remaining black church building. This building was the third occupied by this congregation. The earlier buildings, both of which were situated on this site, were destroyed by fire and storm. Organized in 1880 under the Reverend Parson Stewart, this church has been the hub of social and cultural activity for the black residential neighborhood on Baptist Hill throughout its history. Since its founding, the church has served not only as a place of worship but also as a community social center, a center for community decision making, and an organizing place for local reform movements. Today, First Baptist, the "Mother Church" of all black Baptist congregations in Greenville, is prominent as the sole church building in the neighborhood. [Greenville MRA, A 9/4/86, 86001799]

Theological Building—AME Zion Theological Institute
East Conecuh Street
Greenville

The Theological Building of Lomax-Hannon Junior College is the earliest remaining building associated with black education in Butler County and the only known building associated with the educational efforts of the African Methodist Episcopal (AME) Zion Church. From 1875 through 1915, Alabama churches, both black and white, led the movement to improve higher education by establishing and supporting schools and colleges. The AME Zion Church was the leading black denomination in this movement and by 1911 had attempted three parochial school ventures in Alabama. The Lomax-Hannon Junior College was the second of these schools (it was preceded by Jones University in Tuscaloosa, which closed in 1900, and followed by Zion Institute in Mobile, which became a local project and was renamed the Josephine Allen Institute), and it is the only one that survives. Presently, Lomax-Hannon Junior College serves as the only AME Zion Church institution of learning in the state. [Greenville MRA, A 9/4/86, 86001867]

Ward Nicholson Corner Store
219 West Parmer
Greenville

Ward Nicholson Corner Store, a small neighborhood grocery store, was established in 1885 by the Reverend Frank W. Ward (1857–1925), a prominent African Methodist Episcopal (AME) Zion minister and merchant. Although Ward is best remembered as the proprietor of this store, he was also one of the leading AME Zion ministers involved in stimulating the growth of the denomination in the East Alabama Conference between 1881 and 1892. Ward successfully combined his work as a minister with his business pursuits and by the turn of the century conducted an impressive business. His attempt to achieve economic independence during the late 19th century parallels the movement for economic independence among blacks as a whole. This movement stimulated growth of black-owned businesses during the 1880s and 1890s and subsequently led to the establishment of the National Negro Business League by Booker T. Washington in 1900. [Greenville MRA, AB 11/4/86, 86001870]

CALHOUN COUNTY

Mount Zion Baptist Church
212 2nd Street
Anniston

Mount Zion Baptist Church was the second black church organized in the Anniston area and is the oldest one still in existence. It has been the central social force of the Zion Hill neighborhood, a black residential area characterized as "throwaway land" because it was hilly and not fit for farming. The congregation dates from 1879, when a small group met in a brush arbor near the railroad tracks, southeast of the present location. They raised money for the present lot and for the buildings occupying it. Church members designed and built the current church building. The basement was built in 1890 and used for worship until the first floor was completed in 1894. Mount Zion Baptist Church is a rare surviving church building from the late 19th century associated with the black community in Anniston. [Anniston MRA, CA 10/3/85, 85002875]

West Fifteenth Street Historic District
416–712 West 15th Street
Anniston

The West Fifteenth Street Historic District developed as a secondary business district specifically for the black community. The emergence of a smaller, secondary central business district was unusual in a town the size of Anniston (population in 1900: 9,695). It arose, however, as a result of several demographic, social, and economic factors, including an increase in the share of Anniston's black population at a time when tougher segregation was being imposed; the clustering of the black population around the new coke furnaces and foundries being built in west Anniston; the lack of adequate transportation to the downtown area; and finally, a resurgence of prosperity associated with the Spanish-American War.

The district not only became the primary shopping area for the black community, but served as a social center as well, with meeting halls, a black vaudeville and movie theater, a doctor's office, and a hotel. It became a community within a community, achieving a neighborhood identity that is still retained today. [CA 5/30/91, 91000662]

DALLAS COUNTY

Brown Chapel African Methodist Episcopal Church
410 Martin Luther King, Jr., Street
Selma

Brown Chapel was organized in 1866, when members of a local prayer movement met in the basement of a Selma hotel and decided to discontinue their affiliation with the Methodist Church. The members applied for admission to the African Methodist Episcopal Church and in 1867 were admitted to the Convention. The first frame building was erected on the current site in 1869. In 1908 the present church was constructed.

Brown Chapel is closely associated with the 1965 voting rights campaign of

Brown Chapel African American Methodist Episcopal Church. (David Patrick)

the Southern Christian Leadership Conference (SCLC). In late fall 1964 the SCLC selected Selma as the site of a voting rights campaign. The Dallas County Voters League, which had been organized by the Student Non-Violent Coordinating Committee (SNCC), established a Committee of Fifteen, representing different factions within the black community, to invite Dr. Martin Luther King, Jr., and the SCLC to help in the effort to gain the right to register and vote.

During the first three months of 1965, the church served as the headquarters for the SCLC, the site of rallies conducted by King and other SCLC leaders, and the staging point for demonstrations, including the attempted march to Montgomery on March 7, known as "Bloody Sunday." The campaign directly contributed to the rapid passage of the Voting Rights Act of 1965, an act viewed as the most important and effective piece of civil rights legislation passed in the 1960s. Today Brown Chapel is one of the most widely recognized landmarks

associated with the civil rights movement of the 1960s and is still used for services by the congregation. [CA 2/4/82, 82002009]

First Baptist Church
709 Martin Luther King, Jr., Street
Selma

The First Baptist Church is one of the major landmarks associated with the civil rights rallies and demonstrations of the mid-1960s that led to the passage of the Voting Rights Act of 1965.

The congregation was organized in the early 1840s by a freed slave, Samuel Phillips, and shared its church building with a white congregation. Shortly after the close of the Civil War, the white congregation bought out the claims of the African Americans, who then constructed a new building on St. Phillips Street. During Reconstruction, the congregation was instrumental in establishing Selma University, an early black college and theological school.

In 1894 the congregation constructed a new building on Sylvan Street (now

Martin Luther King, Jr., Street). This building was designed by Dave Benjamin West, a local black contractor. Born in Marion, Alabama, in 1850, West apparently came to Selma sometime after the Civil War. He served as one of the trustees of Selma University and was responsible for constructing some of the early buildings on that campus.

In 1963, under the leadership of the Reverend M. C. Cleveland, First Baptist became the first church in Selma to host the activities and meetings of the Dallas County Voters League. During the next two years, the church was a focal point of the mass meetings and nonviolent teaching sessions sponsored by the Student Non-Violent Coordinating Committee (SNCC). In late 1964 meetings were held in the church to plan the rallies and demonstrations of early 1965 that culminated in the Selma-to-Montgomery march.

During the early months of 1965, Dr. Martin Luther King, Jr., Ralph Abernathy, and other leaders of the Southern Christian Leadership Conference, headquartered in Brown Chapel half a block away, spoke nightly to the youth gathered at First Baptist Church. After the march, the church continued to serve as headquarters for SNCC and as a food and clothing distribution center for needy persons. [CA 9/20/79, 79000383]

JEFFERSON COUNTY

Alabama Penny Savings Bank
310 18th Street North
Birmingham

Constructed in 1913, the Alabama Penny Savings Bank building represents black financial, professional, architectural, and cultural achievements. The bank, founded in 1890, was the first black-owned bank in the state and the second largest black bank in the country in 1907. It financed the construction of homes and churches for thousands of local black citizens.

The bank was built by the Windham Construction Company, a local black construction company. The design of the building suggests that it may also be the work of black architect Wallace A. Rayfield, who created many other buildings for the black community in Birmingham, including the noteworthy Sixteenth Street Baptist Church (1911), only a few blocks away, which was also erected by the Windham Construction Company (see also Sixteenth Street Baptist Church).

From the beginning, the bank's building furnished offices for the black press and professional and businesspeople. When the Alabama Penny Savings Bank folded in December 1915, the building was bought by the Grand Lodge Knights of Pythias, a fraternal service organization to which many black legislators belonged.

This building is in a district that has long symbolized black life in Birmingham. For more than a century, this district was a dynamic center of social life and professional achievement. The vitality of that life in the 1920s and 1930s was captured by author Octavius Roy Cohen in stories read nationwide. Although now diminished by the demolition of some buildings and the dispersal of the black population that has come with integration and suburban expansion, the district retains its identity and association with the black community. [CA 3/10/80, 80004471]

Dr. A. M. Brown House
319 North 4th Terrace
Birmingham

The Dr. A. M. Brown House was the home of Arthur McKinnon Brown

(1867–1939), one of Birmingham's first black doctors, and was constructed around 1908 by Wallace A. Rayfield, an early black architect. Rayfield had moved to Birmingham in 1907 from Tuskegee Institute, where he had taught after his graduation from Pratt Institute. He designed a number of other residences in Birmingham, but he specialized in churches.

Brown attended Lincoln University in Pennsylvania and Michigan Medical School in Ann Arbor, Michigan. In 1891 he graduated with honors in surgery and ophthalmology, and in that year he received a license to practice in Alabama. He began his career in Bessemer and later moved to Birmingham. There, Brown was instrumental in founding Children's Home Hospital, for many years the only facility in the area where black doctors could treat their patients. He was responsible for instituting National Negro Health Week, later changed to National Health Week. Brown also served in the Spanish-American War. After an illness of about a year, Brown died in 1939.

The house remained in the family after Brown's death, and in 1972 Dr. Walter Brown, a son, granted a 50-year free lease to the Birmingham Art Club in memory of his parents. The club uses the building as a community center. [CB 6/20/74, 74000413]

Fourth Avenue Historic District
1600–1800 blocks of 4th Avenue North and part of the 300 blocks of 17th and 18th streets North
Birmingham

The Fourth Avenue Historic District is the only surviving remnant of what was

Students digging the foundation for the C. P. Huntington Memorial Building at Tuskegee Institute, Macon County, c. 1902. Photo courtesy of the Library of Congress (Frances Benjamin Johnston).

the heart of black Birmingham's social and cultural life from around 1908 to 1941. The district's buildings reflect the black community's attempt to fulfill its social and cultural needs within the confines of racial segregation and discrimination. The major buildings remaining are the Colored Masonic Temple (1922), where black service clubs met and debutante balls and black-tie events were held; the Famous Theater (1928) and the Carver Cinema (1941), two distinctive motion picture theaters built for black patrons; and the Alabama Penny Savings Bank (now the Pythian Temple, 1913), a political and professional center and home of *The Birmingham Reporter,* the leading black newspaper of the era.

Many of the city's early black leaders had strong ties to the district. W. R. Pettiford, for example, was one of the founders of the Alabama Penny Savings Bank and pastor of the Sixteenth Street Baptist Church, an important center of black life just beyond the district. Oscar W. Adams, Sr., was editor of *The Birmingham Reporter* and president of the Colored Citizens' League of Birmingham, both of which were located in the Penny Savings Bank building. E. A. Brown, the first black attorney to practice in Birmingham, also had offices in the building. The Windham Brothers, a local black firm that operated for almost 75 years, built the Colored Masonic Temple and the Penny Savings Bank, where they had their offices in the 1910s. *The Colored Laborer* and the *Southern Industrial Fraternal Review,* black newspapers of the 1920s, also had their offices in the bank building. In addition, the building served as headquarters for the Interracial Association of Alabama, the earliest effort in the state at interracial cooperation and the predecessor of the Commission on Interracial Equality.

The Great Depression effectively halted new construction in the district. Although black businesses were still concentrated in the district, the number of black businesses showed a distinct decline. Years later, as segregation laws were dismantled in the 1960s, the district's black customers dispersed into other parts of the city and were never replaced. Today, the district is undergoing revitalization to reflect its black social and business history. [CA 2/11/82, 82002041]

Pratt City Carline Historic District
Avenue U along First Street, Avenue T, and Carline from Avenue W to 6th Street
Birmingham

The Pratt City Carline Historic District was developed in the late 19th century on a tract of 200 acres bordered to the north and west by Alabama's major coal seam, the Pratt seam. The Pratt mines, located just west of the district, achieved prominence as the largest coal-mining development in the South in the late 19th century. Worldwide attention to the Pratt Mines as a result of the New Orleans World Industrial & Cotton Exposition of 1884, where an 11-ton lump of Pratt coal displayed Alabama's mineral resources, later contributed to the influx of immigrants from southern rural areas, northern industrial states, and foreign nations.

Among the new arrivals to the district in the late 19th century were the English, Irish, Scotch, Germans, Austrians, Russians, Welsh, and African Americans. The mining boom town afforded the immigrants opportunities to make money, build and own homes, and become members and leaders of an emerging American middle class. Many African American residents of the district established businesses to serve the black community. Johnny Brooklere, Joe Tucker, Zenous Williams, and Viola McCarroll all became successful entrepreneurs and leaders in the district.

Although Pratt's industrial economy declined during and after the Great Depression, third- and fourth-generation Pratt citizens remain in the town. A neighborhood association has been formed to insure that Pratt's historic significance is recognized and remembered. [CA 3/2/89, 89000118]

Rickwood Field
1137 2nd Avenue West
Birmingham

On the afternoon of August 18, 1910, Birmingham's shops and City Hall closed early. An estimated 10,000 baseball enthusiasts poured through the gates of the newly dedicated Rickwood Field to watch the Birmingham Barons play the Montgomery Climbers. The home team won 3–2. Fourteen years later, the ball park would become home to the two-time pennant-winning Negro League Birmingham Black Barons.

Baseball came to Birmingham largely through the efforts of A. H. "Rick" Woodward, a railroad and mining engineer who provided most of the capital to purchase a minor league team for the city. The Birmingham Barons initially played at Slag Field, a modest ball park, but Woodward insisted on a high-quality facility for the team. After inspecting several ball parks, Woodward modeled Rickwood after Pittsburgh's Forbes Field, no longer standing. The playing field was laid out by baseball great Connie Mack, then the manager of the Philadelphia Athletics. The ballpark was constructed in 1910 at a cost of $75,000.

Birmingham's citizens rallied behind their new home team, cheering the Barons on to win the Southern League

pennant in 1914. Birmingham got its second baseball team in 1920 with the formation of the Birmingham Black Barons, charter members of the Negro Southern League. Black players had been officially barred from organized baseball in 1889. Before this date the International League had had a few black players, but tensions created by their presence forced them out of baseball altogether until the creation of the Negro League.

The Black Barons began playing in Rickwood Field in 1924, alternating weekends with the Barons. When the Barons played, black spectators were required to sit in the unsheltered bleachers 355 feet from home plate. When the Black Barons played, the seating was reversed: black spectators sat in the grandstands, and white spectators sat in the far concrete bleachers. The Black Barons boasted several formidable players during their history. Players such as Mule Suttles, Satchel Paige, Jimmie Crutchfield, Piper Davis, and Willie Mays led the team to win the American Negro League pennant in 1943 and 1948. Davis and Mays were among the Black Barons who followed Jackie Robinson's 1947 lead in crossing the color line into major league baseball.

The high level of performance of the Negro League team made the ball park a source of pride to the African American community of Birmingham. The park has seen some of the best minor league players and major league exhibitions, and it stands as a monument to nation's pastime. [A 2/1/93, 92001826]

Sixteenth Street Baptist Church
Intersection of 6th Avenue and 16th Street
Birmingham

The present sanctuary of the Sixteenth Street Baptist Church was designed by

Wallace A. Rayfield, a local black architect, and constructed in 1911 by a black contractor on land acquired by the congregation in 1873 (see also Alabama Penny Savings Bank).

Wallace A. Rayfield was born in Macon, Georgia, in 1874 and raised in Washington, D.C., where he attended Howard University. He is believed to have received his training in architecture at Pratt Institute in New York City. At the invitation of Booker T. Washington, Rayfield traveled south to teach at Tuskegee Institute in Alabama. In 1907 he left Tuskegee to practice architecture in Birmingham. In addition to the Sixteenth Street Baptist Church, Rayfield designed many houses in Birmingham, including the Dr. A. M. Brown House.

From its construction, Sixteenth Street Baptist Church has served as a center for black community life. On September 15, 1963, during the racial unrest in Birmingham, four children were killed when a bomb exploded near the sanctuary. The tragedy was a turning point in resolving the civil rights protest in Birmingham and became a rallying cry for unity throughout the country. [CA 9/17/80, 80000696]

Smithfield Historic District
Roughly bounded by 8th Avenue North, 6th Street North, 4th Terrace North, and 1st Street North
Birmingham

The Smithfield Historic District is one of Birmingham's earliest black residential neighborhoods. Between 1890 and 1930 Birmingham's industry expanded dramatically, and its population grew from about 26,000 to a quarter of a million, including a substantial number of African Americans. The district illustrates the effects of residential segregation and the consequent development of a black social and economic class system within the black community.

Following the U.S. Supreme Court ruling in the 1896 case *Plessy v. Ferguson,* which upheld the "separate but equal" doctrine, discriminatory and segregation laws were enacted across the country. Based on custom and enforced by city ordinances, many local policies were designed to restrict the economic advancement of African Americans by controlling the quality and quantity of available employment, services, housing, and land resources. In Birmingham segregation policies designated a section of Smithfield as a black neighborhood. In 1926 a local zoning ordinance reaffirmed this designation, and by 1928 83 percent of the residents in the district were black.

The district was also associated with many of Birmingham's most prominent early 20th-century black professionals who made major contributions to the advancement of the city's black community. Dr. Arthur McKinnon Brown, one of Birmingham's pioneer black doctors, was instrumental in establishing Children's Home Hospital, which was for many years the only hospital in the city where black doctors could practice (see also Dr. A. M. Brown House). Professor Arthur Harold Parker is locally noted as one of the city's most outstanding black educators, having served as the principal of Industrial High School for 39 years.

The Reverend R. T. Brown was one of Birmingham's most outstanding and highly respected ministers in the early 20th century. Brown served as the bishop of the diocese of the Colored Methodist Episcopal Church and the chairman of the Board of Trustees of Miles College, a local black liberal arts college. Brown's home was constructed in 1926 and later occupied (1945–56) by entrepreneur A. G. Gaston.

These residents were representatives of the district's black upper middle class. All of them commissioned black architect Wallace A. Rayfield (1870–1941) to design their homes. T. C. Windham (1880–1940), a prolific black contractor, often worked in conjunction with Rayfield to build them (see also Alabama Penny Savings Bank and Sixteenth Street Baptist Church). [CA 10/15/85, 85002899]

West Park
Intersection of 5th Avenue North and 16th Street
Birmingham

Located just northwest of the Sixteenth Street Baptist Church, the Birmingham demonstration headquarters during the civil rights protests of the 1960s, West Park, now known as Kelly Ingram Park, served as the assembly point for many marches, demonstrations, rallies, and prayer services during the spring of 1963.

From April 3 to May 7, 1963, Birmingham was the location of the Southern Christian Leadership Conference's Project "C," a series of marches and rallies to protest segregation in the city. Most notable were the demonstrations held from May 2 to May 7, when the use of fire hoses and dogs by city police against the demonstrators received national media coverage. These demonstrations resulted in the desegregation of Birmingham, and the publicity surrounding the demonstrations caused the federal government to push for legislation that led to the 1964 Civil Rights Act outlawing segregation of public accommodations. [A 5/24/84, 84000636]

Windham Construction Office Building
528 8th Avenue North
Birmingham

Built in 1912, the Windham Building was the home office of the oldest black construction company established in Birmingham. The Windham Brothers Construction Company was organized in Birmingham in 1895 by Thomas C. Windham. In 1897 Thomas's brother, Benjamin L., left New Orleans, where he had received a degree with highest honors from Leland University, and joined his brother's business. Together they established the city's most prolific black construction company, noted for the construction of the most significant buildings in the black community, including residences, churches, and other commercial buildings, as well as prominent buildings in Birmingham's traditional white business section.

Originally built to house a drugstore owned by Thomas Windham's wife, several other small black businesses, and two apartment units, the Windham Brothers Building is an early example of the Windham Brothers Construction Company's workmanship. It served as the home office of the company, which had branches in Chicago, Detroit, Indianapolis, and Nashville, and as the home of Thomas Windham. The company continued business operations in this building until 1966. [A 8/9/84, 84000638]

LEE COUNTY

Ebenezer Missionary Baptist Church
Intersection of Thach Street and Auburn Drive South
Auburn

Ebenezer Missionary Baptist Church, one of the early black churches in Alabama, was organized shortly after the Civil War. It reflected a trend during

Reconstruction in which freedmen gradually withdrew from the white Alabama churches and established their own congregations. In 1870 the present church was built entirely by congregation members.

Founded under the leadership of the Reverend Thomas Glenn, a prominent black preacher in the Auburn area, the church attracted many members and assumed a prestigious role in church organizations. On December 17, 1868, Ebenezer Missionary Baptist Church was one of 27 churches to send delegates to the organizational meeting of the Colored Baptist Convention of Alabama.

The Auburn District Association, consisting primarily of the black Baptist churches in Lee, Macon, and Tallapoosa counties, was organized at the church. The district contributed to the support of the Baptist Colored University in Selma and later to the formation of schools for blacks in Opelika and Lee counties.

In the mid-1970s, Ebenezer Missionary Baptist Church was restored by the Auburn Heritage Association in recognition of its religious and educational contributions to the black community. [AB 4/21/75, 75000317]

LIMESTONE COUNTY

Sulphur Trestle Fort Site
One mile south of Elkmont
Elkmont

In September 1864 Sulphur Trestle Fort was the site of major military action between Confederate General Nathan Bedford Forrest and the Union garrison guarding the railroad trestle over Sulphur Creek. The Union outpost on the rail line was located at Sulphur Trestle, an 80-foot-high wooden bridge nearly 200 yards long. The fort was defended by black troops, the 11th U.S. Colored Troops, under the command of Colonel

Lanthrop. The use of slaves and free blacks was an experiment designed to free up the regular Union troops for front-line duties. Lanthrop was reinforced by 128 men of the Ninth Indiana Cavalry under Colonel Lilly and 60 men of the Third Tennessee Regiment under Colonel J. B. Minnis. On September 25, 1864, Forrest attacked the fort. Colonel Lanthrop was killed and replaced by Colonel Minnis, who surrendered to Forrest. The Confederates killed more than 200 men and captured an additional 800, as well as 700 small arms, two artillery pieces, 16 wagons, 300 horses, and various stores. Forrest had the trestle and fort burned and then moved north to Tennessee. [A 5/8/73, 73000355]

LOWNDES COUNTY

Calhoun School Principal's House
County Route 33
Calhoun

Hampton Cottage, the residence of the principal of the Calhoun Colored School, is the last surviving structure reflecting the influence of the Hampton-Tuskegee vocationalism on black education at the turn of the century. The house, built between 1900 and 1910, was originally one of six teachers' cottages and has been used by the principal only since 1947, when Thorn Cottage, the original residence of the founder and principal, was destroyed by fire.

The Calhoun Colored School was established in 1892, with the support of General Samuel Armstrong and Booker T. Washington, by Charlotte R. Thorn and Mabel Dillingham. The two women had taught together at Hampton Institute. Thorn made Calhoun into one of the most influential black schools in the South. The success of the school was attributed to her program of vocational education and community work, which continued until 1932.

In 1943 the state of Alabama acquired the school, and the Lowndes County Board of Education assumed responsibility for supervising Calhoun as a public school. Today the Calhoun School remains a black rural public school. [B 3/26/76, 76000340]

MACON COUNTY

Tuskegee Institute National Historic Site

One mile northwest of Tuskegee
on U.S. 80
Tuskegee

Founded in 1881 by Booker Taliaferro Washington (1856–1915), Tuskegee Institute (now Tuskegee University) became a major force in launching African Americans into higher education. Washington, a former slave, graduated from Hampton Institute in Virginia in 1875 and returned to Hampton in 1879 to serve as secretary to the principal, General Samuel C. Armstrong. In 1881 Armstrong selected Washington to start a normal and industrial school.

Tuskegee Institute was established by an act of the General Assembly of Alabama on February 12, 1881, and Booker T. Washington, as its founder and first principal, opened the school on July 4 of that year. Between 1881 and 1915 Washington put into practice a program of industrial and vocational education for African Americans. Tuskegee became the symbol of Washington's efforts to ameliorate the economic conditions of African Americans.

Washington's 1895 speech at the Cotton States and International Exposition in Atlanta gave him national recognition as the leader of black people, succeeding Frederick Douglass, who had just died. The Atlanta speech did not advocate integration but instead proposed a policy of mutual progress and cooperation among whites and blacks. Washington's views were opposed by W. E. B. Du Bois and other black intellectuals who felt that he did not sufficiently emphasize political rights and that his stress on industrial education might result in keeping the black race in virtual bondage.

Although it offered courses in a number of technical and professional fields, Tuskegee is most noted for its contributions in the field of agricultural research. George Washington Carver (1861–1943) headed the Agricultural Department from 1896 until 1910 and carried out numerous experiments in the field of scientific farming.

Tuskegee continued its growth and development under Washington's successors, the late Robert Russa Moton (see also Holly Knoll, Gloucester County, Virginia) and Frederick D. Patterson. Most of the existing buildings were constructed after 1900. Buildings of special historic interest at the Tuskegee Institute National Historic Site are The Oaks, Washington's home; the Booker T. Washington Monument; the graves of Washington and Carver; and the Carver Museum. Tuskegee Institute was designated a National Historic Landmark on June 23, 1965. [AB 10/15/66 NHL NPS, 66000151]

MADISON COUNTY

Domestic Science Building

Alabama Agricultural and Mechanical University campus
Normal

The Domestic Science Building is one of the oldest buildings on the campus of Alabama Agricultural and Mechanical University, an early institute for the training of black teachers. Founded by William Hooper Councill, a former slave, the school began as the Huntsville Normal School. The school's charter was approved in 1873, and it opened in 1875. The school remained in Huntsville until 1891, when the campus was relocated to its present site in Normal. That same year the institution became a land-grant college and changed its name to Alabama Agricultural and Mechanical College.

In 1909 Walter S. Buchanan became the second president of the university, and the school expanded under his administration. It was Buchanan who persuaded the Robert R. McCormick family of Chicago to donate funds for the construction of the Domestic Science Building. The imposing Classical Revival style brick building was built in 1911 and was used by the home economics department until 1968. The food-canning services provided under the supervision of faculty and students drew residents to the building from throughout north Alabama. [A 4/11/73, 73000358]

MOBILE COUNTY

Davis Avenue Branch, Mobile Public Library
564 Davis Avenue
Mobile

Built in 1930, the Davis Avenue Branch of the Mobile Public Library was constructed to serve the needs of the black community. The building was modeled after the main branch of the library but constructed on a smaller scale. Black residents helped collect used books for the library and raise funds for the acquisition of new books. The library reflects the social climate of segregation, when African Americans were prevented from participating fully in educational endeavors and provided with separate educational facilities. When the public schools were desegregated and their facilities opened to black students, the branch library became

a repository for government documents. [C 12/22/83, 83003459]

Emanuel AME Church
656 Saint Michael Street
Mobile

Emanuel African Methodist Episcopal (AME) Church, like Mobile's other black congregations of the 19th century, evolved from a desire on the part of black congregations to continue religious services as their white parent churches strove to disassociate themselves from the black membership. Trustees for Emanuel AME Church purchased a vacant lot for their church in 1869, and a frame building was constructed on the site that year. The original frame building was bricked c. 1880, and the building was lengthened and a new facade was added by 1891. Emanuel AME raised enough money to hire a prominent white architect, James F. Hutchisson, for the design of the facade. As a result, the architecture is comparable to contemporary white churches in Mobile and is superior to both black and white rural churches of the period. Unaltered since the 1890s, this building stands as Mobile's only Gothic Revival church constructed for a black congregation. [C 5/29/87, 87000853]

Hawthorn House
352 Stanton Road
Mobile

Built in 1853, the Hawthorn House was the home of the Reverend Joshua Kedar Hawthorn, a white Mobile minister who worked with free black churches. He was pastor of the African Baptist Church, a free black congregation, when it was located at Sandy Bottom, an area near the intersection of Springhill Avenue and Ann Street. A rift in the church resulted in Hawthorn's taking part of the congregation to worship at a location on

Springhill Avenue and Broad Street. By 1859 the congregation had purchased property on Dearborn Street, constructed a church there, and renamed itself the St. Louis Street Baptist Church. In 1860 Hawthorn moved to Baldwin County to minister to another black congregation. [C 5/21/84, 84000671]

Hunter House
504 St. Francis Street
Mobile

The Hunter House was the residence of Bettie Hunter, a former slave who reputedly attained her wealth from a successful hack and carriage business she operated in Mobile with her brother, Henry. The fall of New Orleans (1862) during the Civil War had made Mobile the South's major gulf port.

Transportation of goods to and from the port depended on the city's teamsters and their horse- or mule-drawn wagons. Additionally, a favorite leisure activity of the upper class in Mobile until the 1860s was riding in the country by carriage. Bettie Hunter was part of a group of African Americans who recognized the opportunities in the carriage business and who eventually cornered this part of the transportation market in Mobile.

Built in 1878, the Hunter House is an exceptional example of 19th-century residential architecture for a black-owned home. The two-story Italianate house matches Mobile's white-owned residences of the period in scale, character, and architectural detail.

Hunter died of anemia at the age of 27, one year after the construction of the house. Having no children, she willed her property, including some original furnishings and many of her personal possessions, to her family, which has maintained Hunter House through the years. [CB 3/7/85, 85000446]

Magnolia Cemetery including Mobile National Cemetery
Intersection of Ann and Virginia streets
Mobile

Established on 30 acres of land in 1836, Magnolia Cemetery now comprises the area known as Confederate Rest, three acres set aside as the Mobile National Cemetery, and an area containing a number of black burials. Confederate Rest is an area set aside in 1862 as a burying ground for Confederate soldiers. It contains the graves of 1,100 soldiers killed in action. The three acres designated as the Mobile National Cemetery in 1866 are administered by a department of the Veterans Administration and include the grave of Chappo Geronimo, son of Indian chief Geronimo.

The main portion of the cemetery contains several black interments. While these burial sites are interspersed, one section of the cemetery north of Virginia Street contains graves of prominent African Americans buried since the late 19th century. Included in this portion are the graves of Bettie Hunter, a wealthy and influential 19th-century black businesswoman (see also Hunter House); prominent local black contractor Dave Patton; and 20th-century civil rights leader John LeFlore. [CA 6/13/86, 86003757]

Mount Vernon Arsenal–Searcy Hospital Complex
Coy Smith Highway, one-half mile west of Alabama Route 43
Mount Vernon

The Mount Vernon Arsenal–Searcy Hospital Complex has a long history with documented uses as a 19th-century arsenal (c. 1830–c. 1870), a late 19th-century barracks and prisoner of war camp (1873–1894), and as a mental health hospital for African Americans in the 20th century (1900–1969). On December 11, 1900, the General Assembly of the State Legislature approved the establishment of a mental hospital at Mount Vernon to relieve the overcrowded conditions at Bryce Hospital in Tuscaloosa. In 1902, 318 black patients and 25 employees were transported to the former barracks, which became the state's first mental health facility exclusively for African Americans. Originally called the Mount Vernon Hospital and in 1919 renamed Searcy Hospital, the facility served mentally disturbed black patients exclusively until 1969, when it was ordered to desegregate following the passage of the 1964 Civil Rights Act. [CAB 5/26/88, 88000676]

Dave Patton House
1252 Martin Luther King, Jr., Avenue
Mobile

Constructed in 1915, the Patton House is the only primary structure known to be associated with Dave Patton (1879–1927), a successful black businessman in Mobile in the early 20th century. Patton operated a hauling and wrecking business from a downtown office on Royal Street. Patton was described in 1910 as one of Mobile's most prominent contractors in the dray business. His 14-year-old booming business at that time employed 40 mules and 80 hands.

Patton maintained a close relationship with Booker T. Washington, but the two men apparently did not share the same business philosophy. Patton disregarded the precepts of Washington's National Negro Business League, which advocated the establishment of a separate economy in which blacks would conduct business exclusively with blacks. Patton, however, did not sever his connections with white clients and in fact depended on a largely white clientele. This practice may have insulated his business from the difficulties experienced by many black businesses in the South, for it was during this period that many blacks left Mobile for larger cities. As a result, most of the black businesses dependent predominantly or exclusively on black trade failed. The construction of the Patton House attests to the fact that Patton's business continued to prosper, one of the few successful black-owned businesses in Mobile during that period. [CB 6/12/87, 87000937]

St. Louis Street Missionary Baptist Church
108 North Dearborn Street
Mobile

Built in 1872, the St. Louis Street Missionary Baptist Church is one of only four black congregations established in Alabama before 1865 and the second oldest Missionary Baptist church in Mobile. As early as 1836 a separate black Baptist congregation had been organized in Mobile, where the African Americans of that period had greater freedom than elsewhere in the South. After several years of meeting in a variety of places, the congregation constructed its own church in 1839. By 1854, however, the financially well established Stone Street Baptist Church encountered dissension within its membership. Ten members left that church to organize the St. Louis Street Missionary Baptist Church because they wished to sponsor a statewide missionary program that Stone Street resisted.

The church continued its emphasis on statewide missionary activity under such leaders as the Reverend Charles Leavens, the first black minister to serve the group. It sent congregational organizers all over the state, and many new Alabama congregations and pastors resulted from this effort. In 1874 the congregation sponsored the Seventh Session of the Colored

Baptist Convention, where a resolution was passed to establish the Alabama Baptist Normal and Theological School, which became Selma University in 1908.

St. Louis Street Missionary Baptist Church supplied a number of black church leaders, including a president of the National Baptist Convention, D. V. Jemison, who served as pastor of the church in the late 1920s. [A 10/8/76, 76000347]

State Street AME Zion Church
502 State Street
Mobile

The State Street African Methodist Episcopal (AME) Zion Church, constructed in 1854, is the oldest Methodist church building in Mobile and one of only two black Methodist churches established in the city during the antebellum period. Founded in 1829 for the predominantly black congregation of the African Church of the City of Mobile, the State Street Church was erected after the original building burned.

The congregation was a mission of the Methodist Episcopal Church South until after the Civil War. By 1855 it was one of Alabama's most successful black churches, with 500 full and 50 probationary members.

In 1865 the Methodist Episcopal Church South claimed ownership of the building and challenged the right of the congregation to occupy the structure after it had joined the AME Zion Church. The Reverend Wilbur G. Strong, a pioneer in establishing the AME Zion Church in the gulf states, became the second of many distinguished pastors of the State Street Church. Under Strong's leadership the congregation acquired legal ownership of the property in 1872. Many outstanding ministers who succeeded Strong at the State Street Church were recognized on a

national level for their services to the AME Zion Church. [CA 9/6/78, 78000505]

Stone Street Baptist Church
311 Tunstall Street
Mobile

Built in 1931, Stone Street Baptist Church is an eclectic vernacular mid-19th-century frame church. Stone Street Baptist was the second church building constructed by members of this congregation.

In 1843 the white trustees of Saint Anthony Street Baptist Church purchased a plot of land at the southwest corner of Chestnut and Tunstall streets for the use of the African branch of the church, which became the Stone Street Baptist Church. Twenty-five years later the title to the property was transferred to the black trustees of the Stone Street Baptist Church. Since then, this building has been used continuously by a black congregation of the Baptist denomination.

Today Stone Street Baptist is recognized as one of Alabama's most influential black Baptist churches. It promotes social justice, education, and spiritual enrichment in the black community. This church building, an achievement of laymen who successfully used limited resources available to them, continues to be an inspiration to the historically black neighborhood it serves. [C 8/8/85, 85001749]

MONTGOMERY COUNTY

City of St. Jude Historic District
2048 West Fairview Avenue
Montgomery

The City of St. Jude Historic District pioneered nondiscriminatory health services, education, and social services to African Americans during a time when racial segregation was mandated by law.

Founded by Father Howard Purcell in 1934, the City of St. Jude includes a church, a school, a hospital, a social center, and residential buildings for teaching and nursing staffs, as well as an administration building and a gymnasium. Father Purcell hired African American craftsmen and laborers to construct the buildings, one of whom, Otis Smith, became construction supervisor for the St. Jude School.

Father Purcell's most ambitious undertaking was St. Jude's Catholic Hospital, which opened in early 1951 as the first fully integrated hospital in the Southeast. The hospital received publicity for treating Viola Liuzzo, who had been shot while transporting participants in the voting rights march between Selma and Montgomery.

In the 1950s St. Jude's Church served as a meeting place for two groups of United Church Women, one black and one white, who formed an integrated prayer group. By the 1960s St. Jude's Church had become such a powerful symbol of racial desegregation that Dr. Martin Luther King, Jr., 2,000 participants of the Selma-to-Montgomery march, and supporters of the Voting Rights Act of 1965 used it as a meeting place.

In March 1990 St. Jude served as the site of the 25th anniversary celebration of the Selma-to-Montgomery march. Today St. Jude continues a vital program of social and spiritual service to the black community. [CA 6/18/90, 90000916]

Dexter Avenue Baptist Church
454 Dexter Avenue
Montgomery

Built in 1877, the Dexter Avenue Baptist Church is associated with the civil rights movement in the 1950s and Dr. Martin Luther King, Jr., who first received national and international attention while serving as pastor there. King is most remembered for his leadership of the Montgomery Improvement Association (MIA) and the Southern Christian Leadership Conference. The Dexter Avenue Baptist Church was closely involved with King's activities and those of the MIA.

On December 2, 1955, Mrs. Rosa Parks refused to give up her seat to a white passenger and move to the back of a Montgomery city bus. She was summarily arrested. The anger of the black community was so strong that it formed an organization to fight bus segregation. Black community leaders and hundreds of others crowded into the Dexter Avenue Baptist Church to meet on the issue. E. D. Nixon, a labor leader, called together the city's black civic leaders and initiated the subsequent bus boycott. It was at this meeting that the Reverend Ralph David Abernathy formed the MIA and nominated King as its president.

As president of the MIA, King was responsible for organizing the black community in support of the boycott. He held mass meetings, many of them in the Dexter Avenue Baptist Church, to encourage African Americans to boycott the buses and to arrange voluntary motor pools. The boycott finally ended December 21, 1956, with a Supreme Court decision that held bus segregation to be illegal.

It often has been said that King's success as a black leader in the South was the result of his ability to fuse mass movements and direct confrontation of unjust authority with the black church, which had sustained African Americans since slavery. The Dexter Avenue Baptist Church was part of that fusion. The church was designated a National Historic Landmark on May 30, 1974. [B 7/1/74 NHL, 74000431]

Jefferson Franklin Jackson House. Photo courtesy of the Alabama Historical Commission (Mary A. Neeley).

Jefferson Franklin Jackson House
409 South Union Street
Montgomery

The Jefferson Franklin Jackson House, now known as the Jackson-Community House, is important in black history because of its association with the City Federation of Colored Women and Youth Clubs. Founded in 1939 as the City Federation of Colored Women's Clubs, the organization purchased the house in 1943. The federation was dedicated to strengthening individual clubs in their roles in the community. An integral part of the federation's operation, the Jackson-Community House served not only as its headquarters but also as a library before a public one was available for African Americans and as a Head Start school. It has also served the black community as a home for the elderly and orphans as well as a site for meetings and seminars. [AB 5/17/84, 84000711]

North Lawrence–Monroe Street Historic District
132–148, 216, and 220 Monroe Street and 14, 22, 28–40, and 56 North Lawrence Street
Montgomery

The Monroe Street Historic District reflects early 20th-century development of black-owned, -managed, and -supported businesses in Montgomery. The district was a center of black professional achievement and social life from the early 1900s through the mid-1940s. It illustrates the black community's attempt to fulfill its social, cultural, and economic needs within the confines of racial segregation and discrimination.

Between 1912 and 1919 the number of black businesses was increasing in the Monroe Street area, and by the 1920s there was a heavy concentration of black businesses on North Court Street. Among the businesses located in the area were the offices of the *Emancipator* Newspaper Publishing Company, H. J. Bailey's Shoe Shop, and the Pekin Theatre.

New black businesses appeared throughout the 1920s, and by the 1930s black business activity stabilized. African Americans patronized black doctors, barbers, morticians, hotels and rooming facilities, theaters, and restaurants. Residential segregation and a commitment to supporting black businesses raised the need for black real estate loan and investment firms. The earliest of these was the Montgomery Branch of the Alabama Penny and Savings Bank, which was run for two decades by Victor Tulane and William J. Robinson, who was also general manager for the *Emancipator* newspaper.

The presence of mutual benefit societies was another manifestation of the local black struggle for economic self-sufficiency. Typical of these benefit societies in Montgomery were the People's Mutual Aid Association, Lincoln Reserve, Union Central Relief Association, Liberty Life, North Carolina Mutual, and the Atlanta Mutual Insurance Company.

The district's development and local popularity probably peaked in the 1940s. In 1948 a community service center for African Americans was established at 214 Monroe Street. The center was a project of the Montgomery County Farm Extension Agency supported by local merchants and civic groups.

In the 1950s suburban migration challenged the downtown businesses and resulted in a decline of business activity within the area. During the same period, the black community's mounting dissatisfaction with the "separate but equal" doctrine reached its peak, resulting in the 1955 Montgomery bus boycott, from which sprang the national civil rights movement. Several black businesses in the district offered dispatch services to the boycotters. E. L. Posey's parking lot served as the central dispatch/pick-up station and post for the chief dispatcher. The role played by the black business community in the bus boycott shows the importance of this area as a center of black social and economic life in Montgomery. Today the surviving Monroe area businesses still depend on Montgomery's black consumers for their livelihood. [A 8/30/84, 84000712]

Old Ship African Methodist Episcopal Zion Church

483 Holcombe Street
Montgomery

The Old Ship African Methodist Episcopal (AME) Zion Church houses the oldest black congregation in Montgomery. The church, as reconstructed between 1918 and 1920, is a fine representation of a Classical Revival building. It also contains a portion of the original 1835 building, which was moved to its present site in 1852.

In the early 1850s the Court Street Methodist Church decided to construct a large, masonry building to replace their existing church, which had been constructed in 1835. The Methodists offered the black members their old building on the condition that it would be moved from the site. Under the supervision of Thomas Wilson, a free black contractor, the church was moved to the new location. White ministers served the congregation until 1862, when a slave named Allen Hannon assumed the duties of pastor. The new black church was eventually christened the Old Ship AME Zion Church.

Many of the members of the Old Ship AME Zion Church assumed an active role in community life. The church was a meeting place for prominent black leaders including Frederick Douglass, Booker T. Washington, and Dr. Martin Luther King, Jr. The congregation has also included distinguished local citizens, such as Elijah Cook, the first black undertaker; Dr. Cornelius Dorsett, an early black physician; James and Anne Hale, builders of the city's first hospital for African Americans; and A. C. Caffey, captain of the Capital Guards, a turn-of-the-century black militia unit. [C 1/24/91, 90002177]

Pastorium, Dexter Avenue Baptist Church
309 South Jackson Street
Montgomery

Constructed in 1912, this house was acquired by the Dexter Avenue Baptist Church in 1919 for use as its pastorium. Dr. Martin Luther King, Jr. (1929–68) assumed the pastorship of the church in October 1954 and occupied the house until his move to Atlanta in early 1960. King's occupancy of the house brought it onto the national scene when, on the night of January 31, 1956, it was bombed. The bombing helped focus national attention on the civil rights movement and the Montgomery bus boycott as well as, paradoxically, on King's firm stand on nonviolence and civil rights leadership. Through its association with King and the bus boycott, the Pastorium reflects the role of the black church in the struggle for equal rights for African Americans (see also Dexter Avenue Baptist Church). [CB 3/10/82, 82002064]

Tulane Building
800 High Street
Montgomery

The Tulane Building, built between 1904 and 1908 by prominent black businessman Victor Tulane, is a small monument to the black community in Montgomery. Tulane came to Montgomery around 1893 and opened a grocery store. His business prospered, and he soon expanded into new ventures. He entered the real estate business in the late 1890s and served as cashier of the Montgomery branch of the Alabama Penny Savings Bank (see also Alabama Penny Savings Bank, Jefferson County). He later was elected the first black trustee of the Tuskegee Institute (see also Tuskegee Institute National Historic Site, Macon County).

Tulane conducted his grocery business on the lower level of the Tulane Building and kept his living quarters above the store. When he and his wife moved to a new home, the second floor of the building was used as a club by two of Montgomery's most prominent black social groups. Today the Tulane Building is a symbol of the strength of black enterprise in Montgomery. [CB 3/21/79, 79000398]

PERRY COUNTY

First Congregational Church of Marion
601 Clay Street
Marion

The First Congregational Church is the only Reconstruction-era black church in Marion. It was initially associated with Lincoln Normal School, an important black educational institution established in Marion in July 1867 by a group of freed slaves. In the fall of the following year, the American Missionary Association (AMA) leased the school's small building and grounds and paid the

First Congregational Church of Marion. Photo courtesy of the Alabama Historical Commission (Ellen Mertins).

teachers' salaries. The building provided space for a visiting Congregational minister to preach occasionally. In 1870 the First Congregational Church was organized, and the academy was used for worship. The AMA donated funds for the erection of the present church building, which was completed in late fall 1871.

During the early years of the school, the pastors of the church also conducted classes. In 1873 the school was deeded to the state of Alabama in return for a state promise to make it a normal school and university for African Americans. In 1887 the school was closed by the state, which later reopened the normal school in Montgomery (now Alabama State University). In response to an appeal by the local black community, the AMA reopened the Lincoln Normal School in Marion in a new building and supported it until the 1960s.

The close relationship of the church and school illustrates the role of black churches in providing higher education for African Americans during Reconstruction. Most important, this church is the only 19th-century building remaining that is associated with efforts of the First Congregational Church and the AMA to provide an academic education for African Americans. [CA 12/17/82, 82001614]

Phillips Memorial Auditorium
Intersection of Lincoln Avenue and Lee Street
Marion

The Phillips Memorial Auditorium, constructed between 1915 and 1938, is the last remaining building associated with Lincoln Normal School in Marion. Founded in 1867, the Lincoln Normal School was the last normal school to be established by the American Missionary Association (AMA). The AMA established and administered schools throughout the South to provide African Americans with a private liberal arts academic education that extended beyond industrial and vocational training. The Lincoln Normal School was under the auspices of the AMA for 76 years, although the school received most of its financial support from local contributions.

The school's most significant expansion occurred in the first three and a half decades of the 20th century. During this period, seven academic and residential buildings, including the auditorium, were constructed to accommodate the increased attendance. The auditorium served as the main meeting and social center for the school as well as for Marion's black community.

The Phillips Memorial Auditorium was the last large project undertaken by the Lincoln Normal School before it was incorporated into the Perry County public school system in 1942, ending a significant period of black education in the county. In 1978 the alumni of the Lincoln Normal School purchased and preserved the auditorium, and it now serves as a local meeting hall and social center. [CA 2/13/90, 88003243]

Westwood Plantation (Boundary Increase)
Bounded roughly by Highway 80, Highway 61, Rabbit Yard Road, and Old Uniontown Railroad Spur
Uniontown

The Westwood Plantation is an excellent surviving example of antebellum plantation development in Alabama's Black Belt region. This large tract of land has historically been a part of Westwood Plantation since the 19th century. Included within Westwood's boundaries

are architectural and engineering sites associated with the daily functioning of the plantation, including former slave quarters, hand-dug wells and cisterns, and a mule-driven cotton gin. In addition, documented sites of a number of tenant houses trace the breakup of the plantation system. Some of the current residents of the tenant houses are direct descendants of former Westwood Plantation slaves, and as a result there is a strong tradition of oral history within these families.

Equally important, the site of an interesting former tenant community center, which was once the hub of social life on the property, offers evidence concerning the black social history of the property as it evolved from a mid-19th-century slave society to a 20th-century tenant farm society. [CD 12/10/84, 84000488]

SUMTER COUNTY

Laura Watson House
Epes Road
Gainesville

Constructed around 1900, the Laura Watson House is a good example of the rapidly vanishing folk-type dwellings constructed and occupied by black freeholders at the turn of the century in Alabama. The well-preserved house was built for the Watson family and was occupied by Laura Watson and her son, Booker. [Gainesville MRA, C 10/03/85, 85002928]

TALLADEGA COUNTY

Swayne Hall
Talladega College campus
Talladega

Founded in 1867 by the American Missionary Association (AMA) with the assistance of the Freedmen's Bureau, Talladega College is one of the few black colleges that pursued a strong liberal arts program during a period when vocation-

Swayne Hall. Photo courtesy of the National Historic Landmarks Program.

alism dominated black education. Starting with four teachers and 140 pupils in the elementary grades, Talladega slowly evolved into a full-fledged institute of higher learning.

Talladega's oldest building is Swayne Hall, which was completed in 1857 as a Baptist Men's College. Funds to construct the building were secured by subscriptions among the Baptist community. Some slaveowners consigned slaves to labor on the building in order to work out their subscriptions. When the AMA selected Talladega as the location of one of its schools, it purchased the Baptist Men's College building. It was named Swayne Hall after General Wager B. Swayne of the Freedmen's Bureau, who had helped negotiate the purchase. The

children of the slaves that built Swayne Hall became Talladega's first pupils. Swayne Hall still stands in excellent condition at the center of the campus and serves as the administration building. The building was designated a National Historic Landmark on December 2, 1974. [A 12/2/74 NHL, 74002223]

Talladega College Historic District
Intersection of Battle Street and Martin Luther King Drive
Talladega

Talladega College was founded in 1867 as a joint venture of the Freedmen's Bureau and the American Missionary Association (AMA) as a result of the 1865 Freedmen's Bureau convention in Mobile, at which a resolution was passed to educate the freed slaves. Students originally met in a room in a private home, but enrollment grew so quickly that a frame schoolhouse was constructed within a year. Meanwhile, the AMA and the Freedmen's Bureau searched for a suitable site on which to permanently locate the college. In 1868, they purchased a 34-acre tract of land and the imposing Greek Revival building that stood on it. The building, renamed Swayne Hall, became the first permanent building of the Talladega College campus (see also Swayne Hall).

From 1832 until emancipation, education had been denied to slaves by law in Alabama. When the Talladega College opened, none of the nine counties nearest Talladega had a black public school. Because of a large demand for black education, Talladega College evolved from a one-teacher school in 1867 to a multi-building liberal arts institution predominantly for African Americans.

Despite the need for normal and industrial training, the first principals of Talladega College were committed to the highest quality of liberal education for students. In contrast, the Tuskegee Institute, established in 1881 by the Alabama legislature, under the leadership of Booker T. Washington, advocated industrial education for African Americans.

Henry Swift DeForest, the founder of Talladega College and president from 1879 to 1896, developed a full college-level curriculum offering theological and classical studies in addition to courses in agriculture, industrial arts, domestic sciences, and nursing. Following the development of a full college curriculum, Talladega constructed additional college facilities. Individuals who were instrumental in building the college, both academically and architecturally, were William

Savery, Joseph Fletcher, and Frederick A. Sumner.

William Savery, a slave carpenter and brick mason, constructed Swayne Hall in 1852–53. In 1865, as a freed man, Savery helped organize the first school for African Americans in Talladega County. It was this school that, assisted by the Freedmen's Bureau and the AMA, opened as Talladega College in 1867. As a trustee of the college, he saw its incorporation by charter in 1869. Savery is also credited with the building of Stone Hall (1881) and the President's House (1881) on the campus.

Joseph Fletcher, a 1901 graduate of Talladega College, supervised construction of many of Talladega College's most significant buildings. Among these are Seymour Hall (1923), Callanan Gymnasium (1924), Sessions Practice School (1925), and Fanning Refectory (1927). Fletcher's contributions to the campus culminated with the completion of the quadrangle and the construction of Savery Library (1939).

Frederick A. Sumner, president of Talladega College from 1916 to 1932, had an impressive administration at the school. Under Sumner, many major buildings were constructed on the campus, the college received an "A" rating from the Southern Association of Colleges and Secondary Schools, and a $1 million endowment was created for the college.

Today Talladega College remains a successful example of the movement to educate freed blacks and to place them in an honorable leadership position within society. [CA 8/23/90, 90001316]

TUSCALOOSA COUNTY

First African Baptist Church
2621 9th Street
Tuscaloosa

Built in 1907, the First African Baptist Church is Tuscaloosa's second oldest historically black church. It is also the only known building in the state outside the Tuskegee Institute campus that illustrates the design concepts and themes most commonly attributed to Robert Robinson Taylor, the first black architect to graduate from the Massachusetts Institute of Technology and the first to work on Tuskegee.

The congregation was organized in November 1866 under the leadership of the Reverend Prince Murrell. In August 1963 the congregation received a minister who was to become one of its most celebrated leaders—the Reverend T. Y. Rogers, Jr., a graduate of Alabama State College and the Crozier Theological Seminary in Pennsylvania. The social impact of Rogers's call to Tuscaloosa became evident as early as his installation, which was conducted by Dr. Martin Luther King, Jr.

The late spring and summer of 1964 marked the climax of the most aggressive local civil rights activities in Tuscaloosa. The Tuscaloosa Citizens for Action Committee (TCAC) was formed and launched a campaign to challenge local segregation practices. Rogers was the TCAC's chief spokesperson and the key orchestrator of the local movement.

First African maintains an influential place in the social, political, civic, and community affairs of Tuscaloosa. Under the pastorate of Dr. W. E. Pitts, the congregation preserved the history of black life and culture in the city. [CA 9/28/88, 88001580]

Murphy-Collins House
2601 Paul Bryant Drive
Tuscaloosa

The Murphy-Collins House, constructed in 1923 for Will and Laura Murphy, is one of the few surviving houses of a large segregated downtown residential district. The street on which the house is located marked the dividing line between the black and white areas of the neighborhood, and the house faced a row of white-owned and -occupied buildings. Residents of the Murphys' side of the row were primarily middle-class black professionals. Will Murphy was an undertaker, and Laura Murphy worked as a teacher and served as principal of the 20th Street Elementary School, a nearby black school.

The modest bungalow is one of only two brick houses built in the area and the only brick house built by African Americans. It was constructed by black contractor George Clopton, with bricks from the former state capitol in Tuscaloosa and a previous home owned by Will Murphy. A rare surviving residential building associated with the development of a black middle class in Tuscaloosa, the Murphy-Collins House reflects the aspirations of the Murphys, who served the black community and in turn gained income and high status. [A 1/28/93, 92001824]

ARIZONA

MARICOPA COUNTY

Phoenix Union Colored High School
415 East Grant Street
Phoenix

George Washington Carver High School, originally Phoenix Union Colored High School, was built in 1926 as Arizona's first black high school. Although state laws did not mandate segregation of high schools, increasing antiblack sentiment after World War I led the black community to establish a separate high school. The school first met in the rear of a commercial building and then occupied two other temporary homes. The city's school board then purchased a dump site on which the school was eventually built.

The school enjoyed a reputation for high academic standards. Its teachers were required to hold master's degrees, and the faculty's determination to provide a high-quality education instilled pride in the black community. The name George Washington Carver High School was adopted in 1943. Carver's auditorium was Phoenix's largest public facility for black activities, and it hosted a variety of community events. Many of the school's athletic teams were state championship winners, as was its concert band.

Integration of the state school system in Arizona occurred in 1953, and Carver's doors were closed in 1955. Although no longer in use as a school, the building stands today as a former center of the city's black community and the only building ever constructed exclusively to serve black high school students in Arizona. [A 5/2/91, 91000543]

Phoenix Union Colored High School. Photo courtesy of Arizona State Parks (Jay C. Ziemann).

ARKANSAS

CHICOT COUNTY

New Hope Missionary Baptist Church Cemetery, Historic Section
St. Marys Street
Lake Village

The historic section of this cemetery is the only existing historic property directly associated with the black community of Lake Village between 1870 and 1930. Because the cotton-growing industry dominated the economy of Chicot County both before and after the Civil War, Chicot County had the largest black population in the state until the end of World War I. After World War I, large portions of the black population migrated to urban centers in the North.

Originally built on private land as a plantation church, New Hope Missionary Baptist Church was established at its present location in 1860. With the growth of the black community of Lake Village, particularly after the Civil War, New Hope became the central church, and the New Hope cemetery the principal burial site. The church continues to serve an almost exclusively black congregation but because of the high concentration of burials within the cemetery, few new burials occur. [Ethnic and Racial Minority Settlement of the Arkansas Delta MPS, A 9/21/92, 92001227]

CRAWFORD COUNTY

Henry Clay Mills House
425 North 15th Street
Van Buren

Built by an independent black businessman in 1892, the Henry Clay Mills house represents the social and economic progress made by a limited number of black Arkansans following Reconstruction.

Henry Clay Mills was born a slave in Lauderdale County, Alabama, on June 5, 1847. That same year, Henry's future wife, Harriet Robinson, was born into slavery in North Carolina. After the Civil War both Henry and Harriet lived in Mulberry, Arkansas, where they were married on June 20, 1868. For a number of years Henry and Harriet worked as laborers on a small plantation near Mulberry.

In nearby Van Buren, Henry Mills discovered new business opportunities. Mills began his own moving and transfer company. His venture into small business typified the early movement of black Arkansans from farming to nonagricultural employment. [A 12/16/77, 77000250]

Mount Olive United Methodist Church
Intersection of Lafayette and Knox streets
Van Buren

Mount Olive United Methodist Church represents the oldest black congregation of the United Methodist Church west of the Mississippi River. The church was organized in 1869 by J. G. Pollard and 38 former slaves. Over the next two decades the congregation had grown enough to warrant construction of a new and larger building. Therefore, in 1889, members constructed the present church at a cost of $900. In February 1897 the church hosted the first annual session of the Little Rock Conference of Methodists, and thereafter it hosted the conference four more times. Until the 1950s it was an active and prestigious church with a strong congregation. In addition to its continuous use as a black religious institution, the church is architecturally significant for its simple Gothic Revival design. [CA 7/30/76, 76000401]

DALLAS COUNTY

Hampton Springs Cemetery (Black Section)
Off of Arkansas Route 48
Carthage

Hampton Springs Cemetery is an important part of the heritage and culture of the African Americans of Dallas County. In 1860 black slaves represented 43 percent of the total population of Dallas County. Following the Civil War African Americans settled in what became primarily black communities. Hampton Springs Cemetery, located near Carthage, resembles the traditional black cemeteries of the Southeast. It contains markers of cast concrete, ceramic pipe, oil lamps, wooden stakes, and petrified wood and grave offerings of mussel shells, broken glass, and ceramic jars, bottles, plates, and pitchers. It is the only cemetery in Dallas County and, as of yet, in Arkansas to display traditional African American practices that may have African antecedents. [Dallas County MRA, A 10/28/83, 83003473]

INDEPENDENCE COUNTY

Bethel African Methodist Episcopal Church
895 Oak Street
Batesville

Bethel African Methodist Episcopal Church, the oldest church building in Batesville, housed the city's first black congregation. The formation of the church reflected the freed blacks' desire for independence and pursuit of cultural self-determination during Reconstruction and the Jim Crow era. In 1871 the Batesville Bethel congregation purchased the site of the present church building. The site's location reflected the forced segregation of blacks in Batesville. The original leaders of the Bethel congregation included many local black leaders and two veterans of the 113th Colored Infantry, Samuel Greer and Sandy Willis. Pastor Reuben Johnson headed a fundraising campaign to finance the construction of a church building. In December 1880 the new building was completed, but it burned soon thereafter because of a faulty stovepipe. The congregation borrowed money from Simon Alder, a merchant and banker, to construct the present building, which was completed by 1882 and served as the center of Batesville's black community. [A 10/16/86, 86002875]

MILLER COUNTY

Kiblah School
Route 1
Doddridge

Constructed in 1927, the Kiblah School is associated with the historic black community of Kiblah, homesteaded in 1866 by former slaves and located in present-day Doddridge. The community's

Kiblah School. Photo courtesy of the Arkansas Historic Preservation Program (T. Jones).

name is derived from the word *Ka'aba,* the cubical stone structure in the center of the mosque in Mecca to which Moslems turn their faces in prayer. By 1868, residents of Kiblah had erected log houses and three churches.

There was no school building in the community at the time, but school classes were held in each of the three churches alternately for three months of the school year. In 1870 the state of Arkansas established two school districts in the community. In 1905 the two districts were consolidated, and in 1927 the present Kiblah School building was constructed. The building remained in use until 1970, when the school district was consolidated with a neighboring one and students were sent to a larger school. The Kiblah School building was sold for use as a community center in the 1980s and still serves as one today. [A 11/20/89, 88003210]

MONROE COUNTY

Mount Zion Missionary Baptist Church
409 South Main Street
Brinkley

The Mount Zion Missionary Baptist Church congregation was formed in 1886 and began construction of the present church in 1909. C. A. Getlis, of one of Mount Zion's principal founding families, served as architect and carpenter. The Gothic-influenced design of the church reflects the optimism and prosperity of Mount Zion's founders. The Getlis brothers, along with other Mount Zion church members, were actively involved in the commercial and educational development of the local black community. Mount Zion's members were also instrumental in the formation and growth of the White River Academy, founded in 1893 by J. D. Humphrey. Humphrey was Mount Zion's first pastor and principal of the school for 22 years, as well as architect and general contractor for its Boys Dormitory. White River Academy provided religious and academic training for the black youth of the area until 1955. [A 11/4/86, 86002951]

NEVADA COUNTY

Wortham Gymnasium
Arkansas Route 200
Oak Grove

Wortham Gymnasium was built in the 1920s during a period of great expansion of black educational facilities in southern Nevada County. It is a handsomely balanced design that reveals the skill of the Works Progress Administration (WPA) workers who built it.

In 1920 the African Americans of Oak Grove and southern Nevada County petitioned the county school board to form their own black school district, which later became known as Oak Grove District #4. By 1925 the black community had received permission to establish a public high school for blacks, and a school building was built with help from the Julius Rosenwald Fund. The high school expanded under the principalship of L. W. Johnson, who extended the curriculum to 12 grades, creating a senior high school program, and secured funding for the Wortham Gymnasium. The building was the largest gymnasium in the state of Arkansas and the second gymnasium for African Americans. [CA 4/19/90, 90000667]

PULASKI COUNTY

Dunbar Junior and Senior High School and Junior College
Intersection of Wright Avenue and Ringo Street
Little Rock

Dunbar Junior and Senior High School and Junior College opened in 1929 as the Negro School of Industrial Arts. Dunbar offered outstanding educational opportunities for African Americans from 1929 to its closing in 1955, as reflected in the institution's admittance to the North Central Accreditation Association in 1932. It was one of only two industrial arts schools in the South to acquire junior college rating, and its curriculum was accepted as the basis for admission to colleges and universities throughout the United States. Over the years the school hosted many prominent visitors, including Eleanor Roosevelt, Duke Ellington, Count Basie, and General Benjamin O. Davis, Sr.

In 1943 the school was involved in a dispute concerning equal pay for black and white teachers in the Little Rock school system. The dispute was resolved in the case *Morris v. Williams,* heard before the U.S. Eighth Circuit Court of Appeals, which established the principle of "equal pay based on professional qualifications and services rendered." [CA 8/6/80, 80000782]

Ish House
1600 Scott Street
Little Rock

Constructed in 1880, the Ish House was the home of Jefferson Ish and his son, Dr. G. W. Ish. Jefferson Ish was a progressive educator who devoted his life to ensuring a high-quality education for African Americans. He established the first standardized black school in the area, and he inaugurated departmentalism in the Little Rock public schools. In 1943, after his death, Ish School in Little Rock was named in his honor.

One of Ish's sons, Dr. G. W. Ish, became one of Little Rock's most innovative medical practitioners. In 1926 Dr. Ish became the medical director and chief of the surgical staff at the United Friends of America Hospital. From 1936 to 1965 he was a physician and instructor in health education at Philander Smith

College in Little Rock. In 1968 he was elected president of the General Practitioners Branch of the Pulaski County Medical Society. Dr. Ish's most significant accomplishment, however, was the introduction of the drugs isoniazid and streptomycin in the treatment of pulmonary tuberculosis. [CB 1/3/78, 78000621]

Little Rock High School
Intersection of 14th and Park streets
Little Rock

In the 1950s Little Rock High School, now known as Central High School, became a symbol of the controversy over school desegregation. In 1954 the U.S. Supreme Court's decision *Brown v. Board of Education of Topeka* called for an end to segregated public schools. The Little Rock school board initially refused to comply with the federal constitutional requirement to desegregate. However, a year later on May 24, 1955, the school board presented a plan for gradual desegregation. It would be conducted in three phases. Central High School would be the first to be desegregated, beginning in school year 1957–58. Because there was no provision to ensure that desegregation would occur in a timely manner, the National Association for the Advancement of Colored People and its leader Daisy Bates opposed this plan.

In the summer of 1957 nine African Americans decided to attend previously all white Central High School in the fall. In August 1957 the trouble began. The Capitol Citizens' Council, a Little Rock white citizens' council, and a group calling itself the Mothers' League of Little Rock Central High School agitated throughout the community against integration. On September 2, Arkansas Governor Orval Faubus intervened to prevent integration at the school. By

September 4, when the nine black students arrived at the school to begin classes, the events in Little Rock had attracted the attention of the nation's media. In defiance of the order of the federal district court, Governor Faubus employed the Arkansas National Guard to keep the black students out.

On September 24, 1957, President Eisenhower called the Kansas National Guard to Little Rock to enforce the *Brown* decision. Federal troops remained at Central High School for the remainder of the 1957–58 school year. Governor Faubus, acting under the authority of a state law, ordered the high schools in Little Rock closed for the school year 1958–59. Little Rock Central High School remained empty for a year. The black students who attended Central High School took correspondence courses or attended school outside Arkansas.

The school board reopened the Little Rock high schools in the fall of 1959. In August 1959 four of the original Little Rock nine, this time protected by the local police, returned to Central High School. The building was designated a National Historic Landmark on May 20, 1982. [A 8/19/77 NHL, 77000268]

Main Building, Arkansas Baptist College
1600 High Street
Little Rock

Constructed at the close of the 19th century by black Baptists, Main Building at Arkansas Baptist College is one of the oldest facilities for black higher education in Arkansas. The college was established in 1884 at the annual meeting of the Black Baptist Convention in Arkansas as a school for the training of black ministers and teachers.

In November 1884 the first class was held at Mount Zion Baptist Church in

Main Building, Arkansas Baptist College. Photo courtesy of the Arkansas Historic Preservation Program (Dianna Kirk).

Little Rock. The school operated briefly as the Baptist Institute and was incorporated as Arkansas Baptist College in 1885. After operating the school in various churches in Little Rock, the school's board of trustees purchased land and constructed several frame school buildings. In March 1893 the school's central building was destroyed by fire, and within a short time construction was begun on Main Building. Main Building was the college's first brick building and is Arkansas's oldest remaining black college building.

The early success of Arkansas Baptist

College is attributed to the Reverend Joseph A. Booker, who served as president of the college from 1887 until his death in 1926. Booker's work at the school made him one of the state's most influential black educators. Constructed under Booker's leadership, Main Building stands as one of the most significant buildings associated with black history in Arkansas. [CAB 4/30/76, 76000457]

Mosaic Templars of America Headquarters Building
900 Broadway
Little Rock

This building was constructed in 1911 for the Mosaic Templars of America, a black fraternal organization begun in Little Rock in 1883 by Arkansans John E. Bush and Chester W. Keatts. Although both men were leaders in the black community, Bush is particularly important to black history in Arkansas. His active role in politics made him the acknowledged black Republican leader in the state. In 1898 Bush was appointed receiver of the United States Land Office at Little Rock by President McKinley, a position he continued to hold through the Woodrow Wilson administration. Bush became one of the best-known black figures in the country, and his friendship with Booker T. Washington brought Washington to Little Rock in 1905. Bush's popularity was so great in the black community that there was talk of nominating him for governor in 1914. In addition to his other activities, Bush was for many years vice president of the National Negro Business League.

By the early 1920s the Mosaic Templars of America had become one of the largest and most powerful black fraternal organizations in the country. In the local community it helped develop a strong business block in the historically black West 9th Street area of Little Rock. Today the Mosaic building serves as a visual anchor to the historic West 9th Street area. [CAB 4/19/90, 90000634]

Taborian Hall
Intersection of 9th and State streets
Little Rock

Built in 1916, Taborian Hall is one of the few buildings that remains from the era when West 9th Street, between Izard and Broadway streets in downtown Little Rock, was the hub of black business activity. This commercial area began developing in the 1890s and continued to thrive until the 1950s. Some of the most prominent business establishments in this four-block area were fraternal organizations. These fraternities provided important social and civic outlets for Little Rock's black community, and, more significant, they made available basic insurance protection for the black community. Many of the fraternal groups in the state located their central headquarters on 9th Street. One of these groups, the Arkansas Chapter of the Knights and Daughters of Tabor, a national black fraternity, constructed this building as its new headquarters. Financed with capital from the black community, the building was constructed by a local black contractor, Simeon "Sim" Johnson. Taborian Hall housed businesses and professional offices as well as serving as a social and civic oasis. The hall's ballroom was the scene of performances by famous entertainers such as Louis Armstrong, Count Basie, Cab Calloway, Duke Ellington, and Earl Hines. [A 4/29/82, 82002130]

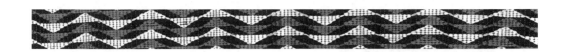

CALIFORNIA

ALAMEDA COUNTY

Liberty Hall
1483–1485 8th Street
Oakland

Liberty Hall was constructed in 1877 for use as a butcher shop and residence. In 1925 the building was sold to the local chapter of the Universal Negro Improvement Association (UNIA). The UNIA, founded by Marcus Garvey in 1914, promoted black self-determination and eventual establishment of an African republic. Although it never achieved the latter goal, the UNIA was able to organize large numbers of African Americans for economic and political action. A 1931 fire and the onset of the Great Depression resulted in a decline in UNIA activity in the region. In 1933 the building was sold to four members of Father Divine's Peace Mission Movement. Like Marcus Garvey, Father Divine, an evangelist turned social activist, led a movement intended to bring about greater social, economic, and political opportunities for African Americans. Divine often located his peace missions in all-white neighborhoods in defiance of restrictive covenants. The mission is best remembered by Depression-era residents for providing hearty meals to the public at little cost. [CA 3/30/89, 89000199]

LOS ANGELES COUNTY

Somerville Hotel
4225 South Central Avenue
Los Angeles

Dr. John Somerville built the Somerville Hotel in 1928 as a hotel for African Americans. Somerville, a pioneer black business, professional, and cultural leader in Los Angeles, was motivated to open the hotel by his own failure to secure lodging upon his arrival in San Francisco from the West Indies. Arriving in California in 1902, he became the first black graduate of the University of Southern California and went on to become the first black graduate of the university's school of dentistry. Somerville and his wife, Vada Jetmore Somerville, were leaders in the local struggle to end discrimination. Their hotel gained instant favor in the black community, hosting within its first year the first national convention of the National Association for the Advancement of Colored People on the West Coast. During the 1930s many nationally prominent members of the black community, such as Joe Louis, Arthur B. Spingarn, and Bessie Smith, either were guests at the hotel or performed there. [A 1/17/76, 76000491]

Sugg House (Bob Brennan).

SAN JOAQUIN COUNTY

Moses Rodgers House
921 South San Joaquin Street
Stockton

Moses Rodgers was born a slave in Missouri but was educated as a mining engineer. In 1849 the gold rush brought Rogers to California, where he built a solid reputation in his field. Investors seeking to purchase mining claims and stocks sought his expertise. Rodgers himself purchased several mines in the Mariposa mining district. In 1890 Rodgers and his wife, Sahra, moved to Stockton so their five daughters could benefit from the high-quality school facilities for African Americans there. In Stockton Rodgers was the first to success-fully drill for natural gas. Inadequate financial backing, however, prohibited him from attaining much monetary success for his efforts. In 1898 the Rodgers built their home on one of the town's finest residential streets, and Moses Rodgers lived there until his death. Members of the Rodgers family retained ownership of the house until 1971. [AB 4/26/78, 78000763]

TULARE COUNTY

Allensworth Historic District
Town of Allensworth and its environs along California Route 43

Allensworth, California, was founded by Colonel Allen Allensworth in 1908 to provide a place for African Americans to live "free from the direct influence of slave-oriented social attitudes." Born a slave, Allensworth managed to pursue a career as a minister, lecturer, and teacher before receiving an appointment as a chaplain in the United States Army. In the military he served with distinction in Cuba and the Philippines. He returned from the army in 1906 and moved to California. Allensworth enjoys the distinction of being the only town in California founded, financed, and governed by African Americans. Politically aware and intellectually oriented, Allensworth was a refuge for black settlers in the West. The California Department of Parks and Recreation has proposed that Allensworth be designated a state historic park. [AB 2/23/72, 72000263]

TUOLUMNE COUNTY

Sugg House
37 Theall Street
Sonora

The Sugg House was built in 1857 by William Sugg, a manumitted slave, and his wife, Mary Elizabeth Sugg. Lured by the gold rush, William Sugg came to California from Raleigh, North Carolina, by wagon train sometime before 1852, working as a muleteer and bullwhacker on the journey. He was manumitted after arriving in California. Mary Sugg made the wagon journey from Johnson County, Missouri, in 1851. The couple were married in 1855 and raised 11 children in the house. The Sugg House is one of the few remaining adobe structures in Toulumne County and is typical of gold rush-era adobes. Despite close quarters, the Suggs found room to take in lodgers when the nearby hotels were full. Members of the Sugg family occupied the house until 1982, 125 years after its construction. [CA 9/13/84, 84001210]

COLORADO

DENVER COUNTY

Barney L. Ford Building
1514 Blake Street
Denver

Barney L. Ford was an escaped slave who became a prominent businessman and Republican political leader in Colorado. Born January 22, 1822, in Stafford, Virginia, Ford escaped to Chicago, where he became active in the abolition movement. In 1860 Ford relocated to Colorado and in 1862 purchased a property at 1514 Blake Street, which was destroyed by fire the next year. He later built the present two-story brick building on the site. The building housed a restaurant and bar, a barbershop, and a hair salon. From this operation, Ford expanded his commercial holdings. He constructed the InterOcean Hotel in Denver at a cost of $53,000 and another InterOcean Hotel in Cheyenne, Wyoming, in 1875 at a cost of approximately $65,000. In 1864 Ford's income was the 14th highest in the state. From the beginning, Ford was an active leader in the civil rights movement in Colorado, and he played a significant role in the admission of Colorado to the union as a free state. Active in the Republican party, he was the first African American to be nominated to the territorial legislature. He was a delegate to the Republican County Convention and Central Committee in 1867, 1872, and 1873. [B 6/24/76, 76000551]

Justina Ford House
3091 California Street
Denver

Built in 1890, this house was the home and office of Dr. Justina Ford, the first black woman doctor in the state of Colorado, from 1912 to 1952. From her arrival in Denver in 1902 until 1952, she remained the city's only female black physician. Ford received her Colorado medical license on October 7, 1902, and established a practice in Denver. Although she always considered herself a family doctor and general practitioner, Ford, like many women doctors of her day, built her practice around obstetrics and gynecology. She generally attracted patients from among African Americans, Mexicans, Spanish, Greeks, Koreans, and Japanese. Ford served not only Denver but many of the surrounding counties as well. She delivered more than 7,000 babies in the 50 years she practiced. Ford became a staff member at Denver General Hospital and was eventually able to join the American Medical Association, an organization that was closed to African Americans for much of her career. In

Barney L. Ford Building (center). Photo courtesy of the National Park Service (Walter Smalling, Jr.).

1951 she was awarded the Human Rights Award from the Cosmopolitan Club of Denver. Ford continued to practice medicine until age 81. [CB 11/23/84, 84000244]

GILPIN COUNTY

Winks Panorama
Southwest of Pinecliffe
Pinecliffe

Winks Panorama was a mountain resort for African Americans founded in an age of discrimination and segregation. In 1922 a group of black promoters formed the Lincoln Hills Development Company to promote the growth of a black community in an area known as Lincoln Hills, near Pinecliffe, Colorado. They were endorsed by Denver groups such as the Shorter African Methodist Episcopal Church and the Young Men's Christian Association and the Lincoln Community Center in Waukegan, Illinois, as well as by many prominent black citizens in the area. In 1925 Winks Hamlet,

who had been involved in the original Lincoln Hills project as a landowner, decided to build a lodge for black vacationers who suffered discrimination in other parts of the United States. He called his lodge Winks Lodge, also known as Winks Panorama.

Even though Winks Lodge suffered financially during the Great Depression and World War II, Winks advertised nationally in *Ebony*, one of the first black magazines in the country, and urged many people to become members. National publicity resulted in a new influx of easterners who were anxious to enjoy the high country. Winks Panorama offered African Americans dignity, peace, quiet, and solitude away from racial problems, the war, and other tensions of the time. Winks Hamlet continued to operate the lodge until 1965. [A 3/28/80, 80000901]

CONNECTICUT

HARTFORD COUNTY

First Church of Christ
75 Main Street
Farmington

The First Church of Christ, built in 1771 and known as the Meeting House, is associated with the Africans famous for the mutiny aboard the Cuban slave ship *Amistad* in the summer of 1839. While the ship was traveling on the coast of Cuba, the Africans on board, led by Joseph Cinque (1817–?), killed the crew and officers learned to operate the schooner on their own. After sailing around the Atlantic, the *Amistad* dropped anchor at Culloden Point in the Long Island Sound, where it was seized by the U.S. brig *Washington*.

For 18 months after the capture of the *Amistad*, the Africans, or Amistads as they had come to be called, were held in New Haven, Connecticut, to be tried on charges of mutiny, piracy, and murder. Abolitionists, such as the wealthy brothers Lewis and Arthur Tappan, protected the African captives and, in so doing, promoted the cause of abolitionism.

The mutiny trial eventually went to the

First Church of Christ. Photo courtesy of the Historic American Buildings Survey (Jack Boucher).

U.S. Supreme Court. After the Supreme Court decision established the fact that Africans, under specific circumstances, were "free native Africans" rather than slaves, the Africans were transported to Farmington to await return passage to Africa. While there, they attended church and community events at the First Church of Christ and became active members of the Farmington community. The church was designated a National Historic Landmark on May 15, 1975. [CA 5/15/75 NHL, 75002056]

Lighthouse Archeological Site (5-37)
Address restricted
Barkhamsted

The Lighthouse Archeological Site (5-37) is a rare example of a historic settlement formed by individuals from very different cultural backgrounds who blended aspects of their cultures to produce a successful community. The settlement, which existed between 1740 and 1860, consisted of displaced Native Americans, whites, and African Americans.

The settlement was established around 1740 by James Chaugham, a Block Island Indian, and Mary Barber, a white woman from Windsor, Connecticut. During the late 18th century, it consisted of 40 dwellings. The villagers raised crops and made baskets to sell to white settlers in the area. By the middle of the 19th century, the village consisted of "four or five huts, or shanties" distributed across the hillside. By 1869 it was abandoned.

At present the site is part of the People's State Forest. The site area, as well as the remainder of the state forest, is used for passive recreation such as picnicking and hiking. [D 4/25/91, 91000445]

Mather Homestead
2 Mahl Avenue
Hartford

Built between 1835 and 1843, the Mather Homestead is owned by the Excelsior Lodge, one of the oldest black organizations in Hartford, which is associated with the Prince Hall movement. The movement originated in Boston in 1784 when a free black abolitionist, Prince Hall (1735–1807), was granted a charter for a black Masonic chapter. In keeping with the Enlightenment ideals of early Freemasonry, Prince Hall lodges became forces for equal education, civil rights, and social welfare in the black community.

From its inception on May 14, 1859, Hartford's Excelsior Lodge included among its members many leaders of Hartford's black community, such as James Ralston, a black leader in both state and local Masonic activities. Ralston was the force behind the Ralston Petition, presented to the state legislature in 1868, which moved the assembly to open state public schools to black children. During its tenure in the Mather Homestead, the lodge has been active in many civil rights causes as well as civic and charitable activities. [CA 4/29/82, 82004426]

NEW HAVEN COUNTY

Goffe Street Special School for Colored Children
106 Goffe Street
New Haven

The Goffe Street Special School for Colored Children is the most notable monument to the history of African Americans in New Haven, a center of abolitionist sentiment before the Civil War.

From 1866 until 1871, when state and local laws were modified to allow for public education for African Americans, the building served as an evening school for the black community. Thereafter the building was used by the black community in various ways. It housed Mrs. Turner's sewing classes (1875); the Boys' Club sponsored by the United Church (1889); Danish Church meetings (1891); Hodson Church (1891); James S. Shell's Masonry School (1891); and Hillhouse Training School, which later became the Olympian Athletic Club.

The Olympian Athletic Club was chartered by the Colored Young Men's Christian Association in 1895. After World War I, St. Luke's Episcopal Church used the building as a parish house and community center for African Americans. In 1929 the Grand Lodge of Negro Masons purchased the building and retains possession of it today. [CA 8/17/79, 79002643]

Prudence Crandall House (Dennis Oparowski)

WINDHAM COUNTY
Prudence Crandall House
Junction of Connecticut Routes 14
and 169
Canterbury

Built in 1805, this home served for a time as a school for black girls. In 1831 Prudence Crandall, age 27 and a graduate of the Society of Friends Boarding School in Providence, was invited by Canterbury residents to head a school there for young girls. She accepted and soon the school was flourishing. When Sarah Harris, a black girl, applied for admission, Crandall accepted her and as a result was the target of much public resentment. Rather than bow to local pressure, Crandall dismissed all of her white pupils and converted her school into one for training black girls to become teachers.

By 1833 Crandall had 20 black girls in residence, and negative public reaction had increased proportionately. Local shopkeepers refused to sell food to the school, and a general boycott developed. So determined and influential were Crandall's opponents that in May 1833 they secured passage by the Connecticut General Assembly of a measure known as the Black Law, which stated that no colored person from outside the state should be permitted instruction in any but the free public school unless a town gave specific approval.

Crandall ignored the law and was arrested and sent to the county jail. She refused to pay the bail for her release and remained one night as a form of protest. After a lengthy court battle, her conviction was set aside by a court of errors on technical grounds. However, the townspeople continued their harassment until the school closed in September 1834. It seemed hopeless to keep the school open with no protection from future attacks.

Crandall married a Baptist minister, the Reverend Calvin Philleo, and moved to Iowa and later to Kansas. Many years later, in 1886, the legislature made belated amends by voting Prudence Crandall Philleo, then living in Kansas, an annuity of $400 a year. The Prudence Crandall House was designated a National Historic Landmark on July 17, 1991. [CA 10/22/70 NHL, 70000696]

DELAWARE

KENT COUNTY

Loockerman Hall

Delaware State College campus
Dover

One of the finest prerevolutionary houses now standing in Delaware, Loockerman Hall is the only remaining building of the former Loockerman plantation. Constructed sometime between 1772 and 1790, the Georgian style house is associated with the Loockerman family, whose members are prominent in Delaware history. Loockerman Hall was also the first building on the campus of Delaware State College.

Established as the State College for Colored Students in May 1891, the school was one of many founded under the 1890 Morrill Land-Grant Act of the United States, which made financial assistance available to states for the creation of colleges for African Americans. The property on which the school was established was at the time a working farm.

Loockerman Hall provided classroom and dormitory space until 1961. After standing vacant for many years, the building was restored, and it now serves as a gallery museum and a center for historical research on early American life in Delaware. [C 6/21/71, 71000218]

Smyrna Historic District

Junction of Delaware Route 6 and U.S. Route 13
Smyrna

An African or African American presence has been recorded in Delaware since the mid-17th century, when the Swedes colonized the area in 1638. In 1655 the Swedes were replaced by the Dutch, who brought African slaves with them, as did the English, who took over the colony in 1664. Slavery in Delaware began to decline in 1790, as farmers moved away from labor-intensive crops and relied more heavily on fertilizers and machinery to grow crops. Delaware was also heavily populated by Quakers, who strongly opposed the institution of slavery. This attitude may account for the relatively low number of slaves in the state and may explain the large number of manumissions recorded in Kent County, the county with the strongest Quaker presence.

After leaving the farms, many African Americans sought work in the cities or left Delaware altogether. A few, however, settled in Delaware's small towns, providing services or working in the small mills and factories established in the 19th century. Within these towns African Americans formed distinct communities and founded their own social, religious, and educational institutions.

Old Fort Church. Photo courtesy of the Bureau of Archeology and Historic Preservation (Richard Jett).

In Smyrna African Americans established a small community on the town's east end. In 1867 they erected the Bethel African Methodist Episcopal (AME) Church, a good example of mid-19th century Gothic Revival architecture. The cemetery surrounding the church has only a few gravestones remaining. Among these is a wooden marker in the shape of a rounded arch. The Bethel AME Church is an important physical reminder of the role African Americans played in the economy of this small town. [African-American Resources in Delaware MPS (AD), CA 5/23/80, 80000930]

New Castle County

Odessa Historic District
Bounded roughly by Appoquinimink Creek, High Street, 4th Street, and Main Street
Odessa

The buildings and sites in the Odessa Historic District are among the few in this area of Delaware to escape major commercial encroachment and significant architectural change. The buildings here are architecturally significant and represent the town's growth and development from 1740 into the 20th century. Among these is the Gothic Revival style Zoar Methodist Episcopal (ME) Church, built in 1881 to serve Odessa's black population. Several stones remain in the church cemetery, which is surrounded by its original brick wall with an iron gate. As in other settlements throughout the 19th and early 20th centuries in Delaware, black residents of Odessa provided a steady work force for the farms, shops, and factories of the community, as well as a labor pool for domestic work. The Zoar ME Church and cemetery are an important reminder of the contributions of African Americans to Odessa's history. [African-American Resources in Delaware MPS (AD), CA 6/21/71, 71000227]

Old Fort Church
Old Baltimore Pike
Christiana

Old Fort Church lies within the boundaries of White Clay Creek Hundred, one of the first areas to be inhabited and developed in New Castle County. The church began as Union African Methodist Church in 1819 near Christiana. By the 1880s membership had increased significantly and consisted primarily of black residents of the village of Christiana Bridge. Church leaders therefore decided to move the church to its present location to better serve its members. In 1897 the 1850 brick church was dismantled and reassembled on the present site. The extent of alterations to the basic one-story gable-front plan, a common plan for small congregations in the 19th century, during its move is unknown. Shortly after the church was moved, its name was changed to Old Fort, signifying the hardships suffered by the congregation and it ultimate triumph in paying the mortgage for the property. [White Clay Creek Hundred MRA, CA 8/19/83, 83001402]

Public School No. 111-C
Delaware Route 7
Christiana

Public School No. 111-C is one of several black schools built in the 1920s and financed by Pierre S. du Pont. Designed by architect James O. Betelle, this simple frame building with Colonial Revival details was designed to symbolize basic democratic virtues perceived to be the foundation of America's greatness. Du Pont had appropriated $900,000 for the construction of black schools in rural Delaware after surveying the poor condition of the state's rural schools. Of the approximately 80 schools built in Delaware for black children during the 1920s, Public School No. 111-C stands as a well-preserved example of the type of segregated school that once served Delaware's black community. [CAB 10/18/79, 79000625]

Sussex County

Harmon School
South of the junction of Route 24 and County Route 297
Millsboro

The Harmon School was built in the early 1920s to replace an earlier one-room frame structure constructed in the 1880s by a separatist Nanticoke faction. The land for the original Harmon School was donated by Isaac Harmon and was used exclusively for Indian students. The current frame Colonial Revival style building is typical of schools constructed for minority communities under school reforms of the early 20th century. After the construction of the new school, the introduction of black students and teachers caused the Indian students to withdraw and form a new school. The property reflects both the Indian separatist movement of the late 19th century and the assimilation of some Indian students into the black community, for some students who claimed Indian descent returned to the school in later years. [Nanticoke Indian Community TR, A 4/26/79, 79003314]

Johnson School

Route 24 between County Routes 309 and 310
Millsboro

The Johnson School is located in the Nanticoke Indian Community on the north shore of the Indian River. The school was built during the early 1920s as a separate educational facility for black students, and its frame Colonial Revival building is typical of schools built for minority communities during school reforms of the early 20th century. The Johnson School was attended by some children whose families claimed Indian descent. The property illustrates the assimilation of part of the Indian River Nanticoke Indian Community into the local black community. [Nanticoke Indian Community TR, A 4/26/79, 79003313]

Lewes Historic District

Ship-carpenter, Front, Savannah, 2nd, 3rd, and 4th streets
Lewes

The Lewes Historic District is significant not only for its architecture, but also for the social history embodied in its development. The district includes a small, historically African American community on the north end of town. The exact date the community was established is unknown. As in many small towns in Delaware, the African American community in Lewes provided the service sector of the economy in the late 19th and early 20th centuries.

Among the institutions built by African Americans in Lewes were St. Paul's ME Church, and St. George's African Methodist Episcopal (AME) Church. St. Paul's was constructed in 1882 in the Gothic Revival style. This church was built to serve an African American congregation that had remained Methodist rather than moving to the AME church. St. George's AME Church, also a Gothic Revival building, was constructed in 1930. The present building is the second to house the congregation, the first having been located on nearby Pilottown Road. The St. George's AME Church Cemetery was laid out next to the original church and remains despite the absence of the original church building. The cemetery contains simple headstones laid out in rows on an elevated rise with a large tree serving as a focal point. The cemetery and the two churches are important reminders of the role of African Americans in the Lewes's development. [African-American Resources in Delaware MPS (AD), CAD 9/19/77, 77000393]

DISTRICT OF COLUMBIA

Asbury United Methodist Church
Intersection of 11th and K streets, N.W.
Washington, D.C.

Asbury United Methodist Church is the oldest black Methodist church in the District of Columbia to remain on its original site. The building, completed in 1916, is the third to house the congregation on the site. Asbury formed when the black congregants of the Foundry Methodist Church purchased the lot in 1836 and erected a Federal style frame building. Although it was housed in a different building from the remaining white congregation, Asbury was not permitted to establish an independent pastorate. In 1845 the original frame building was replaced by a more substantial brick church.

Asbury's congregation grew quickly. Many African Americans favored the Methodist Church for the measure of independence and leadership it afforded them. Of all Protestant denominations, only Baptists and Methodists allowed African Americans to preach, although leadership remained largely white. By 1860 Asbury's congregation had become the largest all-black Methodist church in the District.

The Emancipation Proclamation signaled black independence within the Methodist Church, and Asbury was finally granted its own pastorate in 1864. Planning began in 1902 for the construction of the present structure, which would accommodate the growing congregation and display its prominence among black Methodist churches. [A 11/1/86, 86003029]

Banneker Recreation Center
2500 Georgia Avenue, N.W.
Washington, D.C.

Built in 1934, Banneker Recreation Center was the premier black recreation center in the District of Columbia in the period when municipal facilities were segregated. The center's namesake, Benjamin Banneker, was a black mathematician and astronomer who worked with Andrew Ellicott to survey the District of Columbia before the city was established (see also Benajmin Banneker: SW 9 Intermediate Boundary Stone, Arlington County, Virginia).

The center, located in the Freedmen's Bureau subdivision across from Howard University, was built to provide space for leisure activities for adults and supervised play for children. In addition to the swimming pool, then considered the foremost outdoor facility available for the black community, the center offered track and field events, mothers' centers, and music and dance activities. The center's program was the product of the recreational reform agenda undertaken by the Department of Recreation, which hoped to maintain social order by educating the citizenry and inculcating good habits.

House at 317 T Street, N.W., in the LeDroit Park Historic District. Photo courtesy of the National Capital Planning Commission (William Edmund Barrett).

In 1953 Banneker became one of seven recreation centers to be declared "open" or desegregated. Banneker Recreation Center continues an active, community-based program and remains a focus for the black community. [CA 4/28/86, 86000876]

Mary McLeod Bethune Council House National Historic Site
1318 Vermont Avenue, N.W.
Washington, D.C.

The Mary McLeod Bethune Council House was the residence of Mary McLeod Bethune (1875–1955) from

1943 until 1955. It was also the first national headquarters of the National Council of Negro Women and is the location of the Mary McLeod Bethune Memorial Museum and the National Archives for Black Women's History.

Mary McLeod Bethune was born July 10, 1875, in Maysville, South Carolina. She attended Maysville Mission School and then Scotia Seminary (now Barber-Scotia College) in Concord, North Carolina, and Moody Bible Institute in Chicago. Her ambition was to become a missionary in Africa.

Unable to fulfill this dream, she returned to the South to teach southern blacks. While there, she worked with Lucy Laney, a former slave who had founded the Haines Normal Institute in Augusta, Georgia. Laney inspired her to dedicate her life to education. In 1904 she founded the Daytona Normal and Industrial School for Negro Girls in Daytona, Florida. The school later became a high school and a then junior college and finally merged with Cookman College to become an accredited college for African Americans.

Education was not the only field in which Mary Bethune was a leader. Soon after establishing herself as an educator in Florida, she was elected president of the State Federation of Colored Women's Clubs. She received national recognition as a supporter of the women's club movement when she joined the National Association of Colored Women, and in 1924 she became president of the organization. Her greatest success in the movement occurred on December 5, 1935, when she founded the National Council of Negro Women, an umbrella organization of black women's organizations, and became its president, a post she held until 1949.

In 1930 President Hoover appointed Bethune to the White House Conference on Child Health. The Great Depression years saw her most significant government service. In 1935 President Franklin D. Roosevelt named her director of the Division of Negro Affairs, a key position in the National Youth Administration. In this post she worked with other "black cabinet" members such as Robert Weaver, William Hastie, and Frank Horne.

From 1936 to 1951 Bethune served as president of the Association for the Study of Negro Life and History. Though she was by no means a professional historian and the bulk of the association's administrative duties were performed by Carter G. Woodson, she attracted donors to the association.

Mary Bethune died in Daytona Beach, Florida, in 1955. She is buried on a mound overlooking the Bethune-Cookman College campus. Her Washington, D.C., residence was designated a National Historic Site on October 15, 1982, and added to the National Park system on December 11, 1991 (see also Mary McLeod Bethune Home, Volusia County, Florida). [B 12/11/91 NPS, 82005389]

Blagden Alley–Naylor Court Historic District
Bounded by O, 9th, M, and 10th streets, N.W.
Washington, D.C.

The Blagden Alley–Naylor Court Historic District represents a significant chapter in the history of Washington, D.C. From the time of its founding, Washington had a sizable population of free black citizens. The black population grew steadily throughout the early 19th century and boomed with the onset of the Civil War. Generally unable to afford houses that faced the public streets, a significant number of the District's black residents lived in alley-fronting lots that had been subdivided by the owners. It was in these alleys that many of the District's black residents built their homes, lived, and established communities.

The largest number of alley dwellings were constructed in the 1880s. In 1880, 42 heads of household were reported living in Blagden Alley and 22 in Naylor's Court (now known as Naylor Court). These neighboring alleys were two of the some 500 alleys inhabited by African Americans in the District after the Civil War. Most alley dwellings consisted of two-story houses made of brick and measuring about 12 feet wide and 24 feet deep with one or two rooms on each floor. Naylor's Court housed stables and commercial buildings as well, forming a distinct, isolated alley community.

Living conditions in the alleys were miserable. Overcrowding—four to six persons inhabiting one room—was common. Unsanitary conditions, poorly constructed shelters, and limited economic means combined to produce a high death rate among alley dwellers. Reformers further complained that these conditions fostered immoral behavior.

In 1897 an alley census was made, numbering the black alley dwellers at 16,064 and whites at 1,198. It is believed that even these figures are conservative, for residents may have been unwilling to give accurate accounts to police.

Campaigns to abolish the alley dwellings had been under way since the 1890s. In 1904 humanitarian and urban social reformer Jacob Riis was brought to the city to investigate the problem and advise President Theodore Roosevelt and Congress. In 1909 Charles Weller, secretary of Associated Charities, published a study on Washington's alleys using Blagden Alley as his model. The reform movement grew rapidly, reaching a peak in 1914 when it was spearheaded by First Lady Ellen Wilson.

In 1918 Congress considered legislation that would abolish the alley dwellings, but its efforts were cut short with the advent of World War I. The legislation was not considered again until 1934, with the creation of the Alley Dwelling Authority, which oversaw construction of communities for Washington's low-income black residents (see also Langston Terrace Dwellings). Blagden Alley and Naylor Court were the setting of a life once typical to Washington's black population, and they inspired reformers to eliminate those substandard conditions. [CA 11/16/90, 90001734]

Anthony Bowen YMCA
1816 12th Street, N.W.
Washington, D.C.

Completed in 1912, the Anthony Bowen Young Men's Christian Association (YMCA) building was designed by William Sidney Pittman, one of the first formally trained black architects in the United States (see also E. E. Hume Hall, Franklin County, Kentucky). The Anthony Bowen branch of the YMCA, organized in 1853, was the first chapter established for black men and boys.

Anthony Bowen, the chapter's founder, was born a slave but purchased his freedom and moved to the District of Columbia from a nearby county in Maryland. While working as a U.S. Patent Office clerk, Bowen devoted his life to service to the black community. For example, Bowen was instrumental in pressuring Congress to appropriate funds in 1867 for the construction of a public school for blacks in the District.

Until the construction of Pittman's

building, the chapter held its events at various locations around the city. In the early 1900s a campaign was initiated to raise funds for a permanent building. Grants from Julius Rosenwald and John D. Rockefeller contributed significantly to the building costs, along with $27,000 raised by the District's black community. The campaign marked the beginning of biracial cooperative efforts for the advancement of African Americans in America's cities. [A 10/3/83, 83003523]

Blanche K. Bruce House

909 M Street, N.W.
Washington, D.C.

Blanche Kelso Bruce (1841–98) was born into slavery in Virginia. His master took him as a young child from Virginia to Missouri and back, finally settling in Mississippi, where Bruce worked as a hand in a tobacco field and factory. He also trained in the printing trade before the outbreak of the Civil War, when he escaped to the free state of Kansas. In Kansas he opened and taught in the first state elementary school for African Americans. Bruce returned to Missouri after the emancipation of slaves there in 1865 and taught school while working as a printer's apprentice. Prompted by a speech by James L. Alcorn, a future governor of Mississippi, Bruce settled in Mississippi. He began his career in politics when he was appointed conductor of elections and sergeant-at-arms of the new state senate in 1869.

In 1874 Bruce was elected U.S. senator from Mississippi, becoming the second African American to hold the position and the first to serve a full term. He moved to the District of Columbia in 1875 and quickly established himself as an intelligent and effective politician who addressed a wide range of national concerns. Bruce took up the fight to improve opportunities and conditions for African Americans and spoke and voted on their behalf repeatedly during his term in office. Perhaps his most significant accomplishment was handling the affairs of the Freedmen's Savings Bank after its collapse in 1874. Through Bruce's efforts, investors were able to recover three-fifths of the money they had deposited in the failed venture.

After completing his term in the Senate, Bruce became register of the Treasury under President Garfield in 1881. He remained in this position under President Arthur, moved to the position of recorder of deeds under President Harrison, and resumed the post of register of the Treasury under President McKinley. He remained an active advocate of equal opportunity for African Americans until his death on March 17, 1898. His funeral at Metropolitan African Methodist Episcopal Church in Washington was attended by 3,000 people (see also Metropolitan African Methodist Episcopal Church). Blanche K. Bruce's Washington residence was designated a National Historic Landmark on May 15, 1976. [B 5/15/75, 75002046]

Ralph Bunche House

1510 Jackson Street, N.E.
Washington, D.C.

Designed by noted black Washington architect Hilyard Robinson, this building was the home of distinguished African American diplomat and scholar Ralph Bunche. Bunche's accomplishments are many. He held several positions at the United Nations, including undersecretary general. He had a long association with Howard University, where he organized the Political Science Department. He also served there as professor, adviser to the president, and the school's first black overseer. He also taught at Harvard

University, where he earned his doctorate. Bunche was the first African American to hold a desk at the State Department and to win the Nobel Peace Prize, which he was awarded in 1959 for his role in mediating an Arab-Israeli peace settlement. Bunche subsequently was awarded the Medal Freedom, the nation's highest civilian award, by President John F. Kennedy.

While living in Washington, D.C., and teaching at Howard University, Bunche commissioned Robinson to design his residence. Robinson was the most prolific and successful black architect in Washington until his retirement in the 1960s. Robinson was educated at Columbia University and trained under Vertner Tandy, then New York's only licensed black architect.

In 1924, Robinson came to the District of Columbia to teach at Howard University, where he became director of the School of Architecture in 1932. Robinson's work was greatly influenced by a trip to Europe in 1930. Like the Bunche House, many of his designs are executed in the International Style (see also Langston Terrace Dwellings and Ralph Bunche House, Queens County, New York). [CA 9/30/93 93001013]

Francis L. Cardozo Senior High School

Intersection of 13th and Clifton streets, N.W.
Washington, D.C.

Located on a prominent ridge north of the original boundary of the city of Washington, Francis L. Cardozo High School exemplifies the development of an appropriate building form for schools as the activities that they housed were expanded. The building further serves as a microcosm of public school history in the nation's capital, reflecting the evolution of schools from a racially dual to a unified system.

Completed in 1916 as Central High School, the building was originally intended to teach white students, while Dunbar High School, constructed at the same time, was to serve black students. Central was constructed to replace an older, seriously overcrowded building. A shift in school activities in the early 20th century to include academic clubs, sports teams, and cadet companies also necessitated a change in the design of school buildings. Famed St. Louis architect William B. Ittner was engaged to draw up the plans for the Central High School building. Reflecting the broader functions public schools served, the new building included a stadium, athletic field, swimming pool, gyms, armory, tennis courts, greenhouse, library, and auditorium.

During the 1920s Central enrolled more than 3,000 students. In the 1930s and 1940s, however, enrollment dwindled with the creation of junior high schools and construction of other school buildings in Washington. In 1950 the Board of Education, facing vastly overcrowded black schools and emptying white schools, decided to convert Central to a black school.

Cardozo High School was a black school established in 1888 and later renamed in honor of Francis L. Cardozo, a black educator who served as principal of several District public schools. The school had outgrown several buildings, and by 1949 the school had exceeded its building's capacity by 800 and was operating on a triple shift.

In fall 1950 Cardozo High School was moved to the Central High School building. While the school's curriculum was focused primarily on business education, the expanded facilities permitted the school to bolster its technical and academic programs as well as its student activities and after-school clubs. Cardozo's move to the Central High School building allowed a more complete educational experience for Washington's black students. Cardozo was integrated in the 1950s and remains in use as a high school. [CA 9/30/93, 93001015]

Mary Ann Shadd Cary House
1421 W Street, N.W.
Washington, D.C.

Mary Ann Shadd Cary (1823–93) was born into a Delaware family dedicated to the abolition of slavery. Her father was a prominent member of the American Anti-Slavery Society, and their home often served as a shelter for runaway slaves. Mary Shadd herself became one of the most outspoken proponents of abolition and black equality.

After completing her education at a Pennsylvania Quaker boarding school, Shadd returned to Delaware in 1839 to conduct a private school for black children. With the passage of the Fugitive Slave Law in 1850, Shadd and her brother Isaac emigrated to Canada along with scores of other African Americans. Convinced that Canada offered better opportunities, other members of the family soon joined them.

In 1856 Shadd married Thomas F. Cary, a Toronto barber. The couple contributed regularly to the *Provincial Freeman* newspaper. In 1858 abolitionist John Brown held his secret "convention" in the home of Isaac Shadd, heightening Mary Shadd Cary's devotion to the abolitionist cause. During the Civil War she was appointed by Governor Levi Morton of Indiana to be a recruiting officer for the Union army in his state. Widowed during the war, Mary Shadd Cary and her daughter, Elizabeth, moved to the District of Columbia, where she taught in

the city's school system and at Howard University. At the same time she lectured on women's rights and suffrage and campaigned for the education and moral improvement of the newly emancipated.

In 1869 Mary Shadd Cary began studying law at Howard University. She completed her law degree in 1883, becoming the nation's first black woman lawyer. She practiced law for many years in the District while she contributed to the *New National Era* and the *Advocate* newspapers. She died in 1893 and was interred in Harmony Cemetery in the District. The W Street house where she lived from 1881 until 1885 was designated a National Historic Landmark on December 8, 1976. [B 12/8/76 NHL, 76002128]

Frederick Douglass National Historic Site
1411 W Street, S.E.
Washington, D.C.

Frederick Douglass (1817–95) was born Frederick Augustus Washington Bailey on Maryland's Eastern Shore. Born a slave, he learned to read and write at an early age and escaped to the North, changing his name to Douglass to avoid recapture. After fleeing north, he married Anna Murray, a free black woman, and became active in the abolitionist cause. By 1841 he was the agent of the Massachusetts Anti-Slavery Society. Fearing capture, Douglass fled to England, where Quakers purchased his freedom.

In 1847 Douglass returned to New York, where he became a lecturer, leader of Rochester's Underground Railroad, and editor and publisher of the *North Star*, an abolitionist newspaper. In 1854 he published his famed autobiography, *The Narrative of the Life of Frederick Douglass,* the first and most important of his three autobiographies. In the summer of 1863 he convinced President Lincoln to enlist black men as soldiers in the Union army. Shortly thereafter, his own sons, Lewis and Charles, joined the newly formed 54th Massachusetts Colored Regiment.

In 1872 Douglass came to Washington, D.C., and purchased a home near the Capitol. In March 1874 he became president of Freedmen's Bank, a savings bank established for newly freed slaves. President Hayes in 1877 named him marshal of the District of Columbia, and four years later he was appointed recorder of deeds for the District of Columbia. In 1889 President Harrison appointed him minister-resident and consul general to the Republic of Haiti and chargé d'affaires for the Dominican Republic. Because of his contributions to improving the social welfare of African Americans, Douglass became recognized as the "father of the civil rights movement."

Douglass purchased his Cedar Hill home in Anacostia in September 1877 and made many improvements to the property over the years. Following the death of his first wife, Douglass married Helen Pitts. In 1895 Douglas died of a stroke at Cedar Hill. At Helen Pitts Douglass's request, Congress in 1900 chartered the Frederick Douglass Memorial and Historical Association, to whom Mrs. Douglass bequeathed the house. Joining with the National Association of Colored Women's Clubs, the association opened the house to visitors in 1916. The property was added to the National Park system on September 5, 1962, and was designated a National Historic Site on February 12, 1988. (See also Strivers' Section Historic District and Metropolitan African Methodist Episcopal Church, District of Columbia; Douglass Summer House, Anne Arundel

County, Maryland; Douglass Place, Baltimore Independent City, Maryland.) [B 10/15/66 NHL NPS, 66000033]

Evans-Tibbs House
1910 Vermont Avenue, N.W.
Washington, D.C.

Pioneering black opera diva Lillian Evans-Tibbs was born into a prominent black Washington, D.C., family in 1890. In 1904 her father, Wilson B. Evans, purchased a house on Vermont Avenue that soon became a meeting place for the District's black intelligentsia. Lillian Evans received her bachelor's degree in music from Howard University in 1913 and married her music teacher, Roy Tibbs, in 1918. She began a career in opera in the early 1920s and adopted the name Madame Evanti, combining her maiden and married names. Before World War I black vocalists in the United States were readily accepted as singers of spirituals, minstrel tunes, and blues but were largely excluded from the world of classical music. Evanti was a member of a small pioneering group that opened up the world of opera to black performers. Traveling to Europe to seek out opportunities unavailable to her in the United States, Evanti became the first black performer to sing in an organized European company. Upon her return, her career flourished even though she was not associated with any major American company. She was instrumental in the establishment of the Negro National Opera in 1942, which provided opportunities in opera for black performers in the United States. [B 9/8/87, 86003025]

Charlotte Forten Grimke House
1608 R Street, N.W.
Washington, D.C.

Charlotte Forten Grimke (1838–1914) was born in Philadelphia into a wealthy free black family. While attending school in Salem, Massachusetts, she resided in the home of Charles Lenox Remond, a prominent black follower of William Lloyd Garrison. After completing her education, she secured a teaching position at a local grammar school, where she developed an interest in writing. In a short time, Garrison's *Liberator,* the *National Anti-Slavery Standard,* and the *Evangelist* were publishing her abolitionist poems and essays. In Salem she became a radical activist for the abolitionist cause, joining a circle that included William Lloyd Garrison, John Greenleaf Whittier, Wendell Phillips, William C. Nell, and Lydia Marie Child.

Charlotte Forten later returned to Philadelphia where she became a supporter of the women's rights and suffrage movement, but she sought to be more actively involved in the struggle to aid the enslaved. The outbreak of the Civil War presented the opportunity. In 1862 General Sherman announced that instructors were desperately needed to educate the 10,000 or so slaves in Port Royal, South Carolina, who had been abandoned by fleeing white masters. The white educators who answered the call were unable to gain the trust of the former slaves. Forten arrived in Port Royal in October 1862. She began keeping a detailed journal of her efforts to provide the freedmen of St. Helena Island with a basic education. This journal provides a vivid picture of her students' progress and challenges the assumption of the day that African Americans lacked the capacity to be educated.

In 1878 Charlotte Forten married the Reverend Francis J. Grimke of Washington, D.C., the nephew of abolitionists Sarah and Angelina Grimke. The couple resided in the R Street house while she continued her work for social welfare and education for African Americans. Charlotte Forten Grimke died in 1914. The house was designated a National Historic Landmark on May 11, 1976. [B 5/11/76 NHL, 76002129]

Gen. Oliver Otis Howard House
607 Howard Place, N.W.
Washington, D.C.

Constructed in 1867–69, the General Oliver Otis Howard House is an excellent example of the residential Second Empire style popular in this country after the Civil War. It is located on the campus of Howard University and was the home of the school's founder, Major General Oliver Otis Howard (1830–1909), who was also first president, serving from 1869 to 1873. Howard was a distinguished Union military leader during the Civil War, an army commander on the western frontier in the 1870s, commissioner of the Bureau of Refugees, Freedmen, and Abandoned Lands (the Freedmen's Bureau), a peace commissioner to the Indians of Arizona and New Mexico, board member of the Young Men's Christian Association, and a board member of the Freedmen's Bank. Howard's former residence is closely related to the early history of Howard University.

Howard University was chartered by a bill enacted by Congress on March 2, 1867. Although Howard was founded on the premise that there be no discrimination based on color or sex, it has traditionally been a black university, open to both well-educated and disadvantaged African Americans. The original campus included the University Building, a dormitory, a medical building, and Howard House, now known as Howard Hall. Howard Hall has had varied uses over the past century. For example, from 1936 to 1942, it was the home of Miss LuLu V.

Childers and served as the Conservatory of Music, which she directed. From 1967 to 1972, it housed the African Language Center and the African Studies Department. Presently the building serves as office space for the University. [AB 2/12/74 NHL, 74002163]

Howard Theatre
620 T Street, N.W.
Washington, D.C.

Built in 1910, the Howard Theatre stood for more than 50 years at the forefront of black entertainment by providing talent on a local and national level. Segregation in theaters created obstacles for black performers, restricting their exposure. The Howard, along with the Apollo in New York, the Uptown in Baltimore, and the Pearl in Philadelphia, provided the stage on which many prominent black entertainers made their debut.

In its early years, the theater featured vaudeville, musicals, and local variety and church programs. The theater, which for many years housed Howard University events, became a focal point for the anti-lynching protests by students in 1919. In 1931, however, "Shep" Allen took the theater in new directions by headlining Duke Ellington. The Howard went on to host big bands and introduce new talents in its amateur night contests. Among the winners of these contests were Ella Fitzgerald, Billy Eckstein, and Bill "Ink Spots" Kenny.

In the 1940s the Howard featured Sarah Vaughn with Billy Eckstein's Orchestra, Lena Horne with Noble Sissle's Orchestra, Sammy Davis, Jr., with the Will Masten Trio, comedian George Kirby, "Moms" Mabley, Louis Prima, Woody Herman, and Stan Kenton. In the 1950s and 1960s the Howard featured Motown and rock and roll acts such as the

Platters, the Pearls, Roy Hamilton, Gladys Knight and the Pips, Smokey Robinson and the Miracles, James Brown, the Temptations, and Tammi Terrell. A host of other well-known black personalities appeared at the Howard over the years, including sports figures, actors, and comedians.

With the change in the character of the neighborhood and the increasingly young clientele in the 1960s, many black performers opted to perform in other locations in the city. The theater closed following the riots associated with the assassination of Dr. Martin Luther King, Jr., in 1968. It was rehabilitated and reopened in 1985, only to close two weeks later. It has since been dark. [A 2/15/74, 74002162]

Langston Golf Course Historic District
Anacostia Park north of Benning Road, S.E.
Washington, D.C.

Langston Golf Course opened in 1939 after a long campaign by black golfers to gain access to golfing facilities. Historically, golf had been associated with upper-class white culture, and African Americans had been excluded from the clubs as players. There had, however, been a long tradition of black caddies who knew the courses well and were often excellent players in their own right. It was a black golfer, Dr. George F. Grant, who invented the golf tee and was granted a patent for it in 1899.

Before the establishment of the Langston Golf Course, the only golf facility open to black players in the District was the nine-hole course located in what is now Constitution Gardens and parts of the surrounding area. Black golf enthusiasts were forced to travel as far as Boston, Pittsburgh, Philadelphia, and New York to play on good courses without discriminatory policies.

Largely in response to these conditions, the United Golfers Association (UGA) was formed in 1926. The UGA was an outgrowth of a previous organization for black golfers that had been formed in 1920. The UGA encouraged the establishment of black golf clubs across the country and helped to popularize the sport among African Americans. Among the leaders of the UGA was a group of Washingtonians who also figured prominently in the development of Langston Golf Course.

Drs. Albert Harris and George Adams, both UGA members, organized the first black golf club in Washington in 1927. The club, which became known as the Royal Golf Club, gave birth to the nation's first golf club for black women in 1937, when wives of the members established the Wake Robin Golf Club. Both clubs were hindered by the lack of access to adequate local golfing facilities and became the driving force behind the campaign for construction of a first-class course for black golfers in the District of Columbia.

After 15 years of lobbying, the Langston Golf Course was opened in 1939 as a nine-hole course. The course was not enlarged to 18 holes as initially promised until 1955. While desegregation of Washington's facilities opened several excellent courses to black golfers in the 1950s, Langston continued to be the home course for Washington's black golfing community. The course is still predominantly played by black golfers, whose loyalty has been forged in their struggle for accessible high-quality golfing facilities in the District of Columbia. [A 10/15/91 NPS, 91001525]

Langston Terrace Dwellings
North from Benning Road to H Street, N.E.
Washington, D.C.

The Langston Terrace Dwellings were built by the Public Works Administration (PWA) between 1935 and 1938 and mark the beginning of the federal government's provision of low-rent housing for low-income black residents of the District of Columbia. John Mercer Langston, the project's namesake, was the first African American to hold elective office in the United States and was a staunch advocate of social reform for poor Washingtonians. Langston Terrace was one of 51 projects across the country sponsored by the PWA in the 1930s.

The complex was designed by Hilyard Robinson, then director of Howard University's school of architecture and Washington's most prolific black architect before 1960. Langston Terrace is constructed in the International Style and exhibits the progressive design principles employed in European public housing. The New Deal Treasury Art Program commissioned Dan Olney to sculpt a terra-cotta frieze to adorn the primary entrance to the complex. Entitled "The Progress of the Negro Race," the work represents the theme of rural to urban migration by African Americans. A second sculpture of a mother and two children, also by Olney, emphasizes the PWA's goals of family unity and progress.

Today Langston Terrace, the nation's first federally initiated, funded, and supervised peacetime housing project for low-income black citizens in the District of Columbia, is also a well-preserved example of one of the earliest federally sponsored public housing projects in the nation. [CA 11/12/87, 87001851]

LeDroit Park Historic District

Bounded roughly by Florida and Rhode Island avenues, 2nd and Elm streets, and Howard University
Washington, D.C.

The LeDroit Park Historic District was created as a subdivision in 1873 on land purchased as a site for Howard University. The purchase included more land than was necessary for the university, and the excess land was sold to then acting president of the university, Amzi L. Barber, son-in-law of successful real estate broker LeDroit Langdon, and his brother-in-law, Andrew Langdon. In 1873 Barber resigned his post at Howard to establish LeDroit Park. The architect for the development was James H. McGill, a Washington developer and architect. McGill's sketches and floor plans for the houses were designed in the tradition of A. J. Downing's country houses. The styles varied from Italianate villas to Gothic cottages. The houses were similar in plan, but each possessed a unique facade. By 1887 approximately 64 houses had been built. Of these, approximately 50 remain. In the 1890s and 1900s brick and frame row houses were constructed between the McGill homes, giving the community the character it retains today.

LeDroit Park was originally developed as an exclusive white community. A fence was built around the neighborhood, and guards were posted at the gates to restrict access. The fence became a point of contention between the white and black communities. Black protesters tore down the fence in July 1888, only to find it rebuilt four days later. The incident marked a movement toward integration of the area. In 1893 the first black family moved into the subdivision. Integration was short lived, however, for whites quickly moved out, and the community had become almost totally black by

Sculpture by Dan Olney at Langston Terrace Dwellings (Gary Griffin).

World War I. Among the prominent black residents of LeDroit Park were Judge and Mary Church Terrell (see also Mary Church Terrell House); Paul Laurence Dunbar; and former mayor of Washington, Walter Washington. [CA 2/25/74, 74002165]

Lincoln Memorial

West Potomac Park
Washington, D.C.

The Lincoln Memorial, designed after the temples of ancient Greece, is the United States' foremost memorial to its 16th president. Completed in 1914, the memorial was designed by architect

Henry Bacon, and the statue of Abraham Lincoln was created by sculptor Daniel Chester French. The memorial is also an important symbol to thousands of civil rights supporters, who have rallied on its grounds to demand equal rights for black Americans. On Easter Sunday 1939, 75,000 people attended a free concert on the grounds by black singer Marian Anderson. The concert was arranged by First Lady Eleanor Roosevelt after Anderson was denied the right to perform at Constitution Hall, owned by the Daughters of the American Revolution. Roosevelt, angered by the discriminatory practices of the organization for which she was an officer, resigned over the incident and secured permission for Anderson to perform at the memorial.

Twenty-four years later, on August 28, 1963, Marian Anderson once again performed at the Lincoln Memorial. This time, it was as part of the March on Washington, a civil rights rally organized by Martin Luther King, Jr., that drew 200,000 people from across the nation. It was at this rally that King delivered his "I Have A Dream" speech, now considered the most powerful oration associated with the civil rights movement. Today the Lincoln Memorial, under the supervision of the National Park Service, attracts crowds of people from every part of the world. [C 10/15/66 NPS, 66000030]

Lincoln Theatre
1215 U Street, N.W.
Washington, D.C.

An excellent example of a major first-run neighborhood movie house of the 1920s, the Lincoln Theatre is significant both architecturally and culturally as a major historical element of the Washington, D.C.'s predominantly black U Street commercial corridor.

Constructed in 1921, the theater was designed by Reginald Geare, a local architect who designed several other theater buildings in the region, including the Knickerbocker, the District of Columbia's first "movie palace." The Lincoln was one of a chain of theaters owned by Harry M. Crandall, Washington's foremost movie theater operator in the early days of the motion picture industry. While the Lincoln was only one of a great many movie theaters in Washington, the other large downtown movie houses catered to a white clientele. From the beginning, Lincoln showed primarily first-run movies for black patrons. It was not until after 1927, however, when the Lincoln was sold to another theater magnate, A. E. Lichtman, that it became a luxury movie house.

While Lichtman was not the only white theater owner in Washington, D.C., to serve black patrons, he was unique in his active support of the local black community. Of the 434 employees in his business, only a handful were white, managers and supervisors included. Lichtman recognized both the demand for first-rate movie houses among the District's black residents and the opportunity to develop the Lincoln to meet this need because of its prime location along the U Street corridor.

The U Street commercial corridor developed during the first half of the 20th century as the center for nightlife and entertainment for the District's black community. Known as the "Black Broadway," the section of U Street between 9th and 18th streets was home to numerous black-owned businesses, including banks, restaurants, skating rinks, dance halls, and bowling alleys. Although the Lincoln was one of three theaters along the strip, it was by far the most elegant, and Lichtman's addition of a dance hall at the rear of the theater made it the most popular.

The dance hall, known as the Colonnade, featured nationally known black performers such as Fats Waller, Bessie Smith, the Mills Brothers, and Lena Horne and quickly became a favorite spot of patrons of the strip. The space was also often used by Howard University and various community organizations for dances, meetings, and fund raisers. The most profitable era for both the theater and the ballroom came during World War II, when the massive influx of government workers to the city swelled the audiences. After the war, however, the gradual breakdown of segregation in Washington led to the decline of the U Street corridor and the Lincoln. In 1953 the K-B theater chain opened its theaters to black audiences and encouraged others to do so as well. The Colonnade closed its doors in the late 1950s and was later demolished. The theater continued to operate sporadically and finally closed in the early 1970s. It remained vacant until its restoration in 1992. [CA 10/27/93, 93001129]

Mayfair Mansions Apartments
3819 Jay Street, N.E.
Washington, D.C.

Mayfair Mansions, constructed between 1942 and 1946, was an early effort to provide decent housing for the District of Columbia's black residents during an era of strict segregation, discrimination, and institutionalized racism in the housing industry. The design of this low-rise, suburban-style apartment complex mirrored projects built for white tenants during the era. The project was conceived and designed by Albert I. Cassell (see also Prince Hall Masonic Temple), who was instrumental in the development of Howard University's School of Architecture, the first fully

accredited architecture school in a black university. Cassell's codirector of the Mayfair Mansions project was radio evangelist Elder Lightfoot Michaux, who was able to garner support for the project through his radio connections. The project was undertaken at a time when shortages in housing for African Americans were exacerbated by the influx of government employees with the onset of World War II. Mayfair Mansions was the first housing development for African Americans that met Federal Housing Administration (FHA) construction standards and insurance underwriting criteria. The project was instrumental in making FHA housing available to black residents of the District and nationwide. [A 11/1/89, 89001735]

Metropolitan African Methodist Episcopal Church
1518 M Street, N.W.
Washington, D.C.

Metropolitan African Methodist Episcopal (AME) Church, completed in 1886, was designed by architect George Dearing in the Victorian Gothic style. The impetus for the organization of the church was dissatisfaction among the District of Columbia's black community with the predominantly white Ebenezer Methodist Episcopal Church. The dissenting parishioners of Ebenezer petitioned for the organization of the first AME church in the District. Originally organized as Bethel AME Church, the church was renamed Metropolitan AME Church in 1870. The building that houses Metropolitan was built at a cost of $70,000 and dedicated on May 30, 1886. Among those participating in the dedication ceremonies were Bishop Daniel Payne of the National AME Church, Frederick Douglass, and the Honorable Francis Cardozo. Funeral services for

Metropolitan AME Church. Photo courtesy of Historic American Buildings Survey (Ronald Canedy).

Douglass and Blanche K. Bruce were held at Metropolitan (see also Frederick Douglass National Historic Site and Blanche K. Bruce House). [CA 7/26/73, 73002102]

Miner Normal School
2565 Georgia Avenue, N.W.
Washington, D.C.

Miner Normal School has its origins in Myrtilla Miner's School for Colored Girls established in 1851. Miner opened her school in Washington, D.C., in hopes that it would become a model teaching facility for black girls. Although there were a number of privately run schools for free blacks in the District at that time, Miner's was the only one devoted solely to teacher training.

The Miner School, as it came to be called, operated in several different locations during its first years. Myrtilla Miner

left the school in 1858 because of poor health, planning to recuperate in California. She was never able to resume her duties at the school, however, and she died in Washington in 1864. Meanwhile, in 1863 the school was incorporated as the Institution for the Education of Colored Youth. In 1871 the institution became affiliated with Howard University's Normal Department. This arrangement was short lived, however, and in 1875 the school began once again to function independently. In 1877 the school moved into a building constructed for it by the District of Columbia. After functioning for some 10 years in this semipublic capacity, the Miner School was incorporated into the District's public school system, becoming one of the first publicly funded institutions for the training of black teachers. Although officially renamed Washington Normal School #2, the school continued to be known as the Miner School.

Construction on the present building was begun in 1913. The building was officially dedicated as the Myrtilla Miner Normal School in 1917. In 1929, in response to longstanding demands for the upgrading of teacher-training programs in the District, Congress voted to expand the Miner School into a four-year, degree-granting institution, and the school became Miner Teachers College. With the end of segregation in 1955, Miner merged with the District's white teachers college to become the District of Columbia Teachers College. The college operated until 1977, when it merged with two other institutions to form the University of the District of Columbia. [CA 10/11/91, 91001490]

Mount Zion Cemetery
Intersection of 17th and Q streets, N.W.
Washington, D.C.

Mount Zion Cemetery is composed of two separate adjacent cemeteries, the Old Methodist Episcopal Church Burying Ground and the Female Union Band Society Graveyard, and is located within the boundaries of the Georgetown Historic District. The Old Methodist Episcopal Burying Ground was purchased in 1808 by the Dumbarton Street Methodist Episcopal Church. The membership of the church was almost 50 percent black at that time. Church records show that in 1809 trustees collected $41 for lots "to be laid out for the colored friends." After 1849 the burying ground lost popularity and was sold to Mount Zion African Methodist Episcopal Church, which had been formed in 1814 by the black members of the Dumbarton Street Methodist Episcopal Church. The Female Union Band Society, owner of the remaining part of the cemetery, was a cooperative benevolent society formed by free black women around 1842. Its members pledged to assist one another in sickness and in death. The cemetery illustrates the significant contribution of African Americans to the development of Georgetown and the work of an early benevolent society organized by black women for their own benefit. [A 8/6/75, 75002050]

Mount Zion United Methodist Church
1334 29th Street, N.W.
Washington, D.C.

Mount Zion United Methodist Church is a simple brick building with Gothic style detailing constructed between 1876 and 1884 and located within the boundaries of the Georgetown Historic District. The original members of the Mount Zion United Methodist Church were black parishioners of the Montgomery Street Methodist Church who elected to form their own church in 1814. According to the 1830 city directory, the church was then located in a "small brick building" on Mill Street. The building also housed a black school from 1840 until just before the Civil War and was alleged to have been a stop on the Underground Railroad, a claim somewhat substantiated by church records. Along with the names of parishioners, the church register gives remarks that designate the status of travelers on the Underground Railroad, according to a 1948 article in a Pittsburgh newspaper. The present building was constructed with the help of its members, who contributed materials and labor to hold down costs. The church was dedicated on July 6, 1884, and has since maintained a strong congregation despite changes in the residential patterns of the neighborhood. [CA 7/24/75, 75002051]

M Street High School

128 M Street, N.W.
Washington, D.C.

The M Street High School had its origins in the Preparatory High School for Colored Youth, founded in 1870. Initially located in the 15th Street Presbyterian Church, the school moved to several different locations before 1890, when Congress appropriated $112,000 for the construction of a school building. This building, designed to hold 450 students, was completed in 1891 as one of the first high schools in the nation constructed with public funds to serve black students.

The teachers were unusually well educated, owing in part to the lack of opportunities for black professionals elsewhere. The school offered business and college preparatory classes, and its college preparatory curriculum was considered superior to the first two years of many U.S. colleges and universities. Graduates of M Street were often granted admission to leading northern colleges and universities. Among the school's most distinguished graduates are historians Rayford Logan and Carter G. Woodson. Anna Julia Cooper, Robert Terrell, and Francis L. Cardozo served as principals of the school, and Mary Church Terrell taught Latin there.

By 1915 the school's population had reached 850, far more than the school was built to accommodate. In 1916 the new Dunbar High School was built nearby, and the school was renamed the M Street Junior High School. Dunbar carried on the tradition of academic excellence of the M Street school until integration of the school system in 1954, when the need for an elite school set aside for the black population was no longer pressing. [A 10/23/86, 86002924]

Prince Hall Masonic Temple

1000 U Street, N.W.
Washington, D.C.

Prince Hall organized the first black Free Mason Lodge in America in 1775. His lodge, Hall's African Lodge No. 1, was renamed the Prince Hall Grand Lodge after his death in 1807. The Grand Lodge of the District of Columbia was formed in 1848 and was originally housed in a building purchased from another lodge. The building, however, eventually became a perceived fire hazard, prompting the Grand Lodge to put a down payment on a lot on which to construct a new building.

Construction on the Prince Hall Masonic Temple was begun in 1922. The six-story building was completed in 1929 after three separate phases of construction. It was designed by noted black Washington architect Albert I. Cassell, who later designed Mayfair Mansions, the first housing development for African Americans that met Federal Housing Administration construction standards and insurance underwriting criteria (see also Mayfair Mansions). Cassell's Neoclassical Institutional style building housed a bowling alley, restaurant, ballroom, and office space, thus offering the black community a locale for social and business activities that were otherwise made inaccessible by segregation. [CA 9/15/83, 83001418]

Southern Aid Society–Dunbar Theater Building

1901–1903 7th Street, N.W.
Washington, D.C.

The Southern Aid Society–Dunbar Theater Building was designed in 1919 by black architect Isaiah Hatton. The first floor of the building was occupied by the Dunbar movie theater and retail space. The upper floors contained office space, including the headquarters of the Southern Aid Society, the oldest black life insurance company in the nation, and residences. In the basement was a pool room. When this building was constructed, African Americans in the District of Columbia faced growing prejudice and discrimination institutionalized through Jim Crow laws. Hatton, keenly aware of this situation, had designed the Whitelaw Apartment Hotel (now known as the Whitelaw Hotel, 1918–19), the first hotel in the District to be developed, designed, and constructed by and for African Americans (see also Whitelaw Hotel). Similarly, the Southern Aid Society Building represents the black response to exclusion from white-run businesses, social institutions, and housing. The mixed-use building served the retail, housing, business, and entertainment needs of the District's black community. [CA 11/6/86, 86003071]

St. Luke's Episcopal Church
Intersection of 15th and Church streets, N.W.
Washington, D.C.

St. Luke's Protestant Episcopal Church is among the oldest black Episcopalian congregations in the District of Columbia. Before the construction of St. Luke's, the congregation, known as St. Mary's, met in a chapel of St. John's Episcopal Church. Completed in 1879, St. Luke's was designed in the Early English Gothic style by Calvin T. S. Brent, the District's first black architect, and was organized by the Reverend Alexander Crummell.

Alexander Crummell was one of the most talented and articulate black scholars of the 19th century. Born in New York City in 1819, he attended the famous African Free School in New York but left the city in 1835 to attend the Noyes Academy in New Hampshire. Crummell and several other students were forced out of the academy by racially inspired violence.

Despite this and other racially prompted setbacks, Crummell was admitted to the priesthood in 1844. Unable to establish a black mission in New York, Crummell traveled to England and Africa as a missionary and educator and became a citizen of Liberia.

Upon his return to the United States, Crummell established permanent residency in the District. In 1873 he became rector-elect of St. Mary's, from which St. Luke's emerged. In 1894 he retired from St. Luke's. Three years later he founded the American Negro Academy, a society committed to developing a superior black culture and civilization through "the encouragement of the genius and talent of our race." Notable members of the academy included W. E. B. Du Bois, Archibald and Francis Grimke, Kelly Miller, and Paul Laurence Dunbar. Crummell combined an emphasis on academic education and manual training, maintaining that both elements were essential to the "mental and moral improvement of the race." Alexander Crummell died in September 1898. St. Luke's Episcopal Church was designated a National Historic Landmark on May 11, 1976. [B 5/11/76 NHL, 76002131]

St. Mary's Episcopal Church
730 23rd Street, N.W.
Washington, D.C.

St. Mary's Episcopal Church was the first black Episcopalian church in Washington, D.C. The movement to establish St. Mary's as a parish began in 1865, when the black communicants of Epiphany Church started meeting on their own. Encouraged by Charles Hall, rector of Epiphany Church, they formed their own congregation. Hall was instrumental in procuring a place of worship for the newly founded congregation, imploring Secretary of War Edwin Stanton to save a frame chapel that stood on the grounds of a nearby hospital and was about to be dismantled and to move the structure to the 23rd Street lot donated for the purpose. The first services were conducted in this frame chapel in 1867.

In 1877 the congregation decided to build a new church. In 1886 it secured the services of the New York firm of Renwick, Aspinwall, and Russell to design the church. James Renwick (1818–95) was one of the most prominent architects of his time and designed several buildings in the District, the most well-known of which is the Smithsonian Castle building. The new church, a brick Gothic Revival style building, was opened in 1887. St. Mary's, organized specifically to serve the black community, continues to provide educational and community services. [C 4/2/73, 73002118]

Strivers' Section Historic District

Roughly bounded by New Hampshire and Florida avenues, 17th and 18th streets, along T, U, and Willard streets, N.W.
Washington, D.C.

The Strivers' Section Historic District derives its name from the middle-class black residents of the area, who sought to establish themselves in newly built homes in a respectable community. Located outside the fashionable white Dupont Circle neighborhood, the Strivers' Section was a "community of Negro aristocracy" bordering the black cultural corridor of U Street, a major shopping and theater boulevard for middle-class African Americans.

Since the 1870s the district has been associated with black leaders in business,

education, politics, art, architecture, literature, science, and government. The most prominent was Frederick Douglass, who owned two buildings in a five-house row and probably built three of them (see also Frederick Douglass National Historic Site and Douglass Place, Baltimore Independent City, Maryland). Douglass's son Lewis, who inherited the property after his father's death, lived in one of the buildings until his own death in 1908.

Other black leaders who occupied the neighborhood were Calvin Brent, a late 19th-century architect who designed St. Luke's Episcopal Church (see also St. Luke's Episcopal Church), and James C. Dancy, editor, realtor, and recorder of deeds from 1904 to 1910.

Designed by some of the District's most notable architects, the houses in Strivers' Section represent an architecturally rich period in the development of the nation's capital. From the relatively simply decorated row houses to the more elegant and elaborate apartment buildings, the homes are part of a tradition of community and leadership that continues today. [CA 2/6/85, 85000239]

Charles Sumner School

Intersection of 17th and M streets, N.W.
Washington, D.C.

Dedicated in 1872, the Charles Sumner School was one of the first public schools erected for the education of African Americans in Washington, D.C. The Sumner School was built on the site of a school constructed in 1866 under the auspices of the Freedmen's Bureau. The school was named for Charles Sumner (1811–74), one of the U.S. Senate's most dedicated proponents of abolition and black civil rights. Sumner fought for the abolition of slavery in the District of Columbia, the creation of a Freedmen's Bureau, the admission of testimony from

African Americans in the proceedings of the U.S. Supreme Court, equal pay for black soldiers, and the right of African Americans to ride street cars in the District of Columbia.

The Sumner School is one of a series of award-winning modern public schools constructed by the District of Columbia during a period of municipal improvement in the 1860s and 1870s. The building was designed by prominent Washington architect Adolph Cluss, who addressed in this architecturally distinct building many of the problems arising out of the development of a new building type, the urban public school. The Sumner School remains one of the few architectural reminders of the presence and history of African Americans in one of the most historic areas of the city. [CA 12/20/79, 79003150]

Mary Church Terrell House
326 T Street, N.W.
Washington, D.C.

Mary Church Terrell was born in Memphis, Tennessee, in 1863 and received her A.B. from Oberlin College in 1884. She came to the District of Columbia in 1887 to teach Latin at the M Street High School (see also M Street High School). Following a return to Oberlin to earn her M.A. and a trip to Europe, Mary Church married Robert A. Terrell, a prominent black lawyer and head of M Street High School's Latin department. After her marriage Mary Church Terrell stopped teaching, and in 1895 she became the first black woman in the United States to earn an appointment to the board of education, where she would serve for 12 years.

In 1896 Terrell was chosen president of the newly formed National Association of Colored Women. An outspoken advocate of the women's suffrage movement,

she was invited to speak at the 60th anniversary of the First Women's Rights Convention in Seneca Falls, New York. Perhaps her most famous speech, however, was delivered in Germany in 1903 at the International Congress of Women. Entitled "The Progress and Problems of Colored Women," Terrell's speech launched her on a nationwide lecture circuit.

Mary Terrell's tireless efforts for justice and civil rights included serving as a member of an investigative committee that examined charges of police mistreatment of African Americans during the 1919 riots in the District. In 1949, at the age of 86, she challenged the District's failure to enforce antidiscrimination laws applying to public accommodations. Her suit resulted in the 1953 Supreme Court case *District of Columbia v. John R. Thompson Co.* The court's decision ended segregated public accommodations in the nation's capital.

Mary Church Terrell died in 1954 at her family summer home in Maryland. Her LeDroit Park T Street residence was designated a National Historic Landmark on May 15, 1975 (see also LeDroit Park Historic District). [B 5/15/75 NHL, 75002055]

True Reformer Building
1200 U Street, N.W.
Washington, D.C.

Constructed in 1902, the True Reformer Building was one of the first secular buildings in the United States to be designed, financed, and constructed by African Americans. The four-story brick building was designed by John A. Lankford, the first registered black architect in the District of Columbia.

The United Order of the True Reformers was founded in Richmond in 1881 by former slave and temperance reformer the Reverend William Washington Browne. In addition to providing life insurance services, the fraternal benefit society maintained a home for the elderly, five stores, a hotel, a newspaper, a bank, and a farm.

Over the course of its history, the True Reformer Building has played a significant role in the social and commercial life of the black community. Its offices and auditoriums have held church gatherings, social events, and activities of the local Young Men's Christian Association. From 1937 to 1957, the building was leased by the Boys Club of the Metropolitan Police of the District of Columbia. The club was organized in 1934 to combat juvenile delinquency and provide direction for the District's youth. Located in the heart of Washington's black community, the True Reformer Building provided a focus for black activity in a segregated city. [CA 1/9/89, 88003063]

Phillis Wheatley YWCA
901 Rhode Island Avenue, N.W.
Washington, D.C.

The Phillis Wheatley Young Women's Christian Association (YWCA) was organized in 1905 by members of a black women's literary group. Its activities were held in various locations around the city before the War Work Council appropriated funds for the present structure on Rhode Island Avenue. Construction was completed in 1920. Phillis Wheatley, whose name the organization adopted in 1923, was a black poetess who arrived in the United States on the slave ship *Senegal* in 1761.

During World War I the Wheatley YWCA provided travelers' aid to African Americans who came north to Washington. During World War II the chapter provided United Service Organizations (USO) services to black

soldiers who were denied entrance at white USO centers. Throughout its history, the Wheatley YWCA has offered educational and recreational activities, housing, and community services for the District's black community. Among the notable black Washingtonians who have been associated with the Wheatley YWCA are Mary Church Terrell; Dorothy Height, president of the National Council of Negro Women; and Julia West Hamilton, a former president of the national YWCA. [A 10/6/83, 83003532]

Whitelaw Hotel
1839 13th Street, N.W.
Washington, D.C.

In November 1919 construction was completed on the first luxury hotel for African Americans in the District of Columbia. Built at a cost of $158,000, the Whitelaw Apartment Hotel (now known as the Whitelaw Hotel) embodied the ideal of racial solidarity and self-help espoused by black Washingtonians faced with increasing social and economic restrictions in a climate of rising racial tensions. Relations between black and white residents of the District of Columbia in the first two decades of the 20th century were characterized by growing conflict.

In an era dominated by Jim Crow legislation, African Americans faced institutionalized racism and segregation and a decline in black political appointments. Despite organized efforts by the local chapter of the National Association for the Advancement of Colored People, the largest in the nation in 1916, racial conflict continued to escalate, culminating in the 1919 Washington race riots. It was in this atmosphere that the Whitelaw was conceived. Situated in the solidly black middle-class U Street corridor, the Whitelaw was built by and for the black community, easing the shortage of accommodations, housing, and social facilities and standing as a tangible symbol of black self-help.

John Whitelaw Lewis, one of the most important figures in Washington's black commercial world in that period, was the project's originator. Shortly after arriving in Washington in 1894, Lewis organized a building association that eventually became a realty company. He later founded the Industrial Savings Bank and the National Mutual Improvement Association of America, both undertakings designed to promote racial solidarity and economic self-sufficiency.

To finance the venture, Lewis assembled the Whitelaw Apartment House Corporation, which sold stock to black investors. The building was designed by prominent black Washington architect, Isaiah T. Hatton. A graduate of Washington's prestigious M Street High School, Hatton designed several other buildings for the African American community in Washington (see also the Southern Aid Society–Dunbar Theater Building). The Whitelaw building provided apartment space, hotel accommodations, a ballroom, and a grotto. Within the first five days after its opening, more than 20,000 people visited the building, which quickly became a center for cultural, social, and political gatherings for the black community.

The Whitelaw Apartment Hotel has been rehabilitated for use as an apartment building and now provides low- and moderate-income housing. The Whitelaw is major element of a once-thriving black commercial and entertainment corridor that has lost many of its historic buildings. [CAB 7/14/93, 93000595]

Carter G. Woodson House
1538 9th Street, N.W.
Washington, D.C.

Carter G. Woodson was born the son of former slaves on December 19, 1875, in New Canton, Virginia. Although he had no formal education until the age of 20, when he entered Douglass High School in Huntington, Virginia, Woodson went on to earn his Ph.D. from Harvard University in 1912. He was, after W. E. B. Du Bois, only the second African American to receive a doctorate from Harvard. In 1908 Woodson settled in the District of Columbia, where he taught English, Spanish, and French at the M Street High School (see also M Street High School). Woodson's passion, however, was the study of the history of the African American people, and in 1915 he organized the Association for the Study of Negro Life and History (ASNLH).

Headquartered in Woodson's Washington row house, the ASNLH was organized during an era of Jim Crow laws and segregation in the District. Through the ASNHL and its first publication, *The Journal of Negro History,* Woodson worked to dispel the myth of inferiority that plagued African Americans. Among the prominent black scholars associated with the ASNLH were Charles H. Wesley, Alain Locke, E. Franklin Frazier, Luther P. Jackson, and Charles S. Johnson.

Woodson died in his 9th Street residence on April 3, 1950. The efforts he made to spread a popular understanding and knowledge of black history are continued today in the operations of the ASALH (the organization is now known as the Association for the Study of Afro-American Life and History) and its publications. The Woodson House was designated a National Historic Landmark on May 11, 1976. [B 5/11/76 NHL, 76002135]

Old Dillard High School. Photo courtesy of Research Atlantica, Inc. (Jane Day).

FLORIDA

ALACHUA COUNTY

Pleasant Street Historic District

Roughly bounded by Northwest 8th Avenue, Northwest 1st Street, Northwest 2nd Avenue, and Northwest 6th Street Gainesville

The Pleasant Street Historic District is the earliest and most important black residential neighborhood in Gainesville. Founded immediately after the Civil War, the area represented a transition in the status of black people in Alachua County from that of slave laborers supporting a rural plantation economy to one of freedmen seeking to establish economic independence and cultural self-determination in an urban environment.

Black settlers in the Pleasant Street Historic District founded their own businesses, churches, schools, and social and political organizations. The businesses consisted of grocery stores, clothing stores, theaters, funeral parlors, and bars. Also located in the district were black-operated insurance offices, including the Afro-American Life Insurance Company and the Central Life Insurance Company.

The establishment of black churches stemmed from a desire of freedmen to express their independence and form their own religious institutions free from the influence of their former masters. The Mount Pleasant African Methodist Episcopal (AME) Church (now the Mount Pleasant United Methodist Church) became the leading church organization in the area. Several other churches were organized in the Pleasant Street neighborhood soon after Mount Pleasant, including the Bethel AME Church (1877) and the First Friendship Baptist Church (1884).

Union Academy was established by the Freedmen's Bureau in the district in 1865 to educate both adults and children. The academy continued to be the center of local black education until 1925, when a new building, Lincoln High School, was constructed outside the district. Another black educational institution in the district was the St. Augustine Mission School, organized as an Episcopal mission and school in 1893. It served the community until 1944.

Most of the houses in the Pleasant Street Historic District were built in the first 30 years of this century. Many were inhabited by ordinary working people, but given the segregated society of Gainesville, the area also housed black merchants, professionals, and community leaders. The historic district retains its role as a religious and social center for black residents of Gainesville. [CA 4/20/89, 89000323]

BAKER COUNTY

Olustee Battlefield

2 miles east of Olustee on U.S. Route 90
in Osceola National Forest
Olustee

This site commemorates Florida's major Civil War battle, the Battle of Olustee. On February 20, 1864, approximately 5,500 Union troops under the command of General Truman A. Seymour marched westward from Sanderson. Confederate forces were defending positions near Olustee at Ocean Pond. General Joseph Finegan, the Confederate commander, had acquired reinforcements from Georgia to supplement his meager force of 1,200. By February 18, approximately 5,000 Confederates had gathered near Olustee at Ocean Pond. The later arrival of reinforcements and ammunition tipped the scales in favor of the Confederates. The battle lasted for five hours until Union forces retreated. It was a costly battle for the Union: casualties amounted to an estimated 1,860 Union and 946 Confederate soldiers. Participants in the battle included three all-black infantry regiments: the First North Carolina Colored Infantry, the Eighth U.S. Colored Infantry, and the 54th Massachusetts Colored Infantry. About one-third of the Union troops were African Americans. Although it was a Confederate victory, the battle did not result in the withdrawal of Union troops from Florida; rather, it merely confined them to Jacksonville, Fernandina, and St. Augustine. [A 8/12/70, 70000177]

BROWARD COUNTY

Old Dillard High School

1001 Northwest 4th Street
Fort Lauderdale

Built in 1924, Old Dillard High School, originally known as the Colored School, was the first black high school in Broward County and the symbol of the black community's struggle for equal opportunities in education in Fort Lauderdale and Broward County. Joseph Ely, the first principal, renamed the school after James Hardy Dillard, a white man who supported black education in the South and served as president of the Jeanes Foundation, an organization that funded black rural schools in the South. Clarence C. Walker (1880–1942), the son of a former slave, became principal in September 1937. Walker, who was friends with prominent black leaders such as Booker T. Washington, saw education as the only way for African Americans to advance and black schools as centers of community pride. The building was later converted to an elementary school and renamed Clarence C. Walker Elementary School in recognition of Walker's contributions to black education. In 1974 the building became an administrative annex for the Division of Instruction. Restoration work was completed in the spring of 1990, and the building now serves as the Old Dillard School Community Center. [A 2/20/91, 91000107]

DADE COUNTY

D. A. Dorsey House

250 Northwest 9th Street
Miami

The D. A. Dorsey House, constructed c. 1914, was the residence of Dana A. Dorsey (1872–1940), one of Miami's most prominent black businessmen. Dorsey probably built this house for his second wife, Rebecca Livingston. An early developer of the Colored Town section of Miami, Dorsey is generally recognized as Miami's most famous black resident. Dorsey purchased lots for $25 each in the vicinity of the old Seaboard Station and amassed large parcels of real estate. He advertised himself as the "only colored licensed real estate dealer in the city." In 1918 Dorsey acquired Elliot Key and Fisher Island for the purpose of establishing a resort for African Americans. It is probable that Dorsey acquired the largest real estate holdings ever owned by an African American in the history of Dade County. Equally important, Dorsey helped organize south Florida's first black bank, the Mutual Industrial Benefit and Saving Association. He also served as chairman of the Colored Advisory Committee to the Dade County School Board and as registrar for black men in Dade County during World War I. [Downtown Miami MRA, B 1/4/89, 88002966]

Greater Bethel AME Church
245 Northwest 8th Street
Miami

The Greater Bethel African Methodist Episcopal Church is a Mediterranean Revival style building located in the Overtown (originally known as Colored Town) area of downtown Miami. Organized in 1896, several months before Miami was incorporated, the church is the oldest black congregation in the city. The church's first building was constructed before 1899 and was dubbed "Little Bethel." The present church building was begun in 1927 but, because of limited resources during the Great Depression, was not dedicated until 1943, when construction was completed. Out of financial necessity, the church members responsible for building the church adopted a "pay-as-you-go" policy. The church has included among its members and officers many progressive and influential African Americans. Throughout its existence, the church has served the religious and humanitarian needs of the Overtown community. [Downtown Miami MRA, C 4/17/92, 88002987]

Lyric Theater
819 Northwest 2nd Avenue
Miami

The Lyric Theater is a two-story masonry vaudeville and movie theater built by prominent black entrepreneur Gedar Walker in 1915. Located in Miami's Overtown area, known as Colored Town in the early 20th century, the theater is in a district that was known as Little Broadway during the 1930s and 1940s because its clubs presented such stars as Marian Anderson, Bessie Smith, Hazel Scott, and Nat "King" Cole. The Lyric was owned and operated by African Americans and featured black entertainers and theatrical troupes exclusively. Interestingly, the Lyric Theater was equally, if not more, popular with the local white population than with the blacks. The building also served the Overtown community as a venue for other social events, including political meetings, concerts, dramas, boxing, rallies, beauty pageants, and club activities. The Lyric Theater is a surviving testament to black entertainment and social life in Overtown. [Downtown Miami MRA, CA 1/4/89, 88002965]

St. John's Baptist Church
1328 Northwest 3rd Avenue
Miami

St. John's Baptist Church, an Art Moderne style building with Gothic massing, was constructed in downtown Miami during the Great Depression. Located in Overtown, a historically black section of Miami, the building was designed by the black architectural firm of McKissack and McKissack of Nashville and completed in 1940. St. John's congregation was organized in 1906 and met in a small frame building two blocks from the site of the present church until 1939. With membership then exceeding 1,000, the congregation planned and built its new church at a cost of approximately $75,000.

The main force behind the construction of the church was its pastor, the Reverend W. Drake, one of Overtown's best-known black leaders. Drake was born in 1872 in Oglethorpe County, Georgia, and studied at the Baptist Seminary in Atlanta. He came to Miami in 1912 and transformed the Baptist Church in Overtown into one of the area's leading religious institutions. [Downtown Miami MRA, CA 4/17/92, 88002970]

DUVAL COUNTY

Bethel Baptist Institutional Church
1058 Hogan Street
Jacksonville

Built in 1904, this Neoclassical Revival style building has served as the focal point for the religious and community life of Jacksonville's black citizens. In July 1838 the Reverend James McDonald established the congregation with six charter members, including two slaves. At the time of the church's incorporation in 1841, McDonald served a mixed congregation of African Americans and whites, slaves and slaveowners. After the Civil War many black Baptists formed their own churches. Such was the case at Bethel Baptist, where a dispute arose over possession of the church and a legal battle lasted for several years. Finally a court settlement in 1868 awarded the church property to the white members of the congregation and granted the black members financial compensation and retention of the church name. After the split in the congregation, the Bethel Baptist Institutional Church continued to be the principal influence on the spiritual life of Jacksonville's black community. [CA 4/06/78, 78000938]

Brewster Hospital
915 West Monroe Street
Jacksonville

Brewster Hospital, built in 1885, was Jacksonville's first medical facility for the black community. Brewster Hospital had its beginnings in the Boylan-Haven School, a private establishment for black girls. Around the turn of the century, the school began to provide medical services to the black community. With the assistance of the Women's Home Missionary Society of the Methodist Church, one of Boylan-Haven's superintendents, Miss Hattie Emerson, started a formal nurse training program at Boylan-Haven. The school was deeded in September 1901 to the Women's Home Society of the Methodist Church and served as the Brewster Hospital and Nurse Training School until 1910, when it was sold by the Women's Home Society. Brewster Hospital occupied several buildings between 1910 and its closing in 1966. The passage of the 1964 Civil Rights Act opened all local hospitals to the black community, enabling black patients to go to larger, more modern facilities. [A 5/13/76, 76000588]

Catherine Street Fire Station
14 Catherine Street
Jacksonville

The Catherine Street Fire Station was built in 1902 in the aftermath of the Great Fire of 1901, which destroyed almost all of downtown Jacksonville. Until 1905 the station was manned exclusively by African American fire fighters. Blacks had been involved in fire fighting in Jacksonville since at least the mid-1870s, when fire protection was provided by several organized volunteer fire com-

Centennial Hall–Edward Waters College. Photo courtesy of National Register of Historic Places.

panies, including one composed of African Americans. These companies were disbanded in 1886, when the city established a professional fire department and purchased most of their equipment. Although African Americans were assigned to segregated units, they were not excluded from the ranks of professional fire fighters.

Because the Catherine Street Fire Station had been manned by African American professional fire fighters for a time, it was included in the Florida Black Heritage Trail in 1992. Since 1973 the building has housed a valuable collection of historic fire-fighting equipment and served as the Jacksonville Fire Museum. In 1983 it was designated the official museum of the Florida State Fire Fighters Association. [C 6/13/72, 72000309]

Centennial Hall–Edward Waters College
1658 Kings Road
Jacksonville

Built in 1916, Centennial Hall is the oldest building on the campus of Edward Waters College. The building was named to commemorate the 100th anniversary of the African Methodist Episcopal (AME) Church. It reflects a long effort within the AME Church to establish itself as an independent body capable of ensuring top-quality higher education within the black community. From 1874 to 1883, Florida had no institute of higher learning for African Americans. In 1883, through the efforts of the Reverend W. W. Sampson, East Florida Conference High School was established in Jacksonville. The school expanded rapidly, and in 1885 its name was changed to Florida Normal and Divinity School. On March 12, 1892, the school was renamed Edward Waters College, after the third bishop of the AME Church. Today the college is the culmination of a long history of educational work for African Americans. [CA 5/4/76, 76000589]

Kingsley Plantation
Northern tip of Fort George Island at
Fort George Inlet
Jacksonville

The Kingsley Plantation is the only plantation complex surviving from the Spanish Colonial period in Florida. It contains the most complete and best-preserved assemblage of buildings and structures associated with slave-based agriculture in the early 19th century. The plantation was named for Zephaniah Kingsley, a planter and slave trader who resided on the island from 1813 to 1839.

Kingsley used slave labor to operate the plantation where he produced cotton, sugarcane, sweet potatoes, and citrus crops. He had 10 children by three different women—all of whom had been slaves. Of the three, his only acknowledged wife was a former slave named Anna Madgigine Jai, the daughter of an African chief. The plantation operated under the "task system," which afforded the slaves the opportunity to work at their crafts or in their gardens after their defined task on the plantation was completed. This system purportedly allowed the slaves some measure of control over their lives because they were able to sell their produce or crafts and use their earnings to purchase their freedom.

Today Kingsley Plantation includes two plantation houses, one of which may be 200 years old; a tabby, brick, and frame barn; and the ruins of 23 of the original 32 tabby slave cabins. Kingsley Plantation serves as a reminder of the 19th-century Sea Island plantation system and the institution of slavery. It was added to the National Park System on February 16, 1988, as part of the Timucuan Ecological and Historic Preserve. [CADB 9/29/70 NPS, 70000182]

Masonic Temple
410 Broad Street
Jacksonville

Designed in 1913, the Masonic Temple Building has served as the focal point for the Jacksonville black community's commercial and fraternal activities. As early as 1902, the Masonic Lodge had planned to construct a temple. The lodge received financial assistance through the fund-raising efforts of various organizations, such as the Ladies of the Eastern Star, the Royal Arch Masons, and the Jacksonville members of the National Negro Businessmen's League. In 1916 David D. Powell was inducted as the grand master of the Masons of Florida. By 1921 Powell repaid the entire mortgage for the Temple Building along with other debts, a total of $200,000. At that time the Temple was valued at $500,000. In 1926 it was described as one of the finest buildings owned by African Americans in the country. Black insurance agents, dentists, doctors, attorneys, and hairdressers, at one time or another, established their headquarters in the Masonic Temple Building. In 1946 it was home to the office of the Negro Businessmen's League. In addition to providing office and fraternal spaces, the building became a gathering place where the middle-class black community discussed business and politics. [CA 9/22/80, 80000949]

Mount Zion AME Church
201 East Beaver Street
Jacksonville

Architecturally significant as An early example of Romanesque Revival style architecture in Jacksonville, the Mount Zion African Methodist Episcopal Church is home to the oldest black congregation in the city. Founded after the Civil War by a society of freedmen, the church was officially recognized by the regional diocese in 1866. The congregation's first substantial building was erecting in 1890 but was destroyed by fire in 1901. The present building was constructed between 1901 and 1905 at a cost of $18,000. Styled in the Richardsonian Romanesque tradition, the design is credited to Henry L. Klutho, an important local architect. [Downtown Jacksonville MPS, C 12/30/92, 92001697]

Edwin M. Stanton School
521 West Ashley Street
Jacksonville

The Edwin M. Stanton School was established in 1868 as the first public school for African Americans in Jacksonville. It was named for Edwin M. Stanton, an abolitionist and secretary of war in the cabinet of Abraham Lincoln. The present vernacular building was completed in 1917.

James Weldon Johnson (1871–1938) was a student at Stanton High and served as principal from 1894 to 1902. His mother, Helen Louise Johnson, taught at Stanton and is recognized as the first black school teacher in Florida. During his tenure as principal, Johnson expanded the educational program from nine to 12 grades and, in collaboration with his brother Rosamond Johnson (1873–1954), wrote "Lift Every Voice and Sing," which became popularly known as the Negro national anthem. He also became one of the first African Americans admitted to the Florida Bar Association and organized a newspaper, *The Daily American*. Johnson wrote poetry, published several essays, penned a novel entitled *Autobiography of an Ex-Colored Man*, and in his biography, *Along This Way*, described his experiences at the Stanton School. He served in the U.S. Foreign Service as a consul in Venezuela and Nicaragua and as a special envoy to Haiti. He was an influential leader in the civil rights movement and became of one of the first field secretaries of the National Association for the Advancement of Colored People. His remarkable life was cut short by an automobile accident in 1938. Stanton High remained open until 1971, when the building was vacated by the Duval County Board of Public Instruction. [CAB 9/29/83, 83001446]

ESCAMBIA COUNTY

St. Michael's Creole Benevolent Association Hall
416 East Government Street
Pensacola

St. Michael's Creole Benevolent Association Hall was built in 1895–96 by members of St. Michael's Benevolent Social Club. In 1878 T. N. Durbraca and 19 other Creoles organized the club, which they incorporated on June 9, 1881. For almost a century this club provided financial aid for sick members; paid doctor bills and expenses for medicine; and gave death benefits to members' families.

The meeting hall served as the center for Creole social life for 80 years. Dances, receptions, parties, and youth events such as boxing were held here, as well as the monthly and special meetings of St. Michael's Creole Benevolent Social Club.

In 1928 St. Michael's Benevolent Social Club merged assets and membership with the Creole Catholic Benevolent

Association and formed St. Michael's Creole Benevolent Association. The group continued to be active until the 1960s. [CA 5/3/74, 74000623]

FRANKLIN COUNTY

Fort Gadsden Historic Memorial
Six miles southwest of Sumatra
Sumatra

Fort Gadsden Historic Memorial, also known as Negro Fort and British Fort, is symbolic of the cooperation and friendship that existed between African Americans and Seminoles of the American Southeast in the early 1800s. Fort Gadsden was perhaps the best known of the places where runaway slaves from the plantations of Georgia and the Carolinas fled and received refuge among the Seminoles in Spanish Florida. The ex-slaves lived and worked with the Seminoles and served as interpreters and intelligence agents for the entire community. Southern whites viewed the relationship between African Americans and Seminoles as a threat to slavery; therefore under the leadership of Major General Andrew Jackson, the fort was destroyed in 1816 and approximately 300 men, women, and children were killed. The few survivors were made prisoners and released to Georgia slaveholders, who justified their title to them by saying that their ancestors had owned the ancestors of the prisoners.

The destruction of the Negro fort precipitated the outbreak of the first Seminole War of 1817–18. In 1818 Major General Jackson ordered Lieutenant James Gadsden to build a new fort, which became known as Fort Gadsden, on the site. American forces were garrisoned in the fort until Spain ceded Florida to the United States in 1821, thus making it difficult for slaves to take refuge in Florida among the Seminoles. Fort Gadsden was designated a National Historic Landmark on May 15, 1975. [A 2/23/72 NHL, 72000318]

LEE COUNTY

Paul Lawrence Dunbar School
1857 High Street
Fort Myers

Built in 1927, the Paul Lawrence (sic) Dunbar School was the first and, until 1962, only secondary school for black children in Lee, Collier, and Charlotte counties. It was named after Paul Laurence Dunbar (1872–1906), a black poet and novelist.

Paul Laurence Dunbar was born in Dayton, Ohio, on June 27, 1872. Between 1898 and 1904, Dunbar published four collections of short stories: *Folks from Dixie* (1898), *Strength of Gideon and Other Stories* (1900), *In Old Plantation Days* (1903), and *The Heart of Happy Hollow* (1904). He also published four novels: *The Uncalled* (1898), *The Love of Landry* (1900), *The Fanatics* (1901), and *The Sport of the Gods* (1902). Dunbar died in Dayton, Ohio, on February 9, 1906, at age 34. Beloved as a poet and novelist, many schools and numerous other public buildings are named in his memory.

Dunbar School allowed black students the opportunity to complete 12 grades of schooling without having to travel to other parts of the state. Its graduates went on to make noteworthy contributions in many areas of society. Dunbar School was, and still is, regarded as a symbol of black progress and achievement in southwest Florida. Today, it continues to serve Lee County as an adult educational facility and center for community activities. [A 2/24/92, 92000025]

LEON COUNTY

Carnegie Library
Florida Agricultural and Mechanical
University campus
Tallahassee

The Carnegie Library is one of the oldest buildings on the campus of Florida Agricultural and Mechanical University (FAMU) in Tallahassee. Andrew Carnegie, a prominent industrialist and philanthropist, donated $10,000 for the erection of the library building. It was dedicated in February 1908 and had the distinction of being the only Carnegie library located on a black land-grant college campus. The library typifies the architecture of public libraries of the era, and its presence on the FAMU campus symbolizes the school's ongoing efforts to improve the quality of education for black Floridians. It reflects the important combination of private philanthropy and land-grant funding in overcoming the barriers of a segregated university system. [CAB 11/17/78, 78000949]

John Gilmore Riley House
419 East Jefferson Street
Tallahassee

This house is associated with John Gilmore Riley (1857–1955), an early black educator in Tallahassee. Riley never formally attended school but was taught by "Aunt Henrietta," who had been a schoolteacher. His first teaching jobs were in Wakulla and Gadsden counties. It is likely that he came to Tallahassee to live in 1885, when he bought the land on which the Riley House stands. Riley worked for the local board of public instruction from the 1880s until 1926. During that time and until his death, he was a leader in the black community, serving on the board of the St. James Colored Methodist Episcopal Church and actively participating in the Masons. At the time of his death in 1955 he owned valuable property in Tallahassee, including this house, in which he had lived since the 1890s. Shortly after his death, the Leon County School Board named the elementary school on Indiana Street in Tallahassee the John G. Riley School in his honor. [AB 8/1/78, 78000950]

Union Bank
Intersection of Apalachee Parkway and
Calhoun Street
Tallahassee

Built in 1841, the Union Bank, displaying design features of Federal and Greek Revival architecture, played a major role as a bank for merchants and planters in the territorial period of Florida's history. It was chartered in 1833 by the Territorial Council and formally opened on January 16, 1835. Unsound banking practices, the Panic of 1837, and Indian wars led to its closing in 1843. In 1869 the Union Bank building was leased, and then sold, to the National Freedmen's Savings and Trust Company, and it housed the Freedmen's Bureau and the Freedman's Bank. Authorized under a Congressional act of 1865 that created the Bureau of Refugees, Freedmen, and Abandoned Lands, the Freedman's Banks were intended to benefit refugee whites as well as newly emancipated blacks. The Freedman's Bank in Tallahassee served the local black community until 1874, when the system was disbanded and use of the building as a banking facility ended.

Since closing as a bank, the Union Bank building has housed various businesses and served as a church. In an effort to save the building associated with Florida's oldest banking establishment, ownership of Union Bank was transferred to the state of Florida in 1972, and it was relocated to its present site on the southeast corner of the Apalachee Parkway.

The building, as presently situated, occupies a prominent site one block east of Florida's historic capitol. [CA 2/24/71, 71000242]

MARION COUNTY

Mount Zion AME Church
623 South Magnolia Avenue
Ocala

Mount Zion African Methodist Episcopal (AME) Church is the only surviving brick, 19th-century religious building in Ocala, as well as the first brick church owned by a black congregation in the area. As a result of the devastating fire of 1883 in Ocala, Mount Zion was constructed in 1891. The church was designed and constructed by Levi Alexander, Sr., a black contractor. In Ocala, Alexander constructed several houses in the east section, the old Marion Hardware Building, the original Rheinauers Store, Howard Academy, and the AME Church. In designing the church, Alexander provided for the enormous enclosed space and fine acoustics that have made Mount Zion an ideal site for community functions requiring seating capacity up to 600 persons. Every graduation ceremony for Howard Academy was held at Mount Zion until 1950. State meetings of fraternal organizations, concerts, and other cultural activities were held at the church. Mount Zion continues to serve as a religious, social, and civic center for the black community. [A 12/17/79, 79000683]

MONROE COUNTY

George Adderley House
5550 Overseas Highway
Marathon

Built in 1906, the George Adderley House, a modest one-story, masonry building with a hip roof, is the only extant building surviving from the early 20th-century settlement of black Bahamians at Crane Point and on nearby Old Rachel Key in the Florida Keys. Claimed by the Spanish in 1513, the Florida Keys were a haven for pirates and journeying seamen. A small fishing village was established on Key Vaca in the early 19th century, but large-scale settlement did not occur until after 1900, following the construction of the Florida East Coast Railway from Jacksonville to the middle of the Florida Keys. In 1903 George Adderley, a black Bahamian who immigrated to Florida in 1890, purchased 32 acres on Key Vaca in the area known today as Crane Point. Crane Point and nearby Old Rachel Key are the only known sites in the Florida Keys to have been settled exclusively by African Americans. George Adderley was the only member of the black community at Crane Point to own the land on which he lived. Today, the Adderley House provides a unique source of information on how early 20th-century black settlers lived in the middle of the Florida Keys. [CA 9/10/92, 92001243]

Pigeon Key Historic District
Off U.S. Route 1 at mile marker 45
Pigeon Key

Pigeon Key Historic District, situated in the Florida Keys, is important for its association with the Florida East Coast Railway and the Overseas Highway as a workers camp from 1912 to 1938. The Pigeon Key Camp was one of several such camps established in the Florida Keys between 1906 and 1912. It served as an residential camp for workers on the Florida East Coast Railway, which provided the impetus for the development of the east coast of Florida and, in particular, the Florida Keys.

The work force for the railway averaged 3,000 men and, during periods of peak activity, reached as high as 4,000. Black railroad workers from New York, Philadelphia, and the Caribbean Islands worked for the Florida East Coast Railway. The housing conditions were harsh and isolated. Under the supervision of an engineer, the workers labored in exchange for board and lodging in addition to an average salary of $1.00 a week.

The camp for Florida East Coast Railway workers was manned continuously during the next 23 years. During the 1930s the Civilian Conservation Corps (CCC), in conjunction with the Works Progress Administration, employed World War I veterans and established workers housing at three locations in the Keys, including one at Pigeon Key. In the Labor Day hurricane of 1935, the two other CCC camps were completely destroyed, with a substantial loss of life.

Pigeon Key camp survived the hurricane and became a center for relief personnel. However, the hurricane completely destroyed the Overseas Railway, the 156-mile Key West Extension of the Florida East Coast Railroad, halting further development. The railroad turned over Pigeon Key to the state of Florida, and Pigeon Key subsequently became a retreat and playground for officials of the Overseas Road and Toll Bridge District until the district was dissolved in 1958. In the 1970s Pigeon Key was leased to the University of Miami as a facility for marine research. [CA 3/16/90, 90000443]

PALM BEACH COUNTY

Mickens House
801 4th Street
West Palm Beach

Built in 1917, the Mickens House is one of the oldest continuously black-owned residences in West Palm Beach. It is associated with Alice F. Mickens, a pioneer in education in Florida and a powerful force in society in West Palm Beach. Mickens was founder of the City Association of West Palm Beach, a member of the Board of Directors of the National Association of Colored Women's Clubs, president of the Florida Association of Women's Clubs, founder of the Florida Association of Women's Clubs, and a trustee for Bethune-Cookman College.

Mickens entertained leaders in black education such as Mary McLeod Bethune, Ralph Bunche, Howard Thurman, and Henrine Ward Banks. She also hosted cultural and social leaders such as Asa Philip Randolph, Lois Towles, and Phillipi Schyler. Mickens was chosen Outstanding Woman of the Century at the American Negro Emancipation Convention held in Chicago in 1963 and was named Outstanding Floridian in 1970. [B 4/11/85, 85000769]

Northwest Historic District
Roughly bounded by Tamarind Avenue, 11th Street, Rosemary Avenue, and 3rd Street
West Palm Beach

The Northwest Historic District, settled in 1894, is located in the black community of West Palm Beach. From 1929 until 1960, it consisted of two parts, the Northwest Neighborhood and Pleasant City. The Northwest Neighborhood, the larger of the two, was the residential and commercial core of the black area. Together the two sections formed the city's segregated black community.

The district's first black settler, Willie Melton, arrived in the Palm Beach area in 1885. More black settlers arrived after Melton, most migrating from the South and the Bahamas. Many toiled as field laborers on local pineapple and vegetable farms, while others worked in the tourist industry. The early black settlers lived in a small settlement called the "Styx," located on the east side of Lake Worth in what is now Palm Beach. Between 1885 and 1895 they were forced to relocate to the northwest section of the city. During the 1910s the community joined with a smaller black settlement known as Pleasant City. By 1915 the Northwest Neighborhood was the center of the city's black community.

Residents of the Northwest Neighborhood created their own schools, residential neighborhoods, businesses, churches, social clubs, and civic groups. The majority of the homes and businesses in the Neighborhood were constructed by black builders: Simeon Mather, R. A. Smith, J. B. Woodside, Alfred Williams, and Samuel O. Major. The city's first black architect, Hazel Augustus, designed many of the Neighborhood's buildings between the late 1910s and his death in 1925.

In the early 1920s, Henry Sneed, a successful realtor and part owner of the city's first black-owned lumber company, donated land for the Palmview Elementary School and Pine Ridge Hospital, the only hospital that served the black community until integration in the 1960s.

In 1925 Northwest Neighborhood black women founded the Women's Civic League. The league administered funds to the needy in the black community, providing food and other basic necessities. Civic leader Mamie Frederick established the first home for delinquent and homeless black children in West Palm Beach in the early 1930s. Frederick's sister-in-law, Alice Frederick Mickens, was also a civic leader. She promoted other local clubs that pushed for the betterment of the community: the Emanon Child Welfare Club, the National Association for the Advancement of Colored People, and Church Women United.

Many black leaders visited West Palm Beach in the 1930s and the decades following World War II; they included Mary McLeod Bethune, Howard Thurman, Ralph Bunche, and Charlotte Hawkins Brown. Mickens and her family hosted many of these individuals in their home. (See also Mickens House.)

In 1933 Robert Saunders built the Sunset Cocktail Lounge and Ballroom, which featured famous black entertainers of the day, including Cab Calloway and Fats Waller. It served as the entertainment center for the local black population through the 1950s.

The Northwest Neighborhood has undergone many changes since World War II, but it remains a predominantly black area. With desegregation, it has lost most of its middle- and upper-class black populace to other sections of town. The black community of West Palm Beach is now scattered throughout the city. However, the district still represents the only remaining portion of the original black settlement. [A 1/22/92, 91002005]

SANTA ROSA COUNTY

Mt. Pilgrim African Baptist Church
Intersection of Alice and Clara streets
Milton

Built in 1916, the Mt. Pilgrim African Baptist Church is a one-story Gothic Revival style building. It was designed by Wallace A. Rayfield (1874–1941), one of the most important black architects in the South in the early 20th century, and constructed by members of the church, many of whom were freed slaves.

Mt. Pilgrim African Baptist evolved from the First Baptist Church of Milton. First Baptist was established in 1845 and by 1849 had a membership of 83 whites and 33 African Americans. In 1866 the black members left First Baptist Church and established Mt. Pilgrim African Baptist Church.

In the 1870s and 1880s, Mt. Pilgrim assumed a leadership role by serving as the parent church for four other black Missionary Baptist congregations in Santa Rosa County. In addition, the church was a leader in education. In the late 1890s the church donated money to establish a school for Christian children; this school is now Florida Memorial College, a historically black institution in Miami.

In addition to its prominence in the religious life of Milton's black community, Mt. Pilgrim has served as a center for social and civic activities. On April 23, 1918, for example, a Progressive War Savings Club was established at Mt. Pilgrim. The church also sponsored the Patriotic Freedman's United Emancipation Memorial Association of America, a nonprofit group organized to support indigent African Americans. The church remains an important religious and social center among black citizens of Milton. [CA 5/29/92, 92000634]

SEMINOLE COUNTY

St. James AME Church
819 Cypress Avenue
Sanford

Organized in 1867, St. James African Methodist Episcopal (AME) Church is one of the oldest African American religious organizations in Sanford (then called Melonville). The congregation originally conducted prayer services in an old house on Melonville Street in the Tuckertown section of the settlement.

In 1880 the members of the AME congregation in Sanford purchased the present site of St. James Church from Henry Sanford's Florida Land and Colonization Company. The first wood frame church was erected on the lot a year later. The first pastor of St. James Chapel (as it was known then) was the Reverend Samuel H. Coleman, who served the congregation until 1884.

In 1893 the congregation razed the original building and erected another wood frame church that served the congregation until 1910, when plans for building a brick church were developed. Designed and built by Prince W. Spears, a black builder residing in Sanford, the present church building was completed in 1913. Spears had arrived in Sanford about 1910 and established himself as a builder and brick mason.

African Americans in Sanford owned and operated a variety of businesses, and St. James AME Church reflects the social and economic conditions of the black community in Sanford in 1913. Today, black businesses continue in operation along Sanford Avenue, some of them formerly owned by prominent members of St. James AME Church. [CA 4/24/92, 92000352]

ST. JOHNS COUNTY

Lincolnville Historic District
Bounded by Cedar, Riberia, Cerro, and Washington streets and DeSoto Place
St. Augustine

Persons of African descent—both enslaved and free—were present with Pedro Menendez at the founding of St. Augustine in 1565. The cathedral parish records list the first recorded birth of a black child in North America in St. Augustine in 1606. The city, therefore, not only is the oldest city in the country but also has the oldest black heritage of any continuous settlement in the United States.

The subdivision of Lincolnville was established in 1866 when a group of African Americans was granted a lease from the city of St. Augustine for a tract of land on which to establish a community called Little Africa. The community, which soon became known as Lincolnville, experienced little growth until 1877, when a People's Ticket—led by a reform political group that included black Republican leader D. M. Pappy—swept the St. Augustine city elections. The city rapidly initiated street construction and other improvements to the area, and development in both primarily black and primarily white areas proceeded at a modest pace over the next decade. By the turn of the century, Lincolnville had grown into a major black subdivision, with a high rate of political participation among blacks.

The biggest boost to growth in Lincolnville's black community was the increased discrimination against African Americans during the years immediately following Reconstruction. Black residents were barred from voting and segregated from whites in public facilities, and they endured institutionalized racism codified in Jim Crow laws. By limiting or denying the access of African Americans to existing facilities, the white community spurred the creation of a separate set of institutions created specifically to serve the black community.

A number of residences in the district are associated with prominent black political and civic leaders. Among these leaders are A. A. Pappy, who served as elected tax assessor for St. Augustine in 1885; John Papino, who served in the elected positions of town marshal, street commissioner, and city council member and was the last African American in St. Augustine elected to public office in the 19th century; and Frank B. Butler, an early 20th-century business and civic leader. Butler, president of the Lincolnville Colored Business and Professional Men's League, developed Butler Beach so African

Americans in St. Augustine could enjoy the seashore and donated land for the establishment of Frank B. Butler State Park.

Another prominent resident of Lincolnville was Dr. Robert B. Hayling, a representative of the National Association for the Advancement of Colored People, who organized a campaign in 1963 to end segregation in public facilities in St. Augustine. After arranging some initial demonstrations that failed to produce results, Hayling appealed to the Southern Christian Leadership Conference (SCLC) for help.

The SCLC eagerly joined the campaign, focusing on the issue of the passage of the Civil Rights Act of 1964. Lincolnville's black churches joined the effort. Dr. Martin Luther King, Jr., came to St. Augustine to participate in a sit-in on June 11, 1964. The SCLC prevailed upon black baseball star Jackie Robinson to address a civil rights rally, attracting more than 600 people to St. Paul's African Methodist Episcopal Church. In less than one month the Civil Rights Act was passed by Congress and signed into law. Four days later, King was awarded the Nobel Peace Prize.

Lincolnville's black citizens celebrated the hard-won victory for African Americans and the role they played in the struggle. Ironically, the end of segregation diminished the need for some of the black businesses, which were now forced to compete with better-financed white businesses for customers in the black community. The integration of schools meant the closing of black schools in Lincolnville, and the black business district experienced a general decline. Appreciation for the black heritage of the neighborhood and its architectural resources has not, however, died out. A number of Lincolnville residents have joined together to preserve the physical integrity of the district and its history. [CA 11/29/91, 91000979]

ST. LUCIE COUNTY

Zora Neale Hurston House
1734 School Court
Fort Pierce

This one-story concrete block house is the only known extant dwelling in which Zora Neale Hurston (1901?–60) lived and worked. Born in Eatonville, Florida, an all-black town, Hurston was a folklorist, anthropologist, and the most noted black female writer of the Harlem Renaissance. She was one of the first African Americans to receive a bachelor's degree from Barnard College and a recipient of Rosenwald and Guggenheim fellowships.

Hurston published nearly a dozen short stories before her first novel, *Jonah's Gourd Vine* (1934). In 1935, she published *Mules and Men,* containing folk tales, songs, children's games, prayers, sermons, and voodoo practices. Her most successful book, *Their Eyes Were Watching God* (1937), traces a woman's search for self-fulfillment. Hurston's *Moses, Man of the Mountain* (1939) places Moses in an African American tradition instead of the Judeo-Christian tradition. Her autobiography, *Dust Tracks on a Road* (1942), won the Anisfield-Wolf Award from the *Saturday Review* in 1943. Her last published novel, *Seraph on the Suwanee* (1948), involves white characters, showing her attempt to reach a wider audience.

In 1957 Hurston moved to Fort Pierce and worked as a reporter and columnist for a local black weekly newspaper, *The Fort Pierce Chronicle,* while writing her manuscript for *Herod the Great.* On January 28, 1960, Hurston died in a county welfare home after suffering a stroke. Today she is recognized as an important collector of black folklore and one of the most noted black women authors of this century. The Zora Neale Hurston House, in which she lived from 1957 until her death, was designed a National Historic Landmark on December 4, 1991. [B 12/4/91 NHL, 91002047]

VOLUSIA COUNTY

Mary McLeod Bethune Home
Bethune-Cookman College campus
Daytona Beach

Mary McLeod Bethune (1875–1955) was one of the best-known African Americans in the country between World Wars I and II. Her accomplishments ranged from founding the United Negro Women of America, directing the Division of Negro Affairs in Franklin D. Roosevelt's National Youth Administration, and acting as a consultant on interracial affairs to the first United Nations General Assembly, to earning the National Association for the Advancement of Colored People's Spingarn Medal. The most enduring legacy of Bethune's work for civil rights, however, is Bethune-Cookman College, organized as the Daytona Normal and Industrial Institute for Negro Girls in 1904.

Mary McLeod Bethune's work in education had its roots in her training as a young woman for missionary work in Africa. Unable to secure a position in Africa, she began teaching in black schools in the South. In Sumter, South Carolina, she married a fellow schoolteacher, Albertus Bethune. Despite taking on the role of wife and mother, she continued education work among the black poor.

Shortly after the death of her husband, Mary McLeod Bethune moved to Daytona Beach to organize a school to serve members of the growing black community who had been lured to the town by jobs in railroad construction. Her Daytona Normal and Industrial Institute opened in 1904 with five girls and her son, Albert. Bethune appealed to northern philanthropists who vacationed in the resort town for aid for her school and had solid financial footing by 1910. In 1923 the school merged with the Cookman Institute for Boys of Jacksonville to form a junior college with Bethune as president. In 1941 a four-year degree program and teacher-training program were begun, and in 1947 the college received an "A" accreditation rating from the Southern Association of Colleges and Schools.

Although Bethune stepped down as president of the college in 1947, she lived on the college campus until her death in 1955 at the age of 80. Her home on the Bethune-Cookman College campus is a physical reminder of Mary McLeod Bethune's lifelong dedication to the education of black students. The property was designated a National Historic Landmark on December 2, 1974 (see also Mary McLeod Bethune Council House National Historic Site, District of Columbia). [B 12/2/74 NHL, 74000655]

Old DeLand Memorial Hospital
Stone Street
DeLand

The Old DeLand Memorial Hospital consists of two separate buildings. The primary building is the Old DeLand Memorial Hospital, a two-and-a-half-story masonry building constructed in 1920 in the Italian Renaissance style. The second building, the Old DeLand Colored Hospital, is a one-story, T-shaped, masonry vernacular building constructed in 1926 to meet the medical needs of the African American community at the time.

Before the opening of the Old DeLand Colored Hospital in 1926, African Americans needing medical attention were treated in the office of local physicians and then cared for in the home of Mrs. Mandy Worthy, a midwife and practical nurse. Even after 1926, when a black patient needed surgery, the equipment was wheeled across the parking lot from the main operating room of the Memorial Hospital. The medical staff circumvented this requirement whenever possible by using the basement emergency room and by using the main operating room at night, when the hospital authorities were absent. This surgical policy was changed in the mid-1930s, and African Americans were thereafter operated on in the main surgical room, thus reducing the Colored Hospital to the status of a ward.

In 1948 both buildings of the DeLand Memorial Hospital were closed, and its name and services transferred to the dispensary building at the DeLand Naval Air Station. In 1952 a modern facility, the Fish Memorial Hospital, was opened, and the DeLand Memorial Hospital organization was disbanded. [CA 11/27/89, 89002030]

Howard Thurman House
614 Whitehall Street
Daytona Beach

Built in 1888, this house was the home of Dr. Howard Thurman (1900–81) from his birth until his departure for high school in Jacksonville in 1917. Thurman was the first African American in Florida to receive an eighth-grade diploma and pass the "white" examination for entrance to a Florida public high school. After graduating as valedictorian from Morehouse College in 1923, Thurman entered the Colgate-Rochester School of

Divinity, which at that time admitted only two black students annually. He was ordained a Baptist minister in 1925. Thurman became the first black dean at Boston University, a predominantly white university and the first dean of Rankin Chapel at Howard University. It was in this position that Thurman influenced hundreds of students and traveled broadly, heading Christian missions and meeting world figures such as Mohandas "Mahatma" Gandhi and Sir Rabindranath Tagore in the 1930s. His book summarizing many of these conversations, *Jesus and the Disinherited,* formed a central part of the philosophical foundation of the nonviolent civil rights movement headed by Dr. Martin Luther King, Jr. [AB 2/23/90, 90000100]

White Hall
640 2nd Avenue
Daytona Beach

White Hall is a two-story masonry building constructed in 1916 on the campus of Bethune-Cookman College. In 1904 Mary McLeod Bethune (1875–1955) established the Daytona Educational and Industrial Training School for Negro Girls. Born in Mayesville, South Carolina, and educated in Presbyterian mission schools there and at Scotia Normal School in Concord, North Carolina, Bethune had taught in mission schools in South Carolina, Georgia, and Palatka, Florida. In 1907 her remarkable efforts resulted in the construction of Faith Hall. By 1914 Bethune's school, then known as the Daytona Educational and Industrial Training School, had outgrown the Faith Hall facility.

Construction of a new building was made possible with proceeds of a trust fund bequeathed to the school by Thomas H. White, and the building was subsequently named in his honor. The new building was constructed in an open field adjacent to the Daytona Educational and Industrial Training School. With the growth of the school and its merger with the all-male Cookman Institute in 1923 to form Bethune-Cookman College, the campus gradually expanded. Presently, with the exception of the Mary McLeod Bethune Home, White Hall is the oldest building on the campus. It continues to serve as the administrative center of this major black educational institution in the Daytona Beach area. [CA 7/15/92, 92000849]

GEORGIA

BALDWIN COUNTY

Westover
151 Meriwether Road, N.W.
Milledge

Westover was established about 1822 by Benjamin S. Jordan, a wealthy and influential landowner and planter in rural central Georgia. The plantation's surviving outbuildings include a commissary, smokehouse, and portions of a detached kitchen. Also remaining on the property are four slave cabins, in various states of preservation. A slave cemetery adjacent to the outbuildings is marked by roughly hewn or natural rocks, which were often used as slave grave markers, and depressions on the surface of the ground denoting burials. Family tradition corroborates the use of the site as a slave cemetery. This collection of buildings, sites, and objects illustrates the characteristic development pattern of the nucleated antebellum plantation, which rarely survived post-Civil War decentralization. [CD 2/12/87, 87000094]

Atlanta University Center District, Fulton County. Photo courtesy of the Georgia Department of Natural Resources (Randolph C. Marks).

BARTOW COUNTY

Noble Hill School
Gaddis Road
Cassville

Built in 1923 for black children in Cassville, Noble Hill School was one of two schools in Bartow County built with grants from the Rosenwald Fund. The school was part of Georgia's public school system, and it was established to improve the quality of education for black children. The Rosenwald schools were funded by the state, local citizens, and the Rosenwald Fund, initiated by Julius Rosenwald (1862–1932), a wealthy Chicago merchant who was chairman of the board of Sears, Roebuck, and Company. The purpose of the Rosenwald schools was to provide black children with a high-quality elementary education that included both a traditional curriculum and training in industrial arts. Noble Hill School educated many young blacks in Bartow County who became successful in their chosen careers and continued their education with bachelor's, master's, and doctoral degrees. [CA 7/2/87, 87001103]

BIBB COUNTY

Fort Hill Historic District

Roughly bounded by Emery Highway,
2nd Street Extension, Mitchell and
Morrow streets, and Schaeffer Place
Macon

An intact collection of residential, commercial, and community institutional buildings constructed between 1870 and 1941, the Fort Hill Historic District reflects the growth and development of east Macon. The north side of the district was historically occupied by African Americans and is represented by the development pattern of more modest buildings and the historically black Burdell School. This northern section features characteristics typical of historic black neighborhoods in Georgia communities, including a relatively dense pattern of development, a gridiron pattern of narrow streets and lots, a variety of generally modest vernacular houses, and a number of community facilities such as schools, churches, and stores. These buildings of the working-class black community stand adjacent to the homes of upper-middle-class whites in the district and are an important reminder of the role African Americans played in the history of east Macon. [CA 4/16/93, 93000313]

Pleasant Hill Historic District

Roughly bounded by Sheridan Avenue
and Schofield, Madison, Jefferson,
Ferguson, and Galliard streets
Macon

Pleasant Hill Historic District is one of the most intact historic black neighborhoods in Georgia, featuring excellent examples of vernacular architecture, especially shotgun houses. Many of the houses in the district were constructed by black builders, carpenters, plasterers, and brick masons who lived in the district, including G. Moughton, John Young, L. J.

Max, and Zack Williams. The development of Pleasant Hill into Macon's primary black residential area dates back to the 1870s. At that time, Madison and Monroe streets became home to many of the servants for the wealthy white families who lived along neighboring College Avenue. By the 1880s the historic district was being rapidly subdivided into suburban lots with rows of large houses. The neighborhood grew rapidly in the 1890s and 1910s, expanding from the east and the south in a northwesterly direction. By 1912 almost all the streets in the district were laid out, and by 1925 the majority of historic buildings in the district had been constructed.

A broad spectrum of Macon's black citizens, from attorneys, businesspeople, educators, doctors, lawyers, and ministers to unskilled laborers, lived in the neighborhood. Among the most prominent were Lewis Williams, principal of several schools in the neighborhood; B. S. Ingram, principal of Pleasant Hill School and responsible for introducing manual training to the Macon curriculum; Minnie L. Smith, founder of Beta-Etta College; Albert B. Fitzpatrick, manager of black-organized People's Health and Life Insurance Company; L. J. Max, the owner of Wages and Earners Bank and editor of the "Negro" section of the *Macon Telegraph;* and Sara Bailey, credited with starting the first Girl Scout troop in Macon for black girls.

Pleasant Hill developed into an important education center for African Americans in Macon. A number of public and private schools were located in the neighborhood, including the Ballard Normal School, a high school sponsored by the American Missionary Association; St. Peter Claver School and Church, established in 1912 with money from a wealthy Catholic philanthropist; the

Academy for the Blind; the North Macon Colored School; Beta-Etta College; and two public black elementary schools. [CA 5/22/86, 86001130]

BURKE COUNTY

Hopeful Baptist Church
Winter Road east of Blythe Road
Keysville

Constructed in 1851, the Hopeful Baptist Church is a fine example of the Greek Revival style of architecture for a rural church in the late antebellum period. Before the Civil War, both black and white congregants worshiped here together. While this practice was not necessarily uncommon in the rural South, there remain few documented examples of congregations in Georgia whose membership included both races. At Hopeful Baptist Church, both black and white congregants worshiped in the Baptist faith, and the black members were allowed to have their own preacher once a month. After the Civil War, the black members of the congregation left the church to form the Second Hopeful Baptist Church on land donated by Hopeful and continued to use the building until their own church was completed.

The section of the church that was designated for slaves before 1865 is still intact. The last four rows of pews have straight, unadorned end panels, while the pews for white members have curved armrests. Except for this difference in design, the pews are identical. Although the placement and design of the pews indicate a difference in status between the white and black congregants, the combined church membership did in some way reflect the right of freedom of religion, one of the few freedoms available to a large enslaved populace. [CA 1/11/93, 92001734]

CAMDEN COUNTY

High Point–Half Moon Bluff Historic District
Northeast of St. Marys on Cumberland Island
St. Marys

The High Point–Half Moon Bluff Historic District was a black settlement reflecting the transition of African Americans from slavery to landownership. The cemeteries in which former slaves and their descendants are buried provide vivid reminders of the history of the north end of High Point Island.

According to tradition, after the Civil War the former slaves of High Point Island settled at the north end of the island, known as Half Moon Bluff. These freedmen acquired squatters rights and built simple huts for shelter. They became landowners who transferred lands and properties to their descendants.

At Half Moon Bluff the African American landowners created a community through which to maintain their social values and lifestyles. The focal point of the black community was the First African Baptist Church, which not only served a religious function, but also met the educational needs of the African Americans at Half Moon Bluff. [AD 12/22/78 NPS, 78000265]

CHATHAM COUNTY

Laurel Grove–South Cemetery
37th Street
Savannah

The tombstones and grave markers of Laurel Grove–South Cemetery are the only visible memorial and documented record of many of the most important African Americans in the history of Savannah. In 1852, 15 acres of the Laurel Grove Cemetery were set aside for the burial of "free persons of color and slaves." Laurel Grove–South contains the largest number of graves of free blacks of any cemetery in Georgia. Especially significant are the graves of Andrew Bryan and Andrew Marshall, both of whom were born as slaves and managed to purchase their freedom. In 1783 Bryan was converted to the Baptist faith by black missionary George Liele and in 1788 was ordained by Abraham Mitchell. Thereafter he organized the first black Baptist church in North America. Andrew Marshall was Bryan's nephew and the second pastor of the congregation.

Laurel Grove–South Cemetery also documents a subclass of mulattoes in antebellum Savannah. Many mulattoes were slaves, but in Laurel Grove–South are the graves of members of the free Mirault family. The Miraults came to Savannah in 1790 to escape the slave revolt in Santo Domingo. Also among the mulattoes buried in Laurel Grove–South are members of the Deveaux family. Between 1836 and 1864, Jane Deveaux ran a school for African Americans.

The grave of the Reverend James M. Simms is another important landmark in black history in Savannah and the state. Simms, like Jane Deveaux, educated African Americans in the years preceding the Civil War. In 1867 Simms founded the *Southern Radical and Freedmen's Journal,* the first black publication in Savannah after the Civil War. Simms was also instrumental in organizing the Republican party in Savannah and served in the state senate from 1870 until 1872, when African Americans were expelled from the legislature. Another black Reconstruction legislator buried in Laurel Grove–South is the Reverend Ulysses L. Houston. Houston's grave, with its monolith surrounded by a wrought iron fence, is visible testimony to the impor-

tance of black pastors after the Civil War. [A 9/6/78, 78000972]

Nicholsonville Baptist Church
White Bluff Road
Nicholsonville

Two historic church buildings stand on this property, both built by residents of Nicholsonville, a black community whose founders were freed slaves from St. Catherine's Island. The community, known also as Nicholsonboro, was established in 1868, and the first of the two church buildings was erected in the late 1870s. Nicholsonville's residents grew vegetables for summer market and sold their catches of fish and oysters in the winter. The small rural community apparently prospered, for in 1890 a second, larger church building was erected some 70 feet away from the first. Services are still held in the larger building. Both of the churches are important rural examples of black church construction in Georgia in the late 19th century. [CA 5/22/78, 78000969]

St. Bartholomew's Church
Cheves Road
Burroughs

Built in 1896, this one-story frame Victorian Eclectic style church housed one of 11 black Episcopal congregations in Georgia. St. Bartholomew's Church is the oldest continuing black Episcopal congregation in the Episcopal Diocese of Georgia, and its history goes back to the formation of the congregation in 1832. Former slaves created the town of Burroughs, which developed around the church, and used the church as their religious, social and educational center. St. Bartholomew's Church also served as an important education center for the local black population since 1846. The church operated the day school in Burroughs until 1916, when the Chatham County Board of Education took over its operation. Although several churches of other denominations existed, and still exist, in the Burroughs area, St. Bartholomew's Episcopal Church has always been a focal point in the black community. [CA 6/17/82, 82002391]

CLARKE COUNTY

Chestnut Grove School
610 Epps Bridge Road
Athens

Chestnut Grove School is a one-room schoolhouse built in 1896 to educate black children. The black community provided the land, labor, and many of the materials to build the school. The school is representative of educational practices in rural areas, in which a single classroom teacher is responsible for teaching basic reading, writing, arithmetic, and geography to children of all ages from the nearby countryside. As was common in public schools in rural Georgia, student attendance at the Chestnut Grove School was higher in winter months when black children had no farming-related responsibilities to keep them at home.

Chestnut Grove School was also used as a meeting place for the nearby church congregation and the Baptist Aid Lodge, for social gatherings for the black community at Thanksgiving and Christmas, and for picnics during the summer months. It therefore served its community as a social as well as educational facility and has remained a source of pride for the local black residents. [CA 6/28/84, 84003873]

Morton Building
199 West Washington Street
Athens

The Morton Building has had a long association with the black community.

Over the years the building has housed the offices of many prominent black professionals, a number of black-owned businesses, and the Morton Theater, the major entertainment facility for the city's black population for many years. The lot upon which the building is located was purchased in January 1909 by Monroe Bowers "Pink" Morton, a successful businessperson and prominent figure in Athens history, who erected the building in 1909–10. In 1896 Morton was a delegate to the Republican National Convention and was appointed to the committee that officially informed William McKinley of his nomination as the party's candidate for president. By 1914 Morton was publisher and editor of the *Progressive Era,* a local black newspaper. Morton's most impressive contribution was the Morton Theater, which opened on May 18, 1910, with a classical concert by Alice Carter Simmons of Oberlin, Ohio, attended by both black and white patrons. Among the performers who appeared at the Morton Theater were Louis Armstrong, Cab Calloway, Butterbeans & Susie, and Duke Ellington, along with many other traveling companies. [CA 10/22/79, 79000709]

Reese Street Historic District
Roughly bounded by Meigs, Finley, Broad, and Harris streets
Athens

The Reese Street Historic District reflects the residential, commercial, and institutional development of the black community in Athens and Georgia from the late 19th to the early 20th century. A broad spectrum of Athens's black citizens, from educators, doctors, and lawyers to unskilled laborers, settled in the area because of racially segregated housing patterns. Some of the prominent blacks who lived in the district were Dr. W. H.

Harris, a physician; Dr. Charles Haynes, who founded the nursing department at Athens High and Industrial School in 1918; and Drs. Ida Mae and Lace Hiram, dentists.

Both public and private schools for African Americans were founded in the district. The Knox School, established in 1868, was the first school for African Americans in Athens. A small private high school for blacks, the J. Thomas Heard University, was established around 1912. In 1922 the Athens High and Industrial School was among the first black schools to be accredited by the state.

The Reese Street Historic District is one of the most intact black districts in the state and one of only two black districts identified to date in Athens. [CA 11/10/87, 87001990]

West Hancock Avenue Historic District
Roughly bounded by Hill, Franklin, and Broad streets and the Plaza
Athens

The West Hancock Avenue Historic District is an important historic, urban, black community that was originally in the rural outskirts of Athens and is now entirely within the city limits. It is one of only two black districts in Athens and is among the most intact black districts in the state. The district consists primarily of residential structures that are representative examples of modest vernacular house types, including the saddlebag, the L-shaped cottage, and the square plan with pyramidal roof. West Hancock documents the residential patterns and the commercial and institutional development of the black community in Athens from the late 19th century through the early 20th century. Because of racially segregated housing patterns, West Hancock was the home of a wide cross section of

Athens's black residents. Doctors, lawyers, and educators all lived in the district, along with tradespeople and unskilled laborers. Some of the prominent African Americans associated with the district were T. J. Elder, an educator who owned property within the district, and Dr. Andrew Jones, a physician who resided there. To meet the needs of the black community, residents established grocery stores, churches, and a hospital in the area. [CA 3/30/88, 88000227]

COBB COUNTY
Zion Baptist Church
149 Haynes Street
Marietta

The Zion Baptist Church represents the first social institution formed in Marietta by freedmen and women after emancipation. The oldest black congregation in Marietta, the church was created when newly freed blacks petitioned to leave a white congregation in 1866. In 1888 they bricked in an earlier wooden church to create this church as a permanent meetinghouse for the black Baptists of Marietta. Ephraim Rucker was installed as the first pastor of Zion Baptist Church. The church membership grew between 1891 and 1896 and between 1913 and 1918, when the first revival was held. From 1942 to 1953 the church undertook many improvements to this building, and in 1955 it established a building fund. The congregation continued to use the church building for Sunday school until 1979. [CA 7/11/90, 90001026]

DOUGHERTY COUNTY
Bridge House
112 North Front Street
Albany

Built in 1857, the Classical Italianate style Bridge House is the only known

Zion Baptist Church. Photo courtesy of the Georgia Department of Natural Resources (James R. Lockhart).

extant bridge house in Georgia. It was built by Colonel Nelson Tift following a dispute between Tift and the commissioners of Baker County, which lay across the Flint River. When the commissioners refused to build a bridge, Tift hired Horace King, a well-known black bridge builder of Georgia, to construct a bridge that Tift could also operate as a business. The Bridge House was built at the same time as the bridge, and a tunnel connected the two. The house served as a collection point for tolls on wagons and horses using the bridge. On the second floor of the house, Tift operated a luxurious theater and ballroom known as Tift's Hall that attracted many popular actors and musicians of the time. [CA 11/19/74, 74000672]

EFFINGHAM COUNTY

New Hope AME Church
Alexander Street
Guyton

Built in 1885, New Hope African Methodist Episcopal (AME) Church is the oldest AME church in southeast Georgia and the oldest historic black church in Guyton. In 1869 black Methodists in Guyton formed New Hope AME Church as part of the Sixth Episcopal District of the Georgia AME Conference.

New Hope AME was associated with early black ministers in the area, including the Reverends W. H. Wells, Alexander W. Wayman, and S. E. Scott. Church membership records document the diverse socioeconomic characteristics of Guyton's late 19th-century black community. Early church members earned their living as carpenters, farmers, factory workers in saw mills and turpentine stills, or as domestic workers in Guyton households. One member, Pady Jones, was a lawyer. [CA 3/13/86, 86000364]

ELBERT COUNTY

Dove Creek Baptist Church
Georgia Route 72
Elberton

Built around 1880, Dove Creek Baptist Church began as a small black congregation, many of whose members were former slaves and sharecroppers, that withdrew from the predominantly white Dove Creek Church after the Civil War. The original church land was donated by Al Oliver (1816–1882), a white landowner and former slaveowner in Elbert County. This small black church is representative of the independent black religious community that left the older white church following emancipation, a practice that was common in Georgia and throughout the South in the late 19th century. The congregation consisted of about 50 to 75 members in the late 19th and early 20th centuries, and it is still active today. [CA 7/9/87, 87001154]

FLOYD COUNTY

Chubb Methodist Episcopal Church
Three and a half miles southeast of Cave Spring on Chubbtown Road
Cave Spring

Built in 1870, Chubb Methodist Episcopal (ME) Church (now Chubb Chapel United Methodist Church), located in a rural setting within the unincorporated community of Chubbtown, is the only intact historic structure representing Georgia's few free-black settlements. The church is a fine example of a small, vernacular, Gothic Revival-style church built just after the Civil War. It was established by the free black Chubb family, who arrived in Floyd County in the early 1860s, purchased land, and began settling the area. During the post-Reconstruction period the Chubb brothers continued to purchase real estate. Their holdings constituted the foundation of a self-sufficient community known as Chubbtown. The community had it own post office, general store, blacksmith shop, distillery, syrup mill, cotton gin, casket company, and several farms, all owned and operated by the Chubb family. Chubb ME Church was established in a community that was perhaps unique, developed and owned by African Americans before the turn of the century. [CA 5/04/90, 90000728]

FULTON COUNTY

Atlanta University Center District
Roughly bounded by transit right-of-way, Northside Drive, Walnut, Fair, Roach, West End Drive, and Euralee and Chestnut streets
Atlanta

The Atlanta University Center District includes Atlanta University; Clark, Morehouse, Morris Brown, and Spelman Colleges; and the Interdenominational Theological Center. The presidents of the

Chubb Methodist Episcopal Church. Photo courtesy of the Georgia Department of Natural Resources (James R. Lockhart).

member institutions have played a significant role in establishing and maintaining the viability of their schools. Edmund Asa Ware, first president of Atlanta University (1869–85), encouraged African Americans to pursue a liberal education. Under Horace Bumstead (1888–1907), the university gained national acclaim and recognition. John Hope served as president of both Morehouse (1906–31) and Atlanta University (1929–36). Rufus Clement, who followed Hope in 1937, was influential in the black community and later became the first black member of the Atlanta Board of Education.

Benjamin E. Mays, an internationally renowned figure, was president of Morehouse College from 1940 to 1967. In addition to outstanding presidents, the Atlanta University Center has been served by such nationally known faculty members as W. E. B. Du Bois, Whitney Young, E. Franklin Frazier, and Horace Mann Bond.

The center's institutions produced a long list of alumni whose contributions to American life extended throughout the country. Graduates of Atlanta University include James Weldon Johnson, poet and writer; and Walter White, a crusader for minority rights with the National Association for the Advancement of Colored People. Mordecai Johnson, former president of Howard University; and Dr. Martin Luther King, Jr., 1964 Nobel Prize winner and civil rights leader are Morehouse College alumni. Selina Sloan Butler, founder and first national president of the National Congress of Colored Parents and Teachers; and Matilda Dobbs, an opera singer, graduated from Spelman College. Bishop Harold I. Beardon, a pioneer Georgia leader in civil rights and community affairs, received a degree from Morris Brown College. Dr. Alphonso A. McPheeters, a dean of Clark College (1941–62), educational writer, and scholar, is a graduate of Clark College. Alice Henderson, the first female chaplain in the U.S. Army, is an alumna of the Interdenominational Theological Center.

Atlanta University was founded in 1865 as a liberal education institution. In 1929 it became the graduate school nucleus for an affiliated group of colleges that now make up the Atlanta University Center. The history of these institutions begins with the endorsement by the American Missionary Association of Edmund Asa Ware's idea for the establishment of a centrally located southeastern university to train talented black youth and educate teachers. On October 16, 1867, a corporation known as the Trustees of Atlanta University was created. Between 1869 and 1893 70 acres of land representing nine purchases and costing about $23,335 were acquired. Fifty acres of this land between Hunter, Parsons, Walnut, and Chestnut streets were used for the initial development. The cornerstone for the first building, North (Gaines) Hall was laid on June 1, 1869.

The history of Morehouse College began in 1867, when the school was established as Augusta Institute. Upon moving to Atlanta in 1879, the institution changed its name to Atlanta Baptist Seminary and by 1913 adopted its the present name, Morehouse College. The principal founders of Morehouse included Richard C. Coulter, a former slave; Edmund Turney, organizer of the National Theological Institute for the Education of Freedmen in Washington, D.C.; and William Jefferson White, an Augusta Baptist minister.

Spelman College opened in April 1881 and, like Morehouse College, was initially located in the basement of Friendship Baptist College. Spelman College, an all-female institution, was sponsored by the Women's American Baptist Home Missionary Society. Two members of this society responsible for the school's establishment in Atlanta were Sophia B. Packard and Harriet E. Giles. Beginning in the 1880s John D. Rockefeller began his contributions to Spelman, a tradition that has continued through five generations of Rockefellers. In April 1884 the institution's name was changed from Atlanta Baptist Female Seminary to Spelman College in honor of John D. Rockefeller's wife, Laura E. Spelman Rockefeller.

In 1885 Morris Brown College's first building was constructed at the intersection of Houston Street and Boulevard in northeast Atlanta. The new institution was named for Morris Brown (1770–1849), the second consecrated bishop of the African Methodist Episcopal Church. Morris Brown College moved to the old Atlanta University campus in 1932 and joined in the center affiliation in 1939.

Clark College opened in 1869 under the sponsorship of the Methodist Episcopal Church. The school was named after Bishop Davis W. Clark, the first president of the Freedman's Aid Society of the Methodist Episcopal Church. In 1941 the college became affiliated with the Atlanta University Center and moved to its present site.

The Interdenominational Theological Center is the most recent of the Atlanta University institutions. In 1956 the Morehouse School of Religion, Gammon Theological Seminary, Turner Theological Seminary, and Phillips School of Theology joined together to form the Interdenominational Center. In 1957 the center was established on its present 10-acre site, deeded to the institution by Atlanta University.

In addition to the educational institutions, the Atlanta University Center District includes the Friendship Baptist Church, one of the oldest and most respected black churches in Atlanta, organized in 1862 with the Reverend Frank Quarles as pastor; and the University Homes development, one of the first federally funded low-cost housing projects in the United States. Also important to the district is the building that housed the West Hunter Street Baptist Church. The Reverend Ralph David Abernathy, a follower of Dr. Martin Luther King, Jr., served as pastor of this congregation while he was head of the Southern Christian Leadership Conference (SCLC). The old church building has served the Martin Luther King, Jr. Center for Social Change and presently houses the Atlanta chapter of the SCLC.

The member institutions of the Atlanta University Center and the surrounding residential streets, churches, and housing developments make up a community where African Americans were afforded educational, social, and cultural opportunities unavailable to them elsewhere during the long years of educational and social segregation. [CA 7/12/76, 76000621]

Butler Street Colored Methodist Episcopal Church
23 Butler Street, S.E.
Atlanta

Built in 1920, the Butler Street Colored Methodist Episcopal (CME) Church is Atlanta's third oldest black Methodist congregation. The church was organized in 1882 by the Reverend S. E. Poe and Bishop Lucius H. Holsey (1842–1920), a prominent CME leader who also cofounded Paine College in Augusta and the Holsey Normal and Industrial Academy in Cordele. Pioneer Atlanta developer John T. Grant (1821–87) donated the land on which the church is presently located, south of the Sweet Auburn Historic District that served as a center of black entrepreneurial and social activity from 1880 to 1930. [C 5/9/83, 83000228]

First Congregational Church
105 Courtland Street, N.E.
Atlanta

Founded in 1867, the First Congregational Church was one of the most socially conscious churches in Georgia during the period 1890–1930. The Reverend Hugh Proctor (1868–1933) came to First Congregational in 1894 as its first black minister. Proctor remained in Atlanta until 1920, when the membership of the church had grown from 100 to 1,000, and a new church building was constructed. The builder, Robert E. Pharrow, was a black Atlantan and member of the church.

The church's congregation consisted of predominantly middle-class African Americans. Some the church's past and present members include Norris B.

Herndon, son of the founder of the Atlanta Life Insurance Company; the family of Walter White of the National Association for the Advancement of Colored People; the family of Grace Townes Hamilton, a black female member of the Georgia General Assembly; and Jesse O. Thomas, former director of the Atlanta Urban League. Such individuals were members of the First Congregational Church because of the Congregationalists' emphasis on education.

The First Congregational Church offered a day nursery, domestic science classes, and industrial classes for the blind. In addition, the Atlanta Interracial Commission, formed in 1919; the National Medical Association, organized in 1894; and the city's first black Boy Scout troop were all organized in the church.

The First Congregational Church has offered spiritual leadership and social and humanitarian activities to the black community in Atlanta since its inception in 1867. [CA 1/19/79, 79000720]

Martin Luther King, Jr., Historic District
Bounded roughly by Irwin, Randolph, Edgewood, Jackson, and Auburn avenues
Atlanta

Here within the space of several blocks are the birthplace, church, and grave site of Dr. Martin Luther King, Jr. King was founder and first president of the Southern Christian Leadership Conference. In 1964 he was awarded the Nobel Peace Prize for his endeavors in the civil rights movement. He was the youngest person to receive the prize and the second African American so honored. In April 1968, while conducting one of his crusades in Memphis, Tennessee, he was assassinated.

King had lifelong ties to the Auburn Avenue area. The surrounding historical sites show some of those influences of his early development. King's birthplace, at 501 Auburn Avenue, is a two-story frame Queen Anne style house built in 1895. Across the street from his birthplace are row houses built in 1920 that typify the property rented by African Americans during this period. The backyard of Our Lady of Lourdes Catholic Colored Mission is adjacent to the King birthplace. Constructed in 1912, it was the second mission for black Catholics in Georgia and the first black mission in Atlanta. Fire Station Number 6, constructed in 1894, is located two doors from King's birthplace. It was one of the eight original firehouses in Atlanta. At the corner of Auburn Avenue and Jackson Street is the Ebenezer Baptist Church, which was begun in 1914 and completed in 1922, during the pastorship of King's grandfather, the Reverend Adam D. Williams. In 1960 King became copastor of Ebenezer Baptist Church and served in that capacity until his death in 1968. King's grave site occupies most of the lot east of the Ebenezer Baptist Church to Boulevard Street. In 1976 a memorial park was installed around King's crypt, which is located in the center of a reflecting pool. Across from the church and burial site is the Martin Luther King, Jr., Center for Social Change, created as a tribute to King's work. The Martin Luther King, Jr., Historic District was designated a National Historic Landmark on May 5, 1977, and became a unit of the National Park System in 1980. [CB 5/2/74 NHL, 74000677]

Martin Luther King, Jr., National Historic Site and Preservation District
Roughly bounded by Courtland, Randolph, and Chamberlain streets and Irwin Avenue
Atlanta

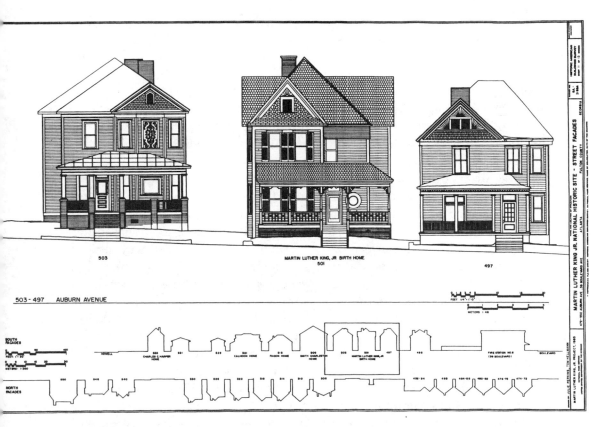

Martin Luther King, Jr., Birth Home (center), 501 Auburn Avenue, in the Martin Luther King, Jr., National Historic Site and Preservation District. Drawing courtesy of the Historic American Buildings Survey (Julie Perkins, Tom Hellman, delineators).

The Martin Luther King, Jr., National Historic Site and Preservation District was established on October 10, 1980. The properties encompassed in the site and district are all related to the life and times of Dr. Martin Luther King, Jr., and the civil rights movement. The park's focus includes King's early life and development in the area and his role in the founding of the Southern Christian Leadership Conference and in the civil rights movement. Located within the boundaries of the Martin Luther King, Jr., National Historic Site and Preservation District are the previously recognized Martin Luther King, Jr., Historic District, the Sweet Auburn

Historic District, and the corridor along Auburn Street connecting the two portions of the National Historic Site that are separated by the I-75 Expressway. The Sweet Auburn Historic District has two periods of significance: the late 19th century through 1930 and 1929–68 (because of the district's association with King). Black social, economic, religious, and political development as manifested in the history of Auburn Avenue provides the context for understanding the significance of King and the civil rights movement. The Martin Luther King Preservation District was designated a National Historic Landmark on May 5, 1977, and became a unit of the national park system in 1980 (see also Martin Luther King, Jr., Historic District). [AB 10/10/80 NPS, 80000435]

Odd Fellows Building and Auditorium
228–250 Auburn Avenue, N.E.
Atlanta

The Odd Fellows Building and Auditorium stands on Auburn Avenue in the heart of Atlanta's black business district. Construction on the building began in 1911, with monies for the project donated by Odd Fellows organizations throughout the state. The Grand United Order of Odd Fellows was one of several fraternal organizations that served the community by providing endowments to the seriously ill and death benefits to widows.

A key individual in the history of the Odd Fellows Building was Benjamin Jefferson Davis, editor of the black newspaper the *Atlanta Independent.* Through his newspaper, Davis promoted the image of the "industrious and thrifty" Auburn Avenue black businesses to counter the white stereotype of the "ignorant and irresponsible" African American. The terra-cotta and stone heads with negroid features that frame the entrances and the upper portions of the building symbolize the proud image and achievement of the race that Davis worked so hard to develop.

In 1913, one year after the opening of the Odd Fellows Building, construction was begun on a two-story addition to the building, which contained an auditorium, stores, and offices. The addition was to provide a meeting place for the black community. The auditorium, large enough to support national conventions as well as local functions, was later converted to a movie theater. Some of the most successful black businesses occupied the retail space. Today the building remains not only a visually interesting architectural form in the urban environment, but also an effective symbol of the achievements of Atlanta's black community. [CAB 5/2/75, 75000594]

Stone Hall, Atlanta University
Morris Brown College campus
Atlanta

Constructed in 1882, Stone Hall served as Atlanta University's administration building and housed some classroom facilities. Recognized for its important role in black education, Atlanta University is associated with distinguished black leaders such as graduate James Weldon Johnson (1871–1938), author of the black anthem "Lift Every Voice and Sing" and leader in the National Association for the Advancement of Colored People (NAACP); and faculty member W. E. B. Du Bois (1868–1963), civil rights and NAACP leader. Founded in 1866 by the American Missionary Association with the financial assistance of the Freedmen's Bureau, Atlanta University offered industrial arts, agricultural training, and academics. In 1929 the school became exclusively a graduate school. Also in 1929, Atlanta University became affiliated with Morehouse and Spelman Colleges, and Stone Hall became one of the buildings Atlanta University leased to Morris Brown College. Morris Brown changed the building's name to Fountain Hall and uses the hall as its administration building. The property was designated a National Historic Landmark on December 2, 1974. [A 12/2/74 NHL, 74000680]

Sweet Auburn Historic District
Auburn Avenue
Atlanta

The phenomenal growth of black commercial enterprise in the post-Civil War period is typified by the Sweet Auburn Historic District. Originally known as Wheat Street, the street became known as Sweet Auburn, a name coined by John Wesley Dobbs. It was called the "richest Negro street in the world." With the rise of segregation and the general acceptance of "separate but equal" as stipulated in the *Plessy v. Ferguson* Supreme Court decision of 1896, the foundation was laid for the black business district of Sweet Auburn.

As Atlanta's black population increased from the late 1890s to the early 1920s, Auburn Avenue's business district attracted black entrepreneurs such as Madame C. J. Walker (see also Madame C. J. Walker Building, Marion County, Indiana; and Villa Lewaro, Westchester County, New York), Asa Spaulding, Robert Abbott, and Alonzo Herndon. Herndon, born a slave, founded the Atlanta Life Insurance Company by uniting nine black insurance societies. In addition, he constructed the Herndon Office Building.

The violent race riots of 1906 indicated the need to build separate institutions within the black community. The first building constructed after the riots was the Henry Rucker Building. Located on Edgewood Avenue, the Municipal Market was built in the 1920s and served as a marketplace for the black community.

Churches also made distinctive contributions to the district. Wheat Street Baptist Church, Big Bethel African Methodist Episcopal (AME) Church, and First Congregational Church sponsored education, extended financial aid, provided shelter, and contributed political leadership. In 1911 Henry Perry, a Texas native, founded the Standard Life Insurance Company in Big Bethel AME Church. Out of this endeavor came the Citizens Trust Company, founded in 1921. Walter White, an Atlanta native

and founder of the Atlanta chapter of the National Association for the Advancement of Colored People, was employed with Standard Life.

Social activity in the black community increased with the rise of businesses and social consciousness. The local Young Men's Christian Association (YMCA) was founded in the basement of Wheat Street Baptist Church. The YMCA provided a source of recreation and guidance for Atlanta's black youth under segregation and was an important meeting place for the adults of the city. Likewise, local fraternal orders, such as the Odd Fellows, the Masons, and the Elks were active in the expansion and development of Auburn Avenue. The Odd Fellows Building, constructed in 1912, provided facilities for concerts and theater. The Royal Theatre attracted to the city Black Patti Company, Bessie Smith, the Rabbit Foot Show, and "Ma" Rainey. The Royal Peacock featured Nat "King" Cole and Cab Calloway, among others.

Events during the 1960s marked the end of segregation, allowing black residents the opportunity to reside and work in other areas of the city and radically changing the area. Yet Auburn Avenue continues as a thriving center of black business and social activity. The Sweet Auburn Historic District was designated a National Historic Landmark district on December 8, 1976. [A 12/8/76 NHL, 76000631]

Booker T. Washington High School
45 Whitehouse Drive, S.W.
Atlanta

Built in 1924, Booker T. Washington High School was the first black high school in Atlanta. The first principal of the school was Charles L. Harper (1875–1955). Under Harper's leadership, the school erected the Booker T.

Washington statue, organized educational tours for honor students, and established the Music Festival and Dramatic Association for Secondary Schools in Georgia. The school offered a standard high school course in academic subjects and in vocational subjects such as automobile mechanics, household management, home nursing, and child care. The excellent training provided at the school prepared students to become local and national leaders in many professions. Some outstanding graduates include Dr. Martin Luther King, Jr. (civil rights leader), Romae T. Powell (judge), and Mabel Smith Lott (psychologist). Today, Booker T. Washington High School remains an important black educational institution. [CA 3/18/86, 86000437]

Yonge Street School
89 Yonge Street
Atlanta

The Yonge Street School, built in 1911, was the first modern brick public school for black students in Atlanta. The school resulted from the passage of a $3 million bond issued by city voters in February 1910. In June 1910 the city of Atlanta purchased the lot on Yonge Street as the school site for $9,000 from Bishop Henry M. Turner, a prominent black leader and Methodist clergyman. During the first school year at Yonge Street, Selena Sloan Butler, with the assistance of the school's principal, Cora Finley, organized the country's first Colored Parents and Teachers Unit. In 1921 the Georgia Congress of Colored Parents and Teachers was created with Butler as president. The Congress of Colored Parents and Teachers merged with the Parents and Teachers Association (PTA) in 1970. This school is therefore the home of the first black PTA unit in the country. In 1955, in memory of Butler's husband and

in honor of her work, Yonge Street School was formally renamed the H. R. Butler School. The 1978–79 school year was the last year of formal operation for the H. R. Butler School. The building now serves as a community center. [A 1/24/80, 80001079]

GLYNN COUNTY

Hamilton Plantation Slave Cabins
Address restricted
St. Simons Island

The Hamilton Plantation Slave Cabins are the remains of one of the several large plantations that existed on St. Simons Island, one of Georgia's large coastal barrier islands. These cabins, built of tabby, a Georgia coastal building material made from oyster shells and lime that had the consistency of cement, and having windows, were among the better-built slave houses in the South. The two surviving cabins were part of a set of four built before 1833. As these cabins show, slaves lived in rows or groups of cabins, or "quarters," on the plantation grounds in an area well away from the Big House. Equally important, the cabins show the use of the double-pen plan, a duplex for more than one slave family and one of the most common slave housing designs in coastal Georgia. [CAD 6/30/88, 88000968]

GREENE COUNTY

Dr. Calvin M. Baber House
Penfield Road
Greensboro

This one-story, wood-framed Craftsman/bungalow style house built about 1925 is associated with Dr. Calvin M. Baber, Greensboro's second black physician, and is the only historic building in the community associated with Greenboro's black physicians. During the late 19th and early 20th centuries it was difficult for many rural and small-town blacks to obtain qualified medical services. Baber came to Greensboro from Alabama in the early 1920s after the death of Dr. A. T. Chisolm, Greensboro's first black physician. Doctors like Chisolm and Baber played crucial roles in the health and well-being of black Georgians. Because of their important role in the community, they were customarily respected figures and community leaders. In addition to practicing medicine, Baber bought, sold, and improved real estate and owned a major commercial building that housed his office and other black professional offices and businesses. [Greensboro MRA, CB 12/17/87, 87001439]

South Street-Broad Street-Main Street-Laurel Street Historic District
South, Broad, Main, and Laurel streets
Greensboro

The South Street-Broad Street-Main Street-Laurel Street Historic District contains a historic lodge building associated with Greensboro's black community. Lodges were centers of social, cultural, and political activity in the black community. Many of these functions had been the exclusive prerogative of black churches, but when African Americans gained the freedom to assemble and organize after the Civil War, lodges assumed an increasingly important community role. Moreover, in Greensboro, few historic resources associated with the black community have survived with integrity. Thus this district symbolizes the larger presence of Greensboro's historic black community.

The district is also important as a residential neighborhood containing the homes of many of Greensboro's black community leaders. Residents from this district have included doctors, lawyers, bankers, merchants, industrialists, and ministers who have been influential in the development of Greensboro. [Greensboro MRA, CA 9/9/87, 87001450]

Springfield Baptist Church
Canaan Circle
Greensboro

Established in 1864, Springfield Baptist Church is recognized as the first black Baptist Church in Greensboro. Its creation after the Civil War as an outgrowth from a white church, the First Baptist Church of Greensboro, is typical of how black churches in both urban and rural areas were created following emancipation. The church was located in the "Canaan" section, one of two black neighborhoods that developed in Greensboro. (The other area is known as "Railroad.") Springfield Baptist Church is also the mother church of Mount Enon Baptist Church.

Springfield Baptist Church illustrates typical cultural patterns of African Americans during Reconstruction. Once freed, African Americans organized into various groups, including educational institutions, fraternal lodges, and churches, independent of their former white counterparts. Black churches in Georgia traditionally have served as centers for social, cultural, and political as well as religious life in the black community because they have remained relatively free from white influence. The large membership of Springfield Baptist Church immediately after Reconstruction (approximately 500) wielded an important measure of local political and social power. This was especially true at the turn of the century, when the present church building was built, a landmark to the relative wealth and influence of this congregation in Greensboro's black community.

The church also was associated with leading individuals in the black community, primarily through its ministers, who served as community leaders: the Reverends Levi Thornton, L. P. Pinkney, and W. M. Jackson. Thornton served as the first minister of the church. Pinkney was the pastor in the early 1900s and also served as the pastor for Thankful Baptist Church in Atlanta and as moderator of the Shiloh Association. In addition to being the pastor of four Baptist churches in Greene County, Jackson was a pastor at the Bethlehem Baptist Church in Atlanta for more than 35 years, editor of the *Georgia Baptist* newspaper, auditor for the General Missionary Baptist Convention of Georgia, and cochair of the Atlanta Negro Voters League. Springfield Baptist Church remains a leading voice in the community. [Greensboro MRA, CA 9/9/87, 87001451]

HABERSHAM COUNTY

Daes Chapel Methodist Church
North Washington Street
Clarkesville

Daes Chapel Methodist Church represents the cultural and religious life of the small black community in Clarkesville. Even though the black citizens of Clarkesville have historically been small in number, they have always been an industrious and substantial force in the community. During the late 19th and early 20th centuries the local black population included landowners, small business owners, and master craftsworkers, as well as laborers, mechanics, and servants. Miss Amanda Daes, a prominent member of the black community, owned land all over the county and ran a restaurant. In the early 1900s Daes donated an acre of land for the church that became Daes Chapel Methodist Church. The church is the only historic building directly and exclusively related to Clarkesville's black community. Today, Daes Chapel continues to serve as a Methodist Church. [Clarkesville MRA, A 8/18/82, 82002430]

HANCOCK COUNTY

Camilla-Zack Community Center District
Route 1
Mayfield

The Camilla-Zack Community Center District was built solely by African Americans for the benefit and betterment of the rural black community. The community began just after the Civil War when three young freedmen, all brothers—Zack Hubert, David Hubert, and Floyd Hubert—bought 165 acres of land for which they paid $1,650 in three years' time. They were the first African Americans in Middle Georgia to purchase land after the war. After establishing a farm, the Hubert brothers built a church and a public school. The descendants and friends of these pioneer African Americans continued the tradition set by their fathers. At its height during the Depression the community included a cooperative store, a health center, a school, and teachers' cottages. The Camilla-Zack Country Life Center was a community center constructed early in the 1930s and named in honor of Zack and Camilla Hubert, who were instrumental in encouraging other African Americans to become landowners and to educate themselves. It was the focal point of the district and was dedicated to providing a more satisfying life for the black community. [CA 12/2/74, 74000685]

HART COUNTY

H. E. Fortson House
221 Richardson Street
Hartwell

The Fortson House is typical of houses

Cooperative Store in the Camilla-Zack Community Center District. Photo courtesy of the Georgia Department of Natural Resources (Van Martin).

built for and occupied by relatively prominent middle-class black citizens of Hartwell in the early 20th century. This building was built in 1913 as the residence of the Reverend H. E. Fortson, minister of the Hartwell First Baptist Church in the early 20th century. He was a prominent black minister and teacher in the Rome section of the town of Hartwell. Traditionally, churches were among the most important social and cultural institutions in black communities, and ministers were thus highly respected figures; the role played by Fortson in the Rome section of Hartwell was no exception. [Hartwell MRA, CB 9/11/86, 86002007]

Jackson Morrison House
439 Rome Street
Hartwell

Built in 1902 by Jackson Morrison as his residence, this house provides valuable commentary on black lifestyles in early 20th-century Hartwell. In many small Georgia towns, influential black residents lived in relatively simple homes. Thus Morrison's house is a simple, one-story frame building. Morrison was a small-town entrepreneur who made money from farming and carpentry as well as real estate speculation. Between 1920 and 1928 Morrison acquired 10 lots in the Rome section of Hartwell. In 1944 he acquired two additional lots. Through

Morrison's real estate transactions, African Americans were able to obtain land for development from white property owners in the area. [Hartwell MRA, CAB 9/11/86, 86002046]

John Underwood House
825 South Jackson Street
Hartwell

This house, the most elaborate residence in the Hartwell area, was built and owned by John Underwood, an African American, on its original 13.4-acre tract. Underwood was employed as an overseer at the Hartwell Cotton Mills. In the early 20th century, it was highly unusual for a small-town black resident to obtain this level of prominence in the operation and management of a major community business. It was also rare for a black citizen to own such a large tract of land. Land ownership of this magnitude and a vocation involving supervisory responsibilities in an important business mark John Underwood as a distinguished black resident of Hartwell. [Hartwell MRA, CB 9/11/86, 86002062]

JEFFERSON COUNTY
Old Market
Junction of U.S. Route 1 and Georgia Route 24
Louisville

Constructed around 1795, the Old Market is a four-sided open-air shed pavilion that was used as a multi-purpose trading house. At the time of its construction, Louisville was the state capital. The market was a focal point of commerce in the city, with streets laid out in a grid around the market square. From the time it was established, the market was used as a site for the sale of slaves. All types of real and personal property were sold here, including land, town lots, furniture and household goods, as well as slaves. For many years the market has been known locally as the "Old Slave Market." It is the only extant structure of its type and purpose in Georgia. [A 2/17/78, 78000991]

LIBERTY COUNTY
Dorchester Academy Boys' Dormitory
Intersection of Georgia Route 38 and U.S. Route 82
Midway

This building is the sole extant building documenting the existence of Dorchester Academy, an important school that for almost 70 years served the needs of the black children of Liberty County and the entire coast. The American Missionary Association, which established this school, played an important role in the education of Southern blacks after the Civil War. With the exception of the Atlanta University complex in Atlanta, very few buildings associated with the association's facilities in Georgia remain, for most were closed in the 1930s and 1940s as public high school education for African Americans began to be offered around the state.

This building also played an important role in the civil rights movement during the 1960s. It was associated with the Southern Christian Leadership Conference, one of the most important civil rights organizations, which was organized in 1957 with Dr. Martin Luther King, Jr., as its president. Dorchester Academy was one of two locations where the SCLC conducted its important Citizenship Education Programs from 1961 to 1970. [CA 6/23/86, 86001371]

LOWNDES COUNTY
Dasher High School
900 South Troup Street
Valdosta

The Dasher High School, a one-story, early 20th-century school building with

Tudor-influenced detailing, is the only survivor of three black high schools in Valdosta. It was named for Robert Dasher, a former Valdosta Board of Education member and mayor of Valdosta, who donated the land for the school.

From 1929, the date of its opening, until 1956, it was the only black high school in Valdosta. The school's first and only principal was the Reverend James L. Lomax (1898–1976), an important civic, religious, fraternal, and educational leader in the black community. Lomax attended Fort Valley State College, Savannah State College, and Syracuse University. He became principal of Magnolia Street School (the black high school in Valdosta that preceded Dasher) in 1923 and continued to serve as a principal in Valdosta until he retired in 1967. In addition, he served for 34 years as pastor of Macedonia First Baptist Church in Valdosta.

Graduates of Dasher High School include many of Valdosta's early to mid-20th-century black leaders as well as a cross section of Valdosta's black community. Among the most noted individuals attending the school were actor and author Ossie Davis (1917–) and Louis Lomax (1923–70), a writer who was James Lomax's adopted son.

At the time of its listing in the National Register, Dasher High served as a senior citizen and community center. [CA 4/18/85, 85000849]

MERIWETHER COUNTY

Greenville Historic District
Bounded by Gresham, Gaston, Woodbury, Talbotton, Baldwin, Bottom, Martin, Terrell, LaGrange, and Newnan streets
Greenville

Greenville Historic District provides a perspective on the lifestyles of African Americans during the 19th and early 20th centuries. Much of Greenville's historic housing illustrates the work of several local black carpenters who made a significant contribution to the rebuilding of the city after the 1893 cyclone. Also, the district features a number of intact resources in three historically black neighborhoods. Methodist Hill, Baldwin Hill, and Baptist Hill located within the district illustrate the pattern of development in black neighborhoods. Within these communities are churches, schools, and businesses that served the needs of the black residents. Two historic black churches, Brinson Chapel African Methodist Episcopal Church and Springfield Baptist Church, both in the Baptist Hill neighborhood, not only served the religious needs of the area but also were important social and educational facilities. This enclave within the historic district represents important aspects of the black community's heritage. [CA 3/16/90, 90000433]

Red Oak Creek Covered Bridge
North of Woodbury on Huel Brown Road
Woodbury

The Red Oak Creek Covered Bridge, a 412-foot lattice-type bridge, was built in 1840 by noted black bridge builder and former slave Horace King. King was given his freedom in 1848 but continued to work for his former master, John Godwin, a contractor. King also built a bridge across the Chattahoochee at Columbus and spent much time in west Georgia building numerous other bridges.

This bridge is believed to be the oldest covered bridge in Georgia and the longest covered bridge span in the state. While the Red Oak Creek Covered Bridge was built during an age when more than 250 covered bridges existed in Georgia, it is one of only some 20 remaining. [CA 5/7/73, 73000632]

MORGAN COUNTY

Madison Historic District (Boundary Increase)
Roughly bounded by Main Street, Old Post Road, Academy Street, Dixie Street, and Washington Street
Madison

The Madison Historic District contains at least two enclaves of small, one-story, frame buildings that represent patterns of development in the town's black neighborhoods. Within the district are churches, schools, and businesses that served the needs of the black residents. Aspects of black history can also be seen in the remaining outbuildings and domestic servant houses located behind many of the district's larger antebellum residences. Also significant to black history are the three historic black churches–St. Paul African Methodist Episcopal Church, Clarke Chapel Baptist Church, and Calvary Baptist. These churches are community landmarks that not only served the religious needs of the area but also were important social and educational facilities. The location, design, and pattern of development of all these resources provide a perspective on the lifestyles of African Americans during the 19th and early 20th century. [CA 1/8/90, 89002159]

MUSCOGEE COUNTY

Building at 1612 3rd Avenue
1612 3rd Avenue
Columbus

This house was the home of George and Cordelia Henry, a black couple who worked as a carpenter and a midwife, respectively. This house probably dates to the 1860s and represents the type of housing built by middle-class African Americans. Members of the Henry family lived here as late as 1912. This structure is also representative of building styles in Columbus during the Civil War era. [Columbus MRA, CA 12/2/80, 80001128]

Colored Cemetery
10th Avenue
Columbus

This cemetery, which is believed to have been set aside in Edward Lloyd Thomas's original plan of the city in 1828 for the burial of Columbus's black citizens, is the oldest public cemetery for African Americans in Columbus. In 1936 the burial ground, which had been called the Colored Cemetery, was renamed Porterdale in honor of Richard P. Porter, an African American who served as the cemetery's sexton from 1878 until 1920. The cemetery has marked graves dating from the early 1840s and includes some marble markers memorializing the burial sites of prominent leaders of the Columbus black community. [Columbus MRA, CA 9/29/80, 80001155]

First African Baptist Church
901 5th Avenue
Columbus

Organized in the 1840s as an offspring of the local Baptist church, the congregation associated with the First African Baptist Church was originally known as the African Baptist Church and was the oldest black congregation in Columbus. The worshipers built the present sanctuary in 1915 at a cost of $75,000, after occupying three previous sanctuaries. An understated example of early 20th-century Gothic Revival style ecclesiastical architecture, the church has the pointed arch window and door openings, quoins, and castellated tower cornices characteristic of this style. [Columbus MRA, CA 9/29/80, 80001165]

Girard Colored Mission
1002 6th Avenue
Columbus

The congregation of the Girard Colored Mission (now the St. James African Methodist Episcopal [AME] Church) is the second oldest AME congregation in Georgia, dating from 1863. The present church was constructed between 1875 and 1876 on land granted to the congregation in 1873 by an act of the Georgia legislature. Built at a cost of $20,000, the church is one of the finest examples of Victorian Gothic Revival style architecture in Columbus. In addition to its role as a religious center for the black community in Columbus, the building, with one of the largest auditoriums available to African Americans in Columbus in before and during the civil rights movement, served as a primary meeting place for most large black assemblies in the city. [Columbus MRA, CA 9/29/80, 80001173]

Liberty Theater
821 8th Avenue
Columbus

One of a few theaters in the state built for African Americans, the 1924 Liberty Theater served as the principal entertainment center for Columbus's black community for more than 50 years. It featured silent movies and "talkies," as well as theatrical and musical performances.

The theater also played an important role during the rise of jazz and blues music in the South. Of special importance were the frequent performances of Gertrude Pridgett "Ma" Rainey (1886–1939), a Columbus native who became known as the "Mother of the Blues." At least once, she performed with Bessie Smith (1894–1937), another great blues singer. The theater also featured Marian Anderson, Ella Fitzgerald, Ethel Waters, Lena Horne, Chick Webb Band, Duke Ellington, Cab Calloway, and Georgia's own Fletcher Henderson (see also Gertrude Pridgett "Ma" Rainey House). [A 5/22/84, 84001208]

Isaac Maund House
1608 3rd Avenue
Columbus

The Isaac Maund House is located in a residential area composed primarily of 1890s shotgun houses. One of the more elaborate houses in this neighborhood, it was probably built by its original owner, Isaac Maund, a black mill worker who later became a carpenter. Located very near residences historically occupied by whites, this house illustrates how close black citizens and whites lived to one another in the late 1800s and early 1900s in some areas of town. [Columbus MRA, CA 12/2/80, 80001179]

William Price House
1620 3rd Avenue
Columbus

This frame cottage was built by William Price, a black subcarrier for the Columbus post office, who lived here with his wife, Maude, as early as 1900. It is a common example of a prevalent housing type occupied by more affluent African Americans in Columbus at the turn of the century. A two-room linear plan with a rear chimney and later additions, the residence embodies a plan commonly used for black housing and servants' quarters on plantations and adapted here for "uptown" living quarters. The house exhibits Queen Anne–influenced decorative features such as the turned posts and decorative spindles on the porch and the fish-scale shingles in the gable above. The house is located within a historically black residential neighborhood with many examples of similar properties. [Columbus MRA, CA 9/29/80, 80001194]

Gertrude Pridgett "Ma" Rainey House
805 5th Avenue
Columbus

In the history of the blues, perhaps no woman is better known than Gertrude Pridgett "Ma" Rainey. Her pioneering work as a woman in her profession and her captivating style earned her the nickname "Mother of the Blues." Born in Columbus, Georgia, in 1886, Rainey made her singing debut in 1900 at the Columbus Opera House. In 1904 she married William "Pa" Rainey, thus acquiring the nickname "Ma." Her career as a blues singer began when she joined the singing and performing circuit with her new husband. The pair performed with various minstrel shows before separating. Afterward Ma Rainey continued touring on her own.

Throughout the 1920s and early 1930s, Ma Rainey worked out of Chicago, where she kept an apartment. She toured extensively in the South, however, performing with the celebrated Rabbit Foot Minstrel Show and acting as her own booking agent. She made her first recording in 1924, and in its advertising the Paramount recording company called her the "Mother of the Blues," a title that remained with her. Many of the songs in her 92 recordings were her own compositions. She sang often of the then taboo subject of the plight of women in relationships with men, in compositions such as "Trust No Man" and "Gone Daddy Blues." Recordings, however, were unable to capture her commanding stage presence and the interaction with live audiences for which she was known.

Ma Rainey continued performing until the 1930s, appearing with the top musicians of her day, including Louis Armstrong, Fletcher Henderson, and another Georgia native, Tom Dorsey. The growing popularity of jazz, and decline of the so-called depressing music of the blues in this time of economic hardship, however, brought her career to an end. She returned to Columbus in 1935 after the death of her sister and her mother to live in the house that she had purchased for her mother in 1920.

The Ma Rainey House has been recently restored, and plans exist to open it as a museum dedicated to Ma Rainey's life and work. Ma Rainey has been honored on a stamp issued by the West African nation of Gambia as part of a series honoring the history of the blues, and in the fall of 1992 she was inducted into the Georgia Music Hall of Fame. [B 11/18/92, 92001530]

William Henry Spencer House
745 4th Avenue
Columbus

The Spencer House is an outstanding example of Neoclassical Revival architecture popular during the early 20th century. Built in 1912, the two-story residence was constructed for William Henry Spencer, a leading black educator in the Columbus public school system. Built at a time when many African Americans did not own their own homes, the house was custom designed for Spencer and his family. Spencer's dedication to the educational development of Columbus is commemorated not only by his home, but also by the naming of a local high school, William H. Spencer Senior High, in his honor. [CB 5/23/78, 78000996]

St. Christopher's Normal and Industrial Parish School
900 5th Avenue
Columbus

Built in 1916, this property was originally known as St. Christopher's Episcopal Church. By 1918 it was called St. Christopher's Normal and Industrial School and St. Christopher's Episcopal Church. Years later the First African Baptist Church purchased the property and converted the building into a child care center. It remained important as an early church-affiliated school in Columbus's black community. [Columbus MRA, CA 9/29/80, 80001201]

John Stewart House
1618 3rd Avenue
Columbus

Built by John Stewart, a black miller who lived here with his wife, Hester, as early as 1900, this frame cottage is a common example of a prevalent housing type occupied by more affluent African Americans in Columbus at the turn of the century. A two-room linear plan with a rear chimney and later additions, the residence embodies a plan commonly used for black housing and servants' quarters on plantations and adapted here for "uptown" living quarters. The house exhibits Queen Anne–influenced decorative features such as the turned posts and decorative spindles on the porch and the fish-scale shingles in the gable above. The house is located within a historically black residential neighborhood with many examples of similar properties. [Columbus MRA, CA 9/29/80, 80001203]

St. John Chapel
1516 5th Avenue
Columbus

Because the cornerstone of the St. John African Methodist Episcopal (AME) Church claims the building was built in 1870 and the basement in 1890, historians speculate that the original building was a frame church built in 1870, which was apparently raised on a new foundation in 1890 and faced with brick. Further evidence suggests the building was re-faced with brick in 1908 during a second renovation. The church's round tower and conical roof are unique architectural features in Columbus.

In its early years, the congregation called its church St. John Chapel. This congregation, which descended from St. James AME Church, the oldest AME congregation in Columbus, later changed the name to St. John AME Church. Thus St. John's houses the second oldest AME congregation in Columbus. [Columbus MRA, CA 9/29/80, 80001202]

RANDOLPH COUNTY

Fletcher Henderson House
1016 Andrew Street
Cuthbert

The Fletcher Henderson House, built in 1888, was the home of Professor Fletcher Hamilton Henderson (1857–1943), a leading black educator in Cuthbert for 64 years. It is also important as the boyhood home of Fletcher Henderson, Jr. (1897–1952) and his brother, Horace Henderson. Fletcher Jr. was one of the first great jazz musicians, known for his keyboard arrangements, compositions, and performances.

Fletcher Jr. became the leader of a number of orchestras in New York and inspired later musicians such as Louis Armstrong, Benny Goodman, and Count Basie. Fletcher Jr. sold his arrangements to Benny Goodman in the mid-1930s after being critically injured in an automobile accident.

In 1938 Horace created arrangements for the Glenn Miller orchestra. He continued to play with Fletcher's band until 1943, and in 1944 he played with Lena Horne.

Fletcher Jr.'s arrangements are classics and are still being played, and his approach remains the foundation of big bands and jazz. Horace played with small combos during the 1950s and 1960s and continued to perform into the 1970s. [AB 6/17/82, 82002460]

RICHMOND COUNTY

Laney-Walker North Historic District
Bounded by D'Antignac, Seventh, Twiggs, Phillips, and Harrison streets, Walton Way, and Laney-Walker Boulevard
Augusta

Laney-Walker North Historic District developed during the 19th century as a multiethnic working-class community that evolved into a vital, self-sufficient black community in response to the South's early 20th-century segregationist policies. The residential buildings are good examples of modest vernacular house types, including the plantation plain, the double pen, the shotgun, the Victorian cottage, and an indigenous Augusta house type. Two of the early 20th-century houses in the district were built by William McNatt, a prominent black builder who lived in the district.

The district's commercial structures document the variety of minority businesses in the community. Two landmark black commercial enterprises are of particular importance in the district. The Pilgrim Health and Life Insurance Company, established in 1898, has become the ninth largest black-owned life

insurance company in the country, and the Penny Savings Bank, established in 1910 by a group of Laney-Walker's most prominent blacks, was one of the few black-owned banks in the state.

Laney-Walker North Historic District contained the homes of many of Augusta's most prominent African Americans, including Frank Yerby, a novelist of international repute; Silas Floyd, a writer and educator; Lucy C. Laney and Charles T. Walker, for whom the neighborhood is named; and numerous black doctors, merchants, builders, and businesspeople.

The district also has a relatively large number of historic black churches, many of which provided educational opportunities to the black community. Trinity Colored Methodist Episcopal Church, one of Augusta's oldest and most important black congregations, was established by slaves in 1840 as an offshoot of Augusta's white Methodist church. Bishop Lucius Holsey, pastor of the church in the late 19th century, was instrumental in establishing Paine Institute (later Paine College) in about 1883, the first of Augusta's well-known schools for African Americans. Harmony Baptist Church (c. 1873) on Hopkins Street is the oldest surviving church building in the district and the location of Augusta's first school for blacks. Tabernacle Baptist Church, established in 1885 and moved to its present building in the Laney-Walker North neighborhood in 1915, is Augusta's largest black congregation and a church with a national reputation. Charles T. Walker (1858–1921), its founder and early pastor, was instrumental in bringing the Walker Baptist Institute to Augusta in 1898. Walker lived in the district on Laney-Walker Boulevard. Also within the district, on Phillips Street, is the home of Lucy C.

Laney-Walker North Historic District. Photo courtesy of the Georgia Department of Natural Resources (James R. Lockhart).

Laney (1854–1933), the noted educator who, about 1883, founded the Haines Normal and Industrial Institute, black Augusta's third important secondary school. [CAB 9/5/85, 85001976]

Springfield Baptist Church (Boundary Increase)
114 12th Street
Augusta

Built in 1801, Springfield Baptist Church is the oldest extant church building in Augusta and one of the oldest in the state. It is a rare example of the late 18th- to early 19th-century nonliturgical or "New England meetinghouse" type of church in Georgia. Originally built to

house Augusta's first Methodist Society, since 1844, it has been the home of Springfield Baptist Church, one of the oldest black congregations in the country; at the time it acquired this building, the congregation was already more than 50 years old.

This congregation, which became independent under the name Springfield Baptist Church in 1787, traces its origins to the 1750 Silver Bluff Baptist Church in South Carolina. Throughout the 19th century, the Springfield Baptist Church played an important role in Augusta's religious history. In addition to serving local black religious, social, and cultural needs, the church helped bridge the transition between slavery and free citizenship in Augusta and stood as the focus of black community life.

The present imposing brick building was built to replace a smaller one on the same location. It is the work of Albert Whitner Todd, an architect living and working in Augusta at the time who later became a charter member of the South Carolina chapter of the American Institute of Architects and served as its president from 1915 to 1916. The Springfield Baptist Church stands today as one of the two last surviving buildings of the historic Springfield's historic black community. [CA 7/5/90, 90000979]

THOMAS COUNTY

Bethany Congregational Church
112 Lester Street
Thomasville

Bethany Congregational Church was built in 1891 by the American Missionary Association (AMA) to serve the religious needs of black students at the Allen Normal and Industrial School (1885–1933). The school and church were built by the AMA, the missionary arm of the United Church of Christ, which after the Civil War became active in providing education for southern blacks. Originally established in Quitman, Georgia, in 1885, the school was relocated to Thomasville in 1886 because of a hostile reception from the white community and the subsequent burning of the school. Both the school and the church played a vital role in educating black youths in Thomasville. The school buildings were razed in 1935 to make way for a housing project, leaving Bethany Congregational Church as the only existing building associated with the former educational complex. Bethany Congregational continues to serve as an important neighborhood church for the surrounding community. [CA 3/7/85, 85000453]

Church of the Good Shepherd
511–519 Oak Street
Thomasville

One of Georgia's few black Episcopal congregations, the Church of the Good Shepherd was organized in Thomasville in 1893 under the leadership of the Reverend Charles LeRoche. The congregation initially consisted of both black and white members, a custom that was not followed in other major denominations in the late 19th and early 20th centuries. The church, which was built in 1894 and is a good example of a late Victorian vernacular church built for a small congregation, also housed a parochial school, which functioned from 1894 to 1964. This school played an extremely important role as one of a handful of private schools in the city that educated black children. The church also provided space for a library, playground, and Boy Scout troop. Through its varied services to the black population of Thomasville, the Church of the Good Shepherd functioned for many years as a religious, social, and educational center for the community. [CA 2/5/87, 86003581]

WASHINGTON COUNTY

Thomas Jefferson Elder High and Industrial School
316 Hall Street
Sandersville

The Thomas Jefferson Elder High and Industrial School dates to 1889, and it is the oldest school building remaining in Washington County. It represents the influential contributions of Thomas Jefferson Elder to the black community. He was "the one man who had meant most to the educational, social and spiritual advancement of the colored people of the county for almost 60 years."

In 1889 Elder formed a trustee group to purchase land and construct a school for classes then being held in Springfield Baptist Church. By the turn of the century, Elder's school was the largest black school in central rural Georgia. It was the first school in this section of Georgia to establish manual training in its curriculum, and it trained teachers for rural black schools. By 1917 a domestic science building was built with the help of the Julius Rosenwald Fund, an educational foundation established to advance southern black education. As early as 1910 Julius Rosenwald, a member of the board of trustees at Tuskegee Institute, showed interest in the improvement of conditions among African Americans. Beginning as a small donor of amounts of $5,000 gifts, he soon became a major contributor to the improvement of educational facilities for southern African Americans.

In 1927–28 the Rosenwald Building was also built with the help of the Rosenwald Fund, although the majority of the costs were paid by local public support and city funds. The support of the Rosenwald Fund for Elder's school speaks for the school's quality. [CA 5/12/81, 81000202]

IDAHO

ADA COUNTY

St. Paul Missionary Baptist Church

124 Broadway Avenue

Boise

Organized in 1909, the St. Paul Missionary Baptist Church first held services in a small building in Boise's commercial district. The present church, a small vernacular building with bungalow design elements, was constructed in 1921 by church members. St. Paul is one of two churches with predominantly black congregations still in existence in the state of Idaho. Early black residents of Boise were primarily domestics and servants for white families and most likely attended services with them in white congregations. St. Paul represents the successful efforts of a group of African Americans, though relatively small in number in the area, to establish their own church. [C 10/29/82, 82000247]

St. Paul Missionary Baptist Church. Photo courtesy of Idaho State Historical Society (Janet McCullough).

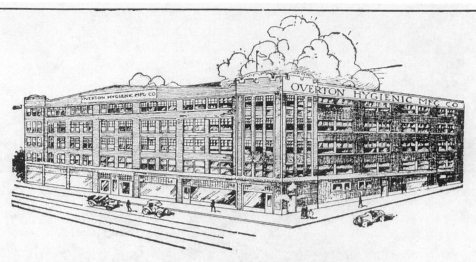

Do You Need Money?

If So, This Is Your Chance.

Most of our agents make more money in three hours than they can make elsewhere in a whole day.

You can earn money as fast as you wish.

HIGH-BROWN Products sell twelve months in the year.

IT'S THE HOUSE BEHIND THE AGENT that means success or failure to the agent in the field.

YOU CAN'T AFFORD TO GAMBLE— Therefore, connect yourself with a reliable institution.

HIGH-BROWN Toilet Preparations are products of proven merit, developed beyond the experimental stage.

They have been used by persons of cultivated tastes and refinement for 25 years.

We Are Offering Unusual Opportunities to Reliable and Energetic Persons.

If you wish to make big money:

If you wish to utilize your spare time profitably:

Or if you wish all-year round steady employment—Opportunity knocks. Write today for agents' terms. If you don't know how to sell, we will teach you.

The Overton-Hygienic Mfg. Co.

Dept. H. C.   Chicago, Ill.

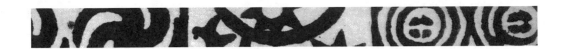

ILLINOIS

BUREAU COUNTY

Owen Lovejoy Homestead
Peru Street (U.S. Route 6)
Princeton

From 1856 until 1864, this property was the home of Owen Lovejoy (1811–64), abolitionist and U.S. representative, who dedicated his life to ending slavery. Lovejoy was born on June 6, 1811, in Kennebec County, Maine. He was the fifth of seven children born to farmer and Congregational minister Daniel B. Lovejoy and his wife. Owen Lovejoy journeyed to Alton, Illinois, at the age of 25 to work with his brother Elijah Lovejoy. Elijah published a newspaper, which he had recently moved to Alton from St. Louis, Missouri.

In St. Louis Elijah Lovejoy's antislavery position had made him extremely unpopular with local residents. In 1836 a mob destroyed his press, forcing him to move across the Mississippi River to the free state of Illinois. His move was to no avail, however, and on November 7, 1837, Elijah Lovejoy was killed while defending his press from mob violence.

Advertisement for the Overton Hygienic Building, Cook County, from Half Century Magazine, *January/February 1924. Courtesy of the Commission on Chicago Landmarks.*

At Elijah Lovejoy's death, Owen Lovejoy swore to dedicate his life to the antislavery cause.

Owen Lovejoy soon became active in the Underground Railroad, establishing his house in Princeton, where he was then living, as a principle depot in Illinois. Aided by his brother Joseph, Owen Lovejoy wrote *Memoir of the Reverend Elijah P. Lovejoy; Who Was Murdered in Defense of the Liberty of the Press at Alton, Illinois, November 7, 1837*. This volume became an important piece of antislavery propaganda.

In 1854, after several unsuccessful campaigns for state office, Owen Lovejoy was elected to the state legislature. In 1857 he was elected to the U.S. Congress, where he campaigned fiercely for the abolitionist cause. On December 14, 1863, Lovejoy introduced a universal emancipation bill that, after much revision and amendment, provided the essence of the 13th Amendment to the Constitution, which was not finally adopted until a year after his death on March 25, 1864. His body was returned to Princeton after his death, and he was buried in the nearby Oakdale Cemetery. [B 5/24/73, 73000690]

COOK COUNTY

Robert S. Abbott House
4742 Martin Luther King, Jr., Drive
Chicago

Formerly the home of black newspaper publisher Robert S. Abbott, the Abbott House is an architectural reminder of a bygone era of sumptuous living on Chicago's South Side. Located on Martin Luther King, Jr. Drive, formerly known as South Parkway, and Grand Boulevard, it lies in the heart of the city's black belt. A community once known for its stately mansions and grand lifestyle, the area no longer ranks as the mecca of black affluence. Today, the Abbott House is but a shell of its former elegance and has been converted into a rooming house.

Robert S. Abbott (1870–1940) created the *Chicago Defender* and led it to a position of national importance in the lives of African Americans, North and South, during the opening decades of the 20th century. Under Abbott, the *Defender* offered hope to tens of thousands of African Americans pushed beyond endurance by the abhorrent acts of racism that were pervasive in the Deep South. According to noted sociologist E. Franklin Frazier, "The *Defender* more than any other Negro newspaper was responsible for stimulating the northward migration of Negroes by picturing the advantages of the North as opposed to southern oppression." In articles and editorials, Abbott encouraged black southerners to seek a haven in the northern cities, particularly in Chicago.

As an entrepreneur, Abbott became the most successful black publisher of his era. Begun in 1905 as a one-man kitchen table operation, the *Defender* by 1929 occupied a three-story building with its own printing press, a large production staff, and a circulation of more than 250,000 copies weekly with readership across the country. The Robert S. Abbot house was designated a National Historic Landmark on December 8, 1976. [B 12/8/76 NHL, 76000686]

Chicago Bee Building
3647–3655 South State Street
Chicago

Centered in the vicinity of State and 35th streets on Chicago's Near South Side are surviving properties of what was once a thriving city-within-a-city created by the black community. Referred to by residents as the Metropolis, the community built its own economic, social, and political establishments, directly supported by black enterprise and capital. The development was firmly established by the turn of the century, and it prospered until the 1930s, when the Depression halted its further evolution.

The last major building to be erected in Black Metropolis, the *Chicago Bee* Building was built by black entrepreneur Anthony Overton to house his newspaper, the *Chicago Bee*. Overton, whose business career began with the Overton Hygienic cosmetics firm, later branched out into other fields, including banking, insurance, and publishing. His first publishing venture started in 1916 with the publication of the *Half Century Magazine*, which featured a variety of short stories, informational articles, and nationwide news reports, as well as providing a prominent advertising forum for the diverse products manufactured by the Overton Hygienic Manufacturing Company.

In 1925 the *Half Century Magazine* was phased out in favor of a new publication, the *Chicago Bee,* a newspaper intended to compete with Robert S. Abbott's *Chicago Defender*. The *Chicago Bee* Building opened in 1931 and housed the newspaper and the Overton Hygienic Manufacturing Company until the early 1940s when the newspaper folded. The cosmetics firm continued to occupy the building, and it still maintains quarters at the State Street address.

The only building designed in the Art Deco style of the late 1920s, the *Chicago Bee* Building is one of the most picturesque of those in the Black Metropolis. [Black Metropolis TR, CA 4/30/86, 86001090]

Oscar Stanton DePriest House
4536–4538 South Dr. Martin Luther King, Jr. Drive
Chicago

Oscar Stanton DePriest (1871–1951) was the first black U.S. representative elected from a northern state, serving from 1928 to 1935. As the only black representative in Congress he became a national spokesperson and worked diligently on issues important to African Americans. He pushed for more equal distribution of government appropriations for education for black children and an increased share of the federal budget for the federally funded Howard University.

Born in Florence, Alabama, on March 9, 1871, DePriest moved to Kansas with his family when he was very young. In 1899 he left Kansas for Chicago, where he established himself as a contractor and painter. An active participant in local politics, he was elected and served two terms as a Cook County commissioner from 1904 until 1908, using his position to educate poor African Americans about local welfare relief resources available to them. Failing to win a third commission term, he returned to his painting and contracting business and began a real estate business, which would eventually amass him a sizable fortune. In 1915 he was the first African American elected as an alderman to the Chicago City Council, where he was principally concerned with finding employment for African Americans. His illustrious career as an alderman was marred by his indictment by a grand jury

with others on conspiracy and bribery charges. Defended by renowned attorney Clarence Darrow, DePriest was acquitted of all charges. In 1924 DePriest was elected to the position of Third Ward committee member, becoming one of the five most powerful politicians in Illinois's First Congressional District. In 1928, following the death of incumbent congressional representative Martin B. Madden after his victory in the Republican primary, DePriest was selected by the five committee members to replace Madden on the Republican ballot. He was elected and seated in the House of Representatives despite the disapproval and objections of several southern representatives.

In January 1934, near the end of his sixth year in Congress, DePriest attempted to desegregate a Capitol Hill dining room supposedly meant for congresspeople and their guests. Although members of the white public had been welcomed and served there, when Depriest's son Oscar Jr. and his confidential secretary, Morris Lewis, attempted to enter to the facility they were turned away. Since the white public was served there, DePriest wanted the same privilege accorded to the black public. DePriest presented a resolution to the House Rules Committee seeking an end to the discriminatory practice. After 30 legislative days with no action on the resolution, DePriest presented a petition to the entire Congress to have the resolution placed on the House floor for discussion and voting. By the middle of April there were enough signatures on the petition to discuss the issue in Congress on April 25. A special five-person committee was convened to investigate the matter–three Democrats chosen by the Speaker and two Republicans chosen by DePriest. Two reports, split along party lines, were issued. The Democrats' majority report stated that the restaurant was not intended for the public and evaded the issue of discrimination. The Republicans' minority report noted that the service practice violated the 14th Amendment rights of African Americans in denying them equal access to the facility. Nevertheless the majority report was accepted, and the restaurant continued its discriminatory practices.

DePriest ran for a fourth term in 1934 but lost to Arthur Mitchell, the first black Democrat elected to Congress. After losing his bid for Congress, Depriest returned to Chicago, where he remained active in local politics, serving as an alderman of the city's Third Ward from 1943 to 1947. He returned to his real estate business after withdrawing from politics following a sharp dispute with fellow party members. DePriest resided in his apartment at this address from 1929, when he purchased the building, until his death in May 1951. For association with DePriest's nationally significant role as a politician and as the first African American elected to Congress following George F. White's term, which ended in 1901, the property was designated a National Historic Landmark on May 15, 1975. [B 5/15/75 NHL, 75000646]

Jean Baptiste Pointe Du Sable Homesite
401 North Michigan Avenue
Chicago

Jean Baptiste Pointe Du Sable (1745–1818) was one of the most prominent pioneers, fur traders, and independent entrepreneurs of the Colonial and Revolutionary eras. By building his trading post at the important portage between the Chicago and the Des Plaines rivers, which is now Pioneer Court, he laid the foundation for the future development of Chicago. Du Sable is represen-

tative of contributions of African Americans in the initial economic and developmental stages of the country's growth.

The home he built at this new trading post was a log cabin; it measured 22 feet by 40 feet and was filled with paintings and fine furniture. During his early years on the site he added two barns, a horse mill, a bakehouse, a workshop, a dairy, a poultry house, and a smokehouse. He built a thriving establishment around which white traders and Indians settled. Besides trading in furs, Du Sable was a miller, cooper, husbandman, and whatever else was needed around the settlement. The Du Sable Homesite was designated a National Historic Landmark on May 11, 1976. [B 5/11/76 NHL, 76000690]

Eighth Regiment Armory
3533 South Giles Avenue
Chicago

Centered in the vicinity of State and 35th streets on Chicago's Near South Side are surviving properties of what was once a thriving city-within-a-city created by the black community. Referred to by residents as the Metropolis, the community built its own economic, social, and political establishments, directly supported by black enterprise and capital. The development was firmly established by the turn of the century, and it prospered until the 1930s, when the Depression halted its further evolution.

The Eighth Regiment Armory was the first armory structure to be erected for a regiment commanded entirely by African Americans. The Eighth Regiment was especially noted for its service record during World War I.

Originally organized as a volunteer regiment drawn from the black community during the Spanish-American War in 1898, the "Fighting Eighth" was established as an infantry section of the Illinois National Guard. Under the command of Colonel Franklin A. Denison, former assistant attorney general of Illinois, the Eighth Regiment saw meritorious service during border conflicts with Mexico in 1916 and later in World War I, when it was incorporated into the 370th U.S. Infantry and served on the major battle-fronts in France. The Fighting Eighth gained special note as the last regiment to drive the German forces from the Aisne-Marne region before the Armistice on November 11, 1918. [Black Metropolis TR, A 4/30/86, 86001096]

Overton Hygienic Building
3619–3627 South State Street
Chicago

Centered in the vicinity of State and 35th streets on Chicago's Near South Side are surviving properties of what was once a thriving city-within-a-city created by the black community. Referred to by residents as the Metropolis, the community built its own economic, social, and political establishments, directly supported by black enterprise and capital. The development was firmly established by the turn of the century, and it prospered until the 1930s, when the Depression halted its further evolution.

Promoted during its construction as "a monument to Negro thrift and industry," the Overton Hygienic Building, erected by Anthony Overton, a former slave, housed a number of enterprises that met the needs of a growing black community in Chicago. They included the Overton Hygienic Manufacturing Company, a pioneering firm in black cosmetics; the Victory Life Insurance Company; the *Chicago Bee,* a major black newspaper; the *Half Century Magazine,* a black-oriented monthly magazine; and the Douglass National Bank, the first

black bank to be granted a national charter. The completion of the Overton Hygienic Building by 1923 provided quarters for Overton's diverse financial empire but also provided the first new rental offices available to black professionals, making the building the prime business address in Black Metropolis.

The Douglass National Bank and Victory Life Insurance Company were on the first floor of the building. Second-floor tenants included the Theater Owners Booking Association, which managed and booked black stage acts; Walter T. Bailey, Chicago's first black architect, who in 1926 designed the 80-story Pythian Temple at State Street and 37th Place; and Overton's son-in-law, Dr. Julian H. Lewis, professor of pathology at the University of Chicago. The Overton Hygienic Manufacturing Company, one of the foremost producers of black cosmetics, with sales distribution extending as far as Egypt, Liberia, and Japan, was housed on the third floor. The Overton Hygienic Building also housed the *Half Century Magazine,* a variety magazine aimed at the black audience that included fiction, news reports, homemaking features, and essays on the problems of succeeding in black business ventures. For his significant business achievements, Anthony Overton was honored with two awards for his advancement of black business, the Spingarn Medal in 1927 and the Harmon Business Award in 1928. The Great Depression, however, caused the demise of the Douglass Bank, leaving Overton with the *Chicago Bee* and his cosmetics firm. [Black Metropolis TR, A 4/30/86, 86001091]

Quinn Chapel of the AME Church
2401 South Wabash Avenue
Chicago

The Quinn Chapel of the African

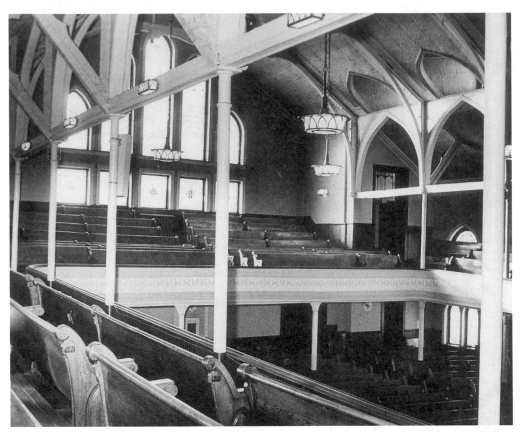

Quinn Chapel of the AME Church. Photo courtesy of the National Register of Historic Places.

Methodist Episcopal (AME) Church is the oldest black congregation in Chicago. In 1844 several black Chicagoans organized a nonsectarian prayer group, which met weekly at the home of one of its members. In 1847 the group organized as a congregation of the AME Church. The church was named Quinn Chapel after Bishop William Paul Quinn, circuit rider and key figure in the western advance of African Methodism. By 1848 Quinn Chapel's congregation had more than 50 members, many of whom were ex-slaves. Not surprisingly, they played an active role in the abolition movement in Chicago.

Along with St. Thomas Protestant Episcopal Church and Grace Presbyterian Church, Quinn Chapel has served as a focal point in the social and humanitarian activities of Chicago's black elite. The congregation founded and nurtured such institutions as the Elam Home, the Provident Hospital, the Wabash Avenue Young Men's Christian Association (YMCA), and the Moseley Playground. Prominent members have included John Day, an early Chicago businessperson and barber; Adelbury H. Roberts, the first African American elected to the Illinois state senate; and Robert R. Jackson, who served 21 years as an alderman on Chicago's City Council (see also Wabash Avenue YMCA). [A 9/4/79, 79000827]

Unity Hall

3140 South Indiana Avenue
Chicago

Centered in the vicinity of State and 35th streets on Chicago's Near South Side are surviving properties of what was once a thriving city-within-a-city created by the black community. Referred to by residents as the Metropolis, the community built its own economic, social, and political establishments, directly supported by black enterprise and capital. The development was firmly established by the turn of the century, and it prospered until the 1930s, when the Depression halted its further evolution.

Beginning in 1917, Unity Hall was the headquarters of the People's Movement Club, a political organization headed by Oscar Stanton DePriest, the primary leader in the drive for fair political representation in the Black Metropolis (see also Oscar Stanton DePriest House). The club was his attempt to establish a new political organization supported from within the black community. [Black Metropolis TR, A 4/30/86, 86001092]

Victory Sculpture

35th Street at King Drive
Chicago

Centered in the vicinity of State and 35th streets on Chicago's Near South Side are surviving properties of what was once a thriving city-within-a-city created by the black community. Referred to by residents as the Metropolis, the community built its own economic, social, and political establishments, directly supported by black enterprise and capital. The development was firmly established by the turn of the century, and it prospered until the 1930s, when the Depression halted its further evolution.

At the close of World War I, movements began within the black community to honor the valorous achievements of the Eighth Regiment of the Illinois National Guard, which served in France under the 370th U.S. Infantry. By the mid-1920s proposals for the erection of a permanent monument in the parkway of Grand Boulevard in the vicinity of 35th Street were met with stiff opposition by the South Park Commission, which had control over the boulevard system. The commission maintained that there was no space available for such a monument but relented after the *Chicago Defender* began actively promoting a "vote no" campaign against the commission board, urging African Americans to defeat any project backed by the commission until the community's war heroes were recognized.

The design was finally prepared in 1926 and consisted of a circular gray granite shaft with three inset bronze sculptural panels, finished with a rich black patina. The panels portray a black soldier, a black woman symbolizing motherhood, and the figure of Columbia holding a tablet that recorded the locations of the regiment's principal battles. In 1936 the figure of a uniformed World War I black doughboy was added to the top of the monument. The sculpture is one of the most famous landmarks of Chicago's black community and is the site of an annual Memorial Day ceremony at which the surviving members of the "Fighting Eighth" gather to honor the memory of their fallen comrades. [Black Metropolis TR, A 4/30/86, 86001089]

Wabash Avenue YMCA

3763 South Wabash Avenue
Chicago

Centered in the vicinity of State and 35th streets on Chicago's Near South Side are surviving properties of what was once a thriving city-within-a-city created by the black community. Referred to by residents as the Metropolis, the community built its own economic, social, and political establishments, directly supported by black enterprise and capital. The development was firmly established by the turn of the century, and it prospered until the 1930s, when the Depression halted its further evolution.

Erected through the efforts of philanthropist Julius Rosenwald, this building was a major social and educational center in the Black Metropolis. The Wabash Avenue Young Men's Christian Association (YMCA) also played an important role in assisting new arrivals from the South during the Great Migration. The staff established comprehensive programs for finding housing and employment for the thousands of southern blacks who arrived in Chicago between 1910 and 1920 seeking greater opportunities. People arriving with no friends or contacts to guide them in the city found a warm welcome at the Wabash Avenue YMCA, where the temporary residence rooms were often filled to capacity. The Wabash Avenue YMCA conducted extensive job training programs that benefited not only the new arrivals but the established neighborhood residents as well. [Black Metropolis TR, A 4/30/86, 86001095]

Ida B. Wells-Barnett House
3624 South Martin Luther King, Jr., Drive
Chicago

Ida B. Wells-Barnett (1862–1931) was a civil rights advocate in Tennessee during the 1890s who dared to speak out against the then common practice of lynching. As editor and co-owner of the weekly *Memphis Free Press,* she carried on a tireless crusade for justice that brought her a wide readership among African Americans and notoriety among whites.

Often first on the scene after a lynching, she carefully documented the facts surrounding each murder. Through a series of speeches and publications, she informed the world that lynching was a heinous crime and a national disgrace. In 1892 she reported that three black Memphis grocers had been lynched merely because they had built successful businesses that effectively competed with white enterprises. The result was the destruction of the offices of her newspaper, forcing her to flee for her life.

Eventually settling in Chicago, she continued to write and crusade against lynching. Wells-Barnett organized women's clubs in New England and Chicago, including the Ida B. Wells Women's Club (1893) and the Alpha Suffrage Club (1913). She was also one of the founders of the National Association for the Advancement of Colored People (NAACP) and an official of the Afro-American Council. Her careful cataloging of lynchings was invaluable for the NAACP's antilynching campaign and for the Dyer antilynching bill. Her outspokenness enabled her to stimulate much social reform for African Americans, and especially for black women. The Ida B. Wells-Barnett House was designated a National Historic Landmark on May 30, 1974. [B 5/30/74 NHL, 74000757]

Dr. Daniel Hale Williams House
445 East 42nd Street
Chicago

Daniel Hale Williams (1856–1931) was born in Hollidaysburg, Pennsylvania. As a young man, he was accepted as an apprentice with Wisconsin's surgeon general, Dr. Henry Palmer. He enrolled in the Chicago Medical College in 1880, completed his courses in March 1883, and opened an office as the fourth black doctor in Chicago. His office soon swelled with patients as his reputation as a practitioner grew.

During this period in medical history, surgeons learned through experience, developing techniques as they operated. As a member of the surgical staff at the South Side Dispensary in Chicago, he frequently performed minor surgery, giving clinical instruction to Chicago Medical College students as he operated. Williams served as a surgeon in several capacities before being appointed to the Illinois State Board of Health in 1891.

Although his own career as a surgeon and general practitioner was quite successful, Williams was concerned that most hospitals were white-controlled and therefore denied opportunities to many black interns, nurses, and physicians, leaving them with little opportunity for training and staff privileges. Resolved to start a hospital that would address the needs of the black community and would-be black professionals, Williams began to collect money for the venture in 1890. The result was the incorporation of the Provident Hospital and Training School Association in January 1891. Provident was the first hospital in the United States founded and fully controlled by African Americans. The hospital soon became a mecca for black interns, nurses, and patients from across the country.

It was at Provident Hospital that Williams gained international prominence. On July 9, 1893, he operated on a black expressman who had sustained a stab wound to the heart. Williams performed exploratory surgery and successfully repaired the puncture in the pericardium, the sac surrounding the heart. Williams's operation is cited in standard texts of medicine as the first fully successful heart operation.

In the years following this highly publicized case, Williams succeeded in many other difficult medical procedures far ahead of his time. These operations were performed without the benefit of modern X-ray, anesthesia, and life-support devices now standard in such procedures. His work at Provident Hospital influenced President Grover Cleveland to appoint him surgeon-in-chief at Freedmen's Hospital in Washington, D.C., in 1894. He is credited with reorganizing and rehabilitating the hospital and the affiliated nursing program at Howard University.

Williams returned to his Chicago practice in 1898. He continued to promote greater access to medical facilities for black doctors and students of medicine. At his insistence, a new hospital was built for black students of the Meharry Medical School in Nashville (see also Hubbard House, Davidson County, Tennessee). Williams died in Idlewild, Michigan, in 1931. The house in Chicago in which he lived from 1905 until two years before his death was designated a National Historic Landmark on June 15, 1975. [B 5/15/75 NHL, 75000655]

MADISON COUNTY

Christian Hill Historic District
Roughly bounded by Broadway, Belle, 7th, Cliff, Bluff, and State streets
Alton

With both commercial and residential buildings surviving from Alton's first period of major growth, the Christian Hill Historic District contains one of the finest and densest concentrations of pre-Civil War architecture in Illinois. The district is important in black history because it includes the site of the murder of abolitionist newspaperman Elijah Lovejoy. Elijah Lovejoy assumed editorial charge of the *St. Louis Observer* in November 1833 but was forced to move his press in

1836 when his antislavery views raised the ire of proslavery residents of St. Louis. Lovejoy moved to Alton in July 1833, only to have his press destroyed the night of his arrival. With contributions from Alton citizens, however, he purchased a new press and printed the first issue of the Alton *Observer* on September 8, 1836. A staunch abolitionist, Lovejoy editorialized in favor of the formation of an Illinois State Anti-Slavery Society. The events precipitated by the editorial led to the destruction of the *Observer*'s press on August 21, 1837. On November 7, 1837, Lovejoy was murdered while he and 19 others were defending a fourth press. The murder and subsequent trials received national attention and were of major importance in the developing conflict over the slavery question (see also Owen Lovejoy Homestead, Bureau County.) [CAB 5/22/78 NHL, 78001165]

Lyman Trumbull House
1105 Henry Street
Alton

From 1849 to about 1863, this 1-1/2 story brick house was the home of Lyman Trumbull (1813–95), who represented the state of Illinois in the U.S. Senate from 1855 until 1873. Born in Colchester, Massachusetts, Trumbull completed all his formal education there at the Bacon Academy and secured a position teaching in nearby Portland, Massachusetts. A few years later he decided to embark on a career in the legal profession. Admitted to the bar in 1836, he entered into a law practice with the governor of Illinois, John Reynolds, an influential Democrat and member of the U.S. House of Representatives. With Reynolds's support, Trumbull won a seat in the Illinois legislature and thereby began a lengthy legal career. During his service in the state legislature Trumbull gained support as a result of his efforts to win repeal of the state's repressive Territorial Indenture Act and Black Codes.

Trumbull entered the national political scene in 1854, when he became involved in spearheading opposition to the Kansas-Nebraska Bill, which would allow the citizens of Kansas and Nebraska to decide whether slavery would be allowed in their respective states and in effect repeal the Missouri Compromise of 1820. During this campaign Trumbull established himself as an effective spokesperson for the anti-Nebraska wing of the Democratic party. In 1855 Trumbull, backed by anti-Nebraska-ites and Whigs, was selected by the Illinois legislature to serve in the U.S. Senate.

Shocked by the deep feelings of sectionalism in the Senate, Trumbull adopted a moderate position. At the same time he was determined to oppose all efforts to extend slavery into the new territories. His position brought him into close alliance with Abraham Lincoln, and both supported the call for an Illinois Republican Convention in 1856. Later that year, Trumbull left the Democratic party completely, attending the Republicans' national convention and campaigning for their candidate in Illinois.

During the next four years Trumbull continued to oppose the spread of slavery. He fought the proposed Lecompton Constitution for the Kansas Territory and spoke against the Dred Scott decision. Trumbull supported Lincoln both in his unsuccessful 1858 Senate race and in his victorious bid for the presidency in 1860. Both felt that the southern secessionist movement should be forcibly crushed. Trumbull urged vigorous prosecution of the Civil War. In 1861 Trumbull became chair of the Senate Judiciary Committee.

To encourage the emancipation of slaves and their use in the war, he wrote and secured enactment of the Confiscation Acts of 1861 and 1862. Trumbull led the fight for the 13th Amendment to the Constitution in order to reinforce Lincoln's power to issue the Emancipation Proclamation.

Following the Civil War and Lincoln's assassination, Trumbull prepared and piloted through the upper chamber much of the country's Reconstruction legislation. He wrote and was the leading proponent of the Freedmen's Bureau Bill of 1866 and the chief supporter of the first Civil Service Act, enacted in 1870. In 1872 he contended unsuccessfully for the Republican presidential nomination. When his third term in the Senate expired, he was not reelected, and he retired to Chicago to practice law. During the remaining years of his life, Trumbull allied himself with William Jennings Bryan, calling for legislative restrictions on monopolies and campaigning for the Populist party. Trumbull died in 1895. His Alton home was designated a National Historic Landmark on May 15, 1975. [B 5/15/75 NHL, 75000667]

PIKE COUNTY

Free Frank McWorter Grave Site
Four miles east of Barry off U.S. Route 36
Barry

The Free Frank McWorter Grave Site is the only remaining property associated with Frank McWorter, a slave who purchased his freedom and became a successful entrepreneur. McWorter was born a slave in Union County, South Carolina, in 1777. While a slave in Pulaski County, Kentucky, in 1910, McWorter was given permission to hire himself out on his own time for extra money. His owner left Pulaski County for Tennessee in 1910, leaving McWorter to manage the farm.

Although there were few opportunities for unskilled black laborers in sparsely settled Pulaski County, McWorter managed find a source of income. He began to manufacture saltpeter, the principal ingredient in gunpowder and an item of daily use on frontier farm settlements. McWorter established his business during the War of 1812, when both the demand and price of the product had increased greatly. His business prospered, and in 1817 McWorter was able to purchase his wife's freedom. Two years later, he purchased his own. After his manumission, McWorter continued his business and began speculating in real estate with his profits. He was able to realize a significant profit from land sales.

In 1830 McWorter moved to Illinois, where he established a profitable farm and continued his real estate speculation. In 1837 he established the town of New Philadelphia on a 360-acre parcel of land that he owned in Hadley Township, Pike County. He began selling lots the same year and with the money he made was eventually able to purchase 13 family members out of slavery. New Philadelphia quickly grew into a prosperous town, reaching its peak in the 1850s, with a population of more than 1,100.

Frank McWorter died in 1854. His entrepreneurial activities, motivated by his desire to purchase the freedom of his family, permitted him to rise above the limitations placed on him by slavery. His grave site stands as a reminder of this remarkable African American pioneer and entrepreneur. [B 4/19/88, 87002533]

Main entrance foyer of the Crispus Attucks High School (Edward Evans).

INDIANA

GRANT COUNTY

J. Woodrow Wilson House
723 West 4th Street
Marion

Locally important for its association with J. Woodrow Wilson, a prominent Marion businessperson, this Neoclassical Revival style building is also significant as the work of black architect Samuel M. Plato, who later was awarded contracts for numerous post offices across the country. Plato was born in Alabama and educated at the State University of Kentucky. He began his career in Marion around 1908, often acting as both architect and contractor. Plato designed and built several residences and commercial buildings, an apartment building, and two churches in Marion before returning to Kentucky about 1914. Plato designed the Wilson House during an era of expanding opportunities for black professionals in Marion. Later Plato became one of the first African Americans to be awarded a federal post office contract and one of only a few to receive a defense housing contract during World War II (see also Broadway Temple AME Zion Church, Jefferson County, Kentucky). [CB 8/11/88, 88001218]

JEFFERSON COUNTY

Eleutherian College
Indiana Route 250
Lancaster

Constructed between 1854 and 1856, Eleutherian College was the second institution in the state of Indiana to admit students without regard to race or gender and was the first in the state to make a college curriculum available to African Americans. The school owed its existence to members of the adjoining community of Lancaster, whose settlers, primarily New England Baptists, held strong abolitionist sentiments. A group of Lancaster residents formed the core of the Neil's Creek Anti-Slavery Society, founded in 1839. A church formed by the society a few years later disavowed slavery in its by-laws and, as a result, was initially denied admission into the Madison Baptist Church Association. It was in a sermon before this church in 1843 that the Reverend Thomas Craven, a visiting preacher form Oxford, Ohio, suggested the establishment of an educational institution open to both black and white students.

Encouraged by the congregation's enthusiastic response, Craven traveled the country raising funds for the school and eventually moved to Lancaster. The school opened in 1848 with 15 students. Classes were initially held in a local meeting hall and later in a log cabin. This cabin, which also served as Craven's home, was constructed on the crest of a hill, providing a physical and symbolic focus for the school visible for miles around. The school also became the focus of hostility by neighboring communities, who burned the homes of black families associated with the school and attempted to convict the school's leaders under an 1851 state law that made it a crime to encourage black migration into the state.

When the present classroom and chapel building were built in 1854, the school changed its name to Eleutherian College, derived from the Greek word *eleutherios,* meaning "liberation" and "equality." At this time the school's programs were expanded to included college-level courses. The school flourished between 1855 and 1861, but local support dwindled after 1861, when Robert Craven, son of Thomas Craven and an instructor at the school, moved away following the death of his father the previous year. Fearing reprisals from local southern sympathizers, most African Americans moved with the onset of the Civil War, and no black students enrolled in the school after 1861.

Lancaster township purchased the building for use as a school building in 1883, and its interior was significantly altered, but many of these alterations were reversed in a 1963 restoration project. Constructed of local materials, the building boasts outstanding stone and wood craftsmanship and is an important physical reminder of the resolve of Lancaster's abolitionist settlers. [CA 2/15/93, 93001410]

MARION COUNTY

Crispus Attucks High School
1140 North Martin Luther King, Jr., Street
Indianapolis

The idea for an all-black high school in Indiana dates back to 1908, when Superintendent of Schools Calvin Kendall identified the integration of the high schools as a problem and stated that it would eventually become necessary to remove black children from the high schools they then attended. Kendall's statement was the catalyst for the construction of Crispus Attucks High School. Originally called Thomas Jefferson High School, the name was changed to honor Attucks, a former slave who was the first to die in the Boston Massacre in 1770. The school was designed by Merritt Harrison (1887–1973), a prominent local architect who later designed the State Boys' School, Lockfield Gardens, and the State Fairground Coliseum. Crispus Attucks High School is Collegiate Gothic in style and features an interior with terra-cotta arcades. [CA 1/4/89, 88003043]

Bethel AME Church
414 West Vermont Street
Indianapolis

Since its founding by William Paul Quinn in 1836, the Bethel African Methodist Episcopal Church has been a significant institution in the black community of Indianapolis. In addition to its importance as the oldest church in the city founded, owned, and operated by and for African Americans, the church was the site of several important events. Church members purportedly participated in the Underground Railroad, aiding escaped slaves in their flight to Canada. The Indianapolis Chapter of the National Association for the Advancement of Colored People was organized there in the early 1900s. On April 27, 1904, the State Federation of Colored Women's Clubs was also organized there. This group later occupied the house at 2034 North Capitol Avenue (see Minor House). [A 3/21/91, 91000269]

Indiana Avenue Historic District
500 block of Indiana Avenue between North, Central Canal, Michigan, and West streets
Indianapolis

This area contains the city's only evidence of a once-thriving commercial strip that served primarily the black community of Indianapolis. Businesses along the avenue, particularly the 400 and 500 blocks, provided food, housing, entertainment, consumer services, and, most important, a sense of identity for black residents. Some businesses are still housed here. These buildings are a link with the cultural contributions made by African Americans to the city during the early years of the 20th century.

Early settlers in the area were composed primarily of hardworking, low-income members of the work force. Most of the African Americans were ex-slaves who had moved to Indianapolis from North Carolina during the 1880s. By 1900 African Americans constituted one-fifth of Indiana Avenue's population.

The earliest businesses in the 500 block of Indiana Avenue catered to the needs of the immigrant community by providing grocery, shoemaking, and tailor services. As early as 1865, two black-operated businesses occupied the 500 block. Samuel G. Smothers operated a grocery store, and William Franklin, a peddler, occupied another building.

Throughout the late 19th and into the 20th centuries, the shop owners were racially integrated, although the clientele was predominately black, for the Indiana Avenue of the 1920s provided goods and services for African Americans not admitted to downtown stores. Segregation led to a cultural identity that was nurtured in an environment reminiscent of the Harlem Renaissance in New York City. Many people, black and white, flocked to the area as Indiana Avenue achieved international recognition for its jazz night clubs and theaters. The avenue was later called "Funky Broadway" and "Yellow Brick Road." [CA 6/12/87, 87000912]

Lockefield Garden Apartments
900 Indiana Avenue
Indianapolis

The Lockefield Garden Apartments were one of the nation's first federally initiated, funded, and supervised peacetime housing projects. The complex was one of 51 housing projects built nationwide by the Public Works Administration (PWA) between 1933 and 1937.

The building were constructed in the International Style and remain the city's most significant example of this style. Their innovative design reflects the European prototypes of large-scale housing and urban design of the 1920s. The complex became an officially recommended model for federally subsidized housing projects across the country.

The apartments were constructed in an area that suffered from a lack of adequate water and sanitation facilities. When the complex was built, it became a source of pride and hope for the local black residents, for it was the only such undertaking in the area solely for their benefit.

Lockefield was one of only three housing developments open to African Americans in Indianapolis and the only one that permitted children. Prospective tenants of Lockefield were carefully screened. Not only did the complex provide housing, but it also promoted a higher standard of living. Interior decorators from local department stores conducted demonstrations for the tenants on how to create an aesthetically pleasing environment for the family. Preschool facilities were available, and adult education classes were offered.

In addition to providing high-quality housing for black families in the area, Lockefield generated business along Indiana Avenue, which became a mecca for the black community from the 1930s to the 1960s (see also Indiana Avenue Historic District). The buildings that survive at Lockefield today are a symbol of the hope the complex provided to the black community and mark the federal government's first direct venture into the welfare of African Americans in Indianapolis. [CA 2/28/83, 83000133]

Minor House
2034 North Capitol Avenue
Indianapolis

Since 1927 the Minor House has served as the headquarters of the Indiana State Federation of Colored Women's Clubs (ISFCWC). The ISFCWC was formed in 1904 to unite the many individual women's clubs in the state and allow them to benefit from their association with one another.

The formation of black women's clubs in northern states was largely influenced by the formation of antislavery, women's rights, and literary societies in the 1830s and 1840s. In both northern and southern states, the clubs that black women formed were concerned with upholding the status of black women and of the race and with the education and welfare of black children.

The federation in Indiana was organized largely through the efforts of Lillian Thomas Fox, the first black

reporter for the *Indianapolis News*. Beginning with 18 participating clubs from six cities in Indiana, the federation grew to 56 clubs from 49 cities by 1933. The statewide federation of clubs helped to stimulate intellectual activity; broadened the scope of the clubs' programs; improved the visibility and credibility of the clubs by giving black women in Indiana a political tool to wield in their favor; and gave club women a forum for exchanging ideas and realizing the importance of their individual club work through the annual meetings.

As the headquarters of the ISFCWC for more than 65 years, the Minor House symbolizes the banding together of black Hoosier women to improve their own status, to elevate the race, and to provide better homes and education for their children. [A 4/7/87, 87000512]

Ransom Place Historic District
Roughly bounded by 10th, St. Clair, West, and Camp streets
Indianapolis

This small pocket of vernacular houses located west of downtown Indianapolis represents an early intact neighborhood associated with the city's prominent and well-established black population. A modest African American presence is documented in Indianapolis as early as the 1830s. From 1850 to the 1880s, the city's black population increased steadily, resulting in the organization of numerous black institutions in the 1880s. There was a corresponding increase in the construction of houses as well, and most of the buildings in the Ransom Place Historic District were built during these years. The houses were occupied by black politicians, physicians, attorneys, ministers, and other professionals.

The neighborhood was integrated during the early 20th century but became

Madame C. J. Walker Building (William Rasdale).

segregated after World War I with the rise of Ku Klux Klan activity in Indiana in the 1920s. By 1930 the area around Ransom Place contained the largest number of black residents in Indianapolis. Redevelopment in the area around the historic district in the late 1930s and 1940s resulted in substantial rehabilitation of the area, which had fallen into disrepair in the early 20th century. Today, the area benefits from continuing revitalization efforts. Modern industrial and commercial expansion surrounding the historic district has left it one of the few reminders of an area once considered a prestigious address by Indianapolis's black community. [A 12/10/92, 92001650]

Madame C. J. Walker Building

617 Indiana Avenue
Indianapolis

Constructed in 1927, the Walker Building was the site of the successful beauty products firm of Madame C. J. Walker. The building also housed a theater, restaurant, ballroom, and pharmacy. In addition, the Walker Building contained the Walker Beauty College, which was responsible for training thousands of successful Walker agents. Architecturally, it is significant for its unique incorporation of African, Egyptian, and Moorish motifs into its Art Deco Style design.

Madame Walker (1867–1919) was the first black woman to open the field of cosmetology as a new and lucrative industry for African Americans. Her experimentation with hair preparations for black women eventually led to the establishment of a thriving business that included not only the manufacturing of 75 beauty products, but also clubs, training programs, beauty schools, and shops throughout the United States. Madame Walker became the first female millionaire in the business world and was known for her generous philanthropy to black charities. The Madame C. J. Walker Building was designated a National Historic Landmark on July 17, 1991 (see also Villa Lewaro, Westchester County, New York). [CAB 7/17/80 NHL, 80000062]

NOBLE COUNTY

Iddings-Gilbert-Leader-Anderson Block
105–113 North Main Street
Kendallville

A fine example of the metal commercial storefronts produced during the late 19th century, the Iddings-Gilbert-Leader-Anderson block is one of three outstanding commercial blocks of this type in downtown Kendallville and is the largest of the three.

One of the four builders, Alonzo Anderson, was an African American. He opened a barbershop in his building at 113 North Main Street. He and his wife, Emma, are the only African Americans known to be buried in Lake View Cemetery, the principal burial ground for the Kendallville community. The building illustrates the commercial success of a black businessman, unusual in a small Indiana town. [CA 7/21/87, 87000544]

PARKE COUNTY

Rockville Historic District
Roughly bounded by Howard Avenue and Jefferson, High, and College streets
Rockville

The Rockville Historic District is a collection of buildings and sites associated with the development of Rockville between 1826 and 1942. Included in the district are the courthouse square and surrounding commercial buildings, as well as a fine collection of vernacular houses and other buildings that are outstanding examples of academic styles. Also contained within the district are buildings associated with the African Americans who migrated to the area in the years after the Civil War and who established a sizable community before their population dwindled in the early 20th century.

In the years after the Civil War, African Americans left the South in great numbers, seeking work in the North. Between 1870 and 1880, Rockville's black population nearly quadrupled, owing in part to a welcome reception by local Quakers. In 1880 African Americans represented nearly 12 percent of Rockville's population, generally living in the same areas as white residents. Among the buildings in the district associated with Rockville's black citizens are the African Methodist Episcopal Church parsonage, built in 1872, and an 1839 brick building that served as a black school from 1874 until 1929. Frederick Douglass spoke in Rockville in the 1870s to raise money for the school.

Rockville's black population decreased in the early 20th century as many rural residents statewide, and especially black residents, moved to larger cities for better job opportunities. Residential areas became increasingly segregated, and the black population dwindled further when the Ku Klux Klan became active in Parke County in the 1920s. The buildings in the Rockville Historic District are among the few extant black resources in rural Indiana and are important reminders of the black community that once thrived in Rockville. [CA 5/27/93, 93000471]

RUSH COUNTY

Booker T. Washington School
614 Fort Wayne Road
Rushville

Built in 1905 to serve the black community of Rushville, the Booker T. Washington School was an educational, cultural, political, social, and fraternal center for the town's black community. The second floor of the school was a political and social center used frequently by the National Association for the Advancement of Colored People as meeting space and to feature local politicians. Around 1919 black educator Mary McLeod Bethune visited the school. Local black chapters of the Odd Fellows and Masons used the second floor of the building, and dances were also held here. [A 5/24/90, 90000809]

VANDERBURGH COUNTY

Liberty Baptist Church
701 Oak Street
Evansville

After the Civil War many former slaves traveled north in hope of a better life. In Indiana, Evansville was the main destination of these immigrants. The Liberty Baptist congregation was organized on June 13, 1865, in a small brick building at Chestnut and Canal streets. Although the deacons and other members were African American, Colonel Woods, a white man devoted to the welfare of former slaves, was the first pastor. He was later replaced by Elder Green McFarland, who served the membership until his death in 1881.

Liberty Baptist is the oldest extant black congregation in Evansville. As immigrants settled primarily around the church, the area became known as "Baptist Town." The church provided leadership in the religious, social, and political life of the city's black community. It continues to serve the local community through day care programs for children, recreational activities for youth, and assistance with low- to moderate-income housing. [CA 12/8/78, 78000058]

VIGO COUNTY

Allen Chapel African Methodist Episcopal Church
224 Crawford Street
Terre Haute

In 1837 Bishop William Paul Quinn founded the Allen Chapel, the oldest black church in western Indiana, which became a focal point for the black community in Vigo County. Several important black figures were associated with the chapel, including Hiram Revels, a former Allen Chapel pastor who later became the first African American elected to the U.S. Senate.

The chapel also served as an Underground Railroad station, housed the first public school for black children in Terre Haute, and sponsored prominent black speakers such as Frederick Douglass. Since 1837 the chapel has been reconstructed twice; the present building was constructed in 1913. [A 9/5/75, 75000030]

WAYNE COUNTY

Levi Coffin House
115 North Main Street
Fountain City

Built in 1837, this house was owned by Levi Coffin (1789–1877), a Quaker abolitionist. Coffin and his wife, Katherine, used the house from 1827 to

1847 as a principal depot on the Underground Railroad, which helped hundreds of runaway slaves escape slavery before the Civil War. It is believed that Coffin helped more than 2,000 fugitive slaves escape to freedom. Because of his outstanding role in the operation of the Underground Railroad, Coffin has been termed its "president."

Coffin also worked with the Committee on Concerns of People of Color. Immediately after the issuance of the Emancipation Proclamation, Coffin worked to aid the freedmen. In 1864 he went to England and was instrumental in the formation of an English Freedmen's Aid Society, which contributed money, clothing, and other articles to newly freed African Americans.

In 1867 Coffin attended the International Anti-Slavery Conference in Paris. Following this event he lived in retirement until his death in 1877. [B 10/15/66 NHL, 66000009]

Old Richmond Historic District
Roughly bounded by C & O Railroad, South 11th and South A streets, and Alley S of South E Street
Richmond

Once called "Little Africa," South 7th, 8th, and 9th streets were the heart of Richmond's free black community before the Civil War. The Bethel African Methodist Episcopal (AME) Church, under the leadership of Bishop William Paul Quinn, served as a religious, social, and educational institution for the city's free blacks. Quinn also developed the church into a stop along the Underground Railroad. He later organized more than 50 AME churches in the Midwest and was active in the founding of Wilberforce University in Ohio. [CAB 6/28/74, 74000025]

IOWA

MONROE COUNTY

Buxton Historic Townsite
Address restricted
Lovilia

The Buxton Historic Townsite is what remains of the town of Buxton, which existed from 1900 to 1924. During this time a large black population resided in Buxton; in fact, for a time a majority of the inhabitants were African American. Iowa was unusual in that it offered relative interracial harmony and allowed African Americans to hold leadership positions in commercial and cultural institutions.

Along with its economic vitality, Buxton had active cultural institutions and social activities. The Buxton Wonders, a predominantly black baseball team, generated community pride. Managed by African Americans, the Young Men's Christian Association (YMCA) contained facilities for diverse social, religious, and recreational activities. Other clubs in Buxton included the Ladies Industrial Club, local chapters of the Federated Women's Club of America and the Sweet Magnolia Club, and fraternal lodges such as the Odd Fellows. Black residents established four churches, St. John's African Methodist Episcopal Church, Mount Zion Baptist Church, the First Congregational Church, and the Church of God.

The Reverend A. L. DeMond of the First Congregational Church was a leading minister who actively participated in national church organizations. Other black leaders in Buxton represented a variety of professional backgrounds. One such leader was Dr. E. A. Carter. Involved in church activities and the YMCA, Carter helped organize and sustain committees on work and education. George Woodson, a law graduate of Howard University, was the primary organizer and first president of the Iowa Black Bar Association and the National Black Bar Association.

Archeological artifacts collected from the Buxton Historic Townsite clearly provide evidence of the social, economic, and cultural lifestyles of Buxton's black community. In social and economic terms, Buxton was truly unique, as never before had so many African Americans lived so comfortably in Iowa. [AD 8/9/83, 83000392]

MUSCATINE COUNTY

Alexander Clark House
203 West 3rd Street
Muscatine

This house was the principal residence of Alexander Clark (1826–91) throughout his productive life. Clark was a prominent political activist who successfully led the fight for the admission of

Buxton Historic Townsite, c.1910 (photographer unknown). Photo courtesy of Dorothy Schweider.

black children in all public schools in Iowa.

Clark's eloquent oratory for black rights and the Republican party gained him a reputation as the "colored orator of the West." In 1868 he led the Colored Convention held in Des Moines that promoted the enactment of a state black suffrage amendment. He served as a delegate to 1869 the National Colored Convention held in Washington, D.C. In 1873 President Grant appointed him consul to Aux Cayes, Haiti, a position he declined because of insufficient salary. Later, in 1890, he accepted President Harrison's appointment to be minister resident and consul general to Liberia.

Also active in benevolent organizations, Clark held the position of grand master in the Masonic Order over the states of Colorado, Iowa, Minnesota, and Missouri throughout the 1870s. He also organized subordinate lodges in Arkansas, Mississippi, and Tennessee. During most of the 1880s Clark also edited and owned the *Chicago Conservator,* a boldly written newspaper supporting black rights. [B 10/14/76, 76000796]

POLK COUNTY

Burns United Methodist Church
811 Crocker Street
Des Moines

Built in 1912, this building has since 1930 been the home of the Burns United Methodist Church, which was organized in 1866 as the first black congregation of its denomination in Des Moines. The church was named for Francis Burns (1809–63), the first black missionary bishop in the Methodist Episcopal Church, who served in the U.S.-created colony for former slaves in Liberia from 1838. The church's creation by the Second Annual Methodist Conference was a recognition of the problems and needs of black people.

From its founding until the purchase of the present church from the German Emmanual Methodist congregation in 1930, the Burns church had six successive places of worship. Throughout these years and afterward, the Burns Methodist congregation displayed cohesion and continuity. Wherever it was located, the church was a focus of community, as well as religious life, for the Des Moines black population. Literary societies, musical evenings, and group dinners were regular activities. During the Great Depression fund-raising activities provided income for the church. Today, Burns United Methodist Church continues to perform important functions in the black community. [A 6/15/77, 77000546]

Fort Des Moines Provisional Army Officer Training School
Fort Des Moines Military Reservation
Des Moines

The creation of the Provisional Army Officer Training School at Fort Des Moines marked both the U.S. Army's first recognition of its responsibility to train black officers and the establishment of a military tradition among African Americans. When the United States entered World War I on April 6, 1917, many black men were anxious to join the army and serve their country. The War Department yielded to the demand that black men be allowed to enlist. This action was followed by further pressure for the army to qualify black officers to lead black soldiers. Strong support for the training of black officers came from the National Association for the Advancement of Colored People and the Central Committee of Negro College Men. Black leaders such as W. E. B. Du Bois urged all African Americans to unite in the push for a training camp for black officers.

On June 17, 1917, 1,000 college men, with 200 noncommissioned officers from existing black military units, were sworn into the Provisional Army Officer Training School by Colonel Charles C.

Ballou. On October 15, 639 men graduated from the course and received their commissions. As the 92nd Division, they received eight weeks of intensive training and first went into action during the last major German offensive, which they helped blunt.

Commanded by the officers from Fort Des Moines, the 92nd Division was an important force in the battles in France from September 1918 to November 11, 1918—the Armistice. This gallant division of black troops received many citations and awards for meritorious and distinguished conduct.

During World War II Fort Des Moines served as a training center for the Women's Army Corps. Graduates of that course included Bernice Gaines Hughes, the first black woman to become a lieutenant colonel in the U.S. armed forces. [A 5/30/74 NHL, 74000805]

SCOTT COUNTY

Bethel AME Church
325 West 11th Street
Davenport

Designed by the architectural firm of Clausen & Clausen, the 1909 half-timber and stucco Bethel African Methodist Episcopal (AME) Church illustrates an unusual adaptation of the Craftsman style for a religious building. Appropriate for a denomination that stresses simplicity and avoidance of ceremony and symbolism, the building has a domestic rather than ecclesiastical character.

Established in 1875, the Bethel AME congregation was one of several black congregations founded after the Civil War to provide separate worship facilities for African Americans. Throughout its history, Bethel AME has served as a religious and social focal point in its turn-of-the-century black neighborhood. [Davenport MRA, CA 7/7/83, 83002401]

KANSAS

GRAHAM COUNTY

Nicodemus Historic District
U.S. Route 24
Nicodemus

During the 1870s a number of African Americans, later named "Exodusters," migrated from the South, where they were greatly dissatisfied with conditions, to the Midwest. One of the principal leaders of this mass migration was Benjamin "Pap" Singleton, a former slave who was responsible for the founding of 11 colonies in Kansas alone between 1873 and 1880. Nicodemus was one of the towns Singleton founded. Established with assistance from a white Tennessee minister, W. T. Hill, and named after a legendary slave, the town of Nicodemus was officially founded on September 17, 1877. By 1880 260 African Americans lived in Nicodemus township. The Exodusters had to cope with many hardships on the Kansas frontier. Few of the settlers had any money. To aid them, the Nicodemus Town Company was established to appropriate food and supplies from across the state and to distribute them to the settlers.

One outstanding member of the Nicodemus community was E. P. McCabe, whose rise to prominence illustrates the opportunities that were available in that frontier society. McCabe served as the county's first county clerk, having been appointed to that temporary position by the state's governor until the county elections of June 1880. He and A. T. Hall operated a land agency in Nicodemus, and in 1882 and 1884 he was elected to the position of state auditor. He was appointed to the same position in the territory of Oklahoma from 1897 to 1907 by Governor G. S. Steel.

By 1881, 35 of the residential and commercial buildings in the Nicodemus Historic District had been constructed. The general store of Z. T. Fletcher, founded in the fall of 1877, was the oldest business in the county. In 1878 a post office was established in a section of the store. In 1879 a livery stable and lumberyard were started. The first church building, of sod construction, was built in 1879 under the auspices of Baptist minister Daniel Hickman. In June 1879 School District No. 1 was established in Nicodemus, with most of the classes taught in peoples' homes.

By the late 1880s Nicodemus showed all the signs of a thriving social center—a baseball team, a literary and benefit society, lodges, and an ice cream parlor. Nicodemus had two newspapers, the *Western Cyclone,* established May 13, 1886, by A. G. Tallman, and the *Enterprise,* established August 17, 1887, by H. K. Lightfoot. By 1887, when the

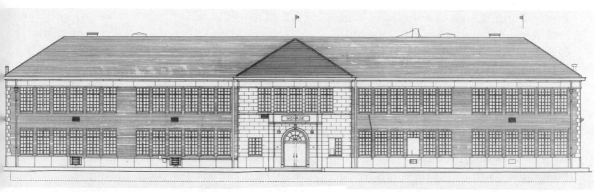

Monroe Elementary School in the Brown v. Board of Education National Historic Site. Drawing courtesy of the Historic American Buildings Survey (Denise A. Hopkins, delineator).

town's first bank was established by a white man, A. L. McPherson, Nicodemus was a recognized social and business center of Graham County.

Nicodemus had probably reached its peak by 1910, when the federal census reported 595 colored inhabitants in the county. By 1950 only 16 people were counted there, and by 1953 the post office was closed, marking the end of Nicodemus's 76 years of existence. The Nicodemus Historic District was designated a National Historic Landmark on January 7, 1976. [AB 1/7/76 NHL, 76000820]

MIAMI COUNTY

John Brown Cabin

John Brown Memorial Park
Osawatomie

Famed abolitionist John Brown came to Osawatomie in October 1855 after five of his sons, who had come in the spring, appealed to him for help against harassment by proslavery elements. While in Kansas, he was involved in a number of incidents in the so-called "Bleeding Kansas" era. The "battle" of Osawatomie on August 30, 1856, was one such skirmish. Although he lived in Kansas for only about 20 months, John Brown's activities have been closely associated with the state.

The John Brown Cabin was built in 1854 by Samuel Glenn, who sold it to Samuel Adair, Brown's brother-in-law. Brown frequented the cabin and occasionally used it as a headquarters for his abolitionist activities. The log cabin originally stood about a mile west of Osawatomie. In 1912 it was dismantled and reassembled in its present location in John Brown Park. In 1928 the state legislature appropriated funds to construct a shelter around the cabin to protect it. The interior of the cabin remains much as it was when Brown was a frequent visitor and contains much of the original furniture (see also John Brown's Headquarters, Washington County, Maryland; John Brown Farm, Essex County, New York; and John Brown House, Franklin County, Pennsylvania; and Harpers Ferry National Historical Park and Jefferson County Courthouse, Jefferson County, West Virginia). [B 3/24/71, 71000319]

NESS COUNTY

George Washington Carver Homestead Site
1.5 miles south of Beeler
Beeler

Former slave and noted scientist George Washington Carver (1860–1943) filed claim to this homestead in 1886 following his unsuccessful effort to enroll in the all-white Highland College in Highland, Kansas. He resided here for two years before leaving to attend college in Iowa. After graduating from Iowa State College, Carver was invited by Booker T. Washington to join the staff of Tuskegee Institute in Alabama and head its newly formed Agricultural Department. He remained there until his death in 1943. During his tenure at Tuskegee he wrote more than 40 technical bulletins and circulars on modern farming techniques that were mainly designed to help the poor black farmers of northern Alabama. Carver's national fame and publicity came after 1921, when he became a national spokesperson for the peanut industry. In recognition of his achievements in biology and plant pathology, the Carver Foundation was established at Tuskegee in 1940 to continue research to aid humanity (see also Tuskegee Institute National Historic Site, Macon County, Alabama; and George Washington Carver National Monument, Newton County, Missouri). [AB 11/23/77, 77000593]

SEDGWICK COUNTY

Arkansas Valley Lodge No. 21, Prince Hall Masons
615 North Main Street
Wichita

Built in 1910, this hall is the last surviving commercial building of the black business community located for many years on Wichita's North Main Street. The Arkansas Valley Lodge No. 21, Prince Hall Masons, chartered in 1885, purchased the lot for the building on November 10, 1905, from a black grocer named G. W. Young. Construction was under way in the spring of 1910. A cornerstone-laying ceremony was held Sunday, April 3, 1910. The building may have been designed by a black architect, Josiah Walker, who had designed other buildings in the black community. The local black newspaper described it as one of the finest buildings owned by a black lodge. Other organizations, such as the Knights of Pythias, Odd Fellows, and Knights of Tabor, rented the hall for their meetings. At times the first floor, as well as the second floor office space, was rented to black businesspeople. Many groups used the facilities for banquets, dances, bazaars, plays, musical shows, and other recreational activities. In many respects the Arkansas Valley Lodge No. 21 was a rallying force in social and cultural life of the black community. [A 8/24/77, 77000596]

Calvary Baptist Church
601 North Water
Wichita

The Calvary Baptist Church is one of the three last significant physical remnants of Wichita's historic black settlement.

Josiah Walker, a black plasterer and architect, probably designed the building, which is an exemplary work of Neoclassical Revival architecture.

The first black settlers in Wichita, freed slaves relocating to the Great Plains from the Civil War–torn South, called themselves "Exodusters." By 1880 almost two dozen black families had settled in the vicinity of North Main Street, primarily in the 500 block, the first area of black residential and business concentration. This area thus became the primary location of cultural, social, business, and religious activities for Wichita's black community, with Calvary Baptist Church as the nucleus. During the years 1917–38, Calvary Baptist Church provided services to the black community of Wichita through sponsorship of a number of organizations within the congregation. The church became nationally known through its pastor, the Reverend S. B. Butler, who was treasurer of the National Baptist Sunday School and the Baptist Young Peoples' Union Congress. Presently Calvary Baptist serves as a source of pride for Wichita's black community. [CA 10/28/88, 88001905]

SHAWNEE COUNTY

Brown v. Board of Education National Historic Site
330 Western Avenue (Sumner School) and 1515 Monroe Street (Monroe School)
Topeka

The Brown v. Board of Education National Historic Site comprises the Sumner and Monroe Elementary Schools, both associated with the 1954 landmark United States Supreme Court case. In its ruling, the court concluded that racially "separate educational facilities are inherently unequal." The decision forced the desegregation of public schools in the 21 states with segregated schoolrooms.

At the center of controversy in the case was the right of Linda Brown, a black student, to enroll at the all-white Sumner Elementary School. Brown had been forced to travel a considerable distance to attend Monroe Elementary School, the black elementary school in Topeka, even though Sumner Elementary was nearby. The refusal of Sumner Elementary to admit her precipitated the court case. The case struck down the 1896 *Plessy v. Ferguson* Supreme Court decision, which provided states had the right to maintain "separate but equal" public facilities.

The *Brown v. Board of Education* decision, written by Chief Justice Earl Warren, had an enormous social and ideological impact. In declaring separate facilities unconstitutional, the court reaffirmed the concept of equal protection under law provided in the 14th Amendment to the U.S. Constitution.

The Sumner and Monroe Elementary Schools symbolize both the harsh reality of discrimination permitted by the *Plessy* decision in 1896 and the promise of equality guaranteed by the Constitution and strengthened by the *Brown* decision. Sumner Elementary School was designated a National Historic Landmark on May 4, 1987. Monroe Elementary School was included in 1991, and the combined designation was added to the national park system in 1993. [A 5/4/87 NHL NPS, 87001283]

Bayless Quarters. Photo courtesy of the Kentucky Heritage Commission (William Gus Johnson).

KENTUCKY

BELL COUNTY

Mt. Moriah Baptist Church
314 North Main Street
Middlesboro

Before the development of planned iron- and coal-producing communities in the late 19th and early 20th centuries, very few African Americans lived in east Kentucky, where the institution of slavery had been rare. Many counties in the area had no black population in the 19th century. The recruitment of miners by large coal-mining concerns resulted in the settlement of large numbers of immigrants and African Americans in an area whose population had consisted almost entirely of Americans of English and Scotch-Irish descent.

Mt. Moriah Baptist Church has played an important role in the history of the religious life of the black community of Middlesboro and is a visible expression of the important role African Americans have played in the settlement and later development of planned communities such as Middlesboro. [A 8/8/85, 85001747]

BOURBON COUNTY

Bayless Quarters
Kentucky Route 13
North Middletown

This bluegrass region contains hundreds of stone spring houses, ice houses, smoke houses, and dairies, but the surviving stone slave quarters are the most striking reminder of the history of the region. Because many of the newly freed blacks continued to work in the same capacity as they did when they were enslaved, they maintained these quarters as housing for a number of years after their emancipation. Other known existing stone slave quarters are the Abner Knox Farm (Boyle County); the John Leavell Quarters (Garrard County); the Stone Quarters on Burgin Road (Mercer County); the Stone Barn on Brushy Creek (Nicholas County); the James Briscoe Quarters, the Ash Emison Quarters, and the Joseph Patterson Quarters (Scott County); and the Hogan Quarters and the Andrew Muldrow Quarters (Woodford County). [Early Stone Buildings of Central Kentucky TR, CA 6/23/83, 83002556]

The Grange
Four miles north of Paris on U.S. Route 68
Paris

An excellent example of Federal style architecture, the Grange was the home of slave trader Edward Stone. Stone used the basement of the Grange as a dungeon for slaves. People sold or gave him slaves that were unruly or had committed crimes. He took them home and chained them to rings set in the walls of the dungeon, leaving them in total darkness and giving them only bread and water until their spirits were broken. Although Stone had developed a lucrative business, he was rejected by the community because of his cruel slave-trading practices. In 1826 Stone announced he would give up trading and become a planter. Loading his last cargo of 77 slaves on a flat-bottomed boat, Stone began his trip down the Ohio River to New Orleans. The armed and desperate slaves surprised and killed Stone and the other white men on board. They weighted the bodies and threw them in the river. The slaves escaped but were soon captured. A Lexington newspaper headed its account of the killings with the words, "Awful Judgment of Heaven upon Slave Traders," reflecting popular opinion of slave traders in Kentucky at that time. [CAB 4/11/73, 73000786]

BOYD COUNTY

St. James AME Church
Intersection of 12th Street and Carter Avenue
Ashland

Ashland was established in the 1840s as an industrial center for northeastern Kentucky. Founded in the 1850s, St. James African Methodist Episcopal Church was one of the first congregations to take advantage of the offer by the Kentucky Iron, Coal and Manufacturing Company to give land to any group that would construct a church in Ashland. [Ashland MRA, A 7/3/79, 79003555]

BOYLE COUNTY

Abner Knox Farm
U.S. Route 150
Danville

This bluegrass region contains hundreds of stone spring houses, ice houses,

smoke houses, and dairies, but the surviving stone slave quarters are the most striking reminder of the history of the region. Because many of the newly freed blacks continued to work in the same capacity as they did when they were enslaved, they maintained these quarters as housing for a number of years after their emancipation.

The Abner Knox Farm includes an uncommon two-story stone building that contained quarters and a kitchen and remains in good condition. Built by Abner Knox in the early 1800s, the building probably originally had a double-pen plan, but the existing building is only one room deep.

Other known existing stone slave quarters are the Bayless Quarters (Bourbon County); the John Leavell Quarters (Garrard County); the Stone Quarters on Burgin Road (Mercer County); the Stone Barn on Brushy Creek (Nicholas County); the James Briscoe Quarters, the Ash Emison Quarters, and the Joseph Patterson Quarters (Scott County); and the Hogan Quarters and the Andrew Muldrow Quarters (Woodford County). [Early Stone Buildings of Central Kentucky TR, CA 6/23/83, 83002583]

CHRISTIAN COUNTY

Freeman Chapel CME Church
137 South Virginia Street
Hopkinsville

Named in honor of steward Peter Freeman, the Freeman Chapel Colored Methodist Episcopal Church was first organized in 1866 by the Reverends B. Newton, David Ratcliffe, and George McClain. It is the second oldest black congregation in Christian County. From 1866 to 1926, the church occupied a building on the southeast corner of 11th and Liberty in downtown Hopkinsville. Since the completion of the present chapel in 1926, Freeman Chapel has served as both a church and a community center for Hopkinsville's black residents. A variety of lodges and fraternal organizations have used this structure for meetings, making it a focal point for both social and religious activities. [Christian County MRA, CA 5/26/83, 83000563]

Poston House
809 Hayes Street
Hopkinsville

Settled in 1785, Christian County is the unofficial capital of the western Pennyrile or Black Patch region of southwestern Kentucky. Although the county had a large slave population, it was not affected by the Civil War like some of the other areas of the South. The county's prosperity was partly due to the growth of the railroad industry there. Even the tobacco industry continued to flourish, as the newly freed slaves worked for low wages.

The new railroad, coupled with the prosperity of the tobacco and coal economy, created a population boom in Hopkinsville, the county seat. Entire neighborhoods were built as speculative developments. The major black neighborhood, located in the Jackson Street area, was very active during the several decades around 1900.

The Poston family lived in this frame bungalow in the historic Jackson Street neighborhood until 1925. Theodore Poston was educated in Hopkinsville and graduated from Tennessee State University in 1928. Moving to New York City, he worked for the *Amsterdam News*, the leading black newspaper in the city. Poston later worked for the *New York Post*. He eventually returned to Hopkinsville, where he died in 1974. [Christian County MRA, B 4/30/79, 79003608]

FAYETTE COUNTY

Chandler Normal School Building and Webster Hall
548 Georgetown Street
Lexington

The Chandler Normal School Building and Webster Hall are the most important buildings associated with the education and culture of African Americans in central Kentucky. The school, which was founded shortly after the Civil War by a northern missionary society, opened in 1889 and continued to serve as a private educational institution for African Americans until it closed in 1923. The most prominent members of the Lexington area's black community received their training at the Chandler Normal School.

Webster Hall, originally a home for the Chandler School's teachers and principal, is also architecturally significant. It is the only campus building that has been identified as the work of Vertner A. Tandy, a native of Lexington and son of a successful black builder at the turn of the century (see also Lincoln Institute Complex, Shelby County). Tandy was one of the earliest and most prolific black architects in the United States, becoming the first black architect registered in New York State and one of the first to be admitted to the American Institute of Architects. He designed many fine homes and institutions in Harlem, New York, including St. Phillips Episcopal Church. He also designed Villa Lewaro, the country home of black millionairess Madame C. J. Walker (see also Villa Lewaro, Westchester County, New York). Tandy was also one of the founders of Alpha Phi Alpha Fraternity, Inc., the nation's oldest black collegiate fraternity. [CA 12/4/80, 80001509]

First African Baptist Church
264–272 East Short Street
Lexington

Built around 1850, the First African Baptist Church is the first African Baptist church to be founded in Kentucky and perhaps the third oldest African Baptist church in the country. The pastors of this congregation, from its beginnings in about 1790, have been men influential in the lives of the black population throughout the state. This tradition of influence began with the first pastor Peter Durrett, a slave who came to Kentucky with his master from Virginia. Durrett's inspirational preaching brought new hope to African Americans in the harsh Kentucky wilderness. More recently, pastors such as Homer Nutter guided many in the African American community through the civil rights struggle of the 1960s. [CA 4/24/86, 86000854]

Lewis O'Neal Tavern
Off U.S. Route 60
Versailles

This building was built on an old stagecoach route that ran between Lexington and Louisville. Used by troops as a fort during the Civil War, it featured a spring that ran beneath it and a cemetery with numbered tombstones. The area around the tavern developed into a community of freed black men and women. [Early Stone Buildings of Central Kentucky TR, CA 6/23/83, 83002766]

Pisgah Rural Historic District
Area northeast of Versailles roughly bounded by South Elkhorn Creek, U.S. Route 60, and Big Sink Road
Lexington and Versailles

Some of the first white settlers in Kentucky brought the institution of slavery with them. This controlled labor force gave owners more hands with which to work stock and crops, perform domestic duties, construct buildings and fences, and process many home-manufactured items. This slave quarter, which also extends into Woodford County, is the only remaining property in Pisgah from that era. It is a rare surviving example of a kind of property once common in the region.

A new class of agricultural worker was established after the Civil War. As newly freed blacks left the quarter for private dwellings, a white tenant class grew alongside the laboring African Americans. The "croppers," both white and black, worked for a portion of the tobacco crop they raised. While whites generally lived in small tenant houses built specifically for their use, African Americans tended to congregate in communities throughout the region. [Pisgah Area of Woodford County MPS, CAD 2/10/89, 88003348]

Redd Road Rural Historic District
Southeast of the intersection of Redd Road and Frankfort Road
Lexington

Slavery was common in rural Fayette County, and a majority of slaveholders owned between one and five black servants. The controlled labor force gave owners more hands with which to produce hemp, corn, grain, livestock, and home-manufactured goods. Relatively rare surviving slave quarters are an important adjunct to an understanding of the historic bluegrass landscape. The Redd Road Rural Historic District, which extends into Woodford County, contains two remaining slave quarters, at the Nathaniel Ashby House and Farm and at Locust Hill. These quarters are the cultural remains of a once prevalent institution that greatly affected bluegrass society during the antebellum period. [CA 2/28/91, 91000153]

FRANKLIN COUNTY

E. E. Hume Hall

Kentucky State University campus
Frankfort

The most important building on the campus of Kentucky State University, E. E. Hume Hall housed the administration offices, library, and chapel for 50 years. It also served as the center for educational, intellectual, and cultural leadership activities for Kentucky's black community. Hume Hall is an important work of prominent black architect William Sidney Pittman, designer of the Anthony Bowen YMCA in Washington, D.C. (see Anthony Bowen YMCA, District of Columbia), the Negro Building for the National Tercentennial at Jamestown, Virginia, and other college buildings at Kentucky State University and Tuskegee Institute. [CA 5/26/83, 83004050]

Jackson Hall, Kentucky State University

East Main Street
Frankfort

Formerly known as Recitation Hall, Jackson Hall was built in 1887 as the first permanent building on the campus of Kentucky State University. The building was named for John H. Jackson, who is thought to be the first black college graduate in the state of Kentucky. Jackson, who graduated from Berea College in 1874, was Kentucky State University's first president. Kentucky State University was founded after the Civil War as a teacher-training school for African Americans. Between 1887 and 1967, when schools were desegregated, the majority of black teacher trainees in Kentucky attended the institution. Among the most notable of its graduates was Whitney M. Young, Jr., who later became a dynamic leader of the National Urban League and whose birth-place is now a National Historic Landmark (see also Whitney M. Young, Jr., Birthplace, Shelby County). Young's father was an instructor at the institution. Jackson Hall, which at various times has housed the chapel, classrooms, science laboratories, school offices, and a basketball court, is the campus building most closely associated with the school's early period, and a reminder of an era of racially segregated education in the state of Kentucky. [CA 4/11/73, 73000802]

Old Statehouse Historic District

Roughly bounded by Broadway, Blanton, St. Clair, Ann, and High streets
Frankfort

An impressive concentration of buildings spanning the full range of 19th- and early 20th-century architectural styles, the Old Statehouse Historic District depicts Frankfort's growth and development. Among the most visually striking of the district's buildings are St. John's African Methodist Episcopal Church and the First Baptist Church. Not only are these buildings fine examples of late 19th-century ecclesiastical architecture, but both are important in Frankfort's black history. St. John's was established in 1839 and was housed in various buildings in the neighborhood before the present Victorian Gothic church was built in 1893. The First Baptist Church was formed by black members who split from a predominantly white Baptist church in 1833. They met in various homes until they raised money to erect a church in 1844. The present Richardsonian Romanesque style edifice was completed in 1904 after a protracted legal battle to obtain permission to build on the site over the objections of white neighbors. The church stands today as a symbol of the congregation's commitment to create and manage its institutions to meet its own needs and desires in the face of white hostility. [C 6/19/80, 80001529]

South Frankfort Neighborhood Historic District
Roughly bounded by U.S. Route 60, Rockland Court, and the Kentucky River
Frankfort

South Frankfort is Frankfort's largest historic residential neighborhood. The varied buildings in the district are evidence of the diverse economic and social standing of its residents from 1833 to 1925. The northeastern section of South Frankfort has historically had a large black population. African Americans provided labor for the industries that developed in Frankfort in the latter part of the 19th century. Of particular historical significance to South Frankfort's black community is the building at 228 East 2nd Street that once housed the Winnie A. Scott Memorial Hospital. The hospital was founded by Winnie Scott, a high school teacher at the Clinton Street School. It was opened to patients in 1910 with seven or eight rooms and an operating room. The facility served black patients until the 1960s, when King's Daughters Hospital began to admit them. The building was converted for use as an apartment house after the closing of the hospital. The building retains its historic appearance and holds symbolic importance as a landmark of segregation in Frankfort. [CB 8/19/82, 82002698]

FULTON COUNTY

Thomas Chapel CME Church
Moscow Avenue
Hickman

Thomas Chapel Colored Methodist Episcopal (CME) Church was organized in 1890 by 17 black citizens of Hickman who were former slaves. The first church building was erected on property donated by the church's builder, first minister, and namesake, the Reverend Warren Thomas, a carpenter and brick mason. The church burned in 1895 and was replaced by the present building. In the design of the new building, special provision was made for a full basement that could accommodate schoolrooms for black children in the community. Before 1910, money allocated for public schools was directly proportional to the amount of property taxes paid by citizens in the communities that they served. Since property in the black community was valued much lower, the amount of money generated for black public schools was very low. It was in this climate that Thomas Chapel CME Church began to provide educational facilities for black students.

For 15 years, the church was the principal educational facility for the black community of Hickman. At one time, all the school's teachers were members of the congregation. Perhaps the best known of the school's former students is Rufus Atwood, a World War I veteran and president of Kentucky State University from 1929 to 1962. Atwood's father was a former slave and founding member of the church. Today Thomas Chapel is recognized as a symbol of the long period of neglect of the education of African Americans in Hickman and throughout Kentucky. [A 1/9/79, 79000988]

GARRARD COUNTY

John Leavell Quarters
Off Kentucky Route 753
Bryantsville

This bluegrass region contains hundreds of stone spring houses, ice houses, smoke houses, and dairies, but the surviving stone slave quarters are the most striking reminder of the history of the region. Because many of the newly freed blacks continued to work in the same capacity as they did when they were enslaved, they maintained these quarters as housing for a number of years after their emancipation.

The John Leavell Quarters is a one-story, two-bay, double-cell slave quarters made of dry stone. After the Civil War, it was occupied by Girt Coomer, a former slave. The building is the only remaining stone slave quarters in Garrard County.

Other known existing stone slave quarters are the Bayless Quarters (Bourbon County); Abner Knox Farm (Boyle County); the Stone Quarters on Burgin Road (Mercer County); the Stone Barn on Brushy Creek (Nicholas County); the James Briscoe Quarters, the Ash Emison Quarters, and the Joseph Patterson Quarters (Scott County); and the Hogan Quarters and the Andrew Muldrow Quarters (Woodford County). [Early Stone Buildings of Central Kentucky TR, CA 6/23/83, 83002779]

GREEN COUNTY

Anderson House
Kentucky Route 1913
Haskingsville

The Anderson House is a one-and-one-half-story brick house built by Garland Anderson around 1819 and is one of the least-altered examples of Federal style architecture in Green County. The property was acquired by Alfred Anderson in 1852 after Garland Anderson's death. Upon receiving the property, Alfred Anderson freed the slaves that were sold with it and gave them their own land, which became known as Anderson Free State. Descendants of freed Anderson slaves still farm in this area. [Green County MRA, CA 8/24/84, 84001496]

HARDIN COUNTY

Embry Chapel Church
117 Mulberry Street
Elizabethtown

The Embry Chapel Church is a fine example of the Romanesque Revival style of architecture. Originally built in 1868 to house the congregation of the Second Presbyterian Church, it was later sold to the local African Methodist Episcopal (AME) congregation in 1891. This AME congregation was formed in 1865 and met in a small frame church (now demolished) before acquiring this property. The church has not been significantly altered since its original construction. [Hardin County MRA, CA 10/4/88, 88001803]

First Baptist Church
112 West Poplar Street
Elizabethtown

During the winter of 1779–80, a group of pioneers came into what is now Hardin County, Kentucky, and established the first permanent settlement. On June 17, 1781, 18 persons formed one of the first Baptist congregations west of the Alleghenies. Of the original members, three were black servants. The original congregation had no building of its own and met either outside in the open or in the homes of members until about 1807, when a log building was erected. The present church was constructed in 1834.

Slavery was a significant issue for the congregation. One of the pastors, Josiah Dodge, was among the first preachers to refuse fellowship with slaveholders. During the 1850s the black members of the community were granted the privilege of holding services of their own under the supervision of the Severn's Valley Church, and they built a log building in which to worship. During this time, the church ordained its first black minister. The black congregants formed their own church in 1866, the First Baptist Church. When the Severn's Valley congregation built a new building in 1897, they sold their church building to the First Baptist congregation.

The church is a tangible reminder of the role of African Americans in the history of Hardin County. [A 12/31/74, 74000879]

JEFFERSON COUNTY

Broadway Temple AME Zion Church
662 South 13th Street
Louisville

Broadway Temple African Methodist Episcopal (AME) Zion Church is a significant work of black architect Samuel Plato. The congregation of AME Zion was organized in 1876 and moved to its present location in 1901. The present church building was constructed in 1915 and a north annex was constructed in 1926. Plato served as both architect and contractor for the church building and most likely for the addition as well.

Plato, a native of Alabama, began his study of architecture through a correspondence course while he was a student at Simmons University in Louisville. After beginning his practice in Marion, Indiana, about 1910, he returned to Louisville several years later. He designed several buildings in Louisville and later became the first African American to receive a federal post office contract. Over the course of his career, Plato designed more than 40 post offices around the country. In addition, he was one of only a few African Americans to be awarded a defense housing contract during World War II. One of his major projects under the program was the construction of Camp Taylor in Louisville.

Broadway Temple is a significant early work. Its reliance on Neoclassical Revival style motifs presages some of his later works. The real interest in AME Zion, however, lies in Plato's imaginative combination of elements, such as varied roof forms and window treatments, unencumbered by any one style or convention. [C 12/8/80, 80001596]

Central Colored School
542 West Kentucky Street
Louisville

The Central Colored School, now the Mary D. Hill School, was first conceived as a permanent, tax-supported facility for the education of Louisville's black children. It served as the only black high school in Kentucky from 1873 to 1894, when the school was moved from 6th and Kentucky streets to 9th and Magazine streets for the exclusive use of white students. It presents a unique reminder of African American progress during the otherwise discouraging post-Reconstruction era. [CAB 9/13/76, 76000901]

Chestnut Street Baptist Church
912 West Chestnut Street
Louisville

Constructed of red brick and richly ornamented with terra cotta, the Chestnut Street Baptist Church is fine example of Gothic Revival style ecclesiastical architecture in Louisville. The building's architect, Henry Wolters, was born in Hanover, Germany, and educated at the Berlin Polytechnic Institute and the famed Ecole des Beaux-Arts in Paris. Wolters worked as an engineer on the Suez Canal before coming to the United States in 1872. The church is the only ecclesiastical building Wolters is known to have designed.

Built around 1884, the church was home to a Baptist congregation until 1910, when it became the Quinn Chapel African Methodist Episcopal (AME) Church. The church was named for Bishop William Paul Quinn, abolitionist and founder of the AME denomination. Organized in 1838, the AME congregation consisted of free blacks who were active in the antislavery movement. The church thus earned the nickname the

Central Colored School in the Limerick Historic District. Photo courtesy of the Kentucky Heritage Commission (Elizabeth F. Jones).

"Abolitionists Church." The congregation was one of the most active in the black community, opening Louisville's first school for black children in the late 1840s. One of the very few historic buildings left in an area of urban renewal, the Chestnut Street Baptist Church is an important part of the history of one of the city's earliest and most important black congregations. [C 12/3/80, 80001598]

Church of Our Merciful Saviour
473 South 11th Street
Louisville

This Gothic Revival church was built after a fire in 1912 destroyed the 1890 building its congregation had previously occupied. The Church of Our Merciful Saviour was very active in the black community; it sponsored the first Boy Scout Troop for black boys in the United States in 1916, only one year after the local Boy Scout Council was founded. [West Louisville MRA, CA 9/8/83, 83002648]

Jeffersontown Colored School
10400 Shelby Street
Jeffersontown

This school was built in 1929–30 as an elementary school for black children who lived in Jeffersontown and the surrounding area. The school had previously been housed in a frame residence beginning in 1912. This is the only black elementary school outside the city of Louisville that is still standing in Jefferson County. [Jefferson County MRA, A 3/29/85, 85002448]

Knights of Pythias Temple
928–932 West Chestnut Street
Louisville

The Knights of Pythias Temple was built in 1914–15 as the state headquarters for the black Knights of Pythias lodge and has long since been associated with the development of the black community in Louisville. The lodges were at their strongest in the early 20th century for the black community. Since their members were generally the better educated and most prominent members of the black community, the groups also served as role models for black youths.

When completed, the building housed a drugstore, a movie theater, and a restaurant. Part of the building also contained hotel rooms that were available for daily or monthly rental by men only. The Knights of Pythias lodges in Louisville became inactive during the Depression. The building continued to be used for offices and apartments, and housed the Davis Trade School for African Americans after World War II. In 1953 the Chestnut Street Branch Young Men's Christian Association purchased the building, and it became known by that name. Today, the building still plays a significant role in the development of the Louisville's black community. [CA 11/29/78, 78001358]

Limerick Historic District (Boundary Increase)
Bounded by Breckinridge, Oak, 5th, and 8th streets
Louisville

Inhabited primarily by the Irish, the Limerick Historic District was also home to a small group of African Americans before the Civil War. They were slaves or servants of local households and resided along the alleys of the Irish district. The L&N Railroad also provided jobs for this community. This concentration of African Americans was most likely the impetus for the establishment of two important black educational institutions during Reconstruction, the Central Colored School and the Municipal College.

Established in 1873, the Central Colored School was the first black high school in Kentucky. Likewise, the Municipal College is indicative of the vigorous pursuit of education for African Americans by both black and white citizens in Louisville.

The architectural fabric of Limerick is rich and varied. It contains a number of elegant Victorian residences as well as unique groupings of unusual architectural types that are concentrated in the area of Municipal College and the Central Colored School (see also Central Colored School and Municipal College Campus, Simmons University). [CA 12/23/83, 83003715]

Louisville Free Public Library, Western Colored Branch
604 South 10th Street
Louisville

Established in 1905, the Louisville Free Public Library, Western Colored Branch, was the first free public library in the United States built exclusively for African Americans. It was financed by Andrew Carnegie, a 19th-century steel magnate, industrialist, and philanthropist. Carnegie established the Andrew Carnegie Library Fund, a national funding program for the construction of libraries, free and open to anyone regardless of race.

The Louisville Free Public Library, Western Colored Branch, played an important role in the advancement of African Americans in Louisville. Much credit for the success of the library is attributed to Thomas F. Blue, the first head of the Western Branch. In 1908 he designed a library science program to train qualified African Americans for library positions. Blue introduced library science to trainees from Cincinnati, Evansville, Houston, Memphis, and a number of other cities. In addition, the Western Colored Branch library served as a community center promoting cultural awareness and a forum for the free exchange of ideas. It housed meetings of the Douglass Debating Club, which sponsored monthly activities with topics of special interest to library patrons. Through the years the black community continued to recognize the importance of the Louisville Free Public Library, Western Colored Branch. [CA 12/6/75, 75000771]

Merriwether House
6421 Upper River Road
Louisville

At the turn of the 20th century, black communities could be found in some half dozen locations in Jefferson County. Most of the settlements were developed by freed blacks at the conclusion of the Civil War. Unlike black urban migration after the Civil War, rural migration to small settlements and farmsteads during the same period has been virtually undocumented.

One such settlement was Harrods Creek, located near the Ohio River. Free blacks established a community in this area during the 1880s and 1890s. The Merriwether family acquired its land near the mouth of the creek on the Ohio in about 1890. In spite of the limited amount of land connected to the house, the Merriwether family engaged in small-scale agriculture, raising and slaughtering hogs, tending a large garden, and the like. The broad curve of the creek and the proximity to the Ohio

River made the site attractive to boaters and vacationers in the early 20th century. The Merriwethers took advantage of this by building and managing docks and cottages at the foot of their property. [Jefferson County MRA, A 3/22/89, 87000361]

Municipal College Campus, Simmons University
1018 South 7th Street
Louisville

Municipal College for Negroes, Simmons University, State University, and Kentucky Normal and Theological Institute all have two historical qualities in common. First, each has been housed at various times on the grassy square below Kentucky Street between 7th and 8th streets near downtown Louisville. Second, they are significant reminders of the course of black higher education in Kentucky.

Two major buildings survive from Municipal College/Simmons University. The older of the two was built in 1909 and originally served as the Girls Dormitory–Domestic Science Building (now the Mary B. Talbert School). The other building is the boy's dormitory (now Steward Hall). It is believed that both of these buildings were built and designed by Louisville's prolific Samuel Plato, one of the most successful local builders of the mid-20th century.

From 1879 to 1951, Simmons University provided higher education for African Americans in Kentucky. As such, it is intricately linked to the heritage and development of African Americans in the state. Today the site, under the ownership of the local school board, provides the community a place for neighborhood meetings, schooling, and recreation. [CA 11/21/76, 76000906]

Russell Historic District

Roughly bounded by South 15th, South 26th, Congress, and West Broadway streets
Louisville

The area known today as Russell became a fashionable residential area during the 1880s. When residential areas south and east of Louisville then became popular in the 1890s, the white population shifted to these outlying areas. Consequently African Americans began to settle in Russell. By 1925 they were well established in Russell, with black professionals owning most of the expensive residences.

An important resource built in response to the rapid influx of black families into Russell is Plymouth Settlement House. Established in 1917 by the Plymouth Congregational Church, the Settlement House provided living quarters for young working women and served as a place of entertainment for children and adults. It also provided classes for adults and teenagers. The Reverend E. G. Harris, a highly respected black minister and founder of the Settlement House, solicited funds for the house from influential white families in Louisville. With their assistance the Settlement House became the area's most vital institution. Today, the name has been changed to the Plymouth Urban Center.

Russell was the home of several black community leaders. Harvey Clarence Russell, for whom the area is named, built his home at 2345 West Chestnut Street in the late 1920s. He was appointed a specialist in black education in the U.S. Office of Education and was elected president of the Kentucky Educational Association. Another resident, Samuel Plato, was one of Louisville's few black architects. Simmons University, the Virginia Avenue School, Zion African Methodist Episcopal Church, and numerous post office buildings throughout the nation are Plato's designs.

Before Russell became a predominantly black community, the alleys were lined with small residences, usually shotgun houses of frame construction. According to oral history these were the dwellings of black families who worked for the white property owners. It has been said that the alleys were always full of activity and were considered the real heart of the black community in those early years.

Russell retains much of its extraordinary 19th-century architectural character through its wealth of brick alleys and sidewalks, cast iron fences and porches, and numerous shotgun houses. The survival of cast iron in the quantities found in Russell is particularly rare. Most local cast iron was lost during World War I when property owners donated it to the war effort. Russell holds an important place in the history of the black community in Louisville because of its role as the cultural, social, residential, and commercial hub of black activity. [CAB 5/7/80, 0001617]

University of Louisville Belknap Campus

2301 South 3rd Street
Louisville

This institution contains remnants of campus plans representing not only the present university, but also two earlier institutions located on the same property, the Louisville House of Refuge and its later incarnation as the Louisville Industrial School of Reform. The House of Refuge, chartered in 1854 for the care of the city's juvenile delinquents and derelicts, made provision for black children as early as 1876. When it became the Industrial School of Reform, the architects built the Black Female Building in 1893. [CA 6/25/76, 76000908]

KENTON COUNTY

Emery-Price Historic District
Roughly bounded by 8th, Greenup, and 11th streets and alley behind west side of Scott Boulevard
Covington

The Emery-Price Historic District is a significant collection of pre-1900 architecture located near downtown Covington. The district has also been a center for Covington's black population, housing many of the city's black professionals since 1900. One of the first schools was located on Robbins Street near Madison (now demolished). The 9th Street Methodist Church, adjacent to the district, has served a black congregation since 1880. One of the major leaders in the black community was the Reverend Jacob Price, who helped establish several churches in the neighborhood and promoted black education. The Jacob Price Homes, located on the eastern edge of the district, are named in his honor. The Lincoln-Grant School was the major black school of the 20th century in Covington and still stands on Greenup Street.

While some demolition and alterations to buildings have occurred within the district, most properties display their original architectural detailing. Within the district are fine examples of Victorian architecture, including the notable Queen Anne Emery Row house on Scott Boulevard. The district continues to be an important center for Covington's black population. [Eastside MRA, CA 2/18/87, 86003484]

MADISON COUNTY

Lincoln Hall
Berea College campus
Berea

Founded in 1855, Berea College was the first college established in the United States for the specific purpose of educating black and white students together. Berea was integrated until 1904, when the Kentucky state legislature mandated that black and white students could not be taught in the same classroom. For four years Berea and its supporters unsuccessfully fought the law in the courts. The U.S. Supreme Court ruled that since Berea was a private organization incorporated by the state of Kentucky, the state had the right to regulate it according to state laws. *Berea College v. Commonwealth of Kentucky* became a landmark case in segregation's constitutional history. The decision was not overturned until the landmark 1954 *Brown v. Board of Education* case, which upheld the right of a black girl to attend an all-white elementary school in Topeka, Kansas.

Of the many buildings on Berea's campus, Lincoln Hall has the deepest associations with the school's history. Constructed in 1887, it has undergone no exterior alteration since it was built and thus possesses a high degree of architectural integrity. Lincoln Hall was designated a National Historic Landmark on December 2, 1974. [A 12/2/74 NHL, 74000892]

McCRACKEN COUNTY

Artelia Anderson Hall
1400 H. C. Mathis Drive
Paducah

Artelia Anderson Hall, located on the old campus of West Kentucky Industrial College, is the most important site in western Kentucky associated with education in the black community. This building stands as a monument to the efforts of Dr. D. H. Anderson, founder of West Kentucky Industrial College, and his wife, Artelia, for whom the building is named. D. H. Anderson founded the college as the West Kentucky Industrial School to provide higher education and technical skills to black students. In 1911 the cornerstone was laid for the first administration and classroom building, with Anderson participating in much of the construction himself.

With state funding he was able to build a girl's dormitory. Completed and dedicated in 1929, it was a milestone in the school's development. The school continued to grow until it was the nation's third largest black junior college in 1938. That year the Kentucky legislature merged the school with the Kentucky State College at Frankfort. The buildings on the old campus, including Artelia Anderson Hall, have sustained a moderate amount of damage as a result of deterioration and vandalism. However, Artelia Anderson Hall is still representative of the money, energy, and talent of African Americans that went into the education of their own. [AB 5/26/83, 83002824]

Lincoln School
South 8th Street between Ohio and
Tennessee streets
Paducah

Consisting of three buildings erected in 1894, 1921, and 1938, Lincoln School was developed to meet the demand for high-quality educational facilities for African Americans. Serving black elementary students, the institution was named in honor of Abraham Lincoln. In 1895 several interested citizens approached the board of education about the need for a higher course of study for the black youth of Paducah. The board immediately established a high school that shared its quarters with the elementary school until 1921, when a new facility was built to meet the growing student population.

In 1927 the most important educator connected to Lincoln School, E. W.

Whiteside, became principal. Whiteside's commitment to the school and community was reflected by the new school motto: Enter to Learn, Depart to Serve. Several important advances were made during Whiteside's tenure, including the addition of government-sponsored adult education classes, a marching band, a school newspaper, and the addition of an auditorium and gymnasium in 1938.

As a result of desegregation efforts in Paducah during the 1960s, Lincoln School merged with Paducah Tilghman, the white high school. Although the old Lincoln School is no longer used as a school, it serves as an important local example of black heritage and achievement. [A 6/23/88, 88000895]

MERCER COUNTY

Stone Quarters on Burgin Road
Kentucky Route 152
Harrodsburg

This bluegrass region contains hundreds of stone spring houses, ice houses, smoke houses, and dairies, but the surviving stone slave quarters are the most striking reminder of the history of the region. Because many of the newly freed blacks continued to work in the same capacity as they did when they were enslaved, they maintained these quarters as housing for a number of years after their emancipation. Other known existing stone slave quarters are the Bayless Quarters (Bourbon County); Abner Knox Farm (Boyle County); the John Leavell Quarters (Garrard County); the Stone Barn on Brushy Creek (Nicholas County); the James Briscoe Quarters, the Ash Emison Quarters, and the Joseph Patterson Quarters (Scott County); and the Hogan Quarters and the Andrew Muldrow Quarters (Woodford County). [Early Stone Buildings of Central Kentucky TR, CA 6/23/83, 83002833]

MONROE COUNTY

Mount Vernon AME Church
North of Gamaliel on Kentucky Route 100
Gamaliel

The Mount Vernon African Methodist Episcopal Church was constructed in 1848 to serve the residents of the small community of Freetown. The community was founded in 1802 when William Howard, a wealthy Monroe County farmer, freed his slaves and gave them each a small piece of land. The former slaves established Freetown, the county's first black community, several miles west of Howard's residence.

Three of the former slaves, along with other Freetown residents, constructed the hand-hewn log church. It was the first black church in Monroe County and also served as a school for black children for 70 years. At the time of its listing in the National Register, the church was used for special events held by the local black community. [A 11/17/77, 77000639]

MONTGOMERY COUNTY

Keas Tabernacle CME Church
101 South Queen Street
Mount Sterling

The Keas Tabernacle Christian Methodist Episcopal Church was formed in 1878 as part of the Reconstruction effort to organize the former slaves who were members of the Methodist Episcopal Church South into a new denomination. It is named after its first minister, Samuel Keas. The building is an excellent vernacular interpretation of the Romanesque Revival style that was popular throughout the region in the late 19th century.

Initially, the church met in a small frame building on the present site. With the help of labor and funds contributed by the congregation, a new church was

Stained-glass window of the Keas Tabernacle CME Church. Photo courtesy of the Kentucky Heritage Commission (William Gus Johnson).

completed in 1893 and has served as an important religious and cultural institution in Mount Sterling ever since. [CA 5/26/83, 83002836]

NELSON COUNTY

Bloomfield Historic District
Central Bloomfield, including parts of Hill, Main, Perry, and Depots streets and Fairfield, Springfield, and Taylorsville roads
Bloomfield

Surviving resources associated with the black population of Kentucky are very rare and are therefore considered cultural artifacts. Slave quarters for urban domestic slaves in Kentucky have been found within main dwellings in basement and attic areas; in detached domestic buildings such as kitchens; and in quarters located within the confines of yard areas. The Bloomfield Historic District includes two surviving slave quarters. The E. B. Miles House is a single-cell log building originally on the grounds of an early 19th-century, center-passage residence. The quarters are in very poor condition but are exceptionally significant because of their rarity. The Miles Quarters are located in a detached kitchen in the grand residence on Taylorsville Road. Both quarters are rare sites representing antebellum black heritage in Bloomfield. [CA 3/18/91, 91000234]

NICHOLAS COUNTY

Stone Barn on Brushy Creek
U.S. Route 68
Carlisle

This bluegrass region contains hundreds of stone spring houses, ice houses, smoke houses, and dairies, but the surviving stone slave quarters are the most striking reminder of the history of the region. Because many of the newly freed blacks continued to work in the same capacity as they did when they were enslaved, they maintained these quarters as housing for a number of years after their emancipation.

Built in the early 19th century, the Stone Barn on Brushy Creek is reputedly connected to the slave trade. According to descendants of former slaves, the building was used as a breeding barn for slaves; and a former owner of the property reported slave chains were once attached to the inside walls of the barn.

Other known existing stone slave quarters are the Bayless Quarters (Bourbon County); Abner Knox Farm (Boyle County); the John Leavell

Quarters (Garrard County); the Stone Quarters on Burgin Road (Mercer County); the James Briscoe Quarters, the Ash Emison Quarters, and the Joseph Patterson Quarters (Scott County); and the Hogan Quarters and the Andrew Muldrow Quarters (Woodford County). [Early Stone Buildings of Central Kentucky TR, CA 6/23/83, 83002840]

PENDLETON COUNTY

Charity's House
108 Montjoy Street
Falmouth

Charity built this house in 1845, shortly after gaining her freedom from slavery. She also built several other houses on the block for her children and grandchildren. Charity is the ancestor of most of Falmouth's black population. Her house is one of the few remaining residences in Falmouth's early black neighborhood known as Happy Hollow. [Falmouth MRA, CA 3/4/83, 83002848]

PULASKI COUNTY

A. Jackson Crawford Building
207 South Main Street
Somerset

Affectionately known as Uncle Jack, A. J. "Jackson" Crawford was well known in Somerset as an attorney for local African Americans. He purchased this property at public auction in 1880 and used it both as a law office and residence until his death in 1915.

The 13th, 14th, and 15th Amendments to the U.S. Constitution completely altered the status of African Americans as slaves and converted them into free men and women and new citizens. Consequently, there was now a need for legal assistance. Crawford, a former slave, filled this need for the black community in Somerset. It seems that during Reconstruction he served as a law clerk

A. Jackson Crawford Building. Photo courtesy of the Kentucky Heritage Commission (Carter Ross, Jr.).

and apprentice in the practice of Thomas Zantzinger Morrow, a prominent attorney in Somerset. He later became the sole provider of legal services for members of the black community from 1880 until his death on July 17, 1915. [B 8/18/80, 80001665]

SCOTT COUNTY

James Briscoe Quarters
Off U.S. Route 25
Delaplain

This bluegrass region contains hundreds of stone spring houses, ice houses, smoke houses, and dairies, but the surviving stone slave quarters are the most striking reminder of the history of the region. Because many of the newly freed blacks continued to work in the same capacity as they did when they were enslaved, they maintained these quarters as housing for a number of years after their emancipation.

The James Briscoe Quarters were built around 1827 and consist of a six-bay, one-story, double dry-stone house, each half having two rooms. The property also includes the brick main house and a log smokehouse, which, along with the slave quarters, form an unaltered part of the plantation complex.

Other known existing stone slave quarters are the Bayless Quarters (Bourbon County); Abner Knox Farm (Boyle County); the John Leavell Quarters (Garrard County); the Stone Quarters on Burgin Road (Mercer County); the Stone Barn on Brushy Creek (Nicholas County); the Ash

Emison Quarters and the Joseph Patterson Quarters (Scott County); and the Hogan Quarters and the Andrew Muldrow Quarters (Woodford County). [Early Stone Buildings of Central Kentucky TR, CA 6/23/83, 83002864]

Ash Emison Quarters
Off U.S. Route 25
Delaplain

This bluegrass region contains hundreds of stone spring houses, ice houses, smoke houses, and dairies, but the surviving stone slave quarters are the most striking reminder of the history of the region. Because many of the newly freed blacks continued to work in the same capacity as they did when they were enslaved, they maintained these quarters as housing for a number of years after their emancipation.

The Ash Emison quarters is a double house of two one-story, dry-stone hall and parlor plans joined end to end. A matching building is said to have existed nearby. The building is a good illustration of dry-laid masonry construction.

Other known existing stone slave quarters are the Bayless Quarters (Bourbon County); Abner Knox Farm (Boyle County); the John Leavell Quarters (Garrard County); the Stone Quarters on Burgin Road (Mercer County); the Stone Barn on Brushy Creek (Nicholas County); the James Briscoe Quarters and the Joseph Patterson Quarters (Scott County); and the Hogan Quarters and the Andrew Muldrow Quarters (Woodford County). [Early Stone Buildings of Central Kentucky TR, CA 6/23/83, 83002866]

First African Baptist Church and Parsonage
209–211 West Jefferson Street
Georgetown

The First African Baptist Church traces its roots to a congregation of Baptists formed in Georgetown in 1810. The congregation was racially mixed, with black slaves baptized as nonvoting members along with their white owners. The first building on the property was a frame structure erected in 1815. In 1829 Kentucky Baptists organized a college in southeast Georgetown. In 1840 Howard Malcolm, president of the college, urged the church to move to the college neighborhood. The move was completed in 1848, and the African Americans in the congregation were given the former lot and building for their own separate congregation, which would operate under the care of the parent white church.

The first pastor of the black Baptist church was the Reverend George Washington Dupee, a slave born in Gallatin County in 1826. He was licensed to preach in 1846 and ordained to the ministry in 1851. On January 1, 1856, Dupee was sold at auction at the Scott County Courthouse. Dr. W. M. Pratt, a Lexington pastor, and others bought him and permitted the black congregation to purchase his freedom.

After the Civil War the congregation reorganized, changing its name from Georgetown Baptist Church to First African Baptist Church. The present building was constructed in 1870 at a cost of $8,250, donated by both the black and white Baptist communities of Georgetown. The parsonage was constructed in 1923 and was at the time described as one of the handsomest buildings constructed for a black congregation in Kentucky. These two buildings today represent the oldest black congregation in the city of Georgetown and one of the oldest black congregations in Kentucky. [CA 3/1/84, 84001985]

Johnson-Pence House
West of Georgetown off U.S. Route 460
Georgetown

The land on North Elkhorn Creek on which the Johnson-Pence House stands was given to Imogene Johnson by her father, Colonel Richard M. Johnson, vice president of the United States under Martin Van Buren. Imogene was the daughter of Johnson and Julia Chinn, a slave Johnson inherited from his father's estate. Children born to black slaves and their white masters were rarely publicly recognized by their fathers. Johnson, however, not only recognized his offspring by a slave, but reared these children in his home, educated them, and gave them large tracts of prime agricultural land when they married. Johnson's refusal to conceal this aspect of his life cost him a great deal politically and is often cited as a factor in his failure to receive a majority of the electoral votes necessary to secure the vice presidency in 1836, whereupon he became the only vice president elected by the U.S. Senate.

Imogene Johnson was born on February 17, 1812, when her father was actively crusading as a "war hawk" in the U.S. Congress and on his way to becoming a hero in the War of 1812. During his political ascendancy, Imogene and her sister, Adaline, were growing up on Richard Johnson's Blue Spring Farm, near the town where their mother worked as a housekeeper. Both girls later married white men and were each deeded a part their father's estate. Adaline was given Blue Spring Farm, and Imogene and her husband, Daniel Pence, received the property on which the Johnson-Pence House now stands. Richard Johnson served inconspicuously as vice president and campaigned in 1840 for renomination to the post. His history, however, proved unacceptable to many, and he

failed in his efforts. He returned to Kentucky to live across the creek from the tract of land he gave to Imogene Johnson and Daniel Pence. He was serving his second term in the state legislature at the time of death in 1850. [CB 11/20/78, 78001397]

Joseph Patterson Quarters
Off U.S. Route 421
Midway

This bluegrass region contains hundreds of stone spring houses, ice houses, smoke houses, and dairies, but the surviving stone slave quarters are the most striking reminder of the history of the region. Because many of the newly freed blacks continued to work in the same capacity as they did when they were enslaved, they maintained these quarters as housing for a number of years after their emancipation.

Other known existing stone slave quarters are the Bayless Quarters (Bourbon County); Abner Knox Farm (Boyle County); the John Leavell Quarters (Garrard County); the Stone Quarters on Burgin Road (Mercer County); the Stone Barn on Brushy Creek (Nicholas County); the James Briscoe Quarters and the Ash Emison Quarters (Scott County); and the Hogan Quarters and the Andrew Muldrow Quarters (Woodford County). [Early Stone Buildings of Central Kentucky TR, CA 6/23/83, 83002869]

SHELBY COUNTY
Bethel AME Church
414 Henry Clay Street
Shelbyville

This one-story brick building was constructed in 1916 to house an African Methodist Episcopal (AME) congregation established in 1858. The AME Church was founded in 1794 by Richard Allen (1760–1831) and grew to be the largest black denomination in the United States in the years before the Civil War (see also Mother Bethel AME Church, Philadelphia County, Pennsylvania). Bethel AME is the best ecclesiastical example of the integration of the Gothic Revival and Classical Revival styles in Shelby County. The sanctuary is also important for its central role in the evolution of black religious life in Shelbyville. [Shelbyville MRA, CA 9/28/84, 84001990]

Lincoln Institute Complex
West of Simpsonville on U.S. Route 60
Simpsonville

Lincoln Institute was the leading secondary education center for African Americans in Kentucky during the period 1908–38. The college was founded by Berea College, located in Madison County, Kentucky, which organized Lincoln Institute in response to a 1904 state law outlawing Berea's policy of biracial education. In 1911 Berea Hall, the first campus building, was erected with money donated by the Carnegie Foundation. Berea Hall was designed by black architects G. W. Foster and Vertner A. Tandy (see Chandler Normal School Building and Webster Hall, Fayette County, and Villa Lewaro, Westchester County, New York).

When Whitney A. Young, Sr., became its director in 1935, he greatly improved the facility by securing additional state and local funding. After a period of growth immediately following World War II, Lincoln Institute became obsolete, as Kentucky's public schools were desegregated in the late 1950s and early 1960s. The campus closed in 1965. [Shelby County MRA, CA 12/27/88, 88002926]

St. John United Methodist Church
College Street
Shelbyville

The best local example of frame Gothic Revival religious architecture, this building is also an important landmark in the evolution of black religious history in Shelbyville. Originally part of the Colored Methodist Episcopal Church, St. John's was the home for many prominent local celebrities, including Verna Chinn, the first black woman to establish a kindergarten in Shelby County; Emma Payne Roland, the first black reporter for the *Shelby Sentinel;* and T. S. Baxter, the first African American to be elected a council member in Shelbyville. [Shelbyville MRA, CA 9/28/84, 84002016]

Whitney M. Young, Jr., Birthplace
Southwest of Simpsonville off U.S. Route 60
Simpsonville

This simple, two-story frame building is the birthplace of Whitney Moore Young, Jr. (1921–71). Executive director of the National Urban League from 1961 to 1971, Young drew unprecedented support for the league's social and economic programs, working for an equality beyond civil rights causes.

Young grew up on the campus of the Lincoln Institute in Kentucky, where his father served on the faculty. At the age of 15, he graduated from Lincoln and enrolled in Kentucky State College for black students.

After graduation he took a job teaching mathematics at a Rosenwald high school in Madisonville, Kentucky. When the United States entered World War II, Young volunteered for service, hoping to study medicine through the Army Specialized Training Program (ASTP). At the time, however, only two medical programs were open to black students, and both were fully enrolled until 1946.

Young instead entered an engineering program at the Massachusetts Institute of Technology. Meanwhile, the ASTP program was ended, and Young was assigned to a road construction company of black soldiers under the direction of southern white officers.

After just three weeks, Young was promoted from private to first sergeant, placing him in a precarious position between the black soldiers and white officers and engendering hostility on both sides. It was then that Young decided on a career in race relations. Returning home after the war, Young enrolled at the University of Minnesota, where his wife, Margaret, was a student. He graduated in 1947 with a master's degree in social work.

In 1948 Young was offered the position of industrial relations director with the Urban League of Minnesota, with which he had volunteered as a student. His success in this position led to his promotion to president of the Omaha, Nebraska, branch of the Urban League in 1950. In this position, he was instrumental in integrating federal housing projects and getting black workers into jobs previously denied them on the basis of race. By the time Young left the post in 1953, he had more than tripled the league's paid membership.

Young accepted the position of dean of social work at Atlanta University in 1954. During his tenure at the school, he became increasingly concerned with the lack of integrated employment opportunities for its graduates. Young supported Atlanta University alumni in their boycott of the Georgia Conference of Social Welfare, which had a poor record of placing African Americans in leadership positions. Young also joined the National Association for the Advancement of Colored people (NAACP) at this time

and eventually rose to become its state president.

The NAACP was much less conservative than the Urban League in pursuing its agenda. As the civil rights movement gathered momentum in the late 1950s and early 1960s, the Urban League was accused of being too timid and was in danger of becoming ineffectual. It was in this climate that Young became director of the National Urban League.

When Young took over the organization in 1961, its loosely coordinated offices had 38 employees and it had an annual budget of $325,000. Under Young's direction, the organization became much more cohesive. By 1964 the budget had increased to $6,100,000, and the organization had 1,600 employees in 93 branches nationwide. He continued working with the league until his death in 1971. During his years with the organization, he initiated numerous programs that resulted in new job and advancement opportunities for minorities. He instituted the Street Academy, an alternative education system that prepared high school dropouts for college entrance exams. Through his New Thrust program, local black community leaders organized to identify and solve problems with the league's assistance. This program helped leaders deal with inadequate housing and health and education disadvantages rather than focusing on joblessness, which was merely the symptom of these conditions.

During his tenure at the National Urban League, Young participated in meetings with Presidents Kennedy and Nixon. In 1968 he was awarded the nation's highest civilian award, the Medal of Freedom, by President Johnson. On March 11, 1971, Young suffered a heart attack and drowned while swimming in Lagos. President Nixon ordered a jet to

Africa to bring home his body. At the funeral the president delivered a eulogy at Young's grave site. The house in which he was born and lived until 1936 stands on the campus of the Lincoln Institute and was designated a National Historic Landmark on April 27, 1984. [B 10/18/72, 72000543]

SPENCER COUNTY

Minor Chapel AME Church
East side of Jefferson Street between Red Row Alley and Reasor Street
Taylorsville

The first inhabitants of Kentucky brought slaves with them from the slave-owning areas of Maryland, North Carolina, and Virginia. The town of Taylorsville had a particularly high percentage of black residents in the years before the Civil War. The 1840 census documents an black population of 107 out of 391, or 27 percent of the entire population. Included in this number were five free blacks. Although many African Americans left Taylorsville in the years immediately after the Civil War, a sizable number stayed and began to build a black community. Minor Chapel is believed to have been constructed around 1895, during a period when several other black churches were being established in the Taylorsville area. Minor Chapel, one other church, and a school constitute the few remaining institutional buildings associated with the late 19th-century development of the Taylorsville black community. At the time of its listing in the National Register, the church remained active with an extremely small congregation. [A 4/2/92, 92000300]

Perry Shelburne House
West side of Railroad Street and north of Red Row Alley
Taylorsville

Constructed around 1882, the Perry Shelburne House is the only remaining residence associated with early black landownership in Taylorsville. The substantial two-story house documents an unusually prosperous lifestyle for a black family of the late 19th and early 20th centuries in the area. Perry Shelburne acquired the property on which the house now stands in 1880 and is credited with building the house. Shelburne and his wife, Amanda, worked for many years as custodians at the Yoder Poignand High School, later Taylorsville High School. Shelburne also worked as a custodian for several churches serving the white community in Taylorsville. At Shelburne's death, his eldest daughter, Sue, inherited the house. She taught school in Spencer County for 42 years, many of them at the black Culpepper School. Shelburne's second daughter also taught school in Spencer County. The house remained in the Shelburne family until after Sue Perry Shelburne's death in the 1960s. The occupations of the Shelburne family were closely associated with important Spencer County educational institutions and help to explain the relative affluence of the family and their ability to build this substantial house. [A 4/2/92, 92000297]

WARREN COUNTY

First Colored Baptist Church
340 State Street
Bowling Green

The First Colored Baptist Church, now called the State Street Baptist Church, was established in 1838 by former slaves as the first formally organized church for African Americans in Bowling Green. This turn-of-the-century Gothic-Romanesque Revival style building is one of the few remaining buildings widely recognized for its link to Bowling Green's 19th-century black community.

[Warren County MRA, CA 12/18/79, 79003524]

WASHINGTON COUNTY

Johnson's Chapel AME Zion Church
East High Street
Springfield

In the mid-19th century, white citizens of Springfield gave the black population a lot on which to build an interdenominational church building. By 1872 the church had divided into Baptist and Methodist groups, and the members of the Methodist congregation moved to a site in a traditionally black neighborhood to build their own church. Johnson's Chapel African Methodist Episcopal Zion Church was built in 1872 by Wise McElroy, a member of the congregation. Constructed in the Gothic Revival style, the church followed the lead of other denominations that built churches in Springfield during the same period. The church, a member of one of the oldest black denominations, was a focal point of Springfield's black community. [Washington County MRA, CA 2/10/89, 88003396]

WOODFORD COUNTY

Hogan Quarters
Off Kentucky Route 33
Versailles

This bluegrass region contains hundreds of stone spring houses, ice houses, smoke houses, and dairies, but the surviving stone slave quarters are the most striking reminder of the history of the region. Because many of the newly freed blacks continued to work in the same capacity as they did when they were enslaved, they maintained these quarters as housing for a number of years after their emancipation.

The Hogan Quarters is a one-and-a-half-story, three-bay, dry-stone house of extra long dimensions. According to local tradition and descendants of slaves, the house was once the slave house. This unusual house features some vernacular Greek Revival–era elements.

Other known existing stone slave quarters are the Bayless Quarters (Bourbon County); Abner Knox Farm (Boyle County); the John Leavell Quarters (Garrard County); the Stone Quarters on Burgin Road (Mercer County); the Stone Barn on Brushy Creek (Nicholas County); the James Briscoe Quarters, the Ash Emison Quarters, and the Joseph Patterson Quarters (Scott County); and the Andrew Muldrow Quarters (Woodford County). [Early Stone Buildings of Central Kentucky TR, CA 8/22/83, 83002899]

Midway Historic District
U.S. Route 62
Midway

A collection of 19th- and early 20th-century buildings and sites, the Midway Historic District encompasses a planned community platted by the Lexington and Ohio Railway and sold off in plots. The first buildings were erected in the 1870s, with a second period of growth in the 1890s. Midway's street arrangement remains much the same today, reflecting the dominance of the railroad. Its orthogonal grid system was later used as model for other railroad towns in Kentucky. Much of the town's social life in the early 20th century was focused on the church. The Midway Historic District contains several substantial churches, three of which were established for black congregations. Of these, the Second Christian Church is of notable historical importance. The congregation is believed to be the oldest black congregation in the state of Kentucky and one of the first in the National Negro Disciples Brotherhood. The building is an important reminder of the role of African Americans in Midway's development. [CA 11/17/78, 78001415]

Andrew Muldrow Quarters
Griers Creek Road
Tyrone

This bluegrass region contains hundreds of stone spring houses, ice houses, smoke houses, and dairies, but the surviving stone slave quarters are the most striking reminder of the history of the region. Because many of the newly freed blacks continued to work in the same capacity as they did when they were enslaved, they maintained these quarters as housing for a number of years after their emancipation.

Other known existing stone slave quarters are the Bayless Quarters (Bourbon County); Abner Knox Farm (Boyle County); the John Leavell Quarters (Garrard County); the Stone Quarters on Burgin Road (Mercer County); the Stone Barn on Brushy Creek (Nicholas County); the James Briscoe Quarters, the Ash Emison Quarters, and the Joseph Patterson Quarters (Scott County); and the Hogan Quarters (Woodford County). [Early Stone Buildings of Central Kentucky TR, CA 6/23/83, 83002907]

Pisgah Rural Historic District
Area northeast of Versailles roughly bounded by South Elkhorn Creek, U.S. Route 60, and Big Sink Road
Lexington and Versailles

See Pisgah Rural Historic District, Fayette County.

Redd Road Rural Historic District
Southeast of the intersection of Redd Road and Frankfort Road
Lexington

See Redd Road Rural Historic District, Fayette County.

Solomon Thomas House
Craigs Creek Road
Salvisa

Between 1785 and 1835, central Kentucky's first settlers constructed numerous stone buildings, many of which are still in existence. The Solomon Thomas House, while typical of this type of architecture, is rare in that it was acquired in 1853 by a black man. Pre-Civil War black ownership was Kentucky highly unusual. [Early Stone Buildings of Central Kentucky TR, CA 6/23/83, 83002914]

LOUISIANA

ASCENSION PARISH

St. Joseph's School
Junction of Louisiana Routes 22 and 44
Burnside

St. Joseph's School was established as the first black Catholic school in Louisiana in 1867. The school was formed as a result of an 1866 decree by the Roman Catholic Church that efforts should be made to establish Catholic schools for the children of newly freed slaves.

Educational opportunities for black children in Louisiana between Reconstruction and the post-World War II era were extremely limited. The state provided public education on a "separate but equal" basis, but in reality black schools were sorely underfunded, lacked adequate facilities, and were staffed by poorly trained teachers. Private parochial schools were often the only places where black children could receive a high-quality, consistent education in rural southern Louisiana.

The building that originally housed St. Joseph's was destroyed by a fallen tree in 1890, and the present building was built in 1892. The building was moved twice, first to the grounds of St. Michael's Church a mile away, and again in 1985 some 10 miles away. Although the setting has been changed, the building itself still conveys its 1892 appearance.

Most rural black schools constructed in Louisiana after the 1920s were built with funds donated by philanthropist Julius Rosenwald and matched by the local communities. St. Joseph's School is a reminder of the historic role of the Roman Catholic Church in black education in the region during the pre-Rosenwald era. [A 11/17/88, 88002651]

AVOYELLES PARISH

St. Paul Lutheran Church
North of Mansura on Louisiana Route 107
Mansura

Constructed in 1916, St. Paul Lutheran Church is important not only as a religious institution, but also in the educational history of the local black community. Educational opportunities for black students in rural Louisiana from Reconstruction to the post-World War II era were limited at best. After Reconstruction, the "separate but equal" public school system was instituted in the state. Black schools, however, were often underfunded and staffed with poorly trained instructors. Classes were often held in churches and lodges, with little money spent on actual school buildings. Schools run by religious denominations were among the few places where black children could receive a decent education.

Parochial schools such as the one at St. Paul Lutheran Church provided a good education with trained, motivated teachers. Initially grades one through seven were taught, and an eighth grade was added in the late 1920s. Teachers were sent by the Lutheran Mission Board and were usually pastors as well as teachers. They taught basic subjects such as history, geography. language, and arithmetic. Although the school primarily served children in Lutherville, students also came from Masura and Markville, each about two miles away. The school, which served as many as 80 students at its peak, operated in the building until the late 1930s. [A 3/1/90, 90000353]

CADDO PARISH

Central High School
1627 Weinstock Street
Shreveport

Constructed in 1917, Central High School was the first high school built for African Americans in Shreveport. Until Central High began operating in September 1917, Shreveport's black population had no opportunity to receive a high school education. Not only did Central High School meet this need within Shreveport, but it also drew students from surrounding parishes and East Texas. It was common practice for local families to rent out rooms to students, and the students boarded in Shreveport during the week in various rooming houses in the neighborhood. The student body grew from 144 in 1919 to more than 1,600 by 1940, graduating 14 students its first year and 215 in 1940. Central High graduated its last class in 1949, when the larger, newly built Booker T. Washington High School opened. Central became a junior high school at that time and is now

an elementary school. [A 5/16/91, 91000606]

CONCORDIA PARISH

Canebrake
Northeast of Ferriday on Louisiana Route 901
Ferriday

The Canebrake plantation complex consists of an overseer's house, slave cabins, and outbuildings including a barn and a chicken house dating from between 1840 and 1860. Between these years, Concordia Parish had become principally a planting province for the planters who resided in Natchez in grand town houses or suburban villa residences. The overseer's house, therefore, is the main house on the plantation and is much smaller in scale than one that would have been constructed for a resident planter.

Despite the modesty of the overseer's house, the relationship between the overseer and slaves is exhibited by physical separation of the house from the "quarter lot" in which the slave houses were located. In addition, the overseer's house is elevated on high brick piers. The five slave cabins remaining on the property are one-story, gable-roofed buildings with central chimneys and unglazed, shuttered windows. The slave cabins, their construction and physical relationship to the overseer's house, the barn, and the cotton fields provide a rare tangible resource for studying the living conditions of the slaves and overseer of a large antebellum cotton plantation. [A 8/29/82, 82002767]

EAST BATON ROUGE PARISH

Leland College
West of Baker off Louisiana Route 19
Baker

The extant buildings on the Leland College campus are important symbols of the development of black higher education in Louisiana. Four of the buildings date from sometime between 1923, when the school opened at the present location, and 1930. Leland College had a significant impact on the education of Louisiana African Americans. It was one of four institutions of higher learning for African Americans chartered in the state either during or shortly after Reconstruction. Leland allowed various upper elementary and secondary schools to become Leland auxiliaries. Graduates of these schools were accepted into Leland without examination, and good students were awarded scholarships. Leland's main efforts were directed toward training educators and ministers. The school's alumni held jobs as teachers, principals, and pastors throughout the state, thereby extending the institution's influence even further. Leland College's educational influence in the black community continued until it closed in 1960. [A 11/10/82, 82000433]

McKinley High School
1500 East Boulevard
Baton Rouge

McKinley High School was the first school in Baton Rouge constructed solely to provide a high school education to area black students. The only school where area African Americans could receive a secondary education from 1914 until McKinley's opening in 1927 was a joint elementary and high school named Baton Rouge High School. When McKinley was completed, the high school program of this school was phased out, and for many years McKinley High School served as the only secondary educational facility for African Americans within a 40-mile radius of Baton Rouge. In 1956 McKinley became an elementary school and then was phased out as a school in 1972. Since that time it has been used by various community groups such as the South Baton Rouge Community Action Service, the South Baton Rouge Health Referral Center, and the South Baton Rouge Head Start Center. [A 11/16/81, 81000292]

Southern University Archives Building
Southern University campus
Scotlandville

The Southern University Archives Building was the first building on the Southern University Baton Rouge campus and stands as a visual reminder of the institution's establishment in Scotlandville in 1914.

In 1879 Pinckney B. S. Pinchback (1837–1921), a black leader who became governor of Louisiana during the Reconstruction era, T. T. Allain (1846–1917), a black businessman and politician in Reconstruction government, and Henry Demas sponsored the movement in the Louisiana State Constitutional Convention (1879) that resulted in the establishment of an institution "for the education of persons of color" in the city of New Orleans. This institution was chartered as Southern University in January 1880 by the general assembly of the state of Louisiana. A 1912 legislative act authorized the closing and sale of the university and its reestablishment on a new site.

On March 9, 1914, Southern University was opened in Scotlandville under the presidency of Joseph Samuel Clark. What is now called the Southern University Archives Building was the only habitable building on the site. At various times this building has served many functions, including a home for the president and his family, conference center, office of the president and his

Holy Rosary Institute. Photo courtesy of Louisiana Department of Culture, Recreation, and Tourism (Jonathan Fricker).

assistants, girls' dormitory, dining hall, hospital, social center, and meeting place for the University Council. As such it was the focus of campus activity for several years. [CA 6/11/81, 81000294]

EAST FELICIANA PARISH

Port Hudson

Port Hudson and environs along U.S. Route 61
Port Hudson

Port Hudson represents the important role of black soldiers in the Civil War. In the spring of 1863 Port Hudson was one of the two Confederate bastions that denied Union forces control of the lower Mississippi. The attack on the Confederate defenses at Port Hudson by the last and Third Regiments of Native Guards on May 27, 1863, was the first major combat action by black troops in the Civil War. Though the attack was repulsed by Confederate forces, the courage of these black Union soldiers was crucial in establishing the success of what had previously been skeptically regarded as a an "experiment"–the recruitment of African Americans to fight for the Union and freedom. After Port Hudson a white Union officer confessed, "You have no idea how my prejudices with regard to negro troops have been dispelled by the battle of the other day. The brigade of negroes behaved magnificently and fought splendidly." Port Hudson was designated a National Historic Landmark on May 30, 1974. [A 5/30/74 NHL, 74002349]

The Carter Plantation. Photo courtesy of the Louisiana Department of Culture, Recreation, and Tourism (Tom Sharp).

LAFAYETTE PARISH

Holy Rosary Institute
421 Carmel Avenue
Lafayette

Holy Rosary Institute was founded in 1913 by the Reverend Philip Keller, a priest of the diocese of Galveston, Texas. At its inception Holy Rosary Institute provided vocational and technical education for black girls, thus embodying the educational philosophy of Booker T. Washington, who remained the dominant spokesperson for African Americans in the United States until his death in 1915. Since 1913 Holy Rosary Institute has been staffed by the Sisters of the Holy Family, a congregation of black religious women founded in New Orleans in the 1850s. Holy Rosary Institute also has served as a normal school to train teachers

for rural black schools and is presently one of the few remaining black Catholic high schools in the United States. [A 12/3/80, 80001734]

LIVINGSTON PARISH

Carter Plantation
Southwest of Springfield on State Route 1038
Springfield

The Carter Plantation is an early 19th-century house associated with a free black man named Thomas Freeman. In 1817 Freeman acquired the land where the property is located. Freeman's ownership and residence in the house are documented in a commissioner's report issued in 1820. According to an article in the *Hammond Vindicator*, Freeman was the first African American to record a legal transaction in the Greensburg district of east Louisiana, and therefore the first black man to own property in what is now Livingston Parish. The article also states that Freeman was a man of considerable wealth and owned a large amount of property. In 1838 Freeman sold the land including the house to W. L. Breed, an important local political figure. [CA 2/23/79, 79001069]

NATCHITOCHES PARISH

Badin-Roque House
South of Natchez
Natchez

Built in the early 19th century, the Badin-Roque House is associated with the Isle Brevelle colony of mulattoes known as the Cane River Creoles of color. The immediate progenitors of this community were Claude Thomas Pierre Metoyer, a Frenchman, and Marie Therese Coincoin (1742–1816?), his slave concubine whom he freed in 1783 (see also Maison de Marie Therese). The several children born of this Franco-African alliance were the beginnings of the Cane River colony of Creoles of color, mixed-blood African Americans famous for owning vast, rich plantations in Louisiana. In the 1850s the Badin-Roque House was occupied by nuns and served as a school for the Cane River Creoles of color. [CA 6/6/80, 80001739]

Magnolia Plantation
North of Derry on Louisiana Route 119
Derry

Set along the Cane River among open flat farmland, the 10-acre Magnolia Plantation complex includes a plantation house, an overseer's house, a row of slave quarters, and a barn containing a cotton press.

The plantation was owned by Ambrose Lecomte, one of the largest slaveholders in Natchitoches Parish, and the largest producer of cotton. At the time of the 1850 census, Lecomte had 182 slaves.

Of the original slave dwellings, eight remain in a double row in the southeast portion of the plantation complex. The buildings are brick, two-room, galleried houses with central chimneys and gable parapets. Each fireplace has an iron lintel.

The quality of construction and architectural refinement exhibited in the slave quarters at Magnolia is extremely high. Moreover, it is unusual for a plantation to retain any slave dwellings at all, and even more uncommon for them to survive in sufficient numbers to constitute a complex, as they do at Magnolia. [CA 3/7/79, 79001071]

Maison de Marie Therese
One mile northwest of Bermuda
Bermuda

The Maison de Marie Therese, a five-room, raised, hipped-roof cottage, was the residence of Marie Therese Coincoin (1742–1816?), a black woman who founded a network of plantations owned by the Cane River region's famous "Creoles of color." Marie Therese Coincoin was born a slave of Louis Juchereau de St. Denis, the founder of Natchitoches. After St. Denis's death in 1744, she remained the slave of his family until 1778, when she was purchased and freed by Claude Thomas Pierre Metoyer, a Frenchman in Natchitoches. She had had several children by him. Marie Therese remained his mistress until 1786, when they ended their alliance and he gave her the land that is the site of the Maison de Marie Therese. Thereafter, she expanded her landholdings and gradually achieved the manumission of her children and grandchildren. With her death she left her descendants a comfortable estate, consisting of at least 16 slaves and more than 1,000 arpents (an old French unit of land measurement approximately equal to an acre) of land. Marie Therese's sons and daughters expanded the property she left into the vast, rich plantations on Cane River (see also Melrose Plantation). [CA 12/6/79, 79001070]

Melrose Plantation
Louisiana Route 119 off Louisiana 493
Melrose

Yucca Plantation, known after 1875 as Melrose Plantation, was established in northwestern Louisiana by an African American named Marie Therese Coincoin. Coincoin had been a slave to a Frenchman in Natchitoches and was freed in 1778. As the mistress of Yucca Plantation, she was a property owner and a wealthy businesswoman at a time when most black women were slaves and most white women had no identity apart from their husbands. The plantation contains what may well be the oldest buildings of French Creole design built by African Americans, for the use of African Americans, in the United States. The original plantation buildings—the Yucca House, the Ghana House, the Big House, and the Barn—were built by Marie Therese. In 1833 the large plantation house, now called Melrose, was built by Marie Therese's grandson, Louis. On the whole, the buildings on the plantation reflect Coincoin's independence and pride in her heritage (see also Maison de Marie Therese). The property was designated a National Historic Landmark on April 16, 1984. [CA 6/13/72 NHL, 72000556]

ORLEANS PARISH

Congo Square
Intersection of Rampart and St. Peter streets
New Orleans

African Americans have played a significant role in the history of New Orleans. While there are many historic properties associated with them, Congo Square is the only known site associated with the retention of their African heritage. A parcel of public land located just across from the French Quarter, Congo Square is where Sunday slave dances were performed in antebellum times. Early on these dances and the accompanying music were African, but by the 1830s and 1840s they revealed an American influence.

Several accounts exist of the slave dances at Congo Square; the most well-known is that of Benjamin Latrobe, who stumbled upon the scene one day in 1819 and writes of hearing "an extraordinary noise," which he first supposed was made by "horses trampling on a wooden floor." He discovered instead "a crowd of some 5 or 600 persons assembled in an open space or public square." Latrobe describes the dances, the instruments, and the singing, concluding "the allowed amusements of Sunday have, it seems, perpetuated here, those of Africa among its inhabitants."

Scholars have noted strong similarities between Latrobe's description of the instruments used and native African instruments and believe that the circular formations that he noted in the dances represent the different tribes of Africa. Various accounts of the dances in subsequent years document increasing American influence in these gatherings, although some purely African elements exist. The last known account of these gatherings came in 1851, the year in which the site became the Place D'Armes, where the military drilled on Sundays. It is believed, however, that the dances continued until the eve of the Civil War.

In 1930 the Municipal Auditorium was constructed abutting the square; the site, however, is still a visually distinct entity and remains, as it was in antebellum times, an open public space. [A 1/28/93, 92001763]

James H. Dillard House
571 Audubon Street
New Orleans

White educator James Hardy Dillard (1856–1940) lived in this house around 1908, when he assumed the directorship of the Negro Rural School Fund from 1908 to 1931. In 1917 Dillard became president of the Slater Fund, a philanthropic foundation that supported county training institutes for black teachers. In addition to his work for the Jeanes and Slater Funds, Dillard was a member of the Southern Education Board, an official of the Phelps-Stokes Fund, and a trustee for some black colleges. He was also active in child welfare and free kindergarten associations, and after becoming president of the public library, he constructed a branch for African Americans. Dillard received many honors, among them honorary doctor of law degrees from Sewanee and Harvard. When Straight University and New Orleans University merged, the new school was named Dillard University. When he retired in 1931, he had contributed significantly to the improvement of black public schools in the South. The property was designated a National Historic Landmark on December 2, 1974. [B 12/2/74 NHL, 74000929]

Flint-Goodridge Hospital of Dillard University
Intersection of Louisiana Avenue and LaSalle Street
New Orleans

Founded in 1911, the Flint-Goodridge Hospital was established and constructed as the medical unit of the newly created Dillard University. This hospital was the only institution in Louisiana in the 1930s offering medical internships to black students, and it was the only place in the state where black nurses could receive professional training. From its opening, the 88-bed hospital was fully accredited, with a staff consisting of 19 white doctors, mostly teachers, and 29 active black staff doctors. Except for Charity Hospital, which served indigent persons, Flint-Goodrich was the only hospital in New Orleans that admitted black patients. The hospital made especially significant contributions to tuberculosis testing and treatment, infant and maternal care, and the treatment of syphilis. [A 1/13/89, 88003139]

St. James AME Church
222 North Roman Street
New Orleans

The St. James African Methodist Episcopal (AME) Church traces its origins to 1844, when a group of free blacks organized themselves into a religious society under the name the AME Church of New Orleans. This action was in response to mistreatment of the group's members by the Wesley Chapel Church, a white congregation that accepted free blacks as members. The new congregation was headed by Thomas Doughty, who spearheaded efforts to construct a permanent building for the congregation. The present church was completed in 1851, and in that year Doughty traveled to the Indiana Conference of the AME Church to bring in the church as a member. He was cordially received and was appointed the first pastor of St. James AME Church. Originally designed with a combination of Greek Revival and Gothic Revival features, in 1903 it was substantially remodeled in the late Victorian Gothic style. [C 10/26/82, 82000449]

St. Peter AME Church

1201 Cadiz Street

New Orleans

St. Peter African Methodist Episcopal (AME) Church is the oldest black congregation in the New Orleans area. The building was constructed in 1858 as the Jefferson City Methodist Episcopal (ME) Church South. African Americans worshiped with the predominantly white Jefferson City ME congregation until after the Civil War, when they were no longer permitted to do so. On March 31, 1877, the white congregation sold the building to the St. Peter AME Church, a black congregation organized in 1850 that Jefferson City's former black members had joined. From its beginning, St. Peter AME played an important role in the black community. In the 1920s the church housed nursing classes taught by the staff of the Touro Infirmary. During the 1930s it provided space for secretarial and business classes. It also made space available for an employment office associated with the relief programs of the New Deal, especially the Works Progress Administration. During the civil rights movement of the 1960s, the church provided classes in voter registration taught by students from Tulane and Loyola Universities. [CA 3/21/79, 79001077]

RAPIDES PARISH

Arna Wendell Bontemps House

1327 3rd Street

Alexandria

This modest Queen Anne Revival style cottage was the birthplace of writer Arna Bontemps, a major figure in the African American literary movement known as the Harlem Renaissance. Bontemps lived in the house from his birth in 1902 until 1906, when his family relocated to California. Bontemps identified strongly with his childhood home, however, returning to the South later in his life and including specific references to the house in his writing.

After earning his bachelor's degree in California in 1923, Bontemps accepted a teaching position at the Harlem Academy in New York, where he remained until 1931. It was during this time that he first published, contributing a poem to the National Association for the Advancement of Colored People's periodical, *Crisis,* in 1924. In 1927 Bontemps was awarded the magazine's poetry prize. In 1926 and 1927 he was awarded the Alexander Pushkin Poetry Prize, and in 1931 he published his first novel, *God Sends Sunday.* Bontemps taught for some time in Huntsville, Alabama, and in Chicago and earned his master's degree in library science from the University of Chicago in 1943. In the same year he became head librarian at Fisk University in Nashville, a position he held until 1965. He spent the final years of his life as professor at the University of Illinois and Yale University, and finally as writer-in-residence at Fisk.

Bontemps's works are numerous and diverse. He wrote 25 books, including novels, children's books, biographies, histories, collections of poems, and plays. He also wrote, edited, or coedited works with other notable Harlem Renaissance figures such as Countee Cullen and Langston Hughes. His childhood home in Alexandria, his early years in Louisiana, and his experiences in the South figure prominently in his work. In the week before his death, Bontemps had made arrangements to travel back to the Alexandria home as part of his research for his autobiography. It would have been at least his second trip back to the house after leaving in 1906. The trip never took place, however, and Bontemps died at his Nashville home on June 4, 1973. His childhood home, which formed such an important part of his identity, is now a museum dedicated to his life and work. [B 9/13/93, 93000886]

ST. CHARLES PARISH

Kenner and Kugler Cemeteries Archeological District
Address restricted
Norco

Kenner and Kugler cemeteries are black burial plots dating from the early 1800s to 1929. They were probably established during the antebellum period as slave cemeteries for the Roseland and Hermitage plantations. Both sites are located on land purchased by the federal government in 1929 for construction of the Bonnet Carré Spillway, a flood control measure for the Mississippi River and its tributaries. The Kenner Cemetery, located on the former Roseland Plantation, is marked by iron and wooden crosses. The Kugler Cemetery, located on the former Hermitage Plantation, is marked by crosses and a metal fence. The artifacts collected from these sites include coffin furniture, coffins, grave markers, cultural remains, and human remains. The two sites have the potential to yield important information about demography, variations in mortuary practices, morbidity, mortality, nutrition, and quality of life of African Americans during the antebellum and Reconstruction eras. [AD 10/16/87, 87001762]

ST. JOHN THE BAPTIST PARISH

Evergreen Plantation
Louisiana Route 18 southeast of
Fiftymile Point
Wallace

This plantation is one of the largest and most intact antebellum plantation complexes in the South. Thirty-seven historic buildings remain on the property, most dating from the antebellum period.

Most notable is a double row of 22 slave cabins. The cabins line both sides of an oak allée and are spaced regularly at 55-foot intervals. Twenty are two-room cabins, while the middle cabin in each row contains four rooms. All are of frame construction with wide drop siding on the facade, interior chimneys, and exposed beams on the gallery and interior. Although the 1860 census lists the owners of the plantation as having 103 slaves in 48 dwellings, an 1876 map shows 22 cabins in the same configuration and location as they are today. While the slave quarters and other plantation buildings have had some of their original building materials replaced over the years, the buildings generally maintain their historic appearance. For its significance in the history of American agriculture, Evergreen Plantation was designated a National Historic Landmark on April 27, 1992. [CA 9/25/91, 91001386]

TANGIPAHOA PARISH

Tangipahoa Parish Training School Dormitory
Off Louisiana Route 38
Kentwood

Tangipahoa Parish Training School, the first county training school in the entire South, pioneered a black educational program that included more than 300 similar schools throughout the South by 1927. A county training school was centrally located and provided instruction for black children in grades one through 10 (or 11) with emphasis on vocational and industrial education at the secondary level. It also provided teacher training to enable its graduates to teach at the rural black schools in the parish. From its founding in 1911 until 1955, it was known as the Tangipahoa Parish Training School and for most of this period was under the leadership of Oliver Wendell

Dillon. From 1955 until 1969, its name was the O. W. Dillon Memorial School. In 1969, with the arrival of integration, it became Kentwood Elementary School. The Old Dormitory, built in the early 1920s, is one of the two oldest remaining buildings associated with Tangipahoa School. It remained a dormitory until 1951, when it was renovated and converted to classrooms. [A 7/27/79, 79001091]

TENSAS PARISH

St. Joseph Historic District
Roughly bounded by Panola Avenue and Front, Hickory, 4th, and Pauline streets
St. Joseph

The St. Joseph Historic District contains 99 buildings that make up the Mississippi River levee town of St. Joseph as it existed 50 years ago. St. Joseph has been the Tensas Parish seat since the parish was created in 1843. Tensas Parish was a Republican stronghold during Reconstruction. About 90 percent of its population and the vast majority of Tensas Republicans were African Americans.

The district is historically significant as the site of an event that led to a nationally publicized and federally investigated race riot in nearby Waterproof in 1878 in which 36 African Americans were killed. The riot at Waterproof occurred because black Republicans had held a preelection meeting at the St. Joseph Courthouse. This meeting, composed entirely of African Americans, was led by Alfred Fairfax, a black Baptist preacher, aspirant for Congress, and the leader of black Republicans in Tensas Parish. Neighboring parishes and Mississippians responded to the Tensas Democrats' call for assistance in putting down this attempt at "Negro rule." This action by the white Democrats led to violence. Fairfax, who had escaped unharmed, wrote a letter to President Hayes, who turned the matter over to the Justice Department. The incident demonstrated the racial political unrest prevalent during Reconstruction. [CA 12/10/80, 80001763]

MAINE

CUMBERLAND COUNTY

Green Memorial AME Zion Church
46 Sheridan Street
Portland

The Abyssinian Congregational Church and Society, now Green Memorial African Methodist Episcopal (AME) Zion Church, was formed in 1842 with the union of two black fellowship groups: the Abyssinian Society, incorporated in 1828; and the Fourth Congregational Church, founded in 1835. The congregation moved to its present location after the construction of this church building in 1914. At the time of its construction, the church was considered one of the most prestigious buildings ever erected for a black congregation in New England. In 1943 the church was renamed in honor of Moses Green, an African American who was born a slave and worked for 52 years at Union Station in Portland, Maine. The Green AME Zion Church is the oldest established black congregation in Maine. [A 1/17/73, 73000115]

John B. Russwurm House
238 Ocean Avenue
Portland

The Russwurm House is the only surviving building closely associated with John Brown Russwurm (1799–1851), who resided there intermittently from 1812 to 1827. Russwurm graduated from Bowdoin College in Brunswick in 1826, becoming the second African American in the nation to receive a college degree. In 1827 in New York City Russwurm founded and co-edited *Freedom's Journal*, the nation's first black newspaper. The newspaper supported both abolition and assimilation at a time when most white abolitionists favored black emigration. In 1829 Russwurm emigrated to Liberia and served as superintendent of education and then colonial secretary, while simultaneously editing the *Liberian Herald*. In 1834 he left Liberia to accept the governorship of the neighboring colony of Las Palmas, under the jurisdiction of the Maryland Colonization Society. Russwurm was the first black governor of a black overseas colony. During his 17-year tenure, Russwurm outlawed slavery, instituted education for females as well as males, and eventually merged Las Palmas with the republic of Liberia. [B 7/21/83, 83000450]

Harriet Beecher Stowe House

63 Federal Street
Brunswick

Completed in 1807, this house was for a time the residence of noted author Harriet Beecher Stowe (1811–96). Harriet Elizabeth Beecher, daughter of well-known Congregational minister Lyman Beecher, was born in Litchfield, Connecticut, on June 14, 1811. In 1832 the family moved to Cincinnati, Ohio, where Lyman Beecher became president of the newly founded Lane Theological Seminary. In 1836 Harriet married Calvin Ellis Stowe, a professor at Lane, who later became a professor at Bowdoin College in Brunswick, Maine. Though the Stowes remained in Brunswick for only two years (1851–52), it was here that Stowe wrote her famous novel on slavery, *Uncle Tom's Cabin* (1852).

John Brown Russwurm (1799–1851). Engraving courtesy of the Smithsonian Institution.

Published as a serial in 1851 in the *National Era,* an antislavery newspaper, and in book form the following year, *Uncle Tom's Cabin* was written primarily as a humanitarian appeal against slavery. Its antislavery message provoked strong reactions throughout the South. The effect of *Uncle Tom's Cabin* was so tremendous that it has been said the Civil War began at 63 Federal Street. Since Brunswick's General Joshua Chamberlain accepted Lee's surrender at Appomattox, the Civil War is also said to have ended in Brunswick.

In response to southern criticism of her portrayal of southern slavery in *Uncle Tom's Cabin,* Stowe wrote *A Key to Uncle Tom's Cabin* (1853), a collection of factual material on slavery intended to justify the charges implied in the novel. With her next work, *Dred: A Tale of Dismal Swamp* (1856), she argued that slave labor contributed to the wastefulness and inevitable deterioration of southern society. After the success of this novel, she led the life of an active writer.

After the Civil War, Stowe purchased an estate in Florida, where she spent many winters. Following the death of her husband in 1886, she lived in seclusion in Hartford, Connecticut, until her own death on July 1, 1896. Her home in Brunswick was designated a National Historic Landmark on December 29, 1962. [B 10/15/66 NHL, 66000091]

MARYLAND

African Methodist Episcopal Church
Intersection of Decatur and Frederick
streets
Cumberland

The African Methodist Episcopal
(AME) Church in Cumberland was built
by a group of free black residents of the
town. The group, who had for many
years worshiped from the balcony of the
Centre Street ME Church, decided in
1847 to leave the predominantly white
congregation and build their own church.
By 1848 a brick building had been completed. This first church was enlarged and
rebuilt in 1871 and enlarged once again
in 1875 in response to growing membership. The present building was built in
1892 in the Methodist configuration,
with the sanctuary on the second floor
and Sunday school rooms below. This
substantial building reflects the level of
prosperity reached by the black community in 1892, as well as the prominent place
of the church in the life of the community. [CA 4/20/79, 79001105]

ANNE ARUNDEL COUNTY

Douglass Summer House
3200 Wayman Avenue
Highland Beach

Built in 1894–95, the Douglass
Summer House is associated with
Frederick Douglass (1817–95) and the
unique African American resort community of Highland Beach. It is one of the
first two cottages built in Highland
Beach, an exclusive resort for wealthy and
prominent African Americans established
in 1893 by Douglass's son, Major Charles
Douglass.

Douglass's summer house at Highland
Beach serves as a reminder of his many
accomplishments as an abolitionist, civil
rights and women's rights advocate, and
statesman (see also Frederick Douglass
National Historic Site, District of
Columbia). The Douglass Summer
House is symbolically and visually the
cornerstone of Highland Beach.

As a summer resort, Highland Beach
attracted prominent African Americans,
particularly from Washington, D.C.
Among the early residents were Paul
Laurence Dunbar, the famous poet and
novelist; Robert Terrell, the first African
American municipal judge in
Washington, D.C.; and Terrell's wife,
Mary Church Terrell, educator, civil liber-
tarian, and author of *A Colored Woman in
a White World*. Frequent visitors to the
resort included Booker T. Washington,
educator and founder of Tuskegee

Frederick Douglass (1817–1895). Engraving courtesy of the National Park Service History Collection.

Institute in Alabama; Paul Robeson, world-famous singer and actor; and poet Langston Hughes.

Major Douglass named the longest street for Frederick Douglass and the two principal streets for Reconstruction-era friends of Frederick Douglass, Bruce Wayman and John Mercer Langston. At the death of Major Douglass in 1921, the responsibility for maintaining Highland Beach fell to his son, Haley Douglass, who long served as a commissioner and mayor. As founders and longtime residents of Highland Beach, the Douglass family has left an indelible mark on the region. Today Highland Beach remains a unique community in African American cultural history. [A 2/20/92, 92000069]

Grassland
Maryland Route 32
Annapolis junction

The Grassland plantation consists of a brick main house, a frame slave house, a stone smokehouse, a frame storage shed, a harness shed, a corncrib, and the ruins of a bank barn. The buildings were erected between 1852 and 1854 by the plantation slaves. Details on the construction of the house and outbuildings are documented in the journal of William Anderson, the original plantation owner. Slaves not only assembled the building materials, but made and fired bricks, hewed timbers, split rails for fences, dug an ice pond, and constructed a dam and icehouse.

Architecturally, the house and outbuildings present a well-preserved example of the type of plantation complex typical of Anne Arundel County during the time of its construction. The survival of such a variety of buildings associated with a plantation of this sort is rare. The brick-nogged frame slave cabin is one of perhaps fewer than a dozen remaining in Maryland. Grassland stands as a testament to the building craft and skill of black slaves in Maryland. [CA 9/13/84, 84001331]

Mt. Moriah African Methodist Episcopal Church
84 Franklin Street
Annapolis

Mt. Moriah African Methodist Episcopal Church lies within the boundaries of the Annapolis Historic District. Built in 1874 in the Victorian Gothic ecclesiastical style, Mt. Moriah is the only building in the Annapolis Historic District associated with black history that retains architectural integrity. The congregation was formed of free blacks by 1803 and possibly as early as 1799. Churches were among the first formally organized institutions created by free blacks. Because African Americans were excluded from many areas of mainstream American life, the church often provided spiritual and moral leadership and the social, civic, and cultural services that sustained the black community. [CA 1/25/73, 73000891]

Stanton Center
92 West Washington Street
Annapolis

The first public school for black children in Anne Arundel County was founded in 1865 by the Freedmen's Bureau. The Stanton School was the second, having been organized around 1868 by trustees who purchased property outside of Annapolis to house the school. The trustees of the Stanton School were to oversee the school until the state instituted a public education system for black children. The trustees were directed by the patrons, supporters, and subscribers of the school. This formal organization of the school was significant. Before the Civil War, the responsibility for educating black children fell to various churches and fraternal organizations in the black community, and no formal curriculum or system of administration existed.

Between 1881 and 1883, the trustees built a two-story frame building on the present site on Washington Street. The building was used as an elementary school. Around the turn of the century, the first stage of the present brick building was completed. Containing eight classrooms, it continued to be used as an elementary school until 1919, when a high school program was added. Thus the Stanton School became the first black high school in Anne Arundel County.

The building housed both primary and secondary classes until 1932, when

Bates High School was constructed in Annapolis. In 1938, with the construction of a new elementary school, the Stanton School was converted to a junior high school, and it remained in this capacity until integration of the county's school system in the mid-1960s.

In 1974 the county board of education turned the school over for use as a community center. The Stanton School building remains a monument to the support local black residents gave to education. In its continued use as a community center, it remains an active part of the community. [CA 12/1/83, 83003627]

BALTIMORE COUNTY

Mt. Gilboa Chapel
Intersection of Oella and Westchester avenues
Oella

Mt. Gilboa Chapel is the site where Oella's most famous resident, Benjamin Banneker, worshiped and attended school. Banneker was born on a farm in Oella in 1731. A self-taught mathematician, he published an almanac from 1796 to 1806 for which he made all the astronomical calculations and weather predictions. Among Banneker's many achievements is his work as a surveyor in preparation for the establishment of the capital city at Washington, D.C. Because Banneker's farm has been subdivided and his exact birthplace is unknown, Mt. Gilboa is the sole above-ground memorial to Banneker in Oella. Although the present building was not built until 1869, the church has served the same community of black families since the 18th century. Today this community continues to look to Mt. Gilboa as its central focus and an important local landmark (see also Benjamin Banneker: SW 9 Intermediate Boundary Stone, Arlington County, Virginia). [CB 10/21/76, 76000978]

St. John's Church
7538 Bellona Avenue
Ruxton

Built in 1886, St. John's Church, along with its accompanying parsonage and social hall, was created as a center for social and religious interaction for the black community in the Bare Hills–Ruxton area of Baltimore County. The congregation was formed in the 1830s but did not acquire the site until 1883. The modest Gothic Revival style building with Queen Anne detailing is typical of churches built in rural Maryland during the late 19th century. Most of the members of the congregation were black domestics and servants who worked for the affluent white population whose houses bordered the church complex.

Despite financial strains, the church managed to stay open and active until the 1950s. At this time changes in transportation patterns, the development of other churches, and the fading practice of keeping live-in servants thinned the congregation's population until the doors were closed permanently. St. John's remains essentially intact as an example of craftsmanship in a late 19th-century rural church building. [CA 3/15/82, 82002807]

BALTIMORE (INDEPENDENT CITY)

Frederick Douglass High School
1601 North Calhoun Street
Baltimore

The old Frederick Douglass High School is significant for its association with the development of high-quality instruction for black children within the Baltimore City public school system. Designed by Owens and Sisco, Architects, and built in 1923–24, it was the first public high school building in the city specifically erected for black students, and believed to be the first in the state of

Maryland. It was also the only secondary school in the Baltimore area open to black students through the 1930s. In its provision of space for "lower" vocational training and classrooms for "higher" academic pursuit, the building's design embodied the prevailing philosophy toward black education at the time. Douglass High remained a "colored" high school until 1954, when the Baltimore school system adopted the desegregation policy mandated by the U.S. Supreme Court, and the high school moved to another location. [A 5/18/89, 89000412]

Douglass Place
516–524 South Dallas Street
Baltimore

Douglass Place is significant for its association with Frederick Douglass (1817–95), famed 19th-century abolitionist, newspaper editor, and statesman. Douglass constructed the five two-story, two-bay brick row houses in 1892 as rental housing for poor African Americans in the Fells Point neighborhood in Baltimore. The property represents Douglass's connection with the neighborhood, where he resided from the 1820s until 1838.

Evidence suggests that Douglass purchased the property, which is located on the site where the Dallas Street Station Methodist Episcopal Church (1773) once stood, for sentimental reasons. Douglass had attended the meetinghouse while he lived in Fells Point as a house servant, on and off, from the 1820s to 1838. From within the walls of the church he received encouragement to believe he had a future in the struggle to better the conditions of African Americans. After the Civil War the black congregation had abandoned the church and moved to another location. Douglass purchased the property for $1,800, razed the church, and "built

housing to replace some of the miserable shacks in which Fells Point African Americans had lived on Strawberry Alley, now renamed Dallas Street." The housing project proved not to be a paying proposition, particularly during the economic slump that followed the panic of 1893. [B 9/15/83, 83004214]

Orchard Street United Methodist Church
510 Orchard Street
Baltimore

Founded as Metropolitan Methodist Episcopal Church, Orchard Street United Methodist Church was built in 1837 as a place of worship for the local black community. Before the construction of the church, Truman Le Pratt, a West Indian, held prayer meetings in his Orchard Street house. Established in 1825, the group grew quickly. Le Pratt, recognizing the group's need for a church, committed money toward its construction. The land on which the church stands was granted by brothers George and Henry Moore, who employed Le Pratt's wife. Despite setbacks caused initially by the brothers' failure to draw up a deed and later by their deaths, the group secured full title to the church and property in 1840.

The building, which displays a mix of Romanesque and Gothic Revival design elements, was enlarged in 1853, 1865, and 1882 to accommodate the growing congregation and the addition of a sabbath school. The Orchard Street United Methodist Church is the oldest surviving building constructed by African Americans in the city of Baltimore. [CA 11/12/75, 75002096]

Public School No. 111
Intersection of North Carrollton Avenue and Riggs Road
Baltimore

Built in 1889 as Colored School No. 9, the Francis Ellen Harper School (now Public School No. 111) is one of the few surviving schools in Baltimore built for black children and staffed by black teachers. The city of Baltimore began providing public education for black students in 1867, and it maintained separate school systems for white and black students until the 1950s. The school was named for Francis Ellen Harper (1825–1911), a Baltimore-born black poet, lecturer, and reformer. As a child in Baltimore, Harper attended the Free Negro School conducted by her uncle. As a member of the Women's Christian Temperance Union, she stressed the need for education for black children. The school building is a simple Romanesque brick building with an ornately detailed brick front facade. [CA 9/25/79, 79003219]

CECIL COUNTY

Snow Hill Site
Address restricted
Port Deposit

Situated within the town of Port Deposit, Maryland, Snow Hill was established as a community for free black merchants and laborers as early as 1847. Martenet's 1858 map of Cecil County identifies Snow Hill as a "colored" community and shows eight residences and one church, the African Methodist Episcopal Church. The official atlas of Cecil County made in 1877 shows the "Colored Methodist Church," some 20 houses, and 46 lots. Land deeds show that the property was owned by whites and leased to free black residents of the area under 99-year renewable lease arrangements. Few of Snow Hill's residents, however, remained in the area for a long period of time.

Archeological investigation of the area produced many 19th-century artifacts and revealed foundations of several buildings and several standing sections of a retaining wall that once stretched along the hillside behind the community. Very little is known about free black settlements in this area of Maryland. This small free black community situated within a thriving white trading town remained intact until the end of the 19th century. [D 4/27/84, 84001758]

DORCHESTER COUNTY

Stanley Institute
South of Cambridge on Maryland
Route 16
Cambridge

Established on its present location in 1867, the Stanley Institute is one of Maryland's oldest schools organized and maintained by the black community. The school was located near Church Creek in Dorchester County. The building, known as Rock School, was moved and reconstructed on its present site in 1867. Its present name was adopted in honor of the school's first board of trustees president, Ezekrial Stanley.

For many years before the establishment of the Rock Methodist Church in the late 19th century, the Stanley Institute served as both church and school. The one-story, gable-roof building is typical of one-room schoolhouses built from the early 19th to the early 20th centuries. [A 9/11/75, 75000888]

HARFORD COUNTY

Berkley School
Junction of Castleton Road and Maryland
Route 623
Darlington

While responsibility for the construction of black schools in the South after the Civil War generally was that of the Freedmen's Bureau, that organization was not able to provide satisfactory facilities in

McComas Institute. Photo courtesy of the Maryland Historical Trust (Natalie Shivers).

Maryland, leaving many communities to seek their own solutions. The Berkley School was constructed largely through the efforts of the prominent black Peaker (also known as Paca) family.

On January 8, 1868, Joseph Peaker and other trustees of the Mount Zion African Methodist Episcopal Church sold one-quarter acre of land to five trustees for the purpose of establishing a black school. The Berkley School, a simple, one-story frame building, was constructed in 1868 for black children in Harford County.

As originally constructed, the building had two floors. The ground floor housed the school, and the upper floor was used by the Hosanna Church. In the early 20th century the upper floor of the building was destroyed by a hurricane, but the first-floor schoolroom survived relatively unscathed. The Berkley School still stands as the first black school in Harford

County and one of the few, in any part of the slaveowning South, built and controlled by African Americans for the purpose of educating black children. [A 7/22/88, 88001011]

McComas Institute
North of Joppa on Singer Road
Joppa

The McComas Institute in Joppa stands as the single most important property in the history of black education in Harford County. Constructed in 1867, it is one of three area schools built by the Freedmen's Bureau after the Civil War and the only one that survives intact. The two-room, one-story frame vernacular building exhibits Greek Revival style influences.

In 1860 Harford County had 4,800 black inhabitants and 1,800 slaves, but before the Civil War there were no publicly supported schools for African

Don S. S. Goodloe House. Photo courtesy of the Prince George's County Historic Preservation Commission (Howard S. Berger).

Americans. The Freedmen's Bureau (formally known as the Bureau of Refugees, Freedmen, and Abandoned Lands) was established on November 9, 1864, to serve the needs of people dislocated by the Civil War, providing them with food, clothing, fuel, medical care, and education. The bureau gave direct aid to establish the first school system for African Americans in Maryland, providing materials, equipment, and money for construction, rental, and repair of schoolhouses.

George and Mary Ann Johnson, described as "colored" in one deed, sold the one acre of land on which the institute was situated for $30 to a group of five trustees "in trust for the purpose of erecting or allowing to be erected thereon a schoolhouse for the use, benefit and education of the Colored People of Harford County."

The Freedmen's Bureau was abolished in 1872, and the Harford County Board of Education took over the support of the bureau's schools. The McComas Institute functioned as a black school until the 1930s, when it officially closed. For some time it has been owned and used by the neighboring Mount Zion Methodist Church. [A 9/8/80, 80001819]

PRINCE GEORGE'S COUNTY

Don S. S. Goodloe House
13809 Jericho Park Road
Bowie

The Don S. S. Goodloe House, a 1915–16 Colonial Revival style building veneered with brick, is significant for its association with Don Speed Smith Goodloe, the first principal of the Maryland Normal and Industrial School. The school, now Bowie State University, was Maryland's first black postsecondary school. As principal of the school from its opening in 1911 until 1921, Goodloe directed and managed this public institution through its formative years, a period characterized by the state's unwillingness to provide adequate funding for the housing and training of the students, while two white normal schools under the state were well funded.

Forced to provide his own housing, Goodloe had this large and commodious house built to accommodate not only his family, but also students for which he received additional income from the state. The house was designed by John A. Moore, a black architect from Washington, D.C. Goodloe occupied the house until his death in 1959. The Goodloe house is the only building from the college's early period still standing. [B 10/13/88, 88001900]

WASHINGTON COUNTY

John Brown's Headquarters
Chestnut Grove Road
Samples Manor

This building, now known as the Kennedy Farmhouse, was the headquarters from which John Brown planned and executed his raid on the federal armory at Harpers Ferry in October 1859. Other than the engine house at Harpers Ferry where Brown staged his final defense, the Kennedy Farmhouse is the building most closely associated with the raid.

Brown arrived in Maryland from Kansas in 1859 and, along with a small band of followers, set out to locate a headquarters for his campaign. He rented the two-story farmhouse located approximately seven miles from Harpers Ferry and owned by the heirs of William Booth Kennedy. Giving his name as "Isaac Smith," Brown posed as a cattle buyer from New York while he spent the next three months pondering maps and vital statistics. He was joined by his family and a few more followers. He began to stockpile military hardware, including 15 boxes of Sharps rifles and Maynard revolvers and hundreds of pikes with which to arm the liberated slaves.

On October 16, 1859, his small band seized the armory and took several hostages. The following day, Colonel Robert E. Lee arrived with a company of United States Marines and cornered Brown and his men in a fire engine house. Surrendering, Brown was brought to trial at Charles Town, Virginia (now West Virginia), for insurrection and treason, found guilty, and hanged on December 2, 1859.

The Kennedy Farmhouse stands as a reminder of the raid, which intensified southern fears of slave rebellion and suspicion of northern intentions, exacerbating the sectional strife that resulted in the Civil War. The Kennedy Farmhouse was designated a National Historic Landmark on November 7, 1973 (see also John Brown Cabin, Miami County, Kansas; John Brown Farm, Essex County, New York; John Brown House, Franklin County, Pennsylvania; and Harpers Ferry National Historical Park and Jefferson County Courthouse, Jefferson County, West Virginia). [B 11/7/73 NHL, 73000941]

MASSACHUSETTS

BERKSHIRE COUNTY

William E. B. Du Bois Boyhood Homesite
Massachusetts Route 23
Great Barrington

This site incorporates the ruins of the boyhood home and adult retreat of William Edward Burghardt (W. E. B.) Du Bois (1868–1963), one of America's most outstanding scholars and black leaders. W. E. B. Du Bois felt a strong attachment to his family home at Great Barrington, where he spent the first 17 years of his life. From 1928 to 1954, he owned the "House of the Black Burghardts" and spent his spare time and quiet moments there. The Burghardt property had been in his family for more than 200 years.

Du Bois was the first African American to receive a Ph.D. degree from Harvard University. Published in 1896, Du Bois's dissertation, *The Suppression of the African Slave Trade,* became the first volume in the Harvard Historical Studies. In 1896 he became a sociology instructor at the University of Pennsylvania and carried out a pioneering sociological investigation that became his second book, *The Philadelphia Negro.* From 1897 to 1910, Du Bois taught at Atlanta University, where he wrote and edited 10 of the 16 monographs of the Atlanta University Studies. He wrote more than 20 books, including *Dusk of Dawn, The Souls of Black Folk, The Quest of the Silver Fleece,* and *Black Reconstruction in America,* as well as several hundred articles and pamphlets.

Equally important, Du Bois was one of the founders of the Niagara Movement and the National Association for the Advancement of Colored People (NAACP), two organizations founded to further the cause of black equality in the United States. As editor of the NAACP's official publication, *The Crisis,* Du Bois protested disenfranchisement, poor housing, and discrimination. He also fostered pan-Africanism, labor solidarity, and black economics. As a result of his efforts to improve conditions for black people, he was recognized throughout the world. Later in life, he tended toward radicalism and died in exile in Ghana in 1963, a self-proclaimed communist. The W. E. B. Du Bois Boyhood Homesite was designated a National Historic Landmark on May 11, 1976. [B 5/11/76 NHL, 76000947]

BRISTOL COUNTY

Paul Cuffe Farm
1504 Drift Road
Westport

This property is associated with Paul Cuffe (1759–1817), one of the most important African Americans of the late 18th and early 19th centuries. Cuffe, a black philanthropist and merchant mariner, was a pioneer in the struggle for minority rights in Massachusetts and was in the vanguard of the movement for black settlement in Africa. He was also involved in projects for black settlement and trade with Sierra Leone. His efforts in this direction won him an international reputation and acquaintance with President James Madison, Secretary of the Treasury Albert Gallatin, and Dr. Benjamin Rush. Cuffe was also influential in the temperance movement among African Americans in New Bedford and Nantucket. In 1808 Cuffe joined the Westport, Massachusetts, Society of Friends Meeting House, a Quaker society dedicated to the antislavery cause. He was active in affairs of the Friends and contributed to the building of a new meetinghouse in 1813. This meetinghouse was involved in the Sierra Leone projects; the members appointed two committees to consult with Cuffe on the projects. Until his death in 1817 he remained a man of great influence and wealth. Cuffe is buried at Central Village Westport, where a monument to his memory was dedicated in 1913. The Paul Cuffe Farm was designated a National Historic Landmark on May 30, 1974. [B 5/30/74 NHL, 74000394]

MIDDLESEX COUNTY

Maria Baldwin House
196 Prospect Street
Cambridge

This property was the home of Maria Louise Baldwin (1856–1922), one of the most distinguished black women educators of the late 19th and early 20th century. She was principal of the Agassiz Grammar School in Cambridge and later master of its secondary school, the only African American and one of only two women in New England to hold such a position.

Maria Baldwin's career at the school was a distinguished one as noted by such people as Charles W. Eliot of Harvard, Julia Ward Howe, and William Monroe Trotter. Her interests and energies extended beyond the classroom into the Boston-Cambridge community, where she was a leader and organizer of numerous educational, literary, and scholarly associations. Maria Baldwin spoke before numerous audiences on a variety of topics, and she earned a reputation nationally as an effective and persuasive speaker.

The tributes paid to her are testimony to the high esteem in which she was held. The 1922 class of the Agassiz School dedicated a memorial table to her. The school's auditorium was named Baldwin Hall, and a scholarship was established in her name. In December 1923 the League of Women for Community Services in Boston formally dedicated the Maria L. Baldwin Memorial Library, and in April 1950 a dormitory for women at Howard University was named after her. Her Cambridge, Massachusetts, home was designated a National Historic Landmark on May 11, 1976. [B 5/11/76 NHL, 76000272]

Howe House
6 Appleton Street
Cambridge

The Howe House is architecturally significant as a design of architect Charles Bulfinch and historically significant as the home of Julia Ward Howe (1819–1910) and her husband, Samuel Gridley Howe (1801–1876), from 1863 to 1866. The Howes played a key role in Boston's abolitionist circles for nearly two decades.

In 1863 the Howes edited an antislavery newspaper, *The Commonwealth*. Their South Boston residence, Green Peace, was a meeting place for abolitionists such as William Lloyd Garrison, Theodore Parker, Wendell Phillips, and Charles Sumner. Samuel Howe headed a Boston vigilante committee dedicated to preventing the return of fugitive slaves and actively supported John Brown's Kansas crusade against slavery. In addition, Howe supported black suffrage and the education of freedmen as essential to their citizenship. Julia Howe also felt strongly on the subject of civil rights for African Americans. She spoke with Frederick Douglass expressing support for civil rights and suffrage for African Americans.

While visiting an army camp in Washington, D.C., Julia composed a poem to the tune "John Brown's Body." She called it "The Battle Hymn of the Republic," and it subsequently brought her enormous recognition. In that same year Samuel Howe assumed leadership of the Massachusetts Board of State Charities, the first institution of its kind in America. For more than 35 years after her husband's death, Julia carried on as a reformer active in the suffrage, peace, and prison reform movements. She died in 1910 at age 91, but her influence and that of her husband continued in many organizations. The Samuel Gridley and Julia Ward Howe House was designated a National Historic Landmark on May 30, 1974. [Cambridge MRA, C 6/30/83, 83000811]

SUFFOLK COUNTY

African Meetinghouse
8 Smith Street
Boston

Constructed in 1806 entirely by black labor, the African Meetinghouse is the oldest known extant African American church building in Boston, and in the entire United States. Before 1805 the black inhabitants of Boston worshipped in the churches of whites. In August 1805 the Reverend Thomas Paul and 20 black members organized the first black church in the city, the First African Baptist Church. At about the same time, Paul helped organize the Abyssinian Baptist Church in New York City, where he preached during the summer of 1808. Paul was installed as the first pastor of the First African Baptist Church and served his congregation until 1829. The church became known as the Independence Baptist Church, Belknap or Joy Street Baptist, and the Abolition Church, for it was here that William Lloyd Garrison organized the New England Anti-Slavery Society on January 6, 1832. As the only sizable meeting place in the city owned by African Americans, the church became a focal point for their community activities as well as their worship. [CA 10/7/71 NHL NPS, 71000087]

Boston African American National Historic Site
Museum of Afro American History,
Dudley Station, Box 5
Boston

The Boston African American National Historic Site, located on the northern slope of Beacon Hill, encompasses the Black Heritage Trail, which introduces visitors to the history and architecture of a free black community active during the 1800s in the abolition movement.

The trail originates at the African Meetinghouse, the oldest extant black-church building in New England. It was here in 1832 that William Lloyd Garrison's New England Anti-Slavery Society issued its Declaration of Anti-Slavery Sentiments. In the ensuing years such prominent abolitionists as Frederick Douglass, Wendell Phillips, and Charles Sumner spoke from the pulpit to denounce slavery. Throughout the 19th century, the meetinghouse hosted musical performances, literary society meetings, socials, political rallies, school classes, and worship services.

Across the street from the meetinghouse are the Smith Court residences, typical homes of black families built between 1799 and 1853. The house at 10 Smith Court, next to the meetinghouse, was built by a black chimney sweeper named Scarlett. William C. Nell (1816–74), a black community leader in school integration and a Revolutionary War historian, once lived at 3 Smith Court.

The Abiel Smith School, built in 1834, is adjacent to the African Meetinghouse. It was the first school to provide primary and grammar school education to Boston's black children. After the Civil War, the school became a center for black veterans of the Grand Army of the Republic.

The next site along the Black Heritage Trail is a small, sturdy, clapboard house built by Colonel George Middleton. Middleton was known for his leadership of the "Bucks of America," an all-black militia in the American Revolution. It is the oldest African American-built house on Beacon Hill.

Many 19th-century African Americans obtained employment along Joy Street to the Boston Common. The edge of the Boston Common features the Robert Gould Shaw–54th Regiment memorial honoring Civil War black soldiers.

The Black Heritage Trail doubles along Joy Street and travels down Pinckney Street to the Phillips School, built in 1824. When state legislation integrated schools in 1855, the formerly white school became the first racially integrated school in the city.

Just one block above Charles Street is the residence of John J. Smith from 1878 to 1893. A barber and a caterer, he served three terms in the state legislature and was later appointed to the Boston Common Council. As an active crusader for the black community, he was involved in the movement to integrate Boston schools and to develop an all-black cavalry during the Civil War.

On Charles Street is located the Charles Street Meeting House, built in 1807 by the Charles Street Baptist Church whose congregation restricted black members to the galleries. In the mid-1830s Timothy Gilbert challenged this rule, and his subsequent expulsion from the church led to the founding of Tremont Temple, Boston's first integrated church. The Charles Street Church was purchased in 1876 by the African Methodist Episcopal Church. It remained a center of black religious activities until 1939, when the congregation moved to Roxbury.

Located on Phillips Street is the home of Lewis Hayden (1815–89). Hayden, an escaped Kentucky slave, and his wife, Harriet, settled in Boston in 1849 and became active in the abolition movement. Their home is the most documented of Boston's Underground Railroad stations, having sheltered many fugitive slaves. A clothing dealer, Hayden helped recruit the all-black 54th Massachusetts Regiment and later served a term in the state legislature.

On the corner of Phillips and Irving streets is the Coburn Gaming House. It was built in 1843–46 for John P. Coburn, a clothing dealer, and his family. Coburn and his brother-in-law also operated a gaming house here.

The Boston African American

William C. Nell House. Photo courtesy of the National Historic Landmarks Program (Brian Pfieffer).

National Historic Site was authorized by Congress October 10, 1980. Its components, coordinated by the National Park Service, remain in federal ownership. [CA 10/10/80 NPS, 80004396]

Charles Street African Methodist Episcopal Church
551 Warren Street
Boston

Built in 1888–89 by the Mount Pleasant Congregational Church, this building, initially named All Souls Unitarian Church, is associated with the black congregation of the Charles Street African Methodist Episcopal (AME) Church. From 1929 to 1933 the church was owned by the Episcopal City Mission and occupied by St. Ansgarius Swedish Church. In 1939 it was acquired by its present owner, the Charles Street AME Church. This congregation had owned the Charles Street Meeting House since 1876. During pre-Civil War days, the congregation's services had been the scene of many stirring abolitionist meetings in which William Lloyd Garrison, Wendell Phillips, Frederick Douglass, and other abolitionists led the fight against slavery. As the last black congregation on Beacon Hill, the move of the Charles Street AME Church to Roxbury reflected the long-term movement of Boston's black population from Beacon Hill to Roxbury and the changing population patterns in 20th-century Boston. [CA 9/1/83, 83000601]

William C. Nell House
3 Smith Court
Boston

This house is associated with William Cooper Nell (1816–74), a prominent black abolitionist, a determined integrationist, and a scholarly historian. Nell learned of the black man's struggle for freedom from his father, William, an associate of David Walker. Walker was the militant black abolitionist who wrote *David Walker's Appeal,* which was banned in several southern states because it encouraged slaves to revolt in order to secure their freedom. Nell was a member of the Massachusetts General Colored Association, an organization founded in 1826 for the purpose of encouraging racial uplift and the abolition of slavery.

An ardent believer in the true meaning of democracy and in the necessity to preserve one's history, William C. Nell published the first history of African Americans in 1855, entitled *The Colored Patriots of the American Revolution.* This book exhibits Nell's appreciation of and historical concern for the support African Americans had given the nation in the Revolutionary War and in the War of 1812.

Nell was a firm advocate of universal brotherhood, the abolishment of slavery, and the participation of African Americans in the Civil War, and he was the first African American to hold a federal position as postal clerk in the city of Boston. He also proved to be an active and successful leader in the effort to desegregate the Boston public school system. William C. Nell fought for the realization of the ideals upon which the United States was based in order to secure those rights for people of African descent. The William C. Nell House was designated a National Historic Landmark on May 11, 1976. [B 5/11/76 NHL, 76001979]

William Monroe Trotter House
97 Sawyer Avenue
Dorchester

This rectangular-plan, balloon-frame house of the late 1880s or 1890s was the primary residence of William Monroe Trotter (1872–1934), who actively and consistently spoke out against racism during the first decade of the 20th century. Although his adult life was one of protest against inequality and injustice, Trotter is best remembered for his opposition to Booker T. Washington. Trotter's opposition to Washington was best exemplified in the confrontation that occurred in Boston on July 30, 1903. Trotter attempted to ask Washington nine questions related to a speech Washington had delivered, and as a result of his aggressive behavior he was arrested. The incident was labeled the "Boston riot" and received widespread coverage.

After the "riot," Trotter formed the Boston Suffrage League. The aim of the group was to place before the American people wrongs against African Americans. In March 1901 Trotter helped to organize the Boston Literary and Historical Association, which served as a forum for militant political opinion expressed by such notables as W. E. B. Du Bois, Oswald Garrison Villard, and Charles Chesnutt. One of Trotter's greatest contributions to black protest came when he and his friend George Forbes founded *The Guardian* in 1901, a weekly newspaper on race relations.

Trotter continued to publish *The Guardian* and to support the cause of African Americans, particularly black soldiers during World War I, for whom he advocated better treatment. During the 1920s Trotter supported the Dyer Anti-Lynching Bill and spoke out against Marcus Garvey's back-to-Africa movement. In 1933 he petitioned Franklin D.

Camp Atwater. Photo courtesy of the Massachusetts Historical Commission (Donald C. Smith).

Roosevelt to end segregation in the District of Columbia.

William Monroe Trotter dedicated his life to bridging the gap between the professed ideals of the nation and its practices concerning the rights of African Americans. He never ceased to view the country from the perspective of its founding documents espousing freedom and equality for all Americans. The William Monroe Trotter House was designated a National Historic Landmark on May 11, 1976. [B 5/11/76 NHL, 76002003]

WORCESTER COUNTY

Camp Atwater
Shore Road
North Brookfield

Camp Atwater was established when Mary Atwater of Springfield donated 60 acres of land to Dr. William DeBerry in memory of her father, David Fisher Atwater, in 1921. During the first season in 1921, 40 black children were enrolled at the camp and enjoyed activities such as tennis, sailing, baseball, and basketball.

In the early years the majority of campers were from families of middle- and upper-class African Americans, primarily from New England. With the camp's rapid increase in popularity, however, campers were soon coming from all over the country. They included many distinguished African Americans, who attributed much of their success to their stay at Camp Atwater and to the cultural and environmental exchanges and strong role models of leadership experienced there. A number of its graduates have distinguished themselves in public life. Camp Atwater's well-known alumni include Coleman Young, mayor of Detroit, and Clifton Wharton, chancellor of the State University of New York. [AD 4/15/82, 82004477]

Liberty Farm
116 Mower Street
Worcester

Liberty Farm, home of the abolitionists Abigail Kelley (1810–87) and Stephen Symonds Foster (1809–81), served as a station on the Underground Railroad, sheltering fugitive slaves on their flight to Canada.

Abigail Kelley Foster's close friendship with abolitionist William Lloyd Garrison and her exposure to the *Liberator* led her into the ranks of abolitionism. Thereafter she lectured throughout the North on the horrors of slavery and the subjugation of women. From 1835 until 1837 Abigail served as secretary of the Lynn Female Anti-Slavery Society. In 1840 she was nominated to a position on the executive committee of the American Anti-Slavery Society. Abigail became close friends with the famed abolitionists Sarah and Angelina Grimke and traveled with them around the state of Massachusetts speaking in schoolhouses and churches against slavery.

Abigail's husband, Stephen Symonds Foster, a prominent reformer who rejected all religious institutions as proslavery, was an extreme abolitionist. Besides abolition, Foster was a strong advocate of women's suffrage, temperance, and world peace and a supporter of the rights of labor.

The Fosters' last public protest took place between 1874 and 1879, when they refused to pay taxes on their farm in retaliation for Abigail's denial of the vote. As a result, the farm was sold at public auction. Fortunately, friends purchased the farm and returned it to the Fosters. Liberty Farm was occupied by the Fosters from 1847 until 1881, and the Federal style farmhouse still stands as a memorial to these two reformers who held steadfast to their vision of a more equitable society. [Worcester MRA, B 9/13/74 NHL, 74002046]

MICHIGAN

LAKE COUNTY

Idlewild Historic District
U.S. Route 10
Idlewild

Idlewild, located in south central Lake County, was one of America's most popular black resorts from 1915 to the 1960s and was associated with many well-known African Americans. Now a vacation and retirement community, Idlewild retains strong ties with its past, since present residents, many of them patrons of the area during its heyday, have worked to revitalize and preserve it.

Because segregation barred African Americans from white resorts, Idlewild developed as a haven for black professionals and small businesspeople. Its location made it accessible for African Americans from urban centers like Chicago, Cleveland, and Indianapolis. Early Idlewild sales pamphlets even boasted a clubhouse on an island in the lake, cottages, a hotel, and plans for a future golf course and ball park.

Two of the most important figures in Idlewild's growth were Dr. Daniel Hale Williams and W. E. B. Du Bois. Williams was a nationally renowned surgeon credited with performing the first successful open heart surgery. In 1919 he built a small cottage on Idlewild Lake and later constructed a hotel on the island. Williams's connection with Idlewild gave potential buyers an additional reason to purchase lots; thus the island became known as "Williams Island." Du Bois, in 1921, brought national recognition to the resort when he featured it an article in *Crisis,* the magazine of the National Association for the Advancement of Colored People (see also Dr. Daniel Hale Williams House, Cook County, Illinois; William E. B. Du Bois Boyhood Homesite, Berkshire County, Massachusetts).

Idlewild's popularity died by 1970 primarily as a result of integration. Federal and state civil rights statutes allowed African Americans access to resorts and clubs that were previously closed to them. Considered by many to be Michigan's "only all-black ghost town," Idlewild is currently being revitalized as a result of the efforts of many local citizens who used to vacation there. [A 6/7/79, 79001160]

WAYNE COUNTY

Breitmeyer-Tobin Building
1308 Broadway Street
Detroit

This building is significant primarily for its historical role as the center of black professional activity in Detroit since the 1930s. The Breitmeyer-Tobin Building is an unusual example of a Beaux Arts style building at the turn of the century. The widespread availability of inexpensive, glazed, terra-cotta architectural elements, which were much less expensive than carved marble or limestone trim, contributed to the popularity of this style, which accommodated the late Victorian taste for ornament while also drawing on sober classical and colonial-inspired designs.

In 1936 the Metropolitan Life Insurance Company, an occupant of the building, allowed African Americans to enter the building to make payments on their insurance policies. This led to an influx of African American patrons. Thereafter black tenants rented office space in the building. As a result, by the late 1940s many of Detroit's prominent black professionals had taken offices in the Tobin Building. Among these were Dr. William H. Lawson and his son, Lloyd, both famed optometrists; five judges, including Damon Keith and Hobart Taylor, Jr., who became associate general counsel to President Johnson and later was appointed to the Board of Directors of the World Bank; and the Brotherhood of Sleeping Car Porters, the largest black union in the United States. Today black professionals are dispersed throughout the city, and the Tobin Building retains its role in fostering the growth and acceptance of black professionalism in Detroit. [CA 3/10/80, 80001918]

Dunbar Hospital
580 Frederick Street
Detroit

Dunbar Hospital had a significant role in the development of the medical profession in the black community of Detroit in the early 20th century. Because of segregation, African Americans, doctors and patients alike, were denied equal access to both private and public hospitals in Detroit. In 1917 there were only 30 black physicians in the city providing home care to the black community. Overworked, they united and formed the Allied Medical Society, forerunner of the present Detroit Medical Society. Its primary objective was to raise funds to establish a hospital to care for the black citizens of Detroit. In 1916 they acquired the Charles Warren House and opened Dunbar Memorial Hospital the following year as Detroit's first black hospital. [CA 6/19/79, 79001172]

Sacred Heart Roman Catholic Church, Convent, and Rectory
1000 Eliot Street
Detroit

The only Italianate style church in the city, Sacred Heart has served Detroit's oldest black Roman Catholic congregation. Organized black Catholicism in Detroit began when Father Joseph Wuest established a black mission at St. Mary's School in Detroit's "Greektown" area on September 1, 1911. Services took place in a converted classroom for the next three years. In 1914 Father Wuest bought a vacant church building on Eliot and Beaubien streets on the lower east side of Detroit. Black migration to the area significantly increased church membership. Today Sacred Heart continues its historic role as the mother church of black Roman Catholicism in Detroit. [CA 6/6/80, 80001926]

Second Baptist Church of Detroit
441 Monroe Street
Detroit

The Second Baptist Church houses Michigan's first black congregation. The

Ossian H. Sweet House. Photo courtesy of the Michigan History Division (Charles C. Cotman).

church was established in 1836, when 13 former slaves decided to withdraw from the First Baptist Church of Detroit because of discriminatory practices there.

The church's political involvement began in 1841. Then a station for the Underground Railroad, Second Baptist's leaders formed the Amherstburg Baptist Association. Through this organization, Baptist churches in Detroit and Canada sought to aid, both spiritually and materially, the ever-increasing number of fugitive slaves arriving from the South. Under the leadership of the Reverend William C. Monroe, Second Baptist developed the Canadian Anti-Slavery Baptist Association. Both associations were of unquestionable value to fugitive slaves and to the abolitionist movement.

Second Baptist Church has been involved in the local community in several capacities. It aided thousands of black migrants in securing homes and work, sponsored social affairs for black citizens, and, from 1842 through 1846, housed Monroe's school for black children. Located in the middle of Detroit's black community, the Second Baptist Church has always been a source of inspiration and encouragement for its members and neighbors. [A 3/19/75, 75000970]

Ossian H. Sweet House
2905 Garland
Detroit

The home of black physician Ossian Sweet is the site of a racial incident that resulted in a nationally publicized 1925 murder trial. Sweet, a graduate of Wilberforce University and Howard University Medical School, purchased the two-story brick house located in an all-white neighborhood in 1925. White residents immediately organized in opposition. In September 1925 Sweet, his wife, and nine associates, each armed with a gun, moved into the house under police escort. The next evening, a large crowd gathered and pelted the house with bottles and rocks, breaking several windows. The crowd then rushed the house, drawing a volley of gunfire from the upstairs windows. One man was killed and another seriously wounded in the exchange, and Sweet and his companions were arrested and charged with first-degree murder.

The National Association for the Advancement of Colored People took up Sweet's cause, asking the controversial attorney Clarence Darrow to undertake Sweet's defense. Darrow, who had gained prominence as the principal defense attorney in the "Scopes Monkey Trial," agreed to take the case. The trial commenced in November 1925 and lasted nearly three weeks. After 26 hours of deliberation, the jury returned on November 25 without a verdict. Presiding Judge Frank Murphy declared a mistrial, dismissed the jury, and released Sweet. A second trial the following year involving Sweet's brother resulted in his swift acquittal, reinforcing the assertion that a citizen has the right to defend his property against mob intervention if he has reasonable cause to believe there is danger. [A 4/4/85, 85000696]

MINNESOTA

HENNEPIN COUNTY

Lena O. Smith House
3905 5th Avenue South
Minneapolis

The Lena O. Smith house is the only surviving building closely associated with its namesake, a prominent local civil rights lawyer and activist. Lena Olive Smith came to Minneapolis in 1907 with her mother, brother, and sister. She graduated from Northwestern College in Minneapolis and passed the Minnesota bar exam in 1927, becoming one of only nine black attorneys to practice law in Minneapolis between 1890 and 1927. For more than 20 years, she was the only black woman to practice law in Minneapolis.

Smith was aggressive in the interest of civil rights issues, playing an active role in the affairs of both the Minneapolis Urban League and the National Association for the Advancement of Colored People (NAACP). She was one of the founding members of the Minneapolis Urban League in 1925. The Urban League, along with black churches, the black press, and the NAACP, was one of the groups that brought civil rights issues to the attention of the public in the 1930s and 1940s.

Smith first represented the NAACP in 1931 as the prosecuting attorney in a case concerning segregation in a south Minneapolis neighborhood. She was also involved in two suits dealing with equal access to public accommodations and was active in ending the policy of segregation of black audiences in the balcony of the Pantages Theater.

In 1932 Smith became the first woman to be elected president of the Minneapolis chapter of the NAACP. She held this position again from 1935 to 1939, at which time she relinquished her post to serve as chair of the joint Twin City Legal Committee for both the Minneapolis and St. Paul NAACP. The committee would provide the impetus for increased participation of the NAACP in legal cases in the Twin Cities for years to come.

The house in which Lena Olive Smith lived from 1925 to 1949 stands as a physical reminder of Lena Smith's service to the black communities of Minneapolis and St. Paul. Smith was active in her practice until her death in 1966 and is remembered by her contemporaries as the most aggressive and vocal civil rights lawyer of her time. [B 9/26/91, 91001472]

OLMSTED COUNTY

Avalon Hotel
301 North Broadway
Rochester

With the growth of the city of Rochester as a national and international center for medicine in the early 20th century, the local hotel and guest house business expanded to serve vast numbers of transient Mayo Clinic patients. Built next to the railroad depot in 1919, the Avalon Hotel was part of this early hotel building boom. It was the only hotel available in Rochester for black patients at the clinic for several decades, until the courts outlawed segregation. It also served as the only hotel available for other black visitors, such as musician Duke Ellington and his band, the musical group the Ink Spots, and boxer Henry Armstrong.

The Avalon Hotel represents the ethnic, social, and geographical diversity of the people brought to Rochester by the presence of the Mayo Clinic, as well as the nature of the social interaction between this population and an otherwise typical Midwestern farming community. Today the Avalon, renamed Broadway Square, continues to function as a rental facility, offering apartments to all visitors. [A 3/19/82, 82002992]

RAMSEY COUNTY

Edward S. Hall House
996 Iglehart Avenue
St. Paul

Edward Stephen Hall came to St. Paul in 1900 from Springfield, Illinois. By 1906 he had married, purchased a home, and established a six-chair barbershop with his brother. Hall operated this business at its original location until 1947, when he moved to a new shop in a nearby location. Hall's business was more than a mere barbershop. Through his service to St. Paul's prominent businesspeople and

politicians, Hall developed important contacts that he used to secure jobs for members of the black community. In 1915 his shop was mentioned in *The Helper,* the weekly bulletin of the St. James African Methodist Episcopal Church, as part of a system in which "tipsters" in the black community would inform "helpers" of job vacancies. This early system of employment referral was effective in securing both short-term and long-term employment but could not fully alleviate the job shortage among African Americans in St. Paul or address jobs outside the service sector. Hall, recognizing this problem and seeking ways to address it, was instrumental in the founding of the St. Paul branch of the Urban League in 1923.

The focus of the St. Paul Urban League was to create opportunities for the advancement of the city's black residents. While Hall believed the issue of employment to be central to the advancement of African Americans in U.S. society, he was also concerned with the need for social fraternity. In 1908 Hall joined with the local Free Masons chapter to which he belonged and the Local Odd Fellows Lodge to organize Union Hall, a meeting place for themselves and the black community. Built in 1914, Union Hall led the way in providing public accommodations for St. Paul's black residents. Working through the Urban League, Hall also helped established the Hallie Q. Brown Community House, a recreation and community center for African Americans. The house in which Hall resided stands as a physical reminder of an individual who made outstanding contributions to St. Paul's black community in so many capacities, exhibiting a lifelong commitment to its members. [B 4/16/91, 91000440]

Harriet Island Pavilion
75 Water Street
St. Paul

Located in a public park on the Mississippi River, the Harriet Island Pavilion is a recreational building constructed by the Works Progress Administration (WPA) in 1941. Executed in the Moderne style with classical detailing, the building is constructed of concrete block with a Kasota limestone veneer. The pavilion is a well-preserved example of the work of Clarence Wesley Wigington, the first black architect for the city of St. Paul, and an important visual component in city's public landscape.

Born in Lawrence, Kansas, and trained as an architect in Omaha, Nebraska, Clarence Wesley Wigington began his career with the city of St. Paul as a draftsperson, later becoming chief design architect. Because all designs from the city architect's office were stamped with the name of the city architect, many of Wigington's works did not bear his name and were not credited to him until later research proved them to be his; this is the case with the Harriet Island Pavilion.

Harriet Island has been used as a recreational area for St. Paul since 1900, when the city's health officer purchased the island and built public baths, ball courts, a pavilion, and other facilities, none of which remain today. The baths were closed in 1919 because of river pollution, and the other facilities deteriorated over the years. In 1929 control of the island was transferred to the city for development as a city park. Further construction was halted, most likely because of the Depression, until the Harriet Island Pavilion was constructed in 1941. Except for its gable roof, the building exhibits all of the design elements of the Moderne style. Both the interior and exterior designs are highly disciplined and show Wigington's refined architectural vocabulary and exceptional skill (see also Highland Park Tower and Holman Field Administration Building). [C 7/10/92, 92000821]

Highland Park Tower
1570 Highland Parkway
St. Paul

A vital part of St. Paul's water system and the only architecturally significant water tower in the city, the Highland Park Water Tower is an important city and neighborhood landmark. The property is additionally significant as the design of Clarence Wesley Wigington, one of St. Paul's few known black architects.

Wigington was born in Lawrence, Kansas, on April 21, 1883. He attended high school in Omaha, Nebraska. After attending architecture school for one year, he went to work for Thomas R. Kimball, a nationally recognized architect who was then president of the American Institute of Architects. While in Omaha, Wigington received a commission to design a church and two apartment buildings and won the competition to design two dormitories for the National Religious Training School in Durham, North Carolina (then an all-black school, now North Carolina State University at Durham).

After relocating to St. Paul, Wigington worked on various projects ranging from creameries to churches. In 1915, after taking the city architectural examination and scoring higher than anyone previously tested, Wigington began working as an architectural draftsperson and designer in the St. Paul Department of Parks, Playgrounds, and Public Buildings. His career with the city of St. Paul lasted 34 years.

The Highland Park Tower was

*Highland Park Tower.
Photo courtesy of the
Minnesota Historical
Society (Patricia
Murphy).*

**Holman Field
Administration
Building**
644 Bayfield Street
St. Paul

The Holman Field Administration Building is one of the most accomplished works of Clarence Wesley Wigington, the first black architect for the city of St. Paul. During his 34-year career with the city, he designed many prominent public buildings that have had a lasting impact on the city landscape. Because his career spanned the New Deal era, many of his designs are associated with the Works Progress Administration (WPA).

The most prominent surviving Wigington designs include the Highland Park Tower, several public schools, the Harriet Island Pavilion, the Keller Golf Course Club House, the Como Park Palm House and the Como Zoo Building, the Ramsey County Boys School, the Public Safety Building, Fire Station No. 17, and a group of WPA-built recreation buildings located in neighborhood parks (see also Harriet Island Pavilion and Highland Park Tower). The Holman Field Administration Building is outstanding

constructed in 1928 at a cost of $69,438. The octagonal tower has a base of smoothly dressed random-cut ashlar Kasota stone, a pressed brick shaft with several windows, and a Bedford stone lookout area. The 134-foot-tall tower is located on the second highest point in the city of St. Paul, and its observation deck affords a dramatic, panoramic view of the Twin Cities metropolitan area. The tower is a dominant feature of the Highland Park neighborhood's skyline and has been preserved in good condition with few alterations (see also Harriet Island Pavilion and Holman Field Administration Building). [C 7/17/86, 86001670] among his designs for its fine execution of the Moderne style, the handsome use of salvaged Kasota stone in a fresh modern design, and its high standard of craftsmanship typical of WPA projects. [CA 8/15/91, 91001004]

Pilgrim Baptist Church
732 West Central Avenue
St. Paul

Built in 1928, the present Pilgrim Baptist Church is the spiritual center for the second oldest black congregation in Minnesota and the oldest one in St. Paul. The church was officially organized in 1866 by a group of former slaves and their leader Robert Hickman. The structure is the third and only surviving church building of the Pilgrim congregation.

Pilgrim Baptist Church developed many leading activists, businesspeople, and politicians. As early as 1870, a core group of self-educated religious and business leaders (as well as members of the laboring class and homemakers) was organizing literary groups, fraternal organizations, and churches in the St. Paul community. Many of these leaders came from Pilgrim.

In later years the Pilgrim Church building was regularly used as a meeting place for the St. Paul National Association for the Advancement of Colored People and Urban League, the Sterling Club, the fledgling Brotherhood of Sleeping Car Porters, and Masonic and other fraternal orders. [AB 4/16/91, 91000438]

ST. LOUIS COUNTY

St. Mark's African Methodist Episcopal Church
530 North 5th Avenue East
Duluth

Founded in 1890, St. Mark's African Methodist Episcopal Church was the first black congregation in the city of Duluth. The church is the only public building in the city built by African Americans for their own use.

St. Mark's membership reflects the small size of the black community in Duluth. Like black churches in other towns, St. Mark's grew to be a key institution in this small community, providing educational and social programs and a forum for public speaking.

A disposition toward social activism grew out of the church community as African Americans struggled with relative isolation within the larger community. Along with another black church, Calvary Baptist Church, black fraternal organizations, and the local chapter of the National Association for the Advancement of Colored People (NAACP), St. Mark's has been at the core of black religious, social, political, and intellectual life for African Americans in Duluth. The church welcomed W. E. B. Du Bois to Duluth in 1921 to encourage the establishment of an NAACP chapter after the lynching of three African Americans on a Duluth street corner. In the 1930s the church alternated with Calvary Baptist as the location of the Sunday Forum, a weekly discussion of issues important to the black community.

The present building was constructed in 1910 to replace a smaller one. Funds for the project were raised through appeal to both the black and white residents of Duluth. In 1934 the church was saved from foreclosure by the sale of a rare photograph of Abraham Lincoln's inauguration donated by a Duluth collector. Since 1890 St. Mark's has nurtured a social consciousness that it shares with Calvary Baptist Church, the NAACP, and the local black Masonic orders. [A 4/16/91, 91000439]

John W. Boddie House. Photo courtesy of the Mississippi Department of Archives and History (Lisa Reynolds).

MISSISSIPPI

ADAMS COUNTY

China Grove Plantation

South of Natchez

Natchez

China Grove Plantation is a rare example of a southern plantation owned by a black family that rose from a position as valued and esteemed slaves to become prosperous citizens of the post-Civil War South. The vernacular, one-and-one-half-story, side-gabled, frame plantation dwelling is fronted by a gallery that has features strongly associated with black architecture of this period: unmolded box columns that were once linked by a railing composed of three horizontal boards. In 1854 white planter James Railey purchased China Grove Plantation, which adjoined his Oakland Plantation. The residence dates from the period 1850 to 1870 and was probably constructed not long after Railey acquired the plantation in 1854. In 1861 Railey specified in his will that his slaves August and Sarah Maziqueand their children were to be exempted from the settlement of his other property and, at the death of his wife, they were to become the property of his brother who "will treat them with kindness, and give them all the comfort they require." The vernacular quality of the house and its proximity to the plantation gin indicate that it was probably con-structed for or by August Mazique, who may have served as Railey's plantation overseer.

In 1869 August Mazique purchased China Grove at public auction after the Raileys' heirs lost the property in a chancery court suit. After purchasing China Grove, the Mazique family prospered to become the largest landowners in southwest Adams County by the end of the 19th century. August Mazique's son, Alexander, eventually purchased Oakland Plantation (see also Oakland Plantation). In 1883, after the death of August Mazique, the 628-acre China Grove Plantation was partitioned by family members, with the present 228-acre tract allotted to widow Sarah and son Otey. This dower portion remained the residence of members of the Mazique family until 1980. [CA 4/7/82 82003089]

Glen Aubin

Off U.S. Route 61

Natchez

Like China Grove, Bourbon, and Oakland Plantations, Glen Aubin was one of several plantations in southwest Adams County that were purchased by former slaves or their children in the years immediately following the Civil War (see also Oakland and China Grove

Plantation). Glen Aubin was constructed as the residence of Adams County planter John Odlin Hutchins and his wife, Aubin, from whom it derives its name, on land acquired by Hutchin's grandfather, Anthony Hutchins, as an English land grant in the early 1780s. Coming to Natchez in 1772, Anthony Hutchins was the area's largest landholder and planter in the late 18th century. The house appears to date from around 1835 to 1845, with the only major changes occurring around 1850, when the roof was raised to accommodate second-story bedrooms.

In 1874 Charlie and Charity Rounds, who were former slaves or free blacks, purchased Glen Aubin. The purchase was arranged by Wilmer Shields, the plantation manager at neighboring Laurel Hill owned by William Newton Mercer. The name Charity appears in a list of slaves owned by Mercer, and it is possible that Charity Rounds had been a Laurel Hill slave who, with her husband, was assisted by Shields in acquiring the plantation. From 1874 until 1894, Glen Aubin served as the residence of the Rounds family, who are responsible for maintaining the architectural integrity of the house, including all original hardware, oak graining, and interior and exterior paint colors. [CA 8/29/85, 85001930]

William Johnson House
210 State Street
Natchez

This house was built under the immediate supervision of William Johnson, a free black entrepreneur and slaveholder, who wrote the first known diary kept by a free black person in the antebellum South. Johnson acted as his own chief contractor in the construction of his house, using the labor of his slaves and local white artisans to construct the

Greek Revival house between 1840 and 1841. His diary, found in 1938 with two missing chapters that were not discovered until 1948, recorded his private observations for the years 1835–51 in Natchez.

Born a slave in 1809, William Johnson was freed at age 11 and assumed the name of the man who freed him. During the 1820s Johnson was an apprentice in a barbershop belonging to his brother-in-law, James Miller, a prominent barber in Natchez. After completing his apprenticeship, Johnson operated his own barbershop at Port Gibson, Mississippi, and later returned to Natchez to buy Miller's establishment.

In addition to Miller's barbershop, Johnson's business enterprises soon expanded to include a bathhouse and two smaller barbershops. Johnson's businesses were operated by both free blacks and slaves working under his direction. Although barbering was Johnson's primary business and money-making venture, he was also engaged in money lending, farming, brokering, real estate rentals, and land speculation. In June 1851 a long-standing boundary dispute with a man named Baylor Winn resulted in the Johnson's murder.

In 1951, exactly 100 years following his death, Johnson's 2,000-page personal and business diary was published under the title *William Johnson's Natchez: The Ante-Bellum Diary of a Free Negro*. The publication of his diary secured for the Natchez barber and businessman a high place in the ranks of American chroniclers. Johnson's published diary provides the most complete account of the life of a free black in the antebellum South. It documents the extraordinary rise of an African American from bondage to freedom and to an established position as a substantial citizen of Natchez, the sym-

Oakland. Photo courtesy of the Historic Natchez Foundation (Mary Warren Miller).

bolic capital of the antebellum cotton kingdom of the Deep South. A biography of Johnson, *The Barber of Natchez,* was published in 1954 by the Louisiana State University Press.

The William Johnson House was added to the National Park System as a part of the Natchez National Historical Park on October 7, 1988. The house serves as a visitor reception center and exhibit area, where the African American history of Natchez is interpreted. The upper floors of the house interpret the life of Natchez's unique diarist. [B 6/16/76, 76001086]

Oakland (Railey House)
Lower Woodville Road
Natchez

Oakland contributes to the study of black history because of its association in the pre–Civil War period and from 1891 to 1955 with the Mazique family, who first came to the Natchez area as slaves. By the late 19th century they had formed a black planting dynasty in southwest Adams County.

Oakland was probably built about 1820, when the property on which it stands was acquired by James and Matilda Railey. James Railey's will in 1861 is the first documentation associating the Maziques with Oakland. The will expresses his concern for his slaves, August and Sarah Mazique, whom he wills to his brother in Kentucky to guarantee them kind treatment. Despite Railey's will, the Maziques remained in Adams County, presumably at Oakland or Railey's adjoining China Grove Plantation (see also China Grove Plantation).

In 1870 James Railey's China Grove Plantation was sold at public auction, and, by a mortgage to Wilmer Shields, a white man who managed neighboring Laurel Hill Plantation, the Maziques became the owners. In 1891 Alexander Mazique, son of August and Sarah, purchased Oakland, where he was born into slavery. Other children of August and Sarah Mazique acquired other plantations, and by 1900 Mazique family members owned approximately a dozen southwest Adams County plantations. The

Mazique family owned Oakland until 1955, when it was sold to its present owners. [CA 6/29/89, 89000781]

Pine Ridge Church
Northeast of Natchez at junction of Pine Ridge Road and Mississippi Route 554
Natchez

Pine Ridge Church is the oldest active Presbyterian church in Mississippi. The beginning of Pine Ridge Church may be traced to the organization in 1807 of Salem Presbyterian Church by missionary James Smylie in the town of Washington, four miles east of Pine Ridge. In 1808 the church was moved to Pine Ridge, and a log church was erected on the site of the present sanctuary. The log sanctuary was replaced in 1828 by a brick one. The brick building was destroyed by a tornado in 1908, and the present church was constructed in 1909.

In the early 1830s the African Branch of the Pine Ridge Church was formed to serve the spiritual needs of the local black population. The black congregation included more than 200 members.

In 1835 Smylie, the first pastor of Pine Ridge Church, gained notoriety with the publication of a proslavery reply to the Reverend John P. Vandyke of the Presbytery of Chillicothe in Ohio, who complained of "the low state of religion in the country," attributing this to the ownership of slaves by Christians in the South. The reply, known as "Smylie's Pamphlet," justified slavery based on Biblical texts and was used extensively by protagonists of slavery all over the South. [CB 12/13/79, 79001296]

Smith-Bontura-Evans House
107 Broadway Street
Natchez

The Smith-Bontura-Evans house, built in stages between 1851 and 1858 by suc-cessful free black businessman Robert D. Smith for his home and livery business, is a remarkably complete and rare regional example of a combined residential and commercial complex. A "free man of Color," Smith was born in Maryland in 1807 and by 1837 was living in Natchez with his wife, Ann, and family. In 1843, having satisfied the County Board of Police that he was of "good character and honest deportment," he was granted a license by the state legislature to reside permanently in Natchez.

Before 1840 the free black population of Natchez and Adams County, which peaked at 283 in 1840, lived free from harassment in various economic circum-stances and maintained distinct intra-group social levels. Among whites, how-ever, fears grew that the free blacks as a class constituted a potential source of slave unrest, and demands for the enforce-ment of laws regulating free blacks esca-lated. Despite the seemingly hostile cli-mate that greatly restricted their mobility, free blacks such as Smith prospered in antebellum Natchez, achieving both social prominence within the black community as well as professional success in the com-munity at large.

Smith became a "hackman" in the 1840s and was established in his own liv-ery business by 1849. His home is a sim-ple, unadorned, brick Greek Revival style town house. Almost as large as the house is the two-story livery section to the rear, where picturesque arched openings pro-vided wide entrances for the carriages that Smith operated in his hack business. Smith ran his business at this location until his death in 1858. His widow, Ann, apparently continued the business until 1860, when, in recognition of the deteri-orating situation of free blacks in Mississippi, she moved with her four minor children to Valparaiso, Chile, to join her oldest son. [CB 3/29/78, 78001585]

BOLIVAR COUNTY

I. T. Montgomery House
West Main Street
Mound Bayou

Located in the Mississippi Delta region of Bolivar County, the town of Mound Bayou was one of a number of black settlements established during the post-Reconstruction period. It represents one of many important attempts by African Americans of that era to establish independent communities in which they could exercise self-government.

The present town of Mound Bayou had its inception in a former black settlement. Isaiah Thornton Montgomery and his cousin Benjamin Green were the slaves of the family of Confederate President Jefferson Davis. As an alternative to slavery, it was Jefferson Davis's idea that blacks be isolated in their own settlements. At the end of the Civil War, in 1865, an actual settlement was established on the former Jefferson plantation of Brierfield at Davis Bend, 20 miles south of Vicksburg on the Mississippi River. The settlement survived for 18 years. Because of recurring floods on the Mississippi, however, the relatives and friends of Montgomery and Green abandoned their settlement and relocated to Vicksburg.

Montgomery founded the town of Mound Bayou in 1887 as a community where African Americans could obtain social, political, and economic rights in the post-Reconstruction South. The town was located along a major railroad line in undeveloped swampland that was part of the fertile Mississippi Delta. Most important though, Montgomery's skilled leadership made the town a success. His talents encompassed the fields of engineering, accounting, and real estate, and he became one of the wealthiest men in Bolivar County. He was active in the Republican party, and he represented Bolivar County in the Mississippi convention of 1890.

Under Montgomery's leadership, Mound Bayou had developed into one of the most prosperous communities in the state by the turn of the century. In 1904 the Bank of Mound Bayou was founded by John Francis and Charles Banks. Numerous shops, stores, fraternal buildings, institutional buildings, and private residences were constructed. It was also during this period, in 1910, that the I. T. Montgomery House was constructed.

In 1912 Montgomery petitioned for a town charter from the governor of Mississippi, and his request was immediately accepted. The I. T. Montgomery House stands as a symbolic tribute to the progress and development of Mound Bayou and to its energetic founder. The house was designated a National Historic Landmark on May 11, 1976. [B 5/11/76 NHL, 76001092]

CLAIBORNE COUNTY

Alcorn State University Historic District
Alcorn State University campus
Lorman

The Alcorn State University Historic District is associated with black education in Mississippi. Prompted by the Morrill Act of 1862, the Mississippi legislature created Alcorn University on May 13, 1871, and in 1878 became the first land-grant school for African Americans in the United States. For its first president, the state selected Hiram R. Revels (1822–1901), who served Alcorn from 1871 until 1882. The President's House, located within the historic district, is the only building in Mississippi known to have been occupied by Revels.

Hiram Revels was one of the country's most distinguished African Americans during the era of Reconstruction. Revels was born a free black in Fayetteville, North Carolina. He attended school in the North and was ordained in the African Methodist Episcopal Church in 1845. During the Civil War Alcorn was active in organizing black troops. Afterward, he moved to Mississippi, where he organized churches and lectured. Revels entered politics in 1868, when he was appointed a city alderman in Natchez. In 1870 he was elected to fill the U.S. Senate seat vacated by Jefferson Davis in 1861, thus becoming the first African American to serve in the United States Congress.

During his one year in the Senate, Revels defended the new rights of African Americans, appointed the first black student to the U.S. Military Academy at West Point, and advocated the readmission of the southern states into the Union. Upon the completion of his term, Revels returned to Mississippi, where he accepted the presidency of Alcorn University in 1871.

The oldest buildings on the Alcorn campus were constructed for Oakland College, a Presbyterian school closed by the Civil War and subsequently purchased by the state in 1871. At the time of purchase by the state, buildings located on the campus included the President's House (c. 1830); Oakland Chapel (c. 1838); Dormitory #2 and Dormitory #3 (both c. 1855); and the Belles Lettres Building (c. 1855).

In 1878, during Revels's last administration, Alcorn became the first black land-grant college in the United States. Following the Revels's resignation, the college grew under the guidance of a succession of black presidents. John H. Burris served as president from 1882 to 1893. His administration, like that of fellow southern black educator Booker T. Washington, emphasized the need to train blacks in the manual arts. During the administration of Witt Lanier from 1899 to 1905, the college enrolled black women. During the first third of the 20th century, Alcorn was governed by two graduates, L. J. Rowan, president from 1905 to 1911 and 1915 to 1934, and J. A. Martin, president from 1911 to 1915. Martin is credited with the initiation of night classes, and Rowan is known for his vigorous campaign for better state funding. During Rowan's term, the new Administration Building (1928) and Harmon Hall (1929) were constructed. The final contributing building of the Alcorn University Historic District, Lanier Hall, was built in 1939 (see also Oakland Chapel). [CAB 5/20/82, 82003098]

Golden West Cemetery
Rodney Road
Port Gibson

Golden West Cemetery in Port Gibson was turned over to local African Americans for use as a burying ground around the turn of the century. The property displays an evocative rural quality and an expression of black folk art in its makeshift monuments. The carved stone monuments used during the early part of this century have been succeeded by cast-concrete slabs with hand-etched inscriptions. Known locally as Port Gibson Negro Cemetery until the 1970s, the property was renamed by Agnes Quigless of the Golden West Cemetery Association. After 1970 a second black cemetery was established in a lot east of Golden West and named Scott Memorial Cemetery. [Port Gibson MRA; Historic Cemeteries in Port Gibson TR, A 7/22/79, 79003417]

Oakland Chapel
Alcorn State University campus
Alcorn

Oakland Chapel was constructed in 1838 as one of the first buildings of Oakland College, an institution serving white students from Mississippi, Louisiana, and Arkansas. In 1871, the Mississippi Reconstruction Legislature authorized the establishment of a college expressly for African Americans in Mississippi. The state purchased the Oakland College campus, and opened Alcorn State University on the site.

Alcorn State University began operations under the guidance of Hiram R. Revels (1822–1901), one of the most distinguished African Americans of the Reconstruction era. During the Civil War he helped organize regiments of black troops to fight in the war. After the Civil War he became involved in politics and religious activities in Mississippi. In 1870 he was elected to the United States Senate, the first African American in history to attain that office. In 1878, while Revels was president of the college, the state legislature reorganized Alcorn, made it a land-grant college, and changed its name to Alcorn Agricultural and Mechanical College. The college was the first land-grant college in the nation founded specifically for African Americans.

John H. Burris was president of the college from the time of Revels's resignation in 1882 until 1893. Burris and those who followed him during the remaining years of the 19th century supported a continuing and growing emphasis on agricultural and industrial education.

The history of the college during the first third of the 20th century was closely tied to the life and career of Dr. L. J. Rowan. During the Rowan era Alcorn became one of the state's most influential institutions. This was an era wherein Booker T. Washington's Atlanta Compromise speech dominated and the college became the state's principal exponent of the "compromise."

In the midst of the Depression, Rowan retired from office and Dr. William H. Bell became president. During Bell's administration the college made improvements in the training of the faculty and the curriculum became more diversified. The college's science department attained high academic excellence. Alcorn State University alumni have distinguished themselves and their alma mater in numerous fields of endeavor (see also Alcorn State University Historic District). Oakland Chapel was designated a National Historic Landmark on May 11, 1976. [CA 12/27/74 NHL, 74001057]

HANCOCK COUNTY

Beach Boulevard Historic District
Roughly bounded by Beach Boulevard, Necaise Avenue, Seminary Drive, and 2nd and 3rd streets
Bay St. Louis

The Beach Boulevard Historic District encompasses a 175-acre area of the city, incorporating almost a two-mile strip of Beach Boulevard, most of the central business core located around Main Street, and adjacent residential properties. The district is a unique collection of architecture dating from 1790 through the 1940s, including vernacular buildings as well as the Greek Revival, Queen Anne, Colonial Revival, Bungalow, and Mission styles. Also unique to the district are the shotgun Creole cottages dating from the 1860s through the 1920s. The thoroughfare from which the district takes its name is lined with large dwellings, many originally constructed as summer homes for

House at 337 Main Street in the Beach Boulevard Historic District. Photo courtesy of the Mississippi Department of Archives and History (Adele Cramer).

prominent New Orleans businesspeople and professionals.

A number of the buildings in the district represent different aspects of black life in Bay St. Louis. Eugene Ray, an African American, was a local builder who constructed three of the c. 1890 Queen Anne style cottages on Railroad Avenue as well as dozens of other cottages in the center of town. These cottages are distinguished by their polygonal bays and decorated vergeboards and were speculatively constructed for the use of summer residents. In addition to his work as a builder, Ray was for a time the only undertaker in Bay St. Louis.

A building associated with religion, education, and black history is the St. Rose de Lima School, established as a private school for black children by missionary priest Father LeDuc in 1868. Also important in the district is the St.

Augustine Seminary. Founded in 1920 in Greenville, Mississippi, by Divine Word Missionaries, the seminary was relocated to Bay St. Louis in 1923. It was the oldest Roman Catholic seminary in Mississippi for the training of young black men for the priesthood, and in 1939 it was the only training school for black Catholic priests in the United States.

The St. Rose de Lima Church, a c. 1926 Mission style building on Necaise Avenue, was constructed for the black Roman Catholics of Bay St. Louis after a separate parish was established for them in 1923. The 100 Men Association Building, constructed in 1922 on Union Street, was established by local community leaders. Organizations such as these were more than social; they provided various benefits such as disability and burial insurance for their members. Other buildings relevant to black history are the houses and two churches that line Sycamore Street. The Velena C. Jones Methodist Episcopal Church is a stucco and brick building built in 1926 on the site of an earlier frame church, the congregation of which was organized in 1892 by the Reverend O. H. Flowers. An even earlier church is the First Baptist Church, organized by the Reverend Taylor Fryerson in 1877. The original church building was destroyed by a 1947 hurricane and replaced by the present brick and stucco building in 1950. [Bay St. Louis MRA, CA 11/25/80, 80002239]

Sycamore Street Historic District
Sycamore Street
Bay St. Louis

The Sycamore Street Historic District is important in the black history of Bay St. Louis and also contains valuable architectural resources dating from around 1860 through the 1920s. The district contains two commercial buildings and eight residences lining the north side of Sycamore Street east and west of the Old Spanish Trail. The district is part of what remains of a small black settlement that once extended east, north, and west of the present district boundaries. Although by 1906 enough black families lived in Bay St. Louis to construct a two-story school (no longer extant), the area west of the Old Spanish Trail was not fully developed as a black community until the 1920s.

The district contains several Bungalow style houses, along with two houses remaining from earlier estates. One of these, located at 531 Sycamore Street, is a vernacular house type that is relatively rare in Mississippi. With multiple entrances, showing a French influence, this five-bay cottage contains doors on each of its middle bays, which provide access to an undercut gallery. It is the only example of its type in Bay St. Louis.

Another important architectural component of the district is the front-gabled commercial building on the corner of St. Francis and Sycamore streets. Built around 1910, it is a good example of a turn-of-the-century vernacular building. Added to an earlier house, it was probably the first large store to be constructed in the neighborhood and illustrates the proximity of the shopkeeper's residence to his business. Although black families lived in nearby residences, an Italian family owned the store and attached residence. [Bay St. Louis MRA, CA 11/25/80, 80002242]

Washington Street Historic District
Washington Street
Bay St. Louis

The Washington Street Historic District comprises the remains of a small black community that had developed in Bay St. Louis by the 1920s. Architecturally, the district furnished excellent visual evidence of the evolution of the shotgun and Creole cottage house types. Washington Street is one of the early through streets leading to the Jordan River, and in the 1800s it also led to Edwards Bayou, where a mill was located. Two houses in the district remain from the early period. The first, at 429 Washington Street, may have been constructed as early as 1875 and is a classic example of the Creole cottage, with central chimney, undercut gallery, and the four-bay facade with two entrances leading to the gallery. The other, at 440 Washington Street, dates from about 1890 and is a distinctive local variation of the shotgun form, displaying a one-bay polygonal facade with rear ell and two-sided undercut porch.

Now residential in character, the Washington Street area contained many more commercial and religious buildings in the 1920s. A black church and a two-story lodge hall were located in the 400 block of Washington Street but are no longer extant. Two important examples of vernacular commercial architecture remain in the district. The first of these is a shotgun building distinguished from a residence by its canopy and orientation to the sidewalk; and the second is the building at the corner of Washington and St. Francis streets, which is a combined residence and business building. [Bay St. Louis MRA, CA 11/25/80, 80002243]

HARRISON COUNTY

Pleasant Reed House
928 Elmer Street
Biloxi

Built around 1887, the Pleasant Reed House is a symbol of the contribution made by the local black community to the history of Biloxi. The building is a remarkably complete example of the shotgun house that became one of the dominant residential types on the Mississippi coast during the late 19th century. Constructed by Pleasant Reed and owned and occupied by members of the Reed family ever since, the Pleasant Reed House is the principal surviving evidence of the saga of this newly freed black family of 13 members. Pleasant Reed was the son of Benjamin and Charlotte Reed, slaves of John B. Reed at Enon on the Leaf River, in Perry County, Mississippi. By the time of Benjamin Reed's death in 1908, the Reed family was the largest black family in Biloxi, and its members became influential in the early development of every segment of local industry considered basic to the area economy, including fishing, lumber milling, railroading, tourism, and fuel supply. [CA 1/11/79, 79001308]

HINDS COUNTY

Ayer Hall
1400 Lynch Street on Jackson State University campus
Jackson

Ayer Hall, constructed in 1903 as the first academic building on the Jackson College (now Jackson State University) campus, is important for its role in the development of education for African Americans in Mississippi. Originally established in Natchez, Mississippi, as Natchez Seminary, Jackson College was the direct outgrowth of a humanitarian movement that had its roots in antislavery sentiment within northern Protestant churches. The movement emerged during and after the Civil War as a missionary commitment to aid the newly freed blacks of the South. In keeping with this spirit, the American Baptist Home Mission Society of New York in 1877 authorized Dr. Charles Ayer (1826–1901) of New York to establish Natchez Seminary for the training of black teachers and preachers who could provide sound leadership within the black community. The founders of Natchez Seminary saw as their broad goal the development of the black sector as a vital force in the political, social, and cultural life of the state.

By 1883 the need for expanded accommodations and a more central location within the state resulted in a move to Jackson, where the society purchased the Campbell property on North State Street, consisting of 52 acres of land with a mansion. Recognizing the importance of a location within the black community, the Mission Society sold the North State Street site to Major Reuben Webster Millsaps in 1902. In 1903 the present site in southwest Jackson on Lynch Street was purchased for $7,800. Ayer Hall, the first building on the site, originally intended for use as a men's dormitory, at various times since 1912 has also housed a chapel, president's office, library, classrooms, and other facilities. [A 7/14/77, 77000788]

Farish Street Neighborhood Historic District
Roughly bounded by Amite, Mill, Fortification, and Lamar streets
Jackson

The Farish Street Neighborhood Historic District, consisting of 695 buildings located in a 125-acre area in downtown Jackson, is the largest black community in Mississippi. By the 1890s the land now located within the historic district became a segregated area for African Americans. The area is historically associated with black professionals who achieved prominence on state, local, and national levels. One of the wealthiest black residents of Jackson was Dr. Sidney D. Redmond, whose house within the district still stands at 229 East Church Street. Physician, businessman, and banker, Redmond was president of the American Trust and Savings Bank, one of two black banks established in Jackson by 1904; a stockholder in three banks controlled by whites and in one of the power-and-light companies; and chairman of the state Republican executive committee. Black businesspeople owned their own shops, and black craftsworkers constructed many of the buildings in the district. The district is an excellent record of vernacular building dating from around 1860 through the 1940s. The majority of the buildings were built between 1890 and 1930, reflecting the growth and prosperity of Jackson and the neighborhood during that period. [CAB 3/13/80, 80002245]

Farish Street Neighborhood Historic District (Boundary Increase)
Roughly bounded by Amite, Lamar, Mill, and Fortification streets
Jackson

The Farish Street Neighborhood Historic District (Boundary Increase) contains one and one-half square blocks with inner courts and approximately 125 buildings similar to those contained in the Farish Street Historic District. As part of the Farish Street neighborhood, the largest economically independent black community in Mississippi, this area was a portion of the residential section of that community and contains many buildings constructed by local black contractors.

Creole cottages built around 1880 remain on Blair and Cohea streets, and a cluster of Queen Anne style cottages is located on West Church Street. Robert Rhodes, Jr., who constructed the stucco Bungalow style cottages in the district, also built his own house on Blair Street. Shotgun cottages from c. 1903 line one block of Farish and Church streets. Lamar Street contains Bungalow style residences as well as the Alex Williams House, a two-story Colonial Revival style house that reflects the prominence of its original owner, one of the first black merchants in the neighborhood (see also Alex Williams House). The buildings in the area are reflective of the same early 20th-century growth and development patterns as the originally listed district. [CB 9/18/80, 80004542]

Mississippi State Capitol
Mississippi Street between North President and North West streets
Jackson

The old Mississippi State Capitol is the site of several important events that make it a symbol of the struggle for civil rights in 19th-century America. In 1865 the building was the location of the passage of Mississippi's "Black Codes," legislation restricting the movement and actions of free blacks in the state. The passage of the codes doomed President Lincoln's moderate Reconstruction policies in Mississippi and in other southern states and led to the passage of both the first federal civil rights law—the Civil Rights Act of 1866—and the 14th Amendment to the Constitution of the United States.

In 1870 the building became the location of the election of Hiram R. Revels to the United States Senate, which—since he was the first African American to serve in Congress—marked the beginning of active black participation in the federal legislature (see also Alcorn State University Historic District, Claiborne County).

Finally, the Old Mississippi State Capitol was the location of the passage of the state's Constitution of 1890, which marked Mississippi as the first state to formally disenfranchise African Americans without ostensible violation of the 15th Amendment. In order to dismantle these disenfranchisement policies during the 1960s, Congress passed the Voting Rights Act of 1965. The old Mississippi State Capitol was designated a National Historic Landmark on December 14, 1990. [CA 11/25/69, 69000086]

Smith Robertson Elementary School
528 Bloom Street
Jackson

Smith Robertson Elementary School is located on the site of the first public school building for African Americans in Jackson, Mississippi, and the "mother school" for all of Jackson's black community. Black public education in Jackson resulted from an 1894 city ordinance providing for the erection of a school build-

ing for black children. Soon after, a wood frame building was constructed on Bloom Street. In 1903 it was named for Smith Robertson, an African American who had served as alderman from the city's Fourth Ward. Robertson was born a slave in Fayette, Alabama, in January 1840. He came to Jackson in 1874 and opened a barbershop, and he soon became widely respected as one of Jackson's outstanding citizens. He served as city alderman from 1893 until his death in 1899. At a time when popular support for black education in Mississippi was drastically on the wane, it was through Robertson's influence that the city fathers moved to establish the school. In 1897 the city government appointed him a trustee of the school.

The original school building was burned on January 3, 1909, but was immediately rebuilt and opened again on September 20, 1909. Subsequent additions to the building occurred throughout the years. The front portion of the building was constructed in 1929 and is an early and sophisticated example of the Art Deco style in Mississippi.

On June 22, 1971, Smith Robertson Elementary School became one of nine city schools closed by an order of the U.S. Fifth Circuit Court of Appeals to achieve racial integration of the Jackson public schools. Through the efforts of interested citizens, the city of Jackson, and the Department of Archives and History, the school building was renovated for use as a museum in 1984. The Smith Robertson Museum and Cultural Center interprets the life, history, and culture of black Mississippians. [CA 12/13/78, 78001601]

West Capitol Street Historic District
Roughly bounded by railroad tracks and Amite, Roach, and Pearl streets
Jackson

The West Capitol Street Historic District reflects the importance of West Capitol Street as a turn-of-the-century commercial center and the subsequent growth and development of black businesses during the 1920s in Jackson. Before 1885 there was little commercial activity on West Capitol Street; the main business center was located near the old Capitol on State Street and extended down East Capitol Street as far as President Street. By 1890 Jackson had recovered from the Reconstruction period. The population had increased, and new houses were built northwest and south of the old section of town. By 1900 brick commercial blocks had been constructed on the north side of West Capitol Street as far east as 214, and the 200 block was entirely completed by 1925. Located on this block, in the building at 232, were the law offices of prominent black attorneys Beadle and Howard. Although attorney Perry Howard (1877–1961) later moved to Washington, D.C., he became the leader of Mississippi's "Black and Tan" Republicans, a group of African Americans sponsoring delegates at the Republican National Conventions until 1956. [CA 3/13/80, 80002248]

Alex Williams House
937 North Lamar Street
Jackson

Built in 1912, the Colonial Revival style Alex Williams House was constructed by George Thomas, a self-taught black contractor well known for his construction of Bungalow style residences in the community. The size of the two-story house and its formalism distinguished it from its neighbors, which were small vernacular cottages or dwellings designed in the Bungalow style. The house was constructed for Alex Williams, a black grocer who owned property that ran 400 feet west along present Lamar Lane and whose store was located immediately north of it. The Ionic columns are said to have been built to Alex Williams's specifications, and the interior was planned with Thomas's assistance by members of the Williams family. By 1922 Harry and Betty Marino owned the house. Harry Marino was a cotton sampler with the W. J. Davis Company, and Betty Marino was a teacher at Smith Robertson Elementary School (see also Smith Robertson Elementary School). The couple resided in the house until 1945. Around 1950 the building became the Greystone Hotel, which it remains today. [C 7/3/79, 79001313]

JACKSON COUNTY

Thomas Isaac Keys House
1017 DeSoto Avenue
Ocean Springs

The Thomas Isaac Keys House is the home of the first black postmaster of Ocean Springs. Keys, a staunch Republican merchant, was first appointed in 1889 during the administration of Benjamin Harrison. He subsequently served during the McKinley, Theodore Roosevelt, and Taft administrations. The last quarter of the 19th century was a period of cooperation between the predominantly white Democratic party and black Republicans in Mississippi. In exchange for black concessions on local and state levels, white Democratic representatives in Washington directed federal patronage toward blacks during Republican administrations. Keys's tenure as postmaster ended in 1911. He remained politically active, however, serving as delegate to the Republican National Convention in Cleveland, Ohio, in 1924. The property has remained in the Keys family, which has maintained a tradition of public service. [Ocean Springs MRA, B 4/20/87, 87000592]

JEFFERSON DAVIS COUNTY

1907 House

East of Prentiss on Fort Stephens Road
Prentiss

Said to have built by slaves as a plantation residence for the Magee family around 1820, this house is the site of the 1907 founding of Prentiss Normal Industrial Institute, one of the oldest educational institutions for African Americans in Mississippi. The Prentiss Normal and Industrial Institute was organized in June 1907 by Jonas Edward and Bertha LaBranche Johnson, who with other ambitious African Americans purchased the former Magee property from W. L. Polk, a white landowner who had bought it from the Magee family in 1901. The 1907 House was used both as living quarters for the Johnsons and as a classroom facility for the school. Jonas Edward Johnson, an Alcorn College graduate, was president from 1907 until his death in 1953. His wife, a graduate of Tuskegee Institute, then became president, and upon her death in 1971, she was succeeded by her son, A. L. Johnson.

Licensed by the state as a private high school in 1909 and as a private junior college in 1931, Prentiss Institute Junior College received county funds for the operation of its elementary and secondary education programs until 1959, at which time a public school was organized in the town of Prentiss to serve the educational needs of the county's black children. Most of the elementary and secondary courses offered by the college were discontinued after 1959, although several are still available through the junior college curriculum. [CA 2/14/79, 79001321]

LAUDERDALE COUNTY

Carnegie Branch Library

2721 13th Street
Meridian

This public library branch was built with the aid of an $8,000 grant from the Carnegie Foundation. The branch was specifically built for "the colored citizens" after a group of black Methodists requested such a library. It is believed that Meridian was the only city ever given a black library by the Carnegie Foundation as a part of an original grant. The church that originally requested the library donated the site to the city, but upon the closing of the branch in 1974, the property reverted to the St. Paul United Methodist Church. [Meridian MRA, A 12/18/79, 79003385]

Masonic Temple

1220 26th Avenue
Meridian

The Masonic Temple was constructed in 1903 and owned jointly by three black fraternal lodges. This two-story, five-bay frame building has a central recessed entrance with a pediment supported by fluted Ionic pilasters that carry an entablature bearing the keystone of Masonry and the insignia of the Shriners. The interior features a reception hall and banquet hall. The 1907 *Guide of the Colored Community* states that "this splendid home is not only a standing tribute to the business capacity and enterprise of the colored people of this city, but also a perpetual monument to their appreciation of and fidelity to the God-given laws and lessons taught by the code and creed of Masonry." Today, it is still being used as a Masonic lodge. [Meridian MRA, A 12/18/79, 79003395]

Meridian Baptist Seminary
Intersection of 16th Street and 31st
Avenue
Meridian

Organized in 1896, Meridian Baptist Seminary was one of the early educational institutions founded for blacks in eastern Mississippi. Classes were initially held in the basement of the New Hope Baptist Church. G. M. Reese was elected president of the school in 1899, a position he held until his death in 1939. A two-story frame building was erected in 1905 to house classrooms. In 1920–21 this frame building was demolished, and the existing brick building was erected on the same site. Local black builders Tom Ware, Albert Gains, and Adam Peterson are believed to have constructed the building. The school flourished during the 1920s and 1930s under the leadership of President Reese. Course offerings included a traditional high school curriculum with college preparatory and vocational programs, as well as black history. After 1949 the seminary offered only two-year high school transfer certificates, and academic offerings were gradually curtailed until the closing of the school in 1972. [A 1/8/79, 79001326]

Merrehope Historic District
Roughly bounded by 33rd Avenue, 30th
Avenue, 14th Street, 25th Avenue, and
8th Street
Meridian

Merrehope Historic District represents black heritage and progress in Meridian during the city's Golden Age development. The black businesses and institutions of this district testify to the black involvement in this area. In 1908 African Americans owned and operated more than 50 businesses in Meridian, including drugstores, funeral homes, real estate corporations, tailoring and millinery stores, hotels, cafes, groceries, the Queen City Savings Bank, and three newspapers, the *Mississippi Monitor, Teacher and Preaching,* and *Meridian Headlight.* In addition, black lawyers, physicians, teachers, and nurses lived in this neighborhood. A black fire company was located at 9th Street and 27th Avenue between 1884 and 1903. Two black churches, both of which have since been demolished, served the neighborhoods—the First Baptist Church on 13th Street and the St. Paul United Methodist Church, first built in 1867 at 26th Avenue and 12th Street and replaced in 1888. Also there were the Haven Institute and the Meridian Academy, formerly located at the present site of the St. Paul United Methodist Church; the Masonic Temple; and the Carnegie Branch Library, the only Carnegie library for African Americans in the country (see also Carnegie Branch Library and Masonic Temple). [Meridian MRA, CA 9/19/88, 88000973]

Wechsler School
1415 30th Avenue
Meridian

Built in 1894, Wechsler School is believed to be the first brick public school constructed for African Americans in Mississippi with funds derived from public school bonds. The two-story brick building acquired its name from Rabbi Judah (Jacob) Wechsler, the leader of Meridian's Congregation Beth Israel from 1887 to 1893, who had had great interest in and influence on black education in Meridian. The building originally housed the first through eighth grades.

In 1921–22 the curriculum at Wechsler expanded to 12 grades with six students graduating that spring. With the addition of the 12th grade, Wechsler became the only public school in east central Mississippi granting black students a high school diploma. During the 1922–23 school year, Wechsler added classes for adults.

In 1929 the Meridian-State Normal for Teachers (Blacks) , a two-month summer normal school program, moved to Wechsler. Teachers with less than a high school education attended the classes in June and July while the elementary students were on summer break. They renewed their teaching licenses until they earned enough credits for a high school diploma. In 1929, 50 teachers graduated from the normal school at Wechsler.

The high school moved from Wechsler to T. J. Harris School in 1937. Thereafter Wechsler was used as an elementary and junior high school until 1971. From 1971 to 1983 Wechsler served as a public kindergarten for both black and white students. Presently Wechsler serves as a nutritional center for senior citizens. [A 7/15/91, 91000880]

LEFLORE COUNTY

Wesley Memorial Methodist Episcopal
800 Howard Street
Greenwood

Wesley Memorial Methodist Episcopal Church (now known as the Wesley United Methodist Church), was organized in 1870. The church was an outgrowth of the desire of the black community to have a greater voice in church affairs by organizing their own churches, distinct from the white churches where they had worshipped as slaves. The present building was built in 1921 and was designed by local architect Frank R. McGeoy. Constructed with a companion gymnasium wing, the church complex, before integration, was the site of such functions as school basketball games and graduation ceremonies. The Wesley United Methodist Church has continued to serve for many years as the center of social activity for the Greenwood black community. [Greenwood MRA, CA 11/4/85, 85003461]

MADISON COUNTY

John W. Boddie House
Tougaloo College campus
Tougaloo

This Italianate style house was built around 1850 for John W. Boddie, a wealthy planter who died at the end of the Civil War and whose house became the nucleus of Tougaloo College, an institution significant in the educational history of black Mississippians. Following the Civil War, education, housing, and employment of freed slaves were major concerns of the United States Freedmen's Bureau and the American Missionary Association (AMA). By 1868 the AMA, in conjunction with the Freedmen's Bureau, had in operation four primary, eight graded, and two normal schools for Mississippi's freedmen. In 1869 the AMA purchased John Boddie's mansion and the surrounding 500-acre plantation for $10,500. The mansion was to become the nucleus of the boarding school that would teach industrial arts and train black teachers. From its inception Tougaloo was coeducational, although courses of study for boys and girls were entirely different: girls were taught housekeeping, millinery, and nursing; boys were taught architectural drawing, farming methods, and woodworking.

In 1889 the college abandoned its primary school and became an academic high school and a normal school. The college department began in 1897, and the first college class graduated in 1901. In 1916 the school became Tougaloo College, for which the Boddie House holds administrative offices. [CA 5/13/82, 82003106]

Catherine Hall in the Mississippi Industrial College Historic District. Photo courtesy of the Mississippi Department of Archives and History (Jack A. Gold).

MARSHALL COUNTY

Mississippi Industrial College Historic District
Memphis Street
Holly Springs

Mississippi Industrial College Historic District consists of five historic buildings located across the street from the campus of Rust College. Established in 1905 as an educational institution for African Americans, Mississippi Industrial College was founded by the Mississippi Conference of the Colored Methodist Episcopal Church, under the leadership of Bishop Elias Cottrell (1855–1937), a prominent theologian in the region.

Catherine Hall was constructed in 1905 at a cost of $35,000. An existing antebellum brick building is said to have been incorporated in to the construction of Catherine Hall. This claim is based on the fact that an expenditure of $10,000 was allocated the same year for repairs to an old building standing on the site of the present Catherine Hall. Thereafter Hammond Hall (1907), Washington Hall (1910), Carnegie Auditorium (1923), and Davis Hall (1950) were built on the same site.

The early educational mission of the school focused on theological, vocational-technical, and musical training for black youths from preschool through college age. Since 1940, the curriculum has been revised, with emphasis placed on college-level teacher training, arts and sciences, and business management. [CA 1/20/80, 80002290]

Oakview
Rust College campus
Holly Springs

Oakview (Rust College Infirmary) is one of the oldest extant buildings associated with black education in the state of Mississippi. Believed to have been built as a kitchen for a plantation planned by Ulysses Ross, a wealthy Holly Springs contractor, Oakview, as well as other

Rust College buildings, is located on the site of the former slave auction grounds of Holly Springs. The outbreak of the Civil War halted construction of the main house and other outbuildings. This is the only 19th-century building remaining on the campus of Rust College, the first black normal institute in the state and the first college established by the Methodist Episcopal Church. The school was founded in 1866 and chartered as Shaw College in 1870. Shaw College represented the earliest effort made during Reconstruction by the Freedman's Aid Bureau, part of the Methodist Episcopal Church (North), to educate black children and train black teachers. In 1892 the school's name was changed to Rust College in honor of Dr. Richard S. Rust, then secretary of the Freedman's Bureau. [Holly Springs MRA, A 6/28/82, 82003110]

MONROE COUNTY

South Central Aberdeen Historic District
Roughly bounded by Locust, Washington, Franklin, and High streets
Aberdeen

Within the boundaries of the South Central Aberdeen Historic District are architecturally significant Greek Revival style cottages dating from Aberdeen's antebellum "flush times"; the town's finest collection of late 19th- and early 20th-century houses along South Franklin Street, which became known as Silk Stocking Row; and bungalows and various 20th-century houses. Also within the district is the most intact cluster of turn-of-the-century residences for middle-class African Americans in Aberdeen.

The growth of this middle-class black neighborhood centered on the intersection of West Jefferson and South Columbus streets. After the Civil War, the former slave Windsor Reynolds acquired the city block bounded by Jefferson, Long, Washington, and Columbus streets. He and his wife, Ann, subdivided the land into lots and sold them to African Americans. Other successful African American businesspeople built homes on Columbus between Jefferson and Madison streets.

Little is known about Aberdeen's black neighborhoods at the turn of the century. Besides the one included in this district, others were located to the north around Vine Street; to the south around Chaffie, Burnett, and Forrest streets; and where Jackson Street intersects Chestnut and Locust streets. Although the population of the neighborhood surrounding Jefferson and Columbus streets is now predominantly white, the buildings reflect the historic period when it flourished as a black residential community. [Aberdeen MRA, CA 4/22/88, 88000134]

OKTIBBEHA COUNTY

Odd Fellows Cemetery
Junction of U.S. Route 82 and Henderson Street
Starkville

The Odd Fellows Cemetery represents the long-standing historical presence of the black community in Starkville by documenting on its gravestones the existence of generations of African Americans. The cemetery appears to have originated about 1911, when the land it occupies was purchased by Lodge No. 2948 of the Grand United Order of Odd Fellows of America, a white organization that donated the land for use as a black burial ground. It soon became the main cemetery for the black community of Starkville. Over the decades the Odd Fellows Cemetery has become the last resting place for the most prominent leaders of Starkville's black community, including the educator E. W. Hazen and businessmen N. F. Daily, Charles Alexander, and Robert Wier. The life of Robert Wier was memorialized in a biography written by his wife, Sadye H. Wier, and published by the University Press of Mississippi. Since 1976 the cemetery has been the subject of a continuing restoration effort that has resulted in the well-maintained appearance of the cemetery today. [A 7/24/90, 90001064]

WARREN COUNTY

Beulah Cemetery
Intersection of Openwood Street and Old Jackson Road
Vicksburg

Beulah Cemetery is one of the most intact historic properties associated with the development and growth of the black community in Vicksburg. The cemetery was established in 1884 by the Vicksburg Tabernacle No. 19 Independent Order of Brothers and Sisters of Love and Charity, a fraternal order that had wide support among African Americans in Vicksburg.

The organization purchased 52 acres along the old Jackson Road for $1,000 for the purpose of establishing the cemetery. Before the development of the cemetery, African Americans were buried in church cemeteries or in private yards. Named for the proverbial land of Beulah of biblical origin, the cemetery documents the existence of generations of African Americans for whom there might otherwise be no surviving material memorial. Some of the locally prominent members of the black community buried at Beulah are Rosa A. Temple, educator and namesake of Rosa A. Temple High School; G. M. McIntyre, principal of Cherry Street School, for whom a school was also named; Robert Banks Marshall, the city's first black postal employee; William Tillmon Jones, grand chancellor of the Knights of Pythias from 1889 until 1906; and members of the Jefferson and Dillon families, founders of local black funeral homes. [Vicksburg MPS, A 10/23/92, 92001404]

Metropolitan AME Zion Church in the Santa Fe Place Historic District, Jackson County. Photo courtesy of the Missouri Department of Natural Resources (Patricia Brown Glenn).

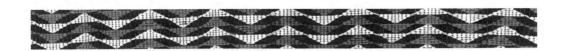

MISSOURI

BOONE COUNTY

John W. Boone House
4th Street between East Broadway and
Walnut
Columbia

John William "Blind" Boone was an internationally renowned black concert pianist and composer during the 1890s and early 20th century. Overcoming obstacles stemming from his race and his blindness, he performed programs ranging from classical selections to humorous camp songs and featuring his own ragtime and popular compositions. Boone occupied this house in Columbia during most of his professional career and was regarded as one of Columbia's most generous and public-minded citizens. His performed fund-raising concerts for many many black churches, schools, and other organizations before his death in 1927. [Social Institutions of Columbia's Black Community TR, A 9/4/80, 80002309]

Frederick Douglass School
310 North Providence Road
Columbia

The history of the Frederick Douglass School can be traced to 1868, when the Cummings Academy opened under the auspices of the local black churches. In 1872 the school received official recognition as the Columbia Black Public School.

In 1885 a new school was built and the name was changed to the Excelsior School. Upon petition from the black community in 1898, the Columbia Board of Education officially changed the name to the Frederick Douglass School. The present building was finished in 1917 and served as the Columbia black high school until 1954, when Columbia's public schools were integrated. [Social Institutions of Columbia's Black Community TR, A 9/4/80, 80002310]

Second Baptist Church
Intersection of 4th Street and Broadway
Columbia

Black congregations in Missouri grew rapidly after the Civil War. Initially many black citizens attended white churches, but they became dissatisfied with being required to sit in specified areas of the church like the back or the gallery. Consequently, black members formed their own congregations and built their own churches. The first black Baptist church in Columbia was organized by the Reverend William F. Brooks in 1866. After worshiping in various locations the congregation moved into the larger present church, which they named the Second Baptist Church, in 1894.

Partially through the help of John William "Blind" Boone, a nationally and internationally renowned concert pianist and composer during the 1890s and early 20th century, the Second Baptist Church grew and, in turn, fostered black education. The church was an important religious, educational, and social institution in the black community (See also John W. Boone House). [Social Institutions of Columbia's Black Community TR, A 9/4/80, 80002313]

Second Christian Church
401 North 5th
Columbia

Although its congregation was smaller than two other black churches in Columbia, the Second Christian Church, formed in 1872 by the Reverend Burrell Basket, played an important part in the social and religious development of black citizens in a segregated society. In addition, it provided financial support for many of the educational activities in Columbia, such as the Frederick Douglass School. [Social Institutions of Columbia's Black Community TR, A 9/4/80, 80002314]

St. Paul AME Church
Intersection of 15th and Park streets
Columbia

African Americans who had belonged to the Methodist Episcopal Church established St. Paul's African Methodist Episcopal Church in 1880. Like the Second Baptist Church, it was built through the determination of the black community. Congregations from both churches sponsored community fairs and dinners and divided the proceeds between the two churches. Through these events they united not only their own congregations, but all Columbia African Americans, spiritually and socially. (See also Second Baptist Church.) [Social Institutions of Columbia's Black Community TR, A 9/4/80, 80002315]

COLE COUNTY

Jefferson City Community Center
608 East Dunklin Street
Jefferson City

The Jefferson City Community Center symbolizes important social, cultural, and educational efforts by local African Americans to improve conditions in their community during and after the Great Depression. The community center was established by the Jefferson City Community Center Association, which was incorporated in 1935. It was located in the midst of one of the greatest concentrations of African American residences and businesses in Jefferson City in the 1930s and 1940s. Its activities included providing food to needy community members, education, charity, recreation, and social activities conducive to good citizenship.

During World War II the Jefferson City Community Center also served as a United Service Organizations (USO) Center for black military personnel, a function it resumed during the Korean conflict. From 1948 until the early 1950s, it provided a nursery school for young children. It served as the heart of the African American community in Jefferson City into the early 1960s.

The Jefferson City Community Center is located only half a block from Lincoln University, a traditionally African American institution of higher education founded during the Civil War and initially funded by African American Missourians who served in the 62nd and 65th Regiments of the United States Colored Infantry. Lincoln University helped form the physical and social context for the Community Center.

Today the Jefferson City Community Center meets the needs of the new community, which is more racially mixed than

Young Hall in the Lincoln University Hilltop Campus Historic District. Photo courtesy of the Missouri Department of Natural Resources (James M. Denny).

previously, and serves as a meeting place for local organizations and various church congregations. [A 5/14/92, 92000503]

Lincoln Univ. Hilltop Campus Historic District
820 Chestnut Street
Jefferson City

The first school named for President Abraham Lincoln was created from the donations of black Civil War soldiers. The 62nd Colored Infantry, most of whom were Missourians, served in Louisiana and Texas until 1866. At Fort McIntosh, Texas, Lieutenants Foster and Adamson, white officers of the regiment, conceived the idea of an institution for discharged African Americans, many of whom had learned to read and write while in the army. Adamson asked Foster if he would be willing to take charge of a school in Missouri if the regiment would give

money to start it. Foster agreed; a collection was taken. The white officers of the regiment raised $1,034.60 while the black soldiers contributed $3,966.50 toward the founding of the school.

It was difficult for Foster to find a suitable building to house the school. The white Methodist church in Jefferson City refused the use of their sanctuary because the pupils would be black; the black Methodist church refused because the teacher would be white. In 1866 Foster settled for an old log cabin on the outskirts of the city at a place called Hobo Hill. He named the school Lincoln Institute. Classes were later moved to the Second Baptist Church.

In 1870 Lincoln Institute, under the leadership of James Milton Turner, became a training facility for black public school teachers. The school acquired a new campus called "The Hill" with state money, and the first building of Lincoln Institute, a general classroom, was completed in 1871. In 1880 Inman E. Page became the first president of Lincoln Institute. Under his leadership and with state funding, construction on the campus increased rapidly. By 1898 the college had five new buildings, including a gymnasium and the president's house.

As a result of legislation sponsored by Walthall M. Moore, Missouri's first black state representative, Lincoln Institute became Lincoln University in 1921. It was to offer black students educational activities as extensive as those of the segregated University of Missouri. [A 4/28/83, 83000978]

COOPER COUNTY

St. Matthew's Chapel AME Church
309 Spruce Street
Boonville

Settled by Colonel Benjamin Cooper in 1808, Boonville was a key riverport on the Missouri River and the chief agricultural center for goods traveling to the Southwest over the Santa Fe Trail. The town, named for Daniel Boone, did not have a significant black population until after the Civil War, but the black population approximately doubled from 1865 to 1875. The increase was in part the result of a statewide migration of African Americans from rural areas to towns in search of increased economic opportunity. In 1869 St. Matthew's Chapel African Methodist Episcopal (AME) Church was established. This followed a trend that began in 1787 when African Americans at Philadelphia's St. George's Church withdrew their membership because of discrimination and eventually established the AME Church in 1794, which began to expand throughout the Midwest in the 1840s. [Boonville Missouri MRA, A 3/16/90, 82005324]

Sumner Public School
321 Spruce Street
Boonville

On January 11, 1865, the Missouri constitutional convention passed an ordinance that required immediate emancipation of the state's remaining slaves. In the spring of 1865 the general assembly rescinded an 1847 constitutional amendment that forbade the education of Missouri African Americans. The following year the assembly enacted a series of measures intended to establish and fund black schools in each township or city. In 1866 the first black school in Boonville, the Elias Buckner School, opened in a house on the northwest corner of 4th and Spruce streets. When this building was destroyed by fire, it was replaced by the Sumner Public School in 1916. In 1939 the Sumner School received accreditation, and a third building, also named the Sumner School, was constructed in east Boonville. The 1916 building remained vacant until 1940, when it was sold to the Spruce Street Investment Corporation and converted to apartments. The building is one of only three historic black public buildings remaining in Boonville. [Boonville Missouri MRA, A 3/16/90, 82005331]

FRANKLIN COUNTY

AME Church of New Haven
225 Selma Street
New Haven

One of the few historic public institutions in Missouri reflecting the state's black heritage, the African Methodist Episcopal (AME) Church of New Haven is one of only 61 black churches identified in a statewide survey, and one of only two in Franklin County. The building is further distinguished by its exceptional state of preservation.

Founded in 1794 and formally organized in 1816, the AME Church is the oldest of the historic black denominations. The AME Church of New Haven was constructed to serve a congregation organized in 1865 by former slave Anna Pryor Bell. The church was originally housed in a log cabin along the Missouri River. The site proved unsuitable because of periodic flooding, prompting Bell and other members of the congregation to solicit funds for the construction of a new church in a more suitable location.

The present building was constructed in 1892. Sometime after Anna Bell's death in 1905, the building became known as Anna Bell Chapel. Through the years, the membership of the AME Church of New Haven has dwindled. The building remains in use, however, with services held twice a month. The New Haven Preservation Society, meanwhile, is working to increase public awareness of the church's place in the black heritage of Franklin County. [A 8/18/92, 92001002]

JACKSON COUNTY

Attucks School
1815 Woodland Avenue
Kansas City

Constructed in 1905, the Attucks School is the oldest continuously occupied school built for Kansas City's black students. The school, named after Crispus Attucks, was established in 1893 in a rented building on East 18th Street and moved to a nearby building on the same street in 1894. During the late 1890s enrollment in the school district increased rapidly, and the school building was deemed inadequate for its many students.

The present Attucks School building was constructed in 1905 at a cost of $36,811. As the black population of the surrounding area grew rapidly over the years, the school once again became overcrowded. In 1922 a two-story wing was added to the building. Over the next several decades the Attucks School was one of the main grade schools for black students in Kansas City. Following the integration of public schools in the 1960s, the Attucks School became a grade school for all races. The building is still used as a school for students in the area, continuing its tradition of service to the community. [18th and Vine Area of Kansas City MPS, A 9/9/91, 91001150]

18th and Vine Historic District
Roughly bounded by 18th Street, Woodland Avenue, 19th Street, and The Paseo
Kansas City

The 18th and Vine Historic District is is historically important as a center for black commerce in the late 19th and early 20th centuries and as the most intact grouping of buildings in Kansas City associated with the growth and development of jazz in the 1920s and 1930s. African Americans began to move to the area from traditional neighborhoods along the Mississippi River in the 1880s. The 18th and Vine area quickly became a residential center for the black community, and by 1900 a commercial area had begun to develop along 18th Street. The steady growth in the black population and the resulting new construction in the early 20th century transformed the area into a dense urban landscape of residences, commercial buildings, theaters, office buildings, and institutional buildings by 1920. Commercial buildings erected during the boom years in the 1920s were key to the area's development as the center for black enterprise and home to the city's most prominent black professionals and businesspeople.

The emergence of the 18th and Vine area as a commercial center coincided with its rise as a center for jazz music and musicians. The 1920s and 1930s saw a proliferation of nightclubs in the area, featuring the Kansas City style jazz that originated around 1920 with the formation of bands led by Bennie Moten. The Lincoln Building, Gem Theater, and New Rialto Theater are among the jazz showcases still standing in the district.

The coming of World War II and the end of the administration of Kansas City Mayor Tom Pendergast, who allowed the prostitution and bootlegging of liquor on which many of the nightclubs thrived, in the late 1930s led to the closing of clubs throughout the city. The influence of jazz in the 18th and Vine area waned, and some of the city's most prominent jazz musicians, such as Count Basie and Charlie Parker, left Kansas City for Chicago and New York.

Modern development in other sectors of the city has drawn much of the black business activity away from the 18th and Vine area. Despite these changes, the 18th and Vine Historic District remains a significant collection of residential and commercial buildings that represent Kansas City's jazz era and its period of thriving black commerce. [18th and Vine Area of Kansas City MPS, A 9/9/91 NHL, 84004142]

Mutual Musicians' Foundation Building
1823 Highland Avenue
Kansas City

Within the first three decades of the 20th century, Kansas City experienced a large increase in its black population following a rapid migration to urban centers. To satisfy the demand for entertainment that grew out of a diverse culture, a separate world of black entertainment evolved, derived principally from minstrel shows, vaudeville, and ragtime, culminating in its greatest product, jazz. Before

World War I, the main center of jazz was New Orleans. In 1917 city authorities closed down the largest club and red-light district in the country, dispersing many performers to other American cities. A number of them arrived in Kansas City. The genesis of Kansas City jazz dates from approximately 1917, following the organization of the Musician's Union Local 627.

The Mutual Musicians' Foundation Building was a second home, a training ground, and a source of jobs for approximately 90 percent of the musicians who created the powerful Kansas City sound of the 1930s and 1940s. Many of the nations's leading jazz musicians were members of the Mutual Musicians' Foundation, Inc. They included Count Basie, Lester Young, Charlie "Bird" Parker, and Julia Lee, one of the most popular vocalists of the 1940s. The building is immortalized in the song "627 Stomp," one of the original boogie-woogie tunes by jazz great Pete Johnson and singer Joe Turner. The building was designated a National Historic Landmark on December 21, 1981. [A 2/7/79 NHL, 79001372]

Paseo YMCA
1824 The Paseo
Kansas City

The branch of the Young Men's Christian Association that became the Paseo YMCA was organized in 1902 for Kansas City's growing black population. In 1907 three small buildings were constructed at a cost of $10,000 for use by the branch. The organization soon outgrew its buildings, though, and began to examine ways in which to raise money for a new facility. In 1910 Chicago philanthropist Julius Rosenwald offered $25,000 to any group that could raise $75,000 for a black YMCA. The black and white residents of Kansas City combined to raise $80,000 to win the grant from Rosenwald. The present building was completed in 1914 and named the Paseo YMCA, as it was located on the broad avenue called The Paseo in the Paseo district, the most densely populated black neighborhood in the city.

Over the course of its service to the black community, the Paseo YMCA provided lodging, a dining hall and cafeteria, and meeting halls; organized basketball, swimming, and other athletic teams; and sponsored youth groups, Boy Scout troops, and Bible study classes. For many years the Paseo YMCA was the only community enterprise entirely supported and operated by African Americans. During the 1920s and 1930s it provided the only meeting place for black clubs and study groups and the only swimming pool for black residents of the community. The building was open 24 hours a day and was the major social center for black Kansas City residents.

The integration of YMCA facilities in the 1960s, coupled with shifting centers of black population, led to a decline in attendance at the facility. By the 1970s the building had become uneconomical to operate. The building was closed and is presently vacant. The Paseo YMCA possesses a lengthy heritage of service to Kansas City's black residents and remains a landmark on The Paseo. [18th and Vine Area of Kansas City MPS, A 9/9/91, 91001151]

Santa Fe Place Historic District
Roughly bounded by 27th Street, Indiana Avenue, 30th Street, and Prospect Avenue
Kansas City

The Santa Fe neighborhood became the first major residential area in Kansas City where middle- and upper-class African Americans found a residential area that reflected their educational and economic background. It is also the only early black middle-class neighborhood in Kansas City to survive with its architectural integrity intact.

Slavery and the Civil War left a legacy of racism that was manifested in the behavior and social patterns of the Kansas City community. From 1870 to the 1930s black and white relations, mirroring national trends, became increasingly dissonant. A rigorous and systematic pattern of discrimination and segregation evolved, especially in housing and real estate development. Through racially restrictive covenants, white community councils, banks, and real estate developers prevented African Americans, regardless of their economic and educational status, from buying or renting property anywhere except for the traditional areas of black or slum housing.

Unable to live in the Santa Fe neighborhood legally, blacks migrated to areas around the neighborhood. By World War II Prospect Avenue, at the edge of the Santa Fe district, had become a main artery for traffic, and African Americans lived on its west side as well as on the northern boundary of the district. World War II brought thousands more blacks from the South to work in the war industries, and the housing shortage reached a crisis. In response, the Santa Fe residents reinforced their restrictive covenants in 1947. The black community was desperate; it shifted its political attention from education issues to challenging the legality of racially restrictive covenants.

With a series of lawsuits originating in St. Louis, the U.S. Supreme Court issued in 1948 a decision against restrictive covenants based on race. Between 1949 and 1953, African Americans moved into Santa Fe four times faster than into any other area of Kansas City where they could purchase property. The migration of black families into the area occurred with relative peace, perhaps because of the cultural and educational background of the African Americans. In 1956 more African Americans in Kansas City had university degrees than did whites.

Today the neighborhood still boasts the addresses of many of the city's black political, business, and religious leaders, while retaining its image as a successful part of the struggle for civil rights. [CA 5/30/86, 86001204]

LEWIS COUNTY

Lincoln School
Missouri Route B
Canton

Built in 1880, the Lincoln School was the first and only black school in Canton, Missouri. It provided the only educational opportunity for the area's black citizens, teaching grades one through eight and at times providing adult education classes as well. The school closed in 1956 after *Brown v. Board of Education,* the landmark 1954 Supreme Court decision that banned segregation in public schools. [A 2/10/83, 83001029]

MARION COUNTY

Eighth and Center Streets Baptist Church
722 Center Street
Hannibal

The congregation of the Eighth and Center Streets Baptist Church was first organized on November 25, 1837, as the Zoar Church in the home of one of its congregants. The group moved to Hannibal in 1841 and was reorganized under the name of Hannibal United Baptist Church. Located on the corner of 4th and Church streets, the church served both black and white members. The ten-

sions leading to the Civil War resulted in a division of the Baptist church in 1853. The white members formed the First Baptist Church, and the black members moved to the present location.

The lot on which the building now stands was purchased on April 22, 1853, and a church building was erected that served black Baptist, Methodist, and other congregations. A school for black children was located in the rear of this building.

From 1861 to 1865, the school was taught by Blanche K. Bruce. Bruce had escaped from slavery to Hannibal, where he organized the school. After the Civil War Bruce served as United States Senator from Mississippi, becoming the only black senator from Mississippi to serve a full term. He later continued public service in Washington, D.C., where his home is now a National Historic Landmark (see also Blanche K. Bruce House, District of Columbia).

The present church was constructed in 1872. Although membership in the Eighth and Center Streets Baptist Church has declined in recent years, dedicated members continue to keep up the church. The building remains important in the heritage of the black community in Hannibal. [C 9/4/80, 80002376]

NEWTON COUNTY

George Washington Carver National Monument
3 miles south of Monument
Diamond

The George Washington Carver National Monument encompasses 210 acres of the original 240-acre Moses Carver farm. The monument was established to preserve the birthplace and commemorate the rise from slavery of Carver, whose life demonstrates the opportunities afforded in the United States to men of ability and energy, regardless of their origins, and whose accomplishments are today a living part of America's heritage.

George Washington Carver was born around 1861 to slave parents on the plantation of Moses and Susan Carver. According to a story told by Carver's owner, Carver and his mother were kidnapped by a gang of nightriders during the Civil War and taken to Arkansas. Moses Carver sent out a search party and was able to retrieve the baby after giving a racehorse as ransom, but the mother was never seen again. Carver was seriously ill with whooping cough at the time of his rescue and remained in frail health as a result of various illnesses for much of his life. His sicknesses prevented him from doing manual labor and afforded him time to spend in the woods inspecting the plant and animal life.

After the Civil War Carver remained with his former owners, learning tasks such as cooking, cleaning, sewing, and laundering and also learning to read. As a teen, Carver traveled to the nearby town of Neosho to attend a school for black children. Afterward he traveled around the Midwest, working various jobs and attending school whenever possible. He finally graduated from high school in Minneapolis, Kansas. During these years Carver continued and broadened his interest in plant life, collecting and recording specimens and learning to sketch and paint them.

In 1886 Carver became a homesteader on government land in Kansas. He mortgaged his claim in 1888 for $300 and opened a laundry in Winterset, Iowa. Encouraged by friends, he enrolled in Simpson College in Indianola, studying natural sciences, music, and art. On the recommendation of one of his professors, Carver was admitted to Iowa State College at Ames in the spring of 1891 to study botany. Carver excelled in his scientific studies and in art as well, receiving an

George Washington Carver. Photo courtesy of Tuskegee Institute (P. H. Polk).

honorable mention for a still life painting at the World's Columbian Exposition in Chicago in 1893. In 1894 Carver was awarded a bachelor's degree, becoming the first African American to receive a degree from Iowa State College.

After Carver's graduation, Louis Pammell, one of Carver's professors, offered him a position as an assistant in the college's agricultural experiment station. While working at the station, Carver studied for his master's degree in botany. He soon became recognized as an expert in mycology and received invitations to lecture throughout the state. He received his master's degree in 1896.

In the spring of that year, he received an invitation from Booker T. Washington, principal of the Tuskegee Normal and Industrial Institute in Alabama (now Tuskegee University; see also Tuskegee Institute National Historic Site, Macon County, Alabama), to establish a department of agriculture at Tuskegee. Carver would have to start the department from scratch—there was neither a curriculum nor laboratory equipment in place–but he accepted the invitation because he felt education was essential to freedom for African Americans. As a result of Booker T. Washington's efforts, an agricultural experimentation station and agricultural school were established at Tuskegee on February 15, 1897, by an act of the Alabama legislature, which appropriated $1,500 annually for operations and maintenance. Carver was named director of the experiment station.

In this new capacity, Carver dedicated himself to discovering a way to restore fertility to soil depleted of nutrients by the repeated planting of a single crop such as cotton or tobacco, as was the case throughout the South. Carver's experiments with organic and chemical fertilizers and nutrient-restoring crops were taken out of the laboratory as he toured rural communities giving lectures and demonstrations. He brought farmers to the experimentation station to show them how his theories worked. In a further outreach effort, he published a series of bulletins explaining his ideas in simple language that semiliterate people could read and understand. Carver also initiated the "movable school" program, in which he and an assistant drove a mule-drawn wagon through the farmlands, teaching farmers improved techniques for growing and storing food.

Carver is best known, however, as a pioneer in the science of chemurgy, the industrial utilization of agricultural products. From the peanut he developed 300 different products, ranging from face powder to wood stains. Appearing before the House Ways and Means Committee in 1921 to demonstrate some of these products, Carver influenced the implementation of the highest protective tariff ever enjoyed by the peanut industry.

Also widely publicized were Carver's experiments with the sweet potato, from which he developed 118 products, and his production of dyes from southern clay and plants. Carver's fame spread worldwide, and he received requests for assistance from several foreign countries. In the early 1920s he received an offer from Thomas A. Edison to join his team of scientists in New Jersey, but Carver declined, saying he preferred to remain in the South where farmers were greatly in need of his skills.

In 1940 Carver contributed his $60,000 in life savings to the establishment of the George Washington Carver Research Foundation, an organization that now has more than 100 faculty and a budget of $5 million to fund scientific research, training, and outreach projects. Carver was elected a fellow of the Royal Society of Arts of Great Britain in 1916. He received honorary doctorate degrees from Simpson College in 1928 and the University of Rochester in 1941. He was awarded the Spingarn Medal in 1923 and the Franklin Delano Roosevelt Medal in 1939.

Carver died at Tuskegee on January 5, 1943, and is buried on the campus next to Booker T. Washington. In 1953 Congress authorized the George Washington Carver National Monument, the first federal monument dedicated to an African American. The George Washington Carver National Monument was added to the National Park System on October 15, 1966 (see also George Washington Carver Homestead Site, Ness County, Kansas). [B 10/15/66 NHL NPS, 66000114]

SALINE COUNTY

Free Will Baptist Church of Pennytown
Off Missouri Highway UU eight miles southeast of Marshall
Marshall

The black community of Pennytown was founded in 1871 when former slave Joe Penny purchased eight acres of land on which to establish a farm. By 1880, Penny had organized a small hamlet of emancipated slaves who purchased land around his into a discrete community. Most newcomers to Pennytown bought small parcels of land from white landowners. A mixed economy of hunting, farming, wage earning, and communal living made it possible for Pennytown's residents to resist poverty. The community soon had the largest concentration of black landowners in Saline County.

The first Free Will Baptist Church of Pennytown building was erected in 1886 on the property of a white landowner, who gave the congregation permission to move a frame house to the site and refashion it into a house of worship. The building also housed a school for black children as well as community events. By 1894 the property had a new owner, who sold the half-acre parcel on which the building stood to the trustees of the church.

The present church building was completed on the same site in 1926, and the frame building was later removed. Pennytown remained a thriving community until after the Great Depression, when most of its residents left the area for seasonal farm work in other parts of the state. Much of the vacated land was bought up by surrounding farms, and remaining Pennytowners left to seek better jobs and new opportunities in a more urban setting. The Free Will Baptist Church of Pennytown is today the only known institutional building that survives at the location of a rural freedmen's hamlet in Missouri. In recent years, former Pennytowners have sought to establish a connection with their past, and an annual "homecoming" celebration is held at the church. [A 4/19/88, 88000388]

ST. CHARLES COUNTY

African Church
554 Madison Street
St. Charles

The African Church is an example of antebellum vernacular architecture and is important in the social, religious, and educational history of the black community in St. Charles. Completed around 1859, the church is believed to be the oldest black church in St. Charles. The land on which the building stands was purchased in 1855 for the purpose of erecting a building to house the black members of the Methodist Episcopal Church South, who elected to form their own congregation. The church was constructed by members of the congregation using hand-hewn timbers and handmade bricks. A school was organized in the building during the week, with classes for children during the day and for adults in the evening. The building served the black community of St. Charles until 1855, when a larger building was erected nearby. The African Church building has been converted for use as a private residence. [CA 11/21/80, 80004366]

ST. LOUIS (INDEPENDENT CITY)

Jefferson National Expansion Memorial National Historic Site
Mississippi River between Washington and Poplar streets
St. Louis

Included within the boundaries of the Jefferson National Expansion Memorial National Historic Site is the Old St. Louis Courthouse, significant in African American history as the location of the second trial of Dred Scott. Scott, plaintiff in the now-famous *Scott v. Sanford* U.S. Supreme Court case, was born a slave in Southampton County, Virginia. In 1818

Scott, known at the time as Sam, was owned by Captain Peter Blow and John Moore. Sam moved with the Blow family to St. Louis in 1831 after Peter Blow's death. In 1833 Blow's son, Charles, acting as executor of the estate, sold Sam to John Emerson, a U.S. army surgeon, for $500. Emerson was transferred in 1834 to Fort Armstrong in Illinois, where slavery was prohibited under the Northwest Ordinance, and in 1836 he was transferred to a post in the Wisconsin Territory, where slavery was barred by the Missouri Compromise. Military personnel, who did not consider themselves citizens of any state, often brought slaves with them into areas where slavery was prohibited by law.

While in the Wisconsin Territory, Sam married a slave woman, and the two were hired out as servants until they returned to St. Louis with Emerson in 1839. Emerson died in 1843, leaving all his property in trust to his wife, Eliza, for the benefit of their minor daughter. Sam, who had by this time taken the name Dred Scott, which is of unknown origin, was hired out to a military officer, who released him in Texas in 1846. Returning to St. Louis, Scott attempted to purchase freedom for himself, his wife, and their two daughters but was refused by Mrs. Emerson, who considered them property left in trust.

Encouraged by two lawyers noted for taking on slave cases, the Scotts unsuccessfully attempted to sue for their freedom, alleging false imprisonment and assault. When the ruling came against them, they moved for a new trial, and the verdict was set aside and a second trial date set. Meanwhile, Mrs. Emerson appealed to the Missouri Supreme Court but was denied because the case was still pending in the lower court. On January 12, 1850, Judge Alexander Hamilton ruled in the Scotts' favor, based on the fact that Dred Scott had been carried into a free state and territory and was therefore legally free.

Mrs. Emerson, who appealed the decision to the state court, remarried and moved to Massachusetts, leaving her legal affairs in the hands of her brother, John F. A. Sanford. While the case was pending in the state court, the Scotts remained in St. Louis and were hired out under the circuit court's jurisdiction. In 1852 the Missouri Supreme Court reversed the judgment of the appellate court and remanded the Scotts to slavery.

In 1853 Scott was urged by lawyer friends for whom he worked as a janitor to bring a new case against Sanford. Scott lost the case and was denied his motion to overrule the decision but appealed to the U.S. Supreme Court on a writ of error because official court documents erroneously stated Scott had been sold to Sanford. On March 6, 1857, the United States Supreme Court ruled that Scott was not free by reason of his removal to Illinois or the Wisconsin Territory. Since he had been judged not free by the state of Missouri, he was not a citizen of Missouri and therefore could not bring suit against Sanford, a citizen of another state. Immediately after the decision, the former Mrs. Emerson transferred the Scotts' title to the heirs of Peter Blow, from whom the Emersons had purchased Dred.

Dred Scott died of tuberculosis on September 17, 1858, never fully understanding the importance of the cases involving him or that they were a partial cause for the Civil War. He was buried in an unmarked grave but later reburied by the Blows. In 1957 members of the Blow family placed a marker on his grave.

The Missouri Historical Society's Dred Scott Collection at the Old St. Louis Courthouse includes all the legal documentation from all the cases and various newspaper articles on the decisions. The Jefferson National Expansion Memorial National Historic Site was authorized in Congress in 1954 and was designated a National Historic Landmark on May 27, 1987. [CA 10/15/66 NHL NPS, 66000941]

Scott Joplin House
2658 Delmar Boulevard
St. Louis

Scott Joplin (1868–1917) is one of America's most notable composers. His work with the musical genre known as ragtime provided important foundations for modern American music, combining elements of midwestern folk and Afro-American melodic rhythm traditions within the structural contexts of Western European musical forms. His work is noted by current music authorities as reflecting the hallmarks of true genius.

The years between 1900 and 1903, during which Joplin resided at the apartment complex on Delmar Boulevard, were some of the most important and creative years of his musical career. Music he composed during this time includes "Peacherine Rag," "The Entertainer," and "Little Black Baby." "The Entertainer" was part of the score for the 1973 movie *The Sting,* helping to popularize Joplin's music after more than 50 years of relative obscurity. This residence is the only building still in existence in the United States that can be positively linked to Joplin and his life. Joplin died in New York City in 1917. His St. Louis residence was designated a National Historic Landmark on December 8, 1976. [B 12/8/76 NHL, 76002235]

Negro Masonic Hall
3615–3619 Dr. Martin Luther King Boulevard
St. Louis

The Negro Masonic Hall, now called the Most Worshipful Prince Hall Grand Lodge #2, was formerly the primary meeting place for St. Louis's black Masons. The lodge bears the name of the 18th-century black New Englander who was the first to organize African Americans in a Masonic lodge and is the earliest extant building owned black Masonic groups in the city.

The Negro Masonic Hall served the African American community during a crucial period of in-migration, racial enmity, increasing segregation, economic change, and social reform between 1909 and 1942. Scholars of African American history have often indicated that benevolent associations such as the Freemasons were second in importance only to the church in building solidarity in the black community. Black Masonic organizations contributed to the progress of the black community by encouraging African Americans to establish and operate businesses. Benevolent fraternal organizations reached their zenith in the black community between the end of the Civil War and the beginning of World War II.

The historical association of the lodge with an elite, ritualistic, community-spirited organization is evident in the high-ceilinged interior spaces used as meeting rooms and in the ornamental facade of the building. The building was constructed around 1886 as a commercial building and was purchased by the Negro Masonic Hall Association in 1909, when black Masonic groups were making a concerted effort to move from rented meeting places into building they owned themselves. Despite alterations carried out in 1942 to preserve the structural soundness of the third-floor meeting space, the building remains much as it was from 1909 until World War II, when it was the primary meeting hall for St. Louis's black Masonic lodges. [A 4/15/93, 93000262]

Homer G. Phillips Hospital
26101 Whittier Street
St. Louis

In the early 20th century St. Louis African Americans became increasingly vocal about their lack of adequate health care or medical training. Taxes from black citizens supported municipal facilities that were open only to whites. Attempts to promote a change in policy whereby blacks and whites could train in the same institutions were met by threats of strikes by white doctors. In 1914 a committee of 17 concerned black physicians convinced city officials to purchase the abandoned Barnes Medical College at Garrison and Lawton avenues. Renamed City Hospital #2, the facility was renovated and opened as a 177-bed health care center for African Americans in 1919. Soon it became apparent that 177 beds could not serve the needs of St. Louis's growing black population.

After several more years of debate, it was agreed that a hospital with adequate facilities would be built to serve the needs of the black community. Constructed between 1932 and 1936, the Homer G. Phillips Hospital, named after the attorney who was most responsible for the successful outcome of this struggle, became one of the few fully equipped hospitals in the country where black doctors, nurses, and technicians could receive training. The lack of municipal support caused administrative and budgetary problems that were hard to overcome, and on August 17, 1979, the Homer G. Phillips Hospital closed its doors as an acute care facility. [CA 9/23/82, 82004738]

Quinn Chapel AME Church
227 Bowen Street
St. Louis

Quinn Chapel African Methodist Episcopal (AME) Church has used one building as a house of worship longer than any other black congregation in the Carondelet district of south St. Louis. Named in honor of William Paul Quinn, the first bishop of the AME Church, this church has been the focal point for many worthwhile activities in the black community since 1882. It is one of the few extant buildings originally commissioned by the once independent city of Carondelet. [CA 10/16/74, 74002277]

Shelley House
4600 Labadie Avenue
St. Louis

In 1930 J. D. Shelley and his family migrated to St. Louis from Mississippi. Like millions of other African Americans, they left the rural South in search of a life that was free of prejudice based on one's skin color and that would offer greater economic opportunity. What they found was a city whose available real estate was characterized by racially restrictive covenants that limited equal access to housing for people of color.

The Shelleys directly challenged this discriminatory policy by purchasing a home at 4600 Labadie Avenue. This house was in a restricted neighborhood, where residents agreed not to sell to any member of the "negro or Mongoloid" race under penalty of suit by the other property owners. The Louis D. Kraemers, owners of other property on Labadie Avenue covered by the restrictive covenant, sued to restrain the Shelleys from moving into the house.

In a 1948 landmark decision, the U.S. Supreme Court ruled that racially restric-

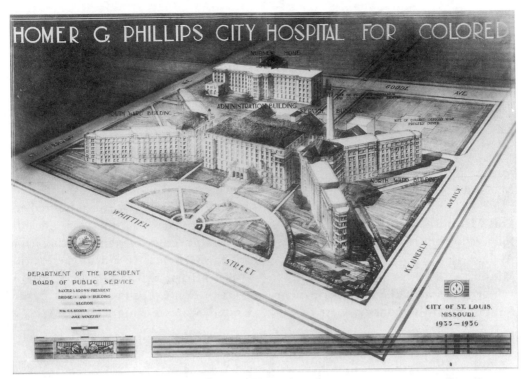

Drawing of the Homer G. Phillips Hospital, c.1936. Photo courtesy of the Landmarks Association of St. Louis, Inc.

tive housing covenants could not be enforced. Although the covenants were not outlawed, the case of *Shelley v. Kraemer* was seminal in reinforcing the 14th Amendment guarantee of equal protection of the laws, which includes rights to acquire, enjoy, and disperse property. The ruling was an important decision leading to the effective integration of African Americans into mainstream American society. The Shelley House was designated a National Historic Landmark on December 14, 1990. [A 4/18/88 NHL, 88000437]

Charles Sumner High School
4248 West Cottage Avenue
St. Louis

Sumner High School, located in the center of the black St. Louis community known as the Ville, served for 18 years as the sole source of secondary education for black St. Louisans. The struggle to secure public education for African Americans in St. Louis, which began before the Civil War, culminated in the establishment of the original Charles Sumner High School in 1875. When the institution moved to its present site in 1909, it became an important source of black pride and a symbol of achievement. The list of Sumner students who have gone on to success and fame includes activist Dick Gregory; opera singers Grace Bumbry and Robert McFerrin–the first black singer at the Metropolitan Opera; pop singers Chuck Berry and Tina Turner; tennis star Arthur Ashe; and past National Association for the Advancement of Colored People President Margaret Bush Wilson. [CA 4/19/88, 88000469]

MONTANA

MISSOULA COUNTY

Fort Missoula Historic District
Intersection of Reserve Street and South
Avenue
Missoula

Fort Missoula, the only permanent
military post in Montana west of the
continental divide, was established
in June 1877. The fort has served in
several capacities over the years, including as a government training school for
skilled mechanics to aid in the World
War I effort, as the largest Civilian
Conservation Corps headquarters in the
United States during the 1930s, as a

detention camp for Italian-American and Japanese-American civilians during World War II, and, for a short time after World War II, as a medium-security prison camp for American soldiers.

The fort is significant in African American history as the headquarters of the black 25th Infantry Regiment. The 25th Regiment arrived at Fort Missoula in May 1888. Headed by cycling enthusiast Lieutenant James A. Moss, the regiment was assigned to evaluate the military possibilities of the bicycle. Moss organized a 1,900-mile trek over rough terrain from Fort Missoula to St. Louis, Missouri, to demonstrate the military usefulness of the bicycle. The regiment was required to demonstrate skills beyond basic riding and to perform drills, scale fences, ford streams and rivers, and travel 40 miles a day carrying all their equipment.

Twenty men left Fort Missoula on the expedition on June 14, 1897. They arrived in St. Louis on July 24. The army, however, was unimpressed by the feat. The bicycle was not adopted as a means of transportation, and the bicycle corps returned to Montana by train. The 25th Infantry Regiment left Fort Missoula in 1898. [CA 4/29/87, 87000865]

Fort Missoula Historic District, c. 1886. Photo courtesy of the Fort Missoula Historical Museum.

NEBRASKA

DOUGLAS COUNTY

Jewell Building
2221–2225 North 24th Street
Omaha

Built in 1923, the Jewell Building is a monument to Omaha's musical, social, and black heritage. The Jewells, an influential black family in the Omaha community, employed John Lof and Sons to construct the building at 24th and Grant streets. It was one of the first commercial buildings constructed in Omaha's black developing neighborhood during the 1920s, and it indicates the beginning of the black movement in Omaha. From the 1920s to the 1960s its Dreamland Ballroom attracted nationally prominent jazz musicians. Among those who appeared on the Dreamland Stage were Duke Ellington, Nat "King" Cole, Count Basie, Lionel Hampton, Charlie Barnet, Dizzy Gillespie, Dinah Washington, Ray Charles, Sarah Vaughn, Earl Hines, and Louis Armstrong. Since its construction, the Jewell Building has served as a meeting place for Omaha's black community. [CA 7/21/83, 83001091]

Malcolm X House Site
3448 Pinkney Street
Omaha

Malcolm X (born Malcolm Little), also known by his adopted religious name, El-Hajj Malik El-Shabazz (1925–65), was born in Omaha, Nebraska, on May 19, 1925, the son of Reverend Earl Little, a Baptist minister and an organizer for Marcus Garvey's Universal Negro Improvement Association (UNIA). He lived at the former house on this site until age four, when his family relocated to Milwaukee and later to Michigan. When Malcolm was six years old his father was murdered in Lansing, Michigan, apparently by a Ku Klux Klan terrorist group. In the years thereafter, Malcolm faced difficult times.

In 1952 he became a follower of the Nation of Islam, headed by Elijah Muhammad, and was made a minister of a mosque in Harlem. He was soon the best-known and most effective evangelist of the Nation of Islam, organizing temples from Connecticut to California and building its following from 400 to perhaps 10,000 registered members. He became a civil rights leader who insisted on the legitimacy of violence in self-defense and black control of institutions and politics in the black community. He also stressed the beauty and worth of blackness and the African past.

In March 1964 Malcolm X left the Nation of Islam because of disagreements with Muhammed and formed two organizations of his own: Muslim Mosque, Inc., and the Organization of Afro-American Unity (OAAU). Malcolm X had originally advocated a "back to Africa" move-

Jewell Building. Photo courtesy of the Omaha City Planning Department (James Krance).

ment. After his pilgrimage to the holy city of Mecca and a long journey to the Middle East and Africa in 1964, however, he converted to orthodox Islam, advocated total economic and social self-sufficiency for African Americans, and modified his philosophy to include different races and nationalities.

During the last 10 years of his life he spoke against racial discrimination in the United States and encouraged blacks to unite internationally. He expressed his views and described his personal transformations in his autobiography, *The Autobiography of Malcolm X* (1965). Assassinated on February 14, 1965, Malcolm X is heralded as a leader of the black nationalist movement. [B 3/1/84, 84002463]

Lizzie Robinson House
2864 Corby Street
Omaha

From 1916 until 1924, this simple frame temple-form house in northeast Omaha was the home of Lizzie Robinson, her husband, Edward D. Robinson, and their daughter. Lizzie and Edward Robinson were founders of the Church of God in Christ (COGIC) in Omaha, the first church of that denomination in the state. Lizzie Robinson was also a national organizer of the women's ministry for COGIC, the largest black Pentecostal denomination in the world (see also Mason Temple, Church of God in Christ, Shelby County, Tennessee).

The Pentecostal movement's roots trace back to the economic, social, and cultural crisis of the late 19th century, caused by industrialization and rapid urban growth and subsequent changes in various Protestant denominations. Headquartered in Memphis, Tennessee, COGIC officially adopted Pentecostal doctrine in 1907. Led by its founder, Charles H. Mason, COGIC grew to include as many white members as black by 1909. A white Pentecostal faction, however, broke away in 1914 and, with Mason's blessing, formed the General Council of the Assemblies of God.

Lizzie Robinson's association with COGIC began while she was working as a matron at the Baptist Academy in Dermott, Arkansas. After becoming acquainted with Charles Mason, she left the Baptist Church and went to work for COGIC in Tennessee. In 1911 Mason appointed her supervisor of the Women's Department of the church in Memphis, where she formed the Prayer and Bible Band, the Sewing Circle, and the Home and Foreign Mission Board. During this time, she met and married Edward Robinson, a COGIC minister.

The Robinsons were evangelists in the western United States until they settled in Omaha and founded their church in 1916. Lizzie Robinson continued her evangelical trips accompanied by church women, while Edward Robinson attended to the duties of the church. The COGIC women's work programs grew quickly, and Lizzie Robinson began state organizations, with her traveling companions acting as state mothers, overseers of COGIC women's programs in the state.

After her husband's death, Lizzie Robinson continued her work, spearheading the national drive to raise funds for COGIC's new headquarters in Memphis. Upon its completion, the women's assembly hall was named in her honor. Lizzie Robinson died on December 12, 1945, having established an auxiliary program through local churches and laid the foundation for the state and national COGIC auxiliary programs. The Corby Street house is the remaining building most closely associated with her from the period of her activity with COGIC. [B 2/25/93, 93000058]

Webster Telephone Exchange Building
2213 Lake Street
Omaha

Built in 1907, the Webster Telephone Exchange Building was constructed as part of the Nebraska Telephone Company during a period of intensive growth partially stimulated by the competition of the independent telephone companies. In 1933 the American Bell Telephone Company donated the Webster Telephone Exchange Building to the Urban League, which converted it into a community center. The community center had a free employment bureau, library, reading room, sewing room, day nursery, medical and dental clinic, adult education center, and theater. The building served as a community center until 1950. In 1952 it was converted to an apartment house, and it is now the Great Plains Black Museum, which has interpreted the black heritage of the area since 1975. [CA 12/5/77, 77000829]

NEVADA

CLARK COUNTY

Moulin Rouge Hotel
900 West Bonanza Road
Las Vegas

From its founding in 1905 until 1930, Las Vegas had a small black population. During the Great Depression, African Americans came to southern Nevada hoping to find employment working on the Hoover Dam but were thwarted by discriminatory hiring practices. The percentage of African Americans in Las Vegas remained low until 1941, when the construction of a major defense plant nearby drew thousands of black workers from the Deep South. The large influx of African Americans coincided with stricter segregation practices, relegating black homes and businesses to the poorly developed west side of town.

After World War II tourism developed rapidly along the Strip and in the downtown area with the construction of major hotels and casinos. African Americans were refused accommodations at these hotels and were denied access to casino and dining areas. Even such nationally prominent entertainers as Sammy Davis, Jr., and Pearl Bailey, who often performed at these establishments, were forced to seek lodging at black boarding-houses on the west side. In response to white exclusion, the Moulin Rouge Hotel project was launched in 1954 by a diverse group of investors.

The site chosen for the Moulin Rouge straddled the line between the predominately white area of the Strip and the nearly all-black west side. Opening with great fanfare on May 24, 1955, the hotel billed itself as "the nation's first major inter-racial hotel." The hotel was integrated in all aspects, from employees to patrons to entertainers. The Moulin Rouge quickly earned a reputation for providing some of the best entertainment in Las Vegas. Among those who performed at the Moulin Rouge or were in attendance were Frank Sinatra, Harry Belafonte, Louis Armstrong, Sammy Davis, Jr., Tallulah Bankhead, Gregory Peck, Dorothy Lamour, Milton Berle, George Burns, Gracie Allen, Jack Benny, and Nat "King" Cole.

Despite its popularity, poor management and financial problems led to the hotel's closing in October 1955. In 1960, however, the property was the site of a meeting that led to the breakdown of segregation on the Strip and downtown. Civil rights activists scheduled a demonstration march on the Strip for March 26,

Moulin Rouge Hotel. Photo courtesy of the Nevada Division of Historic Preservation and Archeology (Don T. Walker).

1960, to protest the racially exclusive policies of resort owners in Las Vegas. In order to avoid the action, hotel owners, city and state officials, and Nevada Governor Grant Sawyer agreed to meet that day at the Moulin Rouge with a group of black community leaders headed by the president of the local chapter of the National Association for the Advancement of Colored People (NAACP). The meeting ended with most of the Las Vegas hotel owners agreeing to end the policy of excluding African Americans from their establishments. The scheduled march was canceled. Today the hotel stands as a reminder of the peculiar nature of the entertainment industry in Las Vegas, which was segregated and integrated at the same time. [A 12/22/92, 92001701]

NEW JERSEY

BERGEN COUNTY

Ackerman-Smith House
171 East Allendale Road
Saddle River

The Ackerman-Smith House occupies a significant place in the history of journalism and African Americans in Bergen County. From 1881 until his death in 1901, Alfred P. Smith published a local monthly newspaper in this building, which also functioned as his home. Smith's newspaper, briefly called *A. P. Smith Paper* before becoming *The Landscape,* was the only newspaper published in this rural area of Bergen County in the late 19th century and the only commercial paper ever published in Saddle River. With the *Princeton Trumpet,* it is among the earliest newspapers published by African Americans in New Jersey.

Alfred Smith's family was descended from an early Bergen County family, the DeGroats. The longevity of his paper was probably due to the fact that it was a general interest paper that was directed to the entire community, not just to a black audience. *The Landscape* is an invaluable resource for research on late 19th-century history in the Saddle River valley. The paper ceased publication upon his death in 1901. [Saddle River MRA, CB 8/29/86, 86001600]

BURLINGTON COUNTY

William R. Allen School
Intersection of Mitchell Avenue and East Federal Street
Burlington

The William R. Allen School reflects the evolution of segregation in southern New Jersey during the period after the Civil War. Segregation in Burlington began with the attempts by Quakers and black community leaders to educate and enfranchise African Americans. The education of African American youth, however, evolved into de facto school segregation characteristic of the Jim Crowism popular in the southern states.

From 1870 to 1900 the Federal Street School served as the only school in the city for the education of its black youth. In 1900 the school was replaced by a new school named for William R. Allen, a well-known businessperson and staunch Unionist mayor during the Civil War. Allen had been instrumental in reorganizing the city's educational system when it was divided from one large district into four smaller neighborhood districts.

From 1914 to 1924, the black population in the city increased dramatically during the Great Migration of southern African Americans to northern cities, thus causing student enrollment to increase at the Allen School. As a result of the increase, the Board of Education in 1923 rented a basement room in the Pearl Street Bethel African Methodist Episcopal Church and expanded the teaching staff. Thereafter, student enrollment continued to rise.

Segregation in Burlington schools remained widespread until the late 1940s when the state constitution forbade it. However, the practice of enrolling students in neighborhood schools meant that the Allen School was an all-black facility until its closure in the 1960s. From the mid-1970s to the early 1980s, the county conducted special classes in the building. Since 1984 the school has been vacant. [CA 8/8/91, 90001450]

CAMDEN COUNTY

Grant AME Church
Intersection of 4th and Washington streets
Chesilhurst

The Grant African Methodist Episcopal Church is probably the oldest extant building in Chesilhurst, a predominantly black community established in the mid-19th century. The church was established through the efforts of Margaret Wilson, evangelist and member of the Women's Might Missionary Society. Aided by about a dozen other Chesilhurst residents, Wilson raised money for the purchase of a lot on which to build the church. The cornerstone of the church was laid in 1897. It quickly became a focal point in the Chesilhurst community and surrounding area. The building was expanded in 1936 to accommodate the growing congregation. In 1974 a new church was erected on a site next to the original building. [A 10/5/77, 77000857]

Solomon Wesley United Methodist Church
291-B Davistown Road/Asyla Road
Blackwood, Gloucester Township

Located in present-day Blackwood, the Solomon Wesley United Methodist Church is one of only a few surviving buildings of the historic black community of Davistown, established by emancipated slaves in the early 19th century. The original community was settled on a parcel of land left by Daniel Bates in his will to his slave, Lindley Davis. He also provided Davis with $200 and her own and her family's freedom. Davistown grew to be a small, close-knit community composed primarily of Davis family members.

Constructed in 1850, the Solomon Wesley United Methodist Church is typical of churches built in rural black communities in the 19th century. As the church grew, camp meeting grounds and a school were established on the property. The Davistown Colored School was the only black school within Gloucester Township. The school no longer exists, and the congregation of the church has dwindled since many founding families left Davistown in the 1920s. Today the church is one of only two remaining black churches in Gloucester Township and is the older of the two. [A 4/10/89, 89000241]

ESSEX COUNTY

Bethany Baptist Church
117 West Market Street
Newark

The former Bethany Baptist Church, now housing Cornerstone Baptist Church but still locally known as "Old Bethany," is the oldest and largest black congregation in Newark. Established in 1871, the building is a symbol of racial progress in one of Newark's bleakest areas, the Third Ward. Consisting of both lower- and middle-class parishioners, Bethany provided the community with many of the early 20th-century black leaders in education, social service, business, and civil rights.

As the black population exploded during the Great Migration, Bethany became essential to the survival and integrity of the community by providing services to the newly arrived migrants. Thus many community and civic groups had their origin within the walls of the church. These include the local branch of the National Association for the Advancement of Colored People (NAACP), the Essex County Urban League, branches of the Young Men's and Young Women's Christian Associations (no longer in existence), and a resident home for elderly people in Montclair.

In the area of politics, the church is significant for its association with the Reverend Dr. William Preston Hayes, pastor of Bethany from 1932 to 1961. Among his many activities, Hayes was a member of the Newark Housing Authority from 1942 to 1953 and president of the Newark branch of the NAACP. In 1954 Hayes was honored when the Public Housing Administration of Washington, D.C., permitted, for the first time, a housing project to be named for a living person. It is known as the Hayes Homes. [CAB 5/10/89, 88000466]

State Street Public School
15 State Street
Newark

Built in 1845, the State Street School is the oldest public school building in continuous use in Newark. Between 1869 and 1873 the building housed the Colored School of Newark under the leadership of principal James Miller Baxter Jr. Baxter, who graduated from the Quaker-operated Philadelphia Institute for Colored Youth with high honors, became the first black principal in Newark's school system at the age of 19. By the time Baxter retired from Newark's Board of Education on July 1, 1909, he had left a permanent mark on the Newark community.

During Baxter's tenure the school met several major objectives. The quality of the work done in the school improved; an evening school was established; the school was moved to improved quarters; African Americans were admitted to public high schools, and all of the city schools were opened to African American children. Before 1872 Newark public schools were segregated. Through Baxter's leadership, Irene Pataquam Mulford, Newark's first black high school student, was admitted to Newark High School.

Baxter's abilities as a principal and teacher came to the attention of the federal government, and in 1881 he was considered for the post of United States minister to Haiti. Baxter, however, chose to remain in Newark. When he retired in 1909 he was considered the dean of Newark's corps of principals. His death the same year left a void in Newark's education system that could not be filled. Baxter's obituary was carried nationwide. [CAB 8/3/90, 90001201]

MONMOUTH COUNTY

Fisk Chapel
Cedar Avenue
Fair Haven

Constructed in 1882, Fisk Chapel was named for General Clinton B. Fisk, benefactor of Fisk University (see also Fisk University Historic District, Davidson County, Tennessee). Fisk Chapel's congregation, organized in 1858, was one of two free black African Methodist Episcopal (AME) congregations formed in the area before the Civil War. Originally known as the AME Bethel Church, the congregation received a $3,000 donation from General Fisk in 1882 to build a new church. Fisk Chapel was formally dedicated on August 20,

1882. In addition to its religious functions, a nearby school for black children used Fisk Chapel for meetings, recitals, concerts, and the yearly June graduation ceremony. The church served the black community well into the 20th century, until segregation ended and the school closed. Fisk Chapel is the oldest religious edifice in Rumson and Fairhaven and one of the few remaining black churches in eastern Monmouth County. It remains a symbol of an era in which the church stood at the center of the black community's religious, educational, and social activities. [A 10/29/75, 75001146]

T. Thomas Fortune House
94 West Bergen Place
Red Bank

Timothy Thomas Fortune (1856–1928) was born a slave in Marianna, Florida. His father, Emanuel Fortune, was elected to the Florida constitutional convention of 1868 and to the lower house of the state legislature. Threats from the Ku Klux Klan forced his father to flee for his life to Jacksonville, Florida, where he and his family started anew.

The young Fortune obtained his education at Freedman's Bureau schools in Marianna and Jacksonville. He picked up a knowledge of the printer's trade while working at the *Marianna Courier*. At the age of 13 he began his political apprenticeship in Tallahassee, where he was a page in the state senate. In 1876 he entered the Preparatory Department of

Howard University with the intention of later studying law, but lack of money forced him to abandon this plan. While in Washington he worked on the *People's Advocate* under its editor John Wesley Cromwell. This was the beginning of Fortune's career in journalism.

In 1879 Fortune moved to New York City and became part-owner of a weekly tabloid, *Rumor*. In 1881 the paper became the *Globe* and Fortune its editor. The aim of the *Globe* was to provide a national forum for African Americans. Its editorials attacked the white press for either neglecting or persecuting blacks and blamed the Republican party for betraying Southern blacks. Its pages encouraged blacks to become politically independent in light of Republican party neglect. As a result of his attacks upon Republicans, black party members withdrew their financial support, and by November 1884 the *Globe* was out of business.

After the *Globe* failed Fortune began publication of the *New York Freeman,* of which he was sole owner. He announced that it was published solely for African-Americans, owned and operated by African-Americans, and free of party politics. By 1886, however, Fortune was forced to enter into a financial agreement with whites because of lack of support from the black community. In 1887 the name of the paper was changed to the *New York Age,* and it once again supported Republican politics. Fortune realized that total alienation of the Republican party could bring financial disaster.

Fortune's other significant activities included organizing the National Afro-American League in 1887, supporting the women's club movement, and assisting Ida B. Wells in her antilynching crusade. By the time he died, he had published more than 20 books and articles and more than 300 editorials in his own newspapers. T. Thomas Fortune also developed alternative answers to the race questions of his times, some of which are still being raised today, involving women's rights, interracial marriage, quality education, racial pride, and the search for identity. The T. Thomas Fortune House was designated a National Historic Landmark on December 8, 1976. [B 12/8/76 NHL, 76001171]

Shadow Lawn
Intersection of Cedar and Norwood avenues
West Long Branch

Shadow Lawn was constructed in 1927 for Hubert T. Parson, a protégé of dime store magnate Frank Woolworth who worked his way up from bookkeeper to president of the Woolworth empire. Constructed in the French Classical tradition, the sprawling residence was completed and furnished at a cost of $7,500,000. The building was designed by the firm of Horace Trumbauer. The chief designer in Trumbauer's firm was Julian Abele. Abele graduated from the University of Pennsylvania School of Architecture in 1902, becoming the first African American to practice architecture professionally in the United States. Trumbauer sent Abele to Paris to study, making him the first African American to study architecture at the Ecole des Beaux-Arts in Paris. Shadow Lawn was the last project on which Trumbauer and Abele collaborated. The 1929 stock market crash resulted in Parson's loss of the property, and today the building is owned by Monmouth College. The building stands as an affirmation of Trumbauer and Abele's talent as architects. Shadow Lawn was designated a National Historic Landmark on February 4, 1985. [C 3/28/78 NHL, 78001780]

NEW MEXICO

VALENCIA COUNTY

Hawikuh

12 miles southwest of Zuni
Zuni Indian Reservation
Zuni

Estevan, or Estevanico as he was called by the famous Cabez de Vaca, is the only known black explorer of the 16th century to make major discoveries in the region of North America that would later become the United States. The first known non-Indian to reach the present American Southwest, Estevanico opened a trail from Mexico into the area that now comprises the states of Arizona and New Mexico.

Estevanico was the slave of Spanish Captain Andres Dorantes. He accompanied Dorantes on the tragic Narvaez expedition of 1528, the first known crossing of the North American continent north of central Mexico by non-Indians. The expedition of 300 men was led by Panfilo de Narvaez, newly appointed governor of Florida, to search for treasures for the Spanish government. As the expedition reached the territory of what is now the southeast United States, most of its members were slain by Indians. All but four of them who escaped slaughter died of malnutrition, dysentery, and fever. Among the four who made it back to safety six years later, four of which were spent in

Indian captivity, were Dorantes and Estevanico.

This experience earned Estevanico a spot on the expedition sent in 1538 by Mexico's Viceroy Mendoza to search for the purportedly rich Seven Cities of Gold, which Indians claimed lay far to the north of Mexico. Because he was black, Estevanico was prohibited from being a party leader, but he was appointed the official guide and interpreter for the party led by Fray Marcos de Niza. His flamboyant personality and his ability to communicate with the Indians soon established Estevanico as the virtual head of the expedition. He defied orders from Fray Marcos and soon forged ahead of Marcos, who had become ill.

Estevanico pushed forward until he reached a region never before traveled by non-Indians. Crossing into what is now Arizona and New Mexico, Estevanico saw from a high elevation the walls of the famous city of Cibola, which the Indians called Hawikuh. As Estevanico and his servants entered the city, its residents, suspicious of the strangers, encircled them and imprisoned them. Estevanico was finally slain. The news reached Fray Marcos, who stopped short of Hawikuh. When Coronado's expedition reached Hawikuh in 1540, he was disappointed to learn that the city of gold was no more than a dusty sandstone village. Despite his tragic demise, Estevanico holds an important place in history as the first black explorer to reach the present American Southwest, preparing the way for the Coronado expedition of 1540. Hawikuh, now part of the Zuni Indian Reservation, was designated a National Historic Landmark on October 15, 1966. [AB 10/15/66 NHL, 66000502]

Site of Hawikuh Pueblo. Photo courtesy of the National Park Service (Peter Greenlee).

NEW YORK

CAYUGA COUNTY

Harriet Tubman Home for the Aged
180–182 South Street
Auburn

Harriet Tubman (1820–1913) escaped from slavery in Dorchester County, Maryland, through the Underground Railroad to Philadelphia in 1849. The next year a new federal Fugitive Slave Law was passed, designed to make it easier for slaveholders to recover runaways. Three months later, in December 1850, Tubman made the first of her 19 journeys into Maryland to bring slaves to freedom via the Underground Railroad. She guided at least 300 persons, including brothers, sisters, and her aged parents, to freedom as far north as Canada. At one point, rewards for her capture totaled $40,000.

In between trips south, Tubman led the rescue of the fugitive slave, Charles Nalle, in Troy, New York, in 1859. She was privy to the plans of John Brown. Both believed they were instruments of God's will, and both preferred action to words in the war against slavery. She contributed to the success of the

Paul Robeson Residence, New York County. Photo courtesy of the National Park Service (Walter Smalling, Jr.).

Underground Railroad during the Civil War by acting as a scout, spy, and nurse in South Carolina and Virginia.

After the war Tubman returned to Auburn to continue her humanitarian work. She raised money for black schools in the South and was active in the women's rights movement and in the African Methodist Episcopal (AME) Zion Church. Having cared for the needy in her home for years, she established a home for the African American aged and destitute on property she purchased at auction and deeded to the AME Zion Church. She died there in 1913 at the age of 93. [B 5/30/74, 74001222]

ERIE COUNTY

Durham Memorial AME Zion Church
174 East Eagle Street
Buffalo

Durham is the oldest surviving church associated with the Buffalo African Methodist Episcopal (AME) Zion congregations. Founded as St. Luke's AME Zion Church in 1906, it was the focal point of the educational, social, political, and religious activities of unskilled southern African Americans who had migrated north at the turn of the century in search of industrial employment.

The AME Zion Church was founded in 1796 when a group of free black members withdrew from New York City's John Street Methodist Church because of discrimination against them regarding seating and the receiving of Communion. Their first church building was constructed in 1800 in New York City, and the AME Zion Church was chartered in 1801. The new denomination, an early advocate of abolition, became popular among free northern African Americans, and AME Zion churches were organized throughout the Northeast. By 1843 there were 19 in New York alone.

The church building now occupied by Durham Memorial was constructed in 1920. The site chosen for the new edifice was in the heart of Buffalo's black community in the Michigan and William streets neighborhood. St. Luke's became Buffalo's first black congregation to build its own place of worship, with many wealthy black Buffalonians subsidizing the construction. During the Great Depression St. Luke's was the focal point of the community as it administered the social programs funded by the Works Project Administration.

Expansion of the congregation in the late 1950s forced the members to relocate to a larger existing structure on Ferry Street. A loyal few members chose to remain in the historic building, and the bishop of their conference granted them permission to do so. In honor of the pastor who oversaw the building program in the 1920s, St. Luke's was renamed the Durham AME Zion Church. [A 9/15/83, 83001670]

Macedonia Baptist Church

511 Michigan Avenue
Buffalo

Founded as the Michigan Street Baptist Church, Macedonia Baptist Church has played a central role in Buffalo's black community since its inception during the abolition movement of the 1830s and 1840s. Buffalo's black population was about 350 when the Michigan Street Baptist Church was built in 1845. Some African Americans who were domestic servants lived scattered throughout the city, but the majority listed in the 1840 census lived in the Michigan-William Street area on the eastern fringe of the downtown commercial district. At the turn of the century two compelling community figures became associated with the church and contributed greatly to the politicization of African Americans in Buffalo.

The Reverend Dr. J. Edward Nash (1868–1957) became pastor of the church in the 1890s and remained there for 61 years. During this time he was instrumental in founding the Buffalo Urban League and the local branch of the National Association for the Advancement of Colored People (NAACP). During the span of Nash's leadership, Buffalo's black population mushroomed from 1,805 in 1900 to 74,813 in 1960. The Michigan-William Street area expanded, displacing the German and Jewish sections of the city to the north and east.

The second prominent figure associated with the Michigan Street Baptist Church was Mary B. Talbert, a neighbor and active parishioner. Her house at 521 Michigan Avenue was one of the meeting places for the Niagara Movement, a conference led by W. E. B. Du Bois that spurred the development of the NAACP. Talbert herself became active in the NAACP by heading one of its groups called the Anti-Lynching Crusaders. Under her leadership the group organized women throughout the Northeast to fight against this heinous crime.

The church has since been renamed Macedonia Baptist Church. Today the

John Brown Farm. Photo courtesy of the New York State Department of Commerce (Sheldon Toomer).

building serves as a reminder of the outstanding leadership that Buffalo contributed to the struggle for civil rights. [A 2/12/74, 74001233]

ESSEX COUNTY

John Brown Farm
John Brown Road
Lake Placid

This isolated property in the Adirondack Mountains was the home of famed abolitionist John Brown from 1850 until his death in 1859. The land on which Brown's small frame house stands was adjacent to a 120,000-acre tract set aside by New York abolitionist and philanthropist Gerrit Smith on which free blacks could establish farms. Brown arrived in the Adirondacks in 1849 to assist the black community in establishing farms in the rough terrain and cold

climate. Brown told Smith that pioneer life appealed to him and that he felt he could be "a kind of father" to the African Americans living there. Brown's original home was a log cabin, but in 1855 he moved into this small frame house built for him by his son.

Although Brown was fond of his wilderness home, his abolition activities frequently required him to travel away from home for long periods of time. In 1859 he traveled to Maryland to organize a raid on the federal arsenal at Harpers Ferry, West Virginia, with the intention of arming the slaves and leading them to rebellion. The plot failed, and Brown was found guilty of treason and executed. Brown was brought back to New York to be buried on the property along with two of his sons and 10 of his followers (see also John Brown Cabin, Miami County,

Kansas; John Brown's Headquarters, Washington County, Maryland; John Brown House, Franklin County, Pennsylvania; and Harpers Ferry National Historical Park and Jefferson County Courthouse, Jefferson County, West Virginia). [AB 6/19/72, 72000840]

KINGS COUNTY

Houses on Hunterfly Road District
1698, 1700, 1702, 1704, 1706, and 1708 Bergen Street
New York

The Houses on Hunterfly Road District is a row of four houses lying on the edge of the former community of Weeksville, an early 19th-century free black community. Weeksville was founded around 1827 after the abolition of slavery in New York and is the earliest documented black community in an area that is now predominantly African American. At the time Weeksville was founded, most free blacks in New York lived in Manhattan, where they established religious and social organizations to meet the needs of their communities. Weeksville's residents followed the pattern of these Manhattan communities, establishing two churches, a school, a home for the aged, and an orphan asylum. Weeksville's population increased dramatically after 1863, when it became a refuge for black families following the New York City draft riots. Among the most prominent of Weeksville's former residents are Susan McKinney-Steward, New York's first black female physician, and Moses P. Cobb, the first black policeman in Brooklyn's Ninth Ward.

The Hunterfly Road houses are among the last buildings erected in Weeksville and the oldest known existing buildings in the Bedford-Stuyvesant area of Brooklyn. The houses, which date from between 1840 and 1883, are now owned by the Society for Weeksville and Bedford-Stuyvesant History and, with the vigorous support of former and current Brooklyn residents, have been restored as the Weeksville African American Museum. [C 12/5/72, 72000853]

John Roosevelt "Jackie" Robinson House
1224 Tilden Street
New York

The years 1945 to 1947 were milestones in the history of African American participation in American sports. John Roosevelt "Jackie" Robinson "broke through the color barrier" in major league baseball when the Brooklyn Dodgers signed him to their minor league team, the Montreal Royals, in 1945 and then to the major league Brooklyn Dodgers in 1947. This made him the first African American to play major league baseball in America. Jackie Robinson led the Dodgers to pennants in 1947, 1949, 1952, and 1953 and finally to a world championship in 1955. He opened the doors for some of baseball's later black greats: Roy Campanella, Frank Robinson, and Hank Aaron.

Jackie Robinson's awards and achievements did not end with his career in baseball. He went on to become a vice presidents of Chock Full O'Nuts, a lunch counter chain and chairman of the board of the Freedom National Bank in Harlem. He was elected to baseball's Hall of Fame in 1962. Jackie Robinson died in 1972 at the age of 53. He was responsible not only for opening baseball's doors to African Americans, but also for inspiring acceptance of other persons of color into professional sports. [B 5/11/76 NHL, 76001226]

NASSAU COUNTY

Valley Road Historic District
South of Manhasset on Community Drive
Manhasset

The Valley Road Historic District encompasses six buildings, a cemetery, and archeological sites, which are the remains of Success, a community of free blacks, former slaves, and Matinecock Indians that was established along the Valley Road in 1829. The history of Success illustrates the fusion of minority cultures in the social development of Long Island during the 19th century.

Before the arrival of Dutch and English settlers in the late 17th century, this area was inhabited by Matinecock Indians. Some of the Matinecock were enslaved and intermarried with African slaves brought to the area by white landowners. According the 1790 census, a sizable population of free blacks, mulattoes, and offspring of Native Americans and African Americans existed in the area. Following the abolition of slavery in New York State in 1827, numerous former slave families bought land and established the community of Success along Valley Road in Manhasset.

The population of Success grew rapidly after 1829, when Moses and Susannah Cross, black religious leaders, brought a large portion of their congregation to settle in the community. The congregation built the African Methodist Episcopal Zion Church in 1883 and established the adjoining cemetery. In 1867 the citizens of Success constructed "Institution, U.S.A.," the first free black school in present Nassau County.

Suburban encroachment after World War I led to the decline of Success. The few buildings and sites encompassed by the Valley Road Historic District are the only remains of this remarkable community that demonstrates the Native American and African American element of Long Island's history. [AD 4/8/77, 77000953]

NEW YORK COUNTY

African Burying Ground
Vicinity of Broadway and Reade Street
New York

The only known preserved urban 18th-century African burying ground in the Americas, this site is nationally significant because of its unprecedented potential to yield information about the lives of African Americans in an 18th-century urban context. To date, the remains of more than 400 individuals have been recovered from the site, which was discovered in 1991 during archeological excavations carried out in advance of a major construction project.

The urban setting of the site is particularly significant. In plantation settings, slave quarters were often set apart from their masters' dwellings and can therefore be easily identified for archeological study. In cities, however, slaves often occupied the same houses as their masters and a separate material record is not easily isolated. For this reason it is, ironically, the burying place of this community that provides the clearest material record of their lives.

The burying ground was used for nearly 100 years and includes burials of both enslaved and free African Americans, as both groups were banned from interment in churchyards. While physical anthropologists studying the remains cannot determine whether any particular individual was enslaved or free, they can distinguish between African-born and American-born individuals. This information will allow researchers to begin to construct a profile of the first generation of the Africans to leave Africa for America.

Examination of the remains will yield information concerning nutrition, disease, physical stress, injury, and even occupation of individuals because, in many cases, these aspects of life leave traces on the bones and teeth that are preserved. These data may be used to answer questions about certain social changes, such as increased restrictions or shifts in the demographic and occupational building of New York's African population. In addition, the orientation and configuration of the burials can yield information about funerary practices and social relations within the community.

The approximately seven acres of land that is occupied by the African Burying Ground is presently a part of New York City's civic center area. Buildings, parking areas, and city streets are now built upon the site, with the burials preserved under 16 to 25 feet of dirt fill. The site is undoubtedly the largest of its kind thus discovered in the United States and is the richest in terms of information potential. For this reason, the African Burying Ground was designated a National Historic Landmark on April 19, 1993. [D 4/19/93 NHL, 93001597]

Apollo Theater
253 West 125th Street
New York

The Apollo Theater historically has been one of New York City's and the nation's leading entertainment centers. Completed in 1914 as a burlesque house, it later became the premier performance hall for African American performers and a symbol of the movement to promote black cultural awareness. The Apollo became notorious as a proving ground for black entertainers. Because Harlem has historically been a mecca for black culture and because Harlemites were considered to be the toughest audience anywhere to

please, it has been said that if a performer can make it at the Apollo, they can make it anywhere. The list of entertainers who performed at the Apollo or were discovered at the theater's popular Amateur Night reads like a list of black who's who in the performing arts: Bessie Smith, Louis Armstrong, Sarah Vaughn, Billie Holiday, Moms Mabley, Redd Foxx, James Brown, Sam Cooke, Diana Ross and the Supremes, Patti LaBelle, Dionne Warwick, Aretha Franklin, Michael Jackson, Public Enemy, New Edition, En Vogue, and hundreds more. Aside from having an extraordinary impact on American culture, the Apollo has become synonymous with Harlem itself. [CA 11/17/83, 83004059]

Will Marion Cook House
221 West 138th Street
New York

Will Marion Cook (1869–1944) has been described as "a musician of international reputation," "one of our most popular composers," and a "pioneer in serious musical comedy" who helped open Broadway to black entertainment. Cook, recognizing the value of black folklore and spirituals, applied his classic musical training to these black idioms and developed an authentic form of musical comedy. He teamed with some of the era's most creative personalities including Paul Laurence Dunbar, James Weldon Johnson, and Bert Williams, to produce a prolific amount of material that are considered classics today. His 1898 production *Clorindy, The Origin of the Cakewalk* is considered by many to be his most memorable.

In 1911 Cook helped James Reese Europe organize the Clef Club's Syncopated Orchestra. Composed of 125 black musicians playing guitars, cellos, basses, and wind instruments, the Clef

Club performed at New York's Carnegie Hall in May 1912. Cook himself played violin with the orchestra. In 1924 Cook became one of the six black charter members of the American Society of Composers, Authors and Publishers (ASCAP). The other black members were Harry T. Burleigh, J. Rosamond Johnson, James Weldon Johnson, Cecil Mack, and Will Tyers. Of these men, Cook was regarded as the "most original genius among all the Negro musicians."

At his death at the age of 75, Cook left an abundance of musical scores that attest to his skill as a musician, composer, and theatrical organizer. The house in which Cook lived from 1918 until his death in 1944 was designated a National Historic Landmark on December 8, 1976. [B 5/11/76 NHL, 76001238]

Dunbar Apartments
Bounded by 7th and 8th avenues and
West 149th and 150th streets
New York

The Dunbar Apartments were created to provide decent housing and services for low-income black residents. Initiated and financed by John D. Rockefeller, Jr., Dunbar was the first cooperative housing enterprise for African Americans. Construction on the Dunbar Apartments was begun in 1926. The complex was designed by architect Andrew J. Thomas, who was known for his progressive views on community planning in urban areas. Thomas's plan for Dunbar consisted of 10 U-shaped buildings with flat sides that faced the street and contained a garden area in the middle of the block. This interior courtyard space allowed light and air to reach every apartment.

Thomas's scheme for the Dunbar Apartments also reflects his views on communal and social organization. Within the complex of the apartment and courtyard were a nursery school, a playground, a clubroom for older children, meeting rooms for adults, retail stores, and a branch of the Dunbar National Bank, Harlem's earliest bank and the first bank to be managed and staffed by African Americans. The Dunbar Apartments constituted, in effect, a self-sustained community and were the first large garden apartment complex in Manhattan. Dunbar won first prize for walkup apartment design from the New York Chapter of the American Institute of Architects in 1927.

Purchase costs higher than those initially projected for its tenants prevented Dunbar from serving the low-income persons for whom it was initially built. Nonetheless, Dunbar became an important Harlem address whose tenants included such influential African Americans such as poet Countee Cullen, reformer W. E. B. Du Bois, labor leader A. Philip Randolph, entertainers Paul Robeson and Bill "Bojangles" Robinson, and explorer Matthew Henson (see also Matthew Henson Residence). [CA 3/29/79, 79001601]

Edward Kennedy "Duke" Ellington House
935 St. Nicholas Avenue, Apartment 4A
New York

Edward Kennedy "Duke" Ellington (1899–1975) was one of America's most important composers and jazz musicians. Ellington's career spanned more than half a century, during which he earned the respect of many classically trained musicians such as composer A. Gunther Schuller, president of the New England Conservatory of Music. Schuller called him "one of America's greatest composers" and ranked him with Stravinsky, Ravel, and Villa-Lobos as an important musical figure of the 20th century.

In 1927 Ellington began his tenure at the Cotton Club, a locale that would sky-rocket him to international fame. His engagement there gave him the public exposure that was necessary for him to secure a recording contract. His popular compositions include "Mood Indigo" and "Take the 'A' Train." He built a reputation not only in jazz, which he legitimized as a serious form of music, but also in popular, classical, and sacred music. The New York house that Ellington occupied from 1931 until 1961 was designated a National Historic Landmark on May 11, 1976. [B 5/11/76 NHL, 76001239]

Harlem River Houses
151st to 153rd Street, Macombs Place, and Harlem River Drive
New York

Harlem River Houses, both historical-ly and architecturally significant, were the first federally funded, federally built, and federally owned housing project in New York City. It was an example of the early collaboration between New York City Housing Authority and the federal gov-ernment and was one of the first efforts undertaken by the Roosevelt administra-tion in recognition of the government's responsibility to provide low-income housing. Recognizing the special and urgent needs of Harlem, the Housing Authority actively involved Harlemites in the planning of the project by having them assist in the development of criteria for tenant selection.

The arrangement of the buildings on the difficult trapezoidal site was extremely effective, drawing high praise from con-temporary critics. The project, to which New York City black architect John Louis Wilson contributed, included courtyards and a plaza enhanced by handsome land-scaping and sculpture. Harlem River Houses not only set a precedent for

public housing across the country, but also offered features that could potentially raise the housing standards of all classes. The venture began in early 1936 and was completed in 1937. [CA 12/18/79, 79001605]

Matthew Henson Residence
246 West 150th Street, Apartment 3F
New York

On April 6, 1909, Matthew Henson, the trailblazer of an expedition team that was commanded by white lieutenant Robert Peary and included four Eskimos, became the first known person to reach the North Pole. Henson and Peary were constant companions on many expedi-tions from 1891 to 1909. Henson brought essential skills and qualities to these journeys. He was popular with the Eskimos, whose language he spoke fluent-ly and who thought of him as a brother because his skin was dark like theirs. Henson also saved Peary's life several times–rescuing him from an ice chasm, killing an angry musk-ox that was charg-ing him, and nursing the lieutenant's frozen feet. Not only Henson's ability and experience were vital to the success of those expeditions, but also his courage and unyielding spirit.

During the 1909 expedition to the North Pole, the five men who accompa-nied Henson and Peary were one by one sent back on their dog sledges with teams of Eskimos, as each had performed his function as part of the support team. Peary selected Henson alone to accompa-ny him on the last leg of the trip. As the trailblazer, Henson traveled ahead of Peary, building igloos at each stopping point, not only marking a path but also providing Peary with a place to rest. Henson knew he had arrived at the North Pole when the compass no longer regis-tered north. Peary soon arrived and gave

Henson the honor of planting the American flag on that historic spot.

Upon returning to the United States, Peary was showered with honors while Henson was ignored and forgotten. He was parking cars in a Brooklyn garage in 1913 when he was discovered by a black politician who secured him a government job as a messenger boy. By the time he retired he was working as a clerk. He was unable to get a federal pension despite his exceptional service to his country in the exploration of the North Pole. He did, however, live long enough to receive some belated appreciation, including a salute from President Harry S Truman in a Pentagon ceremony in 1950.

Matthew Henson died in New York City in 1955 at the age of 88. The Dunbar Apartments, his home after 1928, bears a plaque noting his residence and achievements (see also Dunbar Apartments). His skill and courage helped open part of the world to mankind. Henson's New York residence was designated a National Historic Landmark on May 15, 1975. [CB 5/15/75 NHL, 75001207]

Langston Hughes House
20 East 127th Street
New York

James Langston Hughes (1902–1967) was born February 1, 1902, in Joplin, Missouri, the son of James Nathaniel Hughes and Carrie Mercer Langston Hughes. His family moved frequently when he was young; he attended grammar school in Lincoln, Illinois, and high school in Cleveland, Ohio.

The year 1921 was a crucial one for Hughes. He traveled to Mexico with his father, teaching English in two Mexican schools and publishing his first prose piece, "Mexican Games" in *The Brownies Book,* and his now famous "The Negro Speaks of Rivers" in *The Crisis.* It was also in 1921 that Hughes came to New York to attend Columbia University. Although he remained at Columbia for only a year, later concluding his studies at Lincoln University in Philadelphia, Hughes's days at Columbia were critical to his future. It was during this time that he established friendships with young writers who were participants in the Harlem Renaissance and who would greatly influence his writing.

Hughes traveled extensively, working as a seaman and steward on voyages to Europe and Africa, in 1922 and 1923. He returned to the United States in 1924 to live with his mother in Washington, D.C. In 1925 the "busboy poet" was "discovered" by poet Vachel Lindsay. The following year Hughes entered Lincoln University and published his first volume of poetry, *The Weary Blues.*

Hughes's poetry and prose are dominated by images of Harlem. Nicknamed the "Poet-Laureate of Harlem," Hughes depicts Harlem best in his most notable volume of verse, *Montage of a Dream Deferred* (1951), Hughes's greatest contribution to his field. In early works such as *Fine Clothes to the Jew* (1927), he emphasized blues forms. In later works he experimented with the ballad form, dance rhythms, folk speech rhythms, and jazz forms. As a pioneer in the poetry-to-jazz movement, his most masterful use of these forms occur in *Montage of a Dream Deferred* and *Ask Your Mama: 12 Moods for Jazz* (1961).

Although he is primarily considered a poet, Hughes also was a prolific novelist, playwright, and songwriter. He also established the Harlem Suitcase Theater in 1935, a showcase for plays by black writers with black actors, directors, and production staff. Among the honors accorded him were the Anisfeld-Wolfe

Award in 1953 for the year's best book on race relations and the Spingarn Medal in 1960. He was elected to the National Institute of Arts and Letters in 1961.

Langston Hughes died in May 22, 1967, in New York City. The house on East 127th Street in Harlem where he lived the last 20 years of his life is the only residence he occupied for any significant length of time and is the most tangible symbol of his association with Harlem, so vital to his literary career. [B 10/29/82, 82001198]

James Weldon Johnson House
187 West 135th Street
New York

James Weldon Johnson (1871–1938) was a pioneer and crusading spokesman for full equality for African Americans and the advancement of democracy for all Americans. Johnson received his early education in his hometown of Jacksonville, Florida. After graduating from the public school system, he attended Atlanta University, where he received his bachelor's degree in 1894. Returning to Jacksonville, he became principal of the Stanton Grade School, a position he held for four years. Johnson became involved in two other careers. With a few friends he founded the newspaper *The Daily American,* a venture that lasted only eight months. He then studied law, passing the Florida bar examination in 1897 after only 18 months of informal study.

Accompanied by his musically gifted and talented brother, Rosamond, Johnson visited New York in 1899 to explore the world of theater. In 1900 Johnson wrote what would perhaps become his most notable contribution to music, "Lift Ev'ry Voice and Sing." It became standard in churches, schools, and on all occasions where African Americans assembled throughout the country. It was later adopted by the National Association for the Advancement of Colored People (NAACP) as the black national anthem.

The Johnson brothers later returned to New York and formed a partnership with Bob Cole, a talented black musician, to produce songs and plays. The partnership, which lasted seven years, produced some 200 songs that were sung in various Broadway musicals. Many of these are considered classics, including "Under the Bamboo Tree," "Nobody's Lookin But the Owl and the Moon," and "The Congo Love Song." Their theatrical success was crowned when they signed an exclusive contract with theater mogul A. L. Erlanger. The brothers' success proved that African Americans could compete with the best white composers and make a lasting contribution to American culture.

Returning from a European theatrical tour in 1904, Johnson joined Theodore Roosevelt's presidential campaign, even writing a campaign song for him. For his work, Roosevelt appointed Johnson U.S. consul at Puerto Cabello, Venezuela, in 1907. Two years later he was sent to Nicaragua in the same capacity. While there, he completed his only novel, *The Autobiography of an Ex-Colored Man,* published in 1912. Returning to New York with his wife, Grace Neil, Johnson became contributing editor of the *New York Age,* the oldest black newspaper in New York.

From 1916 to 1930 Johnson served as secretary of the NAACP. In 1917 he organized the Silent Protest Parade, in which a group of 10,000 marched down Fifth Avenue to protest the lynching of African Americans. Johnson also managed to continue publishing and was awarded the coveted Spingarn Medal for *God's Trombones: Seven Sermons in Verse* in 1925. He also wrote *Black Manhattan* (1930) and his autobiography, *Along This Way* (1933).

James Weldon Johnson died in an automobile accident in 1938. He was widely mourned and memorialized. For many years he had been one of the foremost black leaders of the United States and an individual of high rank in literature, music, diplomacy, and public affairs. The New York house in which Johnson resided from 1925 until his death in 1938 was designated a National Historic Landmark on May 11, 1976. [B 5/11/76 NHL, 76001241]

Claude McKay Residence
180 West 135th Street
New York

Born in Jamaica, West Indies, in September 1890, Claude McKay was one of the outstanding figures of American literature during the era known as the Harlem Renaissance. He is known for such works as "If We Must Die"; his autobiography, *A Long Way From Home;* and the first book by an African American to reach the best-seller list, *Home To Harlem*. He traveled and published abroad in such places as England, France, Spain, Morocco, and Russia. He died penniless in 1948 at the age of 58. The New York residence McKay occupied from 1942 until 1946 was designated a National Historic Landmark on December 8, 1976. [B 12/8/76 NHL, 76002143]

Florence Mills House
220 West 135th Street
New York

Florence Mills (1895–1927) was one of the most acclaimed entertainers of the 1920s, appearing in such musicals, plays, and revues as *Plantation Revue, From Dover Street to Dixie,* and *Blackbirds*. She earned a place in the history of American theater by playing the starring role in *Shuffle Along,* the first production composed, directed, and performed by blacks. With a musical score by Eubie Blake and lyrics by Noble Sissle, the show featured such songs as "Love Will Find a Way" and "I'm Just Wild about Harry." Mills died at the age of 32 after a brief illness. Approximately 7,000 mourners attended her funeral. The house in which Florence Mills lived from 1910 until her death in 1927 was designated a National Historic Landmark on December 8, 1976. [B 12/8/76 NHL, 76001244]

Minton's Playhouse
206–210 West 118th Street
New York

Located on the ground floor of the Cecil Hotel in Harlem, Minton's Playhouse played a pivotal role in the development of jazz in the 1940s. The Cecil Hotel was constructed in 1895 as a residential hotel. In 1939 Harry Minton, then owner of the hotel, converted a first floor dining room for use as a club. Minton, a saxophonist, was the first black delegate to Local 802 of the American Federation of Musicians in New York City, playing a significant role in the integration of the union and helping to give black musicians professional status. Minton hired renowned former bandleader Teddy Hill to manage the club in 1950. Hill, seeking to provide opportunities for promising young musicians, hired jazz drummer Kenny Clarke to lead a new house band.

The core of Clarke's band was a group of four innovative musicians who would revolutionize jazz music in the 1940s. Clarke, Thelonius Monk, Dizzy Gillespie, and Charlie Christian forged a new style of jazz that came to be known as bop or be-bop. The "be-bop revolution" that began at Minton's Playhouse was a

New York Amsterdam News Building. Photo courtesy of the National Park Service (Walter Smalling, Jr.).

turning point in the recognition of jazz as a sophisticated art form and of its musicians as serious artists.

This new style of music was built around the jam session, a format that provided each artist the opportunity for extended solos, experimental improvisation, and individual creativity. The jam session freed jazz musicians from the rigidity of big band music and afforded them the opportunity to experiment and learn from one another.

Within a few years of its opening, Minton's Playhouse was known by musicians as the serious meeting place of both progressive innovators and the established masters of earlier jazz styles. Minton's operated continuously through the early 1960s and intermittently until 1974, when a fire in the Cecil Hotel forced its closure. Today, the jam sessions that took place at Minton's are recognized by musicians and historians as fundamental to the transformation of jazz composition from a simple, melodic, and harmonic style to a sophisticated and virtuosic musical form. [A 9/18/85, 85002423]

New York Amsterdam News Building
2293 7th Avenue
New York

Founded in the home of James H. Anderson in December 1909, the *New York Amsterdam News* has become the nation's most prominent and respected black newspaper. Its founding coincided with that of the National Association for the Advancement of Colored People (NAACP). The year 1909 marked the shift from the compromise tactics of Booker T. Washington to a new policy of social action. The editorial policy of the

Amsterdam News paralleled the trends in thought of this new movement.

In 1916 increased circulation, growth, and development necessitated an expanded staff and a move to larger quarters. By 1938 the newspaper had once again outgrown its quarters, and it moved into the present building. Between 1916 and 1938 the *Amsterdam News* grew significantly in circulation and in local and national appeal. It expanded from a local newspaper in Harlem to one that provided national coverage. Although no longer housed in the current building, the paper still enjoys a national reputation among African Americans. The New York Amsterdam News Building was designated a National Historic Landmark on May 11, 1976. [A 5/11/76 NHL, 76001247]

Paul Robeson Home
555 Edgecombe Avenue
New York

Born in Princeton, New Jersey, in 1898, Paul Robeson was one of the outstanding individuals of the 20th century. Possessing numerous talents and skills, Robeson graced stages throughout the world for more than 20 years, giving his most memorable performance in the lead role in *Othello*. His deep baritone voice immortalized such songs as "Ole Man River" from the Broadway musical *Show Boat*. He was a member of the famous Provincetown Players in Massachusetts, becoming a close friend of playwright Eugene O'Neill, who later cast him in lead roles in *All God's Chillun Got Wings* and *Emperor Jones*.

A brilliant Phi Beta Kappa student at Rutgers University in New Jersey, Robeson was chosen all-American in football in 1917 and 1918 and delivered the commencement address at his graduation. He went on to attend Columbia University Law School and set up a law practice in Harlem in 1922, before embarking on a career in theater and music. Robeson's refusal to remain silent about American racism and his ardent desire for full human justice resulted in his ostracism from American society during the McCarthy era of the 1940s and 1950s. This exclusion ended his career in this country, but he remained popular in other countries around the world.

Paul Robeson's death in 1976 marked the loss of one of the world's greatest concert artists, stage and screen actors, athletes, and scholars. It also meant the loss of a valuable humanitarian whose courage and determination to speak the truth and to stand up for what he believed in remains a legacy for all free men and women. The New York residence that Paul Robeson occupied from 1939 until 1941 was designated a National Historic Landmark on December 8, 1976. [B 12/8/76 NHL, 76001248]

Schomburg Center for Research in Black Culture
103 West 135th Street
New York

Formerly called the 135th Street Branch of the New York Public Library, the Schomburg Center for Research in Black Culture is the largest repository in the country for the documentation of the history of the black experience in United States. Since World War I the center has amassed approximately 55,000 volumes, 4,500 phonograph records, 5,000 reels of microfilm, hundreds of thousands of manuscripts, archival records, prints, posters, tape recordings, clippings from periodicals and newspapers, sheet music, and copies of the *Freedom's Journal,* the first black newspaper published in America.

The 135th Street Library opened in 1905, when Harlem was primarily a fashionable white and largely Jewish neighborhood. By World War I Harlem had become the black capital of America. Under the direction of Ernestine Rose, the library developed the Department of Negro Literature and History. In 1926 funds were provided by the Carnegie Corporation of New York to purchase a library collection on black life and history owned by Arthur Schomburg, a famous black bibliophile. His collection is the foundation for the present compilation in the center. The 135th Street Library became the Schomburg Center for Research in Black Culture in 1972. [A 9/21/78, 78001881]

St. George's Episcopal Church
Intersection of 3rd Avenue and East 16th Street
New York

For more than 40 years Harry T. Burleigh (1866–1949) was the baritone soloist at St. George's Episcopal Church in Manhattan. His contributions to the America's musical heritage have been characterized as unique and unsurpassed. From a background of poverty, Burleigh became an internationally esteemed composer, arranger, and artist. It was Burleigh's efforts that brought the Negro spiritual to the attention of the classical musical artists of the day. His greatest composition was "Deep River," which has been said to capture the yearnings of a people. He is considered one of the outstanding songwriters of the early 20th century. [B 12/8/76, 76001249]

St. Nicholas Historic District
West 138th and West 139th streets (both sides) between 7th and 8th avenues
New York

The St. Nicholas Historic District comprises four rows of houses designed by three prominent architectural firms and commissioned by a single builder, D. H. King. An outstanding example of 19th-century urban design, the row houses create a strong cohesive element within the area, while the individuality of approach to the houses prevented the area from succumbing to monotony. The houses were constructed during the apex of the disastrous spurt of overinvesting at the end of the 19th century. While monthly rents typically averaged $10 to $18, rents for these houses started at just below $80 monthly. With the panic of 1904, many of the owners sold the properties at a considerable loss.

In the 20th century the area surrounding the houses developed into the exclusive black area of Harlem, known for its elegance and distinction. Black realtors persuaded the owners to sell or rent the houses to black professionals, and after 1919 the homes were occupied predominantly by black physicians practicing in Harlem. Among these was eminent brain surgeon Dr. L. T. Wright, surgical director of Harlem Hospital from 1938 to 1952 and, at the time, the only black member of the American College of Surgeons. Another resident was Dr. P. M. Murray, dean and professor of surgery at Howard University and one of the first black physicians appointed to the staff of a private hospital. Other prominent residents of the historic district were entertainers W. C. Handy, Eubie Blake, and Noble Sissle. The status of its residents soon earned the area the title of "Strivers' Row," one of several such areas in various cities populated by middle-class African Americans. [C 10/29/75, 75001209]

369th Regiment Armory
2366 Fifth Avenue
New York

Designed by the New York architectural firm of Van Wart and Wein, this remarkably intact Art Deco style armory was constructed around 1933. It is the sole armory built for the only unit of the New York National Guard composed entirely of African Americans. Founded in 1913 as the "Negro Regiment of Infantry," the 369th Regiment was one of only four all-black infantry regiments in the United States. Assigned to the 161st Division of the French Army during World War I, the 369th Regiment was the first all-black unit sent to battle on foreign soil. Known as the "Harlem Hell Fighters," the unit was awarded the *Croix de Guerre* by France and the Legion of Honor, the Distinguished Service Cross, and the Congressional Medal of Honor by the United States. The regiment later served with distinction in World War II and in the Korean War. An interesting coda to the regiment's history is that the 369th Regiment jazz band, which included renowned early jazz musicians from Harlem, is credited with introducing jazz to Europe. Some of the band members remained in France after their service in World War I, popularizing jazz music in Paris. [Army National Guard Armories in New York State MPS, AC 1/28/94, 93001537]

QUEENS COUNTY

Louis Armstrong House
3456 107th Street
New York

Born in New Orleans in 1900, Louis Armstrong's contribution to music was international in scope. He was one of the early shapers of jazz as a trumpeter. Known for his scat singing, he was also a master of improvisation and rhythmic drive and had a captivating instrumental and vocal style. Because of his worldwide popularity, he was named American Ambassador of Goodwill by the U.S. Department of State in the 1960s. Best

remembered for his million-selling rendition of "Hello Dolly," "Satchmo," as he was affectionately called, died in New York City in 1971. The house in New York in which he lived from 1940 until 1971 was designated a National Historic Landmark on May 11, 1976. [B 5/11/76 NHL, 76001265]

Ralph Bunche House
115–125 Grosvenor Road
New York

Ralph Bunche (1904–72) was born in Detroit, Michigan. Both his parents died before he was 12 years old, and he was sent to live with his grandmother in California. Bunche excelled in high school, graduating in the top ten in his class, and entered the University of California at Los Angeles in 1922 on an athletic scholarship. He graduated *summa cum laude* in 1927 and was awarded a fellowship to Harvard University, where he received his master's degree in 1928. That year, he moved to Washington and organized the political science department at Howard University.

Bunche lived in Washington until 1947, teaching and studying race relations through various posts and fellowships. From 1922 to 1923, he was a Julius Rosenwald Fellow in West and North Africa. He earned his Ph.D. from Harvard in 1934. In 1935 he became codirector of the Institute of Race Relations at Swarthmore College. From 1936 to 1938, Bunche did field work in South and East Africa, Malaya, the Netherlands, and the East Indies.

One of his most important achievements came in 1939, when he was recommended by the Carnegie Foundation to assist Swedish sociologist Gunnar Myrdal with a two-year study on the situation of African Americans in the United States. The groundbreaking two-volume study was published in 1944 under the title *The American Dilemma*.

In 1944 Bunche became an area specialist and technical adviser at the State Department, and in 1946 he accepted the post of director of the Trusteeship Council of the United Nations. He accepted a permanent position with the United Nations the following year and moved from Washington, D.C., to New York.

In 1948 Bunche became secretary of the peace-seeking Palestine Commission and successfully mediated a peace settlement that ended the Arab-Israeli War in 1949. For this accomplishment, Bunche was awarded the 1949 Nobel Peace Prize. He was he first African American ever to receive the Nobel Prize.

Bunche continued working with the United Nations throughout the 1950s and 1960s and was eventually appointed undersecretary general. While serving in this capacity, Bunche was awarded the country's highest civilian honor, the Medal of Freedom, by President Kennedy. Meanwhile, he also served as a professor at Harvard University and as adviser to the president at Howard University. In 1959 he became the first black overseer of Howard University.

Bunche retired from his United Nations post in ill health on October 1, 1971, and died three months later. The New York residence in which he lived from 1952 until 1971 was designated a National Historic Landmark on May 11, 1976. [B 5/11/76 NHL, 76001266]

RICHMOND COUNTY

Sandy Ground Historic Archeological District
Address restricted
New York

Sandy Ground is one of the small number of black communities in the New York City area formed by free blacks during the antebellum period. The community had its origins in the first half of the 19th century, when it emerged from several sources: free blacks from the New York and New Jersey area; whites from Staten Island; and free blacks from the Chesapeake Bay area of Maryland, Delaware, and Virginia. In 1850 the Sandy Ground free blacks founded the African Methodist Episcopal Zion Church. The church became well known for holding ox roasts and clam bakes. Most of the community's inhabitants worked in the oyster industry until 1916, when the board of health condemned the oyster beds as sources of typhoid and other diseases. Other members of the community worked as farmers, specializing in strawberries, which grow well in the sandy soil for which the area is named. Sandy Ground is an important archeological site because it provides insight into the cultural patterns of an early black community. [CAD 9/23/82, 82003398]

ST. LAWRENCE COUNTY

Waddington Historic District
Junction of New York Route 37 and La Grasse Street
Waddington

The Waddington Historic District is a highly intact and cohesive collection of residential, civic, and religious architecture that chronicles the development of a small village along the St. Lawrence Seaway between 1816 and 1919.

Although Waddington was a well settled community by 1830, the town did not establish its independence from the larger township of Madrid until 1884. One of the first buildings erected in the newly independent town was the Waddington Town Hall. An unusual stone building that resembles religious more than civic architecture, the Waddington Town Hall was built by Isaac Jackson, an emancipated slave who learned the masonry trade while in slavery in Kentucky. Johnson made his home in Canada and traveled back into border towns such as Waddington to construct several stone buildings. Among these was a four-arch stone bridge that once stood between the towns of Waddington and Madrid but is no longer extant.

The Waddington Town Hall is one of 11 buildings that make up the Waddington Historic District and together represent the development of the village throughout the 19th and early 20th centuries. [CA 5/18/92, 92000457]

SUFFOLK COUNTY

Bethel AME Church and Manse
291 Park Avenue
Huntington

African Americans have been living in the town of Huntington since its founding in the 18th century, primarily as slaves on large plantations. The Bethel African Methodist Episcopal (AME) Church and Manse complex recalls the role that African Americans played in the founding and subsequent growth of the town. The complex was constructed in the 1840s by the local Methodist congregation and exhibits characteristics of Huntington's local building tradition, including wood frame construction, wood sheathing, and an overall utilitarian appearance lacking decorative detail. The church has been used continuously by Huntington's black community and has played a central role in its spiritual life since 1860. The Bethel AME Church and Manse complex is a rare extant historic resource associated with the town's black population. [Huntington Town MRA, CA 9/26/85, 85002490]

TOMPKINS COUNTY

St. James AME Zion Church
116–118 Cleveland Avenue
Ithaca

The African Methodist Episcopal (AME) Zion Church traces its roots to 1796, when a group of black members withdrew from New York City's John Street Methodist Church to escape the discriminatory treatment they received there. By 1822 eight AME Zion churches had formed, and by 1843 New York alone had 19. One of these was Ithaca's congregation, which began in 1825. Built around 1836, St. James AME Zion Church served as an Underground Railroad station. Harriet Tubman, an active member in the AME Zion Church, was a frequent visitor to St. James (see the Harriet Tubman Home for the Aged). Ithaca was an important transfer point on the route from Virginia, through the land of the Pennsylvania Quakers, to Canada and safety. Some fugitives, however, chose to settle in Ithaca because of the support they would receive from the St. James congregation.

St. James remained the focal point for the black community well into the 20th century. It has served as a secular meeting center as well as a religious institution. In fact, it was one of the early meeting places for Alpha Phi Alpha Fraternity, the country's oldest black collegiate fraternity. Alpha Phi Alpha was founded by a group of black students in 1906 at Cornell University in Ithaca. One of these founders, Vertner W. Tandy, went on to become the first black registered architect in New York (see Villa Lewaro, Westchester County; and Chandler Normal School, Fayette County, Kentucky). [CA 7/22/82, 82003407]

WASHINGTON COUNTY

Lemuel Haynes House
Route 149
South Granville

Lemuel Haynes (1753–1833) was the first black clergyman to be ordained a minister by any religious organization in America. He was also the first black minister for a white congregation, the Congregational Church in New England. As a young man he fought in the American Revolution as one of Ethan Allen's Green Mountain Boys. This house was constructed in 1793 and was occupied by Haynes from 1822 until his death in 1833. The house was designated a National Historic Landmark on May 15, 1975. [B 5/15/75 NHL, 75001235]

WESTCHESTER COUNTY

Foster Memorial AME Zion Church
90 Wildey Street
Tarrytown

The present Foster Memorial African Methodist Episcopal (AME) Zion Church has its roots in a small congregation organized by Henry and Amanda Foster, free blacks who settled in Tarrytown around 1837. The original congregation met in Mrs. Foster's confectionary store and later occupied several different temporary quarters as the congregation grew. Mrs. Foster spearheaded efforts to raise money for and build a permanent sanctuary. The present church was constructed by black members of the community in 1865. The congregation was active in the Underground Railroad and provided an important social link for African Americans choosing to settle in Tarrytown in the late 19th and early 20th centuries. The Foster Memorial AME Zion Church survives today as the oldest black church in continuous use in the county and is among the oldest in the state. [A 6/3/82, 82003414]

Villa Lewaro
North Broadway
Irvington

Villa Lewaro, Madame C. J. Walker's residence at Irvington-on-Hudson, was designed by the black architect Vertner Tandy (1885–1949) and completed in 1918. Tandy, a graduate of Cornell University, was New York's first licensed black architect. His Villa Lewaro is a stately example of early Italian Renaissance style skillfully adapted to early 20th-century American architecture. The stately scale of the building resembles Italian palaces. The original four-and-one-half-acre site on which the residence was built had a commanding view of the river. From 1918 to 1934, the house contained 34 rooms. The most impressive were located on the first floor and included the 21-by-32-foot living room and the "Gold Room," which was trimmed in gold and contained a $25,000 organ designed to pipe music throughout the house. The ceilings were decoratively hand painted by European artists.

Villa Lewaro is typical of the architectural skill of Vertner Woodson Tandy. Born in Lexington, Kentucky, Tandy became the first black architect in New York State in 1907. As a youngster, Vertner assisted his father, Henry A. Tandy, a prominent contractor who often acted as his own architect. Vertner designed the Chandler Normal School (see also Chandler Normal School Building and Webster Hall, Fayette County, Kentucky) in Lexington before graduating from Tuskegee Institute's School of Architecture in 1905. He was then admitted to Cornell University as a special student, graduating in 1907.

While he was there he became one of the founders of Alpha Phi Alpha Fraternity, the first black collegiate fraternity in the country.

After graduating from Cornell, Tandy established his architectural office at 1931 Broadway, remaining in New York for his entire 42-year career. His first major project was to design a new home for St. Phillips Episcopal Church in 1910. In 1914 he designed the Harlem town house of cosmetics entrepreneur Madame C. J. Walker, whose daughter, A'Lelia, threw lavish parties there during the Harlem Renaissance. The house became known as the "Dark Tower." He completed Villa Lewaro four years later. Madame Walker died in 1919, leaving Villa Lewaro to A'Lelia. Upon A'Lelia's death in 1931, the property passed to the National Association for the Advancement of Colored People, but upkeep expenses and taxes prevented the organization from accepting it. The expensive interior furnishings were sold at incredibly low prices during a public auction, and the house itself was finally sold for a mere $47,000. Villa Lewaro was designated a National Historic Landmark on May 11, 1976 (see also Madame C. J. Walker Building, Marion County, Indiana). [B 5/11/76 NHL, 76001289]

Union Tavern. Photo courtesy of the National Park Service (Tony Wrenn).

NORTH CAROLINA

ALAMANCE COUNTY

Cooper School
South side of SR 2143, east of junction with SR 2142
Mebane

The Cooper School was established by the American Missionary Association as part of a small educational complex consisting of the Cooper School, Oaks School, and Mary's Grove Congregational Church, which served as the community's first school. The Cooper School is one of two remaining one-room schoolhouses built for black students in Alamance County and is the only surviving building of this educational complex (see also McCray School). The school was probably built around 1900. Few records documenting the early years of the school's history survive. The school operated until 1907, when the Oaks School, a larger facility, was built nearby. In 1907 the school was converted into a parsonage for the ministers of Mary's Grove Congregational Church. The Cooper School represents a tradition of private education for black students that began at Mary's Grove in 1883. [CA 12/15/86, 86003451]

McCray School
Northwest side of North Carolina Route 62, south of junction with SR 1757
Burlington

Built by a local carpenter between 1915 and 1916, the McCray School is one of two remaining one-room schoolhouses in rural Alamance County (see also Cooper School). The school was one of about 24 small rural schools for black students operated by the Alamance County Public School System.

The McCray School served as a strong focal point in the local black community, actively involving parents in school plays, recitals, and fund raisers. When a group of black citizens from McCray petitioned the school board for an addition to the school in 1925, parents were given the responsibility for cutting trees, hauling them to the sawmill, returning the lumber to the site, and hiring a carpenter. The school board agreed to pay for the mill work, nails, locks, hinges, and window frames. When the local black schools were consolidated in a new, modern building in 1928, the McCray School was closed. The building was used as a community center until a fallen tree destroyed the 1925 addition. Members of the black community joined to restore the building, and in 1986 plans were implemented to establish in the building a museum that would depict a one-room schoolhouse of the period in which McCray was built. [CA 12/4/86, 86003438]

BUNCOMBE COUNTY

St. Matthias Episcopal Church
Valley Street
Asheville

St. Matthias Church was founded in 1865 as a mission of Trinity Parish by Jarvis Buxton, an Episcopalian rector who organized the first Episcopalian congregation for free blacks in North Carolina in Fayetteville in 1832. St. Matthias was established to serve the newly freed slaves in the local community, making it the oldest congregation of black Episcopalians in western North Carolina. The original church, a two-story frame building, became too small to accommodate the growing congregation and was replaced by the present building in 1896. At this time the congregation also changed its name to St. Matthias. In addition to its religious functions, St. Matthias established a parochial school shortly after the Civil War, providing educational opportunities for African Americans that may not have been otherwise available.

Built of brick in the Gothic style with elaborate interior woodwork, the church is among the finest constructed for a black or white congregation in North Carolina. As a full-fledged member of the Episcopal diocese of both North Carolina and Western North Carolina, St. Matthias played an important role in the late 19th-century development of black congregations in the denomination. [CA 5/10/79, 79001685]

Young Men's Institute Building
Intersection of Market and Eagle streets
Asheville

The Young Men's Institute (YMI) Building was constructed in 1893 as a community center for the black residents of Asheville. The YMI was founded by George Vanderbilt who intended it to serve the many black construction workers helping build his Biltmore Mansion in Asheville. The two-story pebbledash and brick building was designed by architect R. S. Smith, resident and supervising architect for Biltmore under Richard Morris Hunt. The YMI Building, described by the *Asheville Citizen* as "one of the handsomest buildings in Asheville," housed a meeting room, kindergarten, gymnasium, and bathing facilities on its upper floor. The space often accommodated events sponsored by local black churches, schools, and civic associations and was a focal point of Asheville's black community. The first floor was rented out, and during the course of its history housed several shops and a library. In 1906 Vanderbilt mortgaged the property to YMI, which successfully operated in the building until the Great Depression, when it was forced to close. In 1946 the YMI sold the property to the local Young Men's Christian Association (YMCA) branch, which continued the work of the YMI until the building was closed in 1977. [CAB 7/14/77, 77000994]

BURKE COUNTY

Gaston Chapel
100 Bouchelle Street
Morganton

Gaston Chapel is the oldest extant and first substantial black church in Burke County. Gaston's first black congregation was formed when members of the African Methodist Episcopal congregation founded in Morganton in 1872 left to form their own church around 1881. As the new congregation grew in the 1890s, the small frame church in which they originally worshiped became too small, and they began planning for a new church in 1894. Financial difficulties plagued the congregation's efforts to construct a new church. Much of the manual labor was supplied by the members themselves, and bricks were made on the site.

Completed in 1905, the simplified turn-of-the-century ecclesiastic Gothic building follows the form of many of the white churches built in Burke County in the 1890s. Since the 1880s the church has offered a Sunday School program that has enjoyed high enrollment. The church has historically sponsored a number of clubs that provide services to the congregation and the local black community, and many of these clubs are still active today. [CA 10/11/84, 84000077]

Jonesboro Historic District
Roughly bounded by West Concord, Bay, Jones, Lytle, and South Anderson streets
Morganton

Morganton's oldest black neighborhood, the Jonesboro Historic District was home to a concentration of the town's black residents as early as 1880. Located behind the town's most well-to-do residential neighborhood, the community was made up of laborers, artisans, professionals, and some domestic workers. The Jonesboro area was owned by a few black property holders who subdivided large pieces of land and sold parcels to friends and family. Several of these property holders became prominent citizens in the community. Two of the landowners, Jones Avery and Jones Erwin, are credited with lending their name to the community. The most prominent citizen of Jonesboro, however, was Philo Harbison. Born a slave, Harbison trained as a carpenter after the Civil War and eventually became a prosperous builder and contrac-

tor who built homes for both blacks and whites. Harbison also owned a planing mill and a store on the main street of Morganton. Because Harbison was well respected in both the black and white communities, the city council often consulted him on matters of importance to the black community. [Morganton MRA, A 11/9/87, 87001916]

CASWELL COUNTY

Union Tavern
Main Street
Milton

The Union Tavern is best known not as a tavern but as the workshop of Thomas Day. Day was a free black craftsman who came to Milton in 1823. Shortly thereafter, he established his cabinetmaking studio in the Union Tavern building. He initially trained the slaves of wealthy whites and employed white apprentices to assist him. As the apprentices left his business to work on their own, Day purchased several slaves himself to maintain a permanent staff.

Day quickly built a solid reputation in Milton, designing fine large-scale Empire style furniture with individualistic decoration and interior architectural trim such as newel posts, staircases, and mantels for wealthy clients in the Piedmont area of North Carolina, Virginia, and Georgia. Among his accomplishments are the handsome pews of the Milton Presbyterian Church. Day donated the pews, executed in walnut, yellow poplar, and pine with gracefully curved arms, to the church in exchange for the privilege of sitting in the main area of the church usually reserved for whites only. Through the development of his skills, Day became nationally famous and rose above socially imposed racial restrictions of African Americans. The Union Tavern, which housed Day's workshop, was designated a National

Historic Landmark on May 15, 1975. The building has recently been rehabilitated after sustaining damage in a 1990 fire. [CAB 5/15/75 NHL, 75001245]

CUMBERLAND COUNTY

Evans Metropolitan AME Zion Church
301 North Cool Spring Street
Fayetteville

Founded around 1800 by free black shoemaker and preacher Henry Evans, the Methodist Episcopal Church of Fayetteville served both black and white members of the community. The congregation was mixed until the 1830s, when the predominantly white Hay Street Methodist Episcopal Church drew many of the white congregationists away. Black members of the congregation continued to favor Evans's church, and the group eventually formed their own church known as Evans Chapel. In 1872 Evans Chapel officially became a part of the African Methodist Episcopal (AME) Zion system of churches.

Evans Metropolitan AME Zion Church grew quickly in the years following the Civil War. In 1893 construction was begun on the current church building. Major construction tasks were carried out by black artisans from the local community. The expert skill of these artisans is evident in the brick Gothic Revival building and distinguishes it from other turn-of-the-century churches in Fayetteville. [Fayetteville MRA, C 7/7/83, 83001850]

Orange Street School
500 block of Orange Street
Fayetteville

The Orange Street School was built around 1915 and is believed to be the oldest public education building remaining in Fayetteville. Constructed during a period of reform in black education in North Carolina, the two-story brick building with neoclassical detailing is typical of early 20th-century school architecture in North Carolina. Before its construction, many of the schools that served the black community were small, one-teacher frame buildings.

The Orange Street School exclusively served as an elementary school until 1927, when a high school moved in to occupy the upper floors. At this time, the high school was one of only two black high schools in Cumberland County. The high school moved out in 1929 but returned in 1931. During this period, the school's principal was Armour J. Blackburn, who later became director of personnel for Howard University in Washington, D.C. Blackburn was largely responsible for obtaining accreditation for the school in 1929.

The building continued to be used as a school until 1953 and was abandoned in 1983. In 1986 the property was deeded to the Orange Street School Restoration and Historic Association for the establishment of a museum of public education. [CA 9/22/87, 87001597]

St. Joseph's Episcopal Church
Intersection of Ramsey and Moore streets
Fayetteville

St. Joseph's Episcopal Church in Fayetteville comprises a group of buildings with the chapel, parish hall, and parsonage linked by wooden arcades. The black congregation was formed in 1873 and is the second oldest Episcopal congregation in Fayetteville. The complex was built in 1896 on ground donated by one of the parishioners, replacing the "badly situated and dilapidated edifice" that had formerly housed the congregation. In 1916 all the buildings except the chapel were destroyed in a fire. The complex was soon rebuilt in a style complementing the chapel. The shingled Queen Anne style buildings are accented with English, Spanish, and Gothic features and are rare surviving examples of North Carolina's Queen Anne architecture designed as a whole to create the impression of a quiet country setting.

In recent years St. Joseph's has served as a meeting place for the United Service Organization, the National Association for the Advancement of Colored People, and the Episcopal Society for Cultural and Racial Unity. [CA 6/1/82, 82003447]

Durham County

Emmanuel AME Church

710 Kent Street
Durham

Built in 1888, the Emmanuel African Methodist Episcopal (AME) Church was strongly connected with Richard Burton Fitzgerald, a successful brick maker and respected member of Durham's black community. Fitzgerald had become wealthy in his brick business and had purchased and developed several tracts of land in the area. Fitzgerald's interest in his neighborhood, however, went beyond real estate development, for he played a pioneering role in the establishment of Emmanuel AME Church for the black community.

The church was built on land purchased for a nominal fee and with materials donated by Fitzgerald. Although the name "Emmanuel" was chosen for the church, many members of the congregation referred to it as "the Fitzgerald church." Members of the Fitzgerald family were active members of the congregation, and they donated land a few blocks south of the church to be used as a private cemetery for the family and members of the Emmanuel AME Church. The church

operated until 1971 and was purchased shortly thereafter by the Deliverance Temple Holy Church. [Durham MRA, CAB 8/9/85, 85001775]

Horton Grove Complex

North of Durham on SR 1626
Durham

The Horton Grove complex consists of a small 18th-century dwelling, a great barn or stables, a cluster of tobacco barns, and a row of slave cabins. The row of four nearly identical slave houses is located behind the dwelling house. The slave cabins are two stories high and constructed of heavy timber infilled with brick nogging; they are covered with vertical board-and-batten siding and have gabled tin roofs. Inside, each contains a central stair with a 17-by-17 1/2-foot room on each floor. Chimneys, some of which remain, originally stood at both ends of the cabins. It is unknown how slave families resided in these buildings. These houses were unusually spacious, well-constructed buildings described by former residents as cool in summer and warm in winter.

After the Civil War the owner of the plantation executed a contract with his former slaves, who continued to work for him detailing the responsibilities and expectations of plantation workers and owners alike. Black families continued to occupy the cabins for many years. The wealth of oral and written information about the patterns and continuity of family life at Horton Grove is noted by historian Herbert Gutman in *The Black Family from Slavery to Freedom*. [CADB 3/17/78, 78001946]

North Carolina Central University

Bounded by Lawson Street, Alston Avenue, and Nelson and Fayette streets
Durham

North Carolina Central University had its origins in the National Religious Training School and Chautauqua for the Colored Race, founded in 1910 by Dr. James E. Shepard. Shepard graduated from Shaw University as a registered pharmacist in 1894. After working for many years as a druggist, he accepted the position of field superintendent for the International Sunday School Board. In this capacity Shepard developed strong ideas about the education of African Americans. In 1909 he embarked upon a fund-raising campaign to secure money to build his school. The school's mission was to encourage a firm belief in God and to educate youth so they could work effectively toward landownership, higher standards of living, and political participation.

Shepard's school offered grammar school, high school, and college level programs. Financial difficulties plagued the school throughout its history, however, and in 1923 it was taken over by the state of North Carolina and became the Durham State Normal School. Shepard was retained as the school's principal. In 1923 Shepard began a campaign to convert the school into a four-year liberal arts college for black students. The state general assembly accepted the proposal in 1925, establishing the North Carolina College for Negroes. The school became the nation's first state-supported four-year liberal arts college for black students. Shepard was chief administrator of the new institution.

Since its founding, the college has grown to more than 5,000 students and 50 buildings. In 1969 its name was changed to North Carolina Central University, and in 1972 the school became one of the 16 institutions that make up the University of North Carolina. The buildings of North Carolina Central University stand as a reminder of James E. Shepard's unfailing commitment to high-quality education for black students. [Durham MRA, CAB 3/28/86, 86000676]

North Carolina Mutual Life Insurance Company Building
114–116 West Parrish Street
Durham

Founded in Durham, North Carolina, in 1898, the North Carolina Mutual Life Insurance Company evolved out of a tradition of mutual benefit societies and fraternal organizations that offered life insurance benefits to their members as early as the 18th century. By the 20th century these organizations were among the most important social institutions for African Americans. They represent a tradition of racial solidarity and self-help epitomized at that time by the doctrines preached by Booker T. Washington directing black leadership away from politics and protest into business and education and separate black institutions.

Although the institution was successful in its early years, it developed into the "world's largest Negro business" after it was reorganized in 1900 by Charles Clinton Spaulding, nephew of one of the founders, Dr. Aaron M. Moore. Within a decade the business had achieved legal reserve status and could boast of being the largest black business in the country. By the end of World War I, the company had established branches from Maryland to Florida to Oklahoma.

By 1970 the firm had established branches coast-to-coast throughout the North and South. A resurgent interest in racial solidarity and black capitalism in the 1960s strengthened the company's financial position in the black community. It was during this period that major white corporations such as IBM and General Motors contracted part of their employees' group insurance with North Carolina Mutual. Between 1969 and 1972 the company's assets grew from less than $500 million to more than $1 billion, making it the first black billion-dollar corporation.

The North Carolina Mutual Life Insurance Company Building in Durham stands for racial progress and, apart from Tuskegee University, is one of the nation's most conspicuous landmarks of the ideas of racial solidarity and self-help (see also Tuskegee Institute National Historic Site, Macon County, Alabama). For this reason the building was designated a National Historic Landmark on May 15, 1975. [A 5/15/75 NHL, 75001258]

Scarborough House
1406 Fayetteville Street
Durham

Constructed in 1916 with materials salvaged from one of Durham's finest Queen Anne houses, the Scarborough House represents the accomplishments of J. C. and Clydie F. Scarborough, a prominent black Durham family. Drawn by Durham's reputation as a center for black progress, John Clarence (J. C.) Scarborough moved to the city from Kinston, North Carolina, and in 1906 opened the Scarborough and Hargett Funeral Home, the first funeral home for African Americans in Durham.

Scarborough quickly expanded his interests in the local black community, becoming one of its foremost leaders. When the Mechanics and Farmers Bank was organized in Durham in 1908, he became one of its first directors. He also served on the board of St. Joseph's African Methodist Episcopal Church and as secretary of Scarborough Hospital's board of directors.

After the death of his first wife, Daisy Hargett Scarborough, Scarborough organized a nursery school for the children of the community and accepted them regardless of their families' ability to pay. In 1926 he married Clydie Fulwood, who took over the nursery and added the first licensed kindergarten in North Carolina. She devoted her life to the improvement of day care and early education in the state. The Scarborough's Neoclassical Revival style house stands as an architectural reminder of the couple's commitment and contributions to Durham's black community. [Durham MRA, CAB 8/9/85, 85001779]

St. Joseph's African Methodist Episcopal Church
Intersection of Fayetteville Street and Durham Expressway
Durham

This eclectic Gothic Revival style church was designed in 1898 by Philadelphia architect Samuel L. Leary. St. Joseph's congregation was first organized in 1869 by the Reverend Edian D. Markham. The first building, consisting of four poles covered with a brush roof, was soon replaced by a log church in which Markham taught children during the week and held services on Sunday. The school is reputed to have been the first black school in Durham. A series of buildings had stood on the site when a committee was named to plan this larger, more substantial building in 1890.

The bricks for the new building were fired in the brickyards of Richard B. Fitzgerald, an African American who came to Durham in 1866 and eventually became the first president of the Mechanics and Farmers Bank established in 1907. White tobacco capitalists Washington Duke and Julius S. Carr contributed heavily to the building fund, establishing biracial cooperation in the building of the church. St. Joseph's pioneering congregation was composed of persons who made significant contributions to the commercial, educational, and cultural life of African Americans in North Carolina, and in the 20th century the church became a center for civil rights activities. [CA 8/11/76, 76001319]

FORSYTH COUNTY

S. G. Atkins House
346 Atkins Street
Winston-Salem

Dr. Simon Green Atkins founded the Slater Industrial Academy in Winston-Salem in 1892. The Atkins House, constructed in 1893, was the first house to be constructed in the Columbian Heights neighborhood of Winston-Salem. Atkins was instrumental in establishing the Columbian Heights neighborhood as a community for middle-class African-Americans, who had previously been relegated to living in poorly kept overcrowded areas traditionally assigned to the black population. Atkins saw the neighborhood as a way to attract professional teachers to the school.

Atkins was later involved in the founding of the Columbian Heights High School and the Slater School Hospital for African-Americans in Winston-Salem. He served as president of the Slater Industrial Academy from its founding in 1892 until shortly before his death in 1934. [Slater Industrial Academy Houses TR, AB 7/22/79, 79001704]

St. Philip's Moravian Church
East side of South Church Street near Race Street
Winston-Salem

Built in 1861, St. Philip's Moravian Church is the oldest extant church building associated with a black congregation in Forsyth County and is the only known antebellum mid-19th century black church building remaining in the state of North Carolina. The Moravians settled in the Piedmont area of central North Carolina in 1752, purchasing 100,000 thousand acres on which to establish a community. All aspects of community life were tightly controlled by the church. The church owned all the land and purchased and rented slaves to work in the settlement of Salem. While individuals in the settlement were not permitted to hold slaves, the church leased them to farmers and craftsmen in town. By 1800 the settlement included some 70 slaves and 25 to 30 free blacks.

For a time slaves in the Moravian settlements were treated much more humanely than elsewhere in the South. They lived among the rest of the residents of the community and had been baptized members of the Moravian church since 1771. Changes taking place in the South in the late 18th century, however, altered this heretofore peaceful relationship. As slavery became the basis of Southern agricultural life, the Moravians' treatment of black slaves became more like that of the larger Southern society. Tensions between blacks and whites in the community led to the formation of a separate black Moravian church, St. Philip's, in 1822.

The black Moravian church proved immediately attractive to both free blacks and slaves and quickly became a focal point of black social, religious, and educational life throughout this region of the Piedmont. The present St. Philip's church building was constructed in 1861 to replace the original 1822 log church and was used continuously by the congregation until 1952. [CA 9/3/91, 91001170]

FRANKLIN COUNTY

Dr. J. A. Savage House
124 College Street
Franklinton

The John A. Savage House was constructed around 1880 for use as a classroom or dormitory building on the campus of the Albion Academy in Franklinton, North Carolina. The academy was founded in 1878 by Dr. Moses Aaron Hopkins, a black Virginian, and was funded by the Presbyterian Board of Missions for Freedmen. The school was one of several in Virginia and North Carolina funded by the group to provide training for freed slaves. Its students attended classes from elementary through high school grades. Classes offered vocational training and prepared students in the fields of teaching, farming, nursing, and mechanics.

John A. Savage was appointed principal of Albion Academy around 1895. Shortly after his appointment, the Savage House was renovated for use as his residence. Under Savage's leadership, the school grew and prospered from a small tract of land and a few buildings to a complex of 60 acres with several substantial buildings. At the time of Savage's death in 1933, the school had achieved an "A" rating by the accreditation board of the state board of education.

The Albion Academy joined the public school system shortly after Savage's death. In 1934 the city voted to build a new school instead of repairing damage to Albion caused by a water main break. The buildings were allowed to stand empty and fall into disrepair. Today the Savage House and dining hall are all that remain of this school, which once provided excellent training and education for its black students. [AB 9/22/80, 80002834]

Williamson House
401 Cedar Street
Louisburg

John H. Williamson was born a slave in Covington, Georgia. He came to North Carolina at about 13 years of age as the property of Temperance Perry Williamson, for whom the Williamson House was built. A self-educated man, Williamson remained in Franklin County after the Civil War to pursue a career in politics. He was elected the representative from Franklin County to the North Carolina House in 1868, 1870, 1872, 1876, and 1887. In 1868 he was a member of the Constitutional Convention and in 1872 and 1884 was elected delegate to the National Republican Convention in Philadelphia.

Believing there was no hope for equal justice for African Americans in the North, Williamson introduced a bill in 1877 to the general assembly requesting that North Carolina's delegation to Congress encourage the federal government to reserve the territory beyond the Mississippi "for the sole and exclusive use and occupation of the colored race." Although Williamson's proposal was rejected, the bill attracted considerable attention. In 1881 Williamson founded the *Raleigh Banner*. He sold the paper shortly thereafter and founded the *Raleigh Gazette*, which was among the most influential black newspapers in the state. Both newspapers promoted the "advancement of the educational and industrial status of negroes in the state." [CB 6/20/75, 75001272]

GRANVILLE COUNTY

Central Orphanage
Intersection of Antioch Drive and
Raleigh Road
Oxford

The Central Orphanage of North Carolina was founded in 1883 as the Grant Colored Asylum. In 1887 the orphanage consisted of a dilapidated barn and a small house that sheltered eight children cared for by a matron. In this same year the asylum was incorporated as the Colored Orphanage Asylum of North Carolina and named the Reverend Robert Shepard as its superintendent. Under Shepard's direction, the facility grew in size and stature with help from donations by churches, fraternal orders, private philanthropists, and the state legislature. Its land space was increased from 23 to 148 acres and included a farm on which cotton and food crops were grown.

Shepard remained superintendent until 1907, when he was succeeded by Henry Plummer Cheatham. Under Cheatham's direction, the orphanage became a major institution of statewide importance. He replaced the its frame buildings with buildings made of brick formed and fired by the orphans and gathered funds for the work from numerous sources throughout the state.

The orphanage acquired its present name in 1965. Although much reduced in size in recent years, the orphanage continues to care for black children, the first institution of its kind in the Carolinas. [Granville County MPS, CAB 8/31/88, 88001257]

GUILFORD COUNTY

Agricultural and Technical College of North Carolina Historic District
East side of Dudley Street between
Bluford Street and Headen Drive
Greensboro

The Classical Revival style administrative, academic, and student services buildings of the Agricultural and Technical College of North Carolina Historic District include five of the oldest surviving buildings on North Carolina's first black land-grant university campus. The school was originally established as the Agricultural and Mechanical College for the Colored Race in Raleigh in 1891. In 1893 the campus was moved to Greensboro, where it developed into one of the nation's premier historically black institutions of higher education in the field of agriculture and the technical arts.

Dr. J. O. Crosby, the college's first president, designed the main administration building and made the first brick with which it was constructed. Students in the Department of Industries laid bricks for the campus's three original buildings. A brickyard and kiln were located on the campus.

Despite the early emphasis on mechanical skills, the college expanded to include a high school–level college preparatory curriculum. In 1915, under the administration of James Benson Dudley, the college was renamed the Agricultural and Technical College of North Carolina (A&T). During World War I, Dudley established a military training camp at A&T, beginning a tradition that would continue through World War II. Near the end of Dudley's tenure, the North Carolina legislature appropriated about $615,000 for improvements. The sum was at that time the largest amount of money ever allocated for black education in the South. The money was used to construct several campus buildings between 1922 and 1924, three of which are included in the historic district— Murphy Hall, Morrison Hall, and Noble Hall.

By 1939 the college preparatory curriculum had been phased out as emphasis was placed solely on college-level work. A school of education, a department of home economics, and a school of graduate studies had also been established. It was in this year that the Richard B. Harrison Auditorium, one of the historic district properties, was built by the Works Projects Administration.

The campus continued to grow and prosper, but it gained widespread national

Noble Hall, Agricultural and Technical College of North Carolina Historic District. Photo Courtesy of the North Carolina Division of Archives and History (P.S. Dickinson).

attention in 1960. A group of four A&T students entered Greensboro's Woolworth's store to eat at the lunch counter. When they were refused service, they remained seated until the proprietor closed the counter. These nonviolent sit-ins continued in Greensboro and across the South and were the impetus for widespread student protest in the civil rights movement among black and white students alike. The number of people participating in the sit-ins reached a peak in the summer of 1963, before the March on Washington. One of A&T's students at this time was Jesse Jackson, who would become a respected minister, civil rights leader, and politician.

In 1972 A&T became a part of the University of North Carolina system. The newest campus building, completed in June 1987, is the Ronald E. McNair Engineering Building. The building honors a distinguished alumnus who was the United States's first black astronaut and who was killed in the explosion of the space shuttle *Challenger* in 1986. [CA 10/20/88, 88002046]

Downtown Greensboro Historic District
Elm, South Davie, South Green, and East and West Washington streets
Greensboro

The buildings in the Downtown Greensboro Historic District represent the phenomenon of urbanization, which occurred not only in Greensboro, but in many smaller cities all over the United States during the late 19th and early 20th centuries. Within the boundaries of the district is the Woolworth's building. Constructed around 1929 as the local store for F. W. Woolworth Company, this building has elaborate Greek Revival

Ora Martin and her husband in front of the Kilby Hotel, c. 1925. Photo courtesy of the North Carolina Division of Archives and History.

style ornamentation restated in the Art Deco idiom.

The Woolworth's building is also significant as a landmark of the civil rights movement. At 4 P.M. on February 1, 1960, four black freshmen from Greensboro's Agricultural and Technical College entered the store on North Elm Street and seated themselves in the "white-only" section of the lunch counter, launching the Greensboro sit-ins (see also Agricultural and Technical College of North Carolina). The four young men, Ezell Blair, Jr., Franklin McCain, Joseph McNiel, and David Richmond, had no idea that their protest of segregated and unequal eating facilities in the Woolworth store in Greensboro would trigger a chain reaction. The response by students, mostly African Americans, was swift. Within two weeks, similar sit-ins were staged throughout the state, and by mid-March they had spread throughout the South. The summer of 1960 saw 33 southern cities integrate their eating facilities, culminating in integrated lunch counters and restaurants throughout much of the region. A year later 126 cities had accepted the new practice that began in downtown Greensboro. [CA 6/17/82, 82003458]

Kilby Hotel
627 East Washington Street
High Point

John and Nannie Kilby purchased the land on which the Kilby Hotel stands in 1913. A couple of modest means, John Kilby worked for the Southern Railroad and his wife worked as a nurse and a hairdresser and at one time even sold fish from a horse cart. Their industriousness, frugality, and wise investments allowed them to purchase the property and to build their hotel shortly thereafter. Over the years, Nannie was also able to purchase some 30 other houses in High Point near the hotel.

Early on, part of the hotel was used as an amusement center, serving as the neighborhood's social center. Upon Nannie Kilby's death in 1921, the operations of the hotel were taken over by her daughter, Ora Martin. Martin, a civic leader of High Point, maintained the hotel's use as an important social and economic center of the black community. At Ora Martin's death in 1972, her daughter, Mrs. Marion McElrath, inherited the hotel. Her children, who assist in running the hotel, represent the family's fourth generation to operate the hotel. The hotel's guests have been both permanent residents and visitors serving High Point's black business community. The Kilby Hotel remains one of High Point's most important black-owned businesses. [CAB 4/22/82, 82003460]

Palmer Memorial Institute Historic District

Along U.S. Route 70 west of junction with North Carolina 3056
Sedalia

Charlotte Hawkins was born in Henderson, North Carolina, in 1883. Around 1890 her family moved to Massachusetts, where she attended the Massachusetts Normal School at Salem to prepare for a career in teaching. In 1901 she received an appointment as a teacher at a small rural school near Greensboro, North Carolina, sponsored by the American Missionary Association (AMA). She began teaching at the Bethany Normal School and Industrial Institute, which was housed in the Bethany Congregational Church. In the spring of 1902, however, the AMA withdrew support for the school. Rather than accept a transfer by the AMA, Hawkins instead elected to remain in the area and start her own school.

Hawkins called her school the Palmer Memorial Institute (PMI) in honor of Alice Freeman Palmer, a president of Wellesley College, who had assisted Hawkins in her education. Although they were separate entities, PMI and Bethany Church retained close ties throughout the history of the school. The Reverend Manual Liston Baldwin, pastor of Bethany Church, and his wife deeded 15 acres of land to the trustees of PMI for use by the school, which was to "teach said colored race improved methods of agriculture and industrial pursuits." PMI was officially incorporated on November 23, 1907, and the next year secured a donation of land for a farm.

By 1916 the campus had four primary frame buildings, but fires in these buildings provided the impetus for carrying out all subsequent major construction in brick. The fires and a general shortage of funds had thrown Charlotte Hawkins Brown (she was married to Edward S. Brown in 1911) into the role of fund raiser. She assembled a core of wealthy donors who kept the school functioning. In the late 1920s, in an effort to establish financial stability, Brown succeeded in having the AMA take over the operations of the school. Brown was unable to relinquish control of the school, however, and in 1934 the school was returned to her direction.

As the public school system for African Americans improved in the 1930s, PMI's focus changed accordingly. Having lost a great number of younger children to the public schools, PMI closed its elementary department and began to function largely as a finishing and college preparatory school. PMI was among the first black high schools in the state to be accredited by the Southern Association of Colleges and Secondary Schools.

Charlotte Hawkins Brown stepped down as president of PMI in 1952 after 50 years of service. In January 1961 she died and was buried on the campus near her home. Although the institute continued to operate for a decade after her death, racial integration, the civil rights movement, and student unrest all affected the school. The school was closed in 1971 following the destruction by fire of the main campus building. The remaining 40-acre site was purchased by the state of North Carolina in 1987 for the development of the state's first site commemorating the contribution of African Americans to its history. [AB 10/24/88, 88002029]

William Penn High School
Washington Drive
High Point

This school was founded as High Point Normal and Industrial Institute by Quaker philanthropy in 1891 as a school for African Americans. Under the direction of principal Alfred J. Griffin, appointed in 1897, the school grew quickly in its early years. The institute was a self-sustaining unit. The students maintained a large farm on which they raised corn, wheat, pork, and peas for their own consumption. When steady growth of the student body necessitated expanded facilities in 1900, students in brick making, masonry, and carpentry undertook the construction of a new building and completed it entirely on their own in 1901. Many of the furnishings were made by students as well. Four new substantial brick buildings were built in 1910 following destruction by fire of the 1894 frame building. The oldest remaining buildings on the campus date to this time. Although the school emphasized voca-

tional training, students also received a basic academic education and spiritual training.

As enrollment continued to grow, financial concerns limited the faculty in providing high-quality education, and in 1923 the school was sold to the city of High Point as an accredited school for black students. The first principal of the school after its transfer to the public school system was Ewsebia Cartwright, who had come to the school in 1902. Under his leadership the school grew and prospered. Cartwright constructed new classroom buildings, expanded the library and the staff, and instituted a full athletic program. It was also during Cartwright's tenure that the name was changed to William Penn High School in honor of the Quaker leader.

William Penn High School continued to function until the federal mandate to integrate the schools in the mid-1950s. The school board opted to build a new integrated facility, closing the doors of this important landmark to High Point's black community. [A 11/16/78, 78001959]

IREDELL COUNTY

Center Street AME Zion Church
South Center Street
Statesville

After the Civil War many black churches were organized by black congregants of formerly mixed congregations. Among the most numerous of these were the African Methodist Episcopal (AME) Zion churches. Center Street AME Zion Church, constructed in 1903, is the oldest building associated with a black congregation in Statesville and was formed during this post-Civil War movement. The church is built of brick and executed in the Gothic Revival style with intricate corbeled, paneled, and molded brickwork.

This brickwork is characteristic of many turn-of-the-century churches, especially those erected for black congregations as they prospered and gained prominence. Many of these churches, like the Center Street Church, became focal points for the local black community. [Iredell County MRA, CA 11/24/80, 80002868]

JOHNSTON COUNTY

Boyette Slave House
Northwest of Kenly on SR 2110
Kenly

The Boyette Slave House is a rare, little-altered example of a slave house associated with a small farm in rural antebellum North Carolina. In 1800 George Boyett (later spelled Boyette) purchased the property on which the building now stands. Of the 400 acres deeded to Boyett, he farmed only 100 acres, which he planted primarily with corn and sweet potatoes. At Boyett's death, the property passed to his son, Larkin Boyett, who continued the farm. Records show that in 1860 Larkin Boyett had four slaves.

The building is also significant for its stick and mud chimney. This chimney is built entirely of sticks daubed with mud and attached to the house by board jams. This construction method virtually disappeared from the architectural vocabulary of North Carolina with the end of slavery. Considered a holdover of medieval building methods brought to the southern colonies by English settlers, wood and clay chimneys were soon replaced with more substantial and less flammable ones built of brick or stone. Those that remained were usually attached to slave quarters and were abandoned and allowed to fall into ruin after the end of slavery. Remarkably intact, the Boyette chimney is the only known chimney of this type remaining in the North Carolina. [CA 9/20/79, 79003329]

LINCOLN COUNTY

Tucker's Grove Camp Meeting Ground
North of Machpelah off SR 1360
Machpelah

Tucker's Grove Camp Meeting Ground represents the often overlooked participation of African Americans in the camp meeting movement that flourished in North Carolina in the late 18th and early 19th centuries. Bishop Francis Asbury, who preached to frontier Methodist congregations throughout North Carolina from 1780 to 1816, was especially concerned with the spiritual welfare of slaves. He worried that masters did not allow slaves to worship in the Methodist Church, preventing the church from reaching them. Tucker's Grove Camp Meeting ground was established as a result of the Methodist Church's crusade to reach the slave population.

The meeting ground was founded in the first half of the 19th century by the Methodist Episcopal Church and continued to be used as a campground after the abolition of slavery. When it was listed in the National Register in 1972, it had been operating continuously since 1876 as an African Methodist Episcopal Zion campground under the direction of a board of trustees. The oak grove within which the camp meeting complex is located was donated to the trustees by Mary E. Tucker in 1879.

The complex consists of a central building, called an arbor, set in a large grove and surrounded by frame tents that form almost a complete enclosure. The communal plan of the complex, with individual shelters surrounding a common core, recalls the organization of Native American camps and wagon train encampments, fulfilling the need for both safety and fellowship. The deep roof of the Tucker's Grove arbor symbolizes a

Tucker's Grove Camp Meeting Ground. Photo courtesy of the North Carolina Division of Archives and History (Randall Page).

protective canopy sheltering the congregation assembled in the grove. [A 10/18/72, 72000972]

MECKLENBURG COUNTY

Biddle Memorial Hall, Johnson C. Smith University
Intersection of Beatties Ford Road and West Trade Street
Charlotte

Johnson C. Smith University was founded in 1867 with the recognition that few institutions of higher education existed for the education of African Americans in North Carolina. The school was first named Biddle Memorial Institute in appreciation of the first large cash donation made to the school by tobacco heiress Mary Duke Biddle. The school was originally located in the old Confederate Navy Building but was moved to its current location in 1883.

Biddle Memorial Hall was constructed in 1883 and financed with substantial contributions by the Freedmen's Bureau and Mary Biddle. The building served as the main campus building, providing space for classrooms, a reading room, registrar's quarters, a business office, the president's office, and other vital administrative offices. Students participated in the construction of the building and made bricks on the site. In 1923 the name of the university was changed to Johnson C. Smith University in recognition of a generous gift by Jane Berry Smith in honor of her husband. It was at this time that the monumental Romanesque Revival style building at the center of the campus was renamed Biddle Memorial Hall. [CA 10/14/75, 75001281]

Mecklenburg Investment Company Building

233 South Brevard Street
Charlotte

The Mecklenburg Investment Company was formed in May 1921 by a group of Charlotte's leading black citizens. The firm sought shareholders to contribute money for the construction of an office building in the black neighborhood of Brooklyn. The space in the building was to be rented to black businesses. The three-story brick building was built by William W. Smith, a prominent local black builder and contractor. The building was completed late in 1922 with space for stores on the first floor, offices on the second, and a meeting room and offices on the third floor. The building was occupied immediately by black dentists, lawyers, and other professionals who had been scattered throughout the city and often relegated to unsuitable quarters.

Through the business establishments it housed, the building became a focal point of the Brooklyn community and a meeting place for black fraternal organizations. Social functions sponsored by these organizations were often held in the building as well. The Mecklenburg Investment Company Building stands as a monument to the black middle-class ethic of self-reliance and social, political, and economic separation prevalent at the time it was built. [CAB 8/19/82, 82003486]

POLK COUNTY

Rev. Joshua D. Jones House

South side of North Carolina 1526, 0.4 mile from North Carolina 108
Mill Spring

Joshua D. Jones was born in South Carolina in December 1858 and, according to census records, had moved to Polk County, North Carolina, by 1870. He later settled in the Stony Knoll area near the black community of Mill Spring. Stony Knoll was a black community separated from Mill Spring by a high hill. By 1883 Jones was able to purchase his house and the three and one-half acre lot on which it stood. Jones served as the pastor of the Stony Knoll Colored Methodist Episcopal (CME) Church from around 1890 to 1900. He later served the Langford CME Church in Monroe while maintaining his residence in Polk County. Around the turn of the century he opened a small store on his property and worked as a carpenter in the area.

The Rev. Joshua D. Jones House illustrates the efforts made by African Americans throughout the South after the Civil War to own land, to live in communities of their own race, and to act through their church to improve their condition of life. Today the house is the only substantial building in the Stony Knoll community. [A 9/26/91, 91001476]

ROCKINGHAM COUNTY

First Baptist Church

401 South Scales Street
Reidsville

The first black Baptist congregation in Reidsville was formed in 1874 by the Reverend Samuel Jones. The congregation was composed of black members of the First Baptist Church of Reidsville who elected to form their own church. In 1888 the congregation built a frame church building near the First Baptist Church. In 1900 a split occurred in the church concerning the leadership of the Reverend R. L. Slade. Slade's supporters withdrew from the church and formed the Zion Baptist Church. The remaining congregants formed the First Baptist Church.

In 1916 they constructed this handsome Gothic Revival style building in a predominantly black neighborhood near Reidsville's central business district. The church served the members of First Baptist Church from 1916 until their move to new facilities in 1975. [Reidsville MRA, CA 12/11/86, 86003386]

Mt. Sinai Baptist Church
512 Henry Street
Eden

After the Civil War, a strong movement took hold in the South for black churchgoers to form their own congregations. Of these new churches, the Baptist church fast became the most popular denomination for black churches in North Carolina. It was in this context that Mt. Sinai Baptist church was formed in 1888 in Leaksville (present-day Eden).

The congregation first met in a schoolhouse on nearby Henry Street, but in 1891 it acquired a small lot on which a small frame church was erected. In time the congregation outgrew the sanctuary, and in 1921 it purchased a larger lot to be the site of the new church. The handsome brick Gothic Revival style sanctuary was completed in 1921 and is typical of early 20th century Gothic Revival ecclesiastical architecture. The most architecturally distinctive of Eden's black churches, Mt. Sinai is symbolic of the new prosperity and pride of black churches following emancipation. [CA 6/25/87, 87000914]

North Washington Avenue Workers' House
East side of 300 block of North Washington Avenue
Reidsville

During the late 19th and early 20th centuries, many rural farm workers in North Carolina left the depressed agricultural sector and moved to growing towns seeking work in expanding industries. While whites often found work in textile mills, many black workers were employed in factories in the tobacco industry such as the American Tobacco Company in Reidsville. With the tremendous influx of workers, affordable housing for workers became increasingly scarce. The North Washington Avenue Workers' Houses were built as inexpensive rental housing for the workers of the American Tobacco Company.

The modest frame dwellings derive from single-pen houses of log and frame that were common in North Carolina's rural landscape. Houses like these were usually built in clusters close to the tobacco factory and may once have numbered in the hundreds. The North Washington Avenue Workers' Houses are five houses standing in a row that were probably built in 1915 by Thomas Littleton Gardner, a local druggist. Although many windows and doors have been replaced and electricity and indoor plumbing added, the houses retain much of their original character and are the only surviving, intact group of this particular house type in the area. [Reidsville MRA, CA 12/11/86, 86003388]

ROWAN COUNTY

Livingstone College Historic District
West Monroe Street
Salisbury

Livingstone College was founded as the Zion Wesley Institute in 1879 under the auspices of the African Methodist Episcopal (AME) Zion Church. The school was originally located in nearby Concord on a seven-acre tract of land with a farmhouse. Its goal was the "training of young men and women for religious and educational work in this country and in Africa." Despite support from the church, the school struggled financially and was forced to close eight months into its second year.

The reopening of the school in its Salisbury location was largely due to the work of Joseph Charles Price. Price, a delegate to the Ecumenical Council in London in 1881, embarked on a speaking tour in England to raise money for the school. He returned with $10,000 in 1882. This money was combined with donations from the local white community, and the school was reopened in Salisbury in October 1882 on a 40-acre tract of land. Within a year the school's enrollment had jumped from three to nearly 100.

In 1885 the name of the school was changed to Livingstone College in honor of the noted English missionary, explorer, and philanthropist. As the college grew and prospered, the surrounding area was developed as a residential community for persons connected with the college. Price and his former classmate William Henry Goler, who was a teacher at Livingstone, were largely responsible for this development, forming a partnership to buy the land, lay out streets, and build homes. Some of the buildings in the surrounding neighborhood, such as Price's home, are included in the historic district.

William Henry Goler became president of the college after Price's death in 1893. Under Goler's leadership, the school expanded academically as well as physically. The Industrial Department was expanded significantly, reflecting both a current trend in industrial and self-help education in black education and Goler's own experience as a contractor. Theological courses were strengthened to meet the church's requirements as well. A military department and music course were added to the original theological, classical, normal, and preparatory courses.

Goler retired in 1917 and was succeeded by Daniel Cato Suggs. It was Suggs's successor, however, that turned Livingstone into a modern institution of higher education. William Johnson Trent, Sr., installed in 1925, removed the departmental buildings in place and replaced them with a College of Liberal Arts and Sciences with up-to-date standards for the bachelor of arts and bachelor of science degrees. Under Trent's leadership, the college received an "A" rating from the Southern Association of Schools and Colleges.

Today Livingstone College is housed in 22 buildings on 272 acres of land; it continues to be affiliated with the AME Zion Church. Livingstone takes special pride in its fully black heritage, a symbol of self-help among African Americans in a time when most black colleges were being developed by white missionary societies. [CAB 5/27/82, 82003509]

Mount Zion Baptist Church
413 North Church Street
Salisbury

Mount Zion Baptist Church was founded in 1867 by Harry Cowan, former slave of Thomas L. Cowan, one of Rowan County's largest landowners. Thomas Cowan had encouraged Harry Cowan to take up the ministry to the extent possible as a slave and granted him preaching, baptizing, and marrying privileges in his extensive plantations. Harry Cowan served as preacher for Mount Zion from 1867 until 1891. The congregation probably did not have a church at this time and likely worshiped under brush shelters. In 1893 the congregation purchased the lot on which the church now stands.

The present church was constructed in 1907, replacing a smaller building that stood on the lot. By 1920 the church had been expanded to house a school. The Sunshine School, which served grades one through six, was run by the wife of then pastor Fisher Robert Mason. The school offered both religious and academic training at a time when educational opportunities for black students in North Carolina were extremely limited. Although the school was closed in 1928 because of Mrs. Mason's declining health, the church has maintained a position of social and religious significance in the black community of Salisbury. [A 12/30/85, 85003188]

STANLY COUNTY

West Badin Historic District
Roughly bounded by Sims, Lincoln, Marion, and Lee streets
Badin

The West Badin community is a residential area that was developed for black workers and their families by the Alcoa Aluminum Corporation. The company was the principal business in the town of Badin and was responsible for much of the development in the town. Alcoa made a concerted effort to attract black workers to Badin, stating in a 1920 brochure, "Badin offers greater economic, educational, moral, and social development to the colored laborer than any other community in the United States." While this claim was no doubt exaggerated, the company did build a new $10,000 church and a school. The company also provided services of a black physician, nurse, and welfare worker for its employees and generally offered services comparable to those found in the white community. Although strict racial segregation was maintained and black workers generally held lower-skilled jobs in the company, living conditions, wages, and cultural opportunities for black workers were considerably greater in Badin than at other company towns in the South. [Badin MRA, A 10/12/83, 83004002]

WAKE COUNTY

East Raleigh–South Park Historic District
Roughly bounded by Bragg, East, East Lenoir, Alston, Camden, Hargett, Swain, Davis, and South Blount streets
Raleigh

The East Raleigh–South Park Historic District is the largest historic black neighborhood in Raleigh and one of the largest and most historic, relatively intact urban black residential and cultural concentrations in North Carolina. African Americans first began arriving in Raleigh in large numbers during Reconstruction. They were drawn by the availability of cheap land and the emergence of three black institutions—Second Baptist Church (now Tupper Memorial); Shaw Collegiate Institute (later Shaw University); and the School for the Negro Deaf, Dumb, and Blind.

The Second Baptist Church was organized in 1866 by the Reverend Henry M. Tupper, a philanthropist from Massachusetts. With support from the American Baptist Home Mission Society, Tupper established a school known as the Raleigh Institute. By 1870 he had acquired land a few blocks south and relocated the school there, renaming it the Shaw Collegiate Institute in honor of its largest benefactor, Elisha Shaw (see also Estey Hall). Second Baptist Church became one of the leading institutions in post-war Raleigh's emerging black community, and Shaw University became a magnet attracting African Americans to live in its environs.

Shaw's presence was the impetus for much development in the area around the institution. As a center of black culture, it attracted new black residents to the community. Additionally, its medical school, law department, and pharmacy school produced a significant number of the small class of professionals in the black community.

The third institution that drew African Americans to Raleigh was the Colored Department of the School for the Deaf, Dumb, and Blind. Built in 1874 and located near Shaw, it was the first public school of its kind for black children in the United States. The school remained in Raleigh until 1931.

With the growth and prosperity of the community's professional elite, Raleigh's housing stock began to reflect the area's diversification. Beginning in the 1890s the side-gable cottage with decorative front gable and modest Victorian porch, as well as hip-roofed cottages, eclectic Victorian dwellings, bungalows, and period revival houses began to appear. These housing types reflect the large middle class of professionals, merchants, and artisans that prospered in this area well into the 20th century. These homes stand amid scores of traditional basic house types such as shotgun houses and plain side-gable dwellings that were constructed to house the area's large population of laborers.

The East Raleigh–South Park Historic District is an important tangible representation of Raleigh's black heritage. The district represents the economic strata and tastes that shaped the built environment of Raleigh's largest black community during its emergence and coalescence from the end of the Civil War to the eve of World War II. [CA 10/11/90, 90001527]

Estey Hall
East South Street on Shaw University campus
Raleigh

Shaw University was chartered by the North Carolina General Assembly in 1875 as a school for former slaves and their children. The school had been orga-nized nearly a decade before when Henry Martin Tupper began teaching a small group of black students in a hotel room in Raleigh. When the class had grown to 75 students, the Freedmen's Bureau provided a building for classes. By 1870 property had been purchased for the construction of a new school using money donated by Elijah J. Shaw, for whom the school was later named. By 1873 Shaw University had established the Estey Seminary for women, one of the few educational institutions for black women organized at this time. Estey Hall, an impressive Victorian institutional building constructed in 1873, is Shaw University's oldest surviving building and is of special significance to the history of education for black women in North Carolina (see also East Raleigh-South Park Historic District). [CA 5/25/73, 73001373]

Masonic Temple Building
427 South Blount Street
Raleigh

The Masonic Temple Building, a simple three-story brick block with Italianate features, was built in 1907 to house the Widow's Son Lodge No. 4 and the Excelsior Lodge No. 21 of the Free Masons. The Widow's Son Lodge was organized in 1867 by Bishop James W. Hood, a prominent black missionary and social leader. The Excelsior Lodge, formed in 1879, initially shared quarters with the Widow's Son Lodge on the second floor of the Raleigh Savings Bank Building. When the building was demolished, the lodge members erected the present building. By locating the building in southeast Raleigh, the Masons helped to draw other black institutions, businesses, and residents to the neighborhood to create a close-knit, vital black society. Although it no longer houses either lodge, the Masonic Temple Building represents the social and charitable building established within the black community in the years following the Civil War. [AB 5/3/84, 84002533]

Moore Square Historic District
Roughly bounded by Person, Morgan, Wilmington, and Davie streets
Raleigh

The East Hargett Street area of the Moore Square Historic District was a prosperous black business district in Raleigh in the 1920s and 1930s. Black residents of Raleigh were pushed into the area from the South Wilmington Street vicinity by restrictive covenants forbidding black occupation of residences and commercial buildings. By the late 1920s, the East Hargett Street area had become the hub of the black community. The district contained many successful black-owned and -operated businesses including a fine hotel, a branch of the Farmers and Mechanics Bank, real estate and insurance companies, a foundry, and retail stores. The hotel, the Arcade, was a fashionable, three-story black hotel built by black contractor C. E. Lightner, and it provided a nucleus for the development of the business district. A second important building in the neighborhood was the Richard B. Harrison Public Library, opened in 1935. The library provided a cultural forum that promoted black music and literature. The Moore Square Historic District remains significant today as the locus of nearly all black businesses and professional services in Raleigh during the first half of the 20th century. [CA 8/3/83, 83001924]

Peace College Main Building
Intersection of Peace and Wilmington streets
Raleigh

The Peace Institute of Raleigh was incorporated in 1858 as a Presbyterian school for young women. The handsome Greek Revival style building was only partially complete at the outbreak of the Civil War. In 1862 it was taken over by the Confederate army to be used as a hospital. Raleigh was surrendered to the Union in 1865, and the Freedmen's Bureau used the building to house the headquarters for its central administrative district. The Freedmen's Bureau, established during Reconstruction by the federal government, aided newly freed blacks in the transition from slavery to freedom, offering them employment, education, and housing opportunities and establishing social and medical services. It was met with strong resistance by southern whites but nonetheless managed to operate effectively until 1869, acting as an important force for the welfare of African Americans during these years.

In 1872 the building was finally given over for its intended use as a female seminary. A well-preserved vestige of the character of antebellum Raleigh, the building now stands as the focal point of the Peace College campus. [C 6/19/73, 73001377]

St. Paul AME Church
402 West Edenton Street
Raleigh

The congregation of St. Paul African Methodist Episcopal Church was formed in 1865 by the slave membership of the Edenton Street Methodist Church. The church was housed in a frame building that originally housed the Edenton congregation and that was moved to the present site. During Reconstruction the ministers of St. Paul took a leading role in the organization of black political activity. African Americans in North Carolina held their first lawful assembly at St. Paul in 1865. Delegates from a 200-mile radius gathered at the church and drafted a series of proposals calling for the repeal of racial laws that limited opportunities for advancement in the black community. Throughout the postbellum years, many of North Carolina's most prominent black spokespeople were drawn from the ranks of St. Paul pastorate and congregation.

Construction on the present red brick and frame American Gothic Revival style building began in 1884 but proceeded slowly because of a shortage of funds. The church was nearly complete in 1909 when a fire gutted the building, leaving only the brick walls standing. The community responded with great sympathy. Donations and bank loans coupled with insurance money enabled the congregation to rebuild the building. The church, completed in 1910, still houses the St. Paul's congregation. [CAB 11/5/87, 80004607]

WARREN COUNTY

Sledge-Hayley House
Intersection of Franklin and Hayley streets
Warrenton

The Sledge-Hayley House was built sometime between 1852 and 1855 in the Greek Revival style that was popular in Warrenton's antebellum boom period. The house was built for George R. and Nancy Fleming Sledge. At Mrs. Sledge's death, the property was purchased by A. D. Harris, who in turn sold it to Nancy S. Hayley, wife of Paul F. Hayley, one of Warrenton's leading black citizens.

Paul F. Hayley was born a slave in 1851 and came to Warren County as a schoolteacher for black children. In 1881 he served in the General Assembly of Northampton County. A year later he took a position with the United States Railway Mail service, where he was eventually promoted to chief clerk. He retired after 38 years of civil service and for 28 years of his retirement was a deacon of the Warrenton Baptist Church. At Paul F. Hayley's death in 1948, the house passed to his daughter Maymie, and her husband, Dr. Thomas W. Haywood. Haywood began his medical practice in Warrenton in 1918 and served as the town's only black physician for more than half a century. [CB 4/17/80, 80002904]

Mansfield Thornton House
Southeast of Warrenton
Warrenton

Born in 1850, Mansfield F. Thornton was one of 153 slaves owned by William Eaton of Warrenton. One of Eaton's daughters taught Thornton to read even though education of slaves was prohibited by law. When the Emancipation Proclamation was issued, Thornton, then 15 years old, began to attend a black public school. After moving to Raleigh, where he worked as a janitor in an Internal Revenue Service clerk's office for three years, he returned to Warrenton, where he served as a clerk of the First Baptist Church for several years. In 1879 he was elected register of deeds, an office he held until 1900. Thornton was presented with a testimonial by the townspeople at his retirement. The testimonial praised him for his years of dedicated service and was signed by many prominent local officials and respected members of the community. Thornton constructed this house in 1885 for himself and his wife, and it is a reminder of his historic role in the community. [B 12/2/77, 77001014]

WILSON COUNTY

East Wilson Historic District
Roughly bounded by East Gold and Academy streets, Ward Boulevard, Woodard Avenue, Elvie Street, and Railroad and Pender streets
Wilson

The East Wilson Historic District is a distinctive early 20th-century African American community located in Wilson, a major manufacturing and commercial center in eastern North Carolina. The initial impetus for growth in Wilson was the arrival of the Wilmington and Weldon Railroad in 1840. Wilson's population at this time included a small number of free blacks and black slaves. After the Civil War large numbers of black migrants came north to Wilson, settling in the area east of the railroad tracks. Between 1880 and 1900 tobacco became a major industry in Wilson. Black residential development occurred near tobacco industry warehouses, where many of Wilson's working-class black residents were employed.

As Wilson's black population grew, black businesses sprang up to serve the community, prompted to a great extent by segregation, which made it necessary for African Americans to create their own institutions. Out of this business class grew a small class of professionals in occupations such as preaching, teaching, and the mortuary business. The diversity of housing styles in the community reflects the socioeconomic diversity of the community. The district includes housing types ranging from the vernacular to popular national styles. The domestic architecture was constructed from the community's beginnings around 1890 to the start of World War II.

Although many individuals made contributions to the community, the most prominent of East Wilson's early residents was Dr. Frank A. Hargrave, who established Wilson's first hospital for blacks in 1905. Samuel H. Vick also made significant contributions as a developer, educator, postmaster, and religious leader. Vick was the largest landholder in East Wilson. Of the many black builders who constructed homes in Wilson, the most skilled was stonemason Nestus Freeman. Freeman built numerous modest bungalows as well as a group of five unusual stone houses and sheds between the 1920s and 1940s. His own home is a stone-faced bungalow, and his yard is adorned with an assortment of whimsical concrete creatures.

The East Wilson Historic District is a tangible representation of Wilson's black heritage. It is one of North Carolina's most important intact black neighborhoods and provides perspective and understanding concerning the African American cultural landscape. [CAB 4/11/88, 88000371]

OHIO

ATHENS COUNTY

Mount Zion Baptist Church
Intersection of Congress and Carpenter
streets
Athens

Mount Zion Baptist Church is the
only major building in Athens associated
with the black community. Organized in
1872, the Mount Zion congregation
began with only a few members. Its first
church was a frame building built in
1876. In 1905 the cornerstone of the current building was laid at the intersection
of Congress and Carpenter streets, a
prominent location in Athens. Much of
the construction work was done by the
church members, and the building was
dedicated in 1909. The quality of the
church's architecture reflects the great
effort expended by members of the black
community to build a fine church of their
own and the important role religion
played in their lives. The congregation at
one point numbered 250, but around
World War II the black population in
Athens began to decline. It has continued
to fall, and today many of the church's
members are Ohio University students.
[A 10/3/80, 80002938]

CUYAHOGA COUNTY

Jacob Goldsmith House
2200 East 40th Street
Cleveland

This house built by Jacob Goldsmith
was home to the Cleveland branch of the
Universal Negro Improvement
Association (UNIA), which acquired it in
1923. The UNIA was founded in 1914
by Marcus Garvey (1887–1940), a black
nationalist and reformer from Jamaica.
Garvey created the first mass movement
among blacks in the United States and
abroad, and by 1920 he had thousands of
followers and UNIA branches around the
world. The association promoted unity
among all blacks through education, racial
pride, worldwide black commercial and
business activity, and the development of
states and communities in Africa. The
Jacob Goldsmith House is one of the few
remaining buildings associated with the
efforts of the UNIA in Ohio. The house
is still owned by the UNIA. [CA 3/8/78,
78002039]

FRANKLIN COUNTY

Lincoln Theatre
77 East Long Street
Columbus

Jacob Goldsmith House. Photo courtesy of National Register of Historic Places.

The Lincoln Theatre is one of the best-preserved remaining vestiges of early 20th-century African American history in Columbus. The building was developed by a black fraternal organization, constructed by a black construction company, and managed by a local black entrepreneur. It was a center for stage and screen entertainment for Columbus's black population.

African Americans established communities in Columbus early in the city's history. As early as 1810, there were 43 "free colored" citizens among Franklin County's population of 3,400. The black population increased significantly in the mid-19th century and again in the early 20th century. A thriving downtown commercial district soon developed on the east side of town, where most of Columbus's black residents lived.

The Lincoln Theater was not the first movie house built in the area; three others stood on the east side. The sale of one of these to a chain that refused admission to African Americans angered local black entrepreneur Al Jackson, who determined to build a first-class movie theater especially for Columbus's African Americans. Jackson entered into a partnership with a local black fraternal organization to develop the theater. Originally known as the Ogden Theater, the building opened with great fanfare on Thanksgiving Day in 1929. Despite its somewhat plain exterior, the theater had a lavishly decorated interior designed in the ornate Egyptian Revival style.

Jackson went on to develop other buildings for the black community in

Columbus. Ironically, after his death the Ogden Theater was sold to the very chain whose admissions policy he condemned. Despite the change in ownership, the theater continued to cater to a black clientele. In 1939 the theater's name was changed to the Lincoln. Among the bands that played in the Lincoln Ballroom was the Billy Eckstein Band, which launched the careers of a number of legendary jazz stars such as Dizzy Gillespie, Charlie Parker, and Sarah Vaughn.

Segregation in Columbus in the 1930s and 1940s only strengthened black commercial and cultural development in the neighborhood. Because it contained several black hotels, the area became a refuge for black travelers passing through Columbus, boosting the local entertainment and hospitality industries. The character of the east side changed dramatically in the 1960s, however, as the breakdown of segregation gave neighborhood residents the option to do business elsewhere and a major interstate highway project cut off the downtown from the residential areas. The neighborhood began to deteriorate, and many of the clubs and businesses closed. Today the Lincoln Theater remains one of the few surviving commercial building from the golden period of commercial and cultural development in the area. The building is presently owned by a nonprofit organization that is planning its rehabilitation. [A 10/8/92, 92001355]

GREENE COUNTY

South School
909 South High Street
Yellow Springs

Built in 1856, South School has played an important role in the black community of Yellow Springs. From 1874 until 1887, when Ohio abolished segregated schools, it was the only school for black students. In comparison with other villages in the county, Yellow Springs had a substantial black population in this period: 233 African Americans out of a total population of 1,435 were reported in 1871. The black community built a new wing for the South School when it became apparent that the original one-room schoolhouse would not accommodate the increasing number of black students. In 1881, 80 students were enrolled, and before it closed in 1887 it had a principal and three teachers. Apart from the church at the corner of Whiteman Street and Xenia Avenue, the South School is the only remaining building from this important period in the history of the black community. [CA 10/4/89, 89001459]

Col. Charles Young House
Columbus Pike between Clifton and
Stevenson roads
Wilberforce

This house is associated with Colonel Charles Young (1864–1922), the third black graduate from the United States Military Academy at West Point and the highest-ranking black officer in World War I. Upon graduation from West Point, Young began his career in the Tenth Cavalry, and on October 31, 1889, he was permanently reassigned to the Ninth Cavalry. In 1894 he was assigned as professor of science and military tactics at Wilberforce University in Ohio, where he met with such men as Paul Laurence Dunbar and W. E. B. Du Bois. During the Spanish-American War, Young commanded the Ninth Ohio Volunteer Infantry (a black regiment) before rejoining the Ninth Cavalry. Following distinguished service in the Philippines, Young commanded Troop "1" at San Francisco in 1902 and then was appointed acting superintendent of the Sequoia and

General Grant National Parks, California. Following his service in the West, Young was appointed U.S. military attaché to Haiti by President Theodore Roosevelt. He later served as military attaché and adviser to the Liberian Frontier Force and as commander of the Second Squadron of the Tenth Cavalry, a unit that served under Brigadier General John J. Pershing's 1916 expedition in northern Mexico. Expecting active service with the outbreak of World War I, Colonel Young was instead found medically unfit by army doctors and forced to retire. Rather than accept this verdict, Colonel Young rode 500 miles from his home to Washington, D.C., to personally appeal for a reversal of the army's decision. On November 6, 1918, the Army recalled Young. He was stationed with the Ohio National Guard at Camp Grant, Illinois.

In 1919 he sailed to Monrovia at the request of the State Department, as an adviser to the Liberian government. He died in Liberia in 1922 while on an inspection visit. The Col. Charles Young House was designated a National Historic Landmark on May 30, 1974. [B 5/30/74 NHL, 74001506]

LAWRENCE COUNTY

William C. Johnston House and General Store
Intersection of Washington and Davidson streets
Burlington

One of the few remaining early buildings in Lawrence County, the William C. Johnston Store is an excellent example of combined commercial and residential architecture. Constructed around 1820, the building housed the first licensed

William C. Johnston House and General Store. Photo courtesy of National Register of Historic Places.

store in the county, which was operated by William and Benjamin Johnston until William's death in 1833. Benjamin, who inherited the business, served as postmaster in 1840. The store was used as a post office for some time after Benjamin relinquished the position. The most colorful history surrounding the store, however, is its possible connection with the Underground Railroad. Burlington was a principal crossing of the Underground Railroad, for the route through the town took travelers to Poke Patch, a black settlement beyond Burlington. Although no conclusive evidence has been found, the Johnston store is believed by residents throughout Lawrence County to have been a stop for those fleeing slavery. Local tradition holds that tunnels ran from the store to the riverbank; however, none have been discovered thus far. [A 9/7/76, 76001463]

Macedonia Church
North of Burlington
Burlington

The Macedonia Church is an important religious and cultural institution in Burlington's black community. Burlington was an abolitionist sanctuary for runaway and freed slaves beginning in 1799. In the autumn of 1849, a group of 32 freed slaves arrived in Burlington. They had been part of a group of 37 slaves emancipated by Virginia planter James Twyman in his will. Twyman had also bequeathed $10,000 for the purchase of land and homes for the 37 former slaves in one of the free states. Thirty-two of the former slaves settled in Burlington on farmland deeded to them October 31, 1849. They joined the existing black church, which had been organized in 1820, and affiliated with the Providence Association of Churches organized in 1830 by Burlington's black religious leaders George Bryant, Charles Roberts, and Henry King. In 1849 the congregation built Macedonia Church with lumber supplied by Eli Thayer, a Massachusetts abolitionist congressman. It became the "mother church" of many other Baptist churches and remains as an important reminder of the spiritual idealism and industry of Burlington's freed slaves. [CA 2/7/78, 78002096]

LORAIN COUNTY

John Mercer Langston House
207 East College Street
Oberlin

Built in 1855, this house was the home of John Mercer Langston (1829–97) from 1856 to 1867. In 1844 Langston entered the preparatory department at Oberlin College. He graduated in 1849 and continued at Oberlin, taking the theological course. His real interest, however, was law, and he read the law privately with Philemon Bliss of Elyria, Ohio. In September 1854 he passed the bar and was admitted to practice. Langston built a successful law practice in Brownhelm, Ohio. In 1855 he was elected township clerk of Brownhelm on the Liberty ticket, thereby becoming the first known African American elected to an office in the United States.

In 1869 Langston left Oberlin for Washington, D.C., where he took the position of inspector general of education and abandoned lands for the Freedmen's Bureau. He left this position to organize the Law Department of Howard University, which was established in January 1869 with Langston as its dean. In 1873 Langston was appointed vice president of Howard University and assumed the duties of acting president until 1875, when he left Howard. In 1885 he served as the first president of the newly organized Virginia Normal and Collegiate Institute in Petersburg, Virginia, and in 1888 he became the first black U.S. congressman elected from the state of Virginia. Langston was also a recruiter for the 54th and 55th Massachusetts Regiment during the Civil War; legal counsel to the District of Columbia Board of Health; and resident minister to Haiti and chargé d'affaires to Santo Domingo. The John Mercer Langston House was designated a National Historic Landmark on May 15, 1975. [B 5/15/75 NHL, 75001464]

MIAMI COUNTY

African Jackson Cemetery
North of Piqua on Zimmerlin Road
Piqua

The African Jackson Cemetery is the primary historic resource remaining from the Randolph Slave Settlement, a major freed black community established in the 1840s. John Randolph was a Virginia statesman renowned for his eccentric and idiosyncratic orations in the U.S. Congress in the first decade of the 19th century. He wrote several wills during the 1820s and 1830s that included contrary provisions for the treatment of his slaves upon his death. After prolonged legal proceedings, it was decided that his nearly 600 slaves would be freed and transported to an area in southern Mercer County, Ohio, purchased for their use. The parcel of land was located near the black community of Carthagena, populated by more than 500 freedmen in 1845. About 380 of Randolph's former slaves made the trip to Ohio, only to be thwarted on their first two settlement attempts by white hostility. Eventually the community instead settled in the area that became known as Rossville.

The Jackson Cemetery was formally acquired by the Randolph's former slaves in 1866. A few gravestones, dating from the 1840s to the 1930s, remain. The cemetery retains its 19th-century appearance and has clearly established links to the Randolph slaves.

With the exception of a few obscure articles, the role of these black settlers in the development of antebellum Ohio has gone unnoticed. Some of the descendants of the original Randolph slaves still live in the area and have formed a historical society to promote recognition of their ancestors' role in the community. [A 12/16/82, 82001475]

MONTGOMERY COUNTY

Classic Theater
815 West 5th Street
Dayton

The Classic Theater is a unique building of great importance to the history of black achievement in southwestern Ohio during the age of segregation. The black people of Dayton were limited to inadequate entertainment facilities when full segregation excluded them from downtown theaters in 1921. Social mores prohibited many black people of the prohibition era from visiting the clubs that customarily hosted black entertainers. Therefore, early in 1926 Carl Anderson and Goodrich Giles, recognizing the need for a black entertainment center, planned the Classic Theater. In 1927 the vision and resources of these men gave Dayton its first black-owned and -operated theater, the Classic Theater. The handsomely decorated theater always booked the best movies, but for many the greater attrac-

tion was the classical recital that always preceded the film. Marble steps led to the ballroom, which was noted for its beautiful crystal ball and floating dance floor. The theater hosted the prime social events of the black community. It gave birth to the Mills Brothers' career in 1928 and hosted popular entertainers such as Duke Ellington, Earl Hines, and Ella Fitzgerald. [CA 2/10/75, 75001496]

Dunbar Historic District
North Summit Street
Dayton

The Dunbar Historic District is historically and visually related to Paul Laurence Dunbar (1872–1906), a major black poet. The Paul Laurence Dunbar House (219 North Summit Street) is the historic capstone of the district. Paul Laurence Dunbar was born on Howard Street in Dayton's East Side to Matilda and Josiah Dunbar, both of whom were former slaves. Dunbar's early interest in poetry and his intense desire for education may have stemmed from his mother's stories. In the Dayton of the 1880s few young people continued their education beyond the fifth or sixth grade. Dunbar, however, pursued his education and attended Central High School. He was popular among his classmates despite his mother's misgivings about his being the only black student. His writing ability won him the editorship of the school paper, which led to the publishing of his poetry in the *Journal,* a Dayton newspaper, and in Orville and Wilbur Wright's *West Side News.*

After graduation, Dunbar's job in the shipping department of National Cash Register Company was short-lived because of his poor health, possibly the tuberculosis that later afflicted him. Thereafter, he worked as an elevator operator in the Callahan Building for $4 a week. Dunbar also gave public readings, which were one of the most popular forms of entertainment in the late 19th century. The readings earned him extra income and served to introduce his poetry to the public. Dunbar's first book, *Oak and Ivy,* was published privately with the financial aid of William Blacher. Dr. H. A. Tobey and Charles Thatcher published a second book of Dunbar's poems, *Majors and Minors,* which gained the attention of William Dean Howells, a literary critic for *Harper's Weekly.* Howells's favorable review brought Dunbar national attention.

In 1898 Dunbar married Alice Ruth Moore, a writer and teacher from New Orleans. He relocated to Washington, D.C., and worked at the Library of Congress for almost a year. In the months that followed, Dunbar accepted every speaking engagement offered throughout the East and Midwest, more than 100 in a few weeks. The strain was too great, and Dunbar collapsed with tuberculosis. Compromised by his need to earn a living, he became increasingly frustrated. Upon seeing the stage production of *Malindy,* for which he wrote the lyrics, Dunbar felt that the characters were ridiculous rather than humorous and vowed to do nothing more like it. Dunbar attempted to speak out against discriminatory treatment of African Americans in the poem "The Haunted Oak" and his novel *The Sport of the Gods.* Both were rejected by the public, and his frustration was compounded. The final blow came in 1902 when Dunbar and his wife separated.

Dunbar was lured back to Dayton by the possibility of being close to many of his childhood friends, and the North Summit neighborhood provided the additional stimuli of the nearby seminary and associated educators. Following World War I, southern African Americans were recruited to work in the west side factories, and the west side became the primary black community in the city. Important black institutions, such as the Classic Theater and several Young Men's Christian Associations, were established in the area in response to segregationist Jim Crow laws. The residence of a major black poet like Dunbar was therefore of great importance to the whole community and today is recognized as a source of pride for the neighborhood. [CAB 6/30/80, 80003174]

Women's Christian Association
800 West 5th Street
Dayton

This late 19th-century building is notable for its association with the Women's Christian Association (W.C.A.) in Dayton's black community. Mrs. Ida Price, Mrs. Eugenia Foston, Mrs. H. J. Lawrence, Mrs. Mary Shaw, Mrs. Clara D. Avery, and Mrs. H. Lee organized the W.C.A. in 1889 and incorporated it in March 1909. They purchased this building in May 1909. The W.C.A. provided recreation and reasonably priced rooms for young working women. During World War I Dayton black women used the W.C.A. as the hub of charitable efforts to support the black troops. In 1918 the Dayton Young Women's Christian Association (YWCA) extended its services to the black community. Led by Mrs. Mary Shaw and Mrs. Jessie Hatchcock, the W.C.A. backed the YWCA's efforts and leased its building to the YWCA for a dollar a year. In 1924 the YWCA outgrew the facility and built its own center on Summit Street. For a number of years the building served as a focus for women's social activities in the black community. [A 5/13/76, 76001501]

OKLAHOMA

CARTER COUNTY

Black Theater of Ardmore
536 East Main Street
Ardmore

The Black Theater building is the oldest black theater in Ardmore and one of the oldest still intact in Oklahoma. It is also one of the few remaining commercial buildings in Ardmore that was associated with its black business district. The all-black theater was built in 1922 to serve the entertainment needs of Ardmore's black community of more than 2,000. It was located near other black businesses and the black residential area. During a period of racial separatism, the property provided a valuable service to those excluded from white theaters, and it stands as a significant monument to the once thriving black business district of Ardmore. The building operated as a theater until 1944, when it was purchased by a black church, the Metropolitan African Methodist Episcopal Church, and was converted for use as a house of worship. [A 6/22/84, 84002978]

Douglass High School Auditorium
800 M Street, N.E.
Ardmore

Douglass High School Auditorium is the only educational resource still standing identified with the black Douglass High School in Ardmore. Established in the early 1900s, the school was the first and only black high school in Ardmore. The black youth, however, had no auditorium until 1930, when this building was constructed near the high school. From 1930 to 1969 the Douglass High School Auditorium served as a social, educational, and recreational center for the black community. Hundreds of black youth participated in music programs, dramatic productions, graduation exercises, and athletic contests held in the auditorium. The building was the largest black facility of its type in southern Oklahoma. The only other comparable facility for black high school youth in southern Oklahoma was in the town of McAlester and was constructed in 1934 with Public Works Administration funding. In 1969 Douglass High School was replaced with a new high school complex, which included an auditorium, and the high school system was integrated. [A 7/11/84, 84002981]

Dunbar School
13 6th Street, S.E.
Ardmore

The Dunbar School is the oldest and only remaining educational institution associated with the black community of Ardmore, and it is one of the few black elementary schools left in southern Oklahoma. The school was used continuously to educate young African Americans from 1922 to 1968. Situated in the black residential area of Ardmore, the Dunbar School served as a significant educational and social focal point for the black community. It served as an important agent for solidifying black pride and cohesiveness during an era of segregation. Because of its importance to the history of black education in Ardmore, the school district in the 1950s changed the school's name to the H. F. V. Wilson Center to honor one of Ardmore's outstanding black educators. Wilson had served as principal of Dunbar Elementary and Douglass High School in Ardmore. Since 1968, when the school operations ceased, the building has housed the Ardmore Head Start program. [A 6/22/84, 84002985]

KAY COUNTY

One-hundred-and-one Ranch
12 miles southwest of Ponca City on Oklahoma Route 156
Ponca City

The One-hundred-and-one Ranch, named for its cattle brand "101," was established by Colonel George Washington Miller in 1879. One a leased 100,000-acre tract of land, Miller built the largest diversified farm and cattle ranch in the United States. The One-hundred-and-one Ranch became famous for its farm crops, oil wells, livestock, and manufactured products, as well as its travelling Wild West Show. Miller employed over 200 farmhands, many of whom were black cowboys, to work on his farm and participate in his Wild West Show. Among these were Henry Clay, who taught Will Rogers roping tricks; George Hooker, a trick rider; and Lon Sealey, another expert bulldogger. The most famous of the One-Hundred-and-One ranch hands, however, was the great Bill Pickett (1870–1932).

When Pickett joined the ranch, the One-Hundred-and-One Ranch cowhands were already barred from the annual rodeos in such places as Wichita, Kansas, and Enid, Oklahoma, because they could outride and outrope the other cowboys. By 1904, the year after Miller's death, the ranch cowboys were considered professionals across the country and were thus barred from amateur competition. During the years 1905 to 1910, the ranch and Wild West Show became known from Oklahoma to Canada.

Pickett became one of ranch's star performers and under its auspices attained national and international fame, appearing for a decade all over the United States, Canada, Mexico, Argentina, and England. Pickett was known for his bulldogging technique and his unique method of busting bulls and steers.

The Wild West Show closed down in 1916 as America prepared for war. Pickett returned to the One-Hundred-and-One Ranch, where he worked until the late 1920s, then settled on a ranch he had bought near Chandler, Oklahoma. When the ranch faced serious financial difficulties in 1931, however, Pickett returned to help out. On April 2, 1932, an accident with a stallion cost him his life. With Bill Pickett, the One-hundred-and-one Ranch set the standard for rodeo entertainment across the nation. It was designated a National Historic Landmark on May 15, 1975. [AB 4/11/73 NHL, 73001560]

McINTOSH COUNTY

C. L. Cooper Building
5B and Harrison
Eufaula

The C. L. Cooper Building is the only remaining commercial building associated with the black business district of Eufaula, Oklahoma, and is historically associated with Dr. C. L. Cooper, the first and only black physician in Eufaula from 1908 to the mid-1930s.

Founded in 1902, Eufaula developed a substantial black community from its outset. The area had a large concentration of African Americans who had migrated into the Indian Territories before statehood, as well as a number of free blacks who remained in the area following the Civil War. Before statehood in 1907, approximately 8,000 African Americans moved into Oklahoma and the Indian Territories seeking homesteads.

Shortly after 1907 Dr. C. L. Cooper acquired a lot on Harrison Street, and in 1915 he constructed this two-story brick building. Dr. Cooper's offices were housed on the second floor and a grocery was located on the ground level. He maintained his office in the building until his death in the mid-1930s. The grocery occupied the first floor until the mid-1940s, when the building was converted into the Cooper Eastside Community Center. The building was used as a recreation and social center for the black community from the mid-1940s until 1972. Since then it has been the meeting place for two black organizations, the Anna J. Cooper Chapter of the Federation of Colored Women's Clubs of Oklahoma and the Paradise Lodge #54 of the Prince Hall Masons. [AB 3/22/85, 85000684]

Rock Front
Broadway
Vernon

Built in 1920, the Rock Front building is the only remaining commercial building in the all-black town of Vernon, Oklahoma. It has served the community with a variety of commercial enterprises: it was originally a grocery and dry goods store and later a pool hall and tavern, and it now houses the U.S. Post Office for Vernon.

The town of Vernon was founded in 1895 in Indian Territory as a result of the all-black town movement promoted by E. P. McCabe (1850–1920), former attorney general of Kansas and a black separatist leader. Located about 10 miles southeast of Dustin, an all-white town, Vernon contained several black businesses shortly after statehood in 1907. Vernon served as a rural market center for the surrounding agricultural community, and its population became one of the largest of the 29 all-black towns founded between 1850 and 1907. The Rock Front building stands as a historic monument to the once thriving business district in this historic all-black town. [A 6/22/84, 84003152]

MUSKOGEE COUNTY

First Baptist Church
Intersection of 6th and Denison streets
Muskogee

Built in 1903, the First Baptist Church is the oldest black Protestant church in Muskogee. The First Baptist congregation evolved from a mission established for freed blacks and Native Americans. The congregation purchased land at 6th and Denison streets to construct this building to accommodate increasing membership and to meet the spiritual and social needs of Muskogee's black Baptist population.

Membership peaked in the 1920s at approximately 700 members, one of the largest black congregations in Oklahoma. During the same decade, the church hosted the annual National Baptist Convention, the largest black Baptist organization in the United States. During the Great Depression, the church assumed an active role in providing food for the poor and unemployed by sponsoring a soup kitchen at the church.

Although membership has declined in recent years, the First Baptist Church celebrated its 100th anniversary as a congregation in 1977 and the 80th anniversary of the building in 1983. Throughout its history, the First Baptist Church of Muskogee has been a source of spiritual inspiration and at the heart of social activity for the black community. [Black Protestant Churches of Muskogee TR, A 9/25/84, 84003164]

Manual Training High School for Negroes
704 Altamont Street
Muskogee

Built in 1910, the Manual Training High School for Negroes is the oldest black educational institution in Muskogee and one of the oldest remaining black secondary schools in eastern Oklahoma. In 1910 approximately 31 percent of Muskogee's population was African American. Because of the need for educational facilities for this growing black population and because Oklahoma's state constitution of 1907 mandated separate educational facilities for blacks and whites, a school bond proposal was approved to build an all-black high school. Drawing upon the prevailing philosophy of Booker T. Washington, a black educator who promoted vocational training for African Americans, the new high school was named Manual Training High School for Negroes.

From the outset the school's program not only offered vocational training but also provided a full range of academic subjects, including Latin, mathematics, history, and science. The building housed seventh through 12th grades until 1953, when the ninth through 12th grades were moved to a new location. The seventh and eighth grades, however, remained in the building until 1980,

when the school was closed. [A 6/22/84, 84003168]

Taft City Hall
Intersection of Elm and Seminole streets
Taft

The Taft City Hall is the oldest remaining local government building in any of the 12 all-black towns still in existence in Oklahoma. Constructed in 1910, seven years after the town was founded, the property has served as a meeting place for Taft's city government for more than 80 years. The all-black town of Taft was founded in 1903 in Indian Territory and served as a rural market center for African Americans who migrated from the South as well as those freed blacks who remained in Indian Territory following the Civil War. Taft's population had reached 225 by the time of statehood, and the stability of the community resulted in the formation of a city council. In 1910 the city of Taft built the present building to house local political meetings as well as to serve as a meeting place for other community organizations. Today the Taft City Hall continues to serve the community of Taft as its only local government building. [Historic Government Buildings in Oklahoma's All-Black Towns TR, A 9/28/84, 84003330]

Ward Chapel AME Church
319 North 9th Street
Muskogee

Built in 1904, the Ward Chapel African Methodist Episcopal (AME) Church is the oldest AME church and the second-oldest black Protestant church in Muskogee. The church reflects the early missionary activity among African Americans in Oklahoma by the AME denomination.

The Ward Chapel congregation was organized in 1883. This building was

Ward Chapel AME Church. Photo courtesy of the Oklahoma Historical Society (Bryan Brown).

built to accommodate the growing congregation and to serve the spiritual and social needs of Muskogee's black community, which numbered more than 7,000 at the time of construction.

The Ward Chapel AME Church has played a vital role in the religious and black history of Muskogee. Equally important, it has served as a stabilizing social institution and source of community cohesiveness for black families during the era of racial separatism in Oklahoma. [Black Protestant Churches of Muskogee TR, A 9/25/84, 84003338]

OKFUSKEE COUNTY

Boley Historic District
Roughly bounded by Seward Avenue, Walnut and Cedar streets, and the southern city limits
Boley

Founded in 1903, Boley, an all-black town named for a white official of the Fort Smith and Western Railway who had encouraged its development, began as a camp of black railroad construction workers. Located on fertile farm land that had been allocated to the Creek Freedmen (former slaves adopted into the Creek tribe following the Civil War), the site was a favorable one for starting an all-black community. Thomas M. Haynes was chosen as the town site manager, and the town began building on 160 acres that belonged to Abigail Barnett McCormick, who inherited the land from her father, James Barnett, a Creek Freedman.

T. M. Haynes attracted African Americans to Boley, which was portrayed as a haven from oppression and a place where African Americans could govern themselves. African Americans from Georgia, Texas, Louisiana, Mississippi, Alabama, and Florida began moving to Boley, and on September 22, 1904, the town was formally opened. On May 10, 1905, a petition for incorporation was granted, and immediately thereafter the first election of town officials was held. The election was supported by the town's citizens, many of whom had never been able to participate in a political process before. Booker T. Washington, after a visit to Boley in 1905, declared that it was "the most enterprising, and in many ways the most interesting of the Negro towns in the United States."

The Boley Progress, the town's first newspaper, sustained interest in the city's growth and prosperity. New residents arrived and settled in Boley until the town's population reached 4,000 in 1911. At that time Boley's commercial district included one bank, five grocery stores, five hotels, seven restaurants, four cotton gins, three drugstores, one jewelry store, four department stores, two livery stables, two insurance agencies, an undertaking establishment, one lumberyard, two photographers, and an ice plant.

Among Boley's social institutions and public buildings were numerous churches; schools, including a vocational training school for black boys; and a Masonic Temple to which black Masons in the state made a yearly pilgrimage.

The cotton crop failure in the 1920s and the Great Depression of the 1930s prompted many residents to move away and hindered the migration of new residents. The Boley Historic District was designated a National Historic Landmark on May 15, 1975. [A 5/15/75 NHL, 75001568]

OKLAHOMA COUNTY

Gower Cemetery
Covel Road between Douglas and Post roads
Edmond

The Gower Cemetery is one of the few sites in Oklahoma associated with the African American settlers who moved into the rural area northeast of Edmond and west of Arcadia in north Oklahoma County during around 1889. A church, a school, and farmhouses and buildings, no longer extant, were also built and used by the African American homesteaders.

The Gower Cemetery was established by John and Ophelia Gower in 1889 for the burial of area residents. Over the next 50 years many of the early homesteaders and family members were buried in Gower Cemetery, including six African American males known to have claimed a homestead in Oklahoma County before June 1890.

In the early 1930s Willie T. Gower, the founders' elder son, developed an indigent plot in the cemetery burial ground. The homeless, paupers, and those from the "streets" were buried in common graves in this section of the cemetery.

The gravestones and markers in the Gower Cemetery are excellent examples of those used by the African American community following the land run and through the early 1940s. The stones that remain standing in the Gower Cemetery maintain a high degree of integrity and are an important part of one of the few identified sites associated with the settlement of African Americans in rural Oklahoma. [A 12/27/91, 91001895]

Melvin F. Luster House
300 3rd Street, N.E.
Oklahoma City

The Melvin F. Luster House was built by Sydney Lyons, a highly successful black businessman, and his wife, Mary. Lyons established the East India Toilet Goods Company before coming to Oklahoma in 1889. In 1909 Lyons moved from Guthrie to Oklahoma City and sold his toiletries, primarily a hair grower, from a horse and buggy. He also

Melvin F. Luster House. Photo courtesy of the Harrison-Walnut Neighborhood Association.

owned and operated a grocery store on Northeast 2nd Street, which has been a black shopping area since the opening of Oklahoma Territory. Lyons prospered, ultimately owning much of the northeast area of Oklahoma City. In 1926 he built both the residence and a manufacturing plant on one lot and increased his product line to include face powder, perfume, and bleach. Lyons's products were sold nationally and in many foreign countries. Few African Americans in Oklahoma City were as successful in business as Lyons in the early 20th century. [B 6/7/83, 83002101]

OKMULGEE COUNTY

Eastside Baptist Church
219 North Osage Avenue
Okmulgee

Built in 1921, Eastside Baptist Church houses one of the oldest black congregations in Okmulgee. Founded in 1903 as Zion Bethel Church, the congregation

held its first services in a small frame residence on the present site. Because of membership growth, the frame church became too small, and the present building was constructed. Throughout its history the church has been a community focal point. From 1931 to 1949, baccalaureate and commencement exercises for the all-black Dunbar High School were held at the church. Throughout the church's history membership has fluctuated from 150 to 225 members, making it one of the largest black congregations in eastern Oklahoma. [Black Baptist Churches in Okmulgee TR, A 11/23/84, 84000306]

First Baptist Central Church
521 North Central Avenue
Okmulgee

Built in 1915, the First Baptist Central Church evolved from the oldest black congregation in Okmulgee, the New Hope Baptist group, organized in 1892.

The congregation outgrew its original building, and the present church was completed in 1915 as the first brick church for African Americans in Okmulgee. It is one of the oldest remaining buildings located within the historic black residential area of Okmulgee, which once had the largest black community in Oklahoma outside of Tulsa, Oklahoma City, and Muskogee.

Church membership at First Baptist Central Church has fluctuated between 200 and 250 congregants over the years, making it one of the largest black congregations in eastern Oklahoma. First Baptist Central Church has served the black community of Okmulgee by providing a place of worship and a social outlet for African Americans, particularly when racial separatism prevailed in Oklahoma. [Black Baptist Churches in Okmulgee TR, A 11/23/84, 84000307]

Okmulgee Black Hospital

320 North Wood Drive
Okmulgee

Located in the heart of Okmulgee's black community about two blocks from the black business district, the Okmulgee Black Hospital was constructed in 1922 to serve the medical needs of the more than 3,000 African Americans in Okmulgee. From 1922 to 1956, the Okmulgee Black Hospital served the health care needs of the black community. Since that time the building has housed social and humanitarian institutions, including a nursing facility for African Americans, the Deep Fork Community Action Center, the Okmulgee County Youth Shelter, and the local chapter of the American Red Cross. The Okmulgee Black Hospital is the oldest intact black hospital building in Oklahoma. [A 6/22/84, 84003387]

Okmulgee Downtown Historic District

Roughly bounded by 4th Street, Frisco Avenue, 8th Street, and Okmulgee Avenue
Okmulgee

The Okmulgee Downtown Historic District was the seat of the Creek Indian government from 1878 to 1907, is the center of Okmulgee's commercial activity, and has been the seat of county government from 1907 to the present. The district is also significant in African American history for the role African Americans played in its commercial development. The village that became Okmulgee was established around 1838, when nearly 15,000 Creek Indians were removed from their ancestral lands in Alabama and Georgia according to the Indian Removal Act and relocated to lands west of the Mississippi. After the Civil War the area was officially named Okmulgee, meaning "boiling waters," and was officially designated the Creek national capital.

Approximately 1,000 slaves and an unknown numbers of others of African descent accompanied the Creek Indians when they left Alabama and Georgia for Indian Territory in the mid-1830s. After the Civil War, these former slaves were adopted into the Creek tribe and were known as "Creek Freedmen." In the 1880s and 1890s, the Freedmen were joined by other African Americans migrating from the South. After the tribal court system was abolished in 1898, full-blood Creeks and Creek Freedmen were each given 160 acres of land. While many of the full-bloods chose rural sites, most of the Freedmen elected to stay near Okmulgee and were responsible for some of the early physical development of the city. Although the earliest black commercial buildings are no longer extant, the

Rosenwald Hall. Photo courtesy of the Oklahoma Historical Society (Bryan Brown).

district contains a number of substantial black commercial buildings and the 1928 Masonic Lodge, the only building in Okmulgee to be used as a black lodge. [CA 12/17/92, 92001693]

SEMINOLE COUNTY

J. Coody Johnson Building
124 North Wewoka Street
Wewoka

Built in 1916, the J. Coody Johnson Building is associated with one of the most influential African Americans in the history of Oklahoma. J. Coody Johnson received a law degree from Howard University in the 1880s and established a law practice in Wewoka, Oklahoma. He represented Seminole Indians in several land cases argued before the U.S. Supreme Court. During the period before statehood in 1907, Johnson served as president of the Negro Protection League of Oklahoma, which assumed an active role in civil rights issues. In 1907 he

chaired the Suffrage League Convention held in Muskogee in which African Americans from across the territories met to protest the Jim Crow clauses proposed for the new state constitution.

In 1916 he constructed the Johnson Building, which housed his law office and later the Black Panther Oil Company, the first black-owned petroleum company in Oklahoma. During the same time, Johnson acted as director of the Black State Fair. Also, Johnson sponsored various recreational activities for the black community of Wewoka, including the Black Panther baseball team of the 1920s. Johnson's efforts greatly benefited the black community of Wewoka in the early 20th century. [B 8/5/85, 85001744]

Rosenwald Hall
College Street
Lima

Built in 1921, Rosenwald Hall is the only remaining school in the all-black town of Lima, founded in 1907, and is one of two surviving school buildings in the existing 12 all-black towns in Oklahoma. It was constructed with funds provided by the Julius Rosenwald Foundation, a philanthropic organization that funded educational facilities for African Americans in the South. It is estimated that by 1930 approximately 10 percent of all black children in Oklahoma studied in school buildings constructed with the aid of Rosenwald funds.

Rosenwald served the all-black community of Lima from 1921 to 1966 as the only elementary school. Since 1966 the property has been used as a day care center and is still owned by the Lima School District. Rosenwald Hall stands as an symbol of education for African Americans in the Lima area and continues to play a vital role in the black community. [Educational Resources of All-Black Towns in Oklahoma TR, A 9/28/84, 84003427]

STEPHENS COUNTY

Johnson Hotel and Boarding House
314 West Mulberry
Duncan

The Johnson Hotel and Boarding House is the only remaining commercial building associated with the black community of Duncan, Oklahoma. Fred Johnson, a longtime resident of Duncan's black community, financed and built the only hotel and boardinghouse on "the Hill," as the black section of town was commonly known. Completed in 1924 at the peak of the oil boom, the Johnson Hotel housed African Americans who worked in oil-related industries and the oil fields located in Duncan.

Duncan's black residential section evolved in the early 1900s in the southeast section of town. The discovery of oil fields caused Duncan's black population

to increase significantly to more than 1,000. A separate high school was constructed for African Americans, and lodging facilities for black oil field workers were needed because of racial discrimination in housing,

From 1924 to 1934, the Johnson property served the black community as a hotel and rooming house. During recent years it has been used as a private residence. It stands as a reminder of the period of racial separatism in Oklahoma's history. [A 5/14/86, 86001098]

WAGONER COUNTY

A. J. Mason Building
Lincoln Street
Tullahassee

The A. J. Mason Building is one of the oldest black-owned businesses of masonry construction in any of the 12 existing all-black towns of Oklahoma.

Tullahassee Mission was established in 1850 by the Reverend R. M. Loughridge as an educational institution in the Creek Nation, Indian Territory. Destroyed by fire in 1880, it was rebuilt by the Creek Nation and used to educate their former black slaves. Three African Americans, Henry C. Reed, Snow Sells, and Sugar George, were appointed trustees of the black school. In 1899 the all-black town of Tullahassee was established around the all-black school. Tullahassee served as a rural market center for black farmers residing in the surrounding agricultural community.

The A. J. Mason Building was constructed in 1912, during this period of growth for Tullahassee. The building housed a grocery until the 1950s. Since that time, it has housed a nightclub. As the population of Tullahassee declined to approximately 150, the town's business district declined. Today, the A. J. Mason Building is the only extant historic commercial building in Tullahassee. [A 8/5/85, 85001743]

Miller-Washington School
Market Street
Red Bird

Built in 1920, the Miller-Washington School is the only remaining educational facility associated with the all-black town of Red Bird, founded in 1902. When the school was built Red Bird's population had peaked at approximately 400 and Oklahoma statutes provided for separate high schools for black students. The school served as the town's only high school until the 1950s, when school consolidation forced the transfer of black secondary students to an integrated high school outside Red Bird with a larger enrollment. From the mid-1950s to 1977, the property housed the Red Bird elementary school. In 1977 the elementary school closed due to decreased enrollment. Presently owned by a local nonprofit group, the building is occasionally used for community meetings. [Educational Resources of All-Black Towns in Oklahoma TR, A 9/28/84, 84003448]

Red Bird City Hall
Boston Street
Red Bird

Constructed in 1933, the Red Bird City Hall is the second-oldest local government building located in the 12 historic all-black towns still in existence in Oklahoma. Of the 12 all-black communities that still exist, Red Bird is one of the oldest.

Established in 1902 in Indian Territory, it was one of 27 black communities founded during the Twin Territories Era. By 1907, when Oklahoma entered the Union, Red Bird's population had reached 140 and the town was a rural market center for the black farmers who lived in the rich Arkansas River valley. Red Bird's population peaked during the 1920s at approximately 400. Although the population of the community has fluctuated, Red Bird has managed to retain its own city government, and the focal point for the community has been the historic city hall. The Red Bird City Hall continues to be used not only for local government functions, but also as a meeting place for civic and community groups. [Historic Government Buildings in Oklahoma's All-Black Towns TR, A 9/28/84, 84003450]

PENNSYLVANIA

BERKS COUNTY

Bethel AME Church
119 North 10th Street
Reading

The Bethel African Methodist Episcopal (AME) Church was built in 1837 with funds donated by a small group of people belonging to a church founded by Richard Allen in Philadelphia in 1791. The church was constructed largely through the efforts of Samuel Murray. A free black shoemaker, Murray owned several properties in the area, which he used as collateral to finance the construction of the church. Murray received a license to preach and became the first pastor of the church.

Berks County had a very small black population when the church was built. Most black Berks County residents at this time either were employed in local iron-fabricating establishments or were held as slaves. Thus the construction of a black church using only the resources of the congregation in Reading in 1837 was a significant effort for the AME movement in Pennsylvania.

The church was the anchor of the black community in Reading for many

Mother Bethel AME Church, Philadelphia County. Photo courtesy of the Philadelphia Historical Commission.

years. Church records indicate that the resources of the church were occasionally used to harbor fugitive slaves. Jacob Russ, one of the founders of the church, was himself a runaway slave from Virginia. Today Bethel AME stands as a testament to the efforts of a small black community to build and sustain this important institution despite their limited means. [A 9/7/79, 79002167]

BUCKS COUNTY

Little Jerusalem AME Church
1200 Bridgwater Road
Cornwells Heights

Built in 1830, Little Jerusalem (Bensalem) African Methodist Episcopal (AME) Church is one of the oldest black churches in America and was the only black church in Bensalem Township during the period 1820–1930. The congregation was founded in 1820 by the Reverend James Miller under the supervision of Richard Allen, abolitionist and founder of the Free African Society and the AME Church. Allen also built the pulpit presently located in the sanctuary of the church.

Four black families (the Briggs, Bosleys, Fraziers, and Mounts) were among the original settlers in the Bucks County area and the first members of Little Jerusalem Church. Under the guidance and pastorate of the Reverend John Butler, a Sabbath school was established in 1848 so area African Americans could learn to read and write. In 1896 the original building was remodeled during the pastorate of the Reverend George W. Gibbs. At that time, 50 different pastors were recorded as having served at the church. Surrounding the church is the graveyard containing the tombstones of members of the 19th-century congregation and black Civil War veterans. [A 12/3/80, 80003429]

Slate Hill Cemetery
Intersection of Yardley-Morrisville Road and Mahlon Drive
Lower Makefield Township, Morrisville

The Slate Hill Cemetery was established on June 4, 1690, and is one of the two oldest burial grounds in Bucks County. Virtually all of Bucks County's earliest settlers were Quakers who came to Pennsylvania to escape religious persecution in England. The cemetery was established in the area then known as Lower Makefield by members of the Falls Meeting House, which is located about four miles from the cemetery. While many of the graves are those of early Quaker settlers, the cemetery also includes the graves of free blacks who served in the Volunteer Colored Regiments during the Civil War.

A community of African Americans had existed in the Yardleyville section of Lower Makefield since the early 19th century. Free black communities were rare in this area; most of the African Americans living in Yardleyville were manumitted by Quakers in the area. When the Civil War began, many of the able men of the community volunteered their services to the Union. Six of the volunteers were interred in the Slate Hill Cemetery. These headstones remain in the cemetery and are distinguished by star-shaped markers. [A 4/28/92, 92000397]

White Hall of Bristol College
701–721 Shadyside Avenue
Croyden

Designed by American master architect Alexander Jackson Davis, White Hall was constructed as the principal building of Bristol College, the first college in Bucks County. The building is considered one of Davis's major achievements. Completed in 1835, the building was to be the first of three designed by Davis for the campus. Less than five years after its opening, however, the college closed. The two other building were never constructed.

White Hall had numerous owners and served various functions from its sale in 1837 until the time of the Civil War. In 1865 White Hall was used as a hospital for wounded Union soldiers. The hospital closed on August 1, 1865, and the property became Bridgewater School, a state-supported school for orphans of black soldiers. In 1868 the buildings that housed Bridgewater School, including White Hall, were purchased by the Freedman's Aid Society in response to an act of the Pennsylvania Assembly specifically providing for the care of black soldiers' orphans. Bridgewater was the only publicly funded orphanage in Pennsylvania to accept children of black soldiers. In 1868, 124 students from around the state were enrolled at Bridgewater, a number that rose to 236 by 1876. Students attended the school until they were 16 years old and were then discharged. The school operated until the mid-1880s. The building once housed a public school on a temporary basis but at the time of its listing in the National Register was vacant. [CA 1/12/84, 84003177]

CHESTER COUNTY

Hamorton Historic District
Junction of U.S. Route 1 and SR 52
Kennett Square

Slate Hill Cemetery. Photo courtesy of the Pennsylvania Historical and Museum Commission (John C. Anderson).

A 19th-century crossroads and commercial center, the Hamorton Historic District developed into a "company town" in the early 20th century with the arrival of Pierre S. DuPont, who transformed the area with the construction of roads and employee housing for his nearby Longwood Gardens. The town retains the distinct architecture associated with these two periods of development. The district is additionally significant as a center of abolitionist activity in Chester County in the early to mid-19th century.

During the 19th century, the area in which the district now lies was heavily populated by Quakers, who were known for their strong abolitionist sentiments. The village of Hamorton was founded during the birth of the abolition movement in southeastern Pennsylvania and, given its location near two Quaker meet-ing houses and the homes of several prominent Quaker abolitionists and "conductors" on the Underground Railroad, it became a focal point for antislavery activity.

One of the most prominent Quaker abolitionists in the area was Dr. Bartholomew Fussell. Fussell, a medical doctor by profession, had been a station master on the Underground Railroad in Kennett Square before coming to Hamorton. Upon his arrival in the village, he advertised the opening of a boarding school for girls, "irrespective of color." He also used his house as a meeting place for doctors who later organized the Female Medical College of Pennsylvania. Less than a year after his arrival in Hamorton, he purchased, along with four other trustees, a lot on which he erected Hamorton Hall, a building "dedicated to Free discussion" on the topic of slavery, temperance, capital punishment, and social and political economy. During the 1840s and 1850s, the hall was the site of lectures by such noted abolitionists as William Lloyd Garrison.

Hamorton was also home to a long-running "free store" operated by Sarah Harvey Pearson, who boycotted goods produced by slave labor. Her husband, George Pearson, was also an ardent abolitionists and active in the free soil movement. While several homesteads in Chester County have been conclusively identified as stations on the Underground Railroad, no one town in the county can match Hamorton for its degree of abolition activity and number of remaining associated historic resources. [CA 4/26/90, 90000704]

Oakdale
Hillendale Road
Pennsbury Township, Chadds Ford

Built in 1840, Oakdale farm is associated with Isaac and Dinah Mendenhall, leading abolitionists. In 1853 they were among the abolitionists who established the Society of Progressive Friends at Longwood in response to the abolition cause.

Their farm was the first stop north of the Delaware line on the Underground Railroad, which was used to assist fugitive southern slaves in their escape from slavery. An interesting feature of Oakdale farm is the concealed room in the old carriage house that was used to harbor fugitive slaves. Isaac Mendenhall constructed a square room between the walk-in fireplace and the west wall. The fleeing slaves entered the hideaway through the loft. Oakdale farm remained in Mendenhall family ownership until the mid-1920s. [CA 1/13/72, 72001103]

White Horse Farm
54 South Whitehorse Road
Phoenixville

White Horse Farm was built around 1770, with additions to the building made in 1810 and 1840. In 1915 the house was renovated for use as a country gentleman's estate. This Colonial Revival style design used in the renovation is distinctive to the Schuylkill River valley between Valley Forge and Pottstown during the first decades of the 20th century. In addition to its architectural significance, the property is historically important for its association with prominent Pennsylvania politician and abolitionist Elijah F. Pennypacker (1804–88).

Pennypacker was born at White Horse Farm and lived there his entire adult life. His political career began with his appointment to the Pennsylvania Surveyor General's Office in 1830. He was appointed to the state House of Representatives in 1831 and served until 1836. During his tenure in the state legislature, he played a leading role in the passage of important bills furthering commerce, education, and transportation in both the state and the nation. In 1836 Pennypacker became secretary to the State Board of Canal Commissioners, the most powerful commission in the state at the time, and was later appointed to the board.

In 1839 Pennypacker abruptly ended his successful career in politics to devote his life to the abolitionist cause. He became active in local, county, and state antislavery societies and in 1840 opened his home as a stop on the Underground Railroad. Hundreds of fugitive slaves from three routes on the Underground Railroad were directed to his home. He personally transported slaves to Norristown and points north and east; no fugitives in his care were ever apprehended. Pennypacker also lectured frequently and widely against slavery, often opposing local sentiment, and emerging as one of the leaders of the abolitionist movement in Pennsylvania.

After the end of slavery, Pennypacker rejoined the political arena, taking up the temperance cause and running as the Prohibition party's candidate for state treasurer in 1875. After losing the election, he did not run for public office again. Elijah Pennypacker died in 1888 at the age of 84. White Horse Farm is a reminder of his lifetime commitment to commerce, transportation, education, and humanitarian causes. [CB 7/29/87, 87001206]

DELAWARE COUNTY

Melrose
Hill Drive
Cheyney

Melrose is associated with a locally prominent female doctor, a leading black university, and a nationally prominent black educator and social reformer. In the second half of the 19th century Melrose was the home of Mary H. Cheyney, a pioneering woman doctor in the local area. She is credited with going beyond the treatment of individual ailments to teaching preventive health measures to the black community.

In 1903 Melrose and the farm on which it stood became the home of the Institute for Colored Youth. The Institute, now known as Cheyney State University, already had an extensive history. In 1828 Quaker philanthropist Richard Humphrey bequested funds for a school to educate African Americans. A training farm was established and became the Institute for Colored Youth in 1842, the oldest such school for higher education in the United States.

Melrose was the home and office for the presidents of the university. During the administration of Dr. Leslie Pinckney Hill (1913–51), the institution was transformed from a small local training school to a nationally respected liberal arts college. Hill was a leader in race relations and social reform. He hosted many informal meetings that led to the organization of musical, theatrical, and literary programs in area churches and missionary work in Chester and Philadelphia. [AB 9/4/86, 86001780]

Thompson Cottage
Southeast of Westchester on Thornton Road
Westchester

Thompson Cottage is a simple 18th-century farmhouse built for black tenant farmers. The house was constructed by James Marshall, who owned considerable property in Concord Township. He owned and leased two farm properties, each with a house and outbuildings, and had a large home with outbuildings for himself. The Thompson House is probably one of the smaller tenant farms owned by Marshall.

In 1847 Thompson Cottage, along with two acres, was purchased by Thomas Thompson, a free black man. Thompson and his descendants owned and occupied the house for 124 years. This is the only instance of a black family's owning a tract of land in the township for such a long period of time. Thompson Cottage therefore exemplifies black landownership and tenancy farming. [CA 4/13/77, 77001166]

FRANKLIN COUNTY

John Brown House
225 East King Street
Chambersburg

Abolitionist John Brown occupied an upstairs bedroom in this house from June until October 1859, while he formulated his plan and secured weapons for his ill-fated attack on the federal arsenal at Harpers Ferry, West Virginia, on October 16, 1859. Not until after the news of the rebellion at Harpers Ferry did residents realize that Brown had resided in their midst. Because of his notoriety as an abolitionist and his Kansas escapades, he assumed the name of Dr. Isaac Smith and claimed to be engaged in the development of iron mines. While in Chambersburg, Brown purchased tools from the Lemnos Edge Tool Works and other local businesses and stored them, as well as weapons, at the nearby Oak and Cauffman Warehouse on North Main Street. While he resided here, Brown was visited by several abolitionist leaders, including Frederick Douglass, Shields Green, J. Henry Kagi, and Francis Jackson Meriam (see also John Brown Cabin, Miami County, Kansas; John Brown's Headquarters, Washington County, Maryland; John Brown Farm, Essex County, New York; and Harpers Ferry National Historical Park and Jefferson County Courthouse, Jefferson County, West Virginia). [B 3/5/70, 70000548]

MONTGOMERY COUNTY

Camptown Historic District
Roughly bounded by Penrose Avenue, Graham Lane, Dennis Street, and Cheltenham Avenue
LaMott

The Camptown Historic District, also known as LaMott Historic District, is an unusual example of a racially integrated 19th-century community. It was created as a result of the antislavery teachings and beliefs of noted Quaker abolitionist and suffragette Lucretia Mott and her son-in-law Edward M. Davis, a member of the Society of Friends and a major landholder in Cheltenham Township. Located on a portion of the site of the country's first training camp for the Third Regiment of the U.S. Colored Troops (1863–65), the community of LaMott was developed with the active participation of African Americans.

The community represents the transformation of the social and racial development of residential enclaves in the post-Civil War era. A leading force behind the community's development at the turn of the century was black resident William A. Ritchie. He organized the Fairview Cemetery Company in 1907, serving as its first president. Ten years later Ritchie helped organize the LaMott Building and Loan Association, which helped more than 20 black families purchase homes and assisted in the establishment of four black-owned businesses.

In addition to Ritchie, William Anderson and Aubrey Bowser were locally noted civic leaders. In 1915 Anderson became the first black policeman in Cheltenham. Aubrey Bowser, a descendant of William Bowser, one of LaMott's earliest black landowners, became a judge, achieving national prominence as one of the founding members of the National Association for the Advancement of Colored People. LaMott has created a rich heritage of black leadership and a high standard of living for African Americans that continues today. [A 10/31/85, 85003434]

PHILADELPHIA COUNTY

Frances Ellen Watkins Harper House
1006 Bainbridge Street
Philadelphia

Writer and social activist Frances Ellen Watkins Harper (1825–1911) occupied this house from 1870 until 1911. Harper was born of free blacks in Baltimore, Maryland. She left Baltimore at age 26 and moved to Columbia, Ohio, where she taught domestic science at Union Seminary.

She began her professional career as an abolitionist lecturer in 1854, when she was hired by the Maine Anti-Slavery Society to lecture in New England and lower Canada. During the same year she published her first major book of essays and poetry, *Poems on Miscellaneous Subjects,* to which abolitionist William Lloyd Garrison wrote the introduction.

During the late 1860s she joined the American Equal Suffrage Association, which was committed to the struggle for universal suffrage. She later joined the American Woman Suffrage Association. In 1885 Harper was a director of the Women Congress and an outspoken foe of stimulants and narcotics. To help teach women about the evils of intemperance, she joined the Woman's Christian Temperance Union (WCTU). She also became the Pennsylvania state superintendent for Work among the Colored People. By 1888 she had been appointed the first national superintendent of Work among Colored People of the North.

Her organizational activities did not prevent her from writing about the experiences of African Americans during the late 19th century. Her work includes a book of essays and poems, *Sketches of Southern Life;* a book of verse, *Atlanta Offerings;* and a novel, *Iola Leroy or Shadows Uplifted.* Her last poem was published in 1909.

Frances Ellen Watkins Harper established a national reputation as a black spokeswoman and is remembered as one of the outstanding women of the 19th century for her contributions to American literature and her active struggle to overcome the country's social problems. Her Philadelphia home was designated a National Historic Landmark on December 8, 1976. [B 12/8/76 NHL, 76001663]

Institute for Colored Youth
Intersection of 10th and Bainbridge streets
Philadelphia

The Institute for Colored Youth, now known as the Samuel J. Randall School, was built to house one of the first schools in the country devoted solely to educating black youths. The institute was chartered in the state of Pennsylvania in 1842 and was first located on a site near the present one. In 1866 the institute moved into new facilities including the present building. The school operated here until 1903, when it was moved to Cheney, Delaware. The Philadelphia School Board purchased the building in 1903 and renovated it for use as a public school. [Philadelphia Public Schools TR, CA 12/4/86, 86003324]

Mother Bethel AME Church
419 6th Street
Philadelphia

Mother Bethel African Methodist Episcopal (AME) Church is a memorial to Richard Allen (1760–1831), its founder. Allen is also the founder of the first black organization in America, the Free African Society, and the leader of black protest meetings such as the one held in 1817 to oppose the plans of the American Colonization Society to send free blacks back to Africa.

In 1814, when the British army occupied Washington, D.C., Richard Allen organized 2,500 black men to defend Philadelphia against an invasion. He also organized day and night schools and was co-organizer of the first Masonic Lodge for black men in Pennsylvania.

Allen presided over the first black national convention, which met in 1830 in Philadelphia to consider political matters crucial to African Americans. The convention led to the establishment, in

1831, of the American Society of Free Persons of Color. This organization served an invaluable role in the development of political consciousness and group solidarity among African Americans.

Allen's most impressive achievement, however, was the formation of the African Methodist Episcopal Church, the first black religious denomination. In 1793, with the aid of Dr. Benjamin Rush, Allen purchased a lot at 6th and Lombard streets and built Bethel Church, which in 1794 became the mother church of the AME Church in the United States. The property is thus the oldest real estate continuously owned by African Americans. A basement crypt houses a museum and Richard Allen's tomb. Today the church still serves an active congregation. Mother Bethel AME Church was designated a National Historic Landmark on May 30, 1974. [CAB 3/16/72 NHL, 72001166]

Henry O. Tanner House
2908 West Diamond Street
Philadelphia

This house is associated with Henry Ossawa Tanner (1859–1937), an expatriate painter and the first black artist to win international recognition. He was born on June 21, 1859, in Pittsburgh, Pennsylvania, to Bishop Benjamin Tucker Tanner and Sarah Miller Tanner. In 1866 the Tanners moved to Philadelphia, and by 1872 they had established the Tanner House, where they enjoyed the social status of a black middle-class family.

Tanner developed an interest in painting at an early age. Throughout his teens he sketched, painted, drew, and modeled using landscapes and animals as his subjects. He enrolled at the Pennsylvania Academy of the Fine Arts in 1880 and studied under the noted painter Thomas Eakins. In 1891 he traveled to Europe, and shortly thereafter he made France his home.

Throughout his career, he was internationally known and honored. The National Academy of Design in New York elected him full academician with an associate membership. Tanner's paintings are owned by many prominent museums in the United States, as well as the Luxembourg Gallery in Paris. He is one of the few American artists to receive the coveted Legion of Honor of France. Some of his works include *The Banjo Lesson* (1893), *The Music Lesson* (1894), *The Raising of Lazarus* (1897), *The Two Disciples at the Tomb* (1906), and *The Return from the Crucifixion*. Tanner's notable contribution to American art was unprecedented for a black artist at that time. The Henry O. Tanner House was designated a National Historic Landmark on May 11, 1976. [B 5/11/76 NHL, 76001672]

Union Methodist Episcopal Church
2019 West Diamond Street
Philadelphia

Designed after the style of Henry Hobson Richardson, the Union Methodist Episcopal Church building reflects its congregation's preference for high-style architecture at the time of its construction. Other churches built in the community during the same period for middle-class congregations are similarly styled, suggesting that these congregations found an architectural model that suited their upward mobility. From the time of its construction in 1889 until the early 20th century, the church served a predominantly white middle-class congregation, which was organized in 1801. At that time, changes in the ethnic makeup of the neighborhood led to the sale of the church to the Jones African Methodist Episcopal (AME) congregation, and the church is now known as Jones Tabernacle.

The congregation's founder, Dr. Richard R. Wright was a prominent figure in Philadelphia's black history. Author of an encyclopedia and numerous books and pamphlets, Wright was president of the historically black Wilberforce University from 1932 until 1936. He also served as cofounder and chief financial backer of the Citizens and Southern Banking Company in Philadelphia, instructor in Hebrew and Greek at Payne Theological Seminary, and 57th bishop of the AME Church. [CB 10/15/80, 80003622]

Wesley AME Zion Church
1500 Lombard Street
Philadelphia

Wesley African Methodist Episcopal (AME) Zion is associated with Richard Allen (1760–1831), abolitionist and founder of the Free African Society and the AME Church. With the assistance of Absalom Jones (1746–1818), Allen organized the independent Free African Society, a beneficial and mutual aid society, on April 12, 1787. Shortly thereafter, they encouraged the organization of other Free African Societies in Newport, Boston, and New York.

On July 17, 1794, Allen and Jones established Bethel Church after leaving the white Methodist Episcopal Church. Allen was elected the first bishop of Bethel. In 1820, 30 members walked out of Bethel in dissent and started their own church. This congregation, known as Wesley, joined with the Zion congregation of New York City and four other churches in 1821 to form the AME Zion Church.

In 1885 Wesley AME Zion purchased an existing church at 1500 Lombard, which they used until the construction of the present church in 1925–26. The church was built just before the Great Depression, and as a result the congregation was deeply in debt. Supporting the church's outreach programs for the city's destitute was an additional financial burden. The fact that the congregation survived is a miracle.

By 1950 the church was out of debt, and in 1952 the Reverend Alfred Gilbert Dunston became its pastor. Dunston, one of the top leaders of 400 black Philadelphia pastors, formed the Selective Patronage Program with the aid of his congregation. Through this program of boycotts, selected Philadelphia companies were forced to hire African Americans in nontraditional positions.

In the early 1960s Dunston also helped establish the Opportunities Industrialization Center, an employment training center. Through the years Wesley AME Zion has continued to play an important part in the improvement of social conditions in the black community. [CA 12/1/78, 78002461]

PUERTO RICO

MANATI MUNICIPALITY

Hacienda Azucarera La Esperanza

Northwest of Manati on Puerto Rico
Route 616
Manati

Developed in the 19th century by Don Jose Ramon Fernandez, Marques de La Esperanza (the title he may have purchased), Hacienda La Esperanza became Puerto Rico's most advanced and wealthiest sugar plantation. He purchased the sugar farm and converted it into an industrial complex that produced sugar, molasses, and rum. He also increased the value of his estate by investing heavily in black slaves. It is possible La Esperanza was the only farm in Puerto Rico operated wholly by slaves–other plantations used a combination of slave and free labor. By 1873 the marques was the largest slaveholder in Puerto Rico. By the 1880s, however, the plantation was no longer a success, for the marques was unable to repay loans for the purchase of his sugar mill. After the marques's death in 1886, Hacienda La Esperanza was sold to the highest bidder.

Today Hacienda la Esperanza is an archeological site that demonstrates the life and culture of its aboriginal people and its colonization and settlement by nonindigenous people, Europeans and Africans. [CAB 8/11/76, 76002190]

Hacienda Azucarera la Esperanza. Photo courtesy of the Puerto Rico Conservation Trust (Jack Boucher, Historic American Buildings Survey).

RHODE ISLAND

NEWPORT COUNTY

Battle of Rhode Island Site
Lehigh Hill and both sides of Rhode
Island Route 21 between Medley and
Dexter streets
Portsmouth

The Battle of Rhode Island was the
only engagement of the Revolutionary
War in which African Americans partici-
pated as a distinct racial group. The unit
was the First Rhode Island Regiment, an
all-black unit raised and trained in Rhode
Island in 1778 and the only all-black
American regiment to fight in the
Revolutionary War. With less than three
months' training, the black soldiers joined
Major General John Sullivan's army in
Providence in an effort to capture the
British garrison of 6,000 in Newport.
The Battle of Rhode Island was fought on
August 29, 1778. It ended with General
Sullivan's forces in retreat despite the
heroic actions of 138 black soldiers. The
confrontation did, however, prevent the
British from advancing further into
Newport. Although the first Rhode
Island Regiment performed well, a law
passed in Rhode Island on June 10, 1778,
prohibiting the enlistment of black sol-
diers, remained in effect. The regiment
remained all-black for two years after the
Battle of Rhode Island and was stationed
at various points along the Narragansett
Bay. It was integrated in 1781 and saw
action the following year in the Yorktown
and Oswego campaigns before being disbanded in June 1783. The Battle of
Rhode Island Site was designated a
National Historic Landmark on May 30,
1974. [A 5/30/74 NHL, 74002054]

PROVIDENCE COUNTY

Cato Hill Historic District
Rhode Island Route 44
Woonsocket

Cato Hill Historic District, a mid-
19th-century working-class neighborhood
in Woonsocket, derived its name from
Cato Aldrich, an African American who
bought the property from the Arnold
family, 17th-century founders of the city.
The neighborhood's development paralleled the growth of Woonsocket as Rhode
Island's third-largest industrial center. In
the 1840s Woonsocket was a rapidly
growing community with an economy
based on textile manufacturing, and Cato
Hill became a convenient center city
neighborhood financially accessible to
mill hands and laborers. The second era
of growth for Cato Hill was the period
during and after the Civil War, 1862 to
1875. These two periods were years of
major industrial expansion in Woonsocket
and were accompanied by growth in the
working-class population of the city. New
workers needed new homes, and this was
the impetus for Cato Hill development.
[Woonsocket MRA (AD), CA 8/10/76,
76002255]

Lithograph of the Smithville Seminary. Courtesy of the Rhode Island Historical Society.

Smithville Seminary

Institute Lane

Scituate

Completed in 1840, the Smithville Seminary, now known as the Watchman Industrial School and Camp, has played an important role in black history in Rhode Island in the 20th century. This outstanding Greek Revival style building was designed by prominent regional architect Russell Warren, the leading Greek Revival architect in Rhode Island and Massachusetts in the early 20th century. Smithville Seminary opened during an era of educational reform in the region. The seminary was originally conducted by the Rhode Island Association of Free Will Baptists. Ownership of the building changed several times before the Reverend Willliam S. Holland acquired it in 1920 and turned it into a day camp and trade school for black youth.

Holland, the son of a former Virginia slave, had founded the Watchman Industrial School, located in Providence. The school sponsored baby clinics and a day nursery, community activities usually associated with settlement houses of the era. By 1923 Holland had moved the Watchman's headquarters to the old Seminary building. His educational program was inspired by Booker T. Washington and based on the ideals of the Hampton and Tuskegee Institutes. The program emphasized training black youths in primary vocational skills in addition to academic subjects. Holland often took custody of black youths in trouble with legal authorities as an alternative to the state's reform school or prison.

A series of fires in the 1920s and 1930s reduced the operations of the Watchman School, and the year-round school was closed in 1938, though the summer camp operated under Holland's direction until his death in 1958. The camp was then run by his second wife, Viola Grant Holland, until 1974, when she was forced for financial reasons to close this fixture in the institutional life of Rhode Island's black community. [CA 3/29/78, 78003446]

SOUTH CAROLINA

ABBEVILLE COUNTY

Harbison College President's Home
North of Abbeville on South Carolina Route 20
Abbeville

Founded as the Ferguson Academy in the 1880s, Harbison College was organized by the Reverend and Mrs. Emory W. Williams as a coeducational institution offering a liberal arts education combined with religious, industrial, and agricultural training for black students in South Carolina. The college was moved to its present location in Abbeville in 1898, when Samuel P. Harbison donated money to purchase an 18-acre tract on the outskirts of the city, and the name of the institution was changed to honor its benefactor. Completed in 1907, Harbison Hall was built as the residence of the college president. The two-story brick building is the only remaining building of the Abbeville campus of Harbison College. [A 1/13/83, 83002181]

BAMBERG COUNTY

Voorhees College Historic District
Voorhees College campus
Denmark

The Voorhees College Historic District comprises 13 buildings constructed between 1905 and 1935. The college was founded in 1897 by Elizabeth Evelyn Wright, a graduate of the Tuskegee Institute, who wished to establish a school modeled after her alma mater (see also Tuskegee Institute National Historic Site, Macon County, Alabama). The school was established at its present location in 1901 and was named the Voorhees Industrial School in honor of its benefactor, Ralph Voorhees. Wright initially stressed vocational training, following the ideals of her mentor, Booker T. Washington. However, the school quickly grew and expanded its focus.

A normal and industrial school was established in 1929 as the first step in higher education for teachers. By 1948 the school had become known as Voorhees School and Junior College and was the only high school for black students in Denmark. By 1968 the school had become Voorhees College and offered a fully accredited four-year liberal arts program. Today Voorhees College continues to provide a high-quality education to black students from all over the United States and several foreign countries. [CB 1/21/82, 82003830]

BARNWELL COUNTY

Bethlehem Baptist Church
Intersection of Wall and Gilmore streets
Barnwell

The congregation of Bethlehem Baptist Church was organized by the black members of the Barnwell Baptist Church in 1833. The group was not recognized as a separate unit, however, until

Bethlehem Baptist Church. Photo courtesy of the Lower Savannah Council of Governments.

1868, when the congregation purchased the old 1829 Barnwell Baptist Church, which stood on the present site and had been vacated after the white congregation constructed a new building around 1850. The black congregation worshipped in the building until 1898, when the present church building was built. A vernacular interpretation of the Victorian architecture of the last two decades of the 19th century featuring Queen Anne and Gothic details, the present building was constructed by members of the congregation using materials from the old building.

Promoting the education of African Americans was an early concern of the Bethlehem Baptist Church. According to church tradition, the congregation organized the Bethlehem Association to provide funds for black education. The association helped to found Morris College in Sumter, South Carolina, and to establish a black high school in Barnwell. The church has been in continuous use since its construction and is conscientiously maintained. [CA 7/10/79, 79002374]

BEAUFORT COUNTY

Dr. York Bailey House
U.S. Highway 21, approximately 0.2 mile east of junction with Lands End Road
Frogmore

This intact example of the vernacular American Foursquare house form is significant for its association with Dr. York W. Bailey, a prominent native of St. Helena Island, who was its first black doctor and only resident physician for more than 50 years. Born on the island in 1881, Bailey attended the Penn School and graduated from the Hampton Institute (see also Penn Center Historic

District and Hampton Institute, Hampton Independent City, Virginia). After studying medicine at Howard University, he returned to the island in 1906 and established his practice. During his tenure as the island's only resident doctor he was often paid in livestock or produce, which he sold in Beaufort. Bailey ordered his house by mail-order catalog. It was shipped to Beaufort, and from there he brought it across to the island by boat and assembled it around 1915. He lived in the house until his death in 1971. [Historic Resources of St. Helena Island c. 1740–c. 1935 MPS, CB 10/6/88, 88001726]

Coffin Point Plantation
3 miles east of Frogmore at northeast end of Seaside Road on St. Helena Island
Frogmore

The Coffin Point Plantation was once a prosperous Sea Island cotton plantation belonging to Ebenezer Coffin, a Bostonian who moved to South Carolina around 1801. A plantation journal entry dated October 1801 notes that an agreement was made with carpenters to build "a dwelling house, stable, and Negro Houses" on the site. Union troops occupied Coffin Point and in 1861 reported 260 slaves were found there. It was during this occupation that Coffin Point earned a place of significance in African American history.

The responsibility for collection of property abandoned by fleeing southerners at the time of occupation by Union troops belonged to the Treasury Department. As a result Secretary Salmon P. Chase put forth a plan to educate newly released slaves, who were considered confiscated property or "contraband" of war, in order to prove their effectiveness as free laborers. A precursor of Reconstruction programs, this effort was

known as the Port Royal Experiment. One of the first teachers and labor superintendents brought to St. Helena was Edward S. Philbrick, who soon gained prominence for successfully administering the education program at Coffin Point until 1865. Coffin Point Plantation stands today as a reminder of this chapter in the history of African Americans in the Sea Islands. [CA 8/28/75, 75001687]

Daufuskie Island Historic District
Southwest of Hilton Head
Hilton Head

Daufuskie Island is one of South Carolina's southernmost Sea Islands. Accessible only by boat, it is one of the few islands unconnected to the mainland by either bridge or causeway. Because of its isolated location, Daufuskie has evolved with a minimum of outside influence.

Daufuskie's first heyday lasted from about 1805 until 1842, when expansion of the plantation system spurred its economy. The slave population grew rapidly as cotton production expanded. Ten slave huts remain standing from this period, significant not only as artifacts of the plantation era, but also as examples of tabby construction, now a vanished building method.

During the Civil War, the island was largely unoccupied. As landowners fled, slaves either fled themselves or were taken from the island. Reconstruction saw a tremendous influx of former slaves, who occupied the abandoned slave quarters and worked the land under freedmen's contracts. Many buildings, including several churches and schools, still stand as documentation of the black community that thrived on Daufuskie Island during the postbellum years. The schools were often used for services and "shouts," rhythmic song-dances whose roots extend

One-room schoolhouse in the Daufuskie Island Historic District. Photo courtesy of the South Carolina Department of Archives and History (Rebecca Starr).

back to plantation and African traditions. The Maryfield Cemetery exhibits the holdover of African tradition as well, for decorating graves with household crockery and the decedent's personal possessions is still a common practice. The First Union Sisters and Brothers Oyster Society Hall building, built in the 1890s, indicates the industry that by 1920 was a major source of income for African Americans of Daufuskie Island.

The prosperous years from 1890 to 1930 saw the island's black population swell to about 1,000. It was during this period that the fine examples of folk housing that are included in the historic district were constructed. By the 1940s and 1950s, however, pollution of the Savannah River and competition from mainland farmers forced an exodus from

the island. The outward migration left the population at 59 in 1980. The decline in population, coupled with the difficulty of access, has allowed the unique ambience of Daufuskie Island to remain essentially intact today. [CA 6/2/82, 82003831]

Eddings Point Community Praise House

South Carolina Sec. Road 183, 0.1 mile north of junction with South Carolina Sec. Road 74
Frogmore

Built around 1900, the Eddings Point Community Praise House is one of four known extant praise houses on St. Helena Island (see also Mary Jenkins Community Praise House). Eddings Point Praise House is significant for its central place in the religious and social lives of black islanders. Praise houses, a phenomenon of the Sea Islands, were first established on St. Helena plantations in the antebellum period. Slaves used small frame houses or other buildings in which to meet and worship. After the Civil War the former slaves built praise houses in which they could meet during the week, in between their regular Sunday services at organized churches (see also Moving Star Hall, Charleston County). Community meetings were often held in the praise houses as well. The religious services held during the week often included singing, prayer, and members' testimonies and almost always ended with a "shout," an *a cappella* song style unique to the Sea Islands. The building is also architecturally significant, as it represents the vernacular praise house architectural form that has survived since the antebellum era. [Historic Resources of St. Helena Island c. 1740–c. 1935 MPS, CA 5/19/89, 88001739]

Fish Haul Archaeological Site (38BU805)

Address restricted
Hilton Head Island

The Fish Haul Archaeological Site is the location of one of only two sites in the Sea Islands investigated thus far, associated with free black communities. Of the two, only the Fish Haul site represents a planned community; the other site examines what was essentially a squatters camp. The site and the artifacts associated with Fish Haul contribute to an understanding of the transition of black culture from slavery to freedom.

The site studied at Fish Haul was the community of Mitchellville, created in 1862 as a village for newly freed slaves as part of the Port Royal Experiment. This "experiment" involved parceling off land seized during Union occupation of the Sea Islands and selling the parcels to newly freed slaves, providing them land on which they might subsist as free laborers. The study of Mitchellville links the Port Royal Experiment with actual physical remains of the village.

While there have been abundant archeological studies on sites connected with slavery, before examination of the Fish Haul Site, only one postbellum black community had been studied in its formative stage. Further investigation of these sites may yield valuable information regarding the nature of black culture during slavery and immediately after emancipation, contributing to a better understanding of the nature of adaptive responses of black Americans. [D 6/30/88, 88000976]

Frogmore Plantation Complex

Off South Carolina Sec. Road 77 near junction with South Carolina Sec. Road 35
Frogmore

The Frogmore Plantation Complex was originally owned by Lieutenant Governor William Bull. At Bull's death in 1850, the plantation passed to his son. The house and barn that stand on the property today were built around 1910 by subsequent owners. The plantation changed hands several times before 1868, when it was purchased by Laura Towne and Ellen Murray, teachers and members of the Pennsylvania Freedmen's Relief Association. The two had arrived in St. Helena from Philadelphia to establish a school for freedmen after the Civil War. Although many enterprises of this sort were undertaken by various reformers, Towne and Murray's school, the Penn School was the most acclaimed (see also Penn Center Historic District and The Oaks). The two enlarged the original building and resided in the house until their deaths, Towne in 1901 and Murray in 1908. [Historic Resources of St.

Helena Island c. 1740–c. 1935 MPS, CB 5/26/89, 88001754]

The Green
Intersection of U.S. Highway 21 and
Lands End Road
Frogmore

The Green is an open plot of land, approximately 167 feet by 230 feet, located near the center of St. Helena Island. It is a long-established site of community meetings, celebrations, and other gatherings of the black residents of St. Helena Island. The site initially housed Darrah Hall, an auditorium and community center built around 1885 and owned by the Penn School (see also Penn Center Historic District). The location first became a meeting place in 1893, when homeless refugees of a devastating hurricane gathered at the Green and crowded into the building seeking shelter. A fire built for cooking and warmth inside the hall spread and destroyed the building. Since that time, the Green, still owned by Penn, has continued to serve as a gathering place for the community. Such activities as Emancipation Day, celebrating the adoption of the Emancipation Proclamation of 1863; the annual Farmer's Fair; and community sings were held at the Green. The site also has the potential to offer archeological data from the period before 1893. It is still frequently used by islanders and retains a particularly high degree of historical integrity. [Historic Resources of St. Helena Island c. 1740–c. 1935 MPS, A 10/6/88, 88001759]

Mary Jenkins Community Praise House
South Carolina Sec. Road 74, 2.1 miles north of junction with U.S. Highway 21
Frogmore

Built around 1900, the Mary Jenkins Community Praise House is one of four known extant praise houses on St. Helena Island (see also Eddings Point Community Praise House). Mary Jenkins Praise House is significant for its central place in the religious and social lives of black islanders. Praise houses, a phenomenon of the Sea Islands, were first established on St. Helena plantations in the antebellum period. Slaves used small frame houses or other buildings in which to meet and worship. After the Civil War, the former slaves built praise houses in which they could meet during the week, in between their regular Sunday services at organized churches (see also Moving Star Hall, Charleston County). Community meetings were often held in the praise houses as well. The religious services held during the week often included singing, prayer, and members' testimonies and almost always ended with a "shout," an *a cappella* song style unique to the Sea Islands. Members of the Ebenezer Baptist Church attend services at this praise house today. One of the early fixtures of the building that remains in place is a cow bell, rung for many years to alert members to a service or meeting. [Historic Resources of St. Helena Island c. 1740–c. 1935 MPS, CA 5/19/89, 88001770]

The Oaks
On unpaved road 0.3 mile west of South Carolina Sec. Road 165
Frogmore

The Oaks was built around 1855 by John Jeremiah Theus Pope and his wife, Mary Frances Townshend Pope. The owners fled the island at the time of its occupation by Union troops during the Civil War. Because of its proximity to the island's boat landing, the residence was chosen as a headquarters by Edward L.

Brick Church in the Penn Center Historic District. Photo courtesy of the National Historic Landmarks Program.

Pierce, one of the leaders of the Port Royal Experiment, a program founded by northern missionaries to establish schools in the South for newly freed slaves. The building served in this capacity throughout the war. It was in 1862 in a back room at the Oaks that Ellen Murray opened the school for freedmen that would eventually become the Penn School (see also Penn Center Historic District). Murray and her close friend and assistant, Laura Towne, came not only to teach the freedmen, but to help them adjust to their freedom in all aspects of their lives, a mission carried out through the Penn School. Classes were held at the Oaks for only four months before growing enrollment forced a move to the Brick Church. Murray and Towne, who later

became a director of the school, resided at the Oaks until 1864. [Historic Resources of St. Helena Island c. 1740–c. 1935 MPS, AB 10/6/88, 88001773]

Penn Center Historic District

South of Frogmore on South Carolina Route 37

Frogmore

The Penn School was founded in 1862 and grew out of a movement by a group of northern missionaries and abolitionists who came to the South Carolina Sea Islands after the Union occupation of the area during the Civil War. Classes were initially held in cotton houses, cabins, and deserted plantation houses in various locations around St. Helena Island. Ellen Murray, a worker for the

Pennsylvania Freedmen's Relief Association, arrived on the island in June 1862. Ten days later, assisted by her friend Laura Towne, she opened a school for freedmen in the back room of her house (see also The Oaks).

Enrollment grew rapidly, and the school was moved to the nearby Brick Church, built in 1855 by Baptist planters. In 1864 the Pennsylvania Freedmen's Association sent a prefabricated, ready-to-assemble schoolhouse to the island. It was erected across the street from the Brick Church, and the new institution was named Penn School. Towne lived on the island, supervising the school and providing health services to local residents until her death in 1901. After her death Penn School became Penn Normal, Industrial, and Agricultural School, its curriculum patterned after that of the Hampton Institute (see also Hampton Institute, Hampton Independent City, Virginia).

Penn School provided exceptional education to black students at a time when the public school system for African Americans was sorely inadequate. In addition, Penn dealt with the public health, agricultural, and financial problems of St. Helena's black residents. The school also collected and preserved historical manuscripts, oral history, musical recordings, and island handicrafts, preserving St. Helena's folk culture and unique heritage.

Although the school closed in 1948, the buildings are still used to serve the community. Penn Community Services, Inc., was organized in 1951 as a nonprofit organization dealing with real estate services, business development, child development, and cultural programs. The organization carries on the tradition of political, social, and cultural work for St. Helena's black community. The Penn Center Historic District was designated a National Historic Landmark district on December 2, 1974. [A 9/9/74 NHL, 74001824]

Seaside Plantation
10 miles east of Beaufort on South
Carolina Route 21
Beaufort

Seaside Plantation on St. Helena Island is believed to have been built by members of the Fripp family between 1795 and 1810. Records of the plantation show that in 1850 the plantation produced 22,000 pounds of cotton and claimed 122 slaves. During the occupation of the island by Union troops during the Civil War, Seaside played a significant role in the Port Royal Experiment. Begun by the federal government in March 1862, the Port Royal Experiment was an effort to train and educate newly released slaves to prove their effectiveness as free laborers; it was thus a prototype of programs that would be implemented during Reconstruction. Seaside was one of the plantations that directly participated in the experiment. Richard Soule, general superintendent of the Port Royal Experiment for St. Helena Island, lived at Seaside, as did Charlotte Forten, missionary, teacher, and member of a prominent Philadelphia black abolitionist family (see also Charlotte Forten Grimke House, District of Columbia). [CA 7/16/79, 79002375]

Robert Smalls House
511 Prince Street
Beaufort

Robert Smalls was born a slave in Beaufort, South Carolina, in 1839, and was hired out by his owner in Charleston, where he lived until the outbreak of the Civil War. A skilled sailor and expert coastal pilot, Smalls was employed during the Civil War on the Confederate dispatch boat *Planter*. In May 1862 Smalls and eight other black crew members stole the ship from its dock. With his wife, his two children, and five other passengers, Smalls delivered the ship to the Union blockade. *Planter* was afterward refitted as an armed transport with Smalls as its captain. Smalls led the vessel safely through Confederate fire in 1863. When *Planter* was decommissioned in 1866, Smalls returned to Beaufort and embarked upon a career in politics.

He was elected to the state assembly in 1868 and to the state senate in 1870, where he championed black interests. In 1874 he was elected to the U.S. House of Representatives, where he continued to fight for the protection of rights for African Americans despite the rising tide of white hostility. His clashes with well-known Democrats enhanced his reputation as a tough, unyielding fighter for freedom and drew the grudging admiration of national Republican leaders. The house in Beaufort in which Smalls lived before and after his Civil War service was designated a National Historic Landmark on May 30, 1974. [B 5/30/74 NHL, 74001823]

BERKELEY COUNTY

Cainhoy Historic District
Southeast of Huger
Huger

The Cainhoy Historic District, located on the southeastern pine land section of Berkeley County, is composed of nine major buildings that date from the mid-18th century to the early 20th century. Cainhoy was an early transportation link between Berkeley County and Charleston. The district's relevance to black history derives from an 1876 incident known as the Cainhoy Massacre.

The incident occurred on October 16, 1876, in connection with the heated election of 1876 between Democrat Wade Hampton and Radical Republican David H. Chamberlain. It began with a political meeting of blacks and whites held in a location near Cainhoy. According to a statement by the chairman of the Democratic party in the area, a group of young white men stole guns deposited in a carriage house by black citizens. As the armed whites advanced on the gathering, a group of black men attempted to wrest away the arms, and a fight broke out. Seven men were killed and 16 wounded in the conflict. The incident was unusual among Reconstruction-era racial confrontations in South Carolina because the black group was victorious. [CA 3/11/82, 82003832]

CHARLESTON COUNTY

Central Baptist Church
26 Radcliffe Street
Charleston

Central Baptist Church is thought to be one of the first black churches founded and built solely by African Americans in Charleston. Central Baptist Church was founded in 1891 by black members of the Morris Street Baptist Church. The present building was completed in 1893 and was first used by the congregation in August of that year. During its first 20 years, the church grew and prospered. This prosperity is reflected in the addition of murals depicting the scenes of the life of Christ, painted between 1912 and 1915. These murals, painted by Amohamed Milai, a native of India, are significant works of folk art. After the completion of the paintings, the church continued to grow. The vernacular Carpenter Gothic style church was renovated around 1977. The building was damaged severely by a hurricane in 1989 and was moved across the street from its original location and restored. [CA 8/16/77, 77001217]

Hutchinson House

North side of Point of Pines Road
Edisto Island

The Hutchinson House is the oldest identified intact house on Edisto Island associated with the black community after the Civil War. It was the residence of Henry Hutchinson, a mulatto who, according to local tradition, built and operated the first cotton gin owned by an African American on the island from about 1900 to about 1920. The site of Hutchinson's cotton gin lies about 100 yards west of the house. Hutchinson was born a slave in 1860, the son of James Hutchinson, a mulatto who made notable attempts as both a slave and a freedman to improve conditions for black residents of Edisto Island. Henry Hutchinson is said to have built the one-and-one-half-story frame house at the time of his marriage to Rosa Swinton in 1885 and to have resided there until his death around 1940. [Edisto Island MRA, CA 5/5/87, 86003218]

McLeod Plantation

325 Country Club Drive
Charleston

The McLeod Plantation was constructed in 1858 by Edward McLeod, whose descendants still occupy it and maintain it as a functioning agricultural enterprise. The plantation retains many features associated with antebellum cotton plantations. Among these is the row of five clapboard slave quarters that line the drive to the house. The drive originally ran to a landing on Stono Creek where supplies were unloaded and produce was shipped to market. At the time of the plantation's nomination to the National Register, the small clapboard cabins with corbeled brick gable-end chimneys were maintained in excellent condition and were occupied by the descendants of former slaves. An additional cabin containing two rooms with separate entrances stands on the property as well. A central chimney serves both rooms; one room was used as a kitchen, and the other as a bedroom. [CA 8/13/74, 74001831]

Moving Star Hall

River Road
St. John's Island

The Moving Star Young Association was founded to provide the black community of St. John's Island with a place of worship; a community meeting hall; and social, fraternal, and burial services. Moving Star Hall was built by its membership in 1917. Largely supplanted by churches after emancipation, the praise house represents the survival of a plantation institution into the early 20th century.

The sickness and death benefits offered by the Moving Star Young Association mirrored those offered by mutual aid societies founded by free blacks before the Civil War. These organizations grew in the late 19th and early 20th centuries as African Americans sought to establish institutions that would provide services unavailable to them through the white community. Members served as pallbearers and grave diggers and tended the sick day and night until they got "better or worse."

The membership of the Moving Star Hall Association was interdenominational. Association members were also members in good standing with local black churches and attended regular church services on Sunday. Meetings were held at the hall from one to three times a week and began with prayer and ended with song. These services, in which each member was allowed a turn at preaching or song leading, were an alternative to the more formal liturgy of the churches, as well as an opportunity to exercise leadership.

Music, an integral element in these services, was a temporary release from the harshness of everyday life for slaves. These musical traditions were carried on after the Civil War in praise houses like Moving Star. In the 1960s Moving Star Hall was associated with the rebirth of appreciation of the music of the Sea Islands. A group known as the Moving Hall Singers appeared at local and national folk festivals and recorded three albums of their songs.

At the time of its nomination to the National Register, Moving Star Hall was vacant. Fuller participation in politics and government and assistance to the poor have made many of the hall's former functions unnecessary. Additionally, the loss of the community's young people to the city has greatly reduced its membership. The hall remains standing, however, as a reminder of the important role played by the Moving Star Young Association and other such organizations in the black community. [A 6/17/82, 82003843]

Old Bethel United Methodist Church
222 Calhoun Street
Charleston

Construction on the Old Bethel United Methodist Church was begun in 1797. The church was originally constructed in the meetinghouse style after a design by Francis Asbury and stood at the corner of Pitt and Calhoun streets in Charleston. The church initially served a mixed black and white congregation, which was indicative of the Methodist Church's philosophy of encouraging black membership. A schism developed in 1834, however, and in 1840 the black members seceded to form their own congregation. In 1852 the church was moved to the western portion of the lot on which it stood, to be used by the black congregation. In 1880 the church was given to the black congregation and was moved again, this time to its present location on Calhoun Street. The addition of a gabled portico supported by four fluted Corinthian columns documents changing styles in ecclesiastical architecture. The church presently serves an all-black congregation of about 200 and is an architectural reminder of the significant relationship between African Americans and the Methodist Church in Charleston. [CA 4/21/75, 75001693]

Old Slave Mart
6 Chalmers Street
Charleston

Constructed in 1853 by Thomas Ryan and his partner, the Old Slave Mart was a commercial building used for the auction of slaves and other goods until the Civil War. Located within the Charleston Historic District, the Slave Mart property originally included two additional lots and three additional buildings to the rear, which housed a jail, or "barracoon," to house slaves prior to sale; a kitchen; and a morgue. These building were removed in the 20th century. The building that remains contains Gothic and Romanesque Revival style design features. With its massive octagonal pillars and arched entry, the building is a vital part of the streetscape and contributes to the overall quality of the Charleston Historic District. The building is the only known extant building used as a slave auction gallery in antebellum South Carolina. Today the building houses a museum of black history and a gift shop. [CA 5/2/75, 75001694]

Point of Pines Plantation Slave Cabin
Point of Pines Road
Edisto Island

The one-story, rectangular, weather-board-clad building dates from the first half of the 19th century. The cabin was once a part of a slave street, or row of slave cabins, on a cotton plantation. Most of the other cabins in the row did not survive past the 1930s and 1940s. Slave cabins such as the one on the Point of Pines Plantation were no doubt once numerous on the island, for tax records show that in 1807, the island's population included 2,609 slaves. Nonetheless, the Point of Pines slave cabin is one of the few remaining slave dwellings on the island. [Edisto Island MRA, CA 11/28/86, 86003213]

Slave Street, Smokehouse, and Allée, Boone Hall Plantation
North of Mount Pleasant off U.S. Route 17
Mount Pleasant

The Boone Hall Plantation was developed by the Boone family in many stages beginning in the late 17th century. The slave street at the plantation was probably built in the late 18th or early 19th century and exemplifies the conditions of slavery in South Carolina in the antebellum period. The nine slave houses are identical and arranged in a row, with small parcels of land between houses. Although many of the houses have suffered a great deal of deterioration and decay, they still convey the spartan living conditions of the slaves who once occupied them. Some of the houses, along with a brick smokehouse located on the plantation, show distinctive characteristics of 18th- and early 19th-century brickmasonry in South Carolina. The slave street at Boone Hall Plantation is one of the few surviving slave streets identified in the state. [CA 7/14/83, 83002187]

Stono River Slave Rebellion Site
Off U.S. Route 17 on west bank of Wallace River
Rantowles

The Stono River Slave Rebellion Site marks the starting point of a slave insurrection that took place on September 9 and 10, 1739. The rebellion was led by an Angolan slave named Jemmy who enlisted slaves from among area planters and led an attack on a nearby warehouse. Seizing the weapons stored at the warehouse, the slaves marched toward St. Augustine in the Spanish province of Florida, where they had been promised their freedom. By this time, they had been joined by other slaves, numbering about 80 in all. The group burned plantations and killed all whites they encountered on their way. By the time the militia was summoned and was able to apprehend the group, they had traveled more than 12 miles. During the encounter with the militia, 14 slaves were killed. Within 10 days, about 20 more were killed. The incident exacerbated the fear of rebellion by the slave population among the white population of the province. When the legislative assembly met the same month, it passed the most comprehensive slave codes adopted in the colonies. These codes remained in place virtually intact until after the Civil War. The Stono River Slave Rebellion Site was designated a National Historic Landmark on May 30, 1974. [A 5/30/74 NHL, 74001840]

Denmark Vesey House
56 Bull Street
Charleston

Denmark Vesey (c. 1767–1822) was raised in slavery in the Virgin Islands among newly imported Africans. In 1781 he became one of 390 slaves collected by Captain Joseph Vesey to be sold at Santo Domingo. The officers and crew of the

Outbuilding on Boone Hall Plantation. Photo courtesy of Elias B. Bull.

ship, however, had made a "pet" of Denmark on the trip, saving him from being sold. He was instead kept aboard the ship as Captain Vesey's personal servant. During the 14 years he traveled on the ship, Denmark was exposed to the cruelties of the slave trade and the indignities suffered by the slaves.

As greater restrictions were made on foreign slave trade, Captain Vesey left the trade and settled in Charleston. Denmark remained with him until the turn of the century when, after winning a $1,500 lot-tery, he purchased his freedom. Taking the last name of his former master, Denmark settled into the residence on Bull Street where he opened a carpentry shop. His hard work in his business earned him substantial wealth and great respect in Charleston, especially among Charleston's majority black population. It was from this community that Denmark Vesey carefully chose followers to participate in a black rebellion.

Planning for the rebellion began in December 1821. Denmark Vesey chose leaders for the rebellion and held meetings in his home on Sundays, a day when slaves were allowed to visit each other freely, so as not to arouse suspicion. He set the date for the rebellion for Sunday, July 14, 1822. On May 25, a slave of Colonel John C. Prioleau was informed of the planned insurrection and reported it to his master's wife. The informant was arrested, and two of the organizers were implicated. Although they were released after interrogation, Governor Bennett ordered the militia to be prepared in the event of an uprising. Denmark Vesey changed the date of the strike to June 16, but within 24 hours, 10 leaders of the planned uprising were arrested.

The leaders of the would-be rebellion were placed on trial. For three days, no one could establish Denmark Vesey's role in the plot. Three of his men, however, broke their pledge of secrecy when offered immunity. All three testified against him. Authorities arrested 313 alleged participants and executed 35. Denmark Vesey was sentenced to death 12 days before the coup was to take place. Denmark Vesey's house and place of business on Bull Street stands as a reminder of the man who masterminded a plot with such precision and efficiency that, even though thwarted, it created mass hysteria throughout the Carolinas and the South. The Denmark Vesey House was designated a National Historic Landmark on May 11, 1976. [B 5/11/76 NHL, 76001698]

DARLINGTON COUNTY

Edmund H. Deas House
229 Avenue E
Darlington

Edmund H. Deas moved to Darlington County in the 1870s from Statesburg, South Carolina, and became active in Republican politics. He served as chairman of the Republican Party in 1884 and 1888 and was a South Carolina delegate to the Republican National Conventions of 1888, 1896, 1900, and 1908. A candidate for Congress in 1884 and 1890, Deas served as deputy collector of internal revenue in South Carolina from 1889 to 1894 and from 1897 to 1901.

Deas purchased the one-story frame dwelling at 229 Avenue E from Kitty M. Oakes in 1905. At the time of his death in 1915 at the age of 60, Deas was known to local residents as the "Duke of Darlington" and owned considerable property. His wife, Beulah Anna Deas, lived in the family residence for many years after the death of her husband. [City of Darlington MRA, CB 2/10/88, 88000045]

West Broad Street Historic District
West Broad Street between Dargan and Player streets
Darlington

The West Broad Street Historic District comprises a collection of intact residences constructed between 1890 and 1928. Most of the residences are grand in scale and reflect the prosperity of the individuals who built them. A group of 14 of the houses in the district is of particular significance. The scale, composition, detailing, and design of these buildings reflect a mastery of the builder's trade and are attributed to black master carpenter Lawrence Reese. A native of Bennettsville, South Carolina, Reese moved to Darlington around 1887. He trained his two sons, Harry and Larry Reese, in the carpentry trade and they joined their father in his work. Reese's skill at his craft earned him a position of prominence in the community among black and white residents alike. [City of Darlington MRA, C 2/10/88, 88000063]

DILLON COUNTY

Selkirk Farm

East of Bingham on Old Cashua Ferry
Road
Bingham

Built in 1858, Selkirk Farm was the home of the Reverend James A. Cousar. The original portion of the house was built by Cousar's slave, Case. The son of a Presbyterian minister, Cousar studied at Oglethorpe University and graduated form the Columbia Theological Seminary. Cousar soon became noted for his work with black congregations. Before the Civil War about half of the members of the Harmony Presbytery, for which he served as clerk, were slaves. Cousar became active in the organization of black congregations before emancipation. His policy of helping African Americans build their own churches was controversial, and church property was often destroyed by vigilantes who opposed his practices. Cousar donated land on which to build two black churches, one in nearby Bishopville and one on his own property. After Cousar's death, the farm passed to his descendants. Members of the Cousar family have occupied the house continuously since 1858. [CAB 7/24/74, 74001847]

EDGEFIELD COUNTY

Paris Simkins House

202 Gary Street
Edgefield

Paris Simkins was born a slave in February 1849, the son of Colonel Arthur Augustus Simkins and Charlotte Simkins, one of the colonel's slaves. Paris Simkins was a valet in his father's house and traveled with the Confederate army during the Civil War in that capacity. After the war, Paris Simkins returned to Edgefield and opened a barber shop. Although he received no formal elementary education,

Simkins learned to read and write from members of his family. He purchased some college textbooks and studied them on his own to further educate himself. In 1868 Paris Simkins married Mary Ann Noble and purchased the property on which the Simkins House now stands.

Simkins became active in the black community in Edgefield and in 1872 was elected to the state general assembly, which at that time held a majority of black members. He served as the Edgefield County representative to the assembly until 1876. During his time in Columbia, he attended law school and became one of eight candidates to earn the bachelor of law degree in 1876. Simkins returned to Edgefield at the end of his second term. He was admitted to the South Carolina bar in 1885 and served as law clerk to Governor John C. Sheppard. In addition, Simkins was postmaster general in Edgefield, operated a store, and was an ordained minister. Simkins died in September 1930. His house in Edgefield, which is more substantial than the homes of most black South Carolinians during the period, is a symbol of the aspirations of some freedmen and a physical record of what a few African Americans were able to achieve during Reconstruction. [B 4/5/84, 84002044]

FAIRFIELD COUNTY

Camp Welfare

Off U.S. Route 21
Ridgeway

Camp Welfare is a collection of approximately 100 one-story, frame, weatherboarded cabins, or "tents," located in an isolated portion of northeastern Fairfield County. The tents are centered around a wooden shelter, or "arbor." The grounds also include Zion Church, a small frame building constructed around

1900. Founded shortly after the Civil War, the camp served as the location for the annual camp meeting of Fairfield's large black community. The meeting was held during the last week in August, traditionally the "lay-by" time, the period between final cultivation of cotton and corn crops and harvest time. Several religious services were held in the arbor each day and were the focal point of the meeting. Only slightly secondary to the services was fellowship with friends and family. Many of the families who attended the meetings continued to do so through several generations, passing their tents down through the family. Camp Welfare is significant as an excellent example of a black religious campground and is one of the few historic properties identified in Fairfield County associated with its large black population. [Fairfield County MRA, A 12/6/84, 84000586]

FLORENCE COUNTY

Slave Houses, Gregg Plantation
Francis Marion College campus
Mars Bluff

The two slave houses on what was formerly the Gregg Planation near Florence were built before 1831 and were among seven houses of similar construction placed on opposite sites of a "street" leading to the plantation house. The street pattern for arranging houses was a common one on southern plantations. During Reconstruction many former slave houses continued to be occupied by their residents. Like these Gregg Plantation houses, many cabins were moved from their original locations to form more autonomous communities. The Gregg Plantation slave houses were originally almost duplicate in design, illustrating an early practice of mass production of dwelling units. Many of the cabins were constructed by black craftsmen and artisans, who employed the same craftsmanship that went into the elegant houses of the plantation owners. The high level of craftsmanship of the Gregg Plantation cabins is unusual for slave houses. Constructed of dovetailed, hewn logs, the small houses incorporate many of the architectural elements found in larger southern houses. Both of the houses were occupied continuously from the time of their construction until 1950. [CA 7/22/74, 74001856]

GEORGETOWN COUNTY

Cedar Grove Plantation Chapel
South Carolina Route 255 0.2 mile north of junction with South Carolina Route 46
Pawleys Island

The Cedar Grove Plantation Chapel was built around 1850 and is an intact example of mid-19th-century vernacular architecture. The chapel is associated with All Saints' Episcopal Church, established in 1793, one of the most significant Episcopal churches in the South Carolina low country in the 18th and 19th centuries. The Reverend Alexander Glennie, a native of England and rector of All Saints' from 1830 to 1860, established a ministry to slaves on the rice plantations of Georgetown County. Glennie's work was encouraged and supported by Georgetown County planters, who eventually built 13 slave chapels in which he preached and taught. The Cedar Grove Plantation Chapel is the only known extant slave chapel of these 13. The chapel originally stood on the grounds of the plantation owned by Andrew Hassell but was moved in 1898 and again in 1976. It was moved to its present location on the grounds of All Saints' Church in 1985 and serves as a youth center for the church. [Georgetown County Rice Culture MPS, CA 3/13/91, 91000231]

Keithfield Plantation

Off County Route 52
Georgetown

Keithfield Plantation was named for John Keith, one of its early owners, who served in the South Carolina Senate and as a militia officer in the War of 1812. Keithfield houses an 1830s slave cabin, one of the few extant slave cabins in Georgetown County. Keithfield is also the location of one of the most serious of the postwar uprisings led by freedmen on the Georgetown County rice plantations, which occurred in the spring of 1866. The freedmen who worked at the plantation left the rice fields, refused to work, and threatened the plantation manager with axes, hoes, and sticks, pelting him with bricks and rocks. They finally forced him to jump into the Black River and swim to safety on the other side. In 1885 John P. Hazzard purchased the property and began cultivating rice there. He rented portions of the plantation to black workers, who planted rice and sold it to merchants in Georgetown. This system was in place until about 1920. The plantation remains an exceptionally intact example of historic rice fields in Georgetown County. [Georgetown County Rice Culture c. 1750–1910 MPS, CA 10/3/88, 88000529]

Pee Dee River Rice Planters Historic District

Along the Pee Dee and Waccamaw rivers
Georgetown

The Pee Dee River Rice Planters Historic District includes extant buildings, structures, and rice fields associated with 12 rice plantations along the Pee Dee River and five rice plantations along the Waccamaw River. The rice culture that flourished from around 1750 to around 1910 produced most of the rice grown in South Carolina during that period when the area was the leader in rice production in the United States. The plantations included in the historic district housed a great number of slaves. The planting, cultivation, harvesting, and preparation of rice required an immense labor force. Slaves made up that labor force, and the growth of the rice culture corresponded to a dramatic increase in the numbers of slaves owned by South Carolinians before the American Revolution. Over 85 percent of the population of the Georgetown district was made up of slaves throughout the first half of the 18th century. The emancipation of the slaves after the Civil War created a particularly acute problem for rice planters, as many freedmen were unwilling to remain, even as paid labor, in the location of their enslavement. The loss of this great part of the labor force, combined with other factors, dealt the South Carolina rice culture a blow from which it was never able to recover. [Georgetown County Rice Culture c. 1750–1910 MPS, CAB 10/3/88, 88000532]

Joseph H. Rainey House

909 Prince Street
Georgetown

Joseph Hayne Rainey (1832–87) was born in Georgetown in 1832 to slave parents. Between 1840 and 1850, Rainey managed to purchase his own and his family's freedom and established himself as a barber in Georgetown. During the Civil War, he was drafted by the Confederacy to work in military fortifications in Charleston Harbor, but he succeeded in escaping to Bermuda with his wife, Susan, in 1862. Returning to South Carolina at the end of the war, Rainey became active in local Republican politics. In 1868 he was elected as delegate from Georgetown to the state constitutional convention and was elected to the state senate, where he served as secretary of the finance committee. In 1870 he was elected to Congress to fill the unexpired term of Benjamin F. Whittemore, becoming the first African American to be seated in the U.S. House of Representatives. Despite stiff competition from other candidates in Georgetown's majority Republican district, Rainey was reelected to four consecutive terms before being defeated by Democrat John H. Richardson in 1878. From 1878 to 1881, Rainey served as an internal revenue agent for the U.S. Treasury Department in South Carolina. In 1886 he returned to Georgetown where he died in 1887. Rainey was most likely born in this Georgetown house and lived here until 1846, when his family relocated to Charleston. Rainey returned to live in the house in 1866 and occupied it until 1870. The property remained in the family until its sale in 1896. The house was designated a National Historic Landmark on April 20, 1984. [B 4/20/84 NHL, 84003877]

Richmond Hill Plantation Archeological Sites
Address restricted
Murrell's Inlet

The Richmond Hill Archeological Site represents the remains of a working 19th-century rice plantation complex. The plantation was owned by Dr. John D. Magill, who had a reputation as one of the least efficient planters in the area and the most brutal slaveowner among the Georgetown district rice planters. The Richmond Hill Plantation's crop yield was well below the average for rice plantations along the Waccamaw. This was a direct result of the cruelty with which Magill treated his slaves. Ex-slaves, recalling their treatment some 70 years later, commented not only that Magill fed and clothed them poorly but that their punishments were both frequent and vicious. Slaves often stole rice during harvest and hid it for safekeeping. They ran away often, receiving harsh and often fatal punishments if caught. Ex-slaves recall that Magill shot or hanged captured runaways. When federal gunboats came up the Waccamaw in 1862, 28 slaves escaped, reporting Magill's cruelty to their deliverers. When Magill died in 1864, the plantation passed to his son, who declared bankruptcy and sold it within five years. The plantation house, overseers' houses, and slave houses that stood on the property were all burned by about 1930. [Georgetown County Rice Culture c. 1750–1910 MPS, CA 10/6/88, 88000537]

GREENVILLE COUNTY

Hampton-Pinckney Historic District
Hampton Avenue and Pinckney Street between Butler Avenue and Lloyd Street
Greenville

The Hampton-Pinckney Historic District comprises some 47 buildings dating primarily from the late 19th and early 20th centuries. The district is one of Greenville's oldest neighborhoods. Located within the historic district is the Matoon Presbyterian Church. Constructed in 1887, the two-story handmade brick building is the oldest black church building in Greenville. The congregation of Matoon Church was organized in 1878. The ground floor of the church building originally housed a parochial school for black children in grades one through nine. Community leaders recall the significant role of the church in the cultural life of black residents in the late 19th and early 20th centuries. Around 1929 the Board of Missions discontinued the parochial school program. Recently, the ground floor housed a children's day care center, continuing the tradition of service to Greenville's black community. [CA 12/12/77, 77001226]

John Wesley Methodist Episcopal Church
101 East Court Street
Greenville

The John Wesley Methodist Episcopal Church was organized in 1866 by the Reverend James R. Rosemond. Rosemond had been a "slave preacher" before the Civil War and organized several churches in Greenville, Anderson, and Pickett counties in the postwar years. John Wesley is one of the earliest churches organized by Rosemond and was part of a post-Civil War movement by the ME Church to send preachers and teachers to work among freedmen in the South. The congregation initially met in a building owned by a white congregation. They soon voted to end affiliation with the southern conference of the ME Church and moved to their own log building known as Hopkins Turnout. The lot on which the church now stands was donated to the congregation around 1899. Construction on the present brick vernacular Gothic Revival style sanctuary began in 1899. Although the building was not dedicated until 1903, the congregation occupied the church in 1900. The church remains essentially as it was when it was constructed. At the time of its listing in the National Register, plans were being drawn for the building's restoration with strong support from the local community. [CA 1/20/78, 78002514]

Working Benevolent Temple and Professional Building
Intersection of Broad and Fall streets
Greenville

Constructed in 1922, the Working Benevolent Temple and Professional Building was designed, built, and financed by the Working Benevolent State Grand Lodge of South Carolina, a black health, welfare, and burial benefit society. The lodge built the temple not only to house its administrative offices and headquarters, but also to attract black professionals to Greenville by providing much-needed office space for black businesses. Over the years the temple has provided offices for black doctors, lawyers, dentists, a newspaper, and insurance firms. The building also housed the first black mortuary in Greenville. During the 1960s, the Lodge's meeting rooms became a gathering point for local organizers of Greenville's civil rights movement. Although the building's use declined with desegregation, at the time of its listing in the National Register, the building remained a focal point for the local black community. [Greenville MRA, CA 7/1/82, 82003865]

GREENWOOD COUNTY
Mt. Pisgah AME Church
Intersection of Hackett Avenue and James Street
Greenwood

An eclectic example of the vernacular ecclesiastical architecture of the early 1880s and 1890s, Mt. Pisgah African Methodist Episcopal (AME) Church was erected in 1908 by members of the congregation. The organization of the congregation of Mount Pisgah AME is representative of the growth in membership in the AME Church in South Carolina in the years after the Civil War. By the end of Reconstruction, the AME Church had become the second-largest black religious denomination in South Carolina; by 1890 the state had a larger AME membership than any other state.

Mount Pisgah AME Church has been an important fixture in the black community of Greenwood over the course of its history. Promoting the education of African Americans has been an ongoing concern of the church. As part of this tradition, the congregation has provided financial assistance to Allen University (see also Allen University, Richland County). The church has also given assistance to individual members of the congregation to attend Allen and other institutions, making it central to the educational life of the community as well. [CA 8/16/79, 79002384]

Trapp and Chandler Pottery Site (38GN169)

Address restricted

Kirksey

The Trapp and Chandler Pottery Site was the locale of an antebellum pottery factory and is the last known intact pottery production site. The Trapp and Chandler factory provided necessary goods to the surrounding populace and was a source of income for many of the community residents. Items produced at the factory include jugs, jars, pitchers, butter pots, bowls, and chamber pots. The site consists of a kiln foundation and partial wall structure, an undisturbed waste pile composed of thousands of alkaline glazed and bisque ware sherds, an adjacent clay pit, and an accumulation of quartz rock.

Like many other potteries in the South, the Trapp and Chandler pottery employed both free and enslaved African Americans who took part in every step of the manufacturing process. Little in-depth study of alkaline glaze stoneware has been conducted to date. Future investigation at the Trapp and Chandler site may lead to a better understanding of this craft and how African Americans who worked at the pottery influenced it. [AD 1/6/86, 86000043]

HAMPTON COUNTY

Hampton Colored School

West Holly Street east of Hoover Street

Hampton

The Hampton Colored School is significant both as an intact example of 20th-century vernacular school architecture and for its association with black education in Hampton from 1929 to 1947. The school was built in 1929 by Ervin Johnson, a local black carpenter, to replace the first black school in Hampton, a two-room building that had operated since 1898. Volunteers from Hampton's black community assisted Johnson in the construction of the new two-room school. The school opened for the 1929–30 school year, serving students from the first through eighth grades. Initial scarcity of funds prevented the school from staying open for the full school year. However, donations from the black community soon paid for a September through June school year and allowed the school to later offer high school courses. It remained the only black school in Hampton until 1947, when Hampton Colored High School was built. After the construction of the new building, the Hampton Colored School became the lunch room for the high school. [CA 2/28/91, 91000233]

LANCASTER COUNTY

Clinton AME Zion Church

Intersection of Johnson and Church streets

Kershaw

Clinton African Methodist Episcopal (AME) Zion Church was the first separate black congregation established in Kershaw in the early 20th century. The church was named for Isom Caleb Clinton, a former slave who was a prominent minister in the AME Zion Church and was ordained a bishop in 1892. The

Cabins in the Mount Carmel AME Zion Campground. Photo courtesy of the South Carolina Department of Archives and History (Steve Smith).

present church was built in 1909 and has undergone few alterations since its construction. It stands as an intact example of the Gothic Revival style church architecture common in the period and an early 20th-century institution in Kershaw's black community. [Lancaster County MPS, CA 2/16/90, 90000092]

Mount Carmel AME Zion Campground
South of Lancaster
Lancaster

Mount Carmel African Methodist Episcopal (AME) Zion Church and Campground is one of the earliest sites in South Carolina associated with the establishment of the AME Zion Church. Founded around 1866 by former slave Isom Caleb Clinton, Mount Carmel AME Zion Church and Campground was part of the widespread growth of independent black churches that occurred in the South during the post-Civil War era. Mount Carmel is also among the state's few surviving campgrounds. The rectangular design of the campground shows the typical shape of 19th-century religious encampments, consisting of an open-sided "arbor," the focal point of revival meetings, surrounded by approximately 55 "tents," or cabins. An annual gathering continues to be held on the grounds under the auspices of the AME Zion Church. Mount Carmel is one of the few places in South Carolina where the tradition of the camp meeting is maintained. [CA 5/10/79, 79002386]

Unity Baptist Church

Intersection of Sumter and Hart streets
Kershaw

The congregation of Unity Baptist Church was organized in 1909 as an outgrowth of Kershaw's First Baptist Church. Unity was the second separate black church established in Kershaw in the early 20th century. The congregation originally met in the homes of its various members. The new sanctuary was built by Deacon George L. Shropshire, a local carpenter and contractor. The Reverend A. W. Hill became the church's first full-time minister in 1911 while he was still a student at Benedict College in Columbia (see also Benedict College Historic District, Richland County). Hill's successor, the Reverend L. C. Jenkins was the first pastor to occupy the parsonage adjacent to the church, built around 1922. Unity Baptist Church has undergone few alterations since its construction and stands as a relatively intact example of the Gothic Revival architecture common in the period and an early 20th-century institution in Kershaw's black community. [Lancaster County MPS, CA 2/16/90, 90000098]

LAURENS COUNTY

Charles H. Duckett House

105 Downs Street
Laurens

Built around 1892 by Charles H. Duckett, this vernacular one-story frame residence is significant for its association with its builder, a prominent black businessman. Charlie Duckett, who occupied the house from the time it was built until his death in 1947, was a carpenter, contractor, and lumber dealer in Laurens during the late 19th and early 20th centuries and was highly respected by citizens of both races. Local residents recall that Duckett owned the only lumberyard in

Laurens for a long time. His obituary in a local paper credited him as being the "only Negro in the southern states who operated a retail lumber business" and named him "the city's most outstanding colored citizen." In addition to his lumber business, Duckett operated a funeral home. He also played an active role in the civic affairs of Laurens and in the Bethel African Methodist Episcopal Church. The Duckett House is architecturally outstanding for its level of ornamentation. The house remained in the Duckett family until 1975, when it was sold to its present owner. [City of Laurens MRA, CB 11/19/86, 86003151]

ORANGEBURG COUNTY

Claflin College Historic District

On a portion of Claflin College campus
Orangeburg

The Claflin College Historic District is comprises five educational buildings constructed between 1898 and approximately 1915. The college was founded by two Methodist ministers in 1869 as Claflin University for the purpose of educating newly freed slaves. Money for the venture was obtained largely from northern philanthropy, especially the Claflin family of Massachusetts. The establishment of Claflin led to the development of Orangeburg as the center for the education of black South Carolinians. Because of the paucity of good public schools for black students in South Carolina in the late 19th and early 20th centuries, many students at Claflin were enrolled in elementary and secondary programs. Graduates of Claflin provided leadership for black communities throughout the state, and, along with graduates of South Carolina State College, accounted for the unusually large number of well-educated black members of the local community. [Orangeburg MRA, CA 9/20/85, 85002324]

Dukes Gymnasium
South Carolina State College campus
Orangeburg

Dukes Gymnasium is significant for its association with pioneer South Carolina black architect Miller F. Whittaker and South Carolina State College mechanical arts student John H. Blanche. Constructed in 1931, the building was designed by Blanche as a graduation thesis in the department of mechanical arts under the supervision of Whittaker, South Carolina's first registered black architect (see also Hodge Hall; Lowman Hall, South Carolina State College; and Williams Chapel AME Church for information on Whittaker). Thomas J. Entzminger, a black carpenter from Columbia, was the chief building supervisor, and instructors in mechanical arts courses at the college installed the steel framing, plumbing, and electrical systems and supervised other parts of the construction. The collaboration of Whittaker and Blanche demonstrates the expanding competence of African Americans in the field of architecture and the expansion of the college's educational parameters. The building itself, well proportioned and solidly built, is the tangible evidence of these efforts. [Orangeburg MRA, CA 9/20/85, 85002321]

East Russell Street Area Historic District
Portions of East Russell Street between Watson and Clarendon streets and portions of Oakland Place and Dickson and Whitman streets
Orangeburg

The East Russell Street Area Historic District includes is a collection of substantial one- and two-story brick and frame houses and a number of modest one-story frame houses. The district is a basically intact neighborhood with a wide range of architectural types and socioeconomic levels within a small area. The pattern of neighborhood growth in the district is typical of the city's residential areas, with the more affluent white citizens building larger houses along the primary streets and less affluent black citizens living in close proximity, in more modest houses along the side streets. The black residents of this neighborhood generally worked in a service capacity as laundresses, drivers, and house servants. Built between 1850 and 1930, the modest, vernacular houses in the district reflect the economic status of those African Americans who provided services for the white residents of Orangeburg. [Orangeburg MRA, CA 9/20/85, 85002335]

Maj. John Hammond Fordham House
415 Boulevard
Orangeburg

Constructed in 1903, the Major John Hammond Fordham House reflects the achievements of John Fordham, its original owner. Fordham was a lawyer and prominent black citizen of Orangeburg who was able to take advantage of expanded opportunities for black South Carolinians in the period between the end of the Civil War and the disenfranchisement and Jim Crow legislation at the turn of the century. A native of Charleston, Fordham moved to Orangeburg in 1874 after he was admitted to the bar. Besides practicing law, Fordham served in several appointive governmental positions, including coroner of Orangeburg, postal clerk in the railway mail service, and deputy collector of internal revenue. Fordham was also a leader in the South Carolina Republican party. The Fordham House is additionally significant as an example of the work of William Wilson Cooke, a pioneer black architect (for information on Cooke, see also Tingley

Memorial Hall, Claflin College). [Orangeburg MRA, CB 9/20/85, 85002341]

Hodge Hall
South Carolina State College campus
Orangeburg

Hodge Hall is a significant part of the expanding physical plant of South Carolina State College and reflects the increasing educational capability of that institution. Hodge Hall was designed by pioneer black architect Miller F. Whittaker as part of his master of science degree program at Kansas Agricultural College. Whittaker, South Carolina's first registered black architect, served as director of the department of mechanical arts and later as president of South Carolina State College. Hodge Hall was built to house the agriculture and home economics departments of the college and was erected with help from students at the school. Whittaker, with assistance from student labor and black contractors, not only shaped much of the physical plant of the college, but also made substantial inroads for African Americans in the profession of architecture (see also Dukes Gymnasium; Lowman Hall, South Carolina State College; and Williams Chapel AME Church). [Orangeburg MRA, CAB 9/20/85, 85002320]

Lowman Hall, South Carolina State College
South Carolina State College campus
Orangeburg

Lowman Hall was constructed in 1917 as a men's dormitory. It is the oldest intact building on the campus and is significant as part of the campus's physical development from the insubstantial frame buildings with which the college opened in 1896 to permanent brick construction. Lowman Hall was one of the first designs

of Miller F. Whittaker, who was then on the college faculty. Whittaker's designs for Lowman Hall and several other structures helped set standards for black students aspiring to the architectural profession (see also Dukes Gymnasium, Hodge Hall, and Williams Chapel AME Church). [Orangeburg MRA, CA 9/20/85, 85002346]

Mt. Pisgah Baptist Church
310 Green
Orangeburg

Mt. Pisgah Baptist Church is a turn-of-the-century church building whose brick construction and sophisticated design are noteworthy evidence of the dedication of its congregation during a period when few African Americans made more than a basic living. The church's design and intact interior make it an important example of religious architecture in Orangeburg. The church is also associated with the Reverend Nelson C. Nix, a prominent black citizen of Orangeburg. Nix served as pastor of Mount Pisgah for more than 40 years. In addition, he held the position of dean of the mathematics department of South Carolina State College. Mt. Pisgah was constructed in 1903 by black builder A. W. Thorne. Tradition indicates that this is the second building to house the congregation, which is believed to have been established around the mid-19th century. [Orangeburg MRA, CB 9/20/85, 85002342]

Tingley Memorial Hall, Claflin College
College Avenue
Orangeburg

Tingley Memorial Hall, a two-story brick building constructed in 1908, is the main building on the Claflin College campus (see also Claflin College Historic District). Built to house the English and pedagogical departments, the building originally contained 14 classrooms and an assembly hall. After the main campus building burned in 1913, Tingley became the administration building and has since been the main building on campus. Tingley Hall was designed by black architect William Wilson Cooke, a graduate of the school who served for 10 years as its superintendent of vocational training. Cooke designed most of the Claflin College buildings, and Tingley Hall was his last project before leaving the institution. In 1907 Cooke became the first African American to be appointed a senior architectural designer with the U.S. supervising architect's office in Washington, D.C. Tingley Hall stands as a reminder of Claflin College's contribution to black education in the state of South Carolina and as a reflection of Cooke's knowledge and skill as an architect. [Orangeburg MRA, CA 8/4/83, 83002205]

Treadwell Street Historic District
Portions of Treadwell and Amelia streets
Orangeburg

Treadwell Street Historic District contains the intact sections of an early 20th-century black neighborhood and provides significant information about the history of the black community in Orangeburg during that time. According to local residents, the neighborhood was one of the most well-to-do black neighborhoods in the city. According to the 1920–21 city directory, all residents of the district were black. While most residents were listed as laborers or tradesmen, there were also several professionals and businessmen living in the neighborhood. Among Orangeburg's most prominent black citizens who lived in the Treadwell Street Historic District were Dr. Henry Rowe, a physician and druggist, and the Reverend

Nelson C. Nix, pastor of Mt. Pisgah Baptist Church (see also Mt. Pisgah Baptist Church). Nix was also dean and instructor in the mathematics department at South Carolina State College. Another instructor at South Carolina State and resident of the district, Professor J. A. Pierce, opened his house to a school for black children, which was run by his wife. [Orangeburg MRA, CA 9/20/85, 85002315]

Williams Chapel AME Church
1908 Glover Street
Orangeburg

Williams Chapel African Methodist Episcopal Church, constructed in the Gothic Revival style, was designed by prominent black architect Miller F. Whittaker (see also Dukes Gymnasium; Hodge Hall; and Lowman Hall, South Carolina State College). Its picturesque massing and distinctive detailing attest to the talents of its architect and the ability of black builder I. J. Minger. Construction of the building began in 1915 but was not completed until around 1925, because of the financial difficulties of the congregation. The congregation was organized in 1873 and originally worshipped in a frame building that stood to the northeast of the present church. [Orangeburg MRA, CA 9/20/85, 85002345]

RICHLAND COUNTY

Allen University
1530 Harden Street
Columbia

Founded by the African Methodist Episcopal (AME) Church in 1881, Allen University was the first private black school founded and operated by African Americans in South Carolina. Allen University opened its doors four years after the University of South Carolina was closed to black students, thus it filled the pressing need for black higher education in South Carolina. Allen has its origins in the Payne Institute, established at Cokesbury by the Abbeville District of the AME Church in 1871. Payne was merged into Allen University by the Columbia and South Carolina conferences of the church in 1880, and the university opened in Columbia the following year. Allen University was founded primarily to provide an educated clergy for the AME Church, but it also offered law and vocational degrees. Allen's law department, which remained in place until the early 1900s, was among the few to be established in southern colleges for African Americans. Today the university continues to be chiefly controlled and managed by and for African Americans. [A 4/14/75, 75001705]

Alston House
1811 Gervais Street
Columbia

The Alston House is important for its association with early black businesses in Columbia. The one-story clapboard Greek Revival cottage set on a brick foundation was built around 1872. Possibly as early as 1875, but definitely by 1895, the building was used as a residence and dry goods store by Carolina Alston. Mrs. Alston was a prosperous black businesswoman and was one of only 25 black businesspeople operating in the Columbia area in the late 19th century. As such, she was an important leader of the black business community of her time. In 1906 Alston sold the building to L. M. Keitt, a black businessman who operated a grocery on the site. Following Keitt's ownership of the property, it passed through a series of owners until 1964, when it became the home of McDuffie's Antiques. [Columbia MRA, CA 3/2/79, 79003359]

Barber House
Off County Route 37
Hopkins

The Barber House is significant for its association during the late 19th century with the South Carolina Land Commission, a unique attempt by a southern state to give freedmen the opportunity to own land. Samuel Barber, a former slave, purchased land in 1872 from the commission. In 1879 his wife, Harriet, also a former slave, received title to the land. The family farmed about 24 acres of land, planting Indian corn and cotton. After the death of Samuel and Harriet Barber, their son John, a public school teacher and Baptist preacher, and his wife, Mamie Holly, occupied the house. They raised 11 children in the house. Today the house is occupied by a great-grandson of Samuel and Harriet Barber. The house is significant for the fact that the same family has remained on the property since 1872. Even more significant, however, is the fact that the Barbers were among the few black families who purchased land from the South Carolina Land Commission who were able to gain free title to the land and to prosper. [Lower Richland County MRA, CA 3/27/86, 86000531]

Benedict College Historic District
Roughly bounded by Laurel, Oak, Taylor, and Harden streets on Benedict College campus
Columbia

The Benedict College Historic District comprises five buildings near the center of campus in Columbia. Founded as the Benedict Institute in 1870, the college was established by the American Baptist Home Mission Society to provide education for freedmen and their descendants and was particularly intended to educate

Chappelle Administration Building. Photo courtesy of the National Historic Landmarks Program.

and train ministers and teachers. The school was named for Stephen Benedict, a Rhode Island businessman, Baptist deacon, and abolitionist, who left a bequest to the society at his death. This money, along with additional funds donated by his widow, was used to buy the land on which the institution was established.

Over the course of its first 20 years, greater emphasis came to be placed on helping black students find work. Programs included agriculture, horticulture, and industrial and vocational training. Benedict Institute became Benedict College in 1894, with an enrollment of some 200 students. The college's curriculum was restructured in the mid-1930s, confining degree programs to bachelor of arts, bachelor of science, and divinity in theology. In 1948 a college of liberal arts was added, and the theology degree was discontinued in 1966.

In the years before desegregation, the school served as a center of black activities in Columbia, providing a locale for meetings, lectures, concerts, and other social functions. This, along with its major role in the education of blacks in North Carolina, makes the Benedict College Historic District a property of great importance to black history in South Carolina. [CA 4/20/87, 87000809]

Chapelle Administration Building
1530 Harden Street
Columbia

Built in 1925, the Chapelle Administration Building, designed by John Anderson Lankford (1874–1946), the "dean of black architecture," is the central building of the Allen University campus.

John Anderson Lankford was educated in the fields of mechanical engineering and architecture at Tuskegee Institute and Lincoln Institute, now Lincoln University in Missouri. In 1899 he opened the first African American architectural firm in the United States in Jacksonville, Florida, and became the first registered African American architect. He later completed graduate work in architecture at Wilberforce University in Ohio. Lankford gained recognition as a leading African American architect, and he designed many important buildings in the black community, including buildings located on the campus of Allen University.

Allen University was founded in 1870 by the African Methodist Episcopal (AME) Church as a result of the efforts of Bishop Daniel Alexander Payne (1811–93), a leader in black education. Initially located in Cokesbury, South Carolina, and called Payne Institute, it was renamed Allen University after it was transferred to Columbia. It was named in honor of Bishop Richard Allen (1760–1831), the founder of the AME Church, the first church in America controlled and supported by African Americans. The establishment of Allen University marked the first attempt by African Americans of South Carolina to maintain an institution of higher learning, and Allen University retains its importance as a historically black college (see also Allen University). The Chapelle Administration Building was designated a National Historic Landmark on December 8, 1976. [CB 12/8/76 NHL, 76001710]

Fair-Rutherford and Rutherford Houses
1326 and 1330 Gregg Street
Columbia

The Fair-Rutherford and Rutherford Houses, built in 1850 and 1925 respec-

tively, are significant for their association with the Rutherford family. William H. Rutherford gained his freedom at age 13 with the end of the Civil War. In 1870 he is listed in the census as a servant in the house of a black Republican party leader, speaker of the South Carolina House of Representatives, and U.S. congressman. By the time of the 1880 census, he was working as a barber. From about 1888 to 1895 he taught school, and from 1900 to 1910 he operated two manufacturing companies. His business was no doubt prosperous, for in 1905, he was able to purchase the Fair-Rutherford House, which he used as a rental property.

William H. Rutherford's son, Harry Benjamin Rutherford, Sr., worked for a time as a barber before joining his father's business. He later owned and operated a fleet of limousines. He acquired the property adjacent to his father's, on which the Rutherford House now stands, in 1914. After Henry Benjamin Rutherford's death in 1916, his widow, Carrie B. Rutherford, moved into the Fair-Rutherford House while she had the Rutherford House built. Henry Benjamin Rutherford's son, Harry Benjamin Rutherford, Jr., and his wife, Everetta Sims Rutherford, were also of local prominence. Both were educators in Columbia teaching in the city's now defunct segregated school system.

The Fair-Rutherford House and the Rutherford House are important landmarks in black history in Columbia marking the accomplishments of the members of this family. The Rutherford family progressed, in four generations, from slavery to prominence in the Columbia community, each generation building on the achievements of the previous one. [A 4/5/84, 84002093]

Goodwill Plantation
Off U.S. Route 378
Eastover

The Goodwill Plantation was developed as a plantation beginning around 1795 by Daniel Huger. Huger grew corn, cotton, peas, beans, and sweet potatoes on the plantation, with cotton the largest cash crop. After Huger's death in 1854, the property was purchased by Edward Barnwell Heyward. Heyward generally continued to plant the same crops as Huger had until the Civil War. During the Civil War, the plantation served in an unusual capacity. Heyward's relatives apparently sent their large numbers of slaves to Goodwill to wait out the war. As many as 976 slaves may have resided at Goodwill during this time. After the war the Heywards employed a number of their former slaves as day laborers and took responsibility for their physical welfare. Among the extant resources from the Heywards' occupation of Goodwill are two one-and-one-half-story frame slave cabins, probably built just after the Heywards acquired the property in 1858. [Lower Richland County MRA, CA 3/27/86, 86000528]

Magnolia
Address restricted
Gadsden

Magnolia plantation retains several antebellum buildings, including two slave houses. Slave labor was integral to the plantation economy of the South, as illustrated by period population statistics from Richland County. The county slave population increased greatly between 1800 and the Civil War. In 1840 slaves in Richland County numbered 10,644, representing the largest increase in any one segment of the county's population in the pre-Civil War era, while whites in Richland County numbered only 5,326. The slave cabins at Magnolia, among the relatively few existing examples of slave quarters in the area, illustrate a once common form of African American antebellum housing in lower Richland County. [Lower Richland County MRA, CA 3/27/86, 86000536]

Mann-Simons Cottage
1403 Richland Street
Columbia

The property on which the Mann-Simons Cottage stands originally belonged to Celia Mann, a free black woman who was a professional midwife. Mann, an extremely religious woman, was instrumental in establishing First Calvary Baptist Church, one of the first black churches in the area. The congregation met in Mann's house, holding services in her basement until the property on which to build a sanctuary was acquired. For some time before the church building was erected, the congregation met in a horse barn that stood on the property. Mann's daughter, Agnes Johnson, married Bill Simons, who may have built the Mann-Simons Cottage around 1850. Simons was an accomplished musician who may also have been a contractor and politician, as the city directories list a black contractor named William Simons and a black representative William Simons in the South Carolina General Assembly. The Mann-Simons Cottage is the only historic house still remaining in the Columbia area that was originally owned by African Americans. The house stood in the same neighborhood with the houses of white families, underscoring the fact that successful free blacks often lived harmoniously in the same area with successful whites in the antebellum South. [AB 4/23/73, 73001726]

Saint Thomas' Protestant Episcopal Church

Near junction of U.S. Route 601 and
South Carolina Route 263
Eastover

St. Thomas' Protestant Episcopal Church was founded at the urging of Bishop William Bell White Howe, who sought to address what he saw as a lack of mission work by the Episcopal Church among the black population. The Reverend Thomas Boston Clarkson, son of a prominent Richland County planter, was appointed by Bishop Howe to minister to the black residents of lower Richland County. A chapel was erected on Middleburg, the Clarkson family plantation. The Clarksons eventually sold Middleburg and made their permanent home in their former summer residence in the Sandhills. Here Clarkson's wife, Septima, established a Sunday school for the black children in the community. In 1885 the Reverend James Saul of Philadelphia donated funds for the erection of a church. The new church, named Saul Chapel, was built in the Sandhills with Clarkson as minister. The Saul Chapel burned to the ground in 1891 and was replaced by the present building and renamed St. Thomas' Protestant Episcopal Church. Completed in 1893, the church was served by both black and white priests. Septima Clarkson carried out missionary work at St. Thomas' until her death, at which time her daughter assumed her teaching position. Today the church continues to have an active congregation. [Lower Richland County MRA, CA 3/27/86, 86000539]

Waverly Historic District

Roughly bounded by Hampton, Heidt, Gervais, and Harden streets
Columbia

The historic core of the Waverly neighborhood was originally an early subdivision of an antebellum community of the same name located on the outskirts of Columbia. By the early 20th century, it had evolved into a community of black artisans, professionals, and social reformers, many of whom made significant contributions to the social and political advancement of African Americans in Columbia and statewide.

Black families first began settling in the Waverly neighborhood in the late 19th century, their numbers growing rapidly in subsequent years. By 1903 black residents outnumbered white residents in Waverly by nearly two to one. By the 1920s Waverly had evolved into Columbia's most prominent black community. The neighborhood's importance in black history is reflected by the homes of its residents and by the concentration of institutions that served the black community at a time when racial discrimination denied them access to services available in the white community. The black residents of Waverly created a nearly self-sufficient community of black-owned business, hospitals, churches, and schools that served black residents in Waverly and in the state.

Two institutions that initially drew African Americans to Waverly were Benedict College and Allen University (see also Allen University and Benedict College Historic District). The former was founded in 1870 by the Baptist Home Mission Society, and the latter in 1881 by the African Methodist Episcopal Church. The pattern in which major black urban communities grew up around black colleges and universities was a common one in the South. The gradually growing presence of a large group of black urban professionals in Waverly was directly related to the concentration of schools, churches, and other public institutions that served the black community.

Hospitals and other health care facilities serving the black community were significant in the development of Waverly. Among these were the Benedict Hospital and the Waverly Fraternal Hospital and Nurses Training School. The presence of these institutions accounts for the unusually high number of black doctors and nurses who worked at or trained in Waverly.

Churches, such as the Woodrow Presbyterian Church, and black retail businesses served the community as well, forming the core of the self-supporting network created by the community's members. Waverly's development illustrates important patterns in the shift from biracial coexistence to the strict racial segregation common to early 20th-century urban centers. [CA 12/21/89, 89002154]

UNION COUNTY

Corinth Baptist Church
North Herndon Street
Union

Corinth Baptist Church was constructed in 1894 as the first separate building to house the first black congregation in Union. The congregation was established around 1883 and first held services in the former Old Union Methodist Church. In 1893 the owner of the mill that stood on an adjacent lot purchased the lot and building from the congregation for $600. The congregation purchased the lot on which the Corinth Baptist Church now stands in January 1894, and the building was completed by the end of the year. The church is a late 19th-century vernacular interpretation of architectural styles common to religious buildings in the region. [Union MPS, CA 7/20/89, 89000939]

James Gilliland House. Photo courtesy of the Tennessee Historical Commission (R. Paul Cross).

TENNESSEE

ANDERSON COUNTY

Woodland-Scarboro Historic District
Roughly bounded by Rutgers Avenue,
Lafayette Drive, and Benedict,
Wilburforce, and Illinois avenues
Oak Ridge

The Woodland and Scarboro neighborhoods were constructed as residential
neighborhoods to house workers of the
U.S. nuclear power facility at Oak Ridge,
Tennessee. Although Oak Ridge was initially designed to be a temporary site
functioning only during World War II,
Congress announced in 1947 that peacetime operations would continue under the
direction of the newly created Atomic
Energy Commission. Although racial discrimination was forbidden on all defense
projects, government policy was to obey
local laws, which, in Tennessee, included
segregated housing laws. The Woodland
neighborhood was, therefore, to house
white workers, while black workers were
housed in the Scarboro neighborhood.
Although they occupied separate facilities,
black workers in Oak Ridge were allowed
the rare opportunity to voice their concerns in housing issues.

Before the community was built, black
community leaders were consulted about
the choice of a location. They rejected the
first location offered and chose the pre-

sent site instead. The city largely followed
separate but equal segregation policies by
providing the black workers with housing
that was nearly identical to that in the
white neighborhood of Woodland. The
significant difference between the two
communities was the greater percentage
of single family homes over duplexes in
the Woodland neighborhood. The old
Scarboro School served as the high school
for Scarboro residents and was the first
and only school for black students in
Anderson County. Because it was under
federal jurisdiction, the Oak Ridge school
system in 1956 became the first in the
state of Tennessee and the first in the
Deep South to integrate. The input
afforded the black residents of Scarboro
and the quality of the facilities provided
represent a progressive step in race relations. [Oak Ridge MPS, CA 9/5/91,
91001106]

BEDFORD COUNTY

James Gilliland House
803 Lipscomb Street
Shelbyville

The Gilliland House is an outstanding
example of the craftsmanship of black
stone mason James S. Gilliland. Born in
1858, Gilliland is said to have practiced
his trade until near his 80th birthday. He
began his career by contracting to build

stone foundations, retaining walls, and fences, but his recognized artistic ability soon brought him work on windows, doors, chimneys, and even tombstones. He performed every facet of stonework from quarrying to carving and was an accomplished brick mason as well. His skill earned him a place of prominence and respect in Shelbyville's black community.

Gilliland's work on his own house illustrates his exceptional talent at his trade. The residence that originally stood on the lot was a two-room, log dog-trot. In 1898, while living in the log structure, Gilliland began quarrying, cutting, facing, and laying the stones that make up the four walls of the building. He constructed the walls around his house and removed the log building from inside. This house is the only one of its kind known to exist in the area and is a testament to Gilliland's outstanding craftsmanship. [B 5/12/75, 75001730]

BLEDSOE COUNTY

Lincoln School
Old Tennessee Route 28 near Rockford Road
Pikeville

One of 354 schools built between 1915 and 1932 for African Americans in Tennessee with the aid of the Julius Rosenwald Foundation, the Lincoln School was the only Rosenwald school in Bledsoe County. Completed in 1926, the building is an excellent intact example of the standardized school architecture specified in *Community School Plans,* published in 1924 by the Rosenwald Foundation.

The Rosenwald school program was conceived by Sears Roebuck and Company magnate Julius Rosenwald as a means of developing self-sufficiency in southern rural black communities. The foundation contributed money toward the construction of rural black schools

whose curriculum emphasized vocational education. Additional funds were to be raised by the community in which the school was located. Although the aim of the program was to promote biracial participation, in most cases, almost all of the community money was raised by black residents. In the case of the Lincoln School, the Rosenwald Fund provided $900, the black community raised $1,200, and additional $3,236 was provided by the county and state, since the Lincoln School consolidated two existing segregated schools.

The school was designed to serve the needs of the community as well as its students. The design standards for Rosenwald schools specified that schools should be large enough to accommodate gatherings of the entire community. The Lincoln School has two sets of two adjoining rooms with movable partitions and a raised speaking platform at the north end of each combined space. These rooms housed numerous political rallies and church and community events and served as the local voting precinct until 1968.

The Lincoln School was the only school for black students in Pikeville until segregation officially ended in 1964. The building has been maintained in excellent condition and even contains some historic furnishings. It stands as reminder of the impact of the Rosenwald school program in Pikeville and numerous other rural black communities. [CA 7/15/93, 93000648]

DAVIDSON COUNTY

Capers CME Church
319 15th Avenue North
Nashville

The Capers Colored Methodist Episcopal (CME) Church was one of the best early church designs of the black architecture firm of McKissack and McKissack. Constructed in 1925, the Neoclassical Revival style church has not been significantly altered. The present building is the church's second home. The original church building was built in 1851 and was known as Capers Chapel in honor of its founder, Bishop Capers. In 1870 Capers Chapel became part of the CME Church and helped to establish several other CME churches in Nashville. The congregation chose McKissack and McKissack to design their new home in 1925. The firm went on to design more than 2,000 ecclesiastical buildings after the completion of Capers CME Church. (See also Carnegie Library, Hubbard House, and Morris Memorial Building.) [McKissack and McKissack Buildings TR, CA 1/2/85, 85000045]

Carnegie Library
17th Avenue North, Fisk University campus
Nashville

The Carnegie Library is an early building on the Fisk University campus and is the earliest remaining building designed by Moses McKissack (see also Fisk University Historic District). Built in 1908, the library was financed by a $20,000 gift to the school from Andrew Carnegie. The university board of trustees selected Moses McKissack to design the library, giving him his first large contract. Secretary of War William Howard Taft laid the cornerstone of the simple masonry neoclassical style building on May 22, 1908. The building served as the main library for Fisk University until recent years and is now used as an academic building. (See also Capers CME Church, Hubbard House, and Morris Memorial Building.) [McKissack and McKissack Buildings TR, CA 1/2/85, 85003769]

Fisk University Historic District
Roughly bounded by 16th and 18th avenues and Hermosa, Herman, and Jefferson streets
Nashville

Fisk University was founded at the close of the Civil War by the American Missionary Association (AMA) and the Western Freedmen's Aid Commission. The school was named for General Clinton B. Fisk, administrator of the Freedmen's Bureau in Tennessee. Since receiving its charter in 1867, Fisk University has established a reputation as one of the best black universities in the country. As an academically oriented liberal arts college, Fisk differed from vocationally oriented schools such as the Hampton and Tuskegee Institutes (see also Hampton Institute, Hampton Independent City, Virginia, and Tuskegee Institute National Historic Site, Macon County, Alabama). This academic focus was provided by the AMA

The AMA, a largely congregational religious organization, was founded in 1846 to oppose slavery and to assist African Americans. Of the many religious organizations that supported education for black students after the Civil War, the AMA established more schools, staffed them with better educators, and gave them more lasting support than any other organization. The AMA was guided by the basic philosophy that there were no inherent racial differences in educational potential and therefore established institutions that were guided by the same goals and used the same curriculum as the best schools of higher education in the United States. It was this philosophy that shaped the standard of academics at Fisk.

Fisk has produced many outstanding graduates, including social philosopher W. E. B. Du Bois; sociologist E. Franklin Frazier; historian John Hope Franklin;

Administration Building in the Fisk University Historic District.
Photo courtesy of Berle Pilsk.

jurist Constance Baker Motley; poets James Weldon Johnson, Arna Bontemps, Sterling Brown, and Nikki Giovanni; and tenor Roland Hayes. In proving that race was not a determining factor in educational potential, Fisk graduates posed a direct challenge to the idea of white supremacy. Led by W. E. B. Du Bois, many Fisk graduates rebelled against the idea of special education for black students and insisted instead on quality academic instruction that would lead African Americans to a stronger self-identity and a position of social and economic equality (see also Carnegie Library and Jubilee Hall, Fisk University). [CA 2/9/78, 78002579]

Goodwill Manor
3500 Centennial Boulevard, Tennessee State University campus
Nashville

Tennessee State University was founded as Tennessee State Agricultural and Industrial College for Negroes in 1909. Goodwill Manor is one of the four buildings that were constructed for the college's use between 1909 and 1912. The building was built as the college president's residence and was first occupied by William Jasper Hale. Hale was also founder and president of both the Tennessee Inter-Racial League and the National Conference of Presidents of Land Grant Colleges and vice president of the National Negro Business League. The

Morris Memorial Building. Photo courtesy of Thomason and Associates.

president of the college during its early years was significantly and directly involved with the lives of the students and faculty, organizing campus activities and serving as campus supervisor at all times. For this reason, Goodwill Manor became a focal point of the college campus.

In addition to its campus functions, Goodwill Manor served as a place for black visitors to stay during the era of enforced racial segregation in public accommodations. Among the distinguished black visitors to Nashville who lodged at Goodwill were Marian Anderson, Jesse Owens, and Booker T. Washington. President Herbert Hoover, and President and Mrs. Franklin Roosevelt were entertained at Goodwill as well. Goodwill Manor is the only remaining building of the original campus and stands as an architectural reminder of

the service of the college and its presidents to the black community. [AB 3/25/82, 82003962]

Hubbard House
1109 1st Avenue South
Nashville

Dr. George W. Hubbard came to the South from New Hampshire during the Civil War. In 1876 he was appointed by the Freedmen's Aid Society of the Methodist Episcopal Church to organize a medical department at Central Tennessee College to train African Americans in the fields of medicine, dentistry, pharmacy, and nursing. The medical college remained largely separate from the rest of the college and received its own charter in 1915, establishing itself officially as Meharry Medical College. Meharry was the first medical school in the South established for the education of black physicians.

The Hubbard House was built for Hubbard upon his retirement as president of Meharry in 1921 and was financed by the trustees and alumni. Meharry alumni made up more than half of the black physicians, dentist, and pharmacists in the South during Hubbard's tenure at the school. In 1931 the college was relocated to a new modern plant in northwest Nashville. The Hubbard House is the last remaining building of the original campus and stands as a monument to Dr. Hubbard's efforts and the accomplishments of the students of Meharry. (See also Capers CME Church, Carnegie Library, and Morris Memorial Building.) [McKissack and McKissack Buildings TR (AD), B 8/14/73, 73001760]

Jubilee Hall, Fisk University
17th Avenue North
Nashville

Constructed between 1873 and 1876, Jubilee Hall, an imposing six-story Victorian Gothic building, is an architectural landmark in the city of Nashville. Its primary significance lies in its association with Fisk University (see also Fisk University Historic District). In 1871, five years after Fisk University was established, the school found itself in financial trouble. In an effort to raise funds, school officials assembled a choir to tour the North singing African American spirituals to white groups sympathetic to the education of freedmen. The name Jubilee Singers was given to the choir by George L. White, the schools treasurer and director of the troupe, in memory of the Jewish year of Jubilee.

Although the troupe failed to profit from its first tour, a second trip the following year brought the group immediate acclaim. Their performance at the World

Peace Jubilee in Boston in 1872 brought widespread recognition and was the starting point of an extensive schedule of national and international tours. With the money raised through these tours, Fisk University was able to purchase land and build necessary school buildings. The first of the buildings constructed was Jubilee Hall, named for the singers. Jubilee Hall has become a symbol of Fisk's determination to endure and provide a high-quality education for black Americans. Jubilee Hall was designated a National Historic Landmark on December 9, 1971. [CA 12/9/71 NHL, 71000817]

Morris Memorial Building
330 Charlotte Avenue
Nashville

The Nashville architectural firm of McKissack and McKissack was formed in 1922 when Moses McKissack III formed a partnership with his younger brother Calvin. McKissack and McKissack was the first black architectural firm in the United States and was organized and staffed by black architects and draftspeople. The McKissack brothers had a family heritage of training in carpentry and the building arts, traceable to Moses McKissack, who was brought to America from West Africa and sold into slavery in 1790. Before entering the partnership with his brother, Moses McKissack III had worked privately, receiving his first large commission, the Carnegie Library on the Fisk University Campus, in 1908 (see also Fisk University Historic District). Calvin McKissack had also worked independently, designing several black schools and churches in Texas.

The firm was granted a license by the newly formed Tennessee Board of Architects and Engineers Examiners in 1922. A rising black middle class in Nashville in the 1920s opened up new opportunities for the brothers, and their architectural practice gained statewide recognition. The firm carried on a prosperous business in Tennessee through 1940 and afterward bid on contracts outside the state, receiving licenses in Alabama, Georgia, South Carolina, Florida, and Mississippi. The brothers received international recognition in 1942, when they were hired by the federal government to construct the 99th Pursuit Squadron Air Base at Tuskegee, Alabama (see also Tuskegee Institute National Historic Site, Macon County, Alabama).

In 1942 the firm received the Spaulding Medal, given to the outstanding black business firm in the United States. Through the 1940s the McKissacks gained prominence nationwide through their public housing designs. As a result of these designs, Moses McKissack III was appointed to a conference on housing problems during the Roosevelt administration. At the death of his brother in 1952, Calvin McKissack took over as president of the firm. At his death in 1968, Calvin's son William DeBerry McKissack took over the firm. The company had completed more than 5,000 buildings by 1975 and continues to be an important contributor to the architectural profession. The four buildings that make up the McKissack and McKissack Buildings Thematic Resource represent the best remaining designs executed by the firm before 1930.

The Morris Memorial Building is a large steel and masonry four-story structure that was constructed between 1924 and 1926 in the heart of Nashville's downtown black business district. The building is neoclassical in design and is one of the firm's finest works from the 1920s. It was constructed to house the offices of the National Baptist Convention U.S.A., Incorporated, an organization that publishes religious materials for black Baptist churches. Soon after its completion, the building drew other black businesses including the offices of McKissack and McKissack. Many black businesses moved to other areas of the city during the 1960s, leaving the Morris Memorial Building as the only building still standing that is associated with black businesses in the downtown area. (See also Capers CME Church, Carnegie Library, and Hubbard House.) [McKissack and McKissack Buildings TR, CA 1/2/85, 85000046]

HAMILTON COUNTY

Martin Luther King Boulevard Historic District

Roughly Martin Luther King Boulevard between Browns and University streets
Chattanooga

The Martin Luther King Boulevard Historic District comprises a community that was first settled in the early 1800s. By the time of the Civil War, some black families had built houses in the vicinity. The area was probably undesirable for white settlement since it was low-lying and contained a pond. By the end of the Civil War, a clearly identifiable black community had formed. Growth in the area was gradual until a boom period in the late 1890s. Most of the buildings in the historic district were built between 1900 and 1917. Many of the early residents of the area worked in the iron furnaces and rolling mills, but some found employment as laborers and domestics, and a few were professionals.

The black community of the Martin Luther King Boulevard area was involved with the racial issues of the times. When the Tennessee legislature passed stringent Jim Crow laws for street cars,

Chattanooga's black residents organized their own system of horse-drawn cars that connected this district with other black residential and work areas in Chattanooga. The area was also home to several organizations devoted to the procurement of equal rights for African Americans.

The buildings within the district express an architectural cohesiveness through similarity of design, materials, and scale. The commercial buildings in the district represent vernacular, functional architectural styles adopted by the black community as commerce along Martin Luther King Boulevard began to grow and flourish. The history of the Martin Luther King Boulevard Historic District is an important chapter in the history of Chattanooga and illustrates the role played by the community in developing and supporting black culture and society in southeast Tennessee. [CA 3/20/84, 84003551]

Shiloh Baptist Church
506 East 8th Street
Chattanooga

Organized in 1866, the congregation of Shiloh Baptist Church was made up of former slaves. Services were held in members' homes until a church building was erected near the present property. This first building burned and was replaced by a second one at the same location. Construction on the present building began in 1885 with labor donated by the congregation. The church was completed 10 years later and dedicated on May 10, 1896.

One of the earliest black church buildings in Chattanooga, Shiloh Baptist Church is also one of the few remaining Gothic Revival style churches in the city. The building stands as a tribute to the determination and dedication of former slaves who worked for 30 years to raise the funds to purchase the land and materials and who built this imposing edifice with their own hands. The church has been the religious, cultural, and social center for the descendants of the freedmen who organized the congregation and constructed the building. [CA 1/19/79, 79002442]

Wiley United Methodist Church
504 Lookout Street
Chattanooga

The property on which the Wiley United Methodist Church now stands has long been a significant site in Chattanooga's history. It originally contained a building known as "the little log schoolhouse" where community meetings were held. In 1847 a frame building assembled in Soddy, Tennessee, was floated down the Tennessee River and moved onto the property for use as a Methodist church. The building served the Methodist congregation until the outbreak of the Civil War, when it was used first as a hospital and later as a prison. The building was in poor condition after the war and was sold to a local Negro Methodist Episcopal congregation in 1867 for use as their house of worship.

The foundation of the present brick church was laid in 1886. While the new church was still under construction, the frame building was destroyed by arson. Work on the new church building was accelerated. Both the capital and the labor for building the new brick church were donated by the congregation, and it was completed in 1888 at a cost of $18,000. By 1909 the congregation had purchased a pipe organ, becoming the first black church in Chattanooga to have one. Today it is one of the oldest organs still in use in Chattanooga. As one of Chattanooga's earliest remaining church buildings, Wiley United Methodist Church is a tribute to one of east Tennessee's earliest black congregations. [C 8/1/79, 79002443]

HAWKINS COUNTY

Price Public Elementary School
Intersection of Hasson and Spring streets
Rogersville

In March 1868 several black residents of Hawkins County purchased a lot for the purpose of building a schoolhouse for black children. By 1870 the Price School, a two-room frame and log building, had been constructed. Although there were 115 schools for white children in Hawkins county in 1900, educational facilities for black children were much fewer. The ones that did exist were often poorly funded, and in 1910 they averaged 46 students per class compared with 17 students per class in white schools. It was not until the 1920s that a concerted effort was made to improve educational facilities for black students in Hawkins County. The present Price School was constructed in 1923 after the mayor and board of aldermen appointed a building committee to build a new black elementary school in Rogersville. Built of brick, the new school contained three classrooms, a basement, and an attic.

Although the Price School had always been used as an elementary school, in 1930 black high school students were transported from all over the county to Price when the board of education hired a Johnson City teacher to teach all high school subjects to freshman and sophomore students in one room of the building. The county took this action because there were not enough high schools for black students in the county. The largest such school was Swift Memorial College in Rogersville, a junior college and high school for black students begun by the Presbyterian Church, U.S.A. Few black students in the county, however, could afford the tuition at Swift.

In 1932 the Hawkins County Board of Education entered into an agreement with Swift whereby black students would be taught high school subjects at the college. The Presbyterian Board of National Missions sold the Swift College property to the county, and Price once again became solely an elementary school. As Swift College only accepted students who had completed courses from an accredited school, the high school became a feeder school for the junior college. In 1938, when Price had only three teachers, Swift Memorial College students did their student teaching there.

After 1958 the building was no longer used as a school. It has since served as a community center, cannery, and storage building. As the only known extant black school in Rogersville, Price Public Elementary School is an example of the county's efforts to provide education for black children during the 1920s and 1930s. [A 11/10/88, 88002538]

KNOX COUNTY

Knoxville College Historic District
901 College Street, N.W.
Knoxville

Knoxville College grew out of the McKee School, the first organized school for African Americans in Tennessee, founded by the Reverend J. G. McKee in Nashville. Established in 1862, the McKee School was the first of several such schools organized under the auspices of the Freedmen's Mission of the United Presbyterian Church. In 1872 the church decided to discontinue its support of the schools in order to develop a college for African Americans to prepare them for careers in teaching and the ministry. Knoxville was selected as the site of the new college, as it was located between Nashville and Atlanta, then centers of black education. Knoxville College began operation in 1875 in a former freedmen's elementary school. The school was moved to its present location the following year. In 1914 the College of Arts and Sciences was established. In the years after 1920, the school earned the distinction of being the leading supplier of teachers to black schools in east Tennessee. The college amended its charter in 1954 to admit white students but remains today a predominantly black institution. The Knoxville College continues to contribute significantly to the educational welfare of African Americans in east Tennessee. [A 5/1/80, 80003841]

Mechanicsville Historic District
Off Tennessee Route 62
Knoxville

The Mechanicsville neighborhood was settled around 1880 and soon became the center of industrial activity in Knoxville. The large number of factories located here in the late 19th and early 20th centuries were largely staffed by black and Welsh residents of the area. In addition to working in the factories, members of these two groups owned and operated small businesses in the area.

African Americans have played a particularly significant role in the history of Mechanicsville, first settling in the community around 1890. Although their residences were initially restricted to a small area of the neighborhood, they soon began to establish homes throughout the community. At one time, a majority of workers employed in the community's first and largest industry, the Knoxville Iron Company, were black. The black population found employment as skilled or unskilled laborers in the marble mills and on the railroad as well.

Perhaps the best-known of Mechanicsville's black residents was Professor Charles W. Cansler, a lawyer, author, and educator for whom Cansler Street is named. Cansler's mother was the first black teacher in Knoxville, and many of his family members became teachers in the Knoxville schools. Cansler himself taught in the Austin School during the early 1900s. Cansler was an ardent activist on behalf of black residents in the community, securing for them playgrounds, parks, and a public library.

Blacks and whites, employers and employees, have historically lived side by side in Mechanicsville, a fact attested to by the varied architecture in the community. The historic mix of African American and Welsh still strongly characterizes the community today. [CB 7/18/80, 80003842]

Col. John Williams House
2325 Dandridge Avenue
Knoxville

This two-story Federal style house was built in 1826 as a residence for Colonel John Williams. Williams, a prominent Knoxville politician, lived in the house until his death in 1837. His estate was sold in 1855, and, after passing through the hands of two different owners, the house was leased in 1883 to the state for use by the Negro Division of the Tennessee School for the Deaf and Dumb. In 1885 the Tennessee legislature authorized purchase of the property and the adjoining 27 acres as a permanent home for the school. As the school grew, two additions and a new dormitory were built, and 55 acres were added to the original lot. With the desegregation of public institutions in the 1960s, the Negro Division moved to a new Tennessee School for the Deaf facility in Knoxville. Although a portion of the ceiling collapsed in the 1920s addition to the house, the original house remains intact as an architectural reminder of its function in the black community in an era of segregation. [CAB 12/3/80, 80003843]

LAUDERDALE COUNTY

Fort Pillow
Tennessee Route 87
Fort Pillow

Located on the east bank of the Mississippi River, Fort Pillow was established by the state of Tennessee during the Civil War to bar the passage of Union gunboats south of Plum Point Bend and guard the river approaches to Memphis. On June 5, 1862, this Confederate fort was occupied by Union troops. In April 1864 Fort Pillow was recaptured by Confederate troops under the leadership of Major General Nathan Bedford Forrest.

At the time of the Confederate attack on Fort Pillow, the fort was garrisoned by approximately 570 Union troops, of whom 262 were African Americans. The Union's black units, the First Battalion of the Sixth U.S. Colored Heavy Artillery and Company D of the Second U.S. Colored Light Artillery, were composed of former slaves recruited in Alabama. The Confederates inflicted heavy casualties on the black soldiers and killed a disproportionate number of Union troops. A congressional committee investigated the battle and concluded that Confederate soldiers had committed atrocities against black soldiers.

News of the Fort Pillow massacre had a profound effect on black soldiers in other units. Black troops in Memphis took an oath to avenge the massacre of the black soldiers. Fort Pillow became the "Alamo" of black soldiers, who committed themselves to the Union cause and made "Remember Fort Pillow" their bat-

tle cry. Fort Pillow was designated a National Historical Landmark on May 30, 1974. [A 4/11/73 NHL, 73001806]

W. E. Palmer House
Off U.S. Route 51
Henning

The Palmer House was the residence of Cynthia and Will Palmer, the grandparents of African American author Alex Haley (1921–92). Haley was born in Ithaca, New York, in 1921 and was taken to Henning six weeks later. He and his mother lived with his grandparents while his father completed his graduate studies. During his 20 years of service in the Coast Guard, Haley began his writing career, publishing a few adventure stories before his retirement in 1959. After writing biographical articles for *Reader's Digest* and the first "*Playboy* interview," Haley collaborated with Malcolm X to write the autobiography of the Black Muslim leader.

As a child, Haley sat on the porch of the Palmer House listening to the stories told by his grandmother and his aunts of the family's African ancestors and their sale into slavery in North Carolina. These stories prompted him to begin research into his ancestry in 1964. Haley was able to trace his lineage back seven generations to a small West African hamlet. It was this history that Haley wrote in his 1977 Pulitzer Prize-winning novel, *Roots*.

Roots is a significant work for several reasons. It relates the African American experience from its origins in Africa to the present, employing a framework of documented historical persons and events. The book records the history of a single family while also epitomizing the collective experience of almost all African Americans in a way that readers find meaningful and deeply moving. The eight-part television series based on the novel surpassed almost every previous television-rating record.

Haley's work provided millions of African Americans with a deeper understanding of their own heritage and inspired thousands to laboriously trace their own family history. Haley purchased his grandparents' home in Henning, where he was inspired to write the book that would become so meaningful to so many African Americans. [CB 12/14/78, 78002604]

MAURY COUNTY

Ashwood Rural Historic District
U.S. Route 43 between Columbia and Mount Pleasant
Columbia

The Ashwood Rural Historic District, four miles from downtown Columbia, encompasses approximately 8,300 acres of southern Middle Tennessee farmland and several hundred historic buildings and structures. The district, named after the community of Ashwood, represents the height of the antebellum plantation economy in Tennessee. Several of the plantation complexes are basically intact and retain many of the original agricultural and other related buildings and structures.

The success of this plantation economy was based on slave labor. Because of the labor-intensive nature of the crops produced in the region, slaves made up 40 percent of the county's total population by 1860; the percentage at Ashwood was even higher. A few slave residences remain in the district on the Clifton Plantation. The single-pen log quarters, constructed of one or two rooms with exterior brick or stone chimneys, were typical of others built in the district.

The slaves often attended religious services with their masters. Records of the district's St. John's Episcopal Church show no less than 116 of a local family's servants were baptized at the church where the family worshiped between 1846 and 1848. At death, slaves were accorded Christian burials, and numerous slave cemeteries exist in the district.

After the Civil War, many of the slaves in the Ashwood district became sharecroppers. Some former slaves purchased or rented their own tracts of land and built their own houses, while others occupied their former quarters. Some white planters gave former slaves small tracts of land. Two small black communities were formed in Ashwood after the war. One of these, Canaan, still exists as a black neighborhood with a church, several residences, and an early 20th-century schoolhouse.

The Ashwood Historic District is an important cultural resource in Maury County. The intact plantation complexes and the Canaan community are significant illustrations of life for African Americans in antebellum and postbellum rural Middle Tennessee. [CADB 2/10/89, 88003247]

Lane College Historic District
Lane Avenue
Jackson

Built between 1905 and 1927, these buildings are the oldest remaining on the campus of Lane College. Founded in 1882, the school has provided education to black students for more than 100 years.

Lane College traces its beginning to the efforts of the Colored Methodist Episcopal (CME) Church to offer education to its members. On December 16, 1870, the church held a conference in Jackson, Tennessee, to discuss the role of the church and the need to sponsor a school for its members. In 1879 Bishop Isaac Lane started to work within the Tennessee conference of the church to establish a school in the state.

Lane was born into slavery March 3, 1834, in Madison County on the plantation of Cullen Lane. Although a slave, Lane taught himself how to read and write. He joined the CME Church in Jackson in 1854 and was elected elder in 1866 and bishop in 1873. In the late 1870s he raised money for the creation of a school for the church, and on January 14, 1880, Lane purchased the land for the school.

In 1882 the first building was constructed on the campus and contained the library, chapel, and recitation rooms. Initially known as the CME High School, the school opened on November 12, 1882, under the supervision of Miss Jennie Lane, daughter of Bishop Lane.

In 1883 the Reverend Charles Phillips became principal of the school. The following year the school was named Lane Institute in honor of Bishop Lane. Lane aided the school in its progress throughout the early 20th century. He remained an inspirational force for the school until his death in 1937 at age 103.

One of the mottoes of the school was "Learning without the Christian religion is incomplete." Many of the school's graduates went on to become ministers in the CME Church; several were elected to the rank of bishop and other high offices.

Today Lane College is one of the South's best-known black colleges, with an enrollment of more than 600 students. The school continues to be a major force in the religious educational program of the CME Church in America. [CA 7/2/87, 87001117]

MEIGS COUNTY

Andy Wood Log House and Willie Wood Blacksmith Shop
State Route 1
Georgetown

This log house and blacksmith shop are significant in black history for their association with two African American blacksmiths, Andy Wood and his son Willie Wood. Historically Meigs County has had a very small black population, and there is little physical evidence of black history in the county. Rural blacksmiths like the Woods, however, were important to the county in the 19th century. The 1850 census listed 28 blacksmiths, representing 24.5 percent of the occupations other than farmer. By 1880 the number of blacksmiths dropped to 10. The Wood Blacksmith Shop is the only one still in operation in Meigs County.

The Wood Log House was built around 1890 by Andy Wood. It has not been modernized by the addition of electricity and is the best example of a single-pen log building in the county. The Blacksmith Shop was built in 1912 by Willie Wood and is filled with a variety of tools and equipment. The shop, like the log cabin, has no electricity; the machinery is powered by hand or gasoline engine. Both buildings are still owned by the Wood family. [Meigs County, Tennessee MRA, A 7/6/82, 82004015]

MONTGOMERY COUNTY

St. Peter African Methodist Episcopal Church
518 Franklin Street
Clarksville

The congregation of the St. Peter African Methodist Episcopal (AME) Church was established in Clarksville in 1866, first worshiping in a building on nearby 2nd Street. The present building was constructed in 1873, and the steeple was added in 1890. Materials for the building were donated by the local Methodist church, which had originally intended to use them in the construction of a sanctuary for its own use but abandoned the project for a much larger building. This simple Victorian Gothic style brick building has remained essentially unchanged since it was remodeled in 1890 and remains the most outstanding black church edifice in Clarksville. [19th Century Churches in Clarksville TR, C 4/6/82, 82004034]

PERRY COUNTY

Cedar Grove Furnace
Address restricted
Linden

Built in virtual wilderness, the Cedar Grove Furnace is a massive stone edifice measuring approximately 30 feet high, 30 feet deep, and 50 feet wide. While it is not known whether Wallace Dixon, the founder of the Cedar Grove Iron Works, employed slave labor in building the furnace, it is certain that the furnace was operated by slaves. The iron industry was at one time a vital industry in Tennessee, particularly in Hickman, Lewis, Perry, and Wayne counties. The majority of ironworkers in Middle Tennessee before 1862 were slaves. The largest slaveowner in the state, Montgomery Bell, was not a cotton planter but an ironmaster. The Cedar Grove Furnace is significant not only as a representative of its type in the Tennessee Western Highland Rim but also as a testament to the importance of African Americans in the economy of central Tennessee before the Civil War. [Iron Industry on the Western Highland Rim 1790s–1920s MPS (AD), CA 6/19/73, 73001814]

RUTHERFORD COUNTY

Bradley Academy
415 South Academy Street
Murfreesboro

The Bradley Academy was founded in Murfreesboro in 1811 and served white students until 1848, when it was absorbed by Union University. The original school building, a small log cabin located on the site where the Bradley Academy now stands, was left unoccupied for 37 years. After the Civil War, the area around the school building became a predominantly black neighborhood, isolating the Bradley Academy site from the then all-white school system of Murfreesboro. In 1884 the school was designated for use as an educational institution for black students.

Increasing enrollment over the years necessitated the addition of a curriculum beyond the elementary school level and the construction of a new building. In 1917 a new, modern building was erected. With the opening of the new facility in 1918, the Bradley Academy became a significant social center in the local black community. The building housed not only the community's educational facilities, but also many social events such as musicals, dances, recitals, and community fairs and was used as a public health facility in the 1920s. In 1928 the academy organized a high school department, which became Rutherford County's first accredited high school for African Americans. Enrollment for the high school increased so quickly within the year, the county authorized construction of a separate facility, Holloway High School, to house it.

With the 1954 *Brown v. Board of Education* decision, Bradley lost its identity as an all-black school. The 1917 Bradley Academy building stands today, however, as a reminder of the vital role the school played in the educational, social, and cultural life of the black community of Murfreesboro before integration. [A 6/14/90, 90000914]

SHELBY COUNTY

Beale Street Historic District

Beale Street from 2nd to 4th streets
Memphis

Beale Street's entertainment district is an important site in the history of the blues. The blues, which began as a distinctly African American art form, have had a significant impact on American rock, jazz, pop, and symphonic music. Beale Street is perhaps best known as the home of legendary black bluesman William Christopher (W. C.) Handy (1837–1958), who popularized the style and became a preeminent figure in the establishment of composed blues as a form of American popular song.

Beale Street provided the backdrop from which urban blues drew inspiration. Like other Mississippi River basin towns, such as New Orleans and St. Louis, Memphis drew a significant permanent black community in which African American musical traditions flourished. The culture that thrived in the nightclubs, saloons, gambling establishments, and pawnshops formed the content of Handy's compositions, such as "Memphis Blues" and "Beale Street Blues." Handy worked in Memphis from 1905 to around 1918. His band was headquartered on Beale Street, and he resided there at one time to avoid distractions while he worked on his music.

The nightlife on Beale Street was not limited to saloons and clubs; theaters also held an important place in the life of the district. The largest showhouse for black audiences in the South was the Palace Theater, famous for its Tuesday night amateur shows. The Pastime, opened in 1909, was the first theater for African Americans on Beale Street. The Lincoln, between Hernando and 4th streets, was the first theater in the district established with black capital.

Beale Street's reputation as an entertainment district that nurtured Handy and other black musicians continued until the Great Depression. Today the Beale Street Historic District represents this significant chapter in African American cultural history. The district was designated a National Historic Landmark on October 15, 1966. [A 10/15/66 NHL, 66000731]

Collins Chapel CME Church and Site

678 Washington Avenue
Memphis

Collins Chapel Colored Methodist Episcopal (CME) Church was formed by the black members of the Wesley African Mission, organized in 1841. The ground on which the church now stands was purchased in 1859; a church building was constructed in 1860 and named Collins Chapel in honor of J. T. C. Collins, the first pastor of the congregation. The 1860 church was destroyed by fire during the Memphis race riots of 1866 and was rebuilt in 1867. Three years after the new church was built, the Methodist Episcopal Church South officially recognized the Colored Methodist Episcopal Church as its own denomination. The delegates to the conference at which the CME denomination was organized included two members of Collins Chapel. The conference also established *The Christian Index,* the official publication of the CME Church. The paper was published in Memphis and included, over the course of its history, five of Collins Chapel's pastors among its editors.

The Christian Index reflected the CME Church's growing militancy in civil rights issues in the early 20th century. It strongly supported the newly formed National Association for the Advancement of Colored People in 1917. Six members of the Collins Chapel congregation were

Lorraine Hotel (now more commonly known as the Lorraine Motel) in the South Main Street Historic District. Photo courtesy of the City of Memphis, Division of Housing and Community Development (Lloyd Ostby).

original charter members of the NAACP, and Collins Chapel itself was an institutional charter member. Collins Chapel continued to aggressively support the civil rights cause through the 1960s, when the movement reached its peak. Collins Chapel CME (now Christian Methodist Episcopal) stands as a landmark in the black community and is recognized for its role in championing the cause of freedom and equality for African Americans since its founding. [A 3/29/91, 91000307]

First Baptist Church
379 Beale Avenue
Memphis

The congregation of the First Baptist Church was founded in a series of praise meetings conducted by the Reverend Scott Keys at his Beale Street residence in 1854. In 1863, under the pastorate of the Reverend Morris Henderson, the congregation moved to the basement of a white church. The congregation moved again when that church was destroyed by fire, and it acquired the property on which the First Baptist Church now stands in 1869. The land was donated by a New York Baptist society and constructed by members of the black community. The brick, Gothic-influenced church was built at a cost of $100,000. During Reconstruction, General Ulysses Grant addressed Memphis's black community from its pulpit. The First Baptist Church is an important center of cultural activity for the black community in Memphis. [A 2/11/71, 71000833]

Mason Temple, Church of God in Christ
958 Mason Street
Memphis

Mason Temple and the surrounding world headquarters complex of the Church of God in Christ (COGIC) were constructed in phases between 1940 and about 1960 as the administrative and spiritual center of COGIC. With about 8,000 congregations and roughly 3.7 million members worldwide, COGIC is second only to the National Baptist Convention, USA, in membership among black denominations. The complex is the surviving property most closely associated with the denomination's dynamic founder, Charles Harrison Mason (1862–1961), who incorporated COGIC and brought the church to international prominence. The property is also the site where on April 3, 1968, Dr. Martin Luther King, Jr., delivered his famous "Mountaintop" speech, his final public address before his assassination at the Lorraine Hotel the next day.

Born in Shelby County in 1862, Charles Mason and his family were staunch church supporters. Mason converted to the Missionary Baptist Church in 1880 and was licensed to preach. He parted with the church over doctrinal differences and formed COGIC in 1897. Influenced by religious leader William J. Seymour, the Pentecostalist minister who led the Azusa Street Revivals in California, Mason and other COGIC ministers were baptized as Pentecostalists. In 1907 Pentecostalism, characterized by the practice of glossolalia (speaking in tongues) and the belief in purification, including the removal of original sin after baptism, was officially established as the fundamental doctrine of COGIC.

The spread of Pentecostalism, which had been practiced predominantly in the South, in the early decades of the 20th century is attributed largely to the Great Migration of African Americans out of the rural South into the urban North. Because COGIC was the sole incorporated Pentecostal denomination in the United States between 1907 and 1914, many white preachers were ordained as COGIC ministers. In 1914, with Mason's blessing, a group of white COGIC ministers formed the Assemblies of God denomination, resulting in the end of biracial association in COGIC by 1924.

Mason Temple served as the headquarters for COGIC, housing its annual convocation and other activities. When the original temple was destroyed by fire in 1956, Mason Temple became the national center for COGIC activity. Like many other churches in the black community, Mason Temple became a focal point for black civil rights activities in the 1950s and 1960s. The temple was a meeting place for black sanitation workers and their supporters during the Memphis Sanitation Workers' Strike of 1968. Following a bloody confrontation between marching strikers and the police on March 28, 1968, a court injunction was issued banning further protest action. In April 1968 Dr. Martin Luther King, Jr., and the Reverend Ralph Abernathy of the Southern Christian Leadership Conference came to Memphis to seek a way of overturning the injunction and to take part in a nonviolent protest march to be planned at Mason Temple.

Although Abernathy was the scheduled speaker that night, the crowd of some 3,000 hoped to hear King. Abernathy phoned King at his room in the Lorraine Hotel and asked him to address the assembly. King's speech that evening, known as "The Mountaintop," is now considered one of the most important pieces of oratory in the history of the civil rights movement. The passion generated by King's address turned to sorrow within 24 hours as he was assassinated on the balcony of the Lorraine Hotel on April 4, 1968. In addition to its historical association with Charles H. Mason and COGIC, Mason Temple remains a memorial to King. [AB 4/10/92, 92000286]

Second Congregational Church
764 Walker Avenue
Memphis

Second Congregational Church, founded in 1868, is significant both as the oldest unaltered church in Memphis designed and built by black artisans for a black congregation and as the church associated with LeMoyne-Owen College (see also Steele Hall). Both the church and the college were products of the missionary work of the Congregational Church and the American Missionary Association (AMA) after the Civil War. LeMoyne-Owen College was founded as LeMoyne Normal and Commercial School in 1871 for the education of black students. Both the church and the school were located on nearby Orleans Street. When the college was moved to its present site in 1914, the church was moved as well. Since its founding, Second Congregational Church has held regular Sunday services for students and faculty of LeMoyne as well as for regular members. Since the construction of the present building in 1928, the church has also held the college's weekly chapel programs and periodic special events.

The Second Congregational Church was, until fairly recently, one of the city's few integrated churches. The church has had both black and white pastors, and, in accordance with the philosophy of its founding organization, has historically been active in promoting better race relations in Memphis. [CA 8/26/82, 82004053]

Second Presbyterian Church
280 Hernando Street
Memphis

Completed in 1892, this monumental building was designed by Minneapolis architects Frederick Kees and Franklin B. Long. The design was the winner out of 50 entries in a contest held by the congregation of the Second Presbyterian Church to select an architect for their new church. The church is one of only a handful of 19th-century churches surviving in Memphis. Even rarer is its Romanesque Revival style ecclesiastical architecture.

In 1949 the property was sold to the African Methodist Episcopal (AME) Church, which renamed it Clayborn Temple. It became a focal point for civil rights activities in Memphis in the 1960s. In 1968 Dr. Martin Luther King, Jr., delivered the first organizing speech of the city sanitation workers' strike at Clayborn Temple. The church also provided important services for the local black community. The AME congregation operated a neighborhood service center and one of the few black kindergartens in Memphis before school integration. [CA 9/4/79, 79002478]

South Main Street Historic District
Roughly South Main Street between Webster and Linden and Mulberry between Calhoun and Vance avenues
Memphis

The South Main Street Historic District in Memphis comprises a collection of predominantly commercial buildings and includes the Lorraine Hotel, a building of exceptional significance to African American history. Built around 1920, the Lorraine Hotel had been a typical South Main Street hotel for white travelers until 1942. By the end of World War II, it had become a black establishment, which had among its early guests Cab Calloway, Count Basie, and other prominent jazz musicians. It was later a stopping point for Roy Campanella, Nat "King" Cole, and Aretha Franklin. It was partly because of its significance to the black community of Memphis that Dr. Martin Luther King, Jr., chose to stay at the Lorraine during the 1968 Memphis sanitation workers' strike. It was outside his second-floor room of the 1965 motel addition to the Lorraine that he was assassinated while helping to settle the strike.

For information on the life of Dr. Martin Luther King, Jr., see Martin Luther King, Jr., National Historic Site, Fulton County, Georgia. [CAB 9/2/82, 82004054]

Steele Hall
LeMoyne-Owen College campus
Memphis

LeMoyne College has its origins in a school for "contraband," former slaves who had left plantations during the Civil War and were arriving in Memphis in large numbers. The school, which came to be called the Lincoln School, was established by the American Missionary Association (AMA) in Memphis in 1865. The institution found itself in financial trouble after the war, however, and was rescued by prominent Pennsylvania physician and AMA member, Dr. Francis Julius LeMoyne. LeMoyne contributed $20,000 to found a school in Memphis. The Lincoln School was reorganized and named LeMoyne Normal and Commercial School in 1871. In 1901 a secondary program was added to the curriculum. The program remained the only high school for black students in Memphis until 1923.

The college was established at its present location in 1914. Steele Hall, which served as Memphis's only black high school from its construction in 1914 until 1923, was for many years the only permanent building on the LeMoyne campus. Although Steele Hall has undergone some changes, it remains a key building on campus. The college, which merged with Owen College in 1968 and is now called LeMoyne-Owen College, plans to continue using the building. From its establishment as the only college available to the Memphis black community to the present, the college has served as a training ground for black leaders. (See also Second Congregational Church.) [A 3/23/79, 79002481]

Tri-State Bank
386 Beale Street
Memphis

The Tri-State Bank building was constructed in the early 1900s and became the home of the Tri-State Bank in 1946. The bank was organized shortly before that time by A. Maceo Walker and John A. Walker and has since grown to be one of the largest black financial institutions in Tennessee. The Tri-State Bank building has played an important role in the political activities of African Americans in Memphis. From 1946 to 1965 the building was a meeting place for the political leaders of the local black community. The campaigns of numerous African American candidates for local office were planned in the building. In the 1960s the site was the starting point of many of the civil rights marches and demonstrations that took place in Memphis. [B 2/11/71, 71000836]

Zion Cemetery
Intersection of South Parkway East and Pillow Street
Memphis

Zion Cemetery is the oldest and one of the largest cemeteries for African Americans in the city of Memphis. The land on which the cemetery was established in 1876 was purchased in 1873 by the United Sons of Zion, a black fraternal and benevolent organization. The cemetery was operated on a nonprofit basis until 1893, when a group of members of the United Sons of Zion formed the Zion Cemetery Company and purchased the property.

The historical events associated with the cemetery are many. During the yellow fever epidemic of 1878, numerous black victims were buried in Zion Cemetery. While most white residents left the city, many African Americans stayed behind to care for the sick and protect the city. Among an association of groups that formed a militia to prevent looting and maintain order was the Pallbearers Association of the United Sons of Zion. Zion Cemetery is also the place of burial for three black merchants who were victims of the lynchings that prompted the international antilynching crusade of Ida B. Wells, editor and owner of the Memphis newspaper *Freedom of Speech*. The cemetery is the final resting place of numerous African Americans whose accomplishments and achievements contributed greatly to the development of Memphis, Shelby County, and the state of Tennessee. [A 2/23/90, 90000301]

SUMNER COUNTY

Fairvue
4 miles south of Gallatin on U.S. Route 31E
Gallatin

The Fairvue plantation was the home of Isaac Franklin, who between 1828 and 1836 created the largest slave-trading operation in the antebellum South. Franklin had joined the shipping business with his brothers in 1807, traveling back and forth to New Orleans to exchange goods. He became aware of the increasing migration to the Southwest and the growing demand for slaves in the region. Seeing the opportunity for great financial

profit through the trading of slaves, Franklin began his slave-trading career.

Along with his partner, John Armfield, Franklin established offices in Alexandria, Virginia; Natchez, Mississippi; and New Orleans, Louisiana; and had agents in almost every major southern city. Franklin and Armfield trafficked in thousands of slaves every year, transporting them on their own fleet of sailing ships. Both partners acquired enormous wealth in their business. Franklin retired in 1836, dividing his time between Fairvue and his other plantations.

Fairvue remains essentially intact and retains the flavor of a typical antebellum plantation, reflecting the culture of antebellum planters in the upper South. Four slave houses stand on the property. Originally there may have been as many as 20 of these one-story, red-metal-roofed cabins on the plantation. The four remaining cabins have undergone interior modernization and serve as private residences. Nevertheless, they offer insight into the living conditions of slaves at Fairvue and other plantations. Fairvue was designated a National Historic Landmark on December 22, 1977. (See also Franklin and Armfield Office, Alexandria Independent City, Virginia.) [AB 6/10/75 NHL, 75002162]

WILLIAMSON COUNTY

John Henry Carothers House
Liberty Pike
Franklin

John Henry Carothers purchased the property on which the Carothers House is located for $25 an acre in 1933. For the next four years, the family farmed 14 acres while living in a small house nearby. In 1937 Carothers purchased stock plans for a small house and began construction of the one-and-one-half-story residence with the assistance of his son, Ezeal

Carothers. The Carothers House is an excellent example of a small farmhouse built by a black Tennessee farmer. More than half of the rural black population in Tennessee was in need of some form of relief by the end of 1930 and lived in substandard housing. The Carothers family prospered more than many of their rural counterparts in Tennessee during the Great Depression. In addition to purchasing land and building a house, they planted 14 acres of the property with hay, wheat, tobacco, and a large kitchen garden and raised cows and chickens.

The Carothers House was the first of three stone houses built by John Carothers from stock architectural plans, and it demonstrates local adaptation of stock building plans using native materials. It is the only house that remains standing of the three, all of which were constructed from limestone quarried from the Carothers farm by Ezeal Carothers. [Williamson County MRA, CA 11/27/89, 89002028]

WILSON COUNTY

Rest Hill Cemetery
Tennessee Route 141 east of junction
with Tennessee Route 24 Bypass
Lebanon

Rest Hill Cemetery is an important physical remnant of the African American community established in Lebanon during Reconstruction. The property on which the cemetery rests was purchased by members of the black community in four separate parcels between 1867 and 1869 and was donated to a group of trustees empowered to establish a black cemetery. In 1869 African Americans were barred from burial in the city cemetery, making Rest Hill an even more vital community institution.

Although the cemetery has been maintained only sporadically over the years, it retains much of its historic character. Headstones remain from as early as 1867. It is difficult to determine the exact number of burials in the cemetery because some stones are missing and many graves had either wooden markers that have since decomposed or no markers at all. In addition, several of the older burials were in family plots, one of the cemetery's most interesting features. According to local tradition, families often purchased large rectangular plots where family members would be interred without individual headstones. At least 33 such plots have thus far been identified.

Rest Hill Cemetery was the only cemetery to serve African Americans in Lebanon until 1933, when a modern, fully landscaped cemetery for African Americans was established. Rest Hill is, however, still in use today. It is a significant resource of African American heritage in Lebanon and the only resource remaining from the Reconstruction period, in which Lebanon's black community has its origins. [A 3/25/93, 93000212]

TEXAS

BASTROP COUNTY

Jennie Brooks House
1009 Walnut
Bastrop

This vernacular Greek Revival style house is significant for its association with Jennie Brooks, an early black settler in Bastrop and daughter of a slave. Brooks purchased this lot and built this house around 1890. This house is also one of the oldest houses in Bastrop built by a black family, and Brooks was one of the few black home owners in the growing black community. Although black home ownership was uncommon at the time, the black community in Bastrop founded their own religious, educational, and social institutions. Brooks was probably active in black community events. Brooks's family also contributed to the community:Her daughters were skilled musicians, and her son was a cafe manager. [Bastrop Historic and Architectural MRA, A 12/22/78, 78003317]

Drawing of Buffalo Soldiers and the Rescue of Corporal Scott by Frederic Remington. Courtesy of the Denver Public Library, Western History Department.

Kerr Community Center
1308 Walnut
Bastrop

Built in 1914, this two-story frame building represents the social history of African Americans in Bastrop. Beverly and Lula Kerr, prominent black community leaders and talented music teachers, built the Kerr Community Center and rented out the facility for social activities, lodge meetings, and entertainment events. The building was erected just behind their house, which still stands at 1305 Pine. During World War II the army renovated and refurnished the building to use it as a United Service Organization center. After the Kerrs' deaths, the Kerr Community Center took over ownership of the building, which, at the time of its listing in the National Register, continued to function as a social center for African Americans. [Bastrop Historic and Architectural MRA, A 12/22/78, 78003339]

Beverly and Lula Kerr House
1305 Pine
Bastrop

Built between 1890 and 1895, this raised, one-story, wood frame Victorian house is associated with the Kerr family, a prominent black family known for its community leadership as well as its musical talents. Beverly Kerr was a barber in a white barbershop and a band teacher whose musical group, Kerr's Orchestra, performed for both black and white audiences. Beverly was the first black band teacher in Bastrop. Beverly's wife, Lula, the first black music teacher in Bastrop, taught in the school system for 40 years. Beverly and Lula were active members of Paul Quinn African Methodist Episcopal Church and leaders of the local lodges in the black community. [Bastrop Historic and Architectural MRA, CA 12/22/78, 78003356]

Kohler-McPhaul House
1901 Pecan
Bastrop

Kohler-McPhaul House, with its unique architectural style showing German-influenced proportions, is associated with the McPhauls, a black family that purchased the house around the turn of the century. This house represents black home ownership during a time when few African Americans owned their own homes. Many of the African Americans who owned their homes were active in social and educational institutions in the black community. The McPhauls, for instance, were leaders in the field of education. Annie McPhaul was one of the first teachers at Piney School, a black school in Bastrop, and her daughter, Penny, was also a school teacher. [Bastrop Historic and Architectural MRA, CB 12/22/78, 78003275]

Harriet and Charlie McNeil House
1805 Pecan
Bastrop

Built in 1870, the Harriet and Charlie McNeil House is one of the oldest houses in Bastrop owned by a black family. In the early 20th century, Harriet McNeil, an African American, purchased this house, and it remained the home of Harriet and her son, Charlie, throughout most of this century. At the time, few blacks in the community owned their homes. [Bastrop Historic and Architectural MRA, A 12/22/78, 78003276]

Ploeger-Kerr-White House
806 Marion
Bastrop

This one-story frame house was constructed by Carl Ludwig Ploeger, a native of Prussia, soon after he married in 1863. It was later purchased by Robert Kerr, the first black legislator from Bastrop and one of the few African Americans to hold political office in the years immediately following Reconstruction. Robert Kerr came to Bastrop from the Kerr Creek community, near Victoria, Texas sometime around 1865. Kerr's first job was keeping books for Hasler Grocery on Main Street; later he drove an express wagon and delivered groceries to people around the town. He became a member of Paul Quinn African Methodist Episcopal Church and was active in church affairs and community activities. Most important, Kerr was elected to the state legislature in 1881, and he remained in office until 1883. Robert Kerr and his wife, Sarah, resided at Ploeger-Kerr-White House throughout his career. The house was later sold to Beverly and Lula Kerr, black leaders and educators, as well as the founders of Kerr Community Center in Bastrop. The house remained in the Kerr family for 47 years. [Bastrop Historic and Architectural MRA, B 12/22/78, 78003346]

BELL COUNTY

Mount Zion United Methodist Church
218 Alexander Street
Belton

Built in 1893, the Mount Zion United Methodist Church was constructed by a black congregation and remains one of the few surviving early black churches in Bell County. The church was built during the peak years of the cotton boom around the turn of the century, when the black community of Belton was growing rapidly. The building is situated on the western bank of Nolan Creek in what was at the time one of the largest African American neighborhoods in Belton. Before the Civil War, Bell County had an economy based on ranching and a relatively small black population—21 percent in 1860. After the war, freed blacks encountered tremendous oppression because of the lack of employment. The emergence of cotton as a principal cash crop later in the century provided employment for African Americans, and consequently the black population grew; however, African Americans were forced to reside only in segregated communities in the less desirable areas. Mount Zion served–and continues to serve–as one of the centers of Belton's black community. [Belton MPS, CA 12/26/90, 90001872]

BRAZOS COUNTY

E. A. Kemp House
606 West 17th
Bryan

African Americans have played an important role in the history of Bryan. They initially came to the region as early as the 1830s when permanent settlement by Anglo-Americans first reached the area. The earliest settlement of African Americans in Bryan was known as Freedmanstown. The Kemp House, located within this black settlement, was the home of the E. A. Kemp family beginning in the mid-1920s. E. A. Kemp was Bryan's leading black educator. Kemp worked to train the black community for better employment, for at that time black citizens had relatively few job opportunities and were often relegated to low-paying jobs. Local black leaders such as Kemp worked to overcome problems encountered by the black population and helped to make Bryan a better township for all citizens. [Bryan MRA, CB 9/25/87, 87001636]

DE WITT COUNTY

E. A. Daule House
201 West Newman
Cuero

Black educational efforts have made important contributions to development within the black community. In Cuero, as throughout Texas, black and white students attended separate school systems. Educator E. A. Daule helped develop and upgrade Cuero's black schools, along with C. H. Griggs, the first principal of the local black school, and the Reverend G. W. James. E. A. Daule owned this house from the 1890s through the 1930s. Daule, who graduated from college in Baton Rouge, Louisiana, came to Cuero in 1890 and became principal of the black high school, serving for about 40 years. During his tenure, in 1904, a two-story frame school was built on the outskirts of town. Originally known as the Cuero Colored High School, it was renamed the Daule School in 1948 in honor of Daule. [Cuero MRA, CB 10/31/88, 88001981]

Macedonia Baptist Church
512 South Indianola
Cuero

Churches have been the most important social institutions in Cuero's black community, and Macedonia Baptist Church is one of Cuero's oldest black congregations. Its sanctuary is an outstanding example of vernacular ecclesiastical architecture in Cuero and is an important architectural and social landmark representing black history. Organized in 1891, Macedonia Baptist Church was originally known as the Second Baptist Church of Cuero. The Reverend G. W. James of Lafayette, Louisiana, was instrumental in its founding, and he served as pastor until his death in 1902. The church building was originally constructed for St. Michael's Catholic Church and stood at McLeod and Church streets. When the Catholics planned a new brick facility, members of Macedonia Baptist Church purchased the old frame sanctuary with some furnishings for $300. The church was then dismantled and rebuilt on its present site by Charlie Gallagher, one of the founders of Macedonia Church. [Cuero MRA, CA 10/31/88, 88001967]

ELLIS COUNTY

Building at 441 East Main
441 East Main
Waxahachie

This building is associated with the development of two black fraternal organizations and is one of two surviving buildings in Waxahachie's once active black business center. The lower floor for many years housed the James Funeral Parlor, owned and operated by a locally prominent black family. It was among the longest-lasting black-owned businesses in Waxahachie during the late 19th and early 20th centuries. The upper floor served as the meeting hall for the Knights of Pythias Unity Lodge No. 37, and the black Masonic Lodge, which split into the Pythagoras Lodge No. 87 and the Progressive Lodge No. 432 in the 1940s. [Waxahachie MRA, A 9/24/86, 86002437]

Building at 500–502 East Main
500–502 East Main
Waxahachie

In 1890 the cotton industry inspired local business leaders to form a board of trade to encourage cotton field-workers to move to Waxahachie. As a result, many black workers settled in the eastern part of Waxahachie, especially along East Main and Wyatt streets. This area developed into a separate and independent community within Waxahachie, as African Americans established their own social institutions and businesses. Virtually all of the local black businesses were located along the 400 and 500 blocks of East Main Street. Built in 1900, this building is one of only a few historic commercial buildings to remain within Waxahachie's black commercial district. It is also the least altered of those surviving in the area. [Waxahachie MRA, A 9/24/86, 86002440]

Joshua Chapel AME Church
110 Ailen
Waxahachie

Joshua Chapel African Methodist Episcopal (AME) Church is a prominent architectural, social, and religious landmark for Waxahachie's black population. Organized in 1876, Joshua Chapel AME Church addressed the social, economic, and educational needs of Waxahachie's black community. In 1917 members of Joshua Chapel AME erected this one-story frame church designed by William Sidney Pittman, a black architect from St. Louis, Missouri. A graduate of Tuskegee University of Alabama and a son-in-law of Booker T. Washington, Pittman designed churches for numerous black congregations throughout the South (see also Tuskegee Institute National Historic Site, Macon County, Alabama).

[Waxahachie MRA, CA 9/24/86, 86002345]

Wyatt Street Shotgun House Historic District

East side of the 300 block of Wyatt Street
Waxahachie

The Wyatt Street Shotgun House Historic District contains a row of small, single-family dwellings built about 1918. The houses stand on narrow lots in an area that has historically been Waxahachie's black community. This row of shotgun dwellings reveals much about lower-class black housing of the early 20th century. The origins of the shotgun dwellings, as noted by folklorist John Vlach, can be traced to tribal Africa. Black slaves who resettled in Haiti were responsible for introducing the house form to the Caribbean. Eventually, the shotgun house made its way to the southern United States, as the slave trade flourished before the Civil War. The first examples in this country were constructed in the mid-19th century for black slaves who worked the plantations of the Mississippi Delta region. In subsequent years the shotgun gained widespread acceptance. The shotgun house retained its popularity well into the 1930s, making it a common vernacular house type of the late 19th and early 20th centuries in the United States. [Waxahachie MRA, CA 9/24/86, 86002463]

HARRIS COUNTY

Antioch Missionary Baptist Church

313 Robin Street
Houston

Organized in January 1866, Antioch Missionary Baptist Church was the first black Baptist church in Houston. In addition, the church is associated with several important leaders in the black community and did pioneering work in the field of black education in Houston. The Reverend I. S. Campbell, a black missionary sent by the Baptist Missionary Society, was Antioch's first minister. In 1868 a friend of Campbell's, the Reverend John Henry Yates, was ordained as the first full-time pastor of Antioch. A native of Virginia, Yates was born a slave and moved to Matagorda County, Texas, in 1863 or 1864. Under Yates's leadership Antioch Baptist Church was a pioneer in the field of education. The church's builder, Richard Allen, was born in Virginia and later moved to Texas. A contractor and bridge builder, Allen was also a prominent political figure. During Reconstruction Allen was elected from Harris County to the 12th legislative session in 1870–71, the first Texas legislature in which African Americans served. Allen constructed a one-story brick building for the congregation, completing it in 1879. The building was enlarged to its present form in the 1890s. The second pastor of Antioch, the Reverend Lights, served the Antioch community from 1894 to 1921. Lights became a recognized leader in local, state, and national religious, educational, and civic affairs. Throughout the 20th century the Antioch Baptist Church has continued to provide leadership in religious, educational, and civic activities. [CA 12/22/76, 76002038]

Freedmen's Town Historic District

Roughly bounded by Genesse, West Dallas, Arthur, and West Gray streets
Houston

The Freedmen's Town Historic District is a 40-block residential area that represents the first settlement of the city's freed slaves. Because this area is the oldest and one of the most important black communities in Houston and because it played a central role in the development of the black community in the late 19th and early 20th centuries, the district has long been considered the "Mother Ward for Black Houston." Founded just after emancipation on the southern banks of Buffalo Bayou, the original Freedmen's Town settlement eventually grew to become the economic, spiritual, and cultural focus of Houston's black community. Within its boundaries lay a thriving black business district and residential neighborhood, Antioch Missionary Baptist Church, the original Colored High School, and the black Carnegie Library. This neighborhood is composed for the most part of frame shotgun houses built between 1870 and 1935, the majority of which were erected as inexpensive rental units to house the ward's black population. [CA 1/17/85, 85000186]

Houston Negro Hospital
3204 Ennis Street
Houston

Completed in 1926, the Houston Negro Hospital, now known as the Riverside General Hospital, is a three-story building in Spanish Colonial Revival style, located within the Third Ward of Houston. Before the opening of the Houston Hospital, the black community of Houston had access to only a few health care facilities. The establishment of Union Hospital in 1919 was the first step in fulfilling the need for a hospital that catered to the black community. The idea to establish a larger hospital was first developed and supported by members of the black community, notably I. M. Terrell, the Union Hospital superintendent and later Houston Negro Hospital's first administrator, and several black physicians including B. J. Covington, Rupert O. Roett, and H. E. Lee. The city of Houston, as recommended by its mayor, donated both the land and the furnishings while a wealthy oil man, J. S.

Culligan, built the hospital building in memory of his son, John Halm Culligan. It was the first nonprofit hospital for black patients in Houston, and it provided a place for well-trained black physicians to work. [A 12/27/82, 82004856]

Houston Negro Hospital School of Nursing Building
Intersection of Holman Avenue and Ennis Street
Houston

The Houston Negro Hospital School of Nursing, built in 1931, is an important landmark in Houston's predominantly black Third Ward. The school's contributions were threefold: it helped to provide staff for Houston Negro Hospital, it enabled nursing students to gain valuable experience, and it was an important institution for training black people in the medical profession. The school building was constructed with money donated by the well-known Houston oil man and philanthropist J. S. Culligan, founder of the Texas Company (Texaco). Anxious to help with the education and training of black citizens, Culligan gave money for the hospital complex "to promote self-help, to inspire good citizenship and for the relief of suffering, sickness and disease amongst them." Culligan also cited the depressed economic conditions due to the Great Depression as another factor in his decision to build the school, since many people needed work. When completed, the school was the city's first residential nursing school for black students. [CA 12/27/82, 82004857]

HOUSTON COUNTY

Mary Allen Seminary for Colored Girls, Administration Building
803 North 4th Street
Crockett

Built in 1886, the Administration

Building of the Mary Allen Seminary for Colored Girls represents black education in rural East Texas. During the 19th century, several educational institutions of higher learning were established in Texas for African Americans. Like virtually all of them, Mary Allen Seminary was founded by a religious denomination. It was established as a seminary for black females by the Board of Missions for Freedmen of the Presbyterian Church, which had its headquarters in Pittsburgh.

In 1924 Byrd R. Smith became the first African American president of the seminary. Smith's appointment also changed the administration of the institution, which until that time had been made up of whites. During his tenure student enrollment increased to 134 students. The school also became an accredited coeducational junior college, enabling its graduates to receive teacher's certificates.

In later years decreased student enrollment, the outbreak of World War II, and Smith's death in 1941 resulted in the sale of the college to the General Baptist Convention of Texas. In February 1978, the Baptist Convention sold it to Stowe Lumber Company, thus ending the 92-year history of the institution. [CA 5/12/83, 83004514]

HUDSPETH COUNTY

Archeological Site No. 41 HZ 227
Address restricted
Sierra Blanca

Site No. 41 HZ 227 is a military camp and possible site of an early morning ambush of the 10th Cavalry Buffalo Soldiers by Apaches on October 28, 1880, an encounter that resulted in the death of seven soldiers. The Ninth and 10th Cavalries were created by General Ulysses S. Grant at the conclusion of the Civil War. Colonels Edward Hatch and Benjamin H. Grierson were assigned to command the experimental units, which were composed of white officers and black recruits, many of whom were former slaves. The 10th Cavalry assumed scouting and patrol duties to prevent the entry of hostile Indians into the United States.

Grierson directed his officers, "You will not refer to this regiment as the Tenth Colored Cavalry but as the Tenth Cavalry. Regardless of the color of their skins, they are soldiers of the U.S. Army." The black soldiers, however, proudly accepted the informal title of Buffalo Soldiers, which they received from their Indian adversaries. It is speculated that the title was based on the similarity of the black soldiers' hair to the fur of the buffalo, and because Indians revered the buffalo, it is thought that the label demonstrated respect for the black soldiers. [Indian Hot Springs MPS, AD 1/11/91, 90002024]

Archeological Site No. 41 HZ 228
Address restricted
Sierra Blanca

Site No. 41 HZ 228 is associated with the 10th Cavalry Buffalo Soldiers, an important late 19th-century black unit of the U.S. Cavalry. The Buffalo Soldiers were instrumental in enforcing law and order on the western frontier. They suppressed civil anarchy, captured Indians, apprehended rustlers, guarded stagecoaches, and constructed roads.

Site No. 41 HZ 228 is a possible military cemetery located near the Indian Hot Springs resort. There appear to be seven graves of stacked native stone at the site. Local tradition states that the seven unmarked graves belong to the Buffalo Soldiers killed in this area by Apaches on October 28, 1880. According to military records, seven men—Corporal William Backus and Privates Carter Burns, George

Mills, Jeremiah D. Griffin, James Stanley, Scott Graves, and Thomas U. Roach—lost their lives on that day. [Indian Hot Springs MPS, AD 1/11/91, 90002025]

Archeological Site No. 41 HZ 439
Address restricted
Sierra Blanca

Site No. 41 HZ 439 contributes to understanding the history of black soldiers on the Texas frontier during the late 19th century. Many of the black soldiers were former slaves, and some had previous service with the U.S. Army. The black soldiers of the Ninth and 10th Cavalries were called Buffalo Soldiers by Apache Indians during the period of conflict between the U.S. Army and the Apaches. Under the command of Lieutenant Robert D. Read, Jr., Buffalo Soldiers from Company B of the 10th Calvary performed mounted picket and patrol duty across the river from Indian Hot Springs. Site No. 41 HZ 439 appears to be the military camp used by Buffalo Soldiers for two scouting trips on October 3 and October 19, 1880. The evidence on the site is associated with patrol activities undertaken by Buffalo Soldiers of the 10th Cavalry during the fall of 1880. Located in the foothills of the Quitman Mountains, it contains a variety of metal objects such as cans, horseshoes, horseshoe nails, pistol and rifle cartridge cases, and cooking utensils. [Indian Hot Springs MPS, D 1/11/91, 90002087]

LIMESTONE COUNTY

Booker T. Washington Emancipation Proclamation Park
West side of Lake Mexia, nine miles west of Mexia
Mexia

Booker T. Washington Emancipation Proclamation Park is the location of the annual "Juneteenth" celebration commemorating the day slaves in Texas were freed. Although President Abraham Lincoln signed the Emancipation Proclamation on January 19, 1863, the order was not implemented in Texas until June 19, 1865, when Major General Gordon Granger of the Union army landed at Galveston and issued a declaration that all slaves were free.

Soon after the Proclamation was read in Galveston, Logan Stroud and his wife, Janie, gathered a group of slaves on their plantation in Limestone County and read the document to them, making them aware of their freedom. Each following year, African Americans in Limestone County gathered on the 19th of June to celebrate the anniversary of their freedom.

The land on which the park is located was purchased in 1898 by a group of African Americans seeking a permanent place to hold the annual celebration. The park is located just two and a half miles from the site of the Stroud plantation. An adjacent 20-acre parcel of land was added to the park in 1900. Originally known as the Nineteenth Ground, the park was renamed in honor of Booker T. Washington in the early 20th century. "Juneteenth" remains a day of celebration for African Americans in Texas. [A 5/24/76, 76002046]

NACOGDOCHES COUNTY

Zion Hill Historic District
Roughly bounded by Park Street, Lanana Creek, Oak Grove Cemetery, and North Lanana Street
Nacogdoches

The Zion Hill Historic District comprises an intact collection of small vernacular frame dwellings dating from the late 19th and early 20th centuries, as well as the Zion Hill Baptist Church and founding pastor's residence. The church and

800 Block of Ernest Street in the Zion Hill Historic District. Photo courtesy of Hardy-Heck-Moore (David Moore).

pastor's residence are the only buildings in the district that possess individual architectural distinction. The district represents the nearly self-contained communities of African Americans that developed in Nacogdoches around the turn of the century.

The district's history closely parallels that of other such black enclaves near and in cities in East Texas and throughout the South after the Civil War. Black communities grew along the edges of established, predominantly white communities so that black workers could live as close as possible to places of employment. The Zion Hill area was home primarily to service workers: shop porters, servants, maids, cooks, and grounds keepers for affluent white families, and, in a few cases, small business owners. The vernacular, wood frame, two-room, shotgun, pyramidal roof, and bungalow houses constructed in

Zion Hill reflect housing types and standards similar to those existing in African American communities throughout the South. [Nacogdoches MPS, CA 1/7/93, 92001759]

TERRELL COUNTY

Bullis' Camp Site
Address restricted
Dryden

From 1877 to 1879 this site served as a temporary base camp for Lieutenant John L. Bullis and his Black-Seminole Indian scouts. From this camp, the scouts launched major military operations against the Indians. The Black-Seminole Indian scouts guarded a road allowing travel into the trans-Pecos region. They also participated in building a railroad, which resulted in settlement in the region and the shipment of cattle to markets in Midwest. Lieutenant Bullis commanded

the unit from 1873 until he was transferred in 1881. The scouts were almost
constantly in the field in 1877 in pursuit
of Mescalero Indians and were very active
in 1879 and 1881. Bullis and his scouts
participated in more than 25 extended
scoutings and engagements with Lipan,
Mescalero, Comanche, and Kickapoo
Indians on both sides of the Rio Grande.
This site may reveal aspects of the social
interaction of the Black-Seminole scouts
and their Anglo officers and illuminate
their material culture. [AD 8/2/78,
78002985]

TOM GREEN COUNTY

Greater St. Paul AME Church
215 West 3rd Street
San Angelo

The black history of San Angelo dates
from the assignment of Buffalo Soldiers
to Fort Concho in the 1880s. The Greater
St. Paul African Methodist Episcopal
(AME) Church was organized in 1883 by
the Reverend J. W. Walker, a former soldier at Fort Concho. St. Paul AME was
the first black church in San Angelo and
has helped establish other churches in the
city. Built in 1927 during a period of
rapid growth in the city, this building
replaced a frame church built about the
time of World War I. Located within a
prominently African American and
Hispanic area, it has been an important
community building and a prominent
institution for several generations of black
citizens in San Angelo. [San Angelo
MRA, A 11/25/88, 88002548]

TRAVIS COUNTY

Clarksville Historic District
Bounded by West Lynn, Waterson, West
10th, and MO-PAC Expressway
Austin

Clarksville is a historic black neighborhood, founded as a rural settlement west
of Austin in the 1870s. After the Civil
War the Reverend Jacob Fontaine, a black
leader, made early attempts to secure land
for settlement of freed slaves. On August
11, 1871, Charles Clark, a former slave,
bought two acres of land on what is today
West 10th Street. The land on which
Clark settled was about half a mile south
of a plantation owned by E. M. Pease, the
governor of Texas from 1853 to 1857, a
Union sympathizer during the Civil War,
and later a Reconstruction governor, who
in the 1870s gave several lots in
Clarksville to some of his former slaves.

Many black settlers followed Clark in
the 1870s to the location west of Austin.
Perhaps the oldest house in the district is
located at 1703 Waterston. The property
was purchased January 1, 1875, by a former slave named Peter Tucker, and the
house was probably built shortly afterward. The house was later owned by
Hezekiah Haskell, a Buffalo Soldier, a
member of the black cavalry units that
were brought to Texas in the 1870s and
1880s to fight the Indians. One of the
most prominent black leaders to live in
Clarksville was Elias Mayes, who served
two terms as a state legislator from Brazos
County. Mayes was one of eight black
legislators sent to the 16th legislative session in 1870 and one of only two black
legislators to the 21st session in 1889. In
1921 Willis S. Edmerson, a contractor,
settled in Clarksville and built several
houses and other buildings in the black
community. He also built several churches in Austin, including the First New
Mount Olive Church, Rosewood Church,
St. Peter's Methodist Church, and
McKinley Heights Church. [CA 7/12/76,
76002070]

Evans Industrial Building
Huston-Tillotson College campus
Austin

Early 20th-century view down Sixth Street in the Sixth Street Historic District. Photo courtesy of the National Register of Historic Places.

Built in 1911, Evans Industrial Building is the oldest building remaining on the campus of Huston-Tillotson College. The college, founded as Tillotson Collegiate and Normal Institute (TCNI), was chartered in 1877 and opened in 1881. It was an indirect outgrowth of the benevolent efforts of the Freedman's Bureau and a direct result of the efforts of the Reverend George Jeffrey Tillotson, who established the school through the American Missionary Association. The purpose of TCNI was

to provide a general academic and industrial education to black students. In an effort to accommodate both educational ideologies, Isaac M. Agard, Huston-Tillotson College president from 1905 to 1918, launched an expansion program to include broader liberal arts training. The construction of Evans Hall realized this commitment. Major Ira Hobart Evans, a member of the Huston-Tillotson College Board of Trustees from 1881 to 1920 and its president from 1911 to 1920, as well as a civic and political leader in

Austin and the state of Texas, provided the major funding and backing for the Evans Industrial Building. [A 6/17/82, 82004525]

McKinney Homestead
Southwest of Austin between Texas Route 71 and U.S. Route 183
Austin

Thomas F. McKinney came to Texas in the early 1820s as one of Austin's first 300 colonists and established the first flour mill in the area. The house, stone fences, and flour mill on his homestead were all built with slave labor. Although McKinney was relatively wealthy when he arrived in Texas, he speculated heavily in cotton and was ruined after the Civil War. McKinney died in 1873, and his widow sold the homestead.

Archeological investigation of the McKinney house reveals it was occupied by rural African Americans in the early 20th century. The cisterns, which were in use until around 1900 and later became filled with household waste, also contain artifacts that may reveal information about rural black life. Although their history has been largely ignored until relatively recently, black farmhands made a considerable contribution to the economy of the Blackland Prairies. Further investigation at the McKinney Homestead may illuminate the role of African Americans in rural Texas in the early 20th century. [D 10/16/74, 74002093]

Sixth Street Historic District
Roughly bounded by 5th, 7th, and Lavaca streets and Interstate 35
Austin

The Sixth Street Historic District reflects black business activity in Austin in the late 19th and early 20th centuries. During the 1870s and 1880s, Sixth Street reached the height of its importance as a major commercial district equal to Congress Avenue, which had a reputation as the most fashionable and prestigious shopping location for certain types of businesses. Numerous black businesses grew along Sixth Street during the 1870s to 1900s. A black physician had an office in the 300 block of East Sixth Street and several businesses on the north side of the 400 and 500 blocks were operated by African Americans who catered to the black community. E. H. Carrington, a former slave who was well known as a leader in the black community, operated a highly successful grocery at 522 East Sixth Street from 1873 to 1907. Louis D. Lyons, Carrington's son-in-law, continued the grocery business through the 1920s. [CA 12/30/75, 75002132]

VICTORIA COUNTY

Townsend-Wilkins House
106 North Navarro
Victoria

The Townsend-Wilkins House is associated with prominent black physicians in Victoria. Initially, it served as the residence of black physician Dr. G. R. Townsend. Townsend practiced medicine from his home until the late 1880s; then he established a medical office at 108 West Santa Rosa. He was a prominent member of the black community during his tenure in Victoria until 1904, when he relocated to Los Angeles. Dr. John H. Wilkins, who established the Lone Star Medical Association, took over Townsend's local medical practice and maintained both his residence and offices in this house. His son, Dr. George Wilkins, eventually took over the practice, working as a physician for 52 years until his death in 1969. [Victoria MRA, CB 12/9/86, 86002605]

Victoria Colored School
702 East Convent
Victoria

The Victoria Colored School is associated with the community's early black education. In 1850, 17 percent of the county's black population resided in Victoria. With emancipation, the majority of African Americans settled in less desirable areas of town near and along the Guadalupe River, such as the Diamond Hill area, which had a substantial black population. Diamond Hill's black residents attended the Victoria Colored School, established by the Victoria Independent School District in 1898–99. In 1901 local contractor Bailey Mills constructed Jules Leffland's design for the Victoria Colored School. Prominent local black educator F. W. Gross was the school's first principal, supervising a faculty of eight teachers. In 1923 the name of the school was changed to Gross School in honor of its first principal. Enrollment increased steadily, and eventually the school outgrew the old building. A new Gross School building was constructed in 1938. The old Victoria Colored School, however, provides a vital link to the history of education in Victoria's black community. [Victoria MRA, A 12/9/86, 86002582]

Webster Chapel United Methodist Church
405 South Wheeler
Victoria

Webster Chapel United Methodist Church was founded for the newly freed slaves in Victoria's Diamond Hill area soon after the Civil War. The Diamond Hill area, in the southeast quadrant of Victoria's original town site, had a substantial black population. The two earliest black congregations in Victoria, the Webster Chapel United Methodist Church and the Palestine Baptist Church, met in this neighborhood, and each built a small frame church in the 1860s. Neither building survives, but the congregation of Webster Chapel built the present frame sanctuary in 1889. It was veneered with brick in the 1930s. Since then, the church has been extensively altered, but it remains an important landmark to the black community of Victoria. [Victoria MRA, A 12/9/86, 86002478]

WILLIAMSON COUNTY
Wesley Chapel AME Church
508 West 4th
Georgetown

Founded in 1869, Wesley Chapel African Methodist Episcopal (AME) Church has owned the land on which the present church stands since 1881. The church is believed to have been built by members of the congregation. It is one the very few extant pre-1935 buildings in Georgetown's historic black neighborhoods. Today Wesley Chapel AME remains important in the black community. [Georgetown MRA, C 11/14/86, 86000204]

UTAH

SALT LAKE COUNTY

Trinity AME Church

239 East 600 South
Salt Lake City

The Trinity African Methodist Episcopal (AME) Church was organized in the 1880s as Utah's first black congregation. The congregants initially met in members' homes and in rented quarters; they began construction on a church building on 1891. The project was interrupted, however, by lack of funds, and the congregation returned to meeting in homes and rented accommodations. The church purchased a lot on which to build a new building in 1907, and in 1909 construction began on the present church using money donated by one of the congregation's members and plans drawn up by another.

Because Salt Lake City's African Americans are such a small minority of the total population, Trinity AME Church has served as a cohesive force and a focus of black social, educational, and religious activity in the black community. The history of the Trinity AME Church is thus a major part of black history in Utah. [A 7/30/76, 76001831]

Trinity AME Church. Photo courtesy of the Utah State Historical Society (Harold Carpenter).

VIRGINIA

ALEXANDRIA (INDEPENDENT CITY)

Franklin and Armfield Office
1315 Duke Street
Alexandria

The slave-trading firm of Franklin and Armfield has been characterized by historians as the most eminent slave-trading firm in the South in the years in which it operated. The firm was founded in 1828 when slave trader Isaac Franklin formed a partnership with John Armfield, whom he had trained in the art of buying and selling slaves. The Alexandria office served as the firm's headquarters. Additional offices were located in Natchez, Mississippi, and New Orleans, Louisiana. Franklin and Armfield trafficked in thousands of slaves every year, transporting them in their own fleet of sailing ships. Upon his retirement from the business, Franklin had amassed considerable wealth; his estate was believed to be valued at $1 million.

The slaves who were brought to the offices were held until their sale in pens that once stood to the rear of the house Despite the removal of the slave pens and interior and exterior alterations, the house retains much of its original appearance. Franklin ceased his operations in Alexandria and sold the house in 1836. The building continued to be occupied by slave traders until the fall of Alexandria to Union troops in 1861. During the Civil War, the house served as a prison for captured Confederate soldiers. Besides Franklin's Fairvue Plantation (see Fairvue Plantation, Maury County, Tennessee), the Alexandria office of Franklin and Armfield is the only remaining building associated with the firm and was designated a National Historic Landmark on June 2, 1978. [A 6/2/78 NHL, 78003146]

ARLINGTON COUNTY

Benjamin Banneker: SW 9 Intermediate Boundary Stone
Intersection of 18th and Van Buren streets
Arlington

Benjamin Banneker (1731–1806) spent almost his entire life in Baltimore County, Maryland (see also Mt. Gilboa Chapel, Baltimore County, Maryland). Despite having little formal education, Banneker acquired an extensive knowledge of mathematics. In 1753 he built what is believed to have been the first working wooden clock in America. Before he constructed the clock, the only

Memorial Church at Hampton Institute, Hampton Independent City. Photo courtesy of the National Historic Landmarks Program.

timepieces Banneker had seen were a sundial and a pocket watch. Banneker soon began to investigate the classical works in the field of astronomy. In 1792 he compiled an almanac for which he produced all the mathematical and astronomical calculations. His almanac drew attention from many learned men of science. Banneker's publications continued for six years and included 28 editions.

In 1798 Banneker was chosen to work with Major Andrew Ellicott to survey the future site of the city of Washington, D.C. Banneker's involvement with the siting of the federal city earned him more fame than perhaps any other African American of the late 18th and early 19th centuries. Since all Banneker's manuscripts and the records of his life were destroyed in a fire in his home on the day of his funeral, the SW 9 Intermediate Boundary Stone of the District of Columbia is one of the few tangible representations of Banneker's work. It was designated a National Historic Landmark on May 11, 1976. [AB 5/11/76 NHL, 76002094]

Charles Richard Drew House
2505 1st Street, South
Arlington

Charles Richard Drew (1904–50) was born in Washington, D.C., in June 1904. He attended Dunbar High School, the District's premier black high school, and went on to attend Amherst College. While at Amherst, Drew decided to pursue a career in medicine. After teaching for a time at Morgan College in Baltimore, Maryland, Drew left to attend medical school at McGill University in Montreal, Canada.

At McGill Drew became acquainted with Dr. John Beattie, the renowned English researcher in blood chemistry, who inspired Drew to enter the field of medical research and teaching. In 1932 Drew graduated second in his class from McGill, earning the degrees of doctor of medicine and master of surgery. The ease with which Drew obtained an internship in Canada, a task that was extremely difficult for black interns in the United States, heightened his awareness of the inadequacies of medical education for African Americans in the United States. During his internship at Montreal General Hospital Drew began his research on blood.

After a year's residency in Montreal, Drew returned to the Washington area, accepting a teaching position at Howard University. In 1938 he received a scholarship for two years of study at Columbia University, where he met Dr. John Scudder, who had been researching the use of blood transfusions as a treatment for shock. Scudder made Drew his assistant in the director's office, where Drew and his aides soon discovered that plasma could be kept without spoilage for the purpose of transfusions. The difficulty of keeping blood from decomposing soon after it was removed from the body had long been a stumbling block to effective blood transfusion.

Drew's discoveries came at an opportune moment, for World War II would soon break out in Europe. Shortly after the beginning of the war, Dr. Beattie from McGill organized the Blood for Britain Program. Unable to make the program successful, Beattie resigned as head and recommended Drew for the position, which Drew accepted. As Germany's planned attack on England was thwarted, the program was disbanded. The United States, however, was soon expected to enter the war, and Drew was chosen to head the drive for plasma in the United States. His position was short-lived, as he resigned over the government's policy of segregating the blood of white donors for white soldiers only and the blood of black donors for black soldiers.

Having received his doctor of science degree in surgery from Columbia in 1940, Drew returned to Howard to head the department of surgery. During his years at Howard, Drew fought to improve educational opportunities for black doctors and open white hospitals to black interns. After the army eliminated its blood segregation policy, Drew returned to its service as a surgical consultant, visiting American bases in Europe to make recommendations for improvement.

Drew was killed in an automobile accident on April 1, 1950, en route to a speaking engagement. His efforts as researcher, physician, and educator were lauded on the floor of the U.S. Senate. The house in Arlington, Virginia, in which Drew lived from 1920 to 1939 stands as a memorial to his endeavors and was designated a National Historic Landmark on May 11, 1976. [B 5/11/76 NHL, 76002095]

AUGUSTA COUNTY

Middlebrook Historic District
Junction of Virginia Routes 252 and 876
Middlebrook

Middlebrook grew up around a major north-south route between Lexington and Staunton. The village, which grew substantially in the 19th century, is one of the oldest and best-preserved rural towns in Augusta County. During the second half of the 19th century, a substantial black community developed at the west end of the town. An 1810 map identifies 10 residential buildings, a school, and a church. Several other black residential units were identified on the north side of town. Today only two houses and the church remain. The black Baptist church, Mt. Edward Colored Baptist Church, is a one-story frame building built around 1886 and continues to be used as a church. Surface archeological investigation reveals the location of other houses that once stood in the area. Further subsurface investigation may provide insight into black material culture in the 19th century and could yield important information concerning the social transitions of black society following emancipation. [CAD 2/10/83, 83003259]

BRUNSWICK COUNTY

St. Paul's College
St. Paul's College campus
Lawrenceville

St. Paul's College was established in 1883 by Episcopalian Church deacon James Solomon Russell to serve the educational and spiritual needs of the region's black community. Russell was born into slavery in Mecklenburg County in 1857, but later attended the Hampton Institute (see also Hampton Institute, Hampton Independent City). Shortly after being ordained a deacon in 1882, Russell was sent to Lawrenceville, where he organized the small group of communicants of St. Andrew's Church into a separate congregation. By 1883 a small frame chapel had been constructed for the congregation's use, and a parochial school was organized in the building's vestry room.

The school soon outgrew its quarters, and a three-room building was erected for the school with funds contributed by the Reverend James Saul of Philadelphia. In September 1888 the St. Paul's Normal and Industrial School was opened in the new building, known as the Saul Building. The school was formally incorporated by the Virginia assembly on March 4, 1890, and grew rapidly. A new Memorial Chapel was constructed in 1904. The chapel, along with the Saul Building and the Fine Arts Building constructed in 1900, formed the early core of St. Paul's College.

As enrollment of pupils from outside the Brunswick County area increased, the curriculum expanded. A collegiate department of teacher training was started in 1922 and accredited by the state in 1926. In 1941 the school's charter was amended to allow for a four-year liberal arts curriculum. The following year, degree programs for the bachelor of science and bachelor of arts degrees were instituted.

In 1957 the school's name was officially changed to St. Paul's College. The Saul Building, the Fine Arts Building, and the Memorial Chapel, the campus' earliest buildings, stand today as a visual reminder of the institution's growth from a one-room parochial school to a four-year liberal arts college. [A 6/27/79, 79003032]

BUCKINGHAM COUNTY

Stanton Family Cemetery
East side of Virginia Route 677, 0.4 mile north of Virginia Route 676
Diana Mills
In 1853 Nancy Stanton of Buckingham County, Virginia, purchased 46.5 acres of land, thus becoming one of the few free black landholders in the region. The social and economic status of the Stanton family, headed by Nancy Stanton and her husband, Daniel, continued to grow as they moved into more prominent occupations, purchased additional land, and acquired material possessions. Nancy Stanton became the first known individual interred in the Stanton Family Cemetery when she died in 1853.

Located on the original family estate, the Stanton Family Cemetery once served as the burial ground for the extended Stanton family. Because the farmstead, consisting of approximately 91.5 acres of land acquired in the 19th century by

Nancy Stanton and her son and grandson, has remained in the family, the cemetery has survived 20th-century growth with little change. The condition of the house and other buildings on the property declined after the family moved in the 1930s, making the cemetery a rare surviving resource that represents the family's distinct cultural role in the county and state.

Many African American cemeteries, both free and slave, have been lost to development, forestation, vandalism, neglect, and agriculture. This cemetery, however, appears to exist in its original state. There are at least 36 burial sites, many of which are marked with slate markers. The simple but distinctive slate markers were probably brought to the cemetery by members of the Stanton family who worked in a nearby slate quarry. The markers occupy their original positions, and the surrounding landscape retains its rural character. The cemetery's size and the fact that it remains remarkably intact make it a rare and significant resource in the African American history of Virginia. [A 4/29/93, 93000350]

CHARLES CITY COUNTY

Lott Cary Birth Site
Northwest of Charles City on Virginia Route 602
Charles City
Lott Cary was born a slave during the American Revolution. This typical late 18th-century farmhouse, which served as the plantation house on the estate of his master, John Bowry, is identified by local tradition as Cary's birthplace. The house is the only remaining building associated with the plantation on which Cary was born and lived.

Cary remained on Bowry's plantation until 1804, when he was hired out as a laborer to the owner of a Shockoe Valley tobacco warehouse. For three years, Cary led an unproductive life marked by frequent drunkenness. In 1807 he became a member of the First Baptist Church of Richmond and was converted and baptized. After his religious conversion, Cary taught himself to read and write by memorizing New Testament passages. His conversion led to improved work habits that earned him a promotion. His industriousness secured him cash bonuses and the privilege of selling loose tobacco for his own profit. Cary managed to save $850, which he used to purchase freedom for himself and his children in 1813. That same year, Cary was awarded a license to preach from the First Baptist Church.

Inspired by Luther Rice, a white Baptist missionary, Cary was ordained a minister and organized the Baptist Missionary Society in 1815. He preached for a number of years, but his life was profoundly changed after reading an 1819 publication describing the exploration of Sierra Leone by Samuel John Mills, Jr., an agent of the American Colonization Society. The society had successfully established a small colony of American free blacks in Sierra Leone. Cary was fascinated with the prospect of returning free blacks to Africa, where they could be free from judgment based on the color of their skin. In 1821, under the auspices of the American Colonization Society, he and his colleague Colin Teague gathered a small group of free blacks from Virginia and sailed for Liberia.

Upon his arrival in Liberia, Cary founded the Providence Baptist Church of Monrovia. Soon he extended his missionary work by establishing Christian schools for natives in the interior. He had difficulty, however, as a rift developed between Cary and Jehudi Ashmun, one of the principal white founders of the colony. Tensions were further exacerbated by financial decline and an attack on the colony by native tribespeople in 1822. Cary bravely defended the colony during the attack but for unknown reasons aroused the suspicions of Ashmun. The two eventually reconciled, and Cary agreed to serve as the American Colonization Society's vice-agent and acting governor.

Ashmun left the colony in 1828 and was succeeded by Cary. Cary's leadership of the colony was short-lived, however; he was killed in a gunpowder explosion while again defending the colony on November 10, 1828.

As the only existing property known to be associated with Cary, the house and its unadorned rural setting have become the focal point of local sentiment regarding Cary. The property also represents the important contribution of black Virginians to the commonwealth during the early national period. [A 7/30/80, 80004883]

CHARLOTTESVILLE (INDEPENDENT CITY)

Mount Zion Baptist Church
105 Ridge Street
Charlottesville

The congregation of Mount Zion Baptist Church was organized in 1864, when both enslaved and free African Americans petitioned to leave the white Baptist churches, where they were relegated to the galleries, and form their own church. The group first met in homes of the members and later in an old hotel. In 1878 the hotel was demolished, and the congregation built the present church on the site. Completed in 1884, the church played an especially significant role after the Civil War in preparing the freed blacks for the new society emerging during the Reconstruction era, as the black church became the social center, school, and general meetinghouse for the black community. Mount Zion Baptist Church was built in an area where both black and white families lived. Many of the area's historic resources were obliterated by an urban renewal project in the 1960s. The Mount Zion Baptist Church is the only remaining resource associated with the black members of the community. [A 10/15/92, 92001388]

CHESTERFIELD COUNTY

Azurest South
2900 Boisseau Street
Petersburg

Completed in 1939, Azurest South is one of only a few International Style residences in Virginia. It is the work of Amaza Lee Meredith, one of the country's few black female architects of the time. Amaza Lee Meredith was born near Lynchburg, Virginia, in 1895. She received her teaching certificate from the Virginia Normal and Industrial Institute (later Virginia State University), Virginia's first black state-supported institution for higher education. She returned to the college to earn her teaching degree in 1922. After several years of teaching in rural black schools in Virginia, Meredith moved to New York and attended Columbia University. She received her bachelor's degree in fine arts in 1930 and her master's degree in 1934. While pursuing her degrees, Meredith taught intermittently at Virginia State, becoming the chairman of the art department in 1935. It was in the late 1930s that she began her design for Azurest South.

Azurest South was built as a residence for herself and her companion, Edna Meade Colson, also a faculty member at Virginia State. At the time she designed Azurest South, Meredith had a small architectural practice, designing homes for family and friends. Perhaps the largest

assemblage of her projects can be found at Sag Harbor on Long Island, a resort community for wealthy white families. Here she and her family and friends created Azurest North, an enclave of vacation homes for middle-class African Americans. She continued to work on design commissions at Sag Harbor until the 1970s.

During the early years of her architectural practice, few African Americans received degrees in architecture or had established practices. The number of African American women practicing architecture was even smaller. Meredith's use of the International Style in her design reflects her knowledge of prevailing architectural trends, which were greatly influenced at the time by European modernism. Azurest South was constructed using the most modern building materials available at the time and is a rare example of International Style residential architecture in Virginia.

After her death in 1984, one-half interest in the building was left to Colson and one-half to the Virginia State University National Alumni Association. Following Colson's death in 1986, the university acquired the other half-interest. The house is now used for meetings and social functions held by the alumni association. [C 12/30/93, 93001464]

Vawter Hall and Old President's House
Virginia State University campus
Ettrick

Vawter Hall and the Old President's House are the two oldest institutional buildings on the campus of Virginia State University. Chartered by the Virginia General Assembly in 1882 as the Virginia Normal and Collegiate Institute, the school is the country's oldest state-supported college for black students.

The law incorporating the school provided teacher training of up to three years, as well as a four-year college program in classics, higher mathematics, and other humanities. In February 1883 a 33-acre farm was purchased on which to build the campus. Until the construction of the first building, Virginia Hall, in 1888, classes were held in the farmhouse standing on the property. In the same year, James Hugh Johnston became president of the college. Adhering to the educational philosophy of Booker T. Washington, Johnston emphasized vocational training. Courses in carpentry, cooking, sewing, and shoemaking were added to the curriculum in the 1890s.

Johnston served as president of the college for 26 years. During his tenure, he was able to ward off criticism by opponents of black education and restore funding that had been cut before his arrival at the college. The Old President's House was constructed in 1906 and Vawter Hall in 1908 following full restoration of funding provided in the original 1882 act. These two buildings, along with the no longer extant Virginia Hall and Johnston Hall, formed the academic and administrative heart of the college.

In 1920 the school became a land-grant college. In 1930 the college began to receive federal funds and was renamed the Virginia State College for Negroes. In 1979 the school became Virginia State University. [CA 5/7/80, 80004180]

CULPEPER COUNTY

Madden's Tavern
Virginia Route 610
Lignum

Madden's Tavern is one of the few small rural taverns that survives from the antebellum period in Virginia. Constructed around 1840, the tavern was designed, built, and operated by Willis Madden, a free black. Madden worked his way out of poverty, taking up a variety of trades such as farm laborer, blacksmith, nail maker, distiller, cobbler, and teamster. He purchased the land on which the tavern stands and constructed the building around 1840, becoming a respected proprietor of a business that was traditionally run by whites. Madden's Tavern was the only known black-owned and -operated tavern in the Virginia Piedmont before the Civil War and was a popular stopping place for white travelers to the up-country. The building stands as evidence of early rural Virginia black entrepreneurship, as well as a monument to its ambitious builder. Although troop raids during the Civil War destroyed the outbuildings and dealt the business a blow from which it could not recover, the family continued to use the building as a dwelling. The property remains in the hands of Madden's descendants. [A 8/16/84, 84003526]

DANVILLE (INDEPENDENT CITY)

Downtown Danville Historic District
Roughly bounded by Memorial Drive and High, Patton, and Ridge streets
Danville

Development in downtown Danville from 1793 through the 19th century was a result of the regional expansion of tobacco production and innovations in its cultivation and manufacture. Known as the "Last Capital of the Confederacy" owing to the brief sojourn there of the Confederate government after the evacuation of Richmond, Danville escaped the Civil War relatively unscathed and entered Reconstruction with a competitive advantage over the devastated tobacco centers of Petersburg and Richmond, Virginia. Danville emerged as the dominant tobacco center in Virginia and North Carolina by 1880 and developed a thriving commercial center.

Danville's African American community became active in the commercial life of the downtown at an early date, with the earliest black business, a barbershop, believed to have been established by the 1850s. In the early 1880s, during a period of African American participation in local government, black merchants rented 20 of 24 stalls in the city market. Small black commercial enclaves developed along South Market Street and North Union Street. Among the Union Street businesses was the Danville Savings Bank and Trust Company. Established in 1919 and located at 201 Union Street after 1924, the bank was one of only a few black-owned Virginia banks to weather the Great Depression and today is one of the oldest continuously operating black banks in Virginia. [CA 8/12/93, 93000830]

FAIRFAX COUNTY

Frying Pan Meetinghouse
2615 Centreville Road
Floris

The Frying Pan Meetinghouse was built sometime between 1783 and 1791 to house a local Baptist congregation. The meetinghouse takes its name from nearby Frying Pan Run. The building was erected by members of the congregation without help from an architect or professional builder. The Frying Pan Meetinghouse is particularly significant to black history because it was an early institution that served a mixed congregation. It was customary for 18th- and early 19th-century Baptist congregations to include African Americans as members. From 1791 to 1867 free blacks as well as slaves became members of Frying Pan. They spoke of their religious experiences in congrega-

tional meetings, were baptized in Frying Pan Run, and were buried in the cemetery. By 1840 Frying Pan had 29 black members and 33 white members. The meetinghouse is a rare documented property related to the religious life of 18th- and 19th-century members of the rural community, both black and white. [CA 2/5/91, 91000016]

FLUVANNA COUNTY

Bremo Slave Chapel
North of Bremo Bluff
Bremo Bluff

The Bremo Slave Chapel, which now serves as the parish hall of Grace Episcopal Church, was constructed in 1835 as a slave chapel for Bremo, the vast plantation belonging to John Hartwell Cocke. Although slave chapels were often found on plantations in the Deep South, the Bremo Slave Chapel is the only known existing slave chapel in Virginia. Cocke constructed the chapel out of concern about the religious well-being of his slaves. This concern arose from his attempt to reconcile the moral and practical issues related to the institution of slavery.

Cocke established Bremo Plantation in 1801. Although opposed to slavery in principle, he felt immediate emancipation was impractical. Cocke worked actively in the movement to encourage voluntary emigration of African Americans to Africa. For those who remained enslaved, however, he felt that it was the duty of the slaveholder to prepare slaves for their eventual freedom and that religious instruction was an important element of this preparation.

The slaves at Bremo were assembling for worship as early as 1821. In 1825 Cocke constructed a brick building on the plantation for educational and religious instruction for his slaves. The slaves received instruction from several young missionaries and Cocke's wife, Louisa. Cocke constructed the current building in 1835 and dedicated it to religious worship. After the Civil War, the building fell into disuse.

At Cocke's death in 1866, the plantation passed to his sons. Sometime between 1882 and 1884, the Cocke family gave the building to the Episcopalian community of Bremo Bluff for use as a church, and the chapel was moved to its present location. The chapel housed Grace Church until 1924, when a new church was built. Since then, the chapel has served as Grace Church's parish hall. [CA 3/17/80, 80004189]

FRANKLIN COUNTY

Booker T. Washington National Monument
15 miles east of Rocky Mount on Virginia Route 122
Rocky Mount

Booker T. Washington National Monument commemorates the life of the black leader who achieved international fame as an educator, speaker, and writer. The monument is located on the site of the old Burroughs plantation, a modest plantation at the foot of the Blue Ridge Mountains that was typical of mid-19th-century plantations in the area. It was here that Booker T. Washington was born into slavery in 1856.

Booker T. Washington was nine years old when the Emancipation Proclamation was issued. At the age of 17, he traveled from West Virginia to the Hampton Institute, where he worked as a janitor to pay for his education there (see also Hampton Institute, Hampton Independent City). He went on to become a teacher at the institute, and at age 25 he received an appointment to organize a normal school for black students at Tuskegee, Alabama. It was his dynamic leadership at Tuskegee that brought him international recognition. The Tuskegee Institute was the physical embodiment of Washington's philosophy of self-help through manual training for the advancement of his race. The school was the impetus for the establishment of many manual training schools for African Americans, especially in the South, but also across the nation (see also Tuskegee Institute National Historic Site, Macon County, Alabama).

Congress authorized Booker T. Washington National Monument by an act approved April 2, 1956. The monument features a replica of the cabin in which he was born. The site represents the humble origins from which Washington rose to international fame following his own philosophy of self-help. Booker T. Washington National Monument was designated a National Historic Landmark on October 15, 1966. [B 10/15/66 NPS, 66000834]

GLOUCESTER COUNTY

Holly Knoll
Off RR 662
Capahosic

Holly Knoll is the retirement home of Robert Russa Moton (1867–1940), successor of Booker T. Washington at Hampton Institute and at Tuskegee Institute (see also Hampton Institute, Hampton Independent City; and Tuskegee Institute National Historic Site, Macon County, Alabama). Moton spent the last five years of his life at Holly Knoll, the only existing residence known to be associated with him.

Robert Moton was born on August 26, 1867 in Amelia County, Virginia, the only son of Booker and Emily Brown Moton. As a boy, he lived on the plantation of Samuel Vaughan in Prince

Edward County, Virginia, where his father "led the hands" and his mother was a cook. Upon learning that Moton's mother had begun teaching him to read, Vaughan encouraged the boy's education, providing him with instruction from the Vaughan family's youngest daughter. Although Moton attended a free black school when it opened in the community, his early schooling was punctuated by absences of up to two years as he took on manual labor jobs.

Moton entered Hampton Institute in 1885 at the age of 19. After graduating in 1890, he became commandant in charge of military discipline at the school and held this position for 25 years. Although his title implies a limited scope of responsibilities, Moton's work included serving as Hampton's principal representative in conferences and commissions sponsored by the institute.

After Booker T. Washington's death in 1915, Moton was chosen to succeed Washington as principal of Tuskegee Institute. One of Moton's most significant achievements while at Tuskegee was to use the school's influence to support the establishment of the Colored Officers Training Camp at Fort Des Moines, Iowa, in 1917. Meeting with Secretary of War Newton T. Baker, he secured the appointment of an African American, Emmet J. Scott, as assistant to Baker.

Moton served as an adviser on federal appointees to Presidents Wilson, Harding, Coolidge, Hoover, and Franklin D. Roosevelt. In 1927 he served as a member of the Hoover Commission on the Mississippi Valley Flood Disaster. He traveled to Haiti in 1930 as chairman of the U.S. Commission on Education in Haiti.

Moton was awarded honorary degrees from Oberlin and Williams Colleges and from Harvard, Virginia Union, Wilberforce, and Howard Universities. In 1930 he was honored with the Harmon Award for his contributions to improving race relations, and in 1932 he was awarded the Spingarn Medal. Robert Moton died at Holly Knoll on May 31, 1940, and was buried at Hampton Institute. Holly Knoll was designated a National Historic Landmark on December 21, 1981. [B 12/21/81 NHL, 81000640]

HAMPTON (INDEPENDENT CITY)

Hampton Institute
Northwest of junction of U.S. Route 60 and the Hampton Roads Bridge Tunnel
Hampton

The Hampton Normal and Industrial Institute was founded in 1868 by Samuel Chapman Armstrong. Armstrong, a brigadier general in the Civil War, was appointed an agent of the Freedmen's Bureau in 1866, when he took charge of a large camp of newly freed blacks near the town of Hampton. Armstrong had led black troops during the war and was impressed with their abilities. This experience was the impetus for the founding of his manual training school for freedmen. He convinced the American Missionary Association to purchase a 150-acre estate for the new school, and the Hampton Normal and Industrial Institute opened with two teachers and 15 students in April 1868.

Hampton was coeducational. Before the construction of permanent shelters, the girls lived in wooden barracks and the boys in tents. The students themselves constructed many of the original buildings at Hampton, working to pay their monthly $10 room and board fee. In 1878 the school admitted a group of 17 Native American students as well. Armstrong felt that the Native American students could benefit from instruction that was unavailable to them elsewhere.

The "Wigwam," the dormitory originally built for the Native American students is still known as such. By 1899 there were nearly 1,000 students at Hampton, and of these, 135 were Native Americans.

The Hampton Institute quickly became a model for other schools established during Reconstruction. The most influential and well known of these was the Tuskegee Institute in Alabama, founded by Hampton's most famous alumnus, Booker T. Washington (see also Booker T. Washington National Monument, Franklin County; and Tuskegee Institute National Historic Site, Macon County, Alabama).

Since its founding, Hampton has been a leader in the education of black youth. In the 20th century, the school changed from primarily a vocational school to a fully accredited liberal arts college with an international faculty and student body. Several of the early campus buildings are now a part of a historic district, which was designated a National Historic Landmark district on May 30, 1974. [A 11/12/69 NHL, 69000323]

Little England Chapel
4100 Kecoughtan Road
Hampton

Little England Chapel was constructed by students of the nearby Hampton Institute between 1878 and 1880 for use as a Sunday school for black children. The property on which the chapel stands was part of a larger 35-acre tract that had been donated to the students after 1868 by Daniel F. Cock, a white missionary from New York. Cock was an instructor at the Hampton Institute, where he taught agriculture to Native Americans. The tract was set aside for the purpose of establishing a community for freed blacks, which became known as Cock's Newtown. The chapel was erected to serve the children of the Newtown area. By 1890 its Sunday school, which made quilts for a new hospital in the area, had become renowned as a sewing school.

The school was expanded in 1893 and again in 1910. Hampton students taught in the Sunday school until the mid-1930s. In 1954 Daniel Cock's son deeded the chapel and the land on which it stands to the Newtown Improvement Club, an organization of area black residents. At the time of its listing in the National Register the building was being used by the Church of Jesus for religious services.

Little England Chapel is the only known existing black missionary chapel in Virginia. It not only is representative of the many community institutions established in Hampton by African Americans after the Civil War, but also symbolizes the significant role that the Hampton Institute played in the local African American community. [CA 7/8/82, 82004564]

William H. Trusty House
76 West County Street
Hampton

William H. Trusty was born to free black parents in 1862. In 1871 the family moved to Hampton, where Trusty secured employment at the James A. Watkins General Store at Fort Monroe. Trusty's thrift and diligence allowed him to accumulate capital with which to purchase property in the Phoebus neighborhood of Hampton. This area was considered of great strategic value to Union forces during the Civil War because of its proximity to Fort Monroe. As the area was occupied by the Union army, it became a haven for emancipated slaves. In the decades following the war, the black population increased greatly. Trusty built his Queen Anne style residence on County Street in Phoebus in 1897. In

1901 Phoebus was incorporated as a town, and Trusty was elected to the town council. At this time, Trusty was operating his own bar on property he owned on a nearby street. In addition to his business property and the property on which his home stood, Trusty owned several other residential properties in Phoebus. His elaborately decorated home on County Street is a symbol of Trusty's political, social, and economic success in postbellum Phoebus. [CB 6/22/79, 79003280]

HENRICO COUNTY

Meadow Farm
Intersection of Mountain and
Courtney roads
Glen Allen

Meadow Farm was built in the late 18th century and was the home of the Sheppard family throughout the 19th century. On August 30, 1800, the owner of the property, Mosby Sheppard, was warned by two of his slaves that the slaves on the neighboring farm of Thomas Prosser were planning an insurrection. The plot was devised by a slave named Gabriel, and its ultimate goal was the capture of Richmond. Upon learning of the plan, Sheppard informed Governor James Monroe, who thwarted the rebellion before it could begin. News of the planned insurrection resulted in widespread hysteria among slaveholders in Virginia and across the South and led to the execution of 41 slaves. The two slaves who reported the plot to Sheppard, Pharaoh and Tom, were purchased by the commonwealth of Virginia and granted their freedom. [CA 8/13/74, 74002125]

Virginia Randolph Cottage
2200 Mountain Road
Glen Allen

Built in 1937, the Virginia Randolph Cottage was the home of Virginia E. Randolph (1874–1958), the first Negro Rural School Fund, better known as Jeanes Fund, teacher. The Jeanes Fund was established under the will of Anna T. Jeanes, a wealthy Philadelphia Quaker, to provide black education in southern rural schools.

The daughter of former slaves, Randolph was born in Richmond, Virginia, where she attended the Baker Elementary and Armstrong High Schools for African Americans. Around 1890 she completed a teacher training course, and two years later she accepted a teaching post at Mountain Road School in Henrico County.

While teaching at Mountain Road School, Randolph won the support of county school supervisor Jackson Davis because of her emphasis on industrial, agricultural, and domestic training. Davis and Randolph visited the county's black schools and trained other teachers. When Davis acquired financial assistance from James H. Dillard, director of the newly endowed Jeanes Fund, Randolph became the first Jeanes teacher in 1908 and the model for all those who followed.

In addition to her work as a Jeanes teacher, Randolph devoted time to the Virginia Randolph Training School until her retirement in 1949. In 1969 the Henrico County Board of Education converted the school into a museum honoring her. Following her death in 1958, Randolph was buried on the grounds. The Virginia Randolph Cottage was designated a National Historic Landmark on December 2, 1974. [B 12/2/74 NHL, 74002126]

LOUDOUN COUNTY

Douglass High School
408 East Market Street
Leesburg

Until the construction of the Douglass High School in 1941, black students in Loudoun County occupied quarters within the building known as the Loudoun County Training School. The training school building was an antiquated frame building lacking proper safety features. Only a sparse curriculum was offered; lack of proper equipment made courses in laboratory sciences and even home economics impossible. Because the school lacked any sort of accreditation, black children who hoped to attend college had to seek an education in expensive private schools.

In response to these conditions, the County-Wide League, comprising parent-teacher associations from black schools in the county, was formed. In the late 1930s the league began to seek land on which to construct a new facility. In 1939, after an exhaustive fund-raising campaign, the group was able to purchase eight acres of land on the outskirts of Leesburg. In December 1940 the property was sold to the school board for the nominal sum of $1, with the stipulation that a new facility for black students would be built.

The new building opened in September 1941, but the school board provided only the barest necessities, such as desks, for the classrooms. Once again, it was incumbent upon the County-Wide League to raise money for curtains, laboratory equipment, home economics equipment, musical instruments, and numerous other items.

The building continued in use as a black school until 1968, when all schools in the county were desegregated and it was converted for use as a middle school. Douglass High School's active alumni association boasts a number of prominent graduates who could not have reached their potential had Loudoun County's black citizens not worked so hard to acquire the land and see that the school was built. The school stands as a tangible symbol of the black struggle for equal rights in education in Loudoun County. [A 9/24/92, 92001274]

LYNCHBURG (INDEPENDENT CITY)

Court Street Baptist Church
Intersection of 6th and Court streets
Lynchburg

The congregation of the Court Street Baptist Church was organized in 1843, when the African Baptist Church officially separated from the First Baptist Church. The congregation was housed in several different locations before it purchased the land for the present building in 1878. The site chosen by the congregation was located on one of Lynchburg's most fashionable streets, a fact not ignored by the town's white community. Despite the attempts of many whites to prevent the sale of the property, the black congregation prevailed, and construction on the building began in 1879. The church was designed by white architect R. C. Burkholder. The construction was carried out, however, by exclusively black labor and was completed in 1880. Many of the decorations and furnishings in the church were crafted by black artisans as well. At its completion, the church was the largest edifice in the city, and its spire was the tallest feature in the downtown skyline. Court Street still houses a large and active congregation and stands as Lynchburg's chief black architectural landmark. [CA 7/8/82, 82004569]

Anne Spencer House
1313 Pierce Street
Lynchburg

During her long and productive life, Anne Spencer (1882–1975) was recognized as a lyric poet of considerable talent.

Since her death, she has attained fame not only as a writer, but as a cultural leader. Given that she was both black and female, her achievement of recognition from her intellectual peers was a remarkable feat.

Anne Spencer was born in February 1882 on a plantation in Henry County, Virginia. Her father was a former slave, and her mother was the daughter of a former slave and a wealthy Virginia aristocrat. In 1886 she and her mother moved to Bramwell, West Virginia, where she lived until entering the Virginia Seminary and Normal School in Lynchburg in 1893. At the age of 17, she graduated as valedictorian of her class. In 1901 she married Edward Alexander Spencer, and the couple moved to the house on Pierce Street in Lynchburg.

Anne Spencer's devotion to the cause of cultural enlightenment for African Americans was expressed in her local activities as librarian and educator and in the lively rapport she maintained with many of the nation's most noted black leaders. Among the prominent visitors to the house were Langston Hughes, Countee Cullen, Georgia Douglas Johnston, W. E. B. Du Bois, Dr. Martin Luther King, Jr., Thurgood Marshall, and Adam Clayton Powell, Jr.

The house and the small study in the garden where she worked were built largely by Edward Spencer. Both remain virtually undisturbed, containing original decorations, furniture, books, and personal belongings in place as Anne Spencer kept them. [B 12/6/76 NHL, 76002224]

MONTGOMERY COUNTY

Big Spring Baptist Church
Virginia Route 631, 0.1 mile east of U.S. Route 460/11
Elliston

Big Spring Baptist Church was built around 1880. The nave plan of the church represents a regional architectural style that departs from the plain, boxlike form most typical of rural churches in the region. Big Spring, the first black church in Elliston, was organized with the support of Captain Charles Schaeffer, a northern Quaker educator who came to the area in the post-Civil War era to found a school for the education of freed slaves. Big Spring was one of several Baptist churches founded by Schaeffer in the county. Of the 13 churches in the region built during the period of Big Spring's construction, Big Spring is the largest and most sophisticated in design. With the exception of the Schaeffer Memorial Baptist Church in Christiansburg, also founded by Schaeffer, it is the most substantial church building in the county, reflecting the commitment and high standards of Schaeffer and the black community. [Montgomery County MPS, CA 11/13/89, 89001809]

NEWPORT NEWS (INDEPENDENT CITY)

J. Thomas Newsome House
2803 Oak Avenue
Newport News

Joseph Thomas Newsome was the 16th of the 17 children born to Joseph and Martha Newsome of Sussex County, Virginia. He attended the Virginia Normal and Collegiate Institute and went on to graduate from Howard University as valedictorian of the law school class of 1899. In 1913 he purchased this Oak Avenue house from Dr. William R. Granger, one of the first members of the black professional community in Newport News. Newsome went on to distinguish himself as one of that group.

Newsome was an ardent community activist, instrumental in the founding of Trinity Baptist Church and the construction of Huntington High School. He was committed to local politics and unified the local black community by organizing the Colored Voters League of Warwick County, an endeavor for which he was rewarded with the position of sergeant at arms for the Republican National Convention of 1920. His greatest professional achievement came in 1913, when he became the first black attorney certified to practice before the Supreme Court of Appeals of Virginia. Newsome died in 1942. His home in Newport News stands as an architectural reminder of the town's most distinguished black citizen. [B 12/19/90, 90001831]

NORFOLK (INDEPENDENT CITY)

Attucks Theatre
1008–1012 Church Street
Norfolk

The Attucks Theatre is a rare example of an early motion picture theater in Virginia financed, designed, and built exclusively by and for African Americans. The theater was erected by a group of black businessmen who operated theaters in Portsmouth and Norfolk and financed by two black financial institutions in the Tidewater area. A prominent landmark on Church Street, the fashionable main street of Norfolk's black community between World War I and the Great Depression, the building was meant to accommodate not only the theater, but also various retail shops and professional offices. Erected in 1919, the building was designed by black architect Harvey N. Johnson, who, along with prominent black architect Charles T. Russell, supervised the construction of the building. The theater's original fire curtain, painted with scenes of the death of its namesake Crispus Attucks, an African American and the first American casualty of the Revolutionary War, still

survives in the building. [CA 9/16/82, 82004575]

First Baptist Church
418 East Bute Street
Norfolk

The congregation of the First Baptist Church in Norfolk was organized in 1800 and included whites, free blacks, and slaves. Church membership grew steadily, and by 1816 the church listed a large number of black congregants in its register. The presence of a great number of African Americans in their midst did not set well with a number of the white congregants, who elected to form their own congregation. The black congregation continued to worship in the building and were led by a white pastor. In 1830 three free black trustees of the church purchased the present Bute Street site and erected a sanctuary known as the "Old Salt Box."

The congregation continued to practice in that church during the occupation of Norfolk during the Civil War. In 1862 the Reverend Lewis Tucker became First Baptist Church's first black pastor. For 30 years Norfolk's old downtown area housed the largest concentration of African Americans in the city and was served by the First Baptist Church. The present Romanesque Revival style church building was built in 1906 during a period of substantial local economic growth and was hailed in the *Virginian-Pilot* as the "handsomest church in the South." [CA 7/21/83, 83003297]

First Calvary Baptist Church
1036–1040 Wide Street
Norfolk

First Calvary Baptist Church was organized in 1880, and the congregation rented a small vacant frame church on Church Street for their sanctuary. They worshiped in the rented building until 1916, when the present building was dedicated. The new church was constructed at a cost of $43,065 by the Norfolk firm of Mitchell and Wilcox. Few families that belonged to First Calvary commanded high incomes. Nonetheless the congregation managed to pay the building costs in two years. The Second Renaissance Revival style building is one of only a few such churches found in the Norfolk/Tidewater area. Its most distinctive features are the generous use of terra cotta in its facade and its stained-glass dome supported by massive arches. These features serve to make First Calvary an architectural landmark, placing it among the best early 20th-century black churches in Virginia. The church congregation has grown and prospered among Norfolk's large and active black Baptist community, which continues to regard the church as a major focal point of black cultural and spiritual life in the city. [CA 10/15/87, 87001853]

St. John's African Methodist Episcopal Church
539–545 East Bute Street
Norfolk

The congregation of St. John's African Methodist Episcopal (AME) Church was formed by the black members of the Cumberland Street Methodist Church in 1800. The black congregants obtained their independence in 1863 and became an AME church in 1864. Through its own efforts, the congregation raised enough money to construct the present church in 1888. At the time it was built, St. John's was the largest black church edifice in Norfolk and the earliest in a series of churches erected in the city in the Richardsonian Romanesque style. The church was designed by Charles M. Cassell, hailed as one of Norfolk's leading late 19th- and early 20th-century archi-

tects, and was constructed by African Americans. Since its founding, St. John's has retained an active and influential role in Virginia AME Church affairs. [CA 12/4/86, 86003441]

NORTHUMBERLAND COUNTY

Holley Graded School
U.S. Route 360 north of Virginia Route 614
Lottsburg

The Holley Graded School was established in 1869 as a school for the children of former slaves. It was founded by Sallie Holley, a white New York native who was an ardent abolitionist and advocate of women's rights, temperance, and universal suffrage. Holley opened the school at the suggestion of her friend Emily Howland, who had recently established a school of her own (see also Howland Chapel School).

In 1869 Holley purchased the parcel of land on which the school stands. Along with her friend Caroline Putnam, and assisted by the local black community, she built and maintained the school. The original Holley School, a one-room building constructed in 1869, was replaced in 1878 and again in 1887. The 1887 building was expanded to three rooms by 1910 but had become dilapidated. Putnam, who had been managing the school since Sally Holley's death in 1893, joined with the local black community to plan a new building.

The present school was built with funds, material, and labor supplied completely by the local black community. Farmers in the neighborhood felled large pines on their property and hauled them to the sawmill, where they were cut into boards and timbers and set aside to use for building the school. Members of the community made trips to a nearby wharf to haul concrete blocks used in the

Howland Chapel School. Photo courtesy of the Virginia Historic Landmarks Commission.

building's foundation. Local black carpenters, metal roofers, and electricians volunteered their labor. Their efforts were coordinated by Henry Burgess, a locally prominent black carpenter who constructed the nearby Zion Church and probably influenced the design of the school.

At the time of its completion, the Holley School was the largest black elementary school in the county. It operated as a school until 1959, when a new modern brick consolidated school for black students was constructed in nearby Lottsburg. The school stood empty until the mid-1960s, when it was converted for use as a community gathering place. The building was completely restored in 1988–89 and stands as a testament to the commitment of the black community that built the school to provide a high-quality education for their children despite their limited means. [C 12/19/90, 89001934]

Howland Chapel School

Junction of Virginia Routes 201 and 642
Heathsville

The Howland Chapel School was built in 1867 to serve the children of former slaves and is the oldest standing schoolhouse in Northumberland County. The one-story frame building was erected by New York educator, reformer, and philanthropist Emily Howland. Howland was the daughter of a wealthy Quaker merchant who worked in the abolition movement and whose home served as a stop on the Underground Railroad. Howland herself became active in the abolition movement and moved to Washington, D.C., in 1858 to teach at Myrtilla Miner's School for black girls (see also Miner Normal School, District of Columbia). At the end of the Civil War, Howland took a keen interest in the welfare of the newly freed slaves. The

Howland Chapel grew out of this interest.

Erected by local carpenters and laborers, the school was unusually large and well-built at a time when both black and white Virginia children attended school in cramped, cheaply built structures. Howland Chapel was used continuously as a schoolhouse from 1867 to 1958 and as a Baptist house of worship from 1867 to about 1920. The building has been restored for use as a museum, community center, and adult education facility. [CB 1/25/91, 90002206]

PORTSMOUTH (INDEPENDENT CITY)

Portsmouth Historic District (Boundary Increase)
Intersection of Green and Queen streets
Portsmouth

The town of Portsmouth was founded in 1752, when Colonel William Crawford set aside approximately 65 acres on his plantation on the Elizabeth River to be laid out for a town. The Portsmouth Historic District was listed on the National Register of Historic Places in 1970. The boundaries of the district were increased, however, in 1983 to include a residential neighborhood dating from the late 19th and early 20th centuries. This added area contains a row of five houses that have historically been occupied by black residents. The extension also includes the Emmanuel African Methodist Episcopal (AME) Church, an important post-Civil War black institution. The first church built by and for African Americans in the city, Emmanuel AME houses the oldest black congregation in southeastern Virginia. The extension of the boundaries of the Portsmouth Historic District represents a growing awareness of the need to acknowledge the role of African Americans in the development of Portsmouth and the history of Virginia. [CA 10/6/83, 83004251]

Truxtun Historic District
Portsmouth and Deep Creek boulevards and Manly, Dahlin, Hobson, Dewey, and Bagley streets
Portsmouth

The 43-acre community of Truxtun was developed between 1918 and 1920 as the first wartime government housing project in the United States constructed exclusively for African Americans. The community was built to relieve the severe housing shortage resulting from the expansion of activities and personnel at the nearby Norfolk Naval Shipyard after the outbreak of World War I. Truxtun was built on the west side of the naval yard, and Cradock, a community for white workers and their families, was built to the south. The segregation of the two housing projects was in accordance with federal policy at the time.

A total of 250 five-room units were built in Truxtun. To create diversity in the project's design, Truxtun planners employed a random distribution of housing types, used several slightly different porch styles and exterior colors, and varied the treatment of planting strips between sidewalks and roadbeds. The setback of the units was staggered to eliminate the impression of high density and to create further variation. Although the initial plan for the community also provided for 35 stores, a garage, a theater, a church, a school, and a community center, only the school and a few of the stores were actually built.

At the end of the war, the government sold the homes by sealed bids to two black businessmen, who then resold them primarily to their original tenants. The neighborhood remained cohesive, electing committees that met weekly with the town manager to address community needs such as sanitation, law and order, and neighborhood improvement. The local civic league remained active until the 1950s, when the ward system was converted to a precinct system, dividing Truxtun into two different precincts.

Although the Truxtun neighborhood has changed substantially since it was first developed, the original planning and architectural characteristics of the neighborhood remain easily discernable. Truxtun preserves the distinctive historic quality of its residential area and remains one of Portsmouth's most significant 20th-century landmarks. [CA 9/16/82, 82004581]

RICHMOND
(INDEPENDENT CITY)

First African Baptist Church
Northeast corner of College and East Broad streets
Richmond

Built in 1867, the First African Baptist Church housed one of the oldest black congregations in Virginia. The church is constructed of brick in the late Greek Revival style. The entrance to the temple-form building is framed by two unfluted Doric columns and was originally decorated with tall, semicircular arched windows. The design of the church echoed that of the First Baptist Church at 12th and Broad streets. In 1955 the building was sold to the Medical College of Virginia and now houses offices and classrooms for the college. Although the division of the interior space to form an auditorium, offices, and classrooms leaves little of the original interior of the building, the exterior remains relatively well preserved and stands as a memorial to one of Virginia's first black congregations. [C 4/16/69, 69000348]

Jackson Ward Historic District
Roughly bounded by 5th, Marshall, and Gilmer streets and the Richmond-Petersburg Turnpike
Richmond

The Jackson Ward Historic District is a little-altered 19th-century residential neighborhood that once served as the center of the black community in Richmond. The area was inhabited by the city's black residents as early as the antebellum era, when many free blacks built homes in this neighborhood, then known as "Little Africa." Before the Civil War Richmond had a sizable free black community, which made up more than one-eighth of the total free population of the city. Richmond was also a center for the hiring out of slaves who, along with the free blacks of Richmond, were able to develop skills in business and crafts that would greatly aid the transition to freedom in the antebellum years and accounted for the late 19th-century black renaissance in Richmond.

Much of the population growth of the area before the Civil War occurred around the black churches and their auxiliary beneficial societies. Out of these grew two of Richmond's most successful beneficial societies, the Grand Fountain of the United Order of True Reformers and the Independent Order of St. Luke (see also True Reformer Building, District of Columbia; and St. Luke Building). Both organizations offered insurance services, a bank, weekly publications, and various retail and commercial enterprises.

By the turn of the century, Richmond was considered the foremost black business community in the country. Jackson Ward was not only the locale of these important black beneficial societies, but also the hub of black professional and entrepreneurial activities in the city. The Jackson Ward area was also home to a

Jackson Ward Historic District. Photo courtesy of the National Park Service (Walter Smalling, Jr.).

campus of the Virginia Union University and many of its noted faculty members (see also Virginia Union University).

Although highway construction in the 1950s physically divided the neighborhood and much of the original area was cleared for construction of Virginia Commonwealth University buildings and the Richmond Coliseum, Jackson Ward remains a place of residence, worship, and business for a substantial part of Richmond's black community. In recent years many individuals have made great efforts to preserve the identity and the character of the area. The Jackson Ward Historic District was designated a National Historic Landmark district on June 2, 1978. [A 7/30/76 NHL, 76002187]

St. Luke Building
900 St. James Street
Richmond

The St. Luke Building houses the national headquarters of the Independent Order of St. Luke, a black benevolent society founded in Baltimore after the Civil War by former slave Mary Prout.

Interior of the front parlor of the Maggie Lena Walker National Historic Site. Photo courtesy of the Virginia Historic Landmarks Commission.

The organization was founded to provide guidance and financial aid to struggling freed slaves. Under the later leadership of Maggie Lena Walker (1867–1934), a pioneering black businesswoman, philanthropist, and educator, the society prospered and flourished where similar ventures had failed. The organization helped blacks make the transition from slavery to freedom, easing the financial burdens of illness and death, encouraging savings and thrift, providing an outlet for inexpensive but well-made retail goods, and promoting Walker's ideals for her race through a news weekly. The dignified Edwardian style building was completed in 1903 and is the oldest black-affiliated office building in Richmond. It was remodeled and enlarged between 1915 and 1920.

Maggie Walker's office in the St. Luke Building is preserved as a memorial, maintained as she left it at her death in 1934 (see also Maggie Lena Walker National Historic Site). [CA 9/16/82, 82004589]

Third Street Bethel AME Church
616 North 3rd Street
Richmond

The Third Street Bethel African Methodist Episcopal (AME) Church was built around 1857 to house one of the first congregations in Virginia to join the AME denomination. It was in this simple antebellum Gothic Revival building that the Virginia Conference of the AME was organized in 1867. Although the first conference of AME churches had been founded in Philadelphia in 1816, white Methodist leadership in the South was reluctant to surrender supervision over black Methodist congregations. In 1863 the black Methodists of St. John's Chapel in Norfolk broke with the Methodist Episcopal Church and affiliated themselves with the Baltimore Conference of the AME Church. This move prompted the 1867 meeting establishing the Virginia Conference. The denomination and the congregation prospered, and in 1875 the congregation remodeled the present building. [A 6/5/75, 75002117]

Virginia Union University
1500 North Lombardy Street
Richmond

Virginia Union University was formed in 1896 by the merger of two institutions founded by the Baptist Home Mission Society. The Wayland Seminary in Washington, D.C., and the Richmond Theological Seminary in Richmond had both been founded during the postbellum years to educate the newly freed slaves. In 1896 the mission society decided to combine the resources of the Richmond and Washington, D.C., seminaries. The Wayland building and properties in Washington were sold and the proceeds used to purchase land in Richmond adjacent to the Hartshorn Memorial College, founded in the 1880s as a school for educating young black women.

Construction of the campus buildings was under way by 1899, and in 1900 a lecture hall, dormitory, dining hall, library, chapel, and two residences had been completed. Much of the construction was financed by northern philanthropists, after whom many of the buildings were then named. Further mergers in the 20th century have transformed the school into an important urban university that has consistently graduated outstand-

ing alumni. The buildings of Virginia Union University stand as a tribute to perseverance and excellence in the field of black higher education. [CA 7/26/82, 82004590]

Maggie Lena Walker National Historic Site
110A East Leigh Street
Richmond

Maggie Lena Walker (1867–1934) was born in Richmond, Virginia, the daughter of an ex-slave and a Northern abolitionist author. She attended Richmond public schools and took post-high school courses in accounting and salesmanship while teaching in the public schools. She married Armistead Walker, Jr., a building contractor, in 1886, and the couple had three children.

Maggie Walker had joined the Grand United Order of St. Luke as a girl. The organization, a fraternal and cooperative insurance venture founded in Baltimore in 1867, awarded her a minor position in the company when she was 17. In 1899 she became the company's executive secretary-treasurer. Maggie Walker transformed the organization, which had been on the brink of failure when she accepted the position, making it a leader among black fraternal organizations. In 1902 she began publishing the official organ of the Order of St. Luke, the *St. Luke Herald*. A year later she founded and served as president of the St. Luke Penny Savings Bank.

Her efforts in the self-help movement for African Americans did not end with St. Luke. In 1912 she organized the Richmond Council of Negro Women, which raised money to establish a school and farm for the training of "delinquent" black girls. As the council's president, she raised funds for the black tuberculosis sanitorium at Burkeville and a black nursing home in Richmond. She became president of the state branch of the National Association for the Advancement of Colored People and served on numerous boards and councils for black welfare. Despite an illness that confined her to a wheelchair, she chaired the board of directors of the St. Luke Penny Savings Bank until her death. The Richmond home in which she lived from around 1909 until her death on December 15, 1934, was designated a National Historic Landmark on May 12, 1975, and was added to the National Park System on November 10, 1978. [CB 5/12/75 NHL NPS, 75002100]

ROANOKE (INDEPENDENT CITY)

First Baptist Church
407 North Jefferson Street, N.W.
Roanoke

First Baptist Church was the largest and most prominent black congregation in Virginia west of Richmond from the late 19th until the mid-20th century. It played a vital role in Roanoke's black community and ultimately encouraged its leading members to become active in the community.

Under the leadership of the Reverend Arthur L. James from 1919 to 1958, the First Baptist Church offered an impressive ministry to its members. James had a parish hall built to house youth activities and a children's nursery. In addition, he presided over the church's Helping Hand Club, a women's group that sent charitable donations to the poor; and organized the church's Men's Club, which looked after inmates of the city's Alms House. The Men's Club also published *The Church News,* reportedly the only black newspaper in southwest Virginia at that time.

In 1930 James and the senior choir hosted a weekly radio broadcast program entitled the "Back Home Devotional Hour." By the time of his retirement, James had established an outstanding record of service to the First Baptist Church and the city of Roanoke. After his retirement in 1958, the First Baptist Church continued as a place of worship and fellowship until 1982, when the Reverend Kenneth B. Wright led the congregation to a new building. [CAB 12/6/90, 90001840]

Harrison School
523 Harrison Avenue, N.W.
Roanoke

Lucy Addison was among a handful of educators in post-Civil War Virginia who pioneered efforts to offer secondary academic education to black children. Addison's philosophy represented a departure from the prevailing educational theory that black students should receive only industrial and manual instruction. Before the establishment of the school on Harrison Avenue, black students who wished to pursue academic training beyond the seventh grade were required to travel some distance to the Virginia State College in Petersburg.

The Harrison School was built in 1916 and opened in 1917 with Addison as principal. Addison was responsible for extending the curriculum of the school beyond the seventh-grade level. The first class to complete the four-year high school course graduated in 1924. The Harrison School operated an elementary school until 1960. The school, along with the Addison High School, built later to house the school's growing high school population, are the only two black school buildings in the area that survive from the early 20th century. The Harrison School stands as a significant reminder of the efforts of Lucy Addison on behalf of academic secondary education for black students in the Roanoke area. [A 9/9/82, 82004592]

SOUTHAMPTON COUNTY

Belmont
Northeast of Capron off Virginia
Route 652
Capron

This modest late 18th-century plantation house was the site where the Nat Turner slave rebellion was effectively suppressed on August 23, 1831. The rebellion, organized by Virginia slave Nat Turner, involved about 80 slaves and free blacks. About 60 whites and 70 of the insurrectionists were killed in this short but violent revolt, which prompted the Virginia legislature to pass laws tightening restrictions on slaves and free blacks in Virginia.

The revolt began 15 miles southwest of Belmont at the home of Joseph Travis, the stepfather of Turner's owner. By the time the insurrectionists reached Belmont, their number had been reduced to about 20. Assuming the plantation house was vacant, the group approached the house, only to be met by the plantation owner, Samuel Blunt, his sons, and his slaves, who had elected to assist in the defense of the house. Blunt's group was gathered in the kitchen east of the house, where they killed some of Turner's party and captured others. Turner himself managed to escape but was apprehended on October 30, 1831, tried in court, and executed by hanging.

The Travis plantation, where the revolt began, is no longer extant. Belmont is the only remaining property associated with the Nat Turner rebellion, the last organized effort by slaves to revolt in the South. [CA 10/3/73, 73002061]

SUFFOLK (INDEPENDENT CITY)

Phoenix Bank of Nansemond
339 East Washington Street
Suffolk

The Phoenix Bank of Nansemond originated in a Suffolk drugstore owned by black physician Dr. W. T. Fuller when a group of black men gathered and organized a club to lend money. Fuller suggested that the men form a bank. In 1919 the organization officially became the Phoenix Bank of Nansemond with Fuller as its first president. Fuller headed the bank until his death in 1921, at which time then vice president of the bank J. W. Richardson was elected to fill the position. It was under Richardson's direction that the Phoenix Bank building was built in 1921. At the time of its construction, the building was recognized as one of the handsomest in the area and stood as a symbol of achievement and pride for Suffolk's black community. The bank prospered until 1931, its resource base growing from $13,000 to over $125,000 during its years in operation. Economic hardship brought on by the Great Depression resulted in a steep decline in depositors, and the bank was forced to close in 1931. The Phoenix Bank building remains a testament to black achievement in Suffolk in an era when black professionals gained economic success through cooperative activity. [A 1/24/91, 90002159]

VIRGIN ISLANDS

ST. CROIX

Christiansted Historic District
Roughly bounded by Christiansted
Harbor, New, Peter's Farm Hospital, and
West streets
Christiansted

The buildings, sites, and structures in the Christiansted Historic District commemorate the early colonization of the U.S. Virgin Islands. Although other European countries had made earlier efforts to colonize St. Croix, it was only under Danish rule that the island was successfully developed as a major sugar producer, bound to both Europe and America by close commercial, social, and cultural ties.

Christiansted was founded on the site of an older French settlement. In 1733 the king of France, needing money to carry on a war with Poland, sold the island of St. Croix to the Danish West India and Guinea Company. The island had been virtually abandoned by the French since 1695.

The first colonists brought slaves with them, and as the demand for labor increased, Africans were brought from West Africa and from Danish slave forts on the Gold Coast in what is today the country of Ghana. Christiansted grew quickly, as many St. John planters and their families relocated to St. Croix following the slave rebellion on that island in 1733.

African slaves played a significant role in the development of Christiansted. Slaves were employed as artisans and assisted in constructing many of the buildings included within the boundaries of the Christiansted Historic District. A sizable free black population developed in the town as well and played an important socioeconomic role. One residential area of town, "Free Gut," was established specifically for free blacks. Christiansted experienced a tremendous boom within two decades. By 1755 the population had risen from a few hundred to 10,200, including nearly 9,000 slaves. In 1804 the total number of slaves in St. Croix rose to 27,349.

The prosperity that sugar cultivation brought to St. Croix during the second half of the 18th century would never have been achieved without the large African population that provided the labor to produce the sugar. The buildings in the Christiansted Historic District reflect the prosperity of an era built on the foundation of slavery. (See also Christiansted National Historic Site.) [CA 7/30/76, 76002266]

Residences on Hill Street in the Christiansted Historic District. Photo courtesy of the U.S. Virgin Islands Planning Office (Samuel N. Stokes).

Christiansted National Historic Site
Bounded by King, Queen, and Queens Cross streets and Christiansted Harbor
Christiansted

Christiansted National Historic Site comprises Fort Christiansvern, Government House, the West India and Guinea Company Warehouse, the Old Customs House, the Old Post Office, and the Hamilton Jackson Park. These properties commemorate the early colonization of the U.S. Virgin Islands. Although other European countries made earlier efforts to colonize St. Croix, it was only under Danish rule that the island was successfully developed as a major sugar producer, bound to both Europe and America by close commercial, social, and cultural ties. The Christiansted National Historic Site lies within the boundaries of the Christiansted Historic District (see also Christiansted Historic District). The property was added to the National Park System as the Virgin Islands National Historic Site on March 4, 1952. In 1961 it was redesignated Christiansted National Historic Site. [CA 10/15/66 NPS, 66000077]

Friedensthal Mission
Southwest of Christiansted
Christiansted

Friedensthal Mission was among the first Moravian missions to be established on the island of St. Croix. The Moravians first arrived in the Dutch West Indies in 1732 to provide educational and religious training for the African slave population. Friedrich Moth, the founder of Moravian missions in the West Indies, sought to make them as self-supportive as possible through the purchase and development of plantations such as New Herrnhut and Niesky on St. Thomas (see also Estate Niesky and New Herrnhut Moravian Church, St. Thomas), Bethany on St. John, and Friedensthal.

Although the labor force for the plantation was provided by slaves, the fair treatment and sincere desire on the part of the missionaries for slaves to assume responsible positions within the church created a friendly relationship between the slaves and the white missionaries. The Moravians provided training in manual labor in addition to general religious and educational instruction, in hopes of preparing the slaves for their eventual emancipation.

While the mission at Friedensthal, which means "valley of peace" in German, was established in 1734, the church now located on the property was constructed in 1852 to replace an earlier smaller church. The church and manse are representative of the construction and design employed by the Moravians in all their missions in the Virgin Islands. [CA 8/25/78, 78002719]

ST. JOHN

Emmaus Moravian Church and Manse
West of Palestina
Coral Bay

The property on which the Emmaus Moravian Church and Manse now stand was given to the Moravians in 1782 by Governor Thomas de Malleville after his conversion by Brother Cornelius, an African who had become a missionary of the Moravians. As a master mason, Cornelius is known to have built at least six churches for the Moravians. He also became an accomplished linguist and eloquent preacher.

Moravian missionaries first came to

the Dutch West Indies in 1732 to establish missions for the religious and educational instruction of the African population of the island. They were the only church allowed to minister to the slaves and were instrumental in establishing Dutch Creole as the primary language spoken by masters and slaves to each other.

The original church on the property was built around 1782 but was destroyed by a hurricane in 1790. A second building was destroyed by fire in 1892. The present church was constructed in 1919. Although the exact date of construction of the manse in not known, it was standing by the late 1780s. In addition to being one of the oldest remaining buildings on the island, it reflects almost 250 years of Moravian influence on the culture of the present-day Virgin Islands. [CA 11/7/77, 77001531]

Estate Carolina Sugar Plantation
West of Coral Bay on King Hill Road
Coral Bay

This was the first and richest sugar estate on the island, established shortly after it was settled in 1717 as an official plantation of the Danish West India and Guinea Company. The ruins of Estate Carolina comprise an exceptionally complete collection of buildings necessary for the production of sugar and bay rum. The large animal treadmill with cane crushers dates to before 1725; the stone windmill was built by 1733. The sugar factory has two decks for boiling sugar, extensive cisterns, and curing rooms for processing molasses and sugar.

It was at Estate Carolina that a successful slave rebellion broke out on November 23, 1733. The rebellion spread to adjacent estates and engulfed the entire island of St. John with the exception of Durlo's Plantation (Caneel

Bay). The rebellion could not be suppressed by the Danes and was put down only upon the arrival of 400 French troops from Martinique and six months of hard fighting. [CA 7/19/76, 76002217]

Fortsberg
Southeast of Coral Bay
Coral Bay

Fortsberg is significant as the site of the first successful slave rebellion on the island of St. John. On November 23, 1733, African slaves seized the fort and massacred the garrison to occupy most of the plantations on the island. Many plantation owners fled to Peter Durlo's Caneel Bay plantation, which was fortified, to seek shelter.

The slaves surprised the Europeans with their adept military strategy. Two attempts to suppress the rebellion were unsuccessful. Finally, the governor of Martinique came to the aid of the Dutch, sending 400 French soldiers to the island. The French soldiers were finally able to put down the rebellion, but only after a six-month campaign ending in May 1734. Much of the fort was destroyed during the conflict.

The fort was rebuilt in its present form in 1760; it was occupied by the British in 1801 and from 1807 to 1815 during the Napoleonic Wars. Today the fort is a reminder of the first step in the long struggle for justice faced by Africans in the present-day Virgin Islands. [CAD 9/1/76, 76002218]

Lameshur Plantation
East of Cruz Bay on Little Lameshur Bay
Cruz Bay

During the early years of Danish sovereignty of the Virgin Islands, religious and educational instruction for Africans was left to the missionaries of the Moravian and United Brethren churches. The Moravians were the first to establish missions in the Virgin Islands, beginning with New Herrnhut in 1732 (see also New Herrnhut Moravian Church, St. Thomas). In 1839 the government issued a regulation calling for compulsory education of all African children within the Danish West Indies. The passage of the regulation was one of a series of reform measures initiated by Governor-General Peter von Scholten, who felt the government had a responsibility to educate the slaves to prepare them for emancipation. Von Scholten envisioned emancipation taking place gradually over the period of his tenure as governor-general from 1836 to 1848.

The Lameshur school was one of 17 schools established in the Danish West Indies under the provisions of the regulation. Constructed in the 1840s, it was one of the smallest schools built under the regulation. Funds to build the school and finance its programs were raised through a head tax imposed upon planters who owned slaves. The school was initially staffed by Moravians on the condition that religious education would be interdenominational and that classes would be taught in English. The remains of this modest school are a monument to the reform measures that established free compulsory education for African children. [Virgin Islands National Park MRA (AD), CAD 6/23/78 NPS, 78000271]

Rustenberg Plantation South Historic District
West of Coral Bay off Center Line Road
Cinnamon Bay

Rustenberg Plantation South was one of the most extensive and richest plantations on St. John. It was developed early in the 18th century as a sugar plantation. The remaining plantation buildings mostly date to before 1780 and include several slave cabins. African slave labor and skills were necessary in the daily operation of the plantation system, and slaves made significant contributions in building the infrastructure of the plantation.

The property initially included a horsemill, sugar factory, bagasse shed, rum still, storage building, combined warehouse and residence, oxpounds with stables, the plantation house, and slave quarters. The buildings and structures that remain are of exceptional interest for their early plan type and construction. The property includes well-preserved agricultural buildings rarely seen today. [Virgin Islands National Park MRA, AD 7/23/81 NPS, 81000093]

St. Thomas

Charlotte Amalie Historic District
Roughly bounded by Nytvaer, Berg, and Government Hills and Bjebre Gade and St. Thomas Harbor
Charlotte Amalie

The Danish West India Company established the first permanent European settlement in St. Thomas in 1672. African slaves were present in the colony soon thereafter, despite the fact that Denmark was a relative latecomer to the slave trade. The colony soon developed into one of the largest slave-trading centers in the West Indies and became a refuge for pirates, who often disposed of their loot on the island.

Although Charlotte Amalie was a prosperous port, piracy diverted much of the legitimate trade until about 1700. By 1754 Charlotte Amalie had recovered and grown into an important and prosperous trading center, and by 1799 it was one of the most important trading centers in all of the West Indies.

Charlotte Amalie served briefly as a base for Confederate blockade runners during the Civil War. By 1875 trading and commerce had peaked, and mercantile activity began to decline as a result of direct shipping and communication links between European and Caribbean countries.

In 1916, after two previous attempts, the United States purchased the Danish West Indies for $25 million in gold. The United States' interest in the Virgin Islands arose from the strategic importance of Charlotte Amalie harbor as a deep-water port and the possibility that Germany would take over the harbor as a military base. The island continued under the administration of the U.S. Navy until 1930. [CA 7/19/76, 76001860]

Estate Botany Bay
West of Charlotte Amalie
Charlotte Amalie

Estate Botany Bay is one of the few remaining ruins of a sugar plantation in St. Thomas. The property includes the remains of a sugar factory and slave cabins. While the exact construction dates of the buildings are unknown, deed records show that the plantation was in operation in 1810.

During the 17th and 18th centuries, the Danes joined other European countries in securing colonies in the West Indies. The Danes hoped that their colonies would provide them with permanent sites for their trading and commercial interests. Profits from agriculture were to supplement the income gained through commerce and trading. Cotton and sugar were the major crops cultivated, but as the demand for sugar increased, it became the island's most important agricultural product.

Sugar production in St. Thomas

peaked in 1725. Like nearly all plantations in the West Indies, Estate Botany Bay depended on African slave labor for the production of sugar. Providing all labor necessary to the daily operations of the estate, slaves were the backbone of the plantation system. The ruins of Estate Botany Bay are a reminder of the importance of slaves and sugar cultivation to the economy of the Virgin Islands. [CA 7/30/76, 76001861]

Estate Neltjeberg
Northwest of Charlotte Amalie
Charlotte Amalie

Estate Neltjeberg comprises the remains of an 18th-century sugar plantation. The property includes the sugar factory, an animal mill, a stable, slave quarters, and the plantation boundary walls. The layout of the complex is typical of colonial architecture on St. Thomas. The building materials and methods of construction are representative of the vernacular tradition that emerged in the U.S. Virgin Islands during the early 18th century.

Although sugar production on St. Thomas had reached its peak by 1725, Estate Neltjeberg remained profitable until the 1830s. African slaves were vital in the daily operation of the plantation. In addition to providing labor for sugar production, skilled artisan slaves assisted in the construction of the buildings and other structures on the property.

The ruins of Estate Neltjeberg are significant for understanding the evolution of vernacular architectural traditions in the Virgin Islands and in illustrating the contribution of African slaves to St. Thomas's economy. [CA 2/17/78, 78002729]

Estate Niesky
1.5 miles west of Charlotte Amalie off Harwood Highway
Charlotte Amalie

Estate Niesky was a working plantation purchased by the Moravian Church in 1755 for use as a mission. Moravian missionaries first arrived in St. Thomas in 1732 and established their first mission, New Herrnhut, in 1737 (see also New Herrnhut Moravian Church). Like New Herrnhut, Niesky was a working plantation on which slaves supplied the labor as well as the congregation for the mission. The property includes the church, manse, slave quarters, and a small cemetery dating from the 18th century.

The Moravian missionaries displayed a deep concern for the black slaves' moral and intellectual development. The slaves were provided general religious and academic instruction and often were also trained as artisans. Slaves were encouraged to assume responsible positions within the church and community. The Moravians' goal was to prepare the slaves for their eventual emancipation.

The buildings that remain at Niesky are typical of Moravian architecture in the Virgin Islands and are important physical documents of the work of the Moravians to better the lives of black slaves in the islands. [CA 8/29/78, 78003092]

Fort Christian
St. Thomas Harbor
Charlotte Amalie

Completed around 1680, Fort Christian is the oldest building in continuous use in the Virgin Islands. The fort was originally constructed as a military fortification and has since been used as a governor's residence, place of worship, administrative center, police headquarters, jail, and municipal court. The building presently houses the Virgin Islands Museum.

New Herrnhut Moravian Church. Photo courtesy of the U.S. Virgin Islands Planning Office (Samuel N. Stokes).

The first permanent settlement in the area that is now Charlotte Amalie was established in 1672 by the Danish West India and Guinea Company. Construction of the fort, which was named after King Christian V of Denmark, began in 1674. The fort was constructed under the leadership of Governor Iverson, who acquired an African slave, Simon Lamare, to work for the company. Lamare, a skilled mason, served as clerk of the works for the construction of the fort and served the Danish West India and Guinea Company for seven years. This arrangement may have been a contractual agreement for Lamare's manumission, a practice that was not uncommon in the West Indies for slaves who possessed special skills. The history of the construction of Fort Christian demonstrates the significant role played by Africans in the early history of the Virgin Islands. [A 5/5/77 NHL, 77001329]

New Herrnhut Moravian Church
East of Charlotte Amalie
Charlotte Amalie

New Herrnhut Moravian Church was the first of the Moravian missions established in the Dutch West Indies, the present-day Virgin Islands. Before the arrival of the Moravians to the islands, the Dutch had made no provision for the education of African slaves residing there. The plantation on which New Herrnhut was established was purchased by the Moravian missionary Frederick Martin in 1737. Also known at times as Brethren's Plantation, Brethren's Tutu, and Posaunenberg, the plantation was named after Herrnhut, the mother church in Germany.

The Moravians established their missions for the religious and academic instruction of Africans, and they did not actively recruit whites as converts. The African slaves on the plantation provided labor for crop cultivation and the congregation for the mission. The Moravians provided the slaves with not only education and spiritual tutelage, but also training as artisans to prepare them for their eventual emancipation.

By 1770 New Herrnhut was a thriving plantation supporting mission activities with all the buildings typical of an active plantation. The operations of the plantation and mission continued until a hurricane severely damaged the grounds in 1867, and the complex fell into ruin. New Herrnhut Church still stands, however, along with its original bell, which was rung to summon slaves to meetings and church. [CA 10/8/76, 76001866]

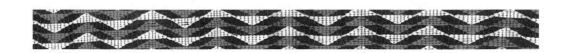

WEST VIRGINIA

CABELL COUNTY

**Douglass Junior and Senior
High School**
Intersection of 10th Avenue and
Bruce Street
Huntington

Built in response to an appeal from leaders in Huntington's black community in 1891, Douglass High School offered a two-year high school course to black students. The school, named for abolitionist and statesman Frederick Douglass, grew rapidly thereafter, both physically and academically. In 1899 the course was expanded to four years, and several new subjects were added. By 1913 the school contained a physics and chemistry laboratory, a domestic science room, a manual training room, a sewing room, a commercial room, a library, and an assembly room and office. It had a faculty of 17 teachers and enrolled 465 students in both graded school and high school. By 1923 Douglass was inspected by the state high school supervisor and found to meet

*Halltown Union Colored Sunday School,
Jefferson County. Photo courtesy of the
West Virginia Department of Culture
and History (Michael J. Pauley).*

all the requirements of a first class high school.

The present Douglass Junior and Senior High School building was completed in 1926 to replace the old Douglass School complex, later renamed the Barnett School. The tradition of academic excellence for black students was carried on in the new location. Many Douglass graduates went on to distinguish themselves on state and national levels in politics, religious life, sports, education, and business. Today the Douglass School stands as a building of local distinction for its service to Huntington's black community. [A 12/5/85, 85003091]

FAYETTE COUNTY

Camp Washington-Carver Complex
County Route 11/3
Clifftop

The Camp Washington-Carver Complex was completed in 1942 by the Works Progress Administration (WPA), which combined federal, state, and local agencies with local manpower in the 1930s to revitalize segments of the national economy during the Great Depression. Construction of the facility grew out of a movement in the late 1930s to provide the state's black youth with outdoor recreational facilities and to

Great Chestnut Lodge of the Camp Washington-Carver Complex. Photo courtesy of the West Virginia Department of Culture and History (C. E. Turley).

establish a complex of the quality of that offered to white youth at the Jackson's Mill 4-H camp.

The black 4-H camp was named Camp Washington-Carver to commemorate black leaders Booker T. Washington and George Washington Carver. The center instructed 400 youth in vocational agriculture, soil conservation, home economics, and 4-H standards. Among the camp's facilities is the Great Chestnut Lodge, the largest log building in West Virginia, built entirely of West Virginia chestnut. The complex of interrelated buildings is constructed entirely of locally fashioned hardwood and native stone to conform to the natural environment. The Camp Washington-Carver Complex survives as a well-preserved example of one of West Virginia's most ambitious WPA projects. [CA 6/20/80, 80004017]

GREENBRIER COUNTY

Maple Street Historic District
107–121 Maple Street
Lewisburg

The Maple Street Historic District consists of six houses on the west side of Maple Street in Lewisburg. The street is situated atop what is locally known as "Gospel Hill," which has historically served as the residential area for most of the town's black population. The buildings were erected between 1890 and 1910 and make up the largest concentration of intact workers' housing for African Americans in Lewisburg. While there was a substantial number of blacks in servitude in Lewisburg before the Civil War, the influence of the community's black population was strongest after 1890. The 1890s brought a great lumber boom, and with it, a need for large numbers of workers.

Employment in the lumber industry brought black workers into a prominent role in Lewisburg's commercial and business life. The black community formed its own schools, churches, and social organizations. Integration came to Lewisburg in the 1950s, changing the character of the Gospel Hill community. The Maple Hill Historic District is a small representative of the former character of Gospel Hill and is all that remains intact of the historic black workers' community of Lewisburg. [CA 4/6/88, 87002529]

Mt. Tabor Baptist Church
Intersection of Court and Foster streets
Lewisburg

The roots of the congregation of this small brick church with early Gothic Revival style detailing date to the 1780s, making it among the oldest Baptist Congregations in southeastern West Virginia. The main section of the present building was constructed in 1832; the gallery and the basement were added in 1844; and the octagonal tower was added in the 1860s.

During the Civil War the building deteriorated substantially. By 1868 church membership dwindled to fewer than a dozen, and the building was in need of repair. In the meantime black congregants, who as slaves had worshiped in the church gallery, requested permission to continue to use the meetinghouse. The request was granted on the condition that they repair the building. Sometime after 1869 a black minister came to the church, an event described as "representative of only one of the many doors now open to people who had once been the possessions of others." During this period, the congregation changed the name of the church from the Lewisburg to the Mount Tabor Baptist Church, and public school classes for black children were held in the basement.

The period from 1884 to 1886 was perhaps the most momentous in the church's history. In 1884 William Foglesong, the only surviving trustee of the church's former white congregation, petitioned the court of Greenbrier County to allow the sale of the church and lot so proceeds could finance the construction of a new church elsewhere for white congregants. The Reverend A. W. Woolsey led the struggle against the repossession of the church, and in 1886 the court denied Foglesong's petition and declared the black congregation the rightful owners of the church. Although such transfers of churches from white to black congregations were common after the Civil War, the court's judgment that the African Americans were rightful successors to the original trustees was an exceptional method of transfer. [A 12/12/76, 76001934]

HARRISON COUNTY

Trinity Memorial Methodist Episcopal Church
420 Ben Street
Clarksburg

Trinity Memorial Methodist Episcopal (ME) Church was built in 1902 to house a black congregation that was formed shortly after the Civil War. Before the Civil War Harrison County had no black churches, and the county's small black population worshiped in the white Methodist church in a separate section reserved for them. The new black congregation initially worshiped in a neighborhood carriage house, in the court house, and in homes of the various church members. Their first church building was built in 1870 on Water Street. Despite their modest number, the congregants were able to raise funds to build the sizable house of worship that stands today on

Ben Street. Built of brick in the late Victorian Gothic Romanesque style, the church is an architectural landmark in a low-density neighborhood composed of frame one- and two-story cottages. The building became a prominent place of fellowship and a center of social activity in the black community. Serving the local black residents from 1902 until 1965, Trinity Memorial ME Church stood for many years as a symbol of black pride in Clarksburg. [CA 4/26/84, 84003584]

JEFFERSON COUNTY

Halltown Union Colored Sunday School
Off U.S. Route 340
Halltown

The Halltown Union Colored Sunday School (now the Halltown Memorial Chapel) was constructed in 1901 in response to a need in the black community for a place of worship in Jefferson County. At the urging of the leaders of the local black community, Daniel B. Lucas donated a parcel of land adjacent to the "colored free school" from his Rion Hall estate on which to build a colored Sunday school. The small stone chapel was built in the Gothic Revival style by local black artisans and workers, who labored on the building after regular working hours and on their days off. The chapel was completed in 1901 and was open to all denominations. It served the black community for more than 60 years as the site of church services, marriages, funerals, and social and community events. In 1982 local residents formed the Memorial Chapel Association to preserve the building. The group has since completely restored this important landmark to black history in Jefferson County. [CA 1/12/84, 84003591]

Harpers Ferry National Historical Park
The confluence of the Shenandoah and Potomac rivers
Harpers Ferry

The town of Harpers Ferry is best known as the scene of the 1859 John Brown raid, an event of great importance leading up to the Civil War. The raid focused the attention of the country on Harpers Ferry. John Brown, an ardent abolitionist and leader in the bloody sectional strife in Kansas, conceived a plan to liberate the slaves by starting a revolution, arming the slaves, and establishing a free black stronghold in the Appalachians. He chose Harpers Ferry because of the stock of weapons at the federal armory there and its location near the mountains.

During the summer of 1859 Brown gathered weapons, supplies, and supporters at the Kennedy Farm, located five miles away in Maryland. On the night of October 16, he set out for Harpers Ferry with 17 men and a wagonload of supplies. The party seized the Potomac bridge watchman and took the armory watchmen into town. Brown cut the telegraph wires and sent out parties to bring in slaves and hostages. An engineer on an eastbound train, however, telegraphed an alarm upon arriving in Monocacy, Maryland, in the early morning.

Brown's men barricaded themselves in armory buildings and began to exchange fire with townspeople. By noon the militia had arrived and secured the Potomac River bridge. The raiders who survived the encounter with the militia managed to take refuge in the fire engine house of the armory's musket factory, where they were stormed by a party of marines on the morning of October 18. Two men were bayoneted and the others captured. John Brown was brought to trial in Charles Town the next week, found guilty of treason, and hanged on December 2, 1859

A group of students in front of Storer College in 1921, Harpers Ferry National Historical Park. Photo courtesy of the National Park Service History Collection.

(see also Jefferson County Courthouse; John Brown Cabin, Miami County, Kansas; John Brown's Headquarters, Washington County, Maryland; John Brown Farm, Essex County, New York; and John Brown House, Franklin County, Pennsylvania).

Harpers Ferry is also significant to black history as the location of Storer College. Storer College was established in the vacated U.S. armory residences in the area known as Camp Hill after the Civil War. The school's support came from northern philanthropists and the Freedmen's Bureau. Begun as an elementary school in 1865, the institution soon became a college focusing on teacher training and expanded to include theology, industrial arts, and home arts. During the college's first 40 years, the student body averaged 176 men and women. The school closed in 1955, but its buildings remain as reminders of one of the earliest institutions established for black education after the Civil War. [A 10/15/66 NPS, 66000041]

Jefferson County Courthouse

Intersection of North George and East Washington streets
Charles Town

The Jefferson County Courthouse in Charles Town, then part of the state of Virginia, was the site of the 1859 trial of John Brown. Brown, an abolitionist from Kansas, had attempted to lead a slave insurrection at the federal armory in Harpers Ferry. The rebellion was quickly put down, and Brown was captured and jailed in Charles Town. Insisting that Brown be tried in a Virginia court, Virginia Governor Henry Wise was largely responsible for establishing Charles Town as the site of Brown's trial. The trial drew great attention, especially from northern sympathizers who campaigned for his acquittal. Brown himself attempted to evade trial by claiming illness, but after examination by a local physician he was proclaimed competent to stand trial. Brown's request to lie on a cot to deliver his testimony, however, was granted. Nevertheless, he was found guilty of conspiring with slaves to rebel, of murder, and of treason against Virginia, and was sentenced to death by hanging. He was hanged nearby, and his body was removed by train to his home state of Kansas (see also Harpers Ferry National Historical Park; John Brown Cabin, Miami County, Kansas; John Brown's Headquarters, Washington County, Maryland; John Brown Farm, Essex County, New York; and John Brown House, Franklin County, Pennsylvania). [A 7/10/73, 73001910]

KANAWHA COUNTY

African Zion Baptist Church
4104 Malden Drive
Malden

The African Zion Baptist Church was first organized in 1865 at Tinkersville, east of its present-day home of Malden. The congregation comprised former slaves who were hired out by their owners in Virginia to work in the local salt production industry. After the Civil War, they quickly established their own community and community institutions. The African Zion Baptist Church was the first black Baptist church established in the new state of West Virginia that was completely owned and controlled by African

Americans and is the mother church of black Baptists in West Virginia. Its founder, Lewis Rice, was a leader in the black community in the Kanawha Valley.

The congregation's first sanctuary was constructed in 1865 with the aid of a local salt entrepreneur. The emerging dominance of the coal industry and corresponding decline of the salt industry by the 1870s, however, prompted the church to move to its present location in Malden, closer to a center for coal production. The current sanctuary was constructed around 1872 and remains essentially unchanged. The church counted among its members the family of Booker T. Washington, whose father labored in a salt-packing house nearby. Washington attended the church from 1865 until 1872, when he left to attend the Hampton Institute (see also Tuskegee Institute National Historic Site, Macon County, Alabama). [AB 12/27/74, 74002010]

Canty House
West Virginia Route 25
Institute

James Canty was born in Marietta, Georgia, in 1863, the son of slave parents. He attended public school in Marietta and graduated from the Tuskegee Institute (see also Tuskegee Institute National Historic Site, Macon County, Alabama). While at Tuskegee, Canty learned blacksmithing and pipe and machinery work. After his graduation, he worked as commandant of students at Tuskegee but soon returned to Marietta to work in a carriage shop and do machine work in furniture factories and a planing mill. In 1893, at the recommendation of Booker T. Washington, Canty was appointed superintendent of mechanics at the West Virginia Colored Institute. In addition to teaching blacksmithing, carpentry, and mechanical drawing, Canty taught in the literary department and constructed a sewage system for the institution. He also began a military training corps at the institute to encourage physical training.

Canty's home in Institute, built in 1923, is one of the most architecturally distinctive buildings in the town and is now owned by the West Virginia State College, the successor of the West Virginia Institute. The house is a monument to one of the college's early and most influential educators. [CB 9/23/88, 88001587]

East Hall
West Quadrangle, West Virginia State College campus
Institute

West Virginia State College was founded as the West Virginia Colored Institute, a black land-grant college, and was among several such schools established under the country's 1890 Land Grant Act for the education and training of black students. East Hall is the oldest building on the West Virginia State College campus. It was built around 1893, originally for use as a boys' dormitory. When a new boys' dormitory was built in 1897, East Hall became the site of the printing department, the library, and the chemistry laboratory. In 1898 East Hall became the residence of principal J. McHenry Jones and was used as the president's house thereafter.

In addition to serving as a residence for the school's many extraordinary educators, East Hall was used for official college entertaining, was the site of student and faculty receptions, and housed numerous guests of the college when public accommodations were still segregated, making suitable accommodations for prominent black visitors hard to find. The list of prominent black leaders who stayed in East Hall includes W. E. B. Du Bois, Channing Tobias, Mary McLeod Bethune, Benjamin Mays, Jessie Faucett, George Washington Carver, Roland Hayes, Carter G. Woodson, and Clarence Cameron White. [A 9/26/88, 88001585]

Garnet High School
422 Dickinson Street
Charleston

Garnet [sic] High School was organized in 1900 by C. W. Boyd. The school, which grew out of a grade school of the same name, was named for escaped slave and abolitionist leader Henry Highland Garnett. Boyd was the school's first principal, serving until 1908, when he became supervisor of Charleston Negro public schools. In 1909 a separate building was constructed for the high school on the same lot as the grade school. Growth in enrollment provided the impetus for the construction of the present building.

Over the years of its service to the black community, Garnet has been famous for the quality of its programs and curriculum. Just before the school closed in 1956, a branch library of the Charleston library system was located at Garnet, making public library resources available to black citizens of the city. Garnet's graduates have attained renown in many fields including dentistry, medicine, law, education, social work, music, and business. Today the school serves as an adult education center, continuing the tradition of excellent educational service to the Charleston community. [A 7/24/90, 90001068]

Elizabeth Harden Gilmore House
514 Broad Street
Charleston

The Elizabeth Harden Gilmore House was built around 1900 in the Classical

Revival style characteristic of homes built in this part of Charleston at that time. The building's primary significance, however, lies in its association with businesswoman and civil rights leader Elizabeth Harden Gilmore. From 1947 until her death in 1986, Gilmore resided and operated her funeral home in the house. She was the first woman to be licensed as a funeral director in Kanawha County, where she opened the business with her husband. In an era when blacks were excluded from using white funeral homes, Gilmore's business offered an important service to Charleston's black community.

Gilmore's greatest contribution to the black community, however, was in her role as a pioneer in the civil rights movement in West Virginia. In 1958 she helped found the local chapter of the Congress of Racial Equality. She led the organization in the sit-ins that opened lunch counters in Charleston to African Americans.

Gilmore also served on the Kanawha Valley Council of Human Relations, which provided a forum for discussion of racial and religious differences and helped black renters find housing. Her push for the passage of an enforceable civil rights law in West Virginia earned her a seat on the West Virginia Board of Regents. She served the board until the late 1970s, serving a term each as vice president and president. The house in which she resided and conducted her business stands as a reminder of a woman whose tireless commitment to the black community won her praise and recognition across the region. [CB 9/17/88, 88001462]

Mattie V. Lee Home
810 Donnally Street
Charleston

In 1915 the Reverend Francis Gow of the St. Paul African Methodist Episcopal Church of Charleston called a number of meetings of local black residents to address the problem of safe and affordable housing for the many young black women arriving in Charleston seeking work. Among those in attendance was Rebecca Bullard, a teacher interested in youth welfare. Bullard assembled a group of citizens to donate funds and opened the Mattie V. Lee Home in October 1915 in a building on Quarrier Street.

The home was named for West Virginia's first black woman physician, who had taken a special interest in the needs of widows and girls in the community. The home, which housed 12 young women, was equipped with recreation facilities and with books, newspapers, and journals. It also served as a meeting place for various women's religious and social groups. Financial support for the home came entirely from annual membership pledges and donations.

The home occupied the Quarrier Street building for five years. In 1920 the executive board began a campaign to raise money for a larger facility. The response from local businesses and individuals was formidable, permitting the purchase of the present building. A home was chartered on January 16, 1920, as the Mattie V. Lee Industrial Home; its stated purpose was to promote the spiritual, intellectual, social, physical, and industrial development of black girls.

The home operated in this capacity until 1958, when it began to receive funds from the United Way and opened its doors to young women of all races. Today the building continues to provide low-cost housing to women and welcomes a variety of community organizations that use the building's meeting rooms. [A 6/16/92, 92000303]

Simpson Memorial Methodist Episcopal Church
607 Shrewsbury Street
Charleston

Simpson Memorial Methodist Episcopal (ME) Church was completed in 1915 to house a congregation organized during the Civil War. The group first worshiped in the basement of the nearby Asbury United Methodist Church. Around 1870 the congregation moved to quarters near the present building and built a small frame sanctuary, which was destroyed by fire in 1887. Work on a new building commenced immediately, and the new church opened for services in 1888. In 1914 the church and lot were sold, and the money was used to finance the present substantial brick building for the growing congregation.

Simpson Memorial ME Church is the oldest black church building in the area. At the time of its construction it stood in a vital black neighborhood. Its size and architectural character made it a prominent neighborhood landmark. Today the church provides a link with the neighborhood's early period of growth and social prominence. [A 8/5/91, 91001011]

Samuel Starks House
413 Shrewsbury Street
Charleston

Samuel W. Starks was born in Charleston, West Virginia, in 1866 and apprenticed as a cooper while attending newly formed schools for black youth in the Kanawha Valley. He took a job as a janitor in the office of the Kanawha and Michigan Railroad, where he became fascinated by telegraphy. Teaching himself to operate the telegraph, he left to work in the telegraph office in Charleston. Discriminatory practices in the office discouraged him, however, and he resigned. Starks moved to Chicago, where he took classes in stenography and bookkeeping. He eventually returned to Charleston and in 1901 earned the distinction of being appointed state librarian by Governor Albert B. White.

Starks was the first African American in the nation to hold the office of state librarian. He was reappointed to the position in 1905 and held the office until his death in 1908. During his tenure, he took a young African American, J. Arthur Jackson, under his wing and trained him as an able library assistant. In 1921 Jackson was appointed West Virginia state librarian, the second African American to hold this position.

In addition to this considerable achievement, Starks also played a significant role in the Knights of Pythias organization. The Knights of Pythias, a secret black fraternal order of which Starks was a member, elected him to their highest office, supreme chancellor, in 1897. Starks had served for 16 years as the grand chancellor for the organization in the state of West Virginia. Under his leadership, the organization grew phenomenally. Between 1897 and 1909, membership grew from fewer than 9,000 to 146,869, including the 38,000 in the women's department, the Order of Calanthe.

Starks's most significant contribution to the Knights of Pythias was to involve the organization in nationwide investment in real estate. Starks saw the acquisition of real estate as a way for African Americans to establish themselves firmly in communities. Through his efforts, the Pythian Mutual Investment Association was formed in 1902 to encourage saving and frugality among its members and encourage black investment in real estate. Starks transformed the organization from a small, relatively obscure group to one of the greatest and most successful of its kind.

Samuel Starks died in 1908 at the age of 42. The large and distinctive home on Shrewsbury Street, which he built just a few years before his death, stands as an impressive physical embodiment of Starks's philosophy. [B 2/1/88, 87002526]

McDOWELL COUNTY

World War Memorial
U.S. Route 52
Kimball

Constructed in 1928, the World War Memorial was erected to honor black veterans of World War I, especially the 1,500 from McDowell County. The monument was built through the efforts of black veterans in the county, many of whom labored in the coal mines.

African Americans had mined coal in the Kanawha Valley as early as 1850 but not in significant numbers until recruiters were sent to the South. Black miners poured into West Virginia, hoping to escape impoverished conditions in the South and lured by company-built housing, access to the company store, and pay equal to that of white miners–a practice unheard of in the South. By 1920, 43 percent of all black miners in the United States were employed in West Virginia, and McDowell County had the highest concentration of black miners in the Appalachian region.

By the outbreak of World War I, McDowell County was the largest bituminous coal producer in West Virginia. The county's coal-mining operations played an instrumental role in the war effort, providing coal and coke to the steel industry for weapons manufacturing. Thousands of miners returned to their jobs in the coal mines after service during the war with a renewed sense of patriotism.

Soon after the war, and during a period of increased political activity in the African American community, McDowell County raised a monument to commemorate its veterans. Black veterans then petitioned to have a memorial building erected to honor their role in the war. The county approved the project and $25,000 was allocated for its construction.

Prominent local architect Hassel T. Hicks designed the monumental Classical Revival style building. Although lavish in exterior detail, the building's interior was simple, with space provided for an auditorium, trophy room, lounge, and library. After its dedication with great fanfare on February 11, 1928, the memorial quickly became a social and cultural center. The building remained in use until the late 1970s and was left in ruinous condition by a fire in 1991. Local residents plan to stabilize the ruins and place a historical marker along the road explaining the site's significance. Despite its current state, the memorial continues to serve as a reminder of role played by African Americans in the history of southern West Virginia. [CA 4/9/93, 93000227]

MERCER COUNTY

Hancock House
300 Sussex Street
Bluefield

Built in 1907 by architect and builder M. H. Pettigo in the American Foursquare style, the Hancock House is a one of Bluefield's most significant examples of its type. The house was commissioned by Charles Hancock, a wealthy businessman and developer, and was sold to the Alpha Phi Alpha fraternity in 1962.

Alpha Phi Alpha is a black fraternity founded in 1906 at Cornell University. It has traditionally promoted understanding, peace at home and abroad, and full participation of men in the spiritual development of mankind. The fraternity's programs include the teaching and guidance of youth, fellowship, wholesome recreation, and community service. The house was purchased to serve as a regional center for these and other community activities.

At the time of its purchase, the house was the largest black-owned building in the area. The Alpha House, as it has come to be known, is the leading privately owned center providing service to the region's black community and has become a cultural mecca. The house, where Duke Ellington performed privately and was later initiated into the fraternity, has been meticulously maintained and retains its original appearance. [CAB 1/17/90, 89001783]

MONROE COUNTY

Union Historic District
Roughly along Main, Dunlap, Pump, and Elmwood streets north from Royal Oak Field, including Paradise and Monument fields
Union

Three buildings in the Union Historic District, the Old Baptist Church, the Bishop Clair House, and the Ames Methodist Church, are significant for their association with Matthew W. Clair, Sr., a prominent figure in black history in West Virginia. Clair was born and raised in Union but later moved to Charleston, where he committed himself to the Methodist faith at Simpson Methodist Episcopal Church, one of West Virginia's largest and most famous black churches (see also Simpson Memorial Methodist Episcopal Church, Kanawha County).

Clair's most famous pastorate was at the Asbury United Methodist Church in Washington, D.C., where he served from 1897 to 1902 and had a hand in the building of the fine Gothic Revival style building (see also Asbury United Methodist Church, District of Columbia).

Known for his excellent speaking ability, Clair always drew large crowds. The Union Historic District includes his home and the two churches in Union at which he preached most often. [CAB 12/6/90, 90001844]

WOOD COUNTY

Bethel AME Church
820 Clay Street
Parkersburg

The Bethel African Methodist Episcopal Church is one of three black churches in Parkersburg. Built in 1887, the two-story, stucco building is a vernacular ecclesiastical interpretation of the Gothic Revival style. Bethel is the oldest black church building in west central West Virginia and is located in a neighborhood of late 19th-century wood frame houses only a block from downtown. Bethel is a quiet sentinel of a settled neighborhood significant in the black history of Wood County. [Downtown Parkersburg MRA, CA 10/8/82, 82001767]

WISCONSIN

DANE COUNTY

East Dayton Street Historic District
649–653 East Dayton Street and 114
North Blount Street
Madison

East Dayton Street Historic District, a group of three frame buildings in a low-income residential area in downtown Madison's industrial/warehouse section, served as an entrance to the black community in Madison for African Americans from Kentucky and other southern states as well as from Chicago, Milwaukee, and other urban centers. Pioneering black families aided newcomers by providing housing and establishing religious, charitable, social, fraternal, and commercial institutions.

The buildings are associated with some of the area's first black families, including the Williamses and the Turners, who are noteworthy for their entrepreneurial spirit. The buildings also housed the Douglas Beneficial Society, a neighborhood commercial center and one of the black community's major social institutions; the Hill grocery store; the parsonage of the African Methodist Episcopal Church (the Thomas house); and the Miller house, a rooming house that housed many black families.

George and Carrie Williams came to Madison in 1850 and operated a barbershop and hairdressing salon, manufac-tured hair goods, ran a "Bazar (sic) of Fashion," and cleaned and dyed clothing. Their shop and residence was located at 120 South Pinckney Street, in the old Opera House building, which George Williams was also in charge of maintaining. Carrie Williams's brother, William Noland, was also a barber by trade who branched out into various entrepreneurial activities. In 1857 Governor Coles Bashford appointed Noland a notary public, making him the first African American to be named a state officer.

Although many African Americans faced poverty in Madison, the Turners, the Millers, and the Hills owned their own homes. John and Martha Turner established the Douglas Beneficial Society to serve as a self-help group for Madison's black families. They also operated a boardinghouse, and in 1900 or 1901 they rented a room to William Miller. In 1902 Turner, Miller, and other African Americans organized the first black church in Madison, the African Methodist Church. In 1909 Mrs. Miller organized the Book Lover's Club, an active but short-lived literary society intended to

Miller House. Photo courtesy of City of Madison Department of Planning and Development (K. H. Rankin).

foster awareness of the accomplishments of African Americans and to encourage self-betterment through recitations of poetry and songs, presentations of essays, and discussions of politics and current topics. [A 12/27/88, 88000217]

Miller House
647 East Dayton Street
Madison

The Miller House is associated with William and Annie Mae Miller, a prominent black middle-class couple active in the improvement of the social conditions of African Americans. From 1908 to 1919 the Miller House served as a boardinghouse for African Americans from the South moving to Madison. William Miller was an active member of the Niagara Movement (1905–8), the National Association for the Advancement of Colored People (NAACP), and a follower of W. E. B. Du Bois. As well as being committed to the improvement of African Americans, Miller actively participated in local and national politics and was respected by Progressive presidential candidate Robert La Follette. Annie Mae Miller was active in community and social organizations in the black community. In the fall of 1909 she organized a literary society called the Book Lover's Club, 10 years before the Harlem Renaissance gained prominence. Annie Mae Miller was also a charter member of the Order of Star, a member of the Madison Council of United Church Women, president of the Minnie Brown Missionary Society, and a founding member as well as treasurer of the Madison chapter of the NAACP. [B 11/8/79, 79000339]

ROCK COUNTY

Fairbanks Flats
205 and 215 Birch Avenue and 206 and 216 Carpenter Avenue
Beloit

Built during World War I, Fairbanks Flats is a rare example of company housing in Wisconsin built exclusively for newly arrived black workers. The economic expansion fostered by the advent of World War I increased the size of Beloit's industrial plant and its industrial work force. In large part, that growth resulted from the expansion of the Fairbanks-Morse Company, the city's largest employer. The company attracted numerous workers, but demand soon outstripped supply, and in the spring of 1917 the company brought hundreds of black workers to be employed at the factory. Under a specially organized subsidiary—Eclipse Home Makers, Inc.—Fairbanks-Morse provided housing for blacks in a segregated area on the outskirts of town, known as the Flats. So central did the Flats become to the black community that shortly after the construction of the apartments, Fairbanks-Morse brought J. D. Stevenson from Tuskegee Institute to found a black Young Men's Christian Association near the Flats. The concentration of black workers in the Flats created the nucleus of a black community that would shape Beloit housing patterns for decades. [Beloit MRA, A 1/7/83, 83003416]

FURTHER READING

Social History and the African American Experience, James O. Horton

Bernstein, Barton J. *Toward a New Past: Dissenting Essays in American History.* New York: Pantheon Books, 1968.

Durham, Philip, and Everett L. Jones. *The Adventures of the Negro Cowboys.* New York: Bantam Books, 1969.

Franklin, John Hope, and Alfred A. Moss, Jr. *From Slavery to Freedom: A History of Negro Americans.* 6th ed. New York: McGraw-Hill, 1988.

Foner, Eric, ed. *The New American History.* Philadelphia: Temple University Press, 1990.

Horton, James Oliver. *Free People of Color: Inside the African American Community.* Washington, D.C.: Smithsonian Institution Press, 1993.

McFeely, William S. *Frederick Douglass.* New York: Norton, 1990.

Novick, Peter. *That Noble Dream: The Objectivity Question and the American Historical Profession.* Cambridge, England: Cambridge University Press, 1988.

Quarles, Benjamin. *Black Abolitionists.* New York: Oxford University Press, 1970.

From Place to Place: African American Migration and Historic Sites, James R. Grossman

Adero, Malaika, ed. *Up South: Stories, Studies, and Letters of This Century's African American Migrations.* New York: New Press, 1993.

Attaway, William. *Blood on the Forge.* 1941. Reprint, Chatham, N.J.: Chatham Bookseller, 1969.

Ballard, Allan. *One More Day's Journey: The Story of a Family and a People.* New York: McGraw-Hill, 1984.

Bontemps, Arna, and Jack Conroy. *They Seek a City.* Garden City, N.Y.: Doubleday, Doran, and Co., 1945.

Crew, Spencer. *Field to Factory: Afro-American Migration 1915–1940.* Washington, D.C.: Smithsonian Institution Press, 1987.

Fisher, Rudolph. "City of Refuge." In Alain Locke, *The New Negro: An Interpretation.* New York: Albert & Charles Boni, 1925.

Grossman, James R. *Land of Hope: Chicago, Black Southerners, and the Great Migration.* Chicago: University of Chicago Press, 1989.

Henri, Florette. *Black Migration: Movement North, 1900–1920.* Garden City, N.Y.: Anchor Press, Doubleday, 1975.

Lawrence, Jacob. *The Great Migration: An American Story.* New York: Harper Collins, 1993.

Lemann, Nicholas. *The Promised Land: The Great Black Migration and How It Changed America.* New York: Knopf, 1991.

Painter, Nell Irvin. *Exodusters: Black Migration to Kansas after Reconstruction.* New York: Norton, 1976.

Redkey, Edwin. *Black Exodus: Black Nationalist and Back-to-Africa Movements, 1890–1910.* New Haven: Yale University Press, 1969.

Trotter, Joe W., ed. *The Great Migration in Historical Perspective: New Dimensions of Race, Class, and Gender.* Bloomington: Indiana University Press, 1991.

Woodson, Carter W. *A Century of Negro Migration.* 1918. Reprint, New York: AMS Press, 1970.

Wright, Richard. *Black Boy: A Record of Childhood and Youth.* New York: Harper and Brothers, 1937.

The African American Legacy beneath Our Feet, Theresa A. Singleton

Ferguson, Leland G. *Uncommon Ground: Archeology and Colonial African America.* Washington, D.C.: Smithsonian Institution Press, 1992.

Harrington, Spencer P. M. "Bones and Bureaucrats: New York's Great Cemetery Imbroglio." *Archeology* 46(2):28–38.

Orser, Charles E., Jr. "Artifacts, Documents, and Memories of the Black Tenant Farmer." *Archeology* 38(4):48–53.

———. *The Material Basis of the Postbellum Tenant Plantation: Historical Archeology in the South Carolina Piedmont.* Athens: University of Georgia Press, 1988.

Singleton, Theresa A. "Buried Treasure: Rice Coast Digs Reveal Details of Slave Life." *American Visions* 1(2):35–39.

———. "The Archeology of Slave Life." In Edward D. C. Campbell and Kym Rice, eds., *Before Freedom Came: African American Life in the Antebellum South.* Charlottesville: University Press of Virginia, 1991.

"Lifting As We Climb": African American Women and Social Activism (1800–1920), Carla L. Peterson

Davis, Angela Y. *Women, Race and Class.* New York: Random House, 1981.

Giddings, Paula. *When and Where I Enter.* New York: William Morrow, 1984.

Harley, Sharon, and Rosalyn Terborg-Penn. *The Afro-American Woman: Struggles and Images.* Port Washington: Kennikat Press, 1978.

Hine, Darlene Clark, Elsa Barkley Brown, and Rosalyn Terborg-Penn, eds. *Black Women in America.* 2 vols. New York: Carlson Publishing, 1993.

Hooks, Bell. *Aint' I a Woman: Black Women and Feminism.* Boston: South End Press, 1982.

Horton, James Oliver. "Freedom's Yoke: Gender Conventions among Antebellum Free Blacks." *Feminist Studies* 12 (Spring 1986): 51–76.

Jones, Jacqueline. *Labor of Love, Labor of Sorrow.* New York: Basic Books, 1985.

Sterling, Dorothy. *We Are Your Sisters.* New York: Norton, 1984.

From the "Mystic Years" to the Harlem Renaissance: Art and Community in African America, A. Lynn Bolles

Du Bois, W. E. B. *Black Reconstruction in America.* New York: New World Publishing, 1935.

Harrison, Daphne Duval. *Black Pearls: Blues Queens of the 1920s.* New Brunswick, N.J.: Rutgers University Press, 1988.

Higgins, Nathan I. *Harlem Renaissance.* New York: Oxford University Press, 1971.

Jones, Leroi (now Amiri Baraka). *Blues People.* New York: William Morrow, 1963.

Lewis, David Levering. *When Harlem Was in Vogue.* New York: Knopf, 1981.

Locke, Alain Leroy. *The New Negro: An Interpretation.* New York: Albert & Charles Boni, 1925.

Reynolds, Gary A., and Beryl Wright. *Against the Odds: African American Artists and the Harmon Foundation.* Newark, N.J.: The Newark Museum, 1989.

Southern, Eileen. *The Music of Black Americans.* 2d ed. New York: Norton, 1983.

Stearns, Marshall and Jean. *Jazz Dance: The Story of American Vernacular Dance.* New York: Schrimer, 1968.

Studio Museum in Harlem. *Harlem Renaissance Art of Black America.* New York: Abrams, 1986.

The Preservation Movement Rediscovers America, Elizabeth A. Lyon and Frederick C. Williamson

Lyon, Elizabeth A. *Cultural and Ethnic Diversity in Historic Preservation.* Information Series, no. 65. Washington, D.C.: National Trust for Historic Preservation, 1992.

National Conference of State Historic Preservation Officers. "Minority Participation in State Historic Preservation Programs Task Force Report." Washington, D.C., 1991.

National Trust for Historic Preservation. Theme Issue "Focus on Cultural Diversity II." *Historic Preservation Forum* 7 (January/February 1993): 4–47.

ABOUT THE CONTRIBUTORS

A. Lynn Bolles is associate professor of Women's studies, and comparative literature at the University of Maryland, College Park. Her research has focused on women in the African diaspora, particularly in the English-speaking Caribbean. Among her works are *My Mother Who Fathered Me nd Others: Gender and Kinship in the English-Speaking Caribbean* (1988), a cowritten volume entitled *In the Shadow of the Sun* (1990), *Without Them, We Wouldn't Have Survived: Women Trade Union Leaders in the Commonwealth Caribbean* (forthcoming), and *Sister Jamaica: A Study of Women and Households in Kingston*.

James R. Grossman is director of the Dr. William M. Scholl Center for Family and Community History, The Newberry Library, Chicago, Illinois. He is author of *Land of Hope: Chicago, Black Southerners, and the Great Migration* (1989). He is currently directing the Labor History Theme Study for the National Park Service. He is the editor of *The Frontier in American Culture*, (University of California Press, 1994).

James Oliver Horton is professor of history and American studies at George Washington University and director of the Afro-American Communities Project of the National Museum of American History at the Smithsonian Institution. He is the author of *Free People of Color: Inside the African American Community* (1993) and coauthor of *Black Bostonians: Family Life and Community Struggle in the Antebellum North* (1979). Horton is currently completing two books, one entitled

Toil, Spirit and Struggle: A History of African Americans to be published in Germany and another called *In Hope of Liberty: African American Communities in the North, 1700-1800* forthcoming from Oxford University Press.

LaVonne Roberts Jackson is a historian of African American history, a former consultant with the National Conference of State Historic Preservation Officers, and a Ph.D. candidate in history at Howard University, Washington, D.C.

Frank W. Johnson, IV, is a historian of African American history, a former consultant with the National Conference of State Historic Preservation Officers, and a Ph.D. candidate in history at Temple University, Philadelphia, Pennsylvania.

John Lewis is serving his fourth term representing Georgia's Fifth Congressional District. He is a member of the House Ways and Means Committee and the Committee on the District of Columbia. He is cochair of the Congressional Urban Caucus. During the height of the civil rights movement from 1963 to 1966, he was the chair of the Student Nonviolent Coordinating Committee and a recognized civil rights leader. For more than 30 years, he has been a champion of human rights in the United States.

Elizabeth A. Lyon is recently retired as the state historic preservation officer for Georgia where she was the chief of the Office of Historic Preservation since 1978. She has served on the Board of the National Conference of State Historic Preservation Officers and as cochair of the conference's special Task Force on Minority Participation in State Historic Preservation Programs. Her writings have examined architectural and landscape history in Atlanta, professional preservation practice, and cultural diversity in historic preservation.

Joan A. Maynard is executive director of the Society for the Preservation of Weeksville and Bedford Stuyvesant History, Brooklyn, New York. She is a trustee emeritus of the National Trust for Historic Preservation.

Carla L. Peterson is associate professor in the Department of English and the Comparative Literature Program at the University of Maryland, College Park. She is the author of essays on Frederick Douglass's journalism, the novels of Frances Harper and Pauline Hopkins, and the African American novel of the 1850s. Her book *'Doers of the Word': African American Women Reformers in the North (1830-1880)* is forthcoming from Oxford University Press.

Rama Ramakrishna is a historian of African American history consulting with the National Conference of State Historic Preservation Officers.

Beth L. Savage is an architectural historian, National Register of Historic Places, Interagency Resources Division, National Park Service, U.S. Department of the Interior.

Carol D. Shull is chief of registration, National Register of Historic Places, Interagency Resources Division, National Park Service, U.S. Department of the Interior.

Theresa A. Singleton is associate curator of historical archaeology, Department of Anthropology, National Museum of Natural History, Smithsonian Institution. She is the author of *The Archaeology of Slavery and Plantation Life* (1985); "An Archaeological Framework for Slavery and Emancipation, 1740 to 1880," in *The Recovery of Meaning: Historical Archaeology in the Eastern United States* (1988); "The Archaeology of the Plantation South: A Review of Approaches and Goals" in *Historical Archaeology* (1990); "The Archaeology of Slave Life," in *Before Freedom Came: African American Life in the Antebellum South* (1991); and "Using Written Records in the Archaeological Study of Slavery, An Example from the Butler Island Plantation" in *Text-Aided Archaeology* (1992).

Frederick C. Williamson has served the state of Rhode Island as its state historic preservation officer since 1969. He also served in the governor's cabinet as the state director of community affairs from 1969 to 1985. Before his state service he was a management analyst for the U.S. Navy. He is past chair and a charter member of the Rhode Island Black Heritage Society. He is a trustee emeritus of the National Trust for Historic Preservation and president emeritus of the National Conference of State Historic Preservation Officers. He served as cochair of the conference's special Task Force on Minority Participation in State Historic Preservation Programs.

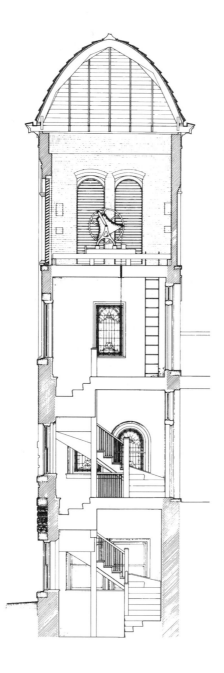

*Sixteenth Street Baptist Church, Birmingham, Jefferson County, Alabama.
Drawing courtesy of the Historic American Buildings Survey (James N.
Ferguson, delineator).*

INDEXES

PENNSYLVANIA

PUERTO RICO

RHODE ISLAND

SOUTH CAROLINA

WEST VIRGINIA

WISCONSIN

School room of Miss Annie Davis' School, c. 1902. Photo courtesy of The Library of Congress (Frances Benjamin Johnston).

INDEX BY OCCUPATION

Tuskegee Faculty Council, 1902. Booker T. Washington seated center, George Washington Carver standing, far right. Photo courtesy of the Library of congress (Frances Benjamin Johnston).

INDEX BY NAMES OF INDIVIDUALS AND ORGANIZATIONS

Allen, Richard
   Antioch Missionary Baptist Church, 481
   Bethel AME Church, 249
   Chapelle Administration Building, 449
   Little Jerusalem AME Church, 409
   Miller House, 538
   Mother Bethel AME Church, 415
   St. Peter AME Church, 263
   Wesley AME Zion Church, 417

Allensworth, Allen
   Allensworth Historic District, 118

Allen, William R.
   William R. Allen School, 337

Allston, Robert F. W.
   Pee Dee River Rice Planters Historic District, 439

Alpha Phi Alpha Fraternity
   Chandler Normal School Building and Webster Hall, 233
   Hancock House, 534
   St. James AME Zion Church, 361
   Villa Lewaro, 362

American Anti-Slavery Society
   Mary Ann Shadd Cary House, 136
   Liberty Farm, 284

American Baptist Home Mission Society
   Atlanta University Center District, 178
   Ayer Hall, 304
   Benedict College Historic District, 448
   East Raleigh–South Park Historic District, 384

American Colonization Society
   Lott Cary Birth Site, 496
   Mother Bethel AME Church, 415

American Medical Association (AMA)
   Justina Ford House, 120

American Missionary Association (AMA)
   Atlanta University Center District, 178
   Bethany Congregational Church, 198
   John W. Boddie House, 310
   Cooper School, 365
   Dorchester Academy Boys' Dormitory, 190
   Evans Industrial Building, 486
   First Congregational Church of Marion, 102
   Fisk University Historic District, 457
   Palmer Memorial Institute Historic District, 377
   Phillips Memorial Auditorium, 103
   Pleasant Hill Historic District, 172
   Second Congregational Church, 472
   Steele Hall, 473
   Stone Hall, Atlanta University, 184
   Swayne Hall, 104

   Talladega College Historic District, 104
   Ward Chapel AME Church, 400
American Negro Academy
   St. Luke's Episcopal Church, 147

American Society of Free Persons of Color
   Mother Bethel AME Church, 415

American Woman Suffrage Association
   Frances Ellen Watkins Harper House, 414

Amsterdam News
   New York Amsterdam News Building, 356
   Poston House, 233

Anderson, Dr. D. H.
   Artelia Anderson Hall, 243

Anderson, James H.
   New York Amsterdam News Building, 356

Anderson, Marian
   Goodwill Manor, 458
   Liberty Theater, 193
   Lincoln Memorial, 141
   Lyric Theater, 155

Anderson, William
   Camptown Historic District, 414

Armfield, John
   Fairvue, 474
   Franklin and Armfield Office, 493

Armstrong, Henry
   Avalon Hotel, 290

Armstrong, Louis
   Apollo Theater, 350
   Louis Armstrong House, 359
   Fletcher Henderson House, 195
   Jewell Building, 332
   Morton Building, 175
   Moulin Rouge Hotel, 335
   Taborian Hall, 116

Armstrong, Samuel Chapman
   Calhoun School Principal's House, 93
   Hampton Institute, 502
   Tuskegee Institute National Historic Site, 94

Asbury, Bishop Francis
   Tucker's Grove Camp Meeting Ground, 379

Ashe, Arthur
   Charles Sumner High School, 329

Association for the Study of Negro Life and History
   Mary McLeod Bethune Council House National Historic Site, 131
   Carter G. Woodson House, 151

Bontemps, Arna Wendell
  Arna Wendell Bontemps House, 263
  Fisk University Historic District, 457

Booker, Joseph A.
  Main Building, Arkansas Baptist College, 114

Book Lover's Club
  East Dayton Street Historic District, 536
  Miller House, 538

Boone, John William "Blind"
  John W. Boone House, 315
  Second Baptist Church, 315

Boston Literary and Historical Association
  William Monroe Trotter House, 282

Boston Suffrage League
  William Monroe Trotter House, 282

Bowen, Anthony
  Anthony Bowen YMCA, 133

Bowie State University
  Don S. S. Goodloe House, 275

Bowser, Aubrey
  Camptown Historic District, 414

Boy Scouts
  Church of Our Merciful Saviour, 239

Brent, Calvin T. S.
  St. Luke's Episcopal Church, 147
  Strivers' Section Historic District, 148

Bristol College
  White Hall of Bristol College, 410

Brotherhood of Sleeping Car Porters
  Breitmeyer-Tobin Building, 285
  Pilgrim Baptist Church, 293

Brown, Dr. Arthur McKinnon
  Dr. A. M. Brown House, 87
  Smithfield Historic District, 91

Brown, Charlotte Hawkins
  Northwest Historic District, 163
  Palmer Memorial Institute Historic District, 377

Browne, William Washington
  True Reformer Building, 149

Brown, James
  Apollo Theater, 350
  Howard Theatre, 139

Brown, John
  John Brown Cabin, 227
  John Brown Farm, 347
  John Brown House, 413
  John Brown's Headquarters, 276
  Mary Ann Shadd Cary House, 136
  Harpers Ferry National Historical Park, 528
  Howe House, 278
  Jefferson County Courthouse, 529
  Harriet Tubman Home for the Aged, 345

Brown, Sterling
  Fisk University Historic District, 457

Bruce, Blanche Kelso
  Blanche K. Bruce House, 134
  Eighth and Center Streets Baptist Church, 322
  Metropolitan AME Church, 143

Bryan, Andrew
  Laurel Grove–South Cemetery, 173

Bryan, William Jennings
  Lyman Trumbull House, 212

Bucks of America
  Boston African American National Historic Site, 279

Buffalo Soldiers
  Archeological Site No. 41 HZ 227, 483
  Archeological Site No. 41 HZ 228, 483
  Archeological Site No. 41 HZ 439, 484
  Clarksville Historic District, 486
  Greater St. Paul AME Church, 486

Bumbry, Grace
  Charles Sumner High School, 329

Bunche, Ralph Johnson
  Ralph Bunche House, 134
  Ralph Bunche House, 359
  Mickens House, 163
  Northwest Historic District, 163

Burleigh, Harry Thacker
  Will Marion Cook House, 350
  St. George's Episcopal Church, 358

Bush, John E.
  Mosaic Templars of America Headquarters Building, 116

Butler, S. B.
  Calvary Baptist Church, 228

Butler, Selena Sloan
  Atlanta University Center District, 178
  Yonge Street School, 186

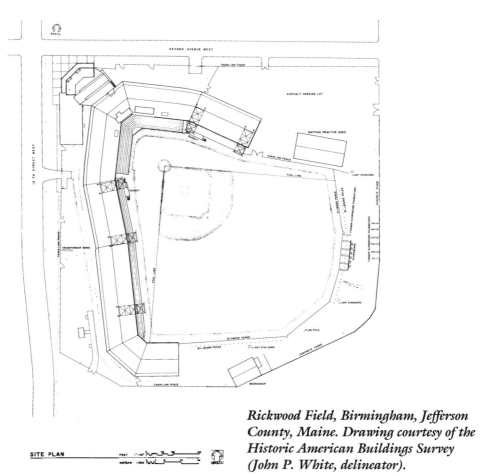

SITE PLAN

Rickwood Field, Birmingham, Jefferson County, Maine. Drawing courtesy of the Historic American Buildings Survey (John P. White, delineator).

INDEX BY SUBJECT

Odessa Historic District, 128

Okmulgee Downtown Historic District, 404

Old Bethel United Methodist Church, 433

Old Fort Church, 128

Old Richmond Historic District, 222

Old Ship African Methodist Episcopal Zion Church, 101

Old Slave Mart, 433

Old Statehouse Historic District, 235

Orange Street School, 368

Orchard Street United Methodist Church, 272

W. E. Palmer House, 465

Pastorium, Dexter Avenue Baptist Church, 102

Joseph Patterson Quarters, 249

Dave Patton House, 97

Peace College Main Building, 386

Pee Dee River Rice Planters Historic District, 439

Phillips Memorial Auditorium, 103

Homer G. Phillips Hospital, 328

Pigeon Key Historic District, 162

Pine Ridge Church, 298

Pisgah Rural Historic District, 234

Pleasant Hill Historic District, 172

Pleasant Street Historic District, 156

Point of Pines Plantation Slave Cabin, 434

Portsmouth Historic District (Boundary Increase), 510

Pratt City Carline Historic District, 89

William Price House, 193

Prince Hall Masonic Temple, 146

Public School No. 111, 272

Public School No. 111-C, 128

Quinn Chapel AME Church, 328

Red Oak Creek Covered Bridge, 191

Redd Road Rural Historic District, 233

Pleasant Reed House, 304

Reese Street Historic District, 175

Smith Robertson Elementary School, 306

Rockville Historic District, 220

Russell Historic District, 242

Sacred Heart Roman Catholic Church, Convent and Rectory, 286

Sandy Ground Historic Archeological District, 360

Santa Fe Place Historic District, 321

Scarborough House, 371

Seaside Plantation, 430

Second Congregational Church, 472

Second Presbyterian Church, 472

Selkirk Farm, 437

Shadow Lawn, 341

Shiloh Baptist Church, 462

Sixteenth Street Baptist Church, 90

Sixth Street Historic District, 488

Slave Houses, Gregg Plantation, 438

Slave Street, Smokehouse, and Allée, Boone Hall Plantation, 434

Sledge-Hayley House, 387

Smith-Bontura-Evans House, 298

Smithfield Historic District, 91

Smithville Seminary, 422

Smyrna Historic District, 126

South Central Aberdeen Historic District, 312

South Frankfort Neighborhood Historic District, 236

South Main Street Historic District, 472

South School, 391

South Street-Broad Street-Main Street-Laurel Street Historic District, 187

Southern Aid Society-Dunbar Theater Building, 146

Southern University Archives Building, 257

William Henry Spencer House, 194

Springfield Baptist Church, 187

Springfield Baptist Church (Boundary Increase), 197

St. Bartholomew's Church, 174

St. Christoper's Normal and Industrial Parish School, 195

St. James AME Church, 165, 262

St. James AME Zion Church, 361

St. John Chapel, 195

St. John United Methodist Church, 250

St. John's African Methodist Episcopal Church, 508

St. John's Church, 271

St. Joseph Historic District, 265

St. Joseph's AME Church, 371

St. Joseph's Episcopal Church, 368

St. Luke Building, 512

St. Mary's Episcopal Church, 147

St. Matthias Episcopal Church, 366

St. Michael's Creole Benevolent Association Hall, 159

St. Nicholas Historic District, 358

St. Paul AME Church, 386

St. Paul Missionary Baptist Church, 200

St. Peter AME Church, 263

St. Peter African Methodist Episcopal Church, 467

St. Philip's Moravian Church, 372

St. Thomas' Protestant Episcopal Church, 452

Stanton Center, 270

Edwin M. Stanton School, 159

State Street AME Zion Church, 98

State Street Public School, 339

John Stewart House, 195

Stone Barn on Brushy Creek, 246

Stone Quarters on Burgin Road, 244

Stone Street Baptist Church, 98

Strivers' Section Historic District, 148

Sugg House, 119

Charles Sumner High School, 329

Charles Sumner School, 148

Sycamore Street Historic District, 303

Talladega College Historic District, 104

Third Street Bethel AME Church, 513

Solomon Thomas House, 254

Thompson Cottage, 413

Estate Nisky, 522
Girard Colored Mission, 193
Golden West Cemetery, 300
Gower Cemetery, 402
Lewes Historic District, 129
Magnolia Cemetery including Mobile National
Cemetery, 96
New Hope Missionary Baptist Church Cemetery,
Historic Section, 110
Odd Fellows Cemetery, 312
Odessa Historic District, 128
Rest Hill Cemetery, 475
Stanton Family Cemetery, 496
Zion Cemetery, 473

Chicago Bee
 Chicago Bee Building, 204
 Overton Hygienic Building, 207

Chicago Defender
 Robert S. Abbott House, 203
 Victory Sculpture, 209

Churches
 African Church, 325
 African Meetinghouse, 279
 African Methodist Episcopal Church, 268
 African Zion Baptist Church, 530
 AME Church of New Haven, 318
 Asbury United Methodist Church, 130
 Ashwood Rural Historic District, 466
 Atlanta University Center District, 178
 Beach Boulevard Historic District, 301
 Bethany Baptist Church, 338
 Bethany Congregational Church, 198
 Bethel African Methodist Episcopal Church, 111
 Bethel AME Church, 216, 249, 409, 535
 Bethel AME Church and Manse, 361
 Bethel Baptist Institutional Church, 156
 Bethlehem Baptist Church, 423
 Big Spring Baptist Church, 506
 Black Theater of Ardmore, 397
 Boston African American National Historic Site,
 279
 Bremo Slave Chapel, 500
 Broadway Temple AME Zion Church, 238
 Brooks, Jennie, House, 477
 Brown Chapel African Methodist Episcopal
 Church, 85
 Burns United Methodist Church, 224
 Butler Chapel AME Zion Church, 83
 Butler Street Colored Methodist Episcopal
 Church, 181
 Buxton Historic Townsite, 223
 Calvary Baptist Church, 228
 Capers CME Church, 456
 Cedar Grove Plantation Chapel, 438
 Center Street AME Zion Church, 378
 Central Baptist Church, 431
 Charles Street African Methodist Episcopal

 Church, 281
 Chestnut Grove School, 175
 Chestnut Street Baptist Church, 238
 Chubb Methodist Episcopal Church, 178
 Church of Our Merciful Saviour, 239
 Church of the Good Shepherd, 198
 City of St. Jude Historic District, 98
 Clarksville Historic District, 486
 Clinton AME Zion Church, 442
 Collins Chapel CME Church and Site, 469
 Corinth Baptist Church, 453
 Court Street Baptist Church, 505
 Daes Chapel Methodist Church, 188
 Daufuskie Island Historic District, 425
 Dexter Avenue Baptist Church, 99
 Dove Creek Baptist Church, 178
 Durham Memorial AME Zion Church, 345
 East Dayton Street Historic District, 536
 East Raleigh-South Park Historic District, 384
 Eastside Baptist Church, 403
 Ebenezer Missionary Baptist Church, 92
 Eddings Point Community Praise House, 426
 Eighth and Center Streets Baptist Church, 322
 Thomas Jefferson Elder High and Industrial
 School, 198
 Emanuel AME Church, 95
 Embry Chapel Church, 237
 Emmanuel AME Church, 381
 Emmaus Moravian Church and Manse, 519
 Evans Metropolitan AME Zion Church, 368
 First African Baptist Church, 107, 192, 234, 511
 First African Baptist Church and Parsonage, 248
 First Baptist Central Church, 403
 First Baptist Church, 84, 85, 237, 381, 399, 470,
 507, 515
 First Calvary Baptist Church, 507
 First Church of Christ, 123
 First Colored Baptist Church, 252
 First Congregational Church, 181
 First Congregational Church of Marion, 102
 Fisk Chapel, 339
 Foster Memorial AME Zion Church, 362
 Free Will Baptist Church of Pennytown, 324
 Freedmen's Town Historic District, 481
 Freeman Chapel CME Church, 232
 Friedensthal Mission, 518
 Frying Pan Meetinghouse, 500
 Gaston Chapel, 366
 Grant AME Church, 338
 Greater Bethel AME Church, 155
 Greater St. Paul AME Church, 486
 Green Memorial AME Zion Church, 266
 Greenville Historic District, 191
 Halltown Union Colored Sunday School, 528
 Hampton-Pinckney Historic District, 440
 Hawthorn House, 95
 High Point-Half Moon Bluff Historic District,
 173
 Hopeful Baptist Church, 173
 Mary Jenkins Community Praise House, 428

Harriet Beecher Stowe House, Brunswick, Cumberland County, Maine. Photo courtesy of the Maine Historic Preservation Commission.

INDEX BY NATIONAL REGISTER LISTING NAME

Negro Masonic Hall, 327
Nell, William C., House, 282
New Herrnhut Moravian Church, 523
New Hope AME Church, 177
New Hope Missionary Baptist Church Cemetery, Historic Section, 110
Newsome, J. Thomas, House, 506
New York Amsterdam News Building, 356
Nicholsonville Baptist Church, 174
Nicholson, Ward, Corner Store, 84
Nicodemus Historic District, 226
1907 House, 308
Noble Hill School, 171
North Carolina Central University, 369
North Carolina Mutual Life Insurance Company Building, 370
North Lawrence-Monroe Street Historic District, 100
North Washington Avenue Workers' Houses, 382
Northwest Historic District, 163
Oakdale, 412
Oakland, 297
Oakland Chapel, 301
Oaks, The, 428
Oakview, 311
Odd Fellows Building and Auditorium, 184
Odd Fellows Cemetery, 312
Odessa Historic District, 128
Okmulgee Black Hospital, 404
Okmulgee Downtown Historic District, 404
Old Bethel United Methodist Church, 433
Old Dillard High School, 154
Old Fort Church, 128
Old Market, 190
Old Richmond Historic District, 222
Old Ship African Methodist Episcopal Zion Church, 101
Old Slave Mart, 433
Old Statehouse Historic District, 235
Olustee Battlefield, 154
O'Neal, Lewis, Tavern, 234
One-hundred-and-one Ranch, 398
Orange Street School, 368
Orchard Street United Methodist Church, 272
Overton Hygienic Building, 207
Palmer Memorial Institute Historic District, 377
Palmer, W. E., House, 465
Paseo YMCA, 320
Pastorium, Dexter Avenue Baptist Church, 102
Patterson, Joseph, Quarters, 249
Patton, Dave, House, 97
Peace College Main Building, 386
Pee Dee River Rice Planters Historic District, 439
Penn Center Historic District, 428
Penn, William, High School, 378
Phillips Memorial Auditorium, 103
Phillips, Homer G., Hospital, 328
Phoenix Bank of Nansemond, 516
Phoenix Union Colored High School, 108
Pigeon Key Historic District, 162

Pilgrim Baptist Church, 293
Pine Ridge Church, 298
Pisgah Rural Historic District, 234
Pleasant Hill Historic District, 172
Pleasant Street Historic District, 156
Ploeger-Kerr-White House, 478
Point of Pines Plantation Slave Cabin, 434
Port Hudson, 258
Portsmouth Historic District (Boundary Increase), 510
Poston House, 233
Pratt City Carline Historic District, 89
Price Public Elementary School, 463
Price, William, House, 193
Prince Hall Masonic Temple, 146
Public School No. 111, 272
Public School No. 111-C, 128
Quinn Chapel AME Church, 328
Quinn Chapel of the AME Church, 207
Rainey, Gertrude Ma Pridgett, House, 194
Rainey, Joseph H., House, 439
Randolph, Virginia, Cottage, 504
Ransom Place Historic District, 218
Red Bird City Hall, 407
Red Oak Creek Covered Bridge, 191
Redd Road Rural Historic District, 233
Reed, Pleasant, House, 304
Reese Street Historic District, 175
Rest Hill Cemetery, 475
Richmond Hill Plantation Archeological Sites, 440
Rickwood Field, 90
Riley, John Gilmore, House, 161
Robertson, Smith, Elementary School, 306
Robeson, Paul, Home, 357
Robinson, John Roosevelt "Jackie", House, 348
Robinson, Lizzie, House, 333
Rock Front, 399
Rockville Historic District, 220
Rodgers, Moses, House, 118
Rosenwald Hall, 405
Russell Historic District, 242
Russwurm, John B., House , 266
Rustenberg Plantation South Historic District, 520
Sacred Heart Roman Catholic Church, Convent and Rectory, 286
Saint Thomas' Protestant Episcopal Church, 452
Sandy Ground Historic Archeological District, 360
Santa Fe Place Historic District, 321
Savage, Dr. J. A., House, 372
Scarborough House, 371
Schomburg Center for Research in Black Culture, 357
Seaside Plantation, 430
Second Baptist Church, 315
Second Baptist Church of Detroit, 286
Second Christian Church, 316
Second Congregational Church, 472
Second Presbyterian Church, 472
Selkirk Farm, 437
Shadow Lawn, 341